Job Titles.

Air Sales Consultant
Cruise Escort

Dictionary for Air Travel and Tourism Activities

✦

More than 7,100 terms on Airlines, Tourism,
Hospitality, Cruises, Car Rentals, GDS,
Geography, Climate, Ecology, Business,
Customs, and Organizations Subjects.

Compiled and commented by
Homero Martínez   *(IATA Dip. TT Snr. Mgt.)*

iUniverse, Inc.
New York   Bloomington

Dictionary for Air Travel and Tourism Activities

More than 7,100 terms on Airlines, Tourism, Hospitality, Cruises, Car Rentals, GDS, Geography, Climate, Ecology, Business, Customs, and Organizations Subjects.

iUniverse books may be ordered through booksellers or by contacting:

iUniverse
1663 Liberty Drive
Bloomington, IN 47403
www.iuniverse.com
1-800-Authors (1-800-288-4677)

ISBN: 978-0-595-52709-0 (pbk)
ISBN: 978-0-595-62762-2 (ebk)

Printed in the United States of America

iUniverse rev. date: 10/14/08

ACKNOWLEDGEMENTS:

To the Superior Intelligence and Its noticeable
or veiled guides showing the path;
To the intimate, yet marvelous family of great
hearts of sons, daughter, and sisters;
To the generous support of nieces, brothers and brethren;
To the publishers' professional advice;
To the encouragement of many who prefer to remain unknown.

ABOUT THE AUTHOR

Homero Martinez is engaged to the travel business for over 30 years, having gathered professional experience by education, training and practice.

He accomplished important executive duties at prestigious airlines. After a successful start with Air France, he was hired by Lufthansa to manage the Sales Department in Ecuador. Some years later Homero became General Manager of Japan Airlines GSA in his country.

While performing his tasks at the airline business he became enrolled by renowned universities such as Catholic University, Technology Equinox University, and University of the Pacific. By special invitation of IATA the author conducted seasonal accreditation courses for Travel Agencies in Venezuela.

Some of his professional qualifications were obtained at Lufthansa School of Seeheim, Germany, and at JAL School of the Americas in San Francisco, California, in addition to IATA Montreal Training Programs.

He is a lawyer specializing in Air Law and the author of many papers, articles and books in the air travel and tourism fields, including the following book titles:

"Basic Glossary for Air Fares",
"Procedures for Fare Calculation",
"The Contract of International Air Transport",
"Commercial Air Transport, Calculation Methodology",
"Universal Geography for Tourism Activities",
"Travel and Tourism Strategies" (A series of 18 titles).

INTRODUCTION

"Knowledge of words leads to knowledge of things" (Plato)

As humankind evolves and progress keeps its pace forward, new processes are adopted, new occupations appear and new concepts are learned. At the same time, a new language is also developed, because emerging activities claim for the arrangement of a terminology that help to configure an effective communication system.

From the scope of manhood history, Air Travel and Tourism are young activities, although it seems tourism has its embryonic roots in travels undertaken by ancient Greek and Roman people. Tourism flourished with the advent of Grand Tour in the seventeenth century, while air travel unfolded along the twentieth century, as planes made their headway.

The two wrongly called "Industries" are expansive and multifaceted systems whose complexity is reflected in the terminology employed to describe them or to operate them. It seems at times that operators and agents communicate by the use of a secretive jargon. Following the idea, the design of a glossary was envisaged to give at least a general understanding of what that language means.

The author was first focused on students in the process of training to become professional actors of travel and tourism, but he later realized that such an explanatory tool could also be an educational resource to assist service suppliers in communicating with their costumers. Furthermore, many people today are minding their own travel business thanks to the Internet assistance. Therefore, why not use the technological tools in a way that resembles the job of the professionals?

The travel business, as it is performed today, is not a simple and restricted activity. It is a system without boundaries, comprising numerous subsystems that are closely concerned with a wide range of human experiences and a variety of fields of knowledge. Geography is connatural to the movement of persons and things. Everything in travel and tourism is related to distances, territories and space. Special emphasis is made on the sustainability feature of tourism nowadays, meaning Ecology can not be excluded from the travel scope. Similar relationships associate travel to Communication, Climate, Business, and many other branches of knowledge. This justifies the need to include concepts which cover a comprehensive array of topics. Transport, hospitality, car rentals, cruising constitute a big group of providers interesting to know through their own jargon. A basic summary is given on technical terminology on air navigation to help understanding how Aircraft fly. Although summary description is included about the continents, the author avoided to include subjects that appertain to the Geography of Tourism.

As to the title, there is a reason why it is not a "Dictionary for Air Travel and Tourism Industries" instead of being a "Dictionary for Air Travel and Tourism Activities". There are strong arguments sustaining that neither Tourism nor Travel is an industry. The simplest reason is that neither one of those activities processes a final manufactured product. This is precisely the interpretation of the World Tourism Organization that prefers to qualify them as "activities," "systems" or "business".

Since some of the objectives of travel and tourism are the communication, the approximation and the understanding of people, the author aspires to give his modest contribution by means of this book. If only a part of this intention is achieved, the work would have deserved the effort.

Calgary, Alberta, Canada
August 2008

HOW TO USE THE DICTIONARY

As explained before, the dictionary is not limited to a list of terms strictly related to travel and tourism, since each of both activities is associated to a wide range of sciences influencing them. The words in cursive letter enclosed in brackets after each term or expression is aimed to classify the terms in the corresponding subject category.

Speaking of air transport, categories such as *Aviation, Airlines, Air Traffic* and *Aeronautics* have been used. *Aviation* comprises general terms and terms mainly related to its history. Words referring to commercial activities and regulatory themes are grouped under *Airlines*. *Air Traffic* encircles all of the vocabulary alluding circulation of aircraft in the air, while *Aeronautics* include those terms allied to the design and construction of aircraft.

Hospitality groups terms pertaining to Hotels, Restaurants and Beverages. When the category is *GDS*, it means the term or expression is used in communication through a Global Distribution System. *Tourism* is a category of differentiated terminology, as well as *Cruises* and *Car Rental*.

Geography, Climate, Ecology, Business, Customs and *Organizations* are categories comprising specific expressions that are clearly understandable.

DICTIONARY FOR AIR TRAVEL AND TOURISM ACTIVITIES

A

A *(Airlines)*: Code for "Alfa", name used to designate the letter "A" in the International Phonetic Alphabet

A *(GDS)*: A code meaning: 1. Aisle (with seat request code); 2. Automatic (with Car Rental Code); 3. Availability (as an entry, it displays flights with seats availability); 4. A surface segment of a trip; 4. Class of service, usually superior, like First Class Discounted.

A/D *(Air Traffic)*: Arrival/Departure

A/FD *(Air Traffic)*: See Airport Facility Directory.

A/G *(Air Traffic)*: See Mandatory Frequency.

A la Carte *(Hospitality)*: French term that literally means "from the menu." In restaurants, it is a menu that has individual dishes and beverages listed at separate prices. By extension, the term refers to travel items that can be purchased separately from a menu list, as opposed to a package product.

A la Carte Bar *(Hospitality)*: Also known as "Cash Bar" or a "No Host Bar" (sometimes spelled No-host Bar or Nohost Bar), the term refers to bar beverages at a social event, which have to be paid by guests. It is opposed to a hosted bar where drinks are paid by the host.

A la Carte Menu *(Hospitality)*: See A la Carte.

AA *(Airlines)*: Two-letter IATA code for American Airlines.

AAA *(GDS)*: An acronym for American Automobile Association.

AAAE *(GDS)*: An acronym for American Association of Airport Executives.

AAD *(GDS)*: An acronym for Agent Automated Deduction.

AAPA *(Organizations)*: An acronym for American Association of Port Authorities.

AAR *(Air Traffic)*: See Airport Acceptance Rate.

AAR *(Organizations)*: An acronym for Association of American Railroads.

AB *(GDS)*: Fare type code meaning Super Apex.

ABA *(Organizations)*: An acronym for American Bus Association, a trade association representing inter-city and charter bus companies.

Abacus *(GDS)*: One of the computer reservation systems *(GDS)* that serves the Asia Pacific Region.

Abaft *(Airlines)*: A term meaning at or near or toward the tail of an airplane.

Abaft *(Cruise)*: A nautical term meaning at or near or toward the stern of a ship.

Abbreviated Briefing *(Air Traffic)*: An updated weather synopsis for pilots with an accurate weather information for their final flight planning.

ABC *(GDS)*: Code meaning Advanced Booking Charter. A charter requiring that bookings are made in advance to the departure date.

ABC Islands *(Geography)*: Collective name for the Netherland Antilles Islands of Aruba, Bonaire and Curacao. They are located just off the northern coast of South America (in front of Venezuela). As tourism destinations, they are perfect for diving, snorkeling, and all types of water sports.

ABCPU Subarea *(IATA Geography)*: The territory comprising **A**rgentina, **B**razil, **C**hile, **P**araguay, and **U**ruguay. See South Atlantic Subarea.

ABD *(GDS)*: Code meaning Aboard.

Abeam *(Airlines)*: At right angles to the length of a plane.

Abeam *(Cruise)*: At right angles to the keel of a ship.

ABF *(Hospitality)*: American Breakfast.

ABI *(Customs)*: See Automated Brokerage Interface.

Abiotic *(Ecology)*: The non living elements or an environment not containing life.

Abiotic Factors *(Ecology)*: Environmental conditions that affect living elements and their interactions, such as temperature, winds, humidity, and other physical or chemical influences.

ABJ *(GDS)*: Three-letter IATA code for Abidjan, capital city of Ivory Coast.

Abonnement *(Tourism)*: Rail ticket available in Europe. It allows unlimited travel within a specified area for a specific period of time.

Abort *(Aeronautics)*: Procedure that fails or terminates prematurely an aircraft operation.

Above Board *(Cruise)*: Cabins above the water level.

Above Ground Level (AGL) *(Air Traffic)*: A measurement of altitude above a specific land mass.

Above Sea Level (ASL) *(Air Traffic)*: Distance of the aircraft above mean sea level.

ABP *(GDS)*: Code meaning Able Bodied Passenger. A passenger without physical impediment who is eligible to sit near the emergency exit on an aircraft.

Absolute Altitude *(Air Traffic)*: The height of an aircraft flying above the actual terrain.

Absolute Ceiling *(Air Traffic)*: The maximum altitude above sea level at which an aircraft can maintain horizontal flight under standard atmospheric conditions.

Absolute Humidity *(Climate)*: A weather element determining the amount of water vapor present in a unit of air volume, usually expressed in kilograms per cubic meter.

Absolute Poverty *(Ecology)*: The lack of minimum income to meet the basic needs of food, clothing, and dwelling. Absolute poverty is measured by comparing a person's total income against the total cost of a specific 'basket' of goods and services including the essentials of daily life.

ABT *(GDS)* Code meaning About.

ABV *(GDS)*: Three-letter IATA code for Abuja, capital city of Nigeria.

AC *(Airlines)*: Two-letter IATA code for Air Canada.

AC *(GDS)*: A code meaning: 1. According, In Accordance; 3. Access Card; 4. Additional Collection; 5. Alternating Current; 6. Air Conditioned (sometimes written "a/c").

AC, A/C or ACFT *(Airlines)*: Codes for Aircraft.

ACA *(GDS)*: Three-letter IATA code for Acapulco, Mexico.

ACAP *(Aeronautics)*: An acronym for Aviation Consumer Action Project.

ACC *(GDS)*: Three-letter IATA code for Accra, capital city of Ghana.

Acceleration *(Aeronautics)*: Rate of change of velocity.

Accelerometer *(Aeronautics)*: An inertial device for measuring acceleration, usually in three orthogonal axes (lateral X, longitudinal Y, and vertical Z).

Access Aisle *(Tourism)*: An aisle at public places necessary for accessing parking spaces.

Access Code *(GDS)*: Password to entry into a computer or a computer file.

Accessibility *(Tourism)*: The possibility to reach a point in the space starting from a given origin. The accessibility measures the facility to access a tourist destination and is one of its main elements.

Accessible Pedestrian Signal *(Tourism)*: A device for transmitting traffic signals in a non-visual manner, such as by sound or vibration.

Accessible Route *(Hospitality)*: A route connecting the accessible parking area to an accessible entrance of the hotel building served by a parking lot.

ACCL *(Cruise)*: An acronym for American Canadian Caribbean Line.

Accommodation *(Hospitality)*: A facility designed to provide lodging. Accommodations may include room and food, and other related services.

Accommodation *(Tourism)*: Any seat, berth, room, or service sold to a passenger.

Accompanied *(Airlines)*: The term denotes a person (infant, child, and deportee) or a thing (baggage) is not traveling alone, but in the company of another person to comply with the rules established for the case. Infants always travel accompanied; children can travel sometimes unaccompanied; many of deportee persons require the company of a guardian.

Accompanied Baggage *(Airlines)*: Baggage that is carried in the same vehicle as the passenger and may be checked or unchecked. Checked is the baggage that travels under the carrier's custody. It is unchecked when it travels under the passenger's custody.

Accountable Document *(Tourism)*: Any piece of paper that, when validated by an authorized body, has a monetary value.

Accountable Manual Documents *(Airlines)*: Blank ARC ticket stock which was used in the past to issue hand-written tickets.

Accounting *(Tourism)*: 1. The process of recording financial transactions and reporting on the financial status of the travel business. 2. The department in the agency that manages the accounting duties.

Accreditation *(Tourism)*: The approval given by authorized organizations to travel agencies allowing the sale of tickets and other travel documents.

Accreditation and Database Management (ADM) *(Organizations)*: A division of the Airlines Reporting Corporation (ARC) that manages the database and accreditation information.

Accrual Method *(Tourism)*: An accounting system that records business income when the sale occurs, order is made, the item is delivered, or the services is rendered, regardless of when the money for them (receivables) is actually received or paid. Expenses are also recorded the moment goods or services are received, even though you may not pay for them until later. The agency doesn't have to wait to see the money, or actually pay money out of its checking account, to record a transaction.

ACCT *(GDS)*: A code meaning: 1. Account, 2. Accounting.

Acculturation *(Tourism)*: Cultural modifications experienced by individuals or social groups who borrow and adopt habits from other cultures. It is a phenomenon resulting from the contact and interrelation between different culture societies. The acculturation generated by tourism can be expressed in terms of adaptation or integration, or in a hostile way (such as aggression or rejection).

ACFT *(Airlines)*: Aircraft Type.

ACI *(Organizations)*: An acronym for Airports Council International.

ACI-NA *(Organizations)*: An acronym for Airports Council International, North America.

ACID *(Air Traffic)*: Aircraft Identification

ACK *(GDS)*: A code that means: 1. Acknowledge, 2. Acknowledged,

3. Acknowledging.

ACKD *(GDS)*: Code meaning Acknowledged.

ACLT *(Air Traffic)*: Actual Calculated Landing Time.

ACM *(Airlines)*: See Agency Credit Memo.

ACON *(GDS)*: Code meaning Air conditioning.

Acoustics *(Hospitality)*: Sound absorption or sound reflection quality of certain materials, usually in ceilings, walls, and floors.

ACPT *(GDS)*: A code meaning Accept, Accepting.

ACPTD *(GDS)*: Code meaning Accepted.

Acquired Immune Deficiency Syndrome (AIDS) *(Tourism)*: Incurable disease caused by a virus that is transmitted through blood or sex practices.

ACRA *(Organizations)*: An acronym for American Car Rental Association.

Acrophobia *(Tourism)*: An irrational fear of heights. Acrophobic people feel in danger and sometimes suffer a panic attack.

Acrylic *(Hospitality)*: Synthetic material used in manufacturing fabric and other fixtures or surfaces.

Act of God *(Tourism)*: An event which is caused by the effect of nature or natural causes, without any interference by humans. It is a natural event over which a travel provider has no control and, hence, no legal responsibility emerges. See also, Force Majeure.

ACTA *(Organizations)*: An acronym for Alliance of Canadian Travel Associations.

ACTE *(Organizations)*: An acronym for Association of Corporate Travel Executives.

Activated Carbon *(Hospitality)*: A type of carbon able to absorb odors and vapors. It is used in several filter systems at hotels.

Active IATA Member *(Airlines)*: A carrier affiliated to IATA which operates international regular services.

Active Layer *(Geography)*: A soil top layer that, located above permafrost, increases warm each summer and refreezes each autumn.

Active Tag *(Airlines)*: An RFID (Radio Frequency Identification) tag that has a transmitter to send back information by means of a battery that sends a signal to a reader. Active tags can be read from a distance of 100 meters (300 feet) or more.

Active Tourism *(Tourism)*: A type of tourism that combines elements of adventure and cultural tourism in a natural environment, making emphasis on low-impact and sustainable elements.

Actor *(Tourism)*: A person who plays a role. In Tourism, the actors are persons or organized groups who take decisive actions and are leaders in a local territory.

Actual Beverage Cost Percentage *(Hospitality)*: Net beverage cost divided by the total bar sales amount.

Actual Flying Time *(Airlines)*: Total time spent in the air since the plane departs to the moment it lands.

Actual Flown Mileage *(Airlines)*: The total amount of miles counted from point of departure to point of arrival, via intermediate points. It is the sum of TPMs (Ticketed Point Mileages).

ACV *(Tourism)*: See Air Cushioned Vehicle or Hovercraft.

AD *(GDS)*: A code meaning: 1. Agent's Discount. When followed by a number, it shows the discount percentage off unrestricted fares. For example: AD75 indicates a discount of 75 percent. 2. Administration.

Ad Hoc *(Tourism)*: A Latin term that means dealing something concerned with one specific purpose. In tourism language it denotes the organization of a tour on a customized basis, usually from existing options.

Ad Hoc Charter *(Airlines)*: A charter operated according to the necessity of an operator or charterer.

Ad Hoc Group *(Tourism)*: A group gathered according to a specific subject or around a specific purpose.

Ad Hoc Schedule *(Airlines)*: A flight or set of flights that are modified for specific dates from the basic schedule.

Ad Valorem *(Customs)*: A term meaning "according to the value" that represents a fixed percentage of the value of goods used to calculate customs duties and taxes.

Ad Valorem Tax *(Hospitality)*: A tax based on the assessed value of the asset itself, usually a fixed percentage of the value.

ADAC *(GDS)*: Code meaning Advise Acceptance.

ADAR *(GDS)*: Code meaning Advise Arrival.

ADB *(GDS)*: Code meaning Advise if Duplicate Booking.

ADC *(Air Traffic)*: Air Data Computer.

ADC *(GDS)*: Code meaning Additional Collection.

ADCOL *(GDS)*: Code meaning Additional Collection.

ADCTC *(GDS)*: Code meaning Advise Contact.

Add/Coll *(Airlines)*: A code used to mean Additional Collection.

Add-on *(Airlines)*: An amount used to construct an unspecified throughfare or an unspecified maximum permitted mileage by adding such an add-on amount to a terminal point of a fare or mileage.

Add-on *(Tourism)*: An option added to travel arrangements, usually at extra cost.

Add-on *(Cruise)*: A supplementary charge added to the cruise fare. Typical add-ons are travel insurance, airline flights to and from the cruise port, pre- and/or post-cruise hotel packages, and pre-or post-cruise land tours.

Add-on(s) *(Tourism)*: Anything optional purchased by a passenger, as in tour arrangements.

Add-on Fare *(Airlines)*: An amount added to a terminal point fare to arrive at a through fare. It is sometimes called Proportional Fare.

Additional Collection *(Airlines)*: Amount collected in addition to the original payment, in case of rerouting, for instance.

Additional Equipment *(Car Rental)*: Based on location availability, the passenger can select certain options for a nominal fee, such as infant and child safety seats or ski racks. Additional equipment or accessories require a reservation of at least 24 hours prior to pick-up date.

Additive *(Hospitality)*: Anything added to a product that is not strictly necessary for its manufacture, but which facilitates the production or enhances certain qualities considered desirable by the producer. For example, brewers use additives to produce more stable and softer foam, greater clarity, and other qualities.

ADDR *(Air Traffic)*: Air Data Dead Reckoning.

Addressability *(Airlines)*: The ability to write data to different fields in the microchip in an RFID transponder.

ADF *(Air Traffic)*: See Automatic Direction Finding.

Adhesion Contract *(Airlines/Tourism)*: A contract that is prepared by one party, whose conditions are accepted by the other party by an act of adhesion. It is a type of contract that heavily restricts one party while beneficiates the other party by the terms pre-stipulated. It implies inequality in bargaining power. Typical examples of this type of contracts are "The Conditions of Carriage" that are part of every airline ticket and the "Terms and Conditions" of cruise and tours that clients must adhere to, at the time of making the payment.

Adiabatic Changes *(Climate)*: A general term referred to changes in temperature with no loss or addition of heat. Adiabatic changes occur in gasses or in the air.

Adiabatic Rate *(Climate)*: A principle stating that temperature decreases as altitude increases.

ADIZ *(Air Traffic)*: See Air Defense Identification Zone.

Adjoining Rooms *(Hospitality)*: Guestrooms located side by side but, although they are next to each other, they have no connecting doors.

Adjuncts *(Hospitality)*: Natural products (such as rice, corn, and wheat flakes), added to malted barley before fermentation.

ADM *(Airlines)*: See Agency Debit Memo.

ADM *(Organizations)*: An acronym for Accreditation and Database Management.

Administrating Carrier *(Airlines)*: The airline that controls the operation of a flight.

ADNO *(GDS)*: Code meaning Advise If Not Ok.

ADOA *(GDS)*: Code meaning Advise On Arrival.

ADPE *(Air Traffic)*: Automated Data Processing Equipment.

ADR *(GDS)*: See Average Daily Rate.

ADS *(GDS)*: A code meaning: 1. Address, Addressing, Addressed. 2. Distribution System. 3. Authorized Destination Status.

ADS *(Air Traffic)*: Code for Automatic Dependent Surveillance.

ADSAP *(GDS)*: Code meaning Advise As Soon As Possible.

ADT *(GDS)*: Code meaning: 1. Adult; 2. Atlantic Daylight Time.

ADTK *(GDS)*: Code meaning Advise If Ticketed.

ADTNL *(GDS)*: Code meaning Additional.

Adult *(Airlines)*: A person who has reached his/her 12th birthday as of the date of commencement of international travel and has to pay full air fare. Some airlines require an accompanying adult for passengers who are not 14 or 16 years old.

ADV *(GDS)*: Code meaning Advise, Advising, Advised.

Advance Purchase Excursion (Apex) *(Airlines)*: The "APEX" fare is a highly discounted excursion fare available on many international routes. This type of fares demands the accomplishment of strict reservations and payment requirements well in advance of departure with varying penalties for cancellation and changes.

Advance Purchase Period *(Airlines)*: The period of time established for payment and ticketing, computed from the date and time of booking confirmation.

Advance Purchase Rate *(Airlines)*: The price for an air transportation paid at specified number of days prior to use.

Advance Purchase Requirement *(Airlines)*: A condition placed on an airfare to oblige travelers to complete the payment at certain number of days ahead of departure, such as 7, 14, or 21 days.

Advance Timetable *(Airlines)*: A timetable issued by a carrier in advance of its period of operation. They are useful for planning purposes but need to advise they are still subject to change.

Advection Fog *(Geography)*: A type of fog formed when warm, moist air moves horizontally over a cold surface and the air is cooled to below its dew point.

Adventure Tour *(Tourism)*: A type of tourism arranged with the specific purpose of activity participation to explore a new experience, often involving perceived risk or controlled danger associated with personal challenges, such as raft riding, ballooning or travel to remote areas, where the traveler should expect the unexpected. This is a combination of physical and mental efforts in a natural environment or exotic outdoor setting. Two types of adventure tours are distinguished: "hard" and "soft", depending on the level of the effort demanded from participants. Adventure tourism is rapidly growing in popularity as tourists seek unusual holidays, different from conventional vacations.

Adventure Travel *(Tourism)* According to the definition of Adventure Travel Trade Association, "Adventure Travel may be any tourist activity including two of the following three components: a physical activity, a cultural exchange or interaction, and engagement with nature". See Adventure Tour.

Advertised Tour *(Tourism)*: A tour package that is advertised after meeting the airline requirements needed to assign an IT (Inclusive Tour) number.

Advisory *(Air Traffic)*: A signal used to give advice on safe or normal configuration, condition of performance, or operation of essential equipment. An advisory also attracts attention and gives information for routine action purposes.

Advisory Capacity *(Airlines)*: A term indicating that a shipper's agent or representative is not empowered to make decisions or introduce changes without the approval of the firm or individual he/she represents.

ADVN *(GDS)*: A code meaning Advise names, Advise as to names.

ADVR *(GDS)*: Code meaning Advise Rate.

ADZY or ADVZY *(Air Traffic)*: Advisory

AED *(GDS)*: Code for Dirham, the national currency of the United Arab Emirates.

AEP *(GDS)*: Three-letter IATA code for Jorge Newbery Airport (formerly Aeroparque), serving the city of Buenos Aires.

Aerobe *(Ecology)*: An organism that uses oxygen in its organic processes that are necessary for living. An "obligate aerobe", for instance, is an organism that needs oxygen to survive.

Aerobatics *(Aviation)*: Flights that typically involve high-performance maneuvers, such as barrel rolls, and spins.

Aerobic *(Ecology)*: 1. An organism that lives or an event that happens only in the presence of oxygen, such as an aerobic bacteria. 2. As an adjective it refers to oxygen consumption by the body, as in aerobic gymnastics.

Aerobic Organism *(Ecology)*: A microorganism that requires free oxygen for its metabolic process.

Aerodrome *(Aeronautics)*: It is an almost obsolete term denoting any location from where aircraft operate. In most cases it has been replaced by terms as Airport or Airfield. In the United States, the word Aerodrome has been modified into Airdrome. In Canada and Australia the term defines any area of land or water used for aircraft operation, regardless of the facilities. Canadian laws state that "...for the most part, all of Canada can be an aerodrome", but they make a difference between "registered aerodromes" and "certified airports". A registered aerodrome must maintain some standards and keep the Minister of Transport (Canada) informed. To become a certified airport the aerodrome must meet certain safety standards to support commercial operations.

Aerodrome of Democracy *(Aviation)*: One of the contributions of Canada to the allied forces during the World War II was through the British Commonwealth Air Training Plan (BCATP), also known as the Empire Air Training Scheme, or Empire Air Training Plan. Although the plan was accorded by Canada, Great Britain, the United States, Australia, and New Zealand, Canada took the responsibility for its costs. For six years, starting 1940, 120 aerodromes were built and operated in Canada and over 120,000 officers were graduated to serve in the air forces of the four Commonwealth nations participating in the plan. As a way to recognize the important contribution of the BCATP to winning the war, United States President Franklin Roosevelt called Canada "The Aerodrome of Democracy."

Aerodynamics *(Aeronautics)*: A field of fluid dynamics that studies how gases, including air, flow and how forces act upon objects moving through air.

Aeronautical Chart *(Air Traffic)*: A map used in air navigation that contains topographical features, hazards and obstructions, navigation aids, navigation routes, designated airspace, and airports.

Aeronautics *(Aeronautics)*: The science, art, theory and practice of designing, building, and operating aircraft through the air or space.

Aerophobia *(Airlines)*: An abnormal and persistent fear of drafts of air and. By extension, it is a fear of flying. Sufferers experience severe anxiety even though they usually realize that the flying does not present a threat compatible with their fear.

Aerosol *(Ecology)*: A suspension of colloidal particles of a solid or droplets of a liquid in a gaseous medium. People identify aerosols as products that use compressed gas to spray from a container. Besides manufactured aerosols, there are natural aerosols such as fog, smoke, and volcanic dust.

Aerospace *(Aviation)*: The earth's atmosphere, its immediate environments, and outer space considered as a whole.

Aerospace Industry *(Aeronautics)*: A set of activities comprising the research, design, manufacture, operation, and maintenance of vehicles moving through air and space. It covers a very diverse field, with a great number of commercial, industrial and military applications.

Aesthetic Balance *(Hospitality)*: The combination of colors, textures, and flavors of foods in meal planning, to make them more pleasant.

AF *(GDS)*: Code meaning: 1. Added Phone; 2. Applicable Fare; 3. Air France.

AFA *(Organizations)*: Acronym for Association of Flight Attendants.

AFCS *(Air Traffic)*: Automatic Flight Control System. See explanation.

Affiliate *(Airlines)*: A company that is controlled by another company.

Affiliate Hosting *(GDS)*: See GDS Hosting.

Affiliate Reservation System *(Hospitality)*: A hotel chain's reservation system in which all participating properties are contractually linked. Each property is present in the computer system database and provides room availability data to the reservation center.

Affiliated Hotel *(Hospitality)*: A hotel that is a member of a chain, franchise, or referral system. An affiliated hotel enjoys special advantages, such as a universal reservation system.

Affinity *(Tourism)*: A condition that links persons on the basis of their common professional or hobby interests.

Affinity Card *(Tourism)*: A credit card marketed by a company or other commercial or social group in association with the credit card company.

Affinity Charter *(Tourism)*: An airplane or ship charter arranged by or for an affinity group.

Affinity Group *(Tourism)*: A group of people linked by a common bond, such as a professional or sport interest.

Affinity Group Airfare *(Airlines)*: A fare set specifically for affinity groups.

Affirmative Philosophy *(Tourism)*: The principle that assumes a business has a responsibility to serve society.

Aflatoxin *(Hospitality)*: A poisonous mycotoxin, which is found worldwide and grows on nuts, corn, wheat, and other grains. Aflatoxin may be found in finished products like bread and peanut butter. Ingestion of aflatoxin usually only causes low-grade fever in humans, but it can produce cancer in trout, rats, and ducks and has been linked to some cases of liver cancer in humans.

AFM or AM *(Airlines)*: A code meaning Actual Flown Mileage. It is the total sum of the TPMs (Ticketed Point Mileages), that is, the distance flown by the passenger from the point of origin to the point of destination through all the intermediate points.

Afrasia *(Geography)*: See Africa-Eurasia.

Africa, Geographical *(Geography)*: Africa is the second largest continent and second most populous, after Asia. It covers around the 22 percent of the total land surface of the Earth, reaching an area of 30,350,000 square kilometers (11,699,000 square miles), including adjacent islands. With over 800 million inhabitants in 53 countries and eight territories, its population means about one tenth of the world human population. Africa is three times bigger than Europe and 50 percent more of the North American territory. The name Africa was first used by the Romans who identified the land of the Afri as *Africa Terra*, extended over the northern part of the continent, where Carthage (Now Tunisia) was located. Most scientists consider that Africa is the home to the oldest inhabited territory on earth, and the origin of humankind, according to the earliest *Homo Sapiens* remains found in Ethiopia.

Africa is separated from Europe by the Mediterranean Sea, and is joined to Asia by the Isthmus of Suez. An axe drawn from Ras ben Sakka in Tunisia to Cape Agulhas in South Africa, measures approximately of 8,050 kilometers (5,000 miles). Another axe from Cape Verde in Senegal to Ras Xaafuun in Somalia measures 7,560 kilometers (4,600 miles). The highest African mountain is the Kilimanjaro, with a height of 5.916 meters. The length of its coast-line is 30.490 kilometers, with few deep indentations of the shore. The continent is surrounded by the Mediterranean Sea to the North, the Atlantic Ocean to the West, the Red Sea to the East, and Indic Ocean to the Southeast. The largest desert in the world, the Sahara, lies to the north. Grasslands cover much of the land, and rainforests are in western Africa near the equator. The Nile River, the longest in the world, (6.695 kilometers long) is in Africa. Lake Victoria is the largest lake of the continent, the world's second-largest freshwater lake, covering an area of 69,490 square kilometers (26,830 square miles). It lies 1,130 meters above sea level and reaches a known depth of 82 meters.

Much of the traditional African cultures have become diminished as a result of years of neglect colonial and neo-colonial regimes, and are considered as synonymous for rural poverty and subsistence farming. Modern Africans are arguably the most diverse people in the world, having more than 3,000 unique ethnic groups been recognized. More than 1,000 different languages are spoken in Africa, some of which have been spoken for hundreds of years. Although most countries in Eastern and Southern Africa have adopted colonial European languages for official government business, most people speak indigenous or local languages.

Africa is the home to many species of exotic animals and live species. Unfortunately, decades of logging, sport hunting, civil wars, pollution, and other human interference have produced a great impact on the wildlife. Although Africans and people from all over the world have depleted animals and habitats, while looking for oil, diamonds, and other resources, National Parks still exist. They preserve wildlife and an incredible natural beauty that attract an ever-increasing number of tourists from around the globe. Most tourist activities develop around Safari Tours (Photo Safari Tours), Mountain Climbing, visits to Lake Victoria and Victoria Falls, or visits to Egypt and other northern African countries to know about ancient cultures.

Africa-Eurasia *(Geography)*: A term that identifies a supercontinent with the world's biggest landmass and around the 85% (approximately 5.6 billion) of the world population living there. It is subdivided into the continents of Africa and Eurasia; the latter subdivided at its turn into Europe and Asia. Speaking of this territory, some geographers and historians refer to as Eurafrasia or Afrasia, but these terms have never been generally accepted. In geopolitical terms, the mainland of Africa-Eurasia (excluding the British Isles, Japan and Madagascar) is known as the World Island, while Africa-Eurasia and its surrounding islands are called the Old World.

Africa Sub-area *(IATA Geography)*: The territory comprising Angola, Benin Botswana, Burkina Faso, Burundi, Cameroon, Cape Verde, Central African Republic, Chad, Comoros, Congo (Brazzaville), Côte d'Ivoire, Democratic Republic of Congo (Kinshasa), Djibouti, Equatorial Guinea, Eritrea, Ethiopia, Gabon, Gambia, Ghana, Guinea, Guinea-Bissau, Kenya, Lesotho, Liberia, Libya, Madagascar, Malawi, Mali, Mauritania, Mauritius, Mayotte, Mozambique, Namibia, Niger, Nigeria, Reunion, Rwanda, Sao Tome and Principe, Senegal, Seychelles, Sierra Leone, Somalia, South Africa, Swaziland, Tanzania, Togo, Uganda, Zambia, and Zimbabwe.

Afro-Eurasia *(Geography)*: Same as Africa-Eurasia.

AFT *(GDS)*: A code that means: 1. After. 2. Actual Flying Time.

Aft *(GDS)*: In lower case, the term refers to the rear end of a ship or toward the rear of a ship (the stern) or an airplane.

Agency *(Business)*: The relationship in which a person (called the agent) acts on behalf of another person, company, or government, known as the principal, in a business dealing with a third party.

Agency *(Tourism)*: A business that attends to the arrangement of transportation, itinerary, accommodation, and collateral services for travelers.

Agency Agreement *(Tourism)*: The contract that rules the relations between IATA or IATAN and travel agencies. It defines the specific duties and areas of responsibility of the agent.

Agency Check *(Tourism)*: A check bearing the agency's name that is drawn against a check account.

Agency Credit Memo (ACM) *(Airlines)*: A credit note issued by a member of the BSP in favor of a travel agency, detailing the amount due by the air carrier.

Agency Debit Memo (ADM) *(Airlines)*: A debit note issued by a member of the BSP detailing the amount due by a travel agency in favor of the air carrier.

Agency List *(Tourism)*: The list of appointed agencies kept in files of the ARC and IATAN.

Agency Manager *(Tourism)*: The person who is engaged to run full time the agency's business and its other activities.

Agency Total Cost *(Tourism)*: The total sum of the cost of all bookings made by a specific travel agency.

Agent *(Business)*: A person who acts on behalf of another person before a third party.

Agent (AGT) *(Tourism)*: 1. An appointed representative who acts on behalf of travel providers. 2. An accredited Passenger Sales Agent location having direct access to one or more System Providers and Servicing Carriers. 3. In a more extensive meaning, an agent is also an employee of a retail travel agency, a carrier employee who sells tickets, or a general agent.

Agent Air Waybill (AWB or MAWB) *(Airlines)*: The document made out by or on behalf of the shipper, giving evidence of the contract existing between the shipper and the carrier(s) for carriage of goods over routes of the carrier(s).

Agent Bypass *(Airlines)*: The practice of suppliers by which they prefer to sell their products directly to customers, avoiding the agent's intermediation.

Agent Coupon *(Airlines)*: Copy of the ticket that remains in the travel agency's files for control.

Agent Eligibility List *(Airlines)*: A list of an agency's employees who are eligible to receive travel benefits, which is submitted to ARC or IATAN by the agency manager. It is also known as "The ARC List."

Agent Reporting Agreement *(Airlines)*: The arrangement concerted by ARC with travel agencies regulating their relationships and dealings.

Agent Sine *(GDS)*: A two-letter identification code assigned to each individual in the agency.

Agentless Booking *(Airlines)*: A booking that is made by means of an automated system ignoring the mediation of a travel agency.

Agile Reader *(Airlines)*: A generic term that usually refers to a Radio Frequency Identification (RFID) reader that can read tags, which operates at different frequencies or uses different methods of communication between the tags and readers.

Aging *(Hospitality)*: A process in the production of alcoholic beverages in which spirits and wines are stored in casks or barrels after fermentation, but before bottling. Its purpose is to improve quality by allowing further chemical reaction to occur with a small amount of air.

AGL *(Air Traffic)*: See Above Ground Level.

Agoraphobia *(Tourism)*: A morbid fear of public or open spaces. Some agoraphobics fear of being caught alone in some public place.

AGR *(Air Traffic)*: Code meaning Air-ground Ranging

AGR *(GDS)*: Code meaning Agree, Agreeing.

AGR Slant Range *(Air Traffic)*: Straight-line distance from the aircraft to a point on the ground.

AGRD *(GDS)*: Code meaning Agreed.

Agreement *(Airlines)*: The act of coming to a meeting of the minds, even without legal obligation. An agreement is accorded between two people who reach an understanding about a particular issue, including their obligations, duties and rights. In law, an agreement is a contract that includes all the elements of a legal contract: offer, acceptance, and consideration (payment or performance), based on specific terms. There are different types of agreements, such as that by which airlines agree the interchangeable use of tickets. Another type of agreement is settled between an air carrier and a travel agency, in which the airline permits the agency the sale of travel products.

AGRMT *(GDS)*: Code meaning Agreement.

Agri-tourism *(Tourism)*: See Agrotourism.

Agricultural Tourism *(Tourism)*: See Agrotourism.

Agroforestry *(Ecology)*: Land management for the simultaneous production of crops and trees, using methods similar to agriculture.

Agrotourism *(Tourism)*: Recreational travel organized around agricultural areas, a farm or any agricultural, horticultural or agribusiness operation, for the purpose of participating in agricultural activities, enjoyment and education. Visitors have the opportunity to work alongside real farmers and to walk with fishermen with the feet immersed in the sea. As a concept, agrotourism is considered to be a branch of ecotourism, which encourages visitors to experience agricultural life. It involves usually hotel, restaurant and recreational services. Agrotourism is strongly supported by rural communities, since they benefit of sustainable tourism development. It is also known as Agritourism, Agri-tourism, Agricultural Tourism, or Farm Tourism.

AGT *(GDS)*: Code meaning Agent.

AH&LA *(Organizations)*: An acronym for American Hotel & Lodging Association.

AHC *(Airlines)*: Acronym for Airport Handling Committee.

Ahead *(Cruise)*: In front of the ship's bow.

AHM *(Airlines)*: Airport Handling Manual.

AHMA *(Organizations)*: An acronym for American Hotel and Motel Association.

Ahoy *(Cruise)*: The traditional greeting onboard ships. The term originated as a Viking battle cry.

AHRS *(Air Traffic)*: Attitude Heading Reference System.

AI *(Airlines)*: Two-letter IATA code for Air India.

AID *(Air Traffic)*: Code meaning: 1. Aircraft Identifier; 2. Aircraft Identification

AIDS *(Tourism)*: See Acquired Immune Deficiency Syndrome.

AIH *(GDS)*: Code meaning Animal in hold.

Aileron *(Aeronautics)*: A control surface located on the trailing edge of each wing tip. Deflection of these surfaces controls the roll or bank angle of the aircraft.

AIM *(Air Traffic)*: Aeronautical Information Manual

Aim *(Air Traffic)*: To strive for a mission objective, such as flying toward a radial of a radio station.

Air Ambulance *(Aeronautics)*: An aircraft equipped to take care of sick or injured people and transport them to a medical facility.

Air Boat *(Tourism)*: A light, flat-bottomed vessel powered by an airplane propeller mounted on the stern and revolving in the air. It is used for tours in swamps or rivers.

Air Boat Line *(Airlines)*: Name of the first commercial airline founded in the United States by Tony Janus, on January 1rst, 1914 to operate services between St. Petersburg and Tampa. Its first flight took place on March 22 of that same year, using a Benoist Model 14 built by St. Louis manufacturer Thomas Benoist. The flying boat was made of three layers of wood; the power was provided by a Roberts 6-cylinder, in-line, liquid-cooled engine; the wings were constructed of spruce framing and covered with linen. The aircraft reached a maximum speed of 64 mph and accommodated one passenger besides the pilot. Several newspapers around Florida were opposed to the airboat operation and questioned its safety when service was begun.

Air Broker *(Airlines)*: A company that intermediates between Tour Operators and Airlines.

Air Cargo Agent *(Airlines)*: A freight forwarder specialized in air cargo who acts on behalf of airlines that pay him a commission or fee. He has to be registered with the International Air Transport Association to obtain his/her operating authorization.

Air Change *(Hospitality)*: Ventilation rate in terms of room or building volume. It is usually expressed as air changes per hour.

Air City *(Cruise)*: The city chosen by the passenger to serve as the origin and termination point for his flights to and from the cruise.

Air Courier *(Airlines)*: An air courier is a person or company whose activity is delivering messages, packages and mail, in such a manner that speed, security, tracking, specialization and individualization of services are featured.

Air-Cushion Vehicle (ACV) *(Tourism)*: It is a craft designed to travel above ground or water, also called a Ground-effect Machine or Hovercraft. It has varied propulsion systems. Some are equipped with a specially designed wing that lifts the craft just off the surface when it reaches a sufficient horizontal speed (the ground effect). Others are supported by fans that force air down under the vehicle to create lift. Air-cushion vehicles can attain higher speeds than ships or land vehicles. Air-cushion vehicles are not regarded as aircraft by the International Civil Aviation Organization (ICAO), and the practice is not ruled yet by governments.

Air Data Computer (ADC) *(Aeronautics)*: A navigation sensor based on atmospheric data sensors that usually measures static pressure, dynamic pressure, and outside air temperature.

Air Defense Identification Zone (ADIZ) *(Air Traffic)*: The area of airspace over land or water, where aircraft need to be indentified, located, and controlled in the interest of national security.

Air Density *(Air Traffic)*: The density of the air in terms of mass per unit of volume.

Air Freedom Rights *(Airlines)*: See Freedoms of the Air.

Air Freight Forwarder *(Airlines)*: A freight forwarder specialized in air cargo. He often consolidates the shipments of many exporters, issuing his own air waybills. He negotiates consolidated rates from airlines, is licensed by the Aeronautics Authority, and has the status of an indirect air carrier. See also Air Cargo Agent, and Forwarder.

Air/Ground Radio (A/G) *(Air Traffic)*: See Mandatory Frequency.

Air Handling Unit *(Hospitality)*: An all-air system through which steam, hot water or chilled water circulates from central boilers and chillers.

Air-inclusive *(Tourism)*: A price or a service package that includes airfare and other components, such as lodging, food and sightseeing.

Air Interface Protocol *(Airlines)*: The rules governing the way bag tags and readers communicate.

Air Law *(Airlines)*: The body of laws, rules, and regulations directly or indirectly concerned with civil aviation. Aviation in this context extends to both heavier-than-air and lighter-than-air aircraft. A 1784 decree of the Paris police forbidding balloon flights without a special permit is considered to be the earliest air law legislation. The development of air transport after World War I upraised the need for regulation, both national and international. The first International Convention for Air Navigation, commonly called the Paris Convention was signed 1919. It recognized the sovereignty of each state over its air space and stated the requirement that each aircraft must have a registered nationality. The second air law body is known as The Warsaw Convention on International Carriage by Air signed in 1929. In the main part of the dispositions, it determined that the owner or operator of the carrier is liable for any injury, death, or damage to baggage and cargo. Other important international agreements were accorded in Chicago in 1944, when 53 countries signed the Chicago Convention that introduced the International Transit Agreement and the International Traffic

Agreement. Additional treaties and agreements have been signed later to regulate the international air transport. Every country has its own sets of air laws governing the use of the space for transport purposes. In the broadest sense, Air Law is concerned to all law connected with the use of the air, including radio and satellite transmissions.

Air Mass *(Geography)*: A very large body of atmosphere defined by essentially similar air temperatures and moisture throughout its horizontal levels.

Air Mile *(Airlines)*: A unit of distance measuring approximately 6,076 feet or 1.6 kilometers.

Air Passenger Duty *(Airlines)*: Charge payable on tickets for flights departing from some countries.

Air Passes *(Airlines)*: Passes for travel flown on the same airlines, created for travelers who need to take many domestic flights in one country. Air passes contain a minimum number of flight coupons and have to be bought outside the country where they will be used.

Air Piracy *(Airlines, Air law)*. The appropriation or hijacking of an aircraft by force during a flight. See Hijacking.

Air Pressure *(Geography)*: 1. The force created by air over a surface. 2. The weight of the atmosphere over a given point that equals approximately to 14.7 pounds (6.8 kg) of force on every square inch at sea level.

Air Rage *(Airlines)*: A phenomenon in which airline passengers express an uncontrolled anger in aggressive or violent behavior.

Air Route Surveillance Radar (ARSR) *(Air Traffic)*: A radar of the Air Route Traffic Control Center (ARTCC) that detects and displays an aircraft's position en route between terminal areas. The ARSR allows controllers to provide air traffic control service when aircraft are in its area.

Air Route Traffic Control Center (ARTCC) *(Air Traffic)*: A Control Center in the United States, which supervises aircraft's navigation in a particular region of airspace at high altitudes between airport approaches and departures.

Air/sea *(Tourism)*: A term referring to arrangements or fares that include both air and land services as in a cruise package with air included.

Air Shuttle *(Airlines)*: Flights operating over regular and frequent routes, not requiring prior reservation.

Air Speed Indicator *(Aeronautics)*: An instrument that measures the air speed of an aircraft through an air mass.

Air Taxi *(Aeronautics)*: A small aircraft operating within a limited range of no more than 250 miles with restricted seating capacity (10, 15, maximum 19 passengers).

Air Terminal *(Airlines)*: A building located in an airport or near an airport where passengers gather before their flight departs or from which they leave after their flight arrives.

Air Traffic *(Aviation)*: Traffic generated by the circulation or movement of aircraft in the air.

Air Traffic Control (ATC) *(Air Traffic)*: A service provided by appropriate authority through ground-based controllers who direct aircraft on the ground and in the air. A controller's main task is to keep aircraft away from each other by use of lateral, vertical and longitudinal separation. Other of their important responsibilities is to ensure safe, orderly and expeditious flow of traffic, and to provide information to pilots, such as weather, navigation information, and Notices to Airmen (NOTAMs). To ensure communication, all pilots and all controllers everywhere are required to speak and understand English. They may use any compatible language in their respective regions, but English must be used if requested. ATC's services are available to all users (private, military, and commercial).

Air Traffic Control System Command Center (ATCSCC) *(Air Traffic)*: Usually known as Command Center, it is the largest and most sophisticated facility of its kind in the world, using the most advanced automation tools enabling the Command Center to manage the US National Airspace System (NAS) in an efficient way. It is aimed to planning and regulating the flow of air traffic in order to reduce delays and avoid congestion while maximizing the overall operation.

Air Traffic Controller *(Air Traffic)*: A person at an air traffic control tower or radar approach control facility that monitors and directs the takeoffs, coordinates the safe, orderly and expeditious flow of air traffic within a delimited airspace, and supervises the landing of airplanes.

Air Transportation *(Aviation)*: The commercial activity to convey people, cargo, and mail by aircraft vehicles.

Air Transportation *(Cruise)*: The optional, extra-cost air travel portion of the cruise package.

Air Transportation Association (ATA) *(Organizations)*: Founded in 1936, it is a trade organization for the principal U.S. airlines. Its core purpose is to support and assist its members by promoting the air transport industry and the safety, cost effectiveness, and technological advancement of its operations, as well as advocating common industry positions before state and local governments.

Air Travel *(Airlines)*: A type of travel made by air, using an airplane. Air travels start and end at a commercial airport, where a set of procedures have to be completed, such as passenger and baggage check-in, security, migration, customs and health controls.

Air Travel Card *(Airlines)*: A credit card sponsored by an airline, good to purchase air travel only. It is also known as the Universal Air Travel Plan Card (UATP)._

Air Travel Organizer's Licence *(Airlines/Tourism)*: A document issued by a Civil Aviation Authority to a business before selling air packages.

Air Walls *(Hospitality)*: Portable flat section panels that are used to divide a large room into smaller areas, as in a meeting saloon.

Air Waybill (AWB) *(Airlines)*: A bill of landing issued to cover the transportation of goods to a specific destination either on international or domestic flights. This is a non-negotiable document of air transportation, stating that the carrier accepts the goods handed by the shipper to carry the consignment to the airport of destination according to specified conditions. According to IATA, the AWB is a contract between the shipper and airline that states the terms and conditions of transportation. There are two types of air waybills:

1. The Airline Air Waybill, with preprinted identification of the issuing carrier; and,

2. The Neutral Air Waybill without preprinted identification of the issuing carrier that can be used by companies other than air

carriers.

Air Waybill Data (MAWB) *(Airlines)*: An electronic "document" that eliminates the need for paper AWB or data re-entry.

Air Waybill Data Message (FWB) *(Airlines)*: Standard Cargo IMP message identifier for electronic Master.

Airborne *(Aeronautics)*: Something supported only by aerodynamic forces, that is, something that is conveyed by or through the air.

Airbridge *(Airlines)*: A covered passage attached to the plane door by which passengers can embark and disembark between an airport terminal and an aircraft.

Airbus *(Aeronautics)*: A European aircraft constructor. Airbus was officially formed in 1970 as a consortium of France's *Aerospatiale* and *Deutsche Airbus*. A short time later Spain's *CASA* joined the consortium. In 1974 the *Airbus Industrie GIE*, as it was known (*Groupe d'Intérêt Economique*) moved its headquarters from Paris to Toulouse. *British Aerospace* joined Airbus Industrie in 1979. Each of the four partners acquired special responsibilities for producing parts of the aircraft that are transported to Toulouse for final assembly. Their initial and successful productions were the A300/A310 Family, the A320 Family and the long-range A330/A340 Family. Airbus put the seal on its successful evolution with the unveiling, in January 2005, of the A380, the world's largest and most advanced passenger aircraft.

Aircraft *(Aeronautics)*: Any vehicle built to travel through the air. Specifically, a transport vehicle certified as airworthy by a competent aeronautical authority.

Aircraft Code *(Airlines)*: An alphanumerical code created by ICAO and IATA to identify types of aircraft. Below is a simple list of IATA and ICAO Aircraft Type Designators.

IATA Code	ICAO Code	Manufacturer and Aircraft Type / Model
340	A340	Airbus A340 all models
380	A380	Airbus A380 pax
733	B733	Boeing 737-300 pax
744	B744	Boeing 747-400 pax
ACP	AC68	Gulfstream/Rockwell (Aero) Commander
B15	BA11	British Aerospace (BAC) One Eleven 500 / RomBAC One Eleven
CCJ	CL60	Canadair Challenger
CCX	GLEX	Canadair Global Express
D1C	DC10	Douglas DC-10-30/40 pax
D95	DC95	Douglas DC-9-50 pax
E70	E170	Embraer 170
E90	E190	Embraer 190
F50	F50	Fokker 50
F70	F70	Fokker 70
IL9	IL96	Ilyushin IL96 pax
L15	L101	Lockheed L-1011 500 Tristar pax
L1F	L101	Lockheed L-1011 Tristar Freighter

Aircraft Configuration *(Airlines)*: An arrangement or layout of an airplane's interior

Aircraft, Narrowbody *(Aviation)*: Single-aisle airplanes, such as Airbus A319 and A320; Boeing 727, 737, and 757; McDonnell Douglas DC9, MD80, MD87, MD90; and all other commercial aircraft not listed as wide bodies.

Aircraft on Ground (AOG) *(Airlines)*: An AOG is an aircraft that has been grounded and is unable to fly for a problem serious enough to prevent the aircraft from flying. It has first boarding priority when it returns to service.

Aircraft Stand *(Airlines)*: An area at an airport where aircraft park.

Airdrome *(Airlines)*: A term once used in the U.S. for Aerodrome. Both terms are considered obsolete.

Airfield *(Airlines)*: A term used in the United Kingdom for

Aerodrome.

Airflow *(Aeronautics)*: The motion of air molecules as they flow around an object, such as a wing.

Airfoil *(Aeronautics)*: Any device that provides reactive force when the plane is in motion relative to the surrounding environment. Airfoils, such as a wing, aileron, or rudder can lift or control a plane in flight.

Airframe *(Aviation)*: The structure of an aircraft including the fuselage, wings, empennage, landing gear, and engine mounts, excluding engines, tires and accessories.

AIRIMP *(GDS)*: Code meaning "ARC, IATAN Reservations Interline Message Procedures." It is the name of a communication system created by ARC and IATAN for reservation purposes.

AIRIMP Codes *(GDS)*: The set of codes used in airline reservation and communication procedures.

Airline *(Airlines)*: Any commercial company providing air transport services for passengers or freight, on the basis of an authorized operating certificate or license. To supply these services, airlines lease or own their aircraft with and may form partnerships or alliances with other airlines for mutual benefit.

Airline Alliance *(Airlines)*: An agreement between airlines to cooperate in the commercial air transport business on defined levels. The extent of cooperation differs according to the type of the alliance. Alliances were born when Lufthansa, United Airlines, and a few other airlines formed the Star Alliance in 1997. Today more than 50 of the world's largest airlines are alliance members. The three largest alliances are, in its order of size: Star Alliance, SkyTeam, and Oneworld. They carry approximately 60 percent of airline traffic globally. Cargo carriers formed recently the WOW Alliance. Alliances provide a wide range of benefits to both international passengers and the airlines themselves. Alliance members benefit mainly by an optimization of their networks, and cost reduction. The benefits for the traveler can consist of: Lower prices due to a decrease of operational costs, more flights to choose, more destinations, a wide range of airport lounges, and mileage rewards by earning miles for a single account on several different carriers. By May 2007, Star Alliance was formed by 32 airlines, transporting 492.8 million passengers to 965 destinations; Sky Team grouped 15 airlines transporting 427.6 million passengers to 841 destinations; Oneworld comprised 11 carriers and transported 320 million passengers to 700 destinations.

Airline Appointed Agency *(Airlines)*. A travel agency qualified by IATA, IATAN, or other authorized body, to sell air transportation services.

Airline Codes *(GDS)*: The two-digit alphabetic or alphanumeric code or the three-digit numeric indicators that identify specifically each airline in GDS systems, tickets, or any means of communication.

Airline Designator *(GDS)*: Two or three-digit alpha, numeric or alphanumeric code assigned to every airline.

Airline Fare *(Airlines)*: Price charged for air transportation between designated points of origin and destination. There is a large amount of airline fare types that change according to the type of class of service, type of trip, season, market conditions, etc. Some of the broad categories are: Normal, Excursion, Promotional, Discounted, and Advance Purchase.

Airline Passenger's Bill of Rights *(Airlines)*: Due to some irregular services airlines provide, a coalition of air travelers are filing a project to obtain from the US congress the establishment of an Airline Passenger's Bill of Rights that protect their rights at present presumably ignored.

Airline Plate *(Airlines)*: A metal plate which was given to travel agencies by Airlines in past times for the purpose to enable them to issue, print, and validate tickets. See also plates.

Airline-related Guests *(Hospitality)*: Airplane crew members and passengers who need emergency accommodations.

Airline Self Service Kiosk (ASSK) *(Airlines)*: Small installation set up by an air carrier for passengers self service.

Airliner *(Airlines)*: A passenger-carrying aircraft operated by an airline.

Airlines Reporting Corporation (ARC) *(Airlines)*: An airline-owned autonomous corporation created to assist the travel industry with financial services, data products and accreditation services, ticket distribution, and settlement in the territory of the United States. It also provides the method to control the disbursement of commissions to travel agencies. ARC provides such services for over 150 air and rail carriers and more than 20,000 ARC-accredited Travel Agency locations and Corporate Travel Departments.

Airplane *(Aeronautics)*: A heavier than air fixed-wing vehicle, driven by a propeller or jet engine and supported by the reaction of the air against its wings.

Airport *(Airlines)*: A place where aircraft regularly take off and land as part of the process of the air transport service. It counts with facilities specially designed to accommodate the landing and taking off operations and buildings for passengers to wait in, board and disembark.

Airport Acceptance Rate (AAR) *(Air Traffic)*: AAR represents the number of arrivals an airport is able to accept each hour. It is also called Airport Arrival Rate.

Airport Access Fee *(Car Rental)*: A fee paid to an airport administration by a car rental company to have the rights of operating its vehicles on the airport grounds, for the costumer's service.

Airport Apron *(Airlines)*: The part of the airport set aside for loading, unloading or maintaining aircraft.

Airport Arrival Rate (AAR) *(Air Traffic)*: See Airport Acceptance Rate.

Airport Art *(Airlines)*: Name given to souvenirs sold at airports.

Airport Capacity *(Air Traffic)*: The maximum number of aircraft operations that can be safely accomplished at an airport.

Airport Codes *(Airlines)*: Three-letter codes used to identify airports. Each airport has a unique three letter code. Cities with only one airport or with a main airport have the same code as the airport. Example: YYC code for city of Calgary and Calgary International Airport. When several Airports serve a city, each airport has its own code. Example: YYZ for Pearson International Airport of Toronto, YTZ for Toronto City Centre Airport, while YTO is the city code for Toronto.

Airport Concession Recovery and Facility Fee *(Car Rental)*: A fee charged by some airports to rental companies for every customer transaction. Rental car companies usually pass this surcharge on to their customers either directly or indirectly.

Airport Embarkation Tax *(Airlines)*: A charge imposed for embarking at an airport.

Airport Facility Directory (A/FD) *(Air Traffic)*: A manual for pilots providing complete information on U.S. airports, and other aviation facilities and procedures. It is published in seven volumes with information from the Federal Aviation Administration (FAA) and the National Aviation Charting Office (NACO), covering the U.S. territory, including Puerto Rico, and the U.S. Virgin Islands.

Airport Facility Fee *(Car Rental)*: See Concession Recovery Fee.

Airport Hotel *(Hospitality)*: A hotel located near a public airport. Although airport hotels vary widely in size and service levels, they are generally full-service and are more likely than other hotels to have in-room entertainment, computerized management systems and call accounting systems.

Airport Identifier *(Aviation)*: A specific combination of four letters or a combination of letters and numbers, assigned by the local authority to each airport as recognition sign.

Airport Lounge *(Airlines)*: Also called Executive Lounge or VIP Lounge, it is a place in the airport where travelers can spend their time after check-in while waiting to board the plane. Most airlines provide such lounges exclusively for Business and First Class passengers.

Airport Surcharge *(Car Rental)*: A fee that is paid for picking up a car at the airport. This can be a flat fee or a percentage of the total rental charge depending on country and supplier. This tax can be avoided by picking up the car at a convenient location in town.

Airport Surveillance Radar (ASR) *(Air Traffic)*: Approach control radar used to detect and display an aircraft's position in the terminal area. ASR provides range and horizontal direction information but not elevation data. Coverage of the ASR can extend up to 60 miles.

Airport Tax *(Airlines)*: A tax levied by airports on air transportation and passed along to passengers.

Airport Traffic Control Tower (ATCT) *(Air Traffic)*: A terminal facility that provides air traffic control services to aircraft operating in the vicinity of an airport or on the movement area. The ATCT authorizes aircraft to takeoff or land at the airport controlled by the tower or to transit the airspace area. A tower may also provide approach control services using radar or non-radar means.

Airport Transfer *(Tourism)*: A transport service provided by a tour operator to a passenger from an airport to a hotel, from a hotel to an airport, from the airport to a pier, or from a pier to an airport. It is usually prepaid as part of a package tour, but available separately as well

Airports Council International (ACI) *(Organizations)*: An entity that groups 580 members operating over 1647 airports in 175 countries and territories. ACI provides members and outside parties with statistical information needed to manage their business strategies and planning. By May 2008, ACI members were handling around 4.4 billion passengers, 86 million metric tones of freight, and 72 million aircraft movements.

Airship *(Aeronautics)*: The generic term for any dirigible or powered lighter-than-air vehicle, including blimps and zeppelins. Until the 1930 years, the word was used to refer to both lighter-than-air and heavier-than-air craft. At present it is used generally for lighter-than-air craft.

Airsickness *(Airlines)*: A motion sickness experienced while traveling by air (especially during turbulence) that appears in visible form of nausea or other discomfort.

Airside *(Airlines)*: Area beyond the passport and security check areas.

Airspace or Air Space *(Aviation)*: Airspace means the portion of the atmosphere extended above the land and maritime territory of a particular country. A basic principle of international air law accepted worldwide is that every state has complete and exclusive sovereignty over the airspace above its territory, including its territorial sea. This principle was unequivocally affirmed in the "Paris Convention on the Regulation of Aerial Navigation" of 1919, and was restated in the "Chicago Convention on International Civil Aviation" of 1944. So, airspace is now generally accepted as an appurtenance of the subjacent territory sharing its legal status. It follows from this principle that every state is entitled to regulate the entry of foreign aircraft into its territory and that persons within its territory are subject to its laws.

Airspeed *(Aeronautics)*: The speed of an aircraft relative to its surrounding air mass.

Airstrip *(Air Traffic)*: A synonym with "runway".

Airway *(Aeronautics)*: An established route for airplanes. See also Jet Way.

Airworthiness *(Aeronautics)*: A term that describes an aircraft is legally and mechanically fit or ready for operation in the air.

Airworthy *(Aeronautics)*: The condition of being capable to fly, usually referring to an airplane's mechanical status.

Airy *(Aeronautics)*: A standard model for computing earth data.

Aka, a.k.a. *(GDS)*: Code meaning Also known as.

AKDT *(Geography)*: See Alaska Daylight Time.

AKL *(GDS)*: Three-letter IATA code for Auckland, important city in New Zealand.

AKST *(Geography)*: See Alaska Standard Time.

Alaska Daylight Time (AKDT) *(Geography)*: AKDT is 8 hours behind of Coordinated Universal Time (UTC). AKDT is used during summer in most of the state of Alaska, except Aleutian Islands west of 169.30 (which use HADT).

Alaska Standard Time (AST) *(Geography)*: AKST is 9 hours behind of Coordinated Universal Time (UTC). AKST is used during winter in most of the state of Alaska, except Aleutian Islands west of 169.30 West (which use HAST).

Albedo *(Climate)*: It is a radiation value which indicates the amount of incoming solar radiation reflected by a surface.

Albergo *(Hospitality)*: Italian name for hotel.

Alberta Clipper *(Geography)*: A storm system so named because it originates in the Canadian Rockies of Alberta, Canada. Also known as Canadian Clipper, it is a fast moving low pressure area which generally affects the central provinces of Canada and parts of the Upper Midwest and Great Lakes regions of the United States, bringing snow, strong winds, and chilly weather. Most clippers occur between December and February, but can also occur occasionally in the month of November.

Alcock and Brown *(Airlines)*: Captain John Alcock and Lieutenant Arthur W. Brown were two British officers, the first persons to make a non-stop transatlantic flight on June 14, 1919. They departed from St. Johns, Newfoundland, and after 16 hours they arrived in Clifton, Ireland, using a modified Vickers Vimy biplane bomber.

Alcoholic Beverage Menu *(Hospitality)*: A menu that lists cocktails, wines, and other alcoholic beverages which can be listed on a separate menu or included on the regular menu. Restaurants with a large selection of wines usually have a separate wine list. Many beverage menus also include no-alcohol or low-alcohol drinks.

Alcoholic Content *(Hospitality)*: The amount of alcohol in a wine or beer.

Alcove *(Hospitality)*: A recess or niche opening in the wall of a room, as for a bed, books, etc. When built outdoors, it usually has a roof or other covering structure

Ale *(Hospitality)*: A brew that is top-fermented at high temperatures and contains more hops than do most beers, resulting in a characteristic bitter taste.

Alert Area *(Air Traffic)*: Airspace with an unusual type of aerial activity, such as a high volume of pilot training exercises that are not hazardous to aircraft. Alert Areas are depicted on aeronautical charts for the information of non-participating pilots. All activities within an Alert Area are conducted in accordance with aeronautical regulations, and pilots of participating aircraft as well as pilots transiting the area are equally responsible for collision avoidance.

Alfa *(Airlines)*: Designator for the letter "A" in the International Phonetic Alphabet.

Alfresco *(Hospitality)*: A term to denote something happening in the open air, as in alfresco dining.

ALG *(GDS)*: Three-letter IATA code for Algiers, capital city of Algeria.

Algotherapy *(Tourism)*: Therapeutic use of heated seaweed wraps in spa treatments to relieve pain and stress. Seaweed is a mild sedative with anti-inflammatory and analgesic properties.

Alien *(Tourism)*: A resident born in a foreign country.

Alignment *(Hospitality)*: The action to bring things into line. See also Orientation.

All-Cargo Aircraft *(Aeronautics)*: A version of an aircraft configured to carry cargo and mail.

All-Expense Tour *(Tourism)*: A tour offering all or most services (such as transportation, lodging, meals, sight-seeing, and so on) for a pre-established price. The term "all-expense" is a concept different to "all-inclusive," since not every tour rate covers everything. The terms and conditions of a tour contract should specify exactly what is covered.

All-in *(Tourism)*: A term meaning "All Inclusive", as in a tour.

All Inclusive *(Tourism)*: A tour package which includes transportation, accommodation, meals and drinks (as specified). In this case, the price covers all listed elements of the package. The term refers also to a resort offering a plan that includes all meals, drinks, tips, service charges, accommodations, entertainment, some water sports, etc.

All-risk Clause *(Airlines)*: An insurance provision that covers goods against loss or damage, except those self caused. See All Risk Insurance.

All Risk Insurance *(Airlines)*: A clause included in insurance policies to cover loss and damage from external causes, such as fire, collision, pilferage, etc. but not against innate defects in the goods, such as faulty or improper packing, nor against war, strikes, riots and civil commotions.

All-suite *(Hospitality)*: A term depicting a hotel where all rooms are suites with a separate living space and/or kitchen facilities.

All-suite Hotel *(Hospitality)*: A hotel configured to feature suites. A suite is an accommodation larger than the typical hotel room, with a living space separate from the bedroom. Sometimes a suite can also have a kitchenette or a whirlpool.

All-terrain Vehicle *(Tourism)*: A powered or unpowered vehicle with large wheels designed for recreational use out of roads, on uneven ground or sand. Their use demands a careful driving, since their circulation can damage notably the vegetation and degrade natural environments.

Alleyway *(Cruise)*: A narrow passage on a ship.

Alliance *(Airlines)*: A term for airlines that have grouped together to reach a stronger identity and larger market share. An alliance permits the associated airlines to collaborate in offering loyalty rewards. Examples are StarAlliance, Oneworld and Skyteam. See

Airline Alliance.

Alliance Fare *(Airlines)*: A fare offered by airlines grouped in an "alliance".

Allocentric *(Tourism)*: The term describes a person who is adventurous, likes to travel to exotic destinations, and who enjoys frequently traveling by unusual forms of transportation. Allocentric travelers generally spend more money than psychocentric travelers.

Allotment *(Airlines/Cruise)*: The number of seats, cabins, berths, etc. assigned for sale by a supplier to an agent.

Allowance, Free Baggage *(Airlines)*: The baggage which may be carried by the passenger without additional payment. See Free Baggage Allowance.

Aloha *(Tourism)*: A Hawaiian term meaning both "hello" and "good-bye."

Alongside *(Cruise)*: A term referring to the side of a ship. It also describes a ship that is located next to a pier or another vessel.

ALPA *(Organizations)*: An acronym for Airline Pilots Association.

Alphabet, Phonetic *(Airlines)*: See Phonetic Alphabet.

Alphanumeric *(Airlines)*: A term referring to codes composed of both letters and numbers, as in a Passenger Name Record.

Alpinism *(Tourism)*: The practice of climbing high mountains either on snow, ice or rock, assisted with suitable equipment.

Alt *(Hospitality)*: A brew much like British ale. Its name derives from a German word that means old, and illustrates it is made by the ancient method of top-fermenting.

Alternate Distribution System *(Airlines)*: 1. Any system that avoids the mediation of travel agents in selling travel products. It is typically used to permit general public to by air tickets through personal computers. 2. The term refers also to a distribution system created to compete with the major GDS suppliers.

Alternative Fuel *(Tourism)*: Any non-conventional fuel that are used to power machines, such as biodiesel, ethanol, butanol, hydrogen, non-fossil methane, non-fossil natural gas, vegetable oil and other biomass sources.

Alternate Operator Service (AOS) *(Hospitality)*: A long-distance telephone operator-service provider that supplies its own operator but leases a network from another common carrier.

Alternate Restaurant *(Cruise)*: A restaurant on a cruise ship where passengers are obliged to pay the full cost of the meal or a service charge. In all-inclusive modality meals are included in the price of the cruise.

Alternative Tourism *(Tourism)*: A type of tourism that seeks to avoid adverse impacts and enhance positive social, cultural and environmental features, which is perceived as alternative to mass tourism. For this reason alternative tourism is sometimes called responsible or green tourism. It is a tourism activity of smaller scale in terms of the number of tourists and the dimensions of tourism development.

Altimeter *(Aeronautics)*: An instrument which displays the altitude above mean sea level (MSL) of an aircraft.

Altiport *(Aeronautics)*: An airport situated in a high location of a mountainous region.

Altitude *(Geography)*: A measure of elevation or height of something above a specific level, specially, above sea level or above the earth's surface.

Altitude Error *(Air Traffic)*: A basic output from guidance to flight director, indicating the difference between actual altitude and desired altitude.

Altocumulus *(Geography)*: White or gray layers or patches of cloud, often with a waved appearance.

Altostratus *(Geography)*: An extended cloud formation of bluish or grayish sheets or layers.

Altruistic Travel *(Tourism)*: A voluntary movement accomplished by conscientious consumers and responsible travel companies who are donors of specific resources, such as economic patronage, time and talent to protect the cultures and environments they visit. It is also called Travel Philanthropy.

Alumni Rates *(Cruise)*: A phrase used for fares reserved for passengers who have previously sailed with a cruise line.

Alumni Rates *(Tourism)*: Fares assigned to tours designed for people who have previously traveled with the tour company. They are also called Reunion Tours.

AM or A.M *(Tourism)*: Ante Meridiem, term used in 12 hour clocks for the period between midnight and midday.

Amadeus *(GDS)*: A European Global Distribution System owned by Air France, Continental Airlines, Iberia and Lufthansa.

Amaxophobia *(Tourism)*: A term used for morbid fear of riding a vehicle or to be in a vehicle.

Ambassador *(Tourism)*: A diplomatic official accredited to a foreign country or government, or to an international organization, who serves as the official representative of his or her own country.

Ambiance *(Hospitality)*: The overall look and feeling or identity of a restaurant, hotel. Also the mood or atmosphere it creates by the combination of decor, lighting, furnishings, and other elements. The term, synonymous with atmosphere, is a feeling or mood associated with a particular place, person, or thing.

Ambient Air Temperature *(Hospitality)*: The surrounding inside air temperature, usually considered ideal for human comfort at 18° to 24°C (65° to 75°F).

Ambient Intelligence (AMI) *(Computing)*: It is a current happening of a vision of the future where we are surrounded by electronic environments, sensitive and responsive to the presence of people. In an ambient intelligence world, devices work in concert to support people in performing their everyday life activities, tasks and rituals in easy, natural way by means of the information and intelligence hidden in the network that connects the devices. As devices develop smaller, more connected and more integrated into our environment, it seems the technology disappears into our surroundings, remaining perceivable only the user interface. For around 40 years individuals had to get adapted to what the computer could do for them, having their thoughts dominated by the PC, keyboard and mouse; now with ambient intelligence the computer must adapt to the individual.

Ambient Lighting *(Hospitality)*: Light element that provides atmosphere and holds together varied components of the decor.

Amenities *(Hospitality)*: In general, it is a feature that increases attractiveness, value, or desirability, and increases the guest's or user's satisfaction. In hospitality, it is a service or item offered to guests. Amenity items are placed in guestrooms for the comfort and convenience of guests, at no extra cost. Examples of guest services offered as amenities are: In-room entertainment systems, automatic check-out, free parking, concierge services, and multilingual staff. Amenities are designed to increase a hotel's appeal, enhance a guest's stay, and encourage guests to return.

Amenity Package *(Tourism)* A bundle of special features, for example, complimentary excursions, bar or boutique credit, or wine at dinner offered to clients on a given tour or cruise, usually as a bonus or extra feature. It is used to induce clients to book through a particular travel agency or organization.

American Association for Nude Recreation *(Organizations)*: The American Association for Nude Recreation is the largest, most long-established organization of its kind in North America. It was created in 1931 and currently has nearly 50,000 members coming from the United States, Canada, Mexico, and beyond. The association advocates nudity and nude recreation in appropriate settings, and educates and informs society of the value and enjoyment of such through on-going member growth. It is based in Kissimmee, Florida.

American Hotel & Lodging Association (AH&LA) *(Organizations)*: AH&LA is the US national association representing all sectors and stakeholders in the lodging industry, including individual hotel property members, hotel companies, student and faculty members, and industry suppliers.

American Hotel & Motel Association (AH&MA) *(Hospitality)*: A federation of state and regional hotel associations that offers benefits and services to hospitality properties and suppliers. AH&MA works over legislation concerning hotels, sponsors seminars and group study programs, conducts research, and publishes Lodging magazines. The Educational Institute of AH&MA is the world's largest developer of hospitality industry training materials.

American Plan *(Hospitality)*: A hotel or resort occupation plan that includes three meals a day (breakfast, lunch and dinner). It is sometimes referred to as Full Plan, commonly abbreviated as "AP".

American Society of Travel Agents (ASTA) *(Organizations)*: A large association of travel professionals, including travel agents and suppliers. Founded in 1931 as the American Steamship and

Tourist Agents' Association, ASTA comprises now the world's largest and most influential travel trade association with over 20.000 members in 140 countries. The mission of ASTA and its affiliated organizations is to facilitate the business of selling travel through effective representation, shared knowledge and the enhancement of professionalism.

AMFORHT *(Organizations)*: An acronym for World Association for Hospitality and Tourism Education and Training.

AMI *(Computing)*: See Ambient Intelligence.

Amidships *(Cruise)*: At or toward the part of a ship halfway between the bow and stern. It is the imaginary line that runs down the center of a ship. Toward the middle of a ship, usually, the most part of the vessel.

Amidships Antebellum *(Tourism)*: The term describes a building and/or period of time prior to the Civil War, such as an antebellum mansion on a cotton plantation in the southern US.

Amphibian, Amphibion or Amphibious *(Tourism)*: Any vehicle with retractable wheels capable of operating on land or sea, such as a Seaplane or a Floatplane.

Amplitude *(Air Traffic)*: The maximum absolute value of a periodic curve measured along its vertical axis (the height of a wave, in layman's terms).

Amplitude Modulation *(Airlines)*: A principal method of transmitting audio, visual, or other types of information using radio waves. The frequency of the carrier wave does not change but its amplitude varies according to the amplitude of the input signal. A higher wave is interpreted as a 1 and a normal wave is interpreted as a zero. By changing the wave, the RFID (Radio Frequency Identification) tag can communicate a string of binary digits to the reader. Computers can interpret these digits as digital information. The method of changing the amplitude is known as amplitude shift keying, or ASK.

AMS *(GDS)*: Three-letter IATA code for Amsterdam, capital city of the Netherlands.

AMT *(GDS)*: Code meaning Amount.

Amtrak *(Tourism)*: Is the National Railroad Passenger Corporation, owned by the U.S. federal government. It was created on May 1,

1971, to provide intercity passenger train service in the United States. "Amtrak" is a blend word resulting from the combination of "American" and "track". It operates passenger service on a 21,000 miles network connecting 500 destinations in 46 states, with some routes serving Canada. According to statistics, Amtrak transported 25.8 million passengers in 2007 and employed 19,000 people.

Amusement *(Tourism)*: An enjoyable activity such as a game, or hobby to keep somebody occupied or entertained, such as a ride, or other attraction found in an amusement park or a video arcade.

Amusement Park *(Tourism)*: An open-air recreational area consisting of stalls, side shows mechanical rides and other forms of active entertainment for a large group of people. Amusement parks appeared for the first time in Europe and evolved from fairs, pleasure gardens, world's fairs, and expositions. Although theme parks are a type of amusement parks, today both terms are often used interchangeably. See also Theme Park.

AN *(GDS)*: Code meaning Added Name.

Anaerobe *(Ecology)*: An organism that can survive in the absence of oxygen. For some organisms, such as "obligate anaerobes," oxygen is a toxic.

Anaerobic *(Ecology)*: Something that lacks or is seriously diminished of oxygen, such as certain types of bacteria that can live without atmospheric oxygen. It is opposite of aerobic.

Analogy Chart *(Geography)*: A graphic organizer which is used to show similarities.

Anchor Ball *(Cruise)*: A black shape hoisted in forepart of a ship to indicate that it is anchored in a fairway.

Anemometer *(Climate)*: It is a weather instrument which measures the speed of wind.

Angle of Attack *(Air Traffic)*: The angle at which the airstream meets the wing.

Anglophone *(Tourism)*: People who speak English, especially native speakers.

Anglosphere *(Tourism)*: A word that describes the group of nations that speak English and share historical, political, and cultural characteristics.

Angular Acceleration *(Air Traffic)*: Rate of change of angular velocity, either scalar or vector.

Angular Velocity *(Air Traffic)*: Rate of change of rotation about an axis, either scalar or vector.

Annual Temperature Range *(Climate)*: Expression referring to a temperature value which indicates the difference between the average temperature of the warmest month and the average temperature of the coolest month.

Annunciator *(Air Traffic)*: Any one of warning, caution, or advisory communications.

ANS *(GDS)*: Code meaning Answer, Answering, Answered.

Answerback Booking *(GDS)*: A booking level that ensures the record locator created in the Airline Reservation System (ARS) is transmitted back to the Computer Reservation System (CRS) for inclusion in the CRS booking file. This assures the booking did reach the ARS.

Antarctic Circle *(Geography)*: The parallel of latitude 66° 33' 39" (or 66.56083°) south of the equator. From this latitude, to the South Pole there are 24 hours of sunlight on the summer solstice (around 22 December), and 24 hours of darkness on the winter solstice (around 21 June).

Antarctica *(Geography)*: Antarctica is a continent almost entirely situated south of the Antarctic Circle, overlying the South Pole. The name Antarctica is a Romanized version of the Greek word *Antarktiké*, meaning "opposite of the Arctic". It is surrounded by the Southern Pacific, Atlantic, and Indian Oceans, and is the fifth-largest continent with an area of 14.4 million square kilometers (5.4 million square mileages). Around 95 percent of the continent is covered by an ice layer measuring an average thickness of 1.6 kilometers (1.0 miles). The coastline measures 17,968 kilometers (11,160 miles) and is mostly characterized by ice formations. Transantarctic Mountains divide the Antarctic continent in two parts. The portion west of the Weddell Sea and east of the Ross Sea is called Western Antarctica, while the remainder territory forms the Eastern Antarctica. The highest peak in this frozen continent is Vinson Massif, at 4,892 meters (16,050 feet), located in the Ellsworth Mountains. There are many volcanoes, but only Mount

Erebus is known to be active. Approximately the 90 percent of the world's ice is found in Antarctica, averaging the 70 percent of the world's fresh water. Antarctica is the coldest and driest place on the earth, with an interior territory that is actually the largest desert in the world. There are no permanent human residents due to the severe indigenous climate conditions. Only cold-adapted plants and animals survive in Antarctica. Some governments maintain scientific research stations with a number of people accomplishing missions for variable periods of time. The continent has no local government and belongs to no country, being regulated by the Antarctic Treaty of 1959 and other related agreements.

Antenna *(Airlines)*: In the process of tracking a bag, the tag antenna is the conductive element that enables the tag to send and receive data. Readers also have antennas, which are used to emit radio waves. The RF energy from the reader antenna is "harvested" by the antenna and is used to power up the microchip, which then changes the electrical load on the antenna to reflect back its own signals.

Antenna Unit *(Computing)*: The part of a system that supports the use of hand-held server terminals. Antenna units relay signals from hand-held terminals to a radio base station.

Anthropisation *(Geography)*: A French term referring to different marks left by human societies over the planet, such as agriculture, urbanization, transport infrastructures, etc.

Anti-collision *(Airlines)*: A general term used to cover methods of preventing radio waves from one device from interfering with radio waves from another. Anti-collision patterns are also used to read more than one tag in the same reader's field.

Anticyclone *(Climate)*: Is a weather phenomenon of circulating air which moves outward from a high-pressure area that forms a system of winds that rotate around a center of low atmospheric pressure. Anticyclone spirals flow in a clockwise direction in the Northern Hemisphere and counter-clockwise in the Southern Hemisphere. Anticyclones are wider systems than depressions, and they usually move slowly, impacting a region for a longer time.

Antipode *(Geography)*: A point on the earth's surface which is diametrically opposite it. It is situated in such a manner that a line drawn from the one point to the other passes through the centre of the earth and forms a true diameter.

Antipodean Day *(Airlines)*: The day "gained" by crossing the International Date Line. It is also called Meridian Day.

Anytime Dining *(Cruise)*: A flexible evening dining program that allows passengers to select from a variety of onboard restaurants during their cruise, as opposed to the "Traditional Fixed Seating" program.

ANZ *(GDS)*: Code meaning Australia and New Zealand.

AOC *(Air Traffic)*: Code meaning: 1. Airline Operations Center or Air Operators Certificate; 2. Operators Committee (Usually one at each Airport and even at each Terminal).

AOC *(Hospitality)*: A French term for *Appellation d'Origine Controllée,* which is a system of laws and rules to regulate French wine production and its quality; it is used to define its origin.

AP *(Hospitality)*: Code for American Plan.

AP *(GDS)*: Code meaning: 1. APEX Fares, Advance Purchase Excursion Fares; 2. Global Indicator for a travel via the Atlantic and Pacific oceans.

APD *(GDS)*: Code meaning Air Passenger Duty.

Aperitif Wine *(Hospitality)*: A wine traditionally served before a meal as an appetizer. Aperitif wines are often fortified and herb-flavored. Vermouth, for instance, is both fortified and flavored with herbal ingredients.

Apex (AP) *(Airlines/GDS)*: **A**dvance **P**urchase **E**xcursion Fare. It is an airline term meaning a fare which must be booked and paid for in advance to the departure date, one of the least expensive fares.

Apex Fares *(Airlines)*: Reduced price fares available on most of the routes. These fares must be purchased a certain number of days in advance to the travel date and are highly restricted.

APHIS *(Organizations)*: An acronym for Animal and Plant Health Inspection Service.

APO *(GDS)*: Code meaning Airport.

Apollo *(GDS)*: A global Distribution System operated by Galileo International in the United States and Mexico.

Appellation Contrôlée *(Hospitality)*: A French term meaning literally "name controlled." This notation on a wine label determines it belongs to the highest classification of French wines and is strictly regulated by a French governmental agency.

APPL *(GDS)*: Code meaning Apply, Applying, Applied.

Applicable Fare *(Airlines)*: The fare to be charged to a specific travel matching passengers' travel needs with observance of all fare construction calculations and conditions.

Application Server *(GDS)*: It is a server program in a computer within a distribution network that provides the business logic for an application program.

Appointment *(Airlines)*: The act by which a corporation, an air carrier or other supplier authorizes a travel agency to exploit a business on its behalf as its agent by exercising powers conferred for the purpose.

APPR *(Air Traffic)*: See Approach.

Approach (APPR) *(Air Traffic)*: To fly towards a point. A basic guidance mode, providing lateral guidance, longitudinal guidance, and vertical guidance to a point at an operator selected groundspeed and radar altitude.

Approach Controller *(Air Traffic)*: The air traffic control personnel responsible for all movement of incoming aircraft before arriving at the final approach.

APPV *(GDS)*: A code meaning Approve, Approved, Approving.

APR *(GDS)*: Code for April

Après-Ski *(Tourism)*: A French Term relating to post-skiing activities at a ski lodge, which comprises any activity that is arranged to operate after skiing.

Apron *(Airlines)*: Any area of an airport assigned for parking, maintenance loading and unloading of aircraft. It is opposed to runways.

APROX *(GDS)*: A code meaning Approximate, Approximately.

APS *(GDS)*: Code meaning Accessible Pedestrian Signal.

APT *(GDS)*: A code meaning: Airport. 2. Apartment, Townhouse. 3. Airline Passenger Tariff.

APU *(Aeronautics)*: Code meaning Auxiliary Power Unit of an aircraft.

Aquaerobics *(Tourism)*: Aerobic exercises performed in a swimming pool, where water provides support and resistance to strengthen muscles.

Aquavit (Akvavit) *(Hospitality)*: National beverage of the Scandinavian countries. It is smooth, light, dry, clear liquor with the flavor of caraway seed.

Aqueduct *(Tourism)*: A structure, often bridge-like, designed to convey water over a long distance. Romans Aqueducts are among the greatest engineering feats of the ancient world. Ancient Rome had eleven major aqueducts, built between 312 B.C. (*Aqua Appia*) and 226 A.D. (*Aqua Alexandrina*). The longest of them was *Anio Novus* with 59 miles long.

AR *(Airlines)*: Two-letter IATA code for *Aerolíneas Argentinas*.

Arbitrary Fare *(Airlines)*: See Add-on Fare.

Arbitration *(Airlines)*: A method of hearing and determination of a dispute by an impartial referee selected or agreed upon by the parties concerned, usually conducted under rules established by the American Arbitration Association in the US. It is intended to avoid the high costs of legal actions.

Arbitration Clause *(Airlines)*: It is a standard clause to be included in some contracts stating that any controversy or claim will be settled by arbitration in accordance with the rules of the pertinent authority, such as the American Arbitration Association in the US.

Arboretum *(Tourism)*: A park-like area in which a varied collection of plants and trees are grown for study or public display.

ARC *(Airlines)*: An acronym for Airlines Reporting Corporation.

ARC Accredited Travel Agency *(Airlines)*: A travel agency that has been qualified by ARC and assigned an identifier number to sell air transport services to retail costumers on a commission basis.

ARC List *(Airlines)*: A list of a travel agency employees entitled for travel benefits submitted to ARC or IATAN. It is also referred to as the Agent Eligibility List.

ARCS *(Air Traffic)*: Airline Routing and Connections Service.

Archimedes *(Airlines)*: Archimedes was the greatest mathematician of the ancient Greece. He was born in 287 BC in Syracuse, Sicily, and died in 212 BC in the same city. His contributions in geometry are still effective; his methods anticipated the integral calculus 2,000 years before Newton and Leibniz. A wide variety of machines including pulleys and the Archimidean screw pumping device are product of his inventions. By the year 200 BC he discovered the principle of buoyancy, stating how and why some objects float in liquids. These discoveries constitute the famous theorem called "Archimedes' Principle", which is contained in his book "On Floating Bodies." His findings were used many years later by men who intended to have hot-air-balloons flying. On the basis of Archimedes' principles, Roger Bacon theorized in 1290 A.D, that something built correctly could be supported by the air.

Archipelago *(Geography)*: A large group or chain of islands in a large body of water.

Architectural Bias *(GDS)*: A discontinued design of a GDS system favoring his sponsor by facilitating his information and booking first.

Archive *(Airlines)*: 1. To transfer data to a tape or disk for long-term storage. 2. A collection of documents or records.

Arctic Circle *(Geography)*: A parallel of latitude 66° 33' 39" (or 66.56083°) North of the equator. It is said that north of the Arctic Circle the sun remains above the horizon at midsummer midnight but never rises at midwinter. In spite of its conditions, trees grow north of the Arctic Circle such as in the Mackenzie Delta.

Area 1 *(IATA Geography)*: All of the North and South American continents and the islands adjacent thereto, Greenland, Bermuda, the West Indies and the Islands of the Caribbean Sea, the Hawaiian Island (including Midway and Palmyra).

Area 2 *(IATA Geography)*: Europe, Africa and the islands adjacent thereto, Ascension Island and that part of Asia west of the Ural Mountains, including Iran and the Middle East.

Area 3 *(IATA Geography)*: Asia and the Islands adjacent thereto (except the portion included in Area 2), the East Indies, Australia, New Zealand and the Islands of the Pacific Ocean (except those included in Area 1).

Area Bank *(Airlines)*: See Area Settlement Plan.

Area Control Center (ACC) *(Air Traffic)*: A facility that is responsible for controlling aircraft en route by instrument flight rules at high altitudes between airport approaches and departures. An ACC usually accepts traffic from, and ultimately passes traffic to the control of a Terminal Control Center or of another Center. The ACC's operations world-wide and the boundaries of the airspace each Center controls are ruled by the International Civil Aviation Organization.

Area Forecast (FA) *(Air Traffic)*: A forecast of VFR clouds and weather condition over an area.

Area Settlement Plan *(Airlines)*: A system managed by ARC to handle all the processing of airline tickets, payments, and disbursement of commissions to travel agencies.

Areas *(IATA Geography)*: IATA has divided the world in three big geographical zones identified by their particular traffic interests. These zones are called Areas and they are: Area 1 (TC1), Area 2 (TC2), and Area 3 (TC3).

ARINC *(Airlines)*: An independent, not-for-profit corporation owned by airlines and created to provide communications and other services to the Airline industry in US.

Armagnac *(Hospitality)*: A great grape brandy produced in a delineated region in southwest France. Probably second only to Cognac, Armagnac is dry, less delicate, and less ethereal than it, but compensates with a fuller body.

ARN *(GDS)*: Three-letter IATA code for Arlanda International Airport, serving the city of Stockholm, Sweden.

ARNG *(GDS)*: A code meaning Arrange, Arranging, Arranged.

ARNK *(GDS)*: Code meaning Arrival unknown. It is used to indicate the land portion of an air itinerary.

Aroma *(Hospitality)*: Part of the total smell derived from the grape fruit due to the effects of the wine maturing.

Aromatherapy *(Tourism)*: The use of essential oils from plants and flowers in spa treatments.

Aromatherapy Massage *(Tourism)*: A massage in which essential oils are applied to the body, usually combined with Swedish massage

ARPT *(Air Traffic)*: Code for Airport.

ARR *(GDS)*: A code meaning Arrive, Arriving, Arrived.

Arrival Times *(Airlines)*: The local time of arrival of a given flight usually published in timetables and GDS.

Arrival Traffic *(Air Traffic)*: Incoming aircraft to an airport.

Arrivals *(Airlines)*: The area of the airport where people pass through immigration, after disembarking, collect their baggage, pass through customs and arrange their transport into the city. On domestic flights, passengers simply collect baggage and leave the airport through Arrivals.

ARS *(Airlines)*: Airline Reservation System, the airline industry version of a CRS.

ARS *(GDS)*: Code for Argentinean Peso, the national currency of Argentina.

ARSR *(Air Traffic)*: See Air Route Surveillance Radar.

ARTA *(Organizations)*: An acronym for Association of Retail Travel Agents.

ARTCC *(Air Traffic)*: See Air Route Traffic Control Center.

Arterial Roads *(Air Traffic)*: Wide streets or major roads that carry large volumes of traffic through a community.

Artificial Beach *(Tourism)*: A beach entirely built by men. It is different to a restored beach.

Artificial Horizon *(Air Traffic)*: An instrument which enables pilots to determine the attitude of the aircraft in relation to the horizon. It helps the pilots to know whether the aircraft is nose-up, nose-down, or banking left or right.

Artificial Light *(Hospitality)*: Any light other than sunlight.

Artificial Boundary *(Geography)*: Terms defining a political boundary which does not follow a natural feature.

ARTS *(Air Traffic)*: Automated Radar Terminal System

ARUNK *(GDS)*: Alternative term for ARNK.

ARVL *(GDS)*: Code meaning Arrival.

AS *(GDS)*: Code meaning Added Segment.

ASAP *(GDS)*: Code meaning As Soon as Possible.

ASC *(GDS)*: Code meaning Advising Schedule Change.

Aseptic Canning *(Hospitality)*: A process of achieving a germ-free condition used for food products that are particularly sensitive to heat. It involves the separate sterilization of containers and contents. Once sterilized, the contents are placed into the containers and hermetically sealed in a sterile environment. This process conserves nutrients, color, taste, odor, and texture but is relatively expensive.

Asia, Geographical *(Geography)*: Asia is the largest and most populous continent of the world, covering about 30 percent of the Earth's landmass. It includes 44 countries, depending territories, and numerous islands extended over an area of 44,390,000 square kilometers (17,139,000 square miles). Its population counts over four billion people, representing around the 61 percent of the world's human population. Asia is a non-homogeneous physical entity. In regard to its size and diversity, Asia is more a cultural concept incorporating a number of regions and peoples. The word *Asia* originated from the Ancient Greek is thought was first used by Herodotus by 440 BC to describe the Persian Empire, as a region different to Greece and Egypt. Other historians say the continent is named after Prometheus' wife, or after Asias, son of Cotys, who assigned his name to a tribe in Sardis.

Mainly located on the eastern and northern hemispheres, Asia may be regarded as part of the landmass comprising Africa and Eurasia. The connection of Asia with Africa is broken by the Suez Canal between the Mediterranean Sea and the Red Sea. It lies east of the Ural Mountains, the Ural River, the Caspian Sea, the Caucasus, the Black Sea, the Bosporus and Dardanelles straits, and the Aegean Sea. Asia is bounded by the Arctic Ocean to the north; by the Bering Sea, the Sea of Okhotsk, the Pacific Ocean, the Sea of Japan, the East China Sea, the Yellow Sea, and the South China Sea to the east; by the Indian Ocean to the south; by the Arabian Sea and the Red Sea to the west. Great peninsulas extend out from the mainland, dividing the oceans into seas and bays, allowing the formation of singular tourism attractions.

Asia is a diversified continent with the highest mount in the world, the Everest (8,850 meters/ 29,035 feet) and the lowest depression, the Dead Sea (397 meters/ 15,000 feet under sea level). The Himalaya range runs from the northwest to the southeast, separating the Indian Subcontinent and the Tibetan Plateau. Although the Himalaya is a barrier for communications, it is also an important influence factor for its geography and history. Other major elevations are the Anatolia Mounts, the Caucasus Range, the Karakorum-Kuenlun Range, the Tien Shan and Altai. In the northern central part of Asia lies the Gobi desert (1,610 kilometers long by 970 kilometers wide).

The Asian continent can be divided into six regions, each with distinctive physical, cultural, economic, and political characteristics:

1. Southwest Asia (Turkey, Iran, and the nations of the Arabian Peninsula) identified by an arid climate and irrigated agriculture, great petroleum reserves, and the ascendancy of Islam;

2. South Asia (Afghanistan and the nations of the Indian subcontinent), a region isolated from the rest of Asia by great mountain barriers;

3. Southeast Asia (the southeastern countries of the peninsula and the Malay Archipelago), a monsoon region marked by the fusion of Indian and Chinese cultures, and a great diversity of ethnic groups, languages, religions, and politics;

4. East Asia, a region comprising China, Mongolia, Korea, and the islands of Taiwan and Japan, located in the mid-latitudes on the Pacific Ocean, constituting the most industrialized region of the continent.

5. Russian Asia, the vast region of Siberia and the Russian Far East.

6. The Central West Asia, a region characterized by desert conditions and ancient traditions of nomadic herding. It is formed by the group of independent former republics of the Soviet Union.

The continent is crossed by rivers, which are among the longest in the world. They generally rise in the high plateaus and flow toward the peripheral lowlands through great chains. The most important of them are: Ob-Irtysh, the Yenisei-Argana, and Lena in Siberia; the Amur, the Huang He, the Yang Tse-Kiang, and the Mekong in Southeast Asia; the Ganges-Brahmaputra, the Indus, and the Tigris-Euphrates in the South and Southwest. Interior drainages of Central Asia empty their waters into inland lakes or disappear into desert sands. The Aral Sea, Lake Baykal, and Lake Balkash are among the world's largest lakes.

Asia is the home to many natural attractions and a numerous expressions of cultures, history and religions that shape Asia's most impressive heritage.

Asia as defined by IATA *(IATA Geography)*: Is the area comprised by the countries of the South Asian Subcontinent, South East Asia, Japan, North Korea and South Korea.

Asian Countries *(IATA Geography)*: Countries located in the Continent of Asia, as defined by IATA.

ASK *(Airlines)*: See Available Seat Kilometers.

ASL *(Air Traffic)*: Above Sea Level.

ASM *(Airlines)*: Ad hoc Schedules Message.

ASP *(GDS)*: Code meaning Area Settlement Plan.

ASR *(Air Traffic)*: See Airport Surveillance Radar.

Assembly Point *(Tourism)*: A point in the itinerary where the group assembles and commences the travel together.

Asset *(Business)*: Any item of property that has monetary value, something valuable that someone owns, benefits from, or has use of, in generating income. There are fixed assets (such as cash, machinery, inventory, land and building), current assets (such as accounts receivable), and such intangibles as business good will and rights to market a product, copyright, patent, or trademark.

Assignment *(Business)*: The transfer of the rights, duties, responsibilities and/or benefits of an agreement, contract, or financial instrument to a third party.

Assimilation *(Tourism)*: The process whereby people become absorbed by a new culture, country, or surroundings. By consequence, it is a condition allowing immigrants to incorporate in the social and economic life of their adoptive countries.

ASSK *(Airlines)*: See Airlines Self Service Kiosk.

Associate Controller *(Air Traffic)*: A person who assists the radar controller.

Associated IATA Member *(Airlines)*: A carrier affiliated to IATA that either operates international non regular services or regular domestic services.

Association *(Business)*: Any group of persons who have decided to join together for a particular purpose, ranging from social to business. It can be formal (with bylaws and rules), or it can be an organization of people without legal structure.

Association *(Ecology)*: A large group of organisms in a particular area, with one or two dominant species. It can also be a group of plants growing together that form a small unit of natural vegetation.

Association of Corporate Travel Executives (ACTE) *(Organizations)*: A not-for-profit association established to provide executive-level global education and networking opportunities. It was founded in 1988 by corporate travel suppliers and buyers seeking to establish equitable representation within the travel management profession. ACTE has offices in Canada, Germany, the United States, Asia, Argentina, Mexico, and South Africa, and provides support to its members in over 50 countries worldwide. It also hosts or co-hosts more than 60 events and reach more than 6,000 executives each year.

Association of Retail Travel Agents (ARTA) *(Organizations)*: ARTA was formed in 1962, by a group of retail travel agents to be the voice of the small and independent travel agents across the United States and Canada. Its two primary activities are centered on providing educational and training opportunities to all levels of agents, and representation of their point of view before industry, government, and consumer organizations.

Association of Travel Agents of America (ATAA) *(Organizations)*: An association of travel agencies, organized to promote professionalism in the travel industry, and to serve as a unified voice for the industry. ATAA is aimed to be the industry leader in providing affordable, innovative and exciting educational opportunities for its members including partnering with other industry sources while creating programs of value to them. ATAA was established as Arizona Travel Agents Association in 1983, but in 2002 it adopted the new name to better reflect the spirit of its membership.

Association of Travel Marketing Executives (ATME) *(Organizations)*: The association was established in 1980 as a non-profit organization. It is a professional organization gathering experienced and innovative travel industry marketers who represent all segments of the industry, including airlines, hotels and resorts, cruise lines, tour operators, online travel companies and initiatives, local, state, and international tourist offices, car rental companies, technology and marketing solution providers, and media executives. ATME is the only worldwide organization of its kind to provide members with an ongoing forum for the exchange of creative ideas and effective marketing solutions within the travel industry.

ASST *(GDS)*: A code meaning Assist, Assisting, Assisted

AST *(Geography)*: See Atlantic Standard Time.

ASTA *(Organizations)*: See American Society of Travel Agents.

ASTA Business Number *(Airlines)*. An alphanumeric code issued by ASTA to its members, keeping a IATA format.

Astern *(Cruise)*: At or towards the stern, the back of a vessel.

Astronomical Latitude *(Air Traffic)*: Latitude measured with respect to vector of apparent gravity.

Astronomical Year *(Geography)*: See Solar Year.

ASU *(GDS)*: Three-letter IATA code for Asuncion, the capital city of Paraguay.

Asylum *(General)*: Refuge given by one country to a citizen of another country, with the purpose to protect that person from arrest or persecution. See Political Asylum.

Asylum Seeker *(General)*: A person who has entered a country (legally or illegally), and who "owing to well-founded fear of being persecuted for reasons of race, religion, nationality, membership of a particular social group or political opinion, is outside the country of his nationality and is unable, or owing to such fear, is unwilling to avail himself of the protection of that country; or who, not having a nationality and being outside the country of his former habitual residence as a result of such events, is unable or, owing to such fear, is unwilling to return to it." (Article 1, (2) of the United Nations Convention Relating to the Status of Refugees).

AT *(GDS)*: Code meaning: 1. Air Traffic; 2. Global Indicator for a travel via the Atlantic Ocean.

ATA *(GDS)*: Code meaning: 1. Actual Time of Arrival; 2. An acronym for Air Transport Association.

ATAA *(Organizations)*: An acronym for Association of Travel Agents of America.

ATB *(GDS)*: Code meaning "Automated Ticket and Boarding Pass." It was an electronically generated ticket including the boarding pass, which was used before May 31, 2008.

ATBP *(Airlines)*: An IATA term meaning Amount to Be Prorated.

ATC *(Airlines)*: Code meaning: 1. Air Traffic Conference of America, the predecessor to ARC; 2. Air Traffic Control; 3. Air Travel Card.

ATCSCC *(Air Traffic)*: An acronym for Air Traffic Control System Command Center.

ATCT *(Air Traffic)*: An acronym for Airport Traffic Control Tower.

ATD *(GDS)*: Code meaning Actual Time of Departure.

ATFDS *(GDS)*: Code meaning Automated Ticket and Fare Determination System.

ATH *(GDS)*: Three-letter IATA code for Athens, capital city of Greece.

Athwart *(Cruise)*: At right angles to a ship's keel.

ATME *(Organizations)*: An acronym for Association of Travel Marketing Executives.

Atmospheric Data *(Air Traffic)*: Environmental data related to the atmosphere at some point of interest.

ATIS *(Air Traffic)*: See Automatic Terminal Information Service.

ATL *(GDS)*: An abbreviation for: 1. Three-letter IATA code for Atlanta, Georgia, USA. 2. Three-letter IATA code for Hartsfield Atlanta International serving the city of Atlanta.

Atlantic Daylight Time (ADT) *(Geography)*: ADT is 3 hours behind of Coordinated Universal Time (UTC). ADT is a daylight saving time effective in summer time zone. It is generally only used during the summer in the following places: Most of the mainland Labrador, part of the province of Newfoundland, New Brunswick, Nova Scotia, and Prince Edward Island.

Atlantic Fares *(Airlines)*: Fares which are applicable between points in Area 1 and points in area 2 and/or area 3 via the Atlantic Ocean.

Atlantic Standard Time (AST) *(Geography)*: A Canadian time zone based on the standard of the 60th meridian, also called Provincial Standard Time. AST is 4 hours behind of Coordinated Universal Time (UTC). AST is used during winter in these Canadian areas: Most of the mainland (Labrador) part of the province of Newfoundland and Labrador, New Brunswick, Nova Scotia, and Prince Edward Island.

ATM *(Air Traffic)*: See Air Traffic Management

ATM *(Business)*: Automated Teller Machine (also known as Cash Point).

ATME *(Organizations)*: Acronym for Association of Travel Marketing Executives.

Atmosphere *(Geography)*: The envelope of mixture of gases encircling an astronomical object. Earth's atmosphere is held near its surface by the earth's gravitational attraction. The divisions of the atmosphere include the troposphere, the stratosphere, the mesosphere, the ionosphere, and the exosphere.

Atmospheric Pressure *(Geography)*: The amount of force exerted over a surface area, caused by the weight of air molecules above it. Atmospheric pressure decreases with increasing height. A column of air of 1 square inch, measured from sea level to the top of the atmosphere would weigh approximately 14.7 pounds per square inch. The standard value for atmospheric pressure at sea level is 29.92 inches or 760 mm of mercury 1013.25 millibars (mb) or 101,325 pascals (pa).

ATN *(Air Traffic)*: Aeronautical Telecommunications Network

ATO *(GDS)*: A code meaning: 1. Airport Ticket Office: 2. Airline Ticket Office; 3. Air Traffic Operations.

Atoll *(Geography)*: A ring-shaped tropical coral reef or string of coral islands surrounding a lagoon.

Atoll Reef *(Geography)*: A circular coral reef which borders an island that has been submerged by a rise in sea level.

ATP *(Airlines)*: Airline Tariff Publishing Company that edited in the past a tariff handbook used among travel agencies.

Atrium *(Cruise)*: An interior, multi-deck and open area of a ship. Atriums are centrally located near elevators, shops, restaurants, cafés, and guest services. By extension, it is a large open space in a building, usually topped by a glass roof, sometimes containing elaborate landscaping and ponds.

Atrium *(Hospitality)*: A guestroom floor configuration in which rooms are laid out off a single-loaded corridor encircling a multistory lobby space; also the multistory lobby space, usually with a skylight. It is a popular style of hotel lobby.

Atrium Cabin *(Cruise)*: Cruise cabins which offer passengers windows that face the ship's interior, overlooking the central atrium or promenade. They are still new to the industry, available only on largest ships.

ATT *(GDS)*: Code meaning Attention.

Attitude *(Aeronautics)*: In simple words, the term refers to the orientation of an aircraft with respect to the direction in which it is traveling or in regard to a point of reference, such as the ground or horizon. The aircraft attitude refers to whether the aircraft is flying straight ahead, climbing, descending, turning or in some combination of these. Most of the possible attitudes are: straight and level (cruise), climbing, descending, takeoff, landing, coordinated banked turn, climbing coordinated banked turn, descending coordinated banked turn, slipping turn, skidding turn.

Attraction *(Tourism)*: A natural place, a facility, and/or protected area provided with an infrastructure where public can find entertainment and/or educational experiences. Some typical examples of attractions are sceneries, aquariums, heritage centers, museums, theme parks, visitor centers, public parks and zoos. In general terms, an attraction is any service or product which tourists would enjoy visiting or using. Attraction is not synonym with "attractor."

Attractor *(Tourism)*: Term defining a significant tourist attraction, which compels visitation. Attractor is a feature or set of features around which a dynamical tourist system of a place evolves. Attractors are the top reasons a tourist would choose to visit in an area.

ATV *(GDS)*: Code meaning All-terrain vehicle.

ATW *(GDS)*: Code meaning Around the World.

ATX *(GDS)*: Code meaning Air Taxi.

Au Complet *(Hospitality)*: A French term used to indicate that a hotel or restaurant is full and has no room available.

Au Pair *(Hospitality)*: A French term denoting a domestic assistant hired to provide child care and some housework in exchange for a modest salary, room, and board with a host family. Usually, au pairs are girls or young women.

AUA *(GDS)*: Three-letter IATA code for Aruba.

Audio Guide *(Tourism)*: A recorded spoken explanation in a visitor's attraction, such as a museum collection or an art exhibition, but also available for self-guided tours of outdoor locations through a handheld device, for instance PDAs and VDAs.

Audio Tour *(Tourism)*: See Audio Guide.

Audit *(Tourism)*: 1. An inspection and verification of a business financial or performance records, conducted by an independent qualified accountant. In tourism activity, Audits of Travel Agency Procedures are carried out in order to identify problems or areas for improvement and apply corrections.

Audit *(Ecology)*: A systematic, objective and documented evaluation performed periodically to verify how well a company, product, program, individual, destination, etc., is doing compared with a set of standards.

Auditorium Style *(Hospitality)*: A seating configuration for a meeting, in which chairs (and tables) are arranged in rows facing a dais or platform, as in a theater.

AUG *(GDS)*: A code for August.

Aurora Australis *(Geography)*: A colorful geomagnetic light display in the sky that is visible near the South Pole. It is known as The Southern Lights, while scientists call it Polar Aurora.

Aurora Borealis *(Geography)*: A colorful geomagnetic light display in the sky that is visible near the North Pole. It is known as The Northern Lights, while scientists call it Polar Aurora. The aurora borealis usually occurs from September to October and from March to April. The Cree Indians call this phenomenon the "Dance of the Spirits."

Australasia *(Geography)*: A term coined by Charles de Brosses in *Histoire des Navigations aux Terres Australes* in 1756 that is used to describe a region of Oceania comprising New Zealand, Australia, Papua New Guinea, and neighboring islands in the Pacific Ocean. It does not include either Polynesia or Micronesia. Geopolitically, Australasia comprises only New Zealand and Australia.

AUTH *(GDS)*: A code meaning Authority, Authorize, Authorizing, Authorized.

Authorized Destination Status (ADS) *(Tourism)*: Agreements accorded by China National Tourism Administration (CNTA) with foreign governments with the purpose to promote people-to-people contacts and boost tourism, removing restrictions on its citizens travelling in groups to other countries.

Auto-caravane *(Tourism)*: A French term referring to a big Caravan that can only park at authorized specific places.

Auto drop PNR *(GDS)*: A passenger Name Record (PNR) that has been signaled for automatic queuing on a GDS.

Auto-ID Center *(Airlines)*: A non-profit alliance held between private companies and academic organizations to develop an Internet-like infrastructure for tracking goods through the use of RFID (Radio Frequency Identification) tags.

Auto Rickshaw *(Tourism)*: Also called "tuk tuk", it is an urban vehicle for hire in cities of the Indian subcontinent and South and East Asia. It is a motorized version of the traditional rickshaw (a type of a cabin three-wheeled cycle driven by a person). Auto rickshaws are primarily used for tourist purpose and are popular in cities where traffic congestion is a major problem, such as in Mumbai, Delhi, and Bangkok.

Autobahn *(Tourism)*: A network of high-speed superhighways in Germany and a few other European countries, equivalent to the US interstate highway system. It is also a German motorway.

Autodial/Auto-Answer *(Hospitality)*: A feature of sophisticated modems that enables a user to place a call to a pre-specified phone number at an exact time, or that sets up the modem in a ready state to receive incoming calls.

Autogyro *(Aeronautics)*: An aircraft that is lift by freely rotating horizontal blades and employs a conventional propeller for forward motion.

Autolysis *(Hospitality)*: The chemical disintegration of food products caused by substances (primarily enzymes) in food.

Automated Brokerage Interface (ABI) *(Customs)*: An electronic system allowing customhouse brokers and importers to interface via computer with the US Customs Service for transmitting entry summary data on imported merchandise.

Automated Commercial System (ACS) *(Customs)*: The electronic system of the US Customs Service, comprising a variety of industry sectors that permits on-line access to information in selected areas.

Automated Manifest System (AMS) *(Customs)*: A US Customs and

Border Protection Agency system allowing carriers, port authority or service center computers to notify the details of shipments loaded onto a specific flight.

Automated People Mover *(Tourism)*: Any of several systems designed for mass transit of people over short distances, such as mechanical stairs, moving sidewalks, automated monorail, and automated driverless cars. They are typically found at airports, downtown districts or theme parks. In short, they are also called People Movers.

Automated Reservation System *(GDS)*: Other name for a Global Distribution System.

Automated Ticket/Boarding Pass (ATB) *(Airlines)*: In the past it was a single copy non-carbonized ticket (normally on card stock) with each coupon imprinted separately. Each coupon used for air transport was comprised of a flight coupon and a detachable passenger coupon and boarding pass for a specific flight. One coupon was issued as the passenger receipt which together with all passenger coupons and boarding passes built up the passenger copy of the passenger ticket and baggage check. It was the form of automated ticket and boarding pass described in IATA Resolutions 722c and 722d.

Automatic Computerized Bar System *(Hospitality)*: A beverage dispenser system that improves control on delivery and inventory, and enhances quality control, accuracy of guest checks and bonding to standard patterns.

Automatic Direction Finding (ADF) *(Air Traffic)*: A basic guidance mode, providing guidance to a radio station.

Automatic Flight Control System (AFCS) *(Air Traffic)*: A system with all equipment to control automatically the flight of an aircraft to a path or attitude described by references internal or external to the aircraft.

Automatic Form Number Reader (AFNR) *(Hospitality)*: A feature of a guest check printer that facilitates order entry procedures. Instead of making manual inputs, the automatic form number reader accesses the account by reading a bar code imprinted on the guest check.

Automatic Identification *(Airlines)*: A general term referring to methods of collecting and entering data directly into computer systems without human involvement. This type of technology includes bar codes, biometrics, RFID and voice recognition.

Automatic Identification of Outward Dialing *(Hospitality)*: A feature of a call accounting system used to identify the extension from which an outgoing call is placed.

Automatic Room *(Hospitality)*: Assignment made in the computer through algorithms based on parameters specified by hotel management. Rooms may be selected according to predetermined floor zones or according to an index of room usage and depreciation. See also Rate Assignment.

Automatic Route Selection *(Airlines)*: A facility of a call accounting system that provides the capability of connecting with a variety of common carriers.

Automatic Slip Feed (ASF) *(Hospitality)*: A feature of a guest check printer that prevents overprinting of items and amounts on guest checks.

Automatic Spell Check *(Hospitality)*: A computer program that helps users to read a proof of documents by automatically checking for spelling errors. The words in the document are electronically compared with entries in the spell checker's dictionary. When a word which appears in the document does not appear in the program's dictionary, it is generally highlighted on the display screen so the operator can correct it.

Automatic Terminal Information Service (ATIS) *(Air Traffic)*: Continuous broadcast of recorded information in selected terminal areas to improve controller effectiveness.

Autopilot *(Aeronautics)*: A navigational device that automatically keeps ships, planes, or spacecraft on a steady preset course. It is a mechanical, electrical, or hydraulic system that works without assistance from a human being.

Autotroph *(Ecology)*: A term meaning "self eater" that refers to organisms capable of producing their own food. An autotroph is a plant capable of synthesizing its own food from simple organic substances. It is opposed to Heterotroph. See Primary Producers.

Auxiliary Heat *(Hospitality)*: A secondary supply of heat provided by a standby heating system when the primary heating system cannot supply heat.

AV *(Airlines)*: Two-letter IATA code for Avianca, the airline of Colombia.

Avail *(Airlines)*: A jargon term for Availability.

Available *(Airlines)*: Something that is accessible or may be obtained. The term qualifies a service which can be the booking object and is applicable to transport seats, hotel rooms, rental cars, or other bookable service.

Available Room Nights *(Hospitality)*: A hotel's inventory consisting of the total number of hotel rooms available, multiplied by the number of days in a given period.

Availability *(GDS)*: The actual inventory of seats, rooms, cabins, or other service that can be sold or reserved. GDSs often publish fares as "available" between two cities, but it does not mean seats at that rate are available. Most websites selling air travel allow the traveler to check whether any particular flight is full or it still has seats available to buy.

Available Room Nights *(Hospitality)*: The total number of hotel rooms available, multiplied by the number of days in a given time period. It represents the hotel's inventory.

Available Rooms *(Hospitality)*: The total of rooms currently available for sale in a hotel, on a given date. Availability excludes occupied rooms or rooms unavailable due to damage, repairs, or other impediment.

Available Seat Kilometers (ASK) *(Airlines)*: An air transport concept indicating the number of aircraft seats available for sale and the kilometers flown. The item corresponds to the total number of seat kilometers that were available to passengers (i.e. aircraft kilometers flown times the number of seats available for revenue passenger use).

Available Seat Miles (ASM) *(Airlines)*: In a general sense, it means one seat transported one mile. It is the most common measure of airline seating capacity or supply. For example, an airliner with 100 passenger seats, flown a distance of 100 miles, represents 10,000 available seat miles (ASMs).

Avalanche *(Geography)*: A large mass of snow, ice or rock that comes loose from a mountain slope and slides or falls downward, becoming a common hazard for ski resort areas.

AVBL *(GDS)*: Code meaning "Available."

AVE *(Tourism)*: The acronym means *Alta Velocidad Española* and identifies the Spanish High Speed Train.

Average Daily Rate (ADR) *(Hospitality)*: A statistical unit often used to evaluate a hotel's pricing scale. The figure is obtained by dividing actual daily revenue by the total number of available rooms and represents the average rental income per occupied room in a given time period.

Average Elapsed Days *(Airlines)*: The average elapsed days between the booking or cancellation date and the flight date for a segment.

Average Length of Stay *(Tourism)*: A statistical figure expressing a tourism relation that is obtained by dividing the total number of overnight stays in a place by the number of arrivals.

Average Occupancy *(Hospitality)*: A ratio that shows rooms sold over a given period of time, representing a percentage of total available rooms in a property over the same period of time.

Average Occupancy per Room *(Hospitality)*: A ratio that shows the average number of paid guests for each room sold. This ratio is obtained by dividing the number of paid room guests by the number of rooms sold. It helps the manager to improve the lodging occupancy.

Average Room Rate *(Hospitality)*: Information that indicates the average room rate. It is useful to know to what extent rooms are being up-sold or discounted. It is calculated by dividing rooms revenue by the number of rooms sold. It is also called Average Daily Rate or ADR.

AVH *(GDS)*: Code meaning Available Hotel Status Message.

Aviation *(Aviation)*: Aviation is a term that currently deals with many activities covering the design, manufacture, use, and operation of heavier-than-air aircraft, including related activities. Based on the purpose of usage, aviation can be divided into civil and military aviation. Civil aviation can be divided into commercial air transport and general aviation. Commercial air transport consists of the operation of commercial airlines servicing both passengers and freight. General aviation comprises activities other than commercial air transport and consists of agricultural, business, instructional, pleasure flying, air taxis, aerial surveying and mapping. Military aviation includes all aviation activity operated by the armed forces, such as military air transport, reconnaissance and combat.

Aviation Trust Fund *(Airlines)*: A program established by the U.S. Congress to raise funds for the nation's air transport system by taxing airline tickets and operations.

Aviator *(Airlines)*: Person qualified to fly an aircraft. Synonymous with Pilot.

AVIH *(GDS)*: Code meaning Animal in Hold.

Avionics *(Aeronautics)*: The science and technology of developing electronic systems and devices for aircraft and spacecraft. In regard to aviation, avionics comprises all of the electronic systems contained in an aircraft.

AVML *(GDS)*: Code meaning Asian Vegetarian Meal.

AVS *(GDS)*: Code meaning Availability Status Messages.

AWB *(GDS)*: Code meaning Air Waybill.

AWOL *(Airlines, Cruise)*: A term meaning to be absent without abandoning. It is used in reference to unauthorized absence of a crew member, as on a cruise ship.

Axis *(Aeronautics)*: An imaginary line, through the center of gravity, around which an aircraft rotates. An aircraft rolls around its longitudinal axis, an imaginary line running through the center of the aircraft, from the nose to the tail.

Ayurveda *(Tourism)*: An ancient Indian holistic system of healing that encompasses diet, massage, exercise and yoga.

AZ *(Airlines)*: Two-letter IATA code for Alitalia, the airline of Italy.

AZA *(Organizations)*: An acronym for American Zoological Association.

AZA-accredited *(Tourism)*: An organization or business that meets standards set by the American Zoological Association for animal care.

Azimuth *(Aeronautics)*: An angle in the horizontal plane, usually measured with respect to body coordinates

Azimuthing Pod Propulsion *(Cruise)*: An advanced and high-tech engine system used by cruise ships aiming to the elimination of ship's vibration. It is also known as "Pod Propulsion".

Azurisation *(Tourism)*: A French term synonymous with "Baléarisation" and "Marbellisation ". It denotes a continued occupation of a littoral space by tourist or residential structures. It implies an unfavorable and degradable concept of the natural environments, as in the Côte d'Azur.

B

B *(Airlines)*: Code for "Bravo", name used to designate the letter "B" in the International Phonetic Alphabet.

B *(GDS)*: Code for Economy/Coach Discounted Class.

B&B *(Hospitality)*: Code for Bed and Breakfast. It is a lodging modality that includes breakfast in the price of lodging, usually a country-style accommodation (even a hotel) with a small number of rooms.

B2B *(Tourism)*: See Business-to-Business.

B2C *(Tourism)*: See Business-to-Customer.

BA *(Airlines)*: Two-letter IATA code for British Airways.

BAA *(Airlines)*: British Airports Authority

Back *(Hospitality)*: Any beverage ordered by a guest, to be served in a separate glass along with his or her drink. Example: Water or Soda Back.

Back of the House *(Hotel Industry/Tourism)*: Service areas of a hotel, restaurant or theme park out of guests' sight. They are functional areas where employees have little or no direct contact with guests, such as kitchen areas, engineering and maintenance, and the accounting department.

Back Office *(Airlines)*: The term identifies business areas where employees perform activities out of the view of guests and passengers.

Back to Back *(Tourism)*: Tours that operate on consistent, continuing bases. For instance, a bus arriving in a city at the end of a tour, finishes the first tour upon arrival, and then starts transport for a second tour back along the same route.

Back-to-back Balcony *(Cruise)*: Also called a verandah, it is an outside porch, usually private, just outside the ship's cabin, used for relaxing.

Back to Back Fares *(Airlines)*: An illegal practice whereby fares are applied to two return trips to the same destination, by the same traveler. It is a forbidden strategy intending to reduce the cost of a round trip when the cost of two excursions is less than the cost of one unrestricted fare. It is also known as. The practice is also called Nested Excursions.

Back to Back Ticketing *(Airlines)*: An illegal practice whereby one air ticket is issued roundtrip to use only one portion. Another one is issued roundtrip again to use only one portion. The passenger intends to use the coupons of one ticket for the outgoing portion of the trip and the coupons of the other tickets for the return portion of the trip. The practice is also called "Cross Ticketing."

Back-to-front System *(Airlines)*: An airplane seating method to fill coach seats in groups from the rear to the front of the plane. Other seating systems are "Open Seating Plan," "Reverse Pyramid System," "Rotating Zone System," and "Wilma."

Backbar *(Hospitality)*: That back part of a bar that is used for storage or display. It is opposite to Underbar.

Background Extinction Rate *(Ecology)*: It is the rate of extinction of species as a result of changes in local environmental conditions and the actions of a natural evolutionary process.

Backhaul (BHC) *(Airlines)*: In air fare calculation for one way trips using normal one way fares, backhaul is a route deviation, by which the passenger goes from an intermediate high-rated point back to a lower-rated point, producing a fare increase. It is the minimum fare for a one way trip which is calculated as per the following formula: HIF - NUC = D; D + NUC = BHC, where HIF is the fare from the point of origin of the trip to the higher rated intermediate point, NUC is the published fare from the point of origin to the point of destination of the trip, D is the difference between the two fares, and BHC is the Minimum One Way Fare to be paid.

Backpacker *(Tourism)*: A traveler or hiker whose only luggage consists of a backpack (a "handbag" that is carried on the back, supported by the shoulders with double handles). Backpackers are travelers who typically stay at hostels or dorm rooms, and use public transport, and other inexpensive services.

Backscatter *(Airlines)*: A device which uses an X-ray technology to see through clothing that is utilized to screen passengers at airports. Some people consider this technology intrusive and humiliating, because it provides a detailed body image.

Backscatter Imaging *(Airlines)*: The usage of backscatter technology.

Backscatting *(Airlines)*: The action to screen a person bye means of a Backscatter.

Backup Drinks *(Hospitality)*: Two drinks purchased at one time by one guest.

Backwash *(Airlines)*: The turbulence caused by the backward flow of air propelled by a jet engine.

Backwash *(Cruise)*: The disturbance caused by the return flow of water by action of a ship's propellers turning in reverse.

Bacon, Roger *(Aviation)*: One of the most famous characters of his time, also known as *Doctor Mirabilis* (Wonderful Doctor). He was a Franciscan friar; an English philosopher who is supposed was born in Somerset, England, presumably in 1220. Bacon performed and described various experiments, made many discoveries, and came near to many others. His book *Opus Majus* contains investigations on mathematics and optics, alchemy and the manufacture of gunpowder, the position and sizes of the celestial bodies, and anticipates later inventions such as microscopes, telescopes, flying machines, hydraulics and steam ships.

Badlands *(Geography)*: Any barren area of severe erosion caused by the action of wind and water. They are usually found in semiarid climates and are characterized by sparse vegetation, poorly cemented sediments, and the presence of canyons, ravines, gullies, and other geological formations. The term "badlands" was first applied to the arid, dissected plateau region of SW South Dakota by Native Americans and fur trappers who found the area difficult to cross.

Baedeker Guides *(Tourism)*: A series of guidebooks published in Germany in the nineteenth century for the use of automobile drivers and tourists, invented by Karl Baedeker in Germany (1835) and by John Murray III in England (1836). The Baedeker guides were very popular and were standard resources for travelers well into the 20th century. At present the guides, often referred to as simply "Baedekers", are written by the specialists, and contain meaningful information on what to do and what to visit.

Baedeker, Karl *(Tourism)*: A German publisher, the first to set the standards for tourism guidebooks. He was born in Essen, Prussia, in November 3, 1801, and started his publishing company in 1827 in Koblenz. His first publication was a handbook for travelers made by J. A. Klein, under the title *Rheinreise von Mainz bis Köln* (Traveling the Rhine from Mainz to Cologne). The red bindings and gilt lettering of Baedeker's style inspired a hallmark, and the content became famous for its detail and accuracy. Baedeker introduced new formats to the travel guides information by including specific details of transportation, accommodation, prices, and other inherent themes. Starting in 1844, he introduced the star ratings for attractions. Baedeker is remembered for his careful work. He died on October 4, 1859.

Bag Drop *(Airlines)*: A place to hold baggage under the custody of an airline or a handling agent.

BAG *(GDS)*: Code meaning Baggage.

Baggage *(Airlines)*: Any number of bags, cases and containers which hold personal belongings necessary or appropriate for the passenger to wear or use for his/her comfort and convenience during his/her trip. Baggage is always carried aboard an airplane where the passenger flies.

Baggage Allowance *(Airlines)*: The luggage allowed by an airline for a passenger to carry in the same flight free of charge. Depending on the route the allowance will either be by piece (numbers of bags or cases) or by weight. Travelers are able to take more luggage by paying an Excess Baggage Charge.

Baggage Allowance *(Cruise):* The amount of bags, generally consisting of the passenger's personal effects, permitted by the cruise line free of charge.

Baggage Check *(Airlines)*: The numbered claim check or receipt issued by a carrier to a passenger for his or her registered luggage handed to the carrier's custody.

Baggage Claim or Baggage Claim Area *(Airlines)*: The area at an air terminal where passengers pick their accompanied checked baggage.

Baggage, Excess *(Airlines)*: A part of the baggage that is in excess of the baggage which is allowed to be carried free of charge. See Excess Baggage.

Baggage Hold *(Airlines)*: The part of the plane where the baggage is stored.

Baggage Liability *(Airlines)*: The carrier's responsibility relating passenger's baggage during its transport.

Baggage Management Improvement Programme (BIP) *(Airlines)*: An IATA program that makes part of the STB (Simplifying the Business) process, which is aimed to reducing the rate of mishandled baggage by improving handling processes to ensure passengers and their baggage are reunited at final destination. Security measures are increasingly added, making the baggage handling process more complex.

Baggage Master *(Cruise)*: Person who controls baggage handling on a ship.

Baggage Tag *(Airlines)*: Personal identification attached to luggage checked by an air carrier.

Baggage, Unchecked *(Airlines)*: The baggage kept under the passenger's custody.

Bagonize *(Airlines)*: A slang term meaning "to agonize" while waiting at the airport luggage carousel for the luggage to appear.

Bagtrack *(Airlines)*: Computerized system used by airlines for tracing lost air passengers luggage.

Bait and Switch *(Airlines)*: An illegal sales practice to attract a customer by advertising a low price offer. Upon market response, people are guided to a higher fare because the "special offer" is sold out or is no longer valid.

BAL *(GDS)*: Code meaning "Balance."

Balanced Forces *(Aeronautics)*: Opposing forces that push or pull against each other with equal force.

Balcony *(Hospitality)*: An open-air space or platform off a room.

Balcony Cabin *(Cruise)*: Any cabin accommodation with a private exterior balcony. The trend is towards more balcony cabins on ships. Some ships now feature balconies in over three-fourths of their cabins.

Balearisation *(Tourism)*: French term which defines a type of space totally specialized in tourism, sensitive to become saturated. The concept introduces the occupation problem when the demand is extremely high. This phenomenon is manifested in different points of the Mediterranean basin, like Marbella and Palma de Majorca. Synonymous with *Marbellisation*.

Ballast *(Aviation)*: Any heavy material, such as sand, placed in the gondola of hot air balloons to control altitude.

Ballast *(Cruise)*: Any heavy material that is placed in the hold of a ship to stabilize a it when it is not carrying cargo.

Balloon *(Aeronautics)*: A non-engine powered vehicle lighter-than-air that is moved by the action of hot air, hydrogen, helium, ammonia or other gas confined. Balloons can be un-tethered and free to drift with the wind or tethered to the ground, in which case they are called Captive or Kite Balloons.

Balneotherapy *(Tourism)*: A general term for water treatments that use hot springs, mineral water or seawater to restore and revitalize the body and ease stress and pain.

Bank Rate *(Airlines)*: The official rate at which banks trade currencies.

Bank Settlement Plan *(Airlines)*: A system administered by IATA or ARC on a regional basis to handle the processing of airline tickets, payments, and the disbursement of commissions to travel agencies.

Banker's Buying Rate (BBR) *(Airlines)*: The rate at which, for the purpose of transfer of funds through banking channels, a bank purchases an amount of foreign currency in exchange for one unit of the national currency of the country in which the exchange transaction takes place.

Banker's Selling Rate (BSR *(Airlines)*: The rate at which, for the purpose of transfer of funds through banking channels, a bank sells an amount of foreign currency in exchange for one unit of the national currency of the country in which the exchange transaction takes place.

Bankruptcy *(Business)*: A federal legal system of statutes by which persons and businesses which are insolvent or face potential insolvency, to place his/her/its financial affairs under the control of the bankruptcy court, while he/she/it reorganizes its finances to survive or liquidate its assets. In the majority of cases bankruptcy is initiated by the debtor (a "voluntary bankruptcy"). Filing a bankruptcy petition automatically suspends all existing legal actions.

Banquet *(Hospitality)*: An elaborate and sometimes ceremonious meal arranged for numerous people, complete with gourmet food, fine wines, and desserts, often including speakers or presentations. The banquet course menu is predefined.

Banquet Contract: *(Hospitality)* See Banquet Event Order (BEO) below.

Banquet Event Order (BEO) *(Hospitality)*: The BEO is a type of contract for the client and serves as a work order for the catering department. The order form states final banquet arrangements, such as time and place of the function, menu, service notes, gratuity, payment, and guarantee clauses. In other words, the BEO is a document providing complete and precise instructions to a hotel for the running of a banquet, meeting, or other event to be held in the hotel. It is also called a "Banquet Function Sheet" or "Banquet Prospectus."

Banquet Menu *(Hospitality)*: A "table d'hôte menu" or a set meal with few choices. Banquet meals are usually elaborate.

Banqueting Room *(Hospitality)*: A large hotel room or hall available for rent to public for functions where food may also be served. It is also called "Function Room".

Banquettes *(Hospitality)*: Upholstered benches usually built in along a wall.

Bar *(Cruise)*: A bar of sand (a sandbar) formed by the action of tides or currents at sea.

Bar *(Hospitality)*: 1. The area in which drinks are prepared and from which drinks are sold. 2. A retail establishment or a counter in a restaurant where alcoholic beverages are sold or dispensed.

Bar and Beverage Operations *(Hospitality)*: A term for all establishments that serve alcoholic beverages. Typical examples are bars and lounges.

Bar Car *(Tourism)*: See Lounge Car.

Bar Code *(Business)*: An automatic identification technology of vertical bars and spaces representing characters that are readable with a scanner. The bar code is the standard method to identify product characteristics that was adopted in the 1970s.

Bar Coded Boarding Passes (BCBP) *(Airlines)*: An automated system created by IATA to enable fast and convenient check-in by allowing the passenger to print the boarding pass in a home printer. He /she can then check-in using a Common Use Self-Service Kiosk and proceed directly to the gate.

Bar Menu *(Hospitality)*: The principal types of beverage operations which the establishment has ready to serve, including draft, wine, mixed drinks, specialty drinks and bottled beer. The bar menu usually includes the drink preferences of the operation's target markets.

Bar Par *(Hospitality)*: The anticipated amount of each beverage type to be stored in the backbar. The Bar Par is generally based on expected consumption.

Bareboat or Bare Boat *(Yacht)*: A sailboat or powerboat for hire without crew. Bareboats were originally rented with no extras, but it is not appropriate today as modern bare boats have all imaginable extras, such as TV's, VCR's, DVD's, air conditioning, microwave ovens, ice makers, blenders, etc. One can also hire a captain, cook or both, turning a bare boat into a Captain Only or Crewed Yacht.

Bare Boat with Crew or Crewed Yacht *(Yacht)*: Crewed charters are sold as package deals, with all costs included. In some cases, alcohol and water toy rentals are extra. Crewed yachts supply all meals and food included in the charter fee, but the user may eat ashore as often as he/she likes, even if a cook is hired.

Bareboat Charter *(Yacht)*: An arrangement whereby a yacht or another vessel is hired without a crew for a specific period. Usually the Bareboat Charter does not include supplies or crew.

Barge *(Cruise)*: A long, large, usually flat-bottom boat used for transporting freight, especially on canals and inland waterways. It is generally unpowered and is towed or pushed by other craft.

Barge Cruising *(Cruise)*: Pleasure cruising along a canal systems, such as in upstate New York or in Europe, operated in converted barges or new ships that resemble them.

Barometer *(Tourism)*: An instrument that is used for measuring atmospheric pressure, generally to determine altitude or weather changes.

Barometric Altitude *(Air Traffic)*: Height with respect to fixed earth references (above mean sea level).

Barometric Pressure *(Geography)*: The atmospheric pressure as indicated by a barometer. It varies according to altitude and weather conditions.

Barrier Island *(Geography)*: A long, relatively narrow island running parallel to the mainland, formed by the action of waves and currents. It usually lies just offshore and serves to protect the main coastline from erosion by surf and tidal surges.

Barrier Reef *(Geography)*: A long, narrow trimming of coral or rock laying parallel to and relatively near a coastline, separated from it by a lagoon.

Barter *(Airlines)*: A method to trade goods or services in exchange for other goods or services, without use of money. Among airlines it is usual to exchange seats for goods or services rendered by various suppliers.

Base Fare *(Airlines)*: The basic price shown on an airline ticket, before adding any taxes, surcharges, airport fees, etc. Generally, commissions are paid on the base fare.

Base Fare Beam *(Cruise)*: A ship's width at its widest point, determining the vessel's ability to pass through the Panama Canal.

Basic Allowance *(Tourism)*: The maximum amount of money that can be drawn from a country with currency restrictions.

Basic Amenities *(Hospitality)*: Term used in lodging or housing, to denote a room or home has the most significant features to make guests comfortable and at ease, such as a bath or shower, hot running water, and a flush toilet.

Basic Environmental Sanitation *(Tourism)*: A requirement demanding to keep the basic sanitary conditions to protect health and hygienic welfare of residents and visitors.

Basic Rate *(Car Rental)*: A type of car rental rate excluding insurance or tax charges. It is opposed to Inclusive Rate.

Basic Utilities *(Tourism)*: Services provided by government or other public entities comprising the minimum requirements for modern living, such as electricity, water, and communication services.

Basing Point *(Airlines)*: A place to and from which air fares are established.

Basis Two *(Hospitality)*: An alternative term for Double Occupancy.

Bassinet *(Airlines)*: A basket (usually hooded) used as portable cradle for an infant.

Batch Mode *(Computing)*: A computer operating mode in which a program requires no input from the user apart from the initial command which actually starts the program. The information necessary for the operation of such a program is gathered slowly and carefully from an initialization file containing specified commands. Ticketing is an example of task performed in a batch mode.

Bath Blankets *(Hospitality)*: A hotel's term for extra-large bath towels in guestrooms. They are also called "bath sheets."

Battery and Tire Surcharge *(Car Rental)*: A car rental tax to cover the state's cost to dispose of worn car batteries and tires, charged by the State of Florida only.

Bathyscaph, Bathyscaphe or Bathyscape *(Tourism)*: A submersible vessel that operates at extreme depths. It is designed to reach ocean depths of over 10000 meters (about 5000 fathoms) and has a flotation compartment with an observation capsule underneath.

BAV *(GDS)*: Code meaning Beds Available.

Bay *(Airlines)*: A compartment in an aircraft used for some specific purpose, as a cargo bay.

Bay *(Cruise)*: A compartment on a ship between decks. It is often used as a hospital.

Bay *(Geography)*: A wide semicircular indentation of a shoreline with a wide mouth at an ocean, sea, or lake surrounded by headlands, capes, or peninsulas. A bay is larger than a cove, but smaller than a gulf.

Bay *(Hospitality)*: The principal compartment of a suite of a space equivalent to a standard guestroom. It is used to describe the size of a suite, which might, for example, be single-bay, double-bay or triple-bay.

Bayou *(Geography)*: A French name for a relatively small, marshy, slow-moving stream running through lowlands or swamps. Bayous are primarily located in the Mississippi River delta region of the southern United States.

BB *(GDS)*: A code that means: 1. Buffet breakfast. 2. Eurobudget fare type.

B/B *(Airlines)*: Code for Break of Bulk Cargo.

BBB Tax *(Hospitality)*: Term for Bed, board, and beverage tax.

BBD *(GDS)*: Code for Barbados Dollar, the national currency of Barbados.

BBML *(GDS)*: A code meaning Baby Meal (Infant or baby food).

BBR *(GDS)*: Code for Banker's Buying Rate.

BCBP *(Airlines)*: See Bar Coded Boarding Passes

BCE *(GDS)*: Code for *Banco Central Europeo* (European Central Bank).

BCHFT *(GDS)*: Code for Beachfront.

BCN *(GDS)*: Three-letter IATA code for Barcelona, important city in Spain.

Beach Club *(Tourism)*: A public club authorized to offer access to private beaches, including amenities on a membership fee basis. Typical examples are Ocean Drive, The Beach Club, and The Lavender Scallion.

Beam *(Cruise)*: The maximum width of a ship (maximum 110 feet) at its widest point, or at the mid-point of its length. Ships exceeding this with can not transit the Panama Canal.

Bearing *(Cruise)*: It is the ship's angular compass direction, such as a "northwest bearing." It is determined by measuring the number of degrees clockwise between north and the required direction, and is always expressed in degrees.

Beaufort Scale *(Cruise)*: An empirical and one of the first scales to estimate wind speeds which was invented by Britain's Admiral Sir Francis Beaufort (1774-1857). The scale measures wind strengths starting from 0 to a force of 12. Today, more sophisticated methods are used, although landsmen and sailors continue to use the legacy of Sir Francis Beaufort.

Beaujolais *(Hospitality)*: A juicy, flavorful red wine made from

Gamay grapes grown in the region of the same name.

Beaujolais Nouveau *(Hospitality)*: A French term denoting the first *Beaujolais* wine to go in the market every year. Its annual release date is the third Thursday in November. It is a refreshing wine, popular throughout the world and available for a few months in the year. It is also called *Beaujolais Primeur*.

Beacon *(Air Traffic)*: A device, usually based on the ground that aids in determining a position or direction.

Bearing (BRG) *(Air Traffic)*: A term meaning Direction on a Compass.

Bed and Breakfast (B&B) *(Hospitality)*: A type of accommodation which is offered often at small hotels or private homes including a room to sleep in and daily breakfast. See also B&B.

Bed Capacity *(Hospitality)*: A ratio determining the lodging capacity of a place. It is obtained by multiplying times two the hotel room number.

Bed Night *(Hospitality)*: A measurement of occupancy used in hotel industry, meaning one person spending one night in a hostelry. Ten persons staying ten nights would be 100 bed nights. It is also a standard measure of overnight tourist traffic.

Bed-Place *(Hospitality)*: A European concept denoting the number of persons a bed can accommodate. For example a queen bed represents two bed-places.

Bed Tax *(Hospitality)*: The tax charged by a local government on hotel stays.

Bed Wars *(Hospitality)*: A jargon term denoting how hotel chains compete to attract customers. Among the most popular bed-war strategies is the offer of better bedding with special mattresses, luxury sheets, and elaborate arrangements of pillows and bolsters.

Bedienung *(Tourism)*: German term meaning "Gratuity Included".

Bedroom *(Tourism)*: 1. A room furnished with beds at a property used for sleeping, typically with amenities. 2. A railway compartment with toilet and sink.

Beer-Clean Glass *(Hospitality)*: A clean glass completely free of grease and soap residues that can cause beer to lose its foam too quickly. A glass that looks clean may not be clean enough to serve beverages.

Beers & Blogs *(Tourism)*: Informal meetings of bloggers to have beers and socialize.

BEI *(Tourism)*: Code for *Banco Europeo de Inversiones* (European Investments Bank).

Bell Captain *(Hospitality)*: The supervisor of a group of bellhops in charge of the shift of guest's luggage.

Bellhop *(Hospitality)*: A person employed to carry luggage around hotels and to perform other services as an errand boy. The term relates to the bell used in hotels to call someone to carry a guest's luggage.

Bellman *(Hospitality):* A person who carries one's luggage to and from a hotel room. Synonymous with Bellhop and Bell Staff.

Bellstaff *(Hospitality)*: See Bellhop.

Belly Cargo *(Airlines)*: Part of the plane below the main deck, where freight is accommodated.

Below *(Cruise)*: Any area located below the main deck of a ship

Benchmarking *(Business)*: It is the practice of establishing goals and target levels of quality, price, or service by comparing performances and processes of other corporations considered the best industry references.

Benelux *(IATA Geography)*: The area comprising Belgium, the Netherlands, and Luxembourg.

BEO *(Hospitality)*: See Banquet Event Order.

BER *(GDS)*: Three-letter IATA code for Berlin, capital city of Germany.

Bereavement Fare *(Airlines)*: A discounted air fare offered to passengers traveling by cause of a death or illness of an immediate relative, on the basis of a Medical Proof.

Bermuda Agreement *(Airlines)*: An agreement signed in 1946 between the United Kingdom and the United States with the purpose to regulate future international air traffic.

Bermuda Plan *(Hospitality)*: An accommodation plan which includes a full breakfast each day with the room rate. It is different to Continental Plan, where the rate includes room and a light daily breakfast.

Bermuda Triangle *(Geography)*: A triangle-shaped area of the

Atlantic Ocean having its apices on Bermuda, Puerto Rico, and the eastern coast of Florida. Numerous watercraft and aircraft are said to have mysteriously disappeared in this area. Many people belief that some of these disappearances are due to paranormal reasons, or by cause of the activity by extraterrestrial beings. However substantial documentation and an analysis of the claimed incidents show that many of them did not even occur within the triangle or were produced by weather conditions, equipment failure, and human error.

Bernoulli's Principle *(Aeronautics)*: Named after Daniel Bernoulli, a Swiss scientist, the principle states that when air speeds up, its pressure is reduced, and when the air slows down, its pressure is increased, meaning that the pressure exerted by a moving fluid is inversely proportional to the speed of the fluid. Moving air reacts in the same way. The faster the air moves through a space, the lower the air pressure; the slower the air moves, the higher the pressure. The wings of an airplane are curved on top and flattened on the bottom and are slanted slightly downward from front to back, facts that make the speed on top differ from that on the bottom. The air passing the wing has to travel a longer distance on top than on the bottom. This causes the air stretches thinner on top of the wing, meaning the air pressure on top of the wing will be lower than that on the bottom of it. Therefore, the force pushing the plane upwards will be higher than the other pushing it downwards. The pressure differential generates the lift, so as the airplane accelerates and the wing moves faster through the air, the greater becomes the lift, eventually overcoming the force of gravity upon the aircraft. Now, how does the plane descend if these forces only tend to lift the aircraft? First of all, speed has to be reduced to slower the airflow. This tends to equal the pressure of the air flowing over the wing and the pressure which flows under the wing. Furthermore, pilots make mechanical maneuvers that bring the plane lower. When they lift the ailerons, for instance, the air passing over the top of the wing creates the pressure that creates a downward and slightly backward force in relation to the aircraft's straightforward movement. These are some of the principles used by aircraft manufacturers when designing and building their huge flying machines.

Berth *(Cruise)*: 1. The dock or place beside a pier where passengers embark or debark from the ship. 2. The bed in a cabin where passengers sleep onboard the ship. 3. By extension, a passenger's stateroom.

Berth Blackout Dates *(Tourism)*: Expression referring to dates on which travel is not available. The expression refers to airline, hotel or car rental arrangements.

Berth Liner Service *(Cruise)*: It is a regular scheduled steamship line with regular published schedules from and to defined ports of call.

Best Practices *(Tourism)*: A term designating highest quality, superior practices, or excellence in a particular field of work performed by a tourism operator.

BEY *(GDS)*: Three-letter IATA code for Beirut, capital city of Lebanon.

Beyond Rights *(Airlines)*: See Freedom Rights.

BDT *(GDS)*: See Bulk Data Transfer.

BFR *(GDS)*: Code for Before.

BG *(GDS)*: Code meaning: 1. Business Group; 2. Bag.

BGM *(Tourism)*: Code for Background Music, a theme park.

BHC *(GDS)*: See One Way Backhaul Check.

Biathlon *(Tourism)*: 1. Any sporting event consisting of two disciplines. 2. A winter sport that combines cross-country skiing and rifle shooting. 3. A summer sport that combines cross-country running and rifle shooting. Not to be confused with duathlon, that is an athletic contest consisting of running and cycling.

BIDT *(GDS)*: Billing Information Data Tapes which are supplied by the CRS on tape or diskette.

Bight *(Geography)*: A long, gradual bend or curved section in a coastline. It can be larger that a bay or a segment of a bay.

BIKE *(GDS)*: Term meaning Bicycle.

Bike Lane *(Tourism)*: The part of a roadway that is located in or beside a street for the exclusive use of bicyclists.

Bike Taxi *(Tourism)*: See Cycle Rickshaws.

Bikeway *(Tourism)*: A road, street, path, trail, or any way that assigned for is specifically designated for bicycle travel.

Bilateral Agreement *(Airlines)*: A convention, treaty, or other written statement signed by two sovereign countries specifying the terms of mutual understanding, policies, and obligations on a particular matter, such as the use of the airspace. It binds only the two signing states with the benefits typically not shared with other (third) countries.

Bilge *(Cruise)*: The lowest compartment on a ship where the two sides meet. It is the bottom part of the interior of the boat where water collects. In seaman's slang, it also denotes a worthless talk.

Bilge Water or Bilgewater *(Cruise)*: A mixture of seawater, oil, chemicals, and other fluids that accumulates in the lowest levels of ships, which does not drain off the side of the deck, during the course of normal navigation. The bilge water must be pumped out if it becomes too full and threatens to sink the ship.

Bilingual *(Tourism)*: 1. A person who speaks or writes two languages. 2. A text written in two languages.

Bill of Fare *(Tourism)*: 1. A list of dishes offer by a restaurant; a menu. 2. A list of events in a presentation; a program.

Bill of Lading *(Airlines)*: A document that states the terms of a contract between a shipper and a carrier by which the freight is to be moved between specified points for a specified charge. It is usually prepared by the shipper on forms issued by the carrier, and serves as a document of title, contract of carriage, and a receipt for goods.

Billboard *(Hospitality)*: A large panel designed to carry outdoor advertising and typically seen along highways, main streets and other high traffic areas.

Billed-to-Room Call *(Hospitality)*: An operator-assisted call. An operator places calls for hotel guests and then registers the charges.

Billing and Settlement Plan (BSP) *(Airlines)*: 1. A method stating the rules for the issuance of traffic documents and settling accounts between airlines and travel agencies. 2. The IATA regional division in charge of such responsibilities.

Billing Clerk *(Hospitality)*: The person responsible for charging to hotel guests all vouchers covering food, beverages, room service, and merchandise purchases.

Bimini *(Cruise)*: A weather-resistant fabric usually mounted on a frame over a portion of the cockpit to provide shade and protection to the pilot and/or passengers against rain or sun. Biminis are an absolute necessity for Caribbean sailing to prevent sunburn or melanoma.

Binnacle *(Cruise)*: The stand on which the ship's compass is mounted, usually located on the wheel's pedestal.

Bioaccumulation *(Ecology)*: The increase in the concentration of a chemical in organs or tissues at a level higher than would normally be accepted.

Biocenoses *(Ecology)*: A group of interacting organisms that form a self-regulating community and live in a particular habitat.

Biocenosis *(Ecology)*: See Biocenosis.

Biocoenosis *(Ecology)*: See Biocenosis.

Bioclimatic Zone *(Ecology)*: Bioclimatic zones are areas characterized by similar climate which are the home to similar plants and animals. Zones are classified according to their geographical position (for example, there are alpine, sub-alpine, mountain, lowland and coastal zones).

Biodegradable: *(Ecology)*: 1. Biodegradable substance is generally an organic material (plant or animal) that has the ability to be broken by natural decomposer processes into simple, stable products that will not harm the environment. In this sense, the term is used to describe "environmentally friendly" products. 2. Anything that can be ingested by an organism without causing that organism harm.

Biodiversity *(Ecology)*: Biodiversity, a contraction of the words "biological diversity," is a complex issue involving many aspects of biological variation. In general terms, it is the number and variety of different biotic factors that are found within a given geographic region. More specifically, biodiversity is the variety and abundance of living organisms in all of their diverse forms and levels of organization, including the diversity of genes, species, communities and ecosystems, as well as the evolutionary and functional processes that sustain them. Four broad categories are distinguished according to this concept:

1. *Genetic Diversity*: The difference among individuals within a

given species;

2. *Species Diversity*: The variety of organisms at the species level;

3. *Cultural Diversity*: The variety among individuals of the same species due to behaviors learned; and

4. *Ecosystem Diversity*: The variety of biomes and habitats occurring in the entire ecosystem of the biosphere.

Biogeography *(Ecology)*: A science that studies the adaptation of organisms to their environment, comprehending such phenomena as their origin, migration and associations. Biogeographical relationships can be understood only from an ecological perspective which would explain the exchanges between an organism and its environment. Biogeography is concerned to the evolution of species, with changes in their ranges and their extinctions. Biogeography is closely related to Geology, Physical Geography, Geomorphology, Climatology, Meteorology, Biology, Taxonomy, Genetics and Physiology.

Biomass *(Ecology)*: The total quantity or weight of organisms in a given area or volume.

Biome *(Ecology)*: A biogeographic region determined by well-defined types of life, and the soil and climate conditions that support them. A biome is a large area with similar flora, fauna, and microorganisms. Animals and plants of a biome cannot generally live outside their specific region. Some types of biome to which we are familiar are deserts, coastal dunes, prairies, taigas, tundras, temperate rain forests, tropical rain forests, cloud forests, bamboo forests, etc.

Biometric *(Tourism)*: A unique and measurable characteristic of a human being that can be measured to identify an individual. Examples of biometrics are fingerprint scanners, retina scans and voice recognition. Biometrics can be used with a smart card to authenticate the user.

Biometric Data *(Airlines)*: It is the set of human characteristics collected with the purpose to secure an individual's identity. Some of these data are: Hand geometry, iris scan, registered traveler program.

Biometrics *(Airlines)*: Biometrics is the science and technology of measuring and analyzing biological data, which are understood as body characteristics, such as fingerprints, eye retinas and irises, voice patterns, facial patterns and hand measurements. The use of biometric is no longer confined to criminal law enforcement. Biometrics provides access to information and entry to buildings. Governments are considering the implementation of biometric identifiers in passports, driver's licenses, and in an eventual ID card. Biometrics is currently used in the following cases:

1. As physical access granting systems:

2. For security scanning and as a way to avoid identity theft;

3. To establish entitlement to services and rights that are limited to certain individuals, including social services, the right to vote, and right of residence and work.

4. For the recording and association of facts, such as employee attendance monitoring, surveillance of public places, archiving and retrieving personal information.

Bionomics *(Ecology)*: A branch of science concerned with the study of an organism and its relation to its environment. Sociologically considered, the term defines a branch of sociology dealing especially with the spatial and temporal interrelationships between humans and their economic, social, and political organization.

Bioregion *(Ecology)*: A type of region defined by its natural and human features that constitutes a natural ecological community.

Biorhythms *(Airlines)*: A hypothetical cycle of the human body, in its physiological, emotional, or intellectual manifestations. In the frame of biorhythms human body is assumed is affected by travel. See also Jet Lag.

Biosphere *(Ecology)*: The part of the earth and its atmosphere where living organisms exist. The concept comprises all of earth's ecosystems included into one single unit. It is also called the Ecosphere.

Biosystem *(Ecology)*: An interacting complex of a community, consisting of plants and/or animals, and its environment functioning as an ecological unit. It is also a living organism or a system of living organisms that can directly or indirectly interact with others.

Biota *(Ecology)*: The total complement of animals and plants living in a particular region, habitat, or geological period.

Bioterrorism *(Ecology)*: A form of terrorism which is practiced by intentional release or dissemination of biological agents such as toxins, viruses, or bacteria.

Biotope *(Ecology)*: A region having uniform environmental conditions to support particular and uniform populations of animals and plants for which it is the habitat. It is the space distinguished by climatic, geographic, chemical, physical, morphological and geological factors in constant or cyclic balance and occupied by living organisms gathered in a specific association. The biotope is the abiotic (non living) component of an ecosystem.

BIP *(Airlines)*: See Baggage Management Improvement Programme.

Biplane *(Aeronautics)*: An airplane which has two wings on each side of the fuselage, one usually slightly forward and above the other.

Bird Dog *(Tourism)*: A jargon term in tourism activities to denote a free-lance person who produces business for a travel agency.

Bistro *(Tourism)*: A French term to define a small and informal restaurant featuring simple menus, where wine is served.

Bitters *(Hospitality)*: A type of spirit, bitter liquors usually made from roots, spices, fruits, or herbs steeped. They are used as cocktail ingredients and have a highly flavorful, aromatic, and bitter taste. Some of the most known bitters are Angostura, Abbot's, and Orange.

BJS *(GDS)*: Three-letter IATA code for Beijing, capital city of the Popular Republic of China.

BK *(GDS)*: A code that means: 1. Book, 2. Booking, 3. Booked

BKK *(GDS)*: Three-letter IATA code for Bangkok, capital city of Thailand.

BL Category *(Cruise)*: On some Cruise Lines, BL is a "Balcony Guarantee" cabin.

Black Box *(Aeronautics)*: A crash-proof device that records data referring an aircraft's flight, such as airspeed, heading, and pilot procedures. It is also called Flight Recorder.

Black Market *(Tourism)*: An illegal usage to trade, commerce, or exchange currency evading taxes, regulations, and governmental supervision, or all.

Black-Water Rafting *(Tourism)*: Also called Cave Tubing, it is a practice of rafting that involves the use of an inflated rubber inner tube, the kind it is normally found in a car or truck tire, as a flotation device to take rafters down river into or through subterranean lands. It began as a special treat for a temerarious few has developed into a huge tourism attraction.

Blacked Out *(Airlines)*: An expression meaning Not Available, to denote that reservations or seats are not obtainable.

Blackout Dates *(Airlines)*: Definite dates when certain types of fares are not available, or travel is not permitted at specified fares.

Blackout Periods *(Airlines)*: Periods of high demand when special rates are not available. Blackout periods usually coincide with holidays and peak travel seasons.

Blackouts *(Airlines)*: Same as Blackout Dates and Blackout Periods.

Blanc de Blancs *(Hospitality)*: A French term meaning literally "white from whites", which denotes a white wine made solely from white grapes, Chardonnay grapes, for instance. A typical example is the Champagne.

Blanc de Noir *(Hospitality)*: A French term meaning literally "white from black", and denotes a white wine made from black (or red) grapes which are fermented with the skins removed. There is a type of Champagne that uses this procedure.

Blanching *(Hospitality)*: The process of exposing a food product to steam or hot water for a short time, setting the color of green vegetables and destroying some microorganisms.

BLCY *(GDS)*: Code meaning Balcony.

Bleach *(Hospitality)*: A chemical product used in laundry operations to remove stains, kill bacteria, and whiten fabrics.

Blended Whiskey *(Hospitality)*: A light-bodied, soft whiskey, mild in flavor and aroma, made as a mixture or blend of neutral spirits and straight whiskey.

Blending *(Hospitality)*: 1. In Wine Industry, it is the use of different types of grapes to make a wine. Also the practice of blending wines of different ages or with different taste characteristics to obtain a new brand of wine. 2. In Whiskey Production, it is the skill of mixing different types of whiskeys. Sometimes whiskeys of the same type differing in age or character are mixed to create a balanced product that should be better than any of its components.

Blériot, Louis *(Airlines)*: Bleriot was a French engineer, born in Cambrai, France on July 1, 1872. He was an inventor, an aircraft designer, and a pilot who is best known for his flight over the English Channel on July 25, 1909. This was the world's first flight over a large body of water in a heavier-than-air craft. In 1900, Bleriot built a motor-powered machine called an *ornithopter*, which was intended to fly by flapping its wings. The experiment failed, but he continued working. In 1903, Blériot associated with Gabriel Voisin, another aircraft designer, to create the *Blériot-Voisin Company*. They built a floatplane glider, which made its first flight in 1905, and developed a biplane powered by an Antoinette motor. The company broke up in 1906, and Blériot began to build and fly aircraft of his own design. The Blériot V was the world's first successful monoplane.

As already said, Blériot made the first flight over the English Channel in 1909, setting a European record of 36 minutes 55 seconds and winning a £1000-prize offered by the London *Daily Mail*. This feat encouraged him to develop his fourth monoplane and first truly successful aircraft, the Blériot XI. Some time later, Blériot became committed to aeronautical design and engineering, founding the company *Société pour les Appareils Deperdussin* in 1914. The company was renamed *Société Pour Aviation et ses Derives* and became one of France's leading manufacturers of combat aircraft. After the war, Blériot formed his own company, *Blériot-Aéronautique*, for the development of commercial aircraft. Blériot died on August 2, 1936.

Blimp *(Aeronautics)*: A non-rigid airship and lighter-than-air airship. It is currently used for advertising purposes or as a camera platform for sporting events, and rarely used for tourist excursions. Without scientific support, it is said the term was coined in 1915 by Lieutenant A. D. Cunningham of the Royal Naval Air Service, as a friendly synonym with a pressure airship. It is believed that this way the word came into common usage.

BLM *(Organizations)*: An acronym for Bureau of Land

Management.

BLML *(GDS)*: Code meaning Bland Meal.

BLND *(GDS)*: A code for Blind Passenger, Passenger is blind.

Block *(Tourism)*: A number of rooms, seats, or space reserved in advance, usually by wholesalers, escorted tour operators, or travel agents having the intention to sell them as components of tour packages.

Block Bookings *(Tourism)*: A block of tourism products put under the control of a tour operator or travel agency by the supplier in order to allow them to confirm reservations without having to refer to the supplier. This arrangement is generally established by negotiation.

Block Spacing *(Airlines)*: An assignation of a number of seats on some of its flights, by one airline to another which then sells them to the traveling public through its own marketing and distribution system.

Blocked Space *(Tourism)*: Airline seats, cruise cabins, or hotel rooms reserved for a group. Such space is usually held speculatively and made available at reduced rates.

Blocked Space Flight *(Airlines)*: A flight for which the operating airline leases some seats or space to other airlines enabling them to sell those seats or space under their own designator. It is the same as Leased Space Flight.

Blog *(Computing)*: An abbreviation of web log created to share on-line updated journals or newsletters that are readily accessible to the general public by posting on a website. Blogs generally accept comments on topics of interest to the author, such as their personal experiences, hobbies, photos, video clips, and the like.

Blue Room *(Airlines)*: A slang term for lavatory on an aircraft.

Blue Train *(Tourism)*: A luxury train operating in South Africa that is widely regarded as one of the world's most luxurious trains. It combines the luxury of the world's leading hotels with the charm of a train travel, running through spectacular Africa's panoramic and enigmatic places. It operates services between Pretoria and Cape Town but the train can be chartered for any other route in South Africa.

Bluetooth *(Computing)*: A short-range radio technology for Internet and mobile devices, aimed at simplifying the share information among them.

BMA *(GDS)*: Three-letter IATA code for Bromma International Airport, serving the city of Stockholm, Sweden.

Board *(Tourism)*: 1. As a verb, the term means getting on a vehicle such as a plane, a train, a bus, or a ship. 2. As a noun, it refers to meals regime, as in a hotel stay.

Board of Directors Setup *(Hospitality)*: A meeting set up of placing chairs around a rectangular or an oval conference table.

Board Point *(Tourism)*: Station of embarkation.

Boarding Gate *(Airlines)*: The entrance to the Jetway ramp that leads to a passenger's aircraft.

Boarding Pass *(Airlines)*: A card or pass that authorizes a passenger to board an aircraft. It usually contains such boarding information as seat assignment, flight number, gate, and departure time, issued by an airline to its passengers. A ticket is not valid unless a boarding pass is issued.

Boat Bite *(Cruise)*: A jargon term for minor injuries experienced while onboard a recreational sailing vessel.

Boat Deck *(Cruise)*: The upper deck on a cruise ship where lifeboats are stored.

Boat Station *(Cruise)*: A ship's space assigned to passengers for training in lifeboat procedures or during an actual emergency.

Boatel *(Tourism)*: 1. A ship moored at a pier or wharf that functions as a hotel. 2. A waterside hotel where for sailing travelers can stay and moor their boats.

BOB *(GDS)*: Code for Boliviano, the national currency of Bolivia.

Bock *(Hospitality)*: A German beer that is darker, richer, somewhat sweeter and contains more alcohol than regular 3.2 percent beer.

Bodega *(Hospitality)*: 1. A Spanish term for wine cellar, a ground level storage hall with a good air conditioning, where wine ripens in barrels; 2. A winery, a wine-making company; 3. A bar or grocery store in some Spanish speaking countries.

Body *(Air Traffic)*: The fuselage of an airplane that holds all the pieces together.

Body *(Hospitality)*: 1. The degree of consistency, texture, firmness, or viscosity of a wine. 2 The aroma and flavor of a spirit. For example, a bodied whiskey has less flavor and aroma than a heavy-bodied whiskey.

Body Coordinates *(Air Traffic)*: Coordinates referenced to the body of the aircraft.

Boeing Company, The *(Airlines)*: Boeing is a major aerospace company maker of large commercial jets and the number two defense contractor behind Lockheed Martin. Boeing has two principal segments: Commercial Airplanes and Integrated Defense Systems. It was originally founded as "Pacific Aero Products Co." in Seattle, Washington, by William E. Boeing, on July 15, 1916. On 17 May 1917, the company was renamed as "Boeing Airplane Company" and began to build navy trainers and the Boeing Model C. Pontoons in the University of Washington's shell house. In 1918 Boeing decided to develop the first commercial flying boat. But times were hard, and to struggle difficulties, the company made furniture, phonograph cases, and fixtures for a corset company. After years of running a timber activity, Boeing created in 1927 an airline named "Boeing Air Transport" that became "United Aircraft and Transport Corp." on February 1, 1929. An agreement with Pan American World Airways (Pan Am) made it possible to develop and build the largest civil aircraft to carry passengers on transoceanic routes. It was the Boeing 314 Clipper, with a capacity of 90 passengers on day flights, and of 40 passengers on night flights. It operated its first flight in June 1938. During the 1950s decade Boeing developed the Boeing 707, the United States first commercial jet airliner. A few years later other versions were added, such as 720, 727 and 737. The Boeing Jumbo 747-100 made its public presentation in 1968, operating the first commercial flight in January 1970. During the 1980 decade, the single-aisle 757 and the larger twin-aisle 767 were built. In April 1994 Boeing introduced the most modern commercial jet aircraft at the time, the twin-engine 777, with a seating capacity of between 300 and 400 passengers in a standard three class configuration. In 2004, Boeing stopped the production of the 757 to focus on the newly-launched 787 Dreamliner as a platform of total fleet rejuvenation.

Boeing, William Edward *(Aviation)*: Boeing was an aviation pioneer who was born in Detroit, Michigan in October 1rst, 1881 to a wealthy German engineer named Wilhelm Böing. After completing his education in Switzerland, he returned to the United States to continue his schooling at the Sheffield Scientific School at Yale but did not graduate. In 1903 at age 22, William E. Boeing left college, and traveled west to Grays Harbor, Washington, where he started a new life and a business of his own. There he combined lumber operations with expeditions to Alaska. By 1910 Boeing was already fascinated with flying machines he saw for the first time during the Alaska-Yukon-Pacific Exposition in 1909. He convinced his close friend George Conrad Westervelt to build better airplanes together. In 1916, Boeing founded "The Pacific Aero Products Co". When USA entered the First World War, the company changed its name to "Boeing Airplane Company" and built 50 planes for the United States Navy. At the end of the war, Boeing concentrated on commercial aircraft, and initiated successful airmail operations. In 1929 he founded the company "United Aircraft and Transport Corp." that was split into three different enterprises in 1934. The US government had enacted antitrust laws accusing the company of monopolistic practices. The same year, in June 20, he was awarded the Daniel Guggenheim Medal for aeronautical achievement. Boeing resigned as chairman and sold his stock. According to his death certificate, William Boeing died on 28 September 1956 at the age of 74, just days before his 75th birthday by cause of a heart attack aboard his yacht.

BOG *(GDS)*: Three-letter IATA code for Bogota, the capital city of Colombia.

Boland Brothers *(Aviation)*: Joseph John Boland (1880-1970), James Paul Boland (1882-1964) and Frank E. Boland (1884-1913) were American aircraft designers who lived in Rahway, New Jersey. Frank provided the enthusiasm; Joseph supplied the mechanical genius; and James had the business sense. They got started as bicycle racers; in 1898 decided to create the "Boland Airplane and Motor Company". They invented the tailless biplane, which was a machine that had no tail, rudder, nor ailerons. It was controlled by two pivoted vertical surfaces at either end of the main planes. Their experiments were approved by mechanical experts. In 1914, upon Frank's death, the surviving brothers sold the manufacturing rights of all Boland airplanes and engines to "Aeromarine Plane and Motor Company" of Avondale, Pennsylvania. Maybe Boland brothers formed a small organization, but their contribution to the early aviation history in the United States was exceptional.

Boland, Frank *(Aviation)*: Frank E. Boland was one of the three brothers (Frank, Joseph and James) who attained important developments during the early days of US aviation. He was born in Rahway, New Jersey in 1884. Before becoming involved in aviation, Frank run a bicycle and garage business in Rahway, in association with his brothers. Frank was an intrepid and temerarious pilot. For two years, he made flight demonstrations at the Old Aeronautical Society's field, Mineola, and at Kuhnert's Aerodrome, Hackensack. The first airplane flight in Venezuela was operated by Frank Boland on 29 September 1912. After accomplishing additional successful flights in this country, he had arranged to perform exhibition flights in Trinidad and Tobago. They could not be completed, because his biplane crashed near Port of Spain the evening of January 24, 1913, while he was making a trial flight.

Boland, Joseph *(Aviation)*: Joseph Boland was one of the three brothers (Frank, Joseph and James) who attained important developments during the early days of US aviation. He was born in Rahway, New Jersey in 1880. Having been an agent for the bicycle and garage business run together with his brothers, he became interested in aviation affairs and left the automobile business to devote his time and considerable money to the development of flying machines. Joseph "Joe" Boland made his first solo flight at Correja Farm, Iselin, New Jersey in December, 1909. Since 1910 he completed other hops in experimental machines taking turns with his two associated brothers. In 1916 he received preliminary infantry training at Plattsburg. From 1942 till the end of World War II he served in the Coast Guard Reserve at the third naval district on a temporary basis without receiving payment. Joseph died in 1970 in Frederick, Maryland.

BOM *(GDS)*: Three-letter IATA code for Mumbay, important city in India.

Bon Voyage *(Tourism)*: A French expression meaning "Have a Good Trip". It is used as a traditional farewell for those departing by ship.

Bond *(Tourism)*: A amount of money guarantee to assure full payment or to indemnify a party against financial loss caused to another by the act or default of a third person or by some contingency over which the third person may have no control.

Bonded *(Tourism)*: Something that is protected or guaranteed by a bond.

Bonded Warehouse *(Airlines)*: A warehouse storage area where imported goods may be stored or processed without payment of customs duties.

Bonding *(Tourism)*: The acquisition of a guarantee of protection for a supplier or a customer. In the travel industry, certain bonding programs are mandatory. Travel Agents are obligated to be bonded to protect the airlines against defaults. Operators and Agents buy bonds voluntarily as a way to protect their clients or for promotional purposes.

Bon d'échange *(Tourism)*: A French expression defining a document to be exchanged for goods or services paid for in advance. It is synonymous with Voucher.

Booking *(Airlines)*: A reservation. The action to set apart an airline seat, a hotel room, a cruise cabin or any other service on a GDS for a guaranteed future use by a specific person at a specific fare.

Booking Engine *(Hospitality)*: An online system used to check availability and make reservations at a hotel.

Booking Fee *(GDS)*: A fee charged by a GDS on a supplier for handling its reservations.

Booking Form *(Tourism)*: Means the document to be completed by purchasers of tours, to provide the operator full particulars about who is buying the tour. It states exact information of what is being contracted, including options. The customer's signature acknowledges the liability clause has been read and understood.

Boosterism *(Tourism)*: An enthusiastic way of "boosting," or promoting a city or destination, with the purpose to improve public perception of it.

Boot *(Car Rental)*: In Great Britain, the trunk of a car.

Booth *(Tourism)*: A small temporary structure or shop at a market or fair, used for selling goods or staging presentations or exhibits.

BOS *(GDS)*: 1. Three-letter IATA code for Logan International Airport serving the city of Boston. 2. Three-letter IATA code for Boston, Massachusetts, USA.

Botel *(Tourism)*: See Boatel.

Bottom Line *(Tourism)*: The figure on the income statement that reflects the net profit or result of a transaction. The bottom line is the profit after all expenses and taxes are paid. 2. By extension, the end result or statement of something, the upshot.

Boundary *(Geography)*: A natural or artificial line dividing two or more territories.

Bouquet *(Hospitality)*: The complex of aromas developed with age in fine wines as a result from the fermentation process; young wines have aroma, not bouquet.

Bourbon *(Hospitality)*: Whiskey distilled from a mixture of corn, malt and rye, and aged in charred oak barrels. Although different formulas exist, the usual ratio is 60 percent corn, 28 percent rye, and 12 percent barley malt.

Bourgogne *(Hospitality)*: A French term used as a wide appellation covering the wine production of the Burgundy Region of France. Some of its types are the Bourgogne Blanc, Bourgogne Rouge and Beaujolais.

Bourse *(Tourism)*: A French term for market or stock market. In Travel Activity, International Travel Bourses are frequent.

Boutique Hotel *(Hospitality)*: A term originated in North America to describe a small, intimate, usually luxurious or fanciful hotel providing enhanced level of personalized service. Sometimes known as "Design Hotels" or "Lifestyle Hotels", boutique hotels began operating in the 1980s in major cities like New York, London, and San Francisco.

Boutique Operation *(Tourism)*: Any business venture committed to providing a high level of service, at a premium price, to a select clientele.

Bow *(Cruise)*: The front part of a ship. The opposite of the bow is the stern.

BP *(GDS)*: A code meaning: 1. Breakfast Plan; 2. Bermuda Plan.

BPR *(GDS)*: Code meaning Boarding Pass Reserved.

BPS *(GDS)*: Code for British Pounds Sterling.

Brand *(Business):* A term denoting the origin of a product and its rights ownership. It is synonymous with Mark and Label.

Branded Boutique *(Hospitality)*: A hotel that intends to combine the intimacy and ambience of a boutique hotel with the effectiveness and marketing features of a chain operation. See also Lifestyle Hotel.

Brandy *(Hospitality)*: Any distilled spirit made from fruit derivatives. Nevertheless, only a spirit distilled from grapes are entitled to be called brandy. If distilled from other fruit, the type of fruit precedes the word "brandy", for example Apple Brandy.

Brasserie *(Hospitality):* Brasserie is an inexpensive French or French-style restaurant tavern, or similar, that serves cheap and simple food, drinks, and especial beer.

Bravo *(Airlines)*: Designator for the letter "B" in the International Phonetic Alphabet.

BRDD *(GDS)*: A code meaning Boarded, Boarding

Break of Bulk Cargo *(Business):* A transportation term referring to the fragmentation of a shipment into smaller amounts for easier shipping.

Breakage *(Tourism)*: Expenses budgeted for a tour but not used or expended, generating additional commercial loss or damage to the tour operator. Typical examples are meals budgeted but not consumed, glasses in a restaurant, or currency fluctuations.

Breakdown *(Airlines)*: 1. An explanatory display or the process of decomposing a whole into its parts. The Fare Breakdown is the part of the ticket where fare composition is explained. 2. An account analyzed into categories.

Break-even-point *(Business)*: The level of a price at which a transaction produces neither a gain nor a loss.

Break-out Room or Breakout Room *(Hospitality)*: A small room, near a larger meeting room that is used when a large group needs to break into sections.

Breathalyzer *(Tourism)*: A portable device to administer breath tests. It is used typically by police to estimate the concentration of alcohol in a person's blood.

Brewing *(Hospitality)*: 1. The production of alcoholic beverages and alcohol fuel through fermentation. This is the method used in beer production, although the term is also common to describe the fermentation process used to produce sake and soy sauce. The term can also be used for mead and wine manufacture. 2. A cooking technique by boiling or simmering food.

Brewpub *(Hospitality)*: A bar or restaurant that brews and serves its own beer for consumption on-premise.

BRG *(Air Traffic)*: See Bearing.

Bridge *(Cruise)*: The navigation and command center of a ship, where the captain stands.

Bridge Officers *(Cruise)*: The officers who are in charge of the navigation tasks of the ship.

Briefer *(Air Traffic)*: An air traffic controller that provides pilots with information on weather conditions and other flight data prior to the flight.

Briefing *(Tourism)*: A talk or meeting at which preparatory information or detailed instructions are given, as for flight or tour operations.

Briefing Tour *(Tourism)*: A tour operated for travel agents, or other industry personnel, with the purpose to familiarize them with a new destination or new procedures.

Brioche *(Hospitality)*: A French term denoting a type of breakfast roll.

Brit *(Geography)*: A citizen of the British Isles. A Briton.

Britannia *(Geography)*: 1. The mythical tutelary goddess of Britain. She became the symbol of the British Empire after being partly fused with the war goddess Minerva. 2. The term originally used by the Romans to refer to the island of Great Britain.

British Dependent Territories *(IATA Geography)*: The territory comprising Anguilla, Bermuda, British Antarctic Territory, British Indian Ocean Territory, Cayman Islands, Gibraltar, Montserrat, Pitcairn Islands, St. Helena and Dependencies, South Georgia and the South Sandwich Islands, Turks and Caicos Islands, and British Virgin Islands.

British Service *(Hospitality)*: A type of food service in which plates are placed in front of guests who help themselves. It is not in effect nowadays.

BritRail *(Tourism)*: The trademarked name of the Association of Train Operating Companies (ATOC) of Britain. BritRail was created by the 26 railway companies of ATOC in order to encourage International travelers to visit Britain and explore its countryside by train. It has a network of 18,500 trains per day serving 2,400 stations. Some of the products BritRail offers to customers are Consecutive Passes to Flexi Passes in either 1st or Standard Class. Discount prices are available for Seniors, Youths, Families, Groups and Off-Season travel.

BRL *(GDS)*: Code for Real, the national currency of Brazil.

BRN *(GDS)*: Three-letter IATA code for Berne, capital city of Switzerland.

Brochure *(Tourism)*: A document used to present the features of a tour program, such as description of destinations, detailed services, booking conditions, prices, liability conditions, etc.

Brown Bagging *(Hospitality)*: The action of providing one's own food or beverage; for example, the ability to bring wine or liquor into a restaurant, when it is not licensed to serve alcohol.

Browser *(GDS)*: A software program used to view, download, upload, surf, or otherwise access documents (for example, Web pages) on the Internet.

Brunch *(Hospitality)*: A meal usually taken late in the morning that combines a late breakfast with an early lunch.

Brussels Tariff Nomenclature Number (BTN) *(Customs)*: The customs duties number published for use in many European countries. In the United States a similar system known as the "Harmonize Tariff Schedule" is used.

BSB *(GDS)*: Three-letter IATA code for Brasilia, the capital city of Brazil.

BSCT *(GDS)*: A code meaning Bassinet, Baby Basket.

BSI *(GDS)*: Code meaning Basic Sine In.

BSO *(GDS)*: Code meaning Basic Sine Out.

BSP *(GDS)*: A code that means Bank Settlement Plan or Billing and Settlement Plan. See Area Settlement Plan.

BSR *(GDS)*: Code meaning Banker's Selling Rate.

BST *(GDS)*: Code meaning British Summer Time. Clocks

are one hour ahead of Greenwich Mean Time (GMT) in the period between the end of March and the end of October.

BTH *(GDS)*: Code meaning Bath.

BTS *(Organizations)*: An acronym for Bureau of Transportation Statistics.

Bubble Car *(Tourism)*: A train car with a transparent dome roof for sightseeing. It is also called a Dome Car.

Bucket Shop *(Airlines)*: 1. A consolidator or any travel agency that sells to the public discounted air tickets. 2. An unofficial and usually illegal betting operation.

BUD *(GDS)*: Three-letter IATA code for Budapest, capital city of Hungary.

Budget *(Tourism)*: 1. A term qualifying hotels, tours, restaurants, etc. which are oriented to a market looking for low prices. 2. A written plan to establish an estimate of income and expenditure for a set period of time. 3. The action to cost out an itinerary or trip.

Budget Airlines *(Airlines)*: Air carriers which operate regular schedules usually for short haul routes, but charging lower fares. They fly sometimes to and from less popular airports and are also known as "No Frills" or "Low Cost Airlines".

Budget Fare *(Airlines)*: A type of fare including substantial discounts, but also subject to severe restrictions.

Budget Hotels *(Hospitality)*: Budget hotels and motels are low priced lodgings. They provide a room with bed, TV, telephone, shower, and most of them, free parking, but usually they do not have room service or a restaurant. This type of accommodation constitutes the fastest growing segment of the U.S. lodging industry.

BUE *(GDS)*: Three-letter IATA code for Buenos Aires, the capital city of Argentina.

Buffet *(Hospitality)*: A meal at which people serve themselves from an assortment of foods featuring several choices in each course, set out on a serving counter or table.

Buffet Service *(Hospitality)*: Hot and cold foods that are arranged on large serving tables in a way that guests walk up to help themselves. Sometimes each course is placed on a separate table. Service personnel, such as carvers, may be required to assist guests.

Buffer Zone *(Geography)*: 1. A border area that acts as a barrier separating or surrounding a protected area designated for special protection providing benefits to nearby human communities or mitigating adverse effects from human activities outside the area. Some buffer zones protect surrounding agricultural areas from damage by wildlife, for example. 2. A neutral area established between hostile or belligerent forces to prevent conflict.

Bug *(Computing)*: A malfunctioning computer program. By extension, any minor problem that causes a temporary setback in a system.

Buginese Schooner *(Cruise)*: A small for- rigged and aft-rigged sailing ship of Indonesian design which originally had two masts. It is used for soft-adventure sailings and accommodates from 12 to 18 passengers. The term is now often applied to similar vessels with three or four masts.

BUH *(GDS)*: Three-letter IATA code for Bucharest, capital city of Romania.

Build Method *(Hospitality)*: A method of preparing drinks by pouring ingredients into the same glass in which the drink is to be served.

Bulk *(Business)*: Cargo of a homogeneous nature that is shipped in loose or unpackaged condition. It can be either dry, such as grain and ore, or liquid, such as petroleum products. Bulk transportation is generally is provided on non-scheduled and special types of ships.

Bulk *(Tourism)*: Something that is of very large size, mass, or volume, or of a large quantity; even an overweight person's body.

BULK *(GDS)*: Code meaning "Bulky Baggage" (An awkwardly large baggage).

Bulk Carrier *(Business)*: A ship specifically designed to transport large amounts of cargo such as sugar, grain, liquefied natural gas, coal, or oil.

Bulk Contract *(Airlines)*: An agreement by which an airline sells large amounts of seats at a discount price for resale by a third party.

Bulk Data Transfer (BDT) *(GDS)*: A function offered by several GDSs in which rate updates are accumulated and then periodically transferred electronically to a specialized company for incorporation in the GDS database. Generally bulk data transfers take place on a daily basis.

Bulk Fare *(Airlines)*: A confidential low net fare negotiated between an air carrier and a tour organizer or a tour operator who purchases a specified block of seats and resells them after marking-up a commission.

Bulk Mail *(Airlines)*: A category of presorted third-class mail of the US Post Office that is mailed at a special low rate.

Bulk Process *(Hospitality)*: An inexpensive process of making champagne and other sparkling wines. It is the same as Charmat Process.

Bulkhead *(Tourism)*: An upright partition or wall dividing a ship or aircraft into sections or compartments.

Bulkhead Seats *(Airlines)*: The airplane seats located immediately after a bulkhead, with limited legroom.

Bulwarks *(Cruise)*: The structure or solid wall that surrounds open, exposed deck areas of a ship, for the protection of persons or objects on the deck.

Bullet Train *(Tourism)*: Known as "Bullet Train" in the West and as Shinkansen in Japan, it is a high speed inter city train network in Japan. The Bullet Train was the world's first high speed train. It started services in 1964 with machines running at speeds at 210 km/h (131mph), the fastest at the time. At present Bullet Trains are running at an average speed of 297 km/h (185 mph). See also Shinkansen.

Bumping *(Airlines)*: The airline practice of denying boarding or removing confirmed passengers who hold tickets on a specific flight, due to an oversold condition. The carrier asks for volunteers to take later flights, and normally provides some sort of compensation in the form of vouchers or tickets for future travel.

Bumping Policy *(Hospitality)*: A policy for accommodating customers whose reservations can not be honored by the hotel due to an over-booked situation. The hotel arranges for alternative accommodation and usually provides some added-value services or compensation to compensate the inconvenience.

Bundling *(Tourism)*: The marketing practice of combining two or more complementary goods or services together for sale at a single price or a package deal.

Bungaloft *(Hospitality)*: A bungalow-style house that also includes a loft or attic. It is primarily of Canadian usage.

Bungalow *(Hospitality)*: A lightweight and tropical house offering independent accommodation with one or more rooms. In hotels, a cottage with a small-house appearance located as a separate building that is usually offered with kitchen or kitchenette, bathroom, a verandah and, eventually, a garden.

Bungee Jumping *(Tourism)*: The sport of leaping usually head-first from a high place, such as a bridge, secured by a bungee around the ankles.

Bunker *(Cruise)*: A ship's compartment usually located on the side and/or bottom where fuel (coal or oil) is stored. The term also refers to the quantity of fuel stored onboard.

Bunkhouse *(Hospitality)*: Generally low cost accommodation with bathroom and laundry, and usually with communal self-catering (cooking) facilities. This type of accommodation is popular among backpackers and students. See Hostel.

Buoy *(Cruise)*: An anchored floating marker used to demarcate channels or warn of danger.

Burg *(Tourism)*: A German suffix denoting a fortified place, or a medieval city.

Burgher *(Tourism)*: 1. A citizen of an English borough or town. 2. A member of the middle class and prosperous solid citizen

Burgomaster *(Tourism)*: The chief magistrate or mayor a municipality of a town in Germany, Holland, Flanders, or Austria.

Bus *(Tourism)*: A vehicle seating many passengers that is used for public transport. When specially designed for carrying tourists, they are also called a "motorcoach".

Bus *(Hospitality)*: A verb meaning to remove used dishes from the table as in restaurants.

Bus Bulb *(Tourism)*: It is a sidewalk configuration by which it is extended or widened to construct a bus stop. In bus bulb stops buses can come to halt in their traffic lanes to board and debark passengers. The name comes from the rounded-shape of some extensions.

Busboy *(Tourism)*: On cruise ship or restaurants, a busboy is a low-level employee who removes dirty dishes from tables during a meal and resets them for a new service. He is also called a "busman" or a "busperson".

Bush *(Geography)*: 1. A woody plant that is smaller than a tree and has many branches growing up from the lower part of the main stem. 2. An unsettled land, wild land, or any rural place.

Bushman *(Geography)*: 1. An Australian dweller of "the bush country". 2. A member of nomadic hunters and gatherers who live in southern Africa.

Business Class *(Airlines)*: A grade of airline seat and service usually between first class and coach available on some commercial airlines designed to offer better seating, food, and service, and check-in facilities. It was originally designed to attract business travelers and is also called Executive Class, Club Class, or Intermediate Class.

Business Class Fare *(Airlines)*: The full fare established for normal, regular or usual service of the intermediate class of service, which is not limited to restricting conditions, such as maximum or minimum stay, or advance purchase requirements.

Business Days *(Tourism)*: Business Days are working days, the period of the week when companies are operating, differentiating from calendar days. Business days vary from country to country.

Business Floor *(Hospitality)*: A floor of a hotel that provides selected service to business or VIP travelers. It is also called an Executive Floor or Tower Concept.

Business Jet *(Airlines)*: A small jet aircraft, generally used by corporation for the use of their executives and employees.

Business Mix *(Hospitality)*: A hotel's combination of business proceeding from various segments such as transit travelers, corporations, leisure, and convention.

Business Mix *(Tourism)*: The percentage of booking transactions made by a travel agency combining leisure and corporate travelers.

Business-to-Business *(Tourism)*: A transaction that takes place between two companies, as opposed to a transaction involving a consumer. The term also describes a company that provides goods or services for another company.

Business-to-Consumer *(Tourism)*: A transaction that takes place between a company and a consumer, as opposed to a transaction between companies. The term also describes a company that provides goods or services for consumers.

Business Travel *(Tourism)*: Travel for commercial, governmental or educational purposes with leisure as a secondary motivation.

Bust-out Operation *(Tourism)*: A case in which an appointed agency sells air transportation services and fails to deposit the funds. The agency is declared in default or delinquency, and goes out of business. The agency owners remain responsible for the funds.

Buyback Agreement *(Car Rental)*: A practice by which rental car companies repurchase their cars at a specified price.

Buyback Car *(Car Rental)*: An automobile bought by a car rental company from a manufacturer on the condition that the manufacturer will buy the vehicle back at an agreed price. It is also called also Risk Car.

Buyer's Market *(Business)*: A market condition in which the offer exceeds the demand, resulting in a decrease of prices favorable for buyers.

Buyer's Remorse *(Business)*: A condition in which a person regrets about a purchase, often ending in a cancellation of the sale.

BVI *(Geography)*: British Virgin Islands.

BVL *(GDS)*: Code meaning Best Value Lodging.

BVU *(GDS)*: Code meaning Bay View.

BWI *(Geography)*: British West Indies.

Bypass *(Tourism)*: A route that takes traffic around the edge of a town avoiding congested roads. By extension, the marketing practice of suppliers to sell directly to the public, without mediation of travel agents.

C

C *(Airlines)*: "Charlie," name used to designate the letter "C" in the International Phonetic Alphabet

C *(GDS)*: Code meaning: 1. Business Class; 2. Car (car rental code); 3. Celsius Degrees (See Celsius Scale).

C&F *(Airlines)*: Cost of goods and Freight included in a quoted price.

C&I *(Airlines)*: Cost of goods and Insurance included in a quoted price.

C of C *(GDS)*: Code for Chamber of Commerce.

CA *(Airlines)*: Two-letter IATA code for Air China International.

CAA *(Organizations)*: An acronym for Civil Aviation Administration.

CAA *(Organizations)*: An acronym for Civil Aviation Authority.

Cab *(Tourism)*: A jargon term for a taxi or the compartment of a vehicle in front of a motor vehicle where driver sits.

Cabana *(Hospitality)*: A term derived from the Spanish *cabaña,* meaning a hotel accommodation which is separate from the main building, with or without sleeping facilities. It is also a shelter on a beach or at a swimming pool.

Cabaret *(Tourism)*: 1. A French term denoting a restaurant or nightclub that provides live entertainment of popular music, singing or dancing. 2. The floor show presented in such a restaurant or nightclub.

Cabin *(Airlines)*: The passenger or cargo compartment of an airplane. According to the plane configuration, there are separate cabins for First Class travelers, Business Class travelers and one for Economy Class travelers.

Cabin *(Cruise)*: The passengers' personal room below deck on a boat. It is also called stateroom

Cabin *(Hospitality)*: A hotel accommodation separate from the main building with an appearance of a rustic wooden small house.

Cabin, Inside *(Cruise)*: A ship's cabin without a window.

Cabin Attendant *(Airlines)*: A member of an airlines crew whose main task is to ensure the safety and comfort of the passengers aboard commercial flights. Other synonymous names are Cabin Crew, Steward or Stewardess, Air hosts or hostesses.

Cabin Cruiser *(Cruise)*: A leisure vessel with one or more cabins providing living and sleeping accommodation.

Cabin Lift *(Tourism)*: Name given to a cable car in USA.

Cabin, Outside *(Cruise)*: A ship's cabin usually providing an outside view.

Cabin Steward *(Cruise)*: An employee responsible for maintaining and cleaning the cabins aboard a ship.

Cabin Steward Cancellation Penalty *(Cruise)*: The penalty charged when travel plans are cancelled, usually after final payment has been made.

Cable *(Cruise)*: A heavy metal chain of great tensile strength usually attached to a ship's anchor. Any strong rope used aboard a ship for another purpose.

Cable *(Tourism)*: 1. A text message or telegram sent by wire (now obsolete). 2. The system of sending television programs or telephone signals along wires under the ground.

Cable Car *(Tourism)*: A hanging vehicle that is moved by an endless cable. It is used to transport people up and down a mountainside.

Cable Length *(Cruise)*: A nautical unit of measure equal to the length of a cable of 100 fathoms (600 feet, or 182.88 meters).

Cablegram *(Cruise)*: A telegram type communication transmitted by undersea cables.

Cabotage *(Airlines)*: The right to operate commercial air transport between two points within a country granted to a foreign airline. See Freedom Rights.

Cabriolet *(Tourism)*: A small two-wheeled carriage with two seats and pulled by a horse.

Cache *(Tourism)*: A hidden place to storage supplies (provisions, money, or weapons). Hiking tourists use caches suspended in the air to store provisions, preventing animals to reach them.

Cachet *(Tourism)*: A French term to define something is charming, alluring, or attractive. It also denotes something that enjoys good reputation.

CAD *(GDS)*: Code meaning: 1. Computer Aided Design; 2. Canadian Dollar.

Café *(Hospitality):* A small restaurant where coffee is served. A Café that offers outdoor seating is named a Sidewalk Cafe.

Cafe au lait *(Hospitality)*: A French expression meaning Coffee with Milk.

Cafe Noir *(Hospitality)*: A French expression for Black Coffee.

Cafeteria *(Hospitality)*: A food service operation in which guests pass through serving lines and help themselves to food items.

Cage *(Customs)*: The transporting of goods by truck to or from a vessel, aircraft, or bonded warehouse, all under customs custody.

CAHS *(Organizations)*: An acronym for Canadian Aviation Historical Society.

CAI *(GDS)*: Code meaning: 1. Computer-assisted Instruction; 2. Three-letter IATA code for Cairo, capital city of Egypt.

Cairn *(Geography)*: A mound of rocks, stones, or other objects piled up as a memorial or to mark a boundary, a path, a trail, an ancient gravesite, or a religious place.

Call Accounting System *(Hospitality)*: An application of the telephone system that prices telephone calls made by hotel guests, which sends the information to the corresponding accounting department for billing.

Call Brand *(Hospitality)*: The specific brand of liquor that is requested by a customer when placing an order. He mentions the liquor name rather than a generic one. These orders are more expensive than house brands.

Call Drink *(Hospitality)*: A drink made from a specific liquor brand.

Call Sign *(Tourism)*: An alphanumeric code that identifies an aircraft or a ship. It is used for radio communication between the vessel and land based stations, or between vessels.

Calling Card *(Hospitality)*: A card used for placing telephone calls.

Calling Card Call *(Tourism)*: A call billed to a code number on a calling card, usually with a surcharge per-call.

CAM *(GDS)*: Code meaning Computer Aided Manufacturing.

Camp *(Tourism)*: 1. A place where people stay in tents or other temporary accommodation structures. 2. An area where people are kept temporarily for a particular training or leisure reason.

Camp, To *(Tourism)*: The action of occupying a Camp.

Camper *(Tourism)*: 1. A person who stays in a tent or in a holiday camp. 2. In United Kingdom, the term also defines a camper van, a motor home. 3. In the US the term is often used for caravan.

Camping *(Tourism)*: 1. To stay in a tent on holiday. 2. The tour option that uses a camp as an accommodation place.

Camping Car *(Tourism)*: A vehicle designed to provide lodging facilities. It is also called Camping Car, Mobil Home, and Motor Home.

CAN *(GDS)*: Three-letter IATA code for Guangzhou, important city in the Popular Republic of China.

Canada and USA *(Airlines)*: For fare construction purposes in international travel Canada and USA are considered one country.

Canada Flight Supplement (CFS) *(Air Traffic)*: Canada's official airport directory, which includes information on every registered Canadian and some North Atlantic aerodromes and certified airports. It is published by NAV CANADA in separate English and French editions, and contains runway data, arrival and departure procedures, ATC and other radio frequencies and services available at each listed airport.

Canada Supplément de Vol *(Air Traffic)*: See Canada Flight Supplement.

Canada-USA Air Transport Agreement *(Airlines)*: An agreement that was signed on March 12, 2007 to replace the 1995 Agreement in its entirety by which any airline of the United States or Canada holding a valid licence for the operation of scheduled or non-scheduled air services continues to have the authorities to operate scheduled or non-scheduled international air transportation respectively to and from points in Canada and the United States as provided in the new Agreement.

Canadian Aviation Historical Society (CAHS) *(Organizations)*: The oldest and largest organization in the world dedicated to the preservation of Canada's flying heritage. It was founded in 1962 by Canadian Aviation enthusiasts from the Toronto area and received a Federal Charter in 1963. It is committed to supporting and encouraging research into Canadian aeronautical history, to promote the collection and diffusion of knowledge, and to stimulate interest and understanding of the influence of aviation on Canada's development and in the world.

Canadian Institute of Travel Counsellors (CITC) *(Organizations)*: A non-profit organization, created in 1968 to raise the level of professionalism within the travel industry by offering a wide range of education and training programs. It is an educational tool of the Canadian travel industry that promotes the professional designations of Certified Travel Counsellor and Certified Travel Manager. Furthermore, CITC keeps an up-to-date listing of certified members in the National Directory of Certified Travel Professionals, and offers value-added services to the associates.

Canadian Owners and Pilots Association (COPA) *(Organizations)*: A not-for-profit association providing information and advocacy services for Canadian pilots. At present, COPA has over eighteen thousand members, which ranks it as the largest aviation association in Canada.

Canadian Transportation Agency (CTA) *(Organizations)*: The Canadian Transportation Agency (*Office des Transports du Canada* in French) is a governmental agency established to administer transportation legislation and Government policies to help achieving an efficient and accessible transportation system by means of the necessary regulation, education, and consultation. The Agency covers all modes of transportation under federal jurisdiction found in various Acts of the Parliament. Among other responsibilities, the Agency licenses air and rail carriers; performs its role as a Canadian Aeronautical Authority by participating in international negotiations and administering bilateral agreements; resolves complaints between shippers and railways concerning rail rates, service and other matters; approves proposed construction of railway lines; protects the interests of Canadian operators when authorizing foreign carriers to operate in Canadian territorial waters or skies.

Canadian Whisky *(Hospitality)*: A blended whisky of Canada, typically light, mild, and delicate. It is distilled from mashes of corn, rye, and is aged in used or re-charred white-oak barrels.

Canal *(Geography)*: An artificial waterway constructed to connect bodies of water navigation, irrigation, water power, or recreational purposes.

Canal Barge *(Tourism)*: A long, large, usually flat bottom boat designed for transporting freight on a canal. Canal barges are usually made for the particular canal in which they will operate. Many of them are nowadays converted to passenger vessel to operate leisure cruising.

Cancel *(GDS)*: To annul, for instance, a reservation.

Cancel Bookings *(GDS)*: Any entry by a Computer Reservation System that causes a direct flight segment to be deleted from a booking file. Cancellations are counted on a per passenger basis, and per direct flight.

Cancellation *(Hospitality)*: A reservation voided by a guest.

Cancellation Charge *(Tourism)*: The charge collected for failing to use a reserved seat or accommodation, without having cancelled such reservations prior to the latest cancellation time specified by the airline or service provider.

Cancellation Clause *(Business):* A contract provision declaring the right to terminate obligations if certain events or conditions occur. Usually previous payment of a penalty is applied for travel contracts.

Cancellation Fee *(Tourism)*: The charge made for failing to use a reserved seat or accommodation, without having cancelled such reservations prior to the latest appropriated time specified by the service provider.

Cancellation Hour *(Hospitality)*: A specific time after which a hotel may release for sale all non-guaranteed reservations, according to property policy.

Cancellation Number *(Hospitality)*: A number issued to a guest who cancels a reservation, proving that a cancellation has been properly made.

Cancellation Penalty *(Tourism)*: The amount charged by the supplier for cancellations not properly or timely transacted.

Cancellation Policy *(Tourism)*: The conditions stated by an airline or hotel detailing the terms under which a booking or reservation may be revoked, the penalties resulting for so doing, and so other related points.

Canoe *(Tourism)*: A small and slender boat pointed at both ends of native origin that is propelled with a paddle.

Canoeing *(Tourism)*: The sport activity using a light boat called a canoe.

CANSO *(Organizations)*: See Civil Air Navigation Services Organization.

Canteen *(Hospitality)*: A school or camp business that sells ice-cream, snacks, and soda pop, as well as postcards, stamps, and other items.

CANX *(GDS)*: A code meaning Cancel, Cancelation, Cancelled.

Canyoning *(Tourism)*: The sport which involves jumping into a fast-flowing mountain stream and being carried down the stream while the participant floats on his back.

Capacity *(Airlines)*: 1. The maximum number of passengers an aircraft can safely transport under given circumstances. 2. The total number of aircraft handled by an airport under given circumstances.

Capacity Controlled *(Airlines)*: The capacity limited to a quantity of airline seats, hotel rooms, or rental cars available under a particular rate or promotional offer.

Capacity Dumping *(Airlines)*: The airlines marketing practice of increasing the frequencies to a route with the purpose to fight competitors intending to drive them out of business or off the route.

Capacity Limitation Agreement *(Airlines)*: An agreement between air carriers, determining the maximum capacity to be offered by each carrier on a particular route.

Cape *(Geography)*: A portion of land projecting into a body of water, usually marking the opening of a bay.

Capital *(Geography)*: The most important city or town of a country that is the seat of government and administrative centre of a country, state or province or a city that is the center of a particular activity.

Capital *(Business)*: Material wealth in the form of money or property that can be used to produce further wealth.

Capitol *(Geography)*: 1. A building or group of buildings in which a state legislature meets and where other state government offices are housed. 2. The white marble domed building in Washington, D.C., where the U.S. congress meets. 3. The decorative portion surmounting a column.

Capstan *(Cruise)*: A device aboard ships consisting of a vertical rotatable drum around which a cable is wound when lifting cargo and other heavy weights.

Capsule Hotel *(Hospitality)*: A Japanese coffin-like sleeping modular typically made of plastic or fiberglass. It provides a reduced room to sleep of about 2 meters long, 1 meter wide, 1.50 meter high. Most of them include a television, an electronic console, and wireless internet connection. Washrooms are communal. The base property usually includes pools, restaurants, or at least vending machines. In Japan it is a hotel system of high occupancy that people call *Kapseru Hoteru*. Some variants with larger accommodation designs are constructed in Kuala Lumpur, London, New York and Amsterdam, calling them "Stay Orange Hotels," "Yotel," "Pod Hotel," or "Citizen M," depending on the place.

Captain *(Tourism)*: 1. The commander of a ship. 2. The pilot in command of a civil aircraft.

Captain Only Yacht Charter *(Yacht)*: A charter with captain only, without a cook, stewardess or deck hand. Captain only charters are available on bare boat yachts only.

Captain's Cocktail Party *(Cruise)*: A shipboard cocktail party hosted by the Captain, usually, the second night into a cruise. All guests are invited and cocktails are generally complimentary. The Captain's Dinner customarily follows the Cocktail Party.

Captain's Dinner *(Cruise)*: Frequently, the second night into a cruise, the Captain invites a dinner in the ship's main dining room. The ship's galley generally tries hard to deliver their finest cuisine.

Captain's Farewell Cocktail Party *(Cruise)*: On 5-nights cruises or longer, a farewell cocktail party is often hosted by the Cruise Director on behalf of the Captain. All passengers are invited to attend and Cocktails are usually complimentary.

Captain's Farewell Dinner *(Cruise)*: On 5-nights cruises or longer, a dinner is offered to all passengers with the best food of the ship.

Capture *(Air Traffic)*: To attain an objective, such as reaching a radial of a radio station.

CAR *(GDS)*: Code for Car Rental.

Car Class *(Car Rental)*: Size and type of rental car. Car classes include small (compact and economy), medium (intermediate and full-size), large (premium and luxury), SUV (intermediate, standard and full-size) and specialty (convertibles, mini vans and 12-passenger vans). Size, style, and rental price have to be specified when renting a car.

Car Ferry *(Tourism)*: A ship designed to transport automobiles and passengers.

Car for Hire *(Car Rental)*: A British term for Rental Car.

Car Pool *(Tourism)*: See High Occupancy Vehicle.

Car Pool Lane *(Tourism)*: See High Occupation Vehicle (HOV) Lane.

Car Rental Agreement *(Car Rental)*: Contract between a car rental vendor and a customer.

Caracalla Thermal Baths *(Tourism)*: A leisure place considered was one of the precedent elements of tourism origin. In 206 A.D. Emperor *Septimus Severus* started the construction of a thermal bath complex which, ten years after, became the largest and most beautiful one in Rome. The remains of the main building that covered eleven hectares can still be observed. Inside thick rectangular walls, the construction comprised some other buildings, such as the library, entertainment and conference rooms, and the gymnasium. The surrounding gardens were decorated with huge cup shaped fountains. An entrance led into the *Frigidarium* (cold water room) and its pool, followed by the *Tepidarium* and the *Calidarium* (hot water room), a 35 square meter room. A huge circular pool was heated by a system called *pannelli radianti* (radiant panels). The accommodation capacity of the Thermal Baths reached up to 2000 people at a time.

Caravan *(Tourism)* 1. In United Kingdom, a large covered vehicle for living or traveling in. It is designed as a mobile home that contains beds and cooking equipment, and is usually pulled by a car. 2. A group of persons traveling together. Typical examples are caravans of desert merchants, especially in northern Africa and Asia that are organized to cross the desert together for safety, usually with a train of camels. 3. A convoy of vehicles such as military vehicles, traveling together.

Caravanning *(Tourism)*: Going on holiday in a caravan.

Carbon Dioxide Equivalent (CO2e) *(Ecology)*: The measure unit that is used to evaluate the global warming potential (GWP) of each of the seven greenhouse gases and their impact.

Carbon Offset *(Ecology)*: The result of any action undertaken to reduce carbon emissions or increase carbon seclusion.

Card Key *(Hospitality)*: A plastic card, similar to a credit card, used in place of a metal key to open a guestroom doors. Card keys work with electronic locks.

Card Mill *(Tourism)*: A term for a malicious practice by which a travel agency recruits outside salespeople offering seductive instant travel benefits said to be obtainable with the photo ID card issued by the agency. It is an illegitimate business of pyramid scheme that sells potentially fake ID cards.

Card-not-present Transaction *(Tourism)*: Usual practice by which a customer pays with a credit card to a supplier who is not in the same place. Such transaction can be made by mail, fax, or Internet.

Cardinal Points *(Geography)*: It is a general term which refers to the four main directions: North, South, East, and West.

Carfare *(Tourism)*: The fare charged for a ride on a bus, taxi or a municipal transportation system.

Cargo (CGO) *(Airlines)*: Goods carried as freight by sea, road or air. Also referred to as "goods", it means any property carried or to be carried on an aircraft, other than mail or other property carried under terms of an international postal convention.

Cargo Accounts Settlement System (CASS) *(Airlines)*: A system of accounting and settling accounts between CASS Airlines and appointed IATA Cargo Agents.

Cargo Agents *(Airlines)*: Cargo Agents approved by IATA for the promotion, sale, and handling of international air cargo on behalf of IATA Member Airlines.

Cargo Charges Correction Advice (CCA) *(Airlines)*: The document used for the notification of changes to the transportation terms, such as charges and/or the method of payment.

Cargo Declaration *(Customs)*: Information submitted prior to departure or arrival of goods, providing the particulars required by Customs.

Cargo Liner *(Airlines)*: An aircraft or ship which transports freight. See also Freighter.

Cargo Manifest *(Airlines)*: A document listing the goods loaded on a flight. It is mainly used for customs entry or exit.

Cargo Receipt *(Airlines)*: It is a receipt of cargo for shipment by a consolidator.

Cargo Services Conference (CSC) *(Airlines)*: An IATA organism that is responsible for the Air Waybill specifications and standards. Its primary objectives are: Setting guidelines for air cargo procedures; developing common standards on broad cargo services; communicating and maintaining contact with other IATA bodies such as Cargo Agency Conference, Cargo Tariff Coordinating Conferences, Passenger Services Conference, Airport Services Committee, IATA Ground Handling Council, and Revenue Accounting Panel. The CSC's functions are based on the following legal instruments:

1. Resolution 600a that provides the governing rules on the use of air waybill, technical specifications, completion instructions, distribution of copies and applicable conditions when transmitting air waybill information electronically; and,

2. Resolutions 600b and 600b (II) that determine the standards for the Conditions of Contract and notices included in the air waybill.

Carhop *(Hospitality)*: An employee who serves food to people in cars at a drive-in restaurant.

Caribbean, The *(Geography)*: The Caribbean is an insular region in the Americas, consisting of the Caribbean Sea and a set of numerous islands. It is located southeast of North America, east of Central America, and to the north and northwest of South America. It covers an area of 2,718,000 square kilometers (1,049,000 square miles) and comprises more than 7,000 islands, islets and cays. The most distinguishable of the islands are the Antilles, divided into the Greater Antilles (Cuba, Jamaica, Hispaniola, and Puerto Rico) and the Lesser Antilles. The Lesser Antilles are also divided into the Windward Islands and Leeward Islands, names that refer to their position relative to the winds that blow from the northeast. The principal islands of the Windward group are Dominica, Grenada, Martinique, Saint Lucia, and Saint Vincent; while the main islands of the Leeward group are Antigua, Guadeloupe, Montserrat, Saint Kitts and Nevis, and the Virgin Islands. The Caribbean islands are a chain extended over 2,482 kilometers (1,543 miles) from the

North to the South with a width of 2,644 kilometers (1,643 miles) from East to West. The Caribbean geography is not uniform, and the climate varies from one island to another, although in general it is a mild tropical climate. Some islands, such as the Bahamas, Barbados, Bonaire, the Cayman Islands and Antigua, have a relatively flat terrain of non-volcanic origin; many others are rugged territories with low mountain-ranges, such as the islands of Cuba, Dominica, Hispaniola, Jamaica, Montserrat, Puerto Rico, Saba, Saint Kitts, Saint Lucia, Saint Vincent and the Grenadines, Trinidad and Tobago, and the Virgin Islands. The Caribbean supports exceptional diverse ecosystems and is considered as a biodiversity hotspot. Sea waters are open and clear, making the Caribbean a major tourist destination. The whole region counts with many popular leisure destinations. It can be said that each island is a destination itself, with its particular allures and features. Major tourist concentrations are in Cuba, Dominican Republic, Jamaica and Puerto Rico.

Caribbean Area Sub-area *(IATA Geography)*: The territory comprising Anguilla, Antigua and Barbuda, Aruba, Bahamas, Barbados, Bermuda, Cayman Islands, Cuba, Dominica, Dominican Republic, French Guiana, Grenada, Guadeloupe, Guyana, Haiti, Jamaica, Martinique, Montserrat, Netherlands Antilles (Bonaire, Curacao, St. Maarten), St. Kitts and Nevis, St. Lucia, St. Vincent and the Grenadines, Trinidad and Tobago, Turks and Caicos Islands, Suriname, Virgin Islands (British).

Caribbean Basin Initiative *(Geography)*: A unilateral and temporary United States program initiated by the 1983 "Caribbean Basin Economic Recovery Act" (CBERA) to promote economic growth in the region through lower tariffs.

Caribbean Islands *(IATA Geography)*: The islands of Anguilla, Antigua and Barbuda, Aruba, Barbados, Cayman Islands, Cuba, Dominica, Grenada, Guadeloupe, Hispaniola (Haiti and Dominican Republic), Jamaica, Martinique, Montserrat, Netherlands Antilles (Bonaire, Curacao, St. Maarten), St. Kitts and Nevis, St. Lucia, St. Vincent and the Grenadines, Trinidad and Tobago, Turks and Caicos Islands, Virgin Islands (British).

Caribbean Tourist Organization (CTO) *(Organizations)*: A regional tourism association formed by government and private sector operatives in the tourism industry across the Caribbean. It collects and disseminates research and data on the development of the regional industry worldwide.

CARICOM *(Geography)*: The Caribbean Community (originally the Caribbean Community and Common Market) was established by the Treaty of Chaguaramas which came into effect on August 1, 1973. The first four signatories were Barbados, Jamaica, Guyana and Trinidad and Tobago. A new Treaty of Chaguaramas was signed by the Heads of Government of the Caribbean Community on July 5, 2001 at their Twenty-Second Meeting of the Conference in Nassau, The Bahamas. It incorporated the Single Market and Economy (CSME) to CARICOM:

Carnet *(Customs)*: 1. A document issued by a US customs office authorizing the transport of a motor vehicle from one country to another without payment of duty. 2. A US customs document authorizing the holder to carry or send merchandise temporarily into a foreign country for display, demonstration, or similar purposes, without paying duties.

Carnet *(Tourism)*: A set of travel tickets or coupons that cost less than the individual tickets purchased separately.

Carnival *(Tourism)*: A public festive occasion of enjoyment and entertainment involving wearing unusual clothes, dancing, street processions, costumes, music, eating and drinking. The period just before Lent begins is also named Carnival, and it is in this time when the most famous events are held, such as the Mardi Gras in New Orleans, the Carnival Parades in Rio de Janeiro and the Carnival celebrations of Trinidad and Tobago.

Carnivore *(Ecology)*: An animal that eats other animals. It is a category of the Trophic Chain that includes also herbivores and omnivores.

Carousel *(Airlines)*: A continuous moving belt at an airport from where passengers collect their bags.

Carriage *(Business)*: Also referred to as "transportation", means the conveyance of passengers and/or baggage or cargo by air, or surface with or without payment.

Carriage, International *(Airlines)*: In the spirit of the Warsaw

Convention, and, according to the contract of carriage, International Carriage is the transportation in which, the place of departure and any place of landing are situated in different sovereign countries.

Carrier *(Airlines)*: In general sense, any company which transports passengers or freight. In the air transportation activity, it is an airline that issues the ticket or the airway bill. Carriers are also all the airlines participating in the transportation of passengers or goods.

Carrier, Common *(Airlines)*: Any firm engaged in the transport of people, goods over land, sea, or through the air, for a specific rate. By regulation, a common carrier is obligated to carry all passengers and goods, provided accommodation is available and the established price is paid.

Carrier Containers *(Airlines)*: The containers over which the carrier has control either by ownership or by leasing from container companies or container suppliers.

Carrier, First *(Airlines)*: The participating airline operating the first sector of the transportation.

Carrier Frequency *(Airlines)*: The main frequency of a transmitter, or RFID reader, which can be changed, or modulated to transmit information.

Carrier, Issuing *(Airlines)*: The airline that issues the ticket or airway bill to be used for the entire journey.

Carrier, Last *(Airlines)*: The participating airline operating the last sector of the transportation.

Carrier, Operating *(Airlines)*: The airline that actually provides carriage or other incidental services inherent to such carriage. The Operating Carrier can be different to the Marketing Carrier.

Carrier, Participating *(Airlines)*: Any carrier over whose routes the transportation is performed under the ticket or airway bill provisions.

Carrig *(Tourism)*: Also called a Jaunting Car, it is an Irish two-wheeled cart drawn by a horse, which is used to operate tourist excursions.

Carrying Capacity *(Airlines)*: The quantity of people or things that an aircraft or other vehicle is designed to carry.

Carrying Capacity *(Tourism)*: The amount of recreational activities a region can accept without deteriorating the environment.

Carrying Capacity *(Ecology)*: The maximum population an area can support without undergoing deterioration.

Carry-on *(Airlines)*: A piece of luggage suitable for being carried aboard an airplane by a passenger.

Carry-on Baggage or Luggage *(Airlines)*: The luggage allowed for a passenger to take aboard an airplane which fits into the space allotted for such luggage. Most carriers state that the bag must fit in the overhead bin or under the seat in front of the passenger. The usual maximum measurements must not exceed 22 x 14 x 9 inches. The term is opposed to Checked Baggage.

Cart Service *(Hospitality)*: A type of table service used by servers for preparing menu items beside the guest's table. Menu items are cooked, and sometimes flambéed in front of the guest. See French Service.

Cartage *(Business)*: The charge assessed for transporting goods for short distances, such as within a commercial area or town. It is also called Drayage or Haulage.

Cartographer *(Geography)*: A person who makes or draws maps.

Cartography *(Geography)*: The science or art of making or drawing maps.

CAS *(GDS)*: Code meaning: 1. Computer-assisted Selling; 2. Three-letter IATA code for Casablanca, important city in Morocco.

Cash Advance *(Tourism)*: 1. An amount given in cash to an employee to cover envisaged expenditures. 2. A loan given by a credit card company, in anticipation that the borrower will be able to repay it.

Cash Bar *(Hospitality)*: Also known as À la Carte Bar or a No Host Bar (sometimes spelled No-host Bar or Nohost Bar). The term refers to bar beverages at a social event, which have to be paid by guests. It is opposed to a Hosted Bar where drinks are paid by the host. By extension, there are a No Host Bar and Menu and a No Host Dinner.

Cash Method *(Tourism)*: An accounting system to record income and expenses at the same time the transaction is completed. See also Accrual Method.

Cashless Cruising *(Cruise)*: A system of payment in which all purchases made onboard (such as drinks, shore tours, etc.) are signed for, and the final bill is presented against a credit card or cash deposit given upon check-in.

Casino *(Tourism)*: A gambling establishment where visitors can find a variety of gaming and/or gambling choices.

Casino Hotel *(Hospitality)*: A smaller hotel with a casino. A type of property that has not or any amenities as in larger resorts of casino resorts.

Casino Resort *(Hospitality)*: A full-service resort with a casino. Generally, casino resorts have several restaurants, retail stores, lounges, showrooms, and convention facilities.

CASMA *(Airlines)*: Acronym for Computerized Airline Sales and Marketing Association.

CASS *(Airlines)*: See Cargo Accounts Settlement System.

Cast Member *(Tourism)*: A cast member is any employee of The Walt Disney Company. The term was coined by Walt Disney, so it is erroneous to refer to employees of other theme parks.

Castaway *(Cruise)*: 1. The survivor of a shipwreck. 2. A person that is rejected by the society.

Castle Road, The *(Tourism)*: A tourist itinerary that runs from Mannheim in Germany to Prague in the Czech Republic. It is a route of 975 kilometer long that features many fortresses and medieval castles.

Casual Courier *(Airlines)*: A person who serves as an air courier on a one-time basis.

Casual Food *(Hospitality)*: The meal consumed at casual restaurants, where formalities are not required, but the offer is not a full table service. Casual food offers higher quality of service and better atmosphere than fast food expenders.

CAT *(Air Traffic)*: Clear Air Turbulence. The disturbance caused to an aircraft when flying through inclement weather or air pockets.

Catamaran *(Tourism)*: A twin hulled ship or boat. The twin hulls run parallel to one another and are connected by a central section which is most often designed with a living and dining area.

Category *(Tourism)*: The category is a concept that joins together the elements permitting to assign a qualification, depending on the service nature of the supplier.

Category *(Cruise)*: A price range of cabins, usually offered from the most expensive to the least expensive. In general, cabins in the same category are on the same deck, and provide similar amenities.

Cater *(Hospitality)*: A verb that means to provide food and drink for a social event, such as a party or reception.

Catering *(Hospitality)*: 1. The business of supplying of food and drink for a social event. 2. The department at a hotel responsible to provide food and drink for a social event.

Catering Manager *(Hospitality)*: A manager in a hotel who promotes and sells banquet facilities on the basis of his expertise to plan, organize, and execute hotel banquets.

Cattle Car *(Tourism)*: A pejorative form to qualify a transport that is filled to capacity or excessively crowded.

Caution *(Air Traffic)*: A signal which alerts the operator to an impending dangerous condition requiring attention, but not necessarily immediate action.

Cay *(Geography)*: A small island in the Caribbean.

Cayley, Sir George *(Airlines)*: Cayley was an English engineer born in Brompton-by-Sawdon, the 27 of December, 1773. He was a pioneer of aeronautical engineering, who is remembered for his flying machines, including his gliders. The experiments led him to build an airfoil and to identify the four vector forces that influence an aircraft flight: thrust, lift, drag, and gravity. His glider model of 1804 resembles a modern aircraft, with a pair of large wings, a smaller tailplane at the back and a vertical fin. By 1849 he designed and built a triplane powered with flappers piloted by an unknown ten-year-old boy. With the continued assistance of his grandson, George John Cayley, and his resident engineer, Thomas Vick, Cayley developed a larger scale glider which flew across Brompton Dale in 1853. At the end of a prolific life, Sir George Cayley died in December 15, 1857.

CBBG *(GDS)*: Code for Cabin Baggage.

CBD *(GDS)*: An American term to describe the commercial area of a town meaning: 1. Central Business District; 2. Commercial Business District.

CBI *(GDS)*: Code meaning Computer-based Instruction.

CBN *(GDS)*: Code for Cabin.

CBP *(Customs)*: See Customs and Border Protection.

CC *(GDS)*: A code meaning Flight Closed, with waiting list closed.

CCA *(Airlines)*: See Cargo Charges Correction Advice.

CCAR *(GDS)*: Code for Compact Car.

CCEF *(Customs)*: Code for Customs Centralized Examination Facility.

CCP *(Airlines)*: Code meaning Currency of Country of Payment.

CCRN *(GDS)*: Code meaning Credit Card Returns Notice.

CCS *(GDS)*: Code meaning Change Segment Status.

CCTE *(GDS)*: Code meaning Certified Corporate Travel Executive.

CCTV *(GDS)*: Code meaning Closed Circuit Television.

CCU *(GDS)*: Three-letter IATA code for Calcutta, important city in India.

CD-ROM *(GDS)*: Code for Compact disc, read-only memory. It is a device that stores computer programs and data.

CDC *(GDS)*: Code meaning Centers for Disease Control and Prevention.

CDD *(Hospitality)*: See Cooling Degree Day.

CDG *(GDS)*: Three-letter IATA code for Charles de Gaulle International Airport, serving the city of Paris, France.

CDM *(Air Traffic)*: See Collaborative Decision Making.

CDR *(Air Traffic)*: See Coded Departure Routes.

CDT *(Air Traffic)*: See Central Daylight Time.

CDW (*Car Rental***)**: See Collision Damage Waiver.

CEAVYT *(Tourism)*: Acronym for *Confederación Española de Agencias de Viajes y Turoperadores*, meaning Spanish Confederation of Travel Agencies and Tour Operators.

Ceiling *(Air Traffic)*: The maximum height above sea level which an aircraft can reach under given standard conditions.

Ceiling *(Hospitality)*: The maximum limit of expenditures set by an establishment.

Celsius *(Climate)*: The centigrade thermometer scale adopted from the Swedish astronomer Anders Celsius (1701-1744). The term "Celsius" is usually preferred to as "centigrade", especially in technical contexts. Celsius is the standard accepted term when citing temperatures.

Celsius Scale *(Climate)*: The metric scale for measuring temperature, in which water freezes at 0 degrees and boils at 100. It is used in most countries of the world, excepting the USA that uses Fahrenheit scale.

Center *(Air Traffic)*: Short for ARTCC.

Center City Hotel *(Hospitality)*: A full-service hotel located in a downtown area.

Center of Gravity *(Aeronautics)*: The point at which all aircraft's weight is considered to be concentrated. It is the point of balance and is located along the longitudinal centerline. Its exact location depends upon the amount of fuel it holds, the place where load is located, and the load's weight.

Central Africa *(IATA Geography)*: The territory comprising Malawi, Zambia and Zimbabwe.

Central America *(IATA Geography)*: The territory comprising Belize, Costa Rica, El Salvador, Guatemala, Honduras, and Nicaragua.

Central America *(Geography)*: It is a geographic region of the American Continent, connecting North America with South America. Central America is a narrow strip of land extended from the Isthmus of Tehuantepec in Mexico to the Isthmus of Panama. Central America has an area of around 592,000 square kilometers. The Pacific Ocean borders to the west, the Caribbean Sea to the east, and the Gulf of Mexico to the northeast. The region is characterized by volcanic eruptions and earthquakes that happen from time to time. Fertile soils constitute productive highland areas that sustain dense populations.

Central America has many places of natural, historical and archeological interest. The following list is a brief summary of some of the outstanding tourist destinations: Guatemala City, the capital of Guatemala, situated in the heart of three magnificent volcanoes, with a history that dates back to the mid 16th century; Panajachel, a charming town situated in the Guatemalan highlands at the lake of Atitlan; Chichicastenango, a Cultural Trade Center, and the Mayan City of Tikal, an archeological site, a must for explores.

Nicaragua has 78 nature reserves covering more than 21,000 km2. Some of the most important places are: Indio-Maíz Biological Reserve, Central America's largest expanse of lowland rain forest reserve, called by UCLA biologists the finest rain forest nature reserve in Central America; Los Guatuzos Wildlife Refuge, a precious wetland, gallery forest and tropical wet forest wildlife park located on the southern shores of Lake Nicaragua and the western shores of the San Juan River; La Flor Wildlife Refuge, a coastal sea turtle nesting site, one of the most important of the Pacific Ocean coast in the Americas. Costa Rica has a great deal of eco-tourism and nature tours to offer. The abundant precipitation helps to create the rivers in this country, some of which offer excellent conditions for whitewater rafting.

Central Daylight Time (CDT) *(Geography)*: CDT is 5 hours behind of Coordinated Universal Time (UTC). CDT is used during summer in these Canadian provinces: Manitoba, Kugluktuk and Cambridge Bay in Nunavut (Other parts use EST/EDT or EST only), most parts west of 90 West of Ontario (Parts east of 90 West is on EST/EDT), Creighton and Denare Beach in Saskatchewan. CDT is used in the summer in these US states: Alabama, Arkansas, North-West parts of Florida, Illinois, part of Indiana, Iowa, Kansas, the Western part of Kentucky, Louisiana, a few Western counties of Michigan, Minnesota, Mississippi, Missouri, Eastern parts of Nebraska, North and Eastern parts of North Dakota, Oklahoma, Eastern parts of South Dakota, Western part of Tennessee, Texas, Wisconsin.

Central Heating System *(Hospitality)*: A system which supplies heat to areas of a building from a central unit through a network of ducts or pipes.

Central Reservation Office (CRO) *(Hospitality)*: Part of an affiliate reservation network which deals directly with the public, processes toll-free telephone reservations and electronic reservations, advertises a central telephone number, provides participating properties with communications technology, and bills them for handling their reservations.

Central Reservation System *(Hospitality)*: A reservation network, external to properties.

Central Standard Time (CST) *(Geography)*: Is 6 hours behind of Coordinated Universal Time (UTC). CST is used during winter in these Canadian provinces: Manitoba, Nunavut (Kugluktuk, Cambridge Bay only, other parts use EST/EDT or EST), Ontario - most parts west of 90 West, Saskatchewan - only Creighton and Denare Beach. CST is used all year in these Canadian provinces: A few communities of Ontario, most of Saskatchewan. CST is used during winter in these US states: Alabama, Arkansas, North-West parts of Florida, Illinois, Few north-western counties of Indiana near Chicago, Iowa, Kansas, except four western counties, Western part of Kentucky, Louisiana, A few western counties of Michigan, Minnesota, Mississippi, Missouri, Eastern parts of Nebraska, North and Eastern parts of North Dakota, Oklahoma, Eastern parts of South Dakota, Western part of Tennessee, Texas, Wisconsin.

Centralized Billing *(Tourism)*: A system in which a travel agent issues a single invoice for travel made by several persons of a corporation.

Centralized Commissions *(Tourism)*: A system in which a supplier pays commissions from a central office, rather than having properties paying commissions individually.

Centralized Payment Plan *(Tourism)*: See Centralized Commissions.

CEO *(Business)*: See Chief Executive Officer.

Certificate of Airworthiness *(Airlines)*: Document issued by a national civil aviation authority to certify that an aircraft satisfies requirements for safe operations and other demands.

Certificate of Analysis *(Customs)*: It is a certificate required by some countries attesting the quality and/or composition of food or pharmaceutical products.

Certificate of Free Sale *(Tourism)*: A certification released by an official office declaring that a product may be freely sold to the public because it meets safety and health requirements and thus.

Certificate of Inspection *(Customs)*: A document certifying the products were in good condition the time prior to shipment.

Certificate of Manufacture *(Customs)*: A statement in which a producer gives evidences on the place his products were manufactured, the manufacturing completion, and confirms the goods are at the buyer's disposal.

Certificate of Origin *(Customs)*: A document often required by certain countries indicating that the goods to be shipped are originated and were produced in the exporter's country.

Certificate of Seaworthiness *(Cruise)*: A document issued by a national maritime authority to certify that a ship satisfies its requirements for safe navigation.

Certificated Airport *(Air Traffic)*: Any airport serving scheduled or unscheduled air carrier aircraft that operate under strict approval of the aeronautic authority which attests that the airport meets minimum standards in accordance with established regulations.

Certification *(Business)*: 1. The act of validating the authenticity of something or someone. 2. A document emitted by an authorized office attesting that a person or an organization meets minimum standards or qualifications in a specified area.

Certified Tour Professional (CTP) *(Tourism)*: A certification given to tour professionals after completing academic study, professional service, escorted travel employment, and evaluation requirements. The CTP Program is administered by the National Tour Foundation and is open to individuals employed in any segment of the travel industry.

Certified Travel Associate (CTA) *(Tourism)*: A travel professional certified by the Institute of Certified Travel Agents, who has passed a series of demanding tests, assuring the traveling public of professional competence.

Certified Travel Counselor (CTC) *(Tourism)*: Ultimate designation of professional competence attesting to a travel agent's successful completion of a study program. It is granted by the Institute of Certified Travel Agents to travel professionals with five year's or more industry experience. The CTC certification can be compared to the "Master's Degree "of the industry.

CES *(Customs)*: Customs Examination Station

CF *(Airlines)*: Code for Constructed Fare.

CFCs *(Ecology)*: The code means Chlorofluorocarbons, some chemical components responsible for the diminution of the layer of ozone. They are found in aerosol sprays, refrigerators, and air conditioners, among other products.

CFM *(GDS)*: A code meaning Confirm, Confirming.

CFMD *(GDS)*: Code for Confirmed.

CFO *(Business)*: Chief Financial Officer. He is the corporate officer primarily responsible for managing the financial affairs of the agency, and for its financial planning and record-keeping.

CFS *(Air Traffic)*: See Canada Flight Supplement.

CFY *(GDS)*: A code that means Clarify, Clarifying, Clarified.

CGO *(GDS)*: Code for Cargo.

CH *(GDS)*: A code meaning: 1. Child, 2. Charter.

CHA *(GDS)*: Acronym for Caribbean Hotel Association.

Chain *(Hospitality)*: A group of hotels linked by a common name, common policy, common ownership and common marketing practices.

Chain *(Geography)*: A series of islands usually grouped by political, cultural, or economic interests.

Chain Operating Company *(Hospitality)*: A firm that operates several properties and provides both a trademark and a reservation system to all managed properties. Typical hotel chain examples are Intercontinental Hotels, Hilton Hotels Corporation, Holiday Inn Worldwide, Best Western, among others.

Chain Restaurant *(Hospitality)*:   A multi-unit organization involving several restaurants. Chain restaurants often share the same menu, purchase supplies and equipment cooperatively, and follow operating procedures that are standardized for every restaurant in the chain.

Chaining Recipes *(Hospitality)*: A particular menu item that includes a number of sub-recipes which can be maintained as a single record in the food service computer system.

Chair Lift *(Tourism)*: A transport system of chairs hanging from an endless overhead cable. It is also called a "Ski Lift" and is used at ski resorts for transporting passengers up or down a mountainside.

Chalet *(Hospitality)*: Also called Swiss Chalet, it is a detached house or villa with a sloping roof and wide eaves very common in the ski regions of Europe.

Chalet-hôtel *(Hospitality)*: A French term meaning a comfortable refuge that provides lodging services. Chalet-hôtels are usually accessible by a car route.

Chalet-Loisir *(Hospitality)*: A French term denoting a recent type of French accommodation. It is commonly located in natural environments, where tourists can practice sport activities.

Chambermaid *(Hospitality)*: A maid who is employed to clean and care for rooms at a hotel.

Chambre d'hôte *(Hospitality)*: A French expression synonymous with Guest-house meaning lodging in rural places that include room and breakfast in the price.

Champagne Method *(Hospitality)*: The traditional method of making champagne, known as the *French Méthode Champenoise*. In this method the second fermentation takes place in the bottle in which the champagne is sold.

Change of Equipment *(Airlines)*: A scheduled change of aircraft occurring at least once en route between origin and destination, not changing the flight number.

Change of Gauge *(Airlines)*: Same as above. A single flight number is used.

Channel *(Cruise)*: 1. Any navigable course over a body of water. 2. A passage in a harbor assigned for a safe transit of ships.

Channel *(Geography)*: The bed of a river, stream, or canal. 2. A relatively narrow sea path between two land masses, such as the Venice Channels or the English Channel.

Channel *(Tourism)*: 1. A means to access, or to communicate. 2. A part of the distribution system used by a supplier to reach a customer, such as storefront travel agencies, brochures, web sites, etc.

Channel-based Pricing *(Airlines)*: A price charged for a product or service, depending on the means of delivery. For instance, GDS companies charge airlines lower fees per-segment to encourage them to use a specific booking tool.

Channeler *(Tourism)*: Often called a Specialty Channeler, he is a professional specializing in a type of travel who intermediates between a provider and the ultimate consumer of a product.

Chaptalization *(Hospitality)*: A method of adding sugar to the must prior to or during fermentation when natural grape sugars aren't high enough to produce reasonable alcohol levels.

Chapter IV Aircraft *(Airlines)*: Any of the last generation's jet airplanes that meet noise standards set by the ICAO.

Charbroiler *(Hospitality)*: A kitchen tool with a bed that radiates heat produced by burners just below it. A grill above the bed holds the food, giving an appearance and a flavor similar to that achieved with a charcoal fire.

Charge *(Airlines)*: 1. An amount to be paid for a special or contingent service related to the carriage of a passenger or baggage. 2. An amount or rate to be paid for the transportation of goods or excess baggage.

Charge, Cancellation *(Tourism)*: The charge collected for failing to use a reserved seat or accommodation, without having cancelled such reservations prior to the latest cancellation time specified by the airline or service provider.

Chargé d'affaires *(Airlines)*: A diplomatic agent who is head of a diplomatic mission in the absence of the accredited ambassador. Usually, a Chargé d'affaires is appointed in cases when diplomatic relations are delicate between his country and the receiving state, and is recognized under the Vienna Convention on Diplomatic Relations of 1961.

Charge, Excess Baggage *(Airlines)*: The charge collected for baggage exceeding the baggage allowance.

Charge, Joint *(Airlines)*: A charge applied for carriage over the routes of the participating carriers, published as a single amount.

Charge, Local *(Airlines)*: A charge applied for carriage over the routes of a single carrier. Same as On-line Charge

Charge, On-line *(Airlines)*: Same as Local Charge.

Charge, Published *(Airlines)*: The amounts specifically announced in the carrier fare publications.

Charge, Through *(Airlines)*: The total amount charged from point of origin to point of destination.

Charge, Valuation *(Airlines)*: A charge on the baggage transported, based on the declared value of such baggage.

Charges, Combination of *(Airlines)*: An amount resulting from the sum of two or more charges.

Charlie *(Airlines)*: Designator for the letter "C" in the International Phonetic Alphabet.

Charmat Process *(Hospitality)*: An inexpensive process of making champagne and other sparkling wines. It is the same as Bulk Process.

Chart, Nautical *(Cruise)*: A map of navigable waters, pointing depths and hazards.

Chart, Weather *(Climate)*: An outline map that shows weather patterns.

Charter *(Airlines)*: 1. A contract to rent or lease an aircraft or other vehicle for personal or special use, or for the use of a group. 2. Any aircraft or vehicle so used or any trip taken by such means.

Charter *(Business)*: A document incorporating a company, which includes the articles of incorporation, the certificate of incorporation, and the specification of its rights.

Charter Airlines *(Airlines)*: Airlines that operate non scheduled flights. Most scheduled airline companies also operate charter flights but are not considered or classified as charter airlines.

Charter Flight *(Airlines)*: A type of flight operated exclusively for the use of a person or a specified group of passengers.

Charter, Inclusive-Tour (ITC) *(Tourism)*: A type of group excursion which travels by a chartered aircraft and has tour services included in the price.

Charter Operations *(Airlines)*: The expression comprises all of the transportation procedures for groups using charter services, which are organized by someone other than the carrier.

Charter Party *(Airlines)*: The carrier and the individual or company participating in a chartering contract.

Chartering *(Tourism)*: The hiring or leasing of aircraft or any other vehicle for the exclusive, temporary use of a group of travelers.

Chateau *(Tourism)*: French term for a large or country house in France, often one that has a vineyard attached and gives its name to wine produced there. They are sometimes remodeled or built in such a style to be used as a hotel.

Chauffeur *(Car Rental)*: A person hired to drive a privately owned car, usually of a limousine.

CHD *(GDS)*: Code for Child.

Check *(Airlines)*: 1. The act of verifying the existence of a reservation by a counter-register, as at an airline check-in counter.

2. To give something to someone, such as a carrier, for temporary safekeeping and later retrieval upon presentation of a receipt, as when checking-in a luggage.

Check *(Business)*: 1. A draft upon a bank account to order the bank to pay a certain amount to the payee. 2. To compare any paper with its counterpart or to ascertain its authenticity. 3. A mark that shows something has been noted or completed.

Check *(Hospitality)*: A synonymous with a bill in a restaurant.

Check In or Check-In *(Tourism)*: 1. The process of registering on arrival at a hotel or airport. Check-in requires the presentation of certain documents, such as tickets, proof of reservation, identification, and payment in case of hotel check-in. 2. The place where people check-in at a hotel or airport.

Check-in Time *(Airlines)*: Latest time before a scheduled departure at which a passenger may show at the airline counter without losing his or her reserved seat. It is usually two hours for international or long-haul flights and one hour for domestic or short-haul flights.

Check-in Time *(Hospitality)*: The time set by the hotel for a guest to take his reserved room.

Check-Out *(Hospitality)*: Procedure by which a guest settles his/her account and leaves the hotel. Many hotels now offer Express Check Out in which the bill is settled automatically with the guest's credit card.

Check-out Time *(Hospitality)*: The latest time a guest can vacate a hotel room without being charged for another night's lodging.

Checked Baggage *(Airlines)*: Baggage given by a traveler to the temporary care of the carrier. It is the luggage that travels in the same flight as the passenger free of charge if it fits into the allowance limits, but in a separate compartment.

Checkpoint *(Tourism)*: A place where people or vehicles can be stopped for inspection purposes.

Checker *(Tourism)*: A person who receives baggage, coats, or other items for check in.

Checksum *(Airlines)*: A code added to the data contents stored on an RFID microchip to determine whether the data is corrupted or lost.

Chef de Partie *(Hospitality)*: A French term indicating the chef in charge of a particular food production area in the kitchen.

Chef du Rang *(Hospitality)*: A French term denoting the employee responsible for taking orders, serving drinks, preparing food at the table, and collecting sales income. The *Chef du Rang* is also the person who may serve wine when the establishment has no sommelier or wine steward.

Chevron Setup *(Hospitality)*: An arrangement for a meeting, in which tables and chairs are aligned in a "V" along a central aisle.

CHF *(GDS)*: Code for Swiss Franc, the national currency of Switzerland.

CHI *(GDS)*: Three-letter IATA code for Chicago, Illinois, USA.

Chicago Convention *(Organizations)*: At the end of World War II the nature of the airline industry began to concern various countries in regard to the utilization of the skies. While sovereignty was affirmed in the "Paris Convention on the Regulation of Aerial Navigation" of 1919 and subsequently by various other multilateral treaties, the United States advocated an "open skies" policy. Strongly opposed to the US' viewpoint was the Great Britain, which argued that freedom of the skies actually was inapplicable. Aspiring settle this matter, the US convoked in 1944 an International Convention to be held in Chicago, in order to establish the framework for all agreements relating the use of international air spaces. In response to this invitation, representatives of 52 countries met at Chicago from November 1 to December 7, 1944, to make arrangements to establish provisional air routes and services. The Conference would be also committed to the adoption of a new aviation convention.

The principle of sovereignty was restated in a document named "Chicago Convention on International Civil Aviation" signed on December 7, 1944 in Chicago, Illinois, by 52 signatory states. By this convention, airspace is then generally accepted as the territory belonging to the subjacent country. It received the requisite 26th ratification on March 5, 1947 and went into effect on April 4, 1947. This last date, the International Civil Aviation Organization (ICAO) was created, and became a specialized agency of the United Nations Economic and Social Council (ECOSOC) in October of the same year. The Convention has been revised eight times since the date it was agreed (in 1959, 1963, 1969, 1975, 1980, 1997,

2000 and 2006).

Chief Executive Officer (CEO) *(Business)*: The highest-ranking executive in a company or organization who is responsible for managing a corporation, company, or agency, for carrying out the policies of the board of directors, and for reporting to the board of directors on a day-to-day basis.

Chief Operating Officer (COO) *(Business)*: A high rank officer responsible for managing the daily activities and operations of a corporation.

Child *(Tourism)*: A person who has reached his/her second birthday but not his/her 12th birthday at the date of commencement of transportation, and pays the applicable child fare. This designation is used in travel industry to determine fares and other rates. The precise definition varies from carrier to carrier and from hotel to hotel.

Child Seat *(Car Rental)*: A seat required in most countries for children under a certain age to be secured in a child seat. When renting a car, a child seat can be reserved in advance.

Children's Fare *(Airlines)*: The price a child passenger has to pay to be transported on an airplane.

Children's Menu *(Hospitality)*: A menu for children comprising simple, nutritious food served in small portions. Children's menus are frequently designed to entertain the child with games, story books, etc.

China National Tourism Administration (CNTA) *(Organizations)*: A public entity of the People's Republic of China, responsible for developing, promoting and regulating China tourism activity. Some of the main responsibilities of CNTA are: Studying out guidelines, policies and plans for the tourism development; Studying out strategies to explore and develop international tourism market; Organizing important promotions and publicizing the whole identity of the national tourism; and Directing tourism education and training. CNTA has set up 16 overseas representative offices in 13 important tourist generating countries and regions, they are: China National Tourism Administration Tokyo Office, Osaka Office, Singapore Office, Kathmandu Office, Seoul Office, New York Office, Los Angeles Office, Toronto Office, London Office,

Paris Office, Frankfurt Office, Madrid Office, Zurich Office, Sydney Office, Moscow Office and Asia Tourism Exchange Center Limited in Hong Kong.

China, Glassware, Silver, and Linen *(Hospitality)*: The assemblage of equipment, machines, kitchenware, implements, forming the asset account of hospitality firms.

Chinook *(Climate)*: It is a term referring to the wet, warm coastal "Chinook Winds" which occur in the northwestern region of North America. They originate in the Pacific Northwest and blow to Canadian Prairies and Great Plains; descend from the Rocky Mountains, heating the air very quickly. Because of this, they are called "Snow Eaters." Chinook is a Native American term.

Chit *(Tourism)*: 1. The bill or check in a restaurant stating the amount owed for food and drink. 2. A short letter, a note.

CHML *(GDS)*: Code meaning Child Meal.

CHNG *(GDS)*: Code meaning Change.

CHNT *(GDS)*: Code meaning Change Name To.

Chocotherapy *(Tourism)*: The therapeutic use of chocolate in beauty and health treatments.

CHRIE *(Organizations)*: An acronym for "Council on Hotel, Restaurant, and Institutional Education."

Chronological Order *(Tourism)*: The sequence by time of happening to make an arrangement.

Chronology *(Tourism)*: The definition of the actual temporal sequence how past events occurred.

Chronometer *(Tourism)*: Any device that measures time, such as a watch. Specifically, a chronometer is a watch is a watch certified to meet certain precision standards.

CHTR *(GDS)*: Code meaning Charter.

Chuckwagon *(Tourism)*: A wagon drawn by horses or other draft animals, and equipped with food and cooking utensils, as on a ranch or in a lumber camp.

Chunnel *(Tourism)*: The term is an abbreviation of the words Channel Tunnel. It is a railroad tunnel, opened in 1994, that runs underneath the English Channel and links Folkestone in England with Coquelles near Calais in France. The Eurostar train passes through it.

Churning *(GDS)*: The irregular practice of making the same booking repeated times to avoid a ticketing deadline.

CI *(GDS)*: Code meaning: 1. Check-In; 2. Two-letter IATA code for China Airlines.

CIA *(GDS)*: Three-letter IATA code for Ciampino Airport, serving the city of Rome, Italy.

CIEE *(Organizations)*: An acronym for "Council on International Educational Exchange."

CIF *(Business)*: 1. A term commonly used in international trading when ocean transport is used. It means Cost, Insurance, and Freight.

CIF *(Organizations)*: An acronym for Canadian Institute of Forestry.

Cinder Cone *(Geography)*: A conical hill formed by the accumulation of volcanic materials around a vent.

CIP *(GDS)*: Code meaning Commercially Important Person.

CIQ *(GDS)*: Code meaning Customs, Immigration, Quarantine.

CIR *(GDS)*: A code for Circular, Circulate.

Circle Pacific Fare *(Airlines)*: A special fare offered by some Pacific carriers allowing passengers to fly to Pacific Rim destinations (Australia, Asia, North and South America), usually including few stopovers. Additional stopovers are available at an extra cost.

Circle Trip *(Airlines)*: A return journey in which the point of origin is also the point of final destination, where the passenger returns to, after stopping on intermediate points located in foreign countries. The circle trip is formed by two or more fare components, each of which has its individual calculation procedure.

Circle Trip Minimum *(Airlines)*: The lowest allowable fare for a circle trip, which cannot be less than the higher round trip fare produced from the point of origin to any intermediate stopover point.

Circuit *(Tourism)*: A journey completed in a number of stages, using various types of transportation for visiting several touristic places.

Circumnavigate *(Tourism)*: To sail or fly around a place such as the world or an island.

Cirrocumulus *(Geography)*: Clouds appearing as small white puffs that resemble flakes or patches of cotton without shadows.

Cirrostratus *(Geography)*: A uniform layer of dark veiled clouds.

Cirrus *(Geography)*: Clouds located at high level (16,000 feet or more), composed of ice crystals that appear in the form of white, delicate filaments.

CIS *(GDS)*: Code meaning Confederation of Independent States.

Citadel *(Tourism)*: Term derived from the French term *citadelle*, which means a fortress protecting or dominating a city.

CITC *(Organizations)*: An acronym for Canadian Institute of Travel Counselors.

City Break *(Tourism)*: A short vacation package spent or based in a particular city, including hotel accommodations and, often, transportation.

City by Night *(Tourism)*: A city tour operated in night time.

City Codes *(Airlines)*: Three-letter codes used to uniquely identify cities and/or airports. Example: TYO for Tokyo, UIO for Quito, LAX for Los Angeles, CCS for Caracas. When a city is served by only one airport, the code is the same both for the city and the airport. Example: MIA for City of Miami and for the International Miami Airport. When a city is served by more than one airport, individual codes are used for the city and for the airports. Example: PAR is the code for the city of Paris, France. CDG is the code for Charles De Gaulle Airport, ORY is the code for Orly Airport and LBG is the code for Le Bourget Airport.

City Pair *(Airlines)*: 1. The origin and destination cities of a travel made by air. 2. The departure and arrival points on a fare component.

City Terminal *(Airlines)*: The CRS terminal located in the airline's city office. See City Ticket Office.

City Ticket Office *(Airlines)*: An airline sales and ticketing office situated at any place outside the airport.

City Tour *(Tourism)*: A sightseeing trip designed to visit a city.

City-wide *(Tourism)*: An expression used to designate a large convention or event that needs many hotels and multiple venues.

Civic Tourism *(Tourism)*: Civic Tourism is that type of tourism which helps protect historic neighborhoods, save the environment, and preserve culture, besides strengthening the economy.

Civil Aeronautics Administration (CAA) *(Organizations)*: A US agency created in 1940 to be responsible for ATC, airman and aircraft certification, safety enforcement, and airway development. It transferred its functions to the newly created agency Federal Aviation Administration by disposition of the Federal Aviation Act of 1958.

Civil Aeronautics Board (CAB) *(Organizations)*: A US agency created in 1940 to be responsible for safety rulemaking, accident investigation, and economic regulation of the airlines. The CAB ceased to exist at the end of 1984, as an indirect consequence of the Airline Deregulation Act of 1978.

Civil Air Navigation Services Organization (CANSO) *(Organizations)*: A global body representing the interests of the Air Navigation Service Providers (ANSPs) worldwide, committed to the provision of safe, efficient and cost effective services. Members of CANSO are divided into two categories: Full Members (organizations providing Air Navigation Services), and Associate Members (any other related organization, such as suppliers of goods and services, academic institutions and Aircraft Operators). It was founded in 1996, is based in Amsterdam, the Netherlands, just outside Schiphol Airport. CANSO supports a European Regional Office in Brussels and an office in Montreal, Canada, and has other regional offices in Africa, Asia, Pacific, the Americas and Eurasia.

Civil Aviation *(Airlines)*: Also called Commercial Aviation, it refers to any activity related to air transport of persons or goods, usually conducted by the private sector. It is opposed to military aviation.

Civil Aviation Authority (CAA) *(Airlines)*: The generic name given to the national body governing civil aviation in a country.

Civil Law *(Business)*: The law concerning common citizens, apart from criminal, military, or religious affairs, and regulating relations between and among individuals and corporations.

Civilization *(Tourism)*: A system or stage that represents a relatively high level of cultural and technological development attained by a community or several communities, often on a nation scale.

CK *(GDS)*: A code meaning Check, Checking, Checked.

CL *(GDS)*: Code meaning Closed. The flight is closed but is available to accept waiting list bookings.

Claim Check *(Airlines)*: The receipt or stub, issued by a carrier to a passenger for his/her checked luggage.

Claim PNR Booking *(GDS)*: A practice occurs when a travel agency issues a ticket on the base of a reservation made directly by the passenger to the airline.

Class *(Airlines)*: 1. The onboard seating selected by the passenger to make his/her travel according to the fare paid, and the facilities and services offered. 2. The one letter code for the class in which the air segment is being booked.

Class *(Cruise)*: Type of accommodation offered by Cruises that provide concierge service, private lounges or specific dining venues available to those passengers who choose more expensive accommodations.

Class A Fire *(Hospitality)*: The combustion of ordinary flammable materials such as wood, paper, and cloth that can be extinguished by throwing water, or applying general chemicals.

Class B Airspace *(Air Traffic)*: The airspace as measured from the earth's surface to 10,000 feet height surrounding a country's busiest airports in terms of airport operations or passenger enplanements.

Class B Fires *(Hospitality)*: Fires generated by flammable liquids such as gasoline, paints, and other oils that can be extinguished by eliminating the air supply, not by using water.

Class C Airspace *(Air Traffic)*: The airspace as measured from the earth's surface to 4,000 feet height surrounding those airports that have an operational control tower, that are serviced by a radar approach control, and that have a certain number of IFR operations or passenger enplanements.

Class C Fires *(Hospitality)*: Electrical fires, usually involving motors, switches, and wiring which can be extinguished with chemicals that do not conduct electricity. Water should never be used.

Class of Service *(Airlines)*: The division determined by the fare paid and the level of amenities provided. 2. The single-letter code used for booking a seat.

Class Override *(Airlines)*: The act of nullifying a previous class.

Class Rates *(Airlines)*: A large group of various items under one general heading makes up a class. The freight rates that apply to all items in the class are called class rates.

Class I to VI *(Tourism)*: A classification system for rating the difficulty of rapids in whitewater rafting. The practice is harder as the Roman numeral is higher.

Classification *(Customs)*: The arrangement of items under the correct number in the customs tariff for duty purposes.

Claused Bill of Lading *(Airlines)*: A bill of lading with exemptions to the receipt of merchandise in the notations "Apparent Good Order".

Clean & Cool *(Hospitality)*: The expression is used to denote small hotel, hostels and lodgings that are cheap and clean, and are focused to young professionals or independent travelers.

Clearance *(Tourism)*: 1. An official authorization for something to take place, as for an airplane to take off; 2. The distance measured between the highest point on a ship and the lower point on a bridge.

Clearance Delivery *(Air Traffic)*: The controller stationed at the ATCT who gives the pilots the approval of their flight plan and then hands them off to the local controller for push-back and taxiing procedures.

Cleat *(Cruise)*: A T-shaped wooden or metal fixture attached to a flat surface to which ropes can be tied for the purpose of securing the vessel.

CLIA *(Organizations)*: An acronym for Cruise Lines International Association.

CLIA Accredited Travel Agency *(Cruise)*: A member that has been qualified by the Cruise Lines International Association and assigned an identifier number to sell cruise line services to retail costumers on a commission basis.

Click Contract *(Business)*: A sort of contract of adhesion by which users of a web site agree to its terms and conditions by clicking or checking a box.

Client *(Airlines)*: A term for a customer, meaning a person who uses the services of a person or corporation, and holds an on-going relationship with his/her supplier.

Clientele *(Airlines)*: A collective of clients or customers. In tourism terms, the clientele is characterized by some identity elements, such as geographic origins, social levels, holiday interests, etc.

Climagraph *(Geography)*: A type of graph that combines a line and bar graph to show information on the average monthly temperature and precipitation scales for a location.

Climate *(Climate)*: The general weather patterns (humidity, precipitation, temperature, wind velocity, etc.) prevailing in a geographical large region over a long period that can help describing its average conditions to a reasonable degree of accuracy.

Climate Change *(Ecology)*: The term is commonly used for "Global Warming" and "The Greenhouse Effect", and refers to the buildup of man-made gases in the atmosphere, which cause changes in weather patterns on a global scale. The effects include changes in rainfall standards, sea level rise, habitat loss, and heat stress.

Climatology *(Climate)*: The scientific study of climates.

Climatotherapy *(Tourism)*: Outdoor therapy typically found in spas that use the climate conditions such as air purity, hot weather, low mountain range, high mountain range, sea climate to relieve respiration, rheumatism or other diseases according to indications and severe regulations.

Climb Rate *(Air Traffic)*: The rate of ascent in feet per nautical mile.

Clos de Vougeot *(Hospitality)*: A grand vineyard in the French district of *Côte de Nuits* of the Burgundy region that produces a red wine of the *Pinot Noir* variety.

Closed Dates *(Tourism)*: Dates on which a travel supplier or a hotel are unavailable to accept bookings.

Clouds *(Geography)*: A visible collection of minute particle matter, such as water droplets and/or ice crystals, in the free air.

CLP *(GDS)*: Code for Chilean Peso, the national currency of Chile.

CLSD *(GDS/Air Traffic)*: Code for Closed.

Club Car *(Tourism)*: A car on a passenger train in which liquor and refreshments are served. See also Lounge Car.

Club Floor *(Hospitality)*: A separate hotel floor designed to provide a superior level of service and security, including the efficiencies of a contemporary office environment, and the amenities and technologies the guest would require conducting his/her business. It is also called Concierge Floor or Concierge Level.

Club Manager *(Hospitality)*: The hired professional responsible for managing all of the elements of a private club's operation.

Clustering *(Hospitality)*: A group of similar things that are close together. By extension, it is a business strategy by which a number of properties are located in the same geographic area.

CMA *(GDS)*: Code meaning Comma.

CMAA *(Organizations)*: An acronym for Club Managers Association of America.

CMP *(Tourism)*: 1. Certified Meeting Professional. 2. Complete Meeting Package.

CMPLT *(GDS)*: A code meaning Complete, Completing, Completion

CNEE *(Customs)*: See Consignee.

CNF *(GDS)*: Code meaning Conference Room.

CNL *(GDS)*: Code for Cancel.

CNS *(GDS)*: Code meaning Cargo Network Services, an IATA company.

CNTR *(GDS)*: Code for Center.

CNY *(GDS)*: Code for Chinese Yuan Renminbi, the national currency of the Popular Republic of China.

Co-host Carrier *(Airlines)*: An airline that has its schedules and availability stored on the system of another airline, having the right to display those flights in a preferential way. Additional features can be added to a co-host agreement.

Coach *(Airlines)*: The economy section on an airplane designated for passengers paying economy class fares. It is also referred to as Tourist Class.

Coach *(Tourism)*: A motor coach.

Coach Tour *(Tourism)*: A guided bus tour for a group of holiday makers that follows a scheduled itinerary.

Coaching Inns *(Hospitality)*: Small hotels of coaching tradition, which were located along stagecoach routes, where travelers could procure food, drink, and lodging. They not only fed travelers, changed horses and provided beds, they were vital to link the coaching system throughout Britain.

Coastal Cruise *(Cruise)*: A journey on a cruise ship with a route close to the coastline, very popular for scientific expeditions. Cruises of this type are opposed to cruises in open sea water, and are often conducted by biologists, geographers, geologists, or historians.

Costal Line *(Geography)*: A line following the contour of the coast.

COC *(GDS)*: Code meaning Country of Commencement of International Air Transportation.

Coche d'eau *(Tourism)*: See House Boat.

Cockpit *(Tourism)*: 1. A compartment in the front of the airplane where the flight crew performs their job of flying the aircraft; 2. A compartment where steering wheel or tiller is situated.

Cockpit Queen *(Airlines)*: A slang term for an airline stewardess who spends her time socializing with the flight crew but neglects to care for the passengers.

Cockpit Voice Recorder (CVR) *(Airlines)*: A device that records all the sounds audible in the cockpit, all radio transmissions made and received by the crew, and all intercom and public announcements made in the aircraft.

COD *(GDS)*: Code meaning Cash on Delivery.

Code *(Airlines)*: A system of words, figures, or symbols used to represent words and concepts, sometimes for purposes of secrecy. In the air transport industry, codes are abbreviated words used to facilitate transmitting messages and information.

Code Share or Codeshare *(Airlines)*: The term refers to flight operations shared by two or more airlines in which a single flight code is used for part of all of a flight. The term "code" relates to the identifier used in flight schedules, which is formed by the 2-character IATA airline designator and the flight number. There can be more than one flight numbers, but only one aircraft. It is a marketing practice in which two or more airlines sell each other's flights using their own codes in GDS/CRS, sharing resources, efforts and results. Passengers usually benefit from a pooled frequent-flyer mileage. Most major airlines today have code share partnerships with other airlines, and code sharing is a key feature of the major airline alliances. The term Code Share seems to be used for the first time in 1990 when the Qantas Airways and American Airlines combined services between US cities and Australian cities.

Code-sharing *(Airlines)*: See Code Share.

Coded Departure Routes (CDR) *(Air Traffic)*: Routes that are of predefined use to guide air traffic around areas of severe weather

Codeshare Agreement *(Airlines)*: An agreement in which participating airlines state the terms and conditions governing a Code share operation. Under a code sharing agreement, the airline that actually operates the flight (the one providing the plane, the crew and the ground handling services) is called the "operating carrier". The company or companies that sell tickets for that flight but do not actually operate it are called "marketing carriers."

Codex Alimentarius *(Ecology)*: It is a term derived from Latin, meaning Food Code or Food Book, which is a collection of international voluntary standards, codes of practice, guidelines, recommendations and other issues that affect consumer food safety and food production under the patronage of consumer protection. The Codex is recognized by the World Trade Organization as an international reference tool for the resolution of disputes concerning food safety and consumer protection. It is developed and updated by the "Codex Alimentarius Commission."

Codex Alimentarius Commission *(Organizations)*: A body created in 1963 by the Food and Agriculture Organization of the United Nations (FAO) and the World Health Organization (WHO). Its main objective is the protection of consumers' health and assurance of fair practices in the international food trade.

Coffee Maker *(Hospitality)*: An automatic or semi-automatic machine used for making coffee and dispensing it into a coffee pot or into individual cups.

Cog Railway *(Tourism)*: A railway system designed to operate on short steep slopes with a series of teeth on the rail mesh to insure traction. It is also called Rack Railway.

Cognac *(Hospitality)*: A fine brandy of France, with great aroma and the bouquet of grapes that is produced in a legally delineated area surrounding the ancient city of Cognac, in the southwest region of France. According to French laws, only brandy distilled from wine made from grapes grown within this district may be called Cognac.

Cohost Booking *(Airlines)*: It is a type of booking allowing a carrier to display, sell and ticket its services through the Computer Reservation System (CRS), which transmits all of the transactions to the Airline Reservation System (ARS), via standard teletype (ST).

Cohost Carrier *(Airlines)*: See Co-host Carrier.

COLA *(GDS)*: Code meaning: 1. Cost of Living Allowance; 2. Cost of Living Adjustment.

Cold Call or Cold calling *(Tourism)*: A sales approach to a prospective client without prior contact, typically via telephone. The action is named cold, because for the customer it is an unexpected call that can disturb him/her, while a "warm call" is made to a person someone known to the sales person, who can expect the call.

Cold Front *(Climate)*: The transition zone where a cold air mass moves generally from northwest to southeast to replace warmer air mass.

Cold Water Cure *(Tourism)*: A therapeutic regime of cold water drinking and application by means of wet sheet packing, douches and immersion, combined with diet and exercise in fresh air.

Cold Wave *(Climate)*: It is a period of abnormally cold weather marked by excessive cooling of the air over a large area. A cold wave may also occur with extended cold weather accompanied by high winds that cause extreme wind chills.

Colors *(Cruise)*: A jargon term for the flag or ensign flown from the mast or stern of a ship.

COLL *(GDS)*: A code for Collect, collecting, or collected.

Collaborative Decision Making (CDM) *(Air Traffic)*: A joint effort between various government and industry components of air transportation, in order to exchange information for better decision making.

Collateral *(Tourism)*: Materials such as brochures, posters, and other that are used to support the promotion of tourism.

Collective Tourist Accommodation *(Tourism)*: A term, common in Europe, to denote lodging larger than a private home where accommodation service is provided, such as a hotel.

Collision Damage Waiver (CDW) *(Car Rental)*: It is a provision in a car rental contract in which the rental company charges an extra fee to the renter and in turn agrees to waive its right to recover losses due to damage inflicted upon the vehicle. This is an international version of the U.S. Loss Damage Waiver (LDW) and defines the car rental insurance covering any damage to a rental vehicle.

Colony *(Geography)*: The term designates a territory depending from an overseas State. It is administered by metropolitan representatives, and has no international juridical personality.

COM *(GDS)*: 1. Code for Comment; 2. See Country of Origin Minimum Check.

Combi *(Airlines)*: An aircraft whose main deck is divided into two sections, one of which is fitted with seats and one which is used for cargo.

Combination of Charges *(Airlines)*: An amount resulting from the sum of two or more charges.

Combination of Fares *(Airlines)*: The amount that is obtained by combining two or more fares. Such combinations are permitted under specified terms.

COMI *(GDS)*: Code meaning Commercial Invoice.

COMM or COMMS *(GDS)*: Code for Commission.

Commercial Agency *(Tourism)*: A travel agency specialized in corporate travel, having little or no walk-in clientele.

Commercial Airline *(Airlines)*: An airline organized to operate commercial services.

Commercial Aviation *(Airlines)*: The business of operating aircraft to carry passengers or goods by commercial companies.

Commercial Duplicate Flight *(Airlines)*: A flight where the operating airline releases seats for the sale by one or more airlines. All participants to such an agreement sell their seats on that flight under their own flight designator.

Commercial Food Service Operation *(Hospitality)*: Any operation, such as independent, chain, or franchise properties, that sell food and beverages for profit.

Commercial Hotel *(Hospitality)*: A property, usually located in a downtown or business area, that makes much of its business with corporate clients. It is also called a Transient Hotel.

Commercial Invoice *(Airlines)*: Shipper's document which describes the goods being shipped and its value. It must accompany all international shipments.

Commercial Rate *(Hospitality)*: A special rate agreed upon by a company and a hotel. By this agreement the hotel usually supplies rooms of a specified quality or better at a flat rate.

Commercial Service Airport *(Airlines)*: An airport owned by a public entity, which operates scheduled commercial services, and has to move at least 2,500 passengers per year.

Commercial Travel *(Tourism)*: Travel for business purposes, not for pleasure.

Commercial Tourism *(Tourism)*: A set of tourist companies with commercial vocation aimed to lucrative results, as opposed to social tourism.

Commis du Rang: *(Hospitality)*: A French term denoting the employee who assists the *Chef du Rang*. A *Commis du Rang* may take food orders to the kitchen, pick up the food when it is ready, take it to the cart at tableside for further preparation, deliver drink orders and serve food to guests.

Commissary *(Airlines)*: A main supply kitchen from which comestibles are distributed to serving points or airline's catering operations.

Commissary *(Hospitality)*: 1. A central food production area from which food is transported for final preparation, or service. 2. An employee store or dining facility.

Commission *(Tourism)*: A percentage of the sale price or the sum of money that suppliers pay to intermediaries (travel agents or salespersons) in return for the service of promoting and selling the suppliers' products or services.

Commission Cap *(Tourism)*: The limit established on commissions payable to travel agents by an airline or other supplier, regardless of the actual price of the service or the commission ranks established.

Commission Split *(Tourism)*: An agreement for sharing a commission income between two or more intermediaries.

Commissionable *(Tourism)*: A term that defines the price on which a commission is calculated. The commission percentage or amount is calculated excluding taxes, or other surcharges. Hotels usually commission only room rates, and tour operators frequently exclude supplements and tour add-ons.

Commissionable Tour *(Tourism)*: A tour designed for sale through retail and wholesale travel agencies, on which the seller perceives a commission.

Commodity *(Airlines)*: Description of goods being shipped.

Common Carrier *(Airlines)*: Any firm organized to transport people and goods over land, sea, or through the air, for a specific rate. By regulation, a common carrier is obligated to carry all passengers and goods provided accommodations are available and the established price is paid.

Common Interest Group *(Tourism)*: Adult passengers who have bona fide common interest to travel together by the same routing to the same destination.

Common Market *(Geography)*: An expression related to an Economic Community of countries.

Common Point Minimum Check *(Airlines)*: A minimum price check to insure that a normal open jaw fare (NOJ) is no lower than the highest one way fare from/to the common ticketed point in the itinerary.

Common Rated Points *(Airlines)*: A term describing identical air fares for two or more different city pairs.

Common Ticketed Point (CTP) *(Airlines)*: In return journeys, the CTP is the city that appears both in the outgoing and the incoming components.

Common Use Self-Service (CUSS) *(Airlines)*: It is a service offered at shared kiosks located throughout the airports to offer convenient passenger check-in while allowing airlines to maintain branding and functionality. CUSS initiative intends to alleviate congestions and improve passenger flow.

Commonalty *(Tourism)*: See Commune.

Commonwealth *(Geography)*: A voluntary association of 53 independent states with the purpose to consulting and co-operating in the promotion of international understanding. The association is not ruled by a written constitution, but has a series of agreements setting out its objectives. The first and fundamental of the mentioned agreements is the "Declaration of Commonwealth Principles" which was issued at the 1971 summit in Singapore. The British Commonwealth joins a group of countries which once were British colonies.

Commonwealth of Independent States (CIS) *(IATA Geography)*: The voluntary association of countries comprising the following nations: Armenia, Azerbaijan, Belarus, Georgia, Kazakhstan, Kyrgyzstan, Moldova, Russia, Tajikistan, Turkmenistan, Ukraine, and Uzbekistan.

Commune *(Tourism)*: It is the smallest territorial collectivity ruled by consensus decisions under the guidance of a local authority. It is the base for certain types of tourism.

Communication *(Tourism)*: A general term to identify any flow of information linking people or places.

Community *(Ecology)*: An integrated group of populations of the same species living together in a particular area at a particular time, in a prescribed habitat. The organisms within a community influence one another's distribution, abundance, and evolution.

Community Based or Community-based Tourism *(Tourism)*: It is a type of tourism socially sustainable that is initiated and usually operated by local people. The activity allows people share leadership emphasizing community well-being over individual profit. Community tourism should be necessarily run with the involvement and consent of local communities, give a fair share of profits back to the local community, be environmentally sustainable, respect traditional culture and social structures, and keep visitor groups small to minimize cultural or environmental impact.

Community Tourism *(Tourism)*: See Community Based Tourism.

Commuter *(Airlines)*: A person who of travels daily between his/her place of residence and regular place of work. Students are referred to as commuters when they are enrolled at a college or university but live off-campus.

Commuter Airlines *(Airlines)*: There is no unanimity to define commuter airlines, since the concept changes as the activity evolves. In general, they are airlines operating regional scheduled services. A definition accepted in the 1980s described a commuter airline as a carrier that operated aircraft for 30 or fewer passengers and a payload capability of 7500 pounds or less, on at least five round trips per week according to its published flight schedules. Nowadays, in the USA the term refers to air carriers that operate regional services using aircraft with a maximum capacity of 60 seats. The tendency is to circumscribe the commuter airline concept to air carriers operating commuter aircraft. They are sometimes called Puddle-Jumpers.

Commuter Aircraft *(Airlines)*: A small aircraft with a passenger capacity of 30 or fewer.

Commuter Carriers *(Airlines)*: See Commuter Airlines.

Commuter Concierge *(Hospitality)*: A hotel employee who provides special advice, recommendations, and other services related to guests comfort, such as restaurant reservations.

Commuter Flights *(Airlines)*: Usually short flights to and/or from small airports.

Comp *(Tourism)*: A jargon term for complimentary denoting something is granted without charge.

Comp Rooms *(Hospitality)*: Rooms provided without charge based on a total number of sleeping rooms occupied by a group. See Complimentary Room.

Companion Fare *(Airlines)*: Promotional airfare whereby a second ticket is purchased at a discount provided both persons travel together.

Companionway *(Cruise)*: An interior stairway connecting two decks on a ship.

Compartment *(Airlines)*: A section of an area within an aircraft, a railroad, car, ship, or other vehicle is partitioned for the carriage of passengers or dead load.

Compass *(Aeronautics)*: A device with a magnetic needle that is horizontally mounted or suspended and free to pivot until aligned with the magnetic field of the earth. It is used to find a geographic direction.

Compass *(Cruise)*: A magnetic instrument containing a magnetized pointer which shows the direction of magnetic north. It is used to determine a direction aboard a ship.

Compass Course *(Aeronautics)*: A bearing as indicated by the horizontal angle between the compass needle and the centerline of the aircraft.

Complimentary *(Tourism)*: Something that is given free of charge.

Complimentary Occupancy Percentage *(Hospitality)*: A ratio representing the number of occupied rooms that are complimentary and generate no revenue. The figure is obtained by dividing complimentary rooms for a period by total available rooms for the same period. It is also called "Complimentary Occupancy".

Complimentary Room *(Hospitality)*: A complimentary or Comp Room is an occupied room for which the guest pays no charge. A hotel may offer complimentary rooms to a group in ratio to the total number of rooms paid.

Composting *(Ecology)*: A process whereby organic wastes decompose naturally, resulting in a product rich in minerals that is ideal for gardening and farming.

Compressor *(Airlines)*: A fan-like disk located at the front end of a jet engine that draws air into the engine and compresses it. The compressed air is mixed with fuel and is burned, producing thermodynamic energy.

Computer *(Computing)*: An electronic device capable of accepting, processing, and storing information, which performs prescribed mathematical and logical operations at high speed, in accordance with a predetermined set of instructions.

Computer Generated Document Number *(Airlines)*: A document number that is computer generated and printed on the document at the time of issue. The airline code and form code may be pre-printed, but the serial number will be computer generated.

Computer Reservations System (CRS) *(Airlines)*: The original term used for a Global Distribution System (GDS). Now it is used in travel industry to refer to an interactive electronic system linking individual travel agencies to a central airline-owned computer which contains information about schedules, availability, fares and related services. It is used to make booking reservations and/ or issue tickets. Its current denomination is Global Distribution System.

Computer Virus *(Airlines)*: A dangerous and destructive program producing malfunctioning of a computer.

Computerized Reservation Terminal or CRT *(GDS)*: A Computer Display Terminal. It is also referred to as Video Display Unit (VDU), Video Display Terminals (VDT) or Monitors.

Concentrated Hub *(Airlines)*: An airport where a single airline centers its operations and controls most of the passenger capacity.

Concentrator *(Airlines)*: A device connected to several RFID readers to gather tags data from the readers.

Concept Map or Concept Mapping *(Business)*: A Concept Map is a technique used to make diagrams on which various relationships among concepts are represented. Concepts are linked by arrow lines, in a branching hierarchical structure. The technique of Concept Mapping was developed as a means of representing the emerging science knowledge of students and is used as a tool to increase meaningful learning, to stimulate the generation of ideas, and is believed to aid creativity.

Concession *(Tourism)*: A right to operate a subsidiary business granted by means of a contract. Typical concessions are those granted to any business located within an airport or onboard a cruise ship in return for a fee.

Concession Recovery Fee *(Car Rental)*: A charge transferred to costumers by car rental companies to recover their cost of taxes imposed by the airport or other authority for enjoying the privilege of operating their vehicles on the Airport grounds. It is sometimes called an Airport Facility Fee or Airport Access Fee.

Concierge *(Hospitality)*: An employee in a hotel whose basic task is to attend guests' special needs, such as non-hotel attractions, facilities, services, and activities.

Concierge Floor or Concierge Level *(Hospitality)*: See Club Floor.

Concorde *(Aeronautics)*: It was a supersonic jet jointly developed by Great Britain and France. It started operations in January 21, 1976, primarily for transatlantic travel. The Concorde was targeted to premium first class market. After 27 years of operations, with the aircraft approaching 30 years of age, a large investment program would be required to update many of the systems on board the aircraft. There was no hope of the airlines being able to fund this investment and keep the aircraft in profit. Consequently, the Concord was retired in May, 2003.

Concourse *(Airlines)*: The section of the airport where gates are located.

COND *(GDS)*: Code for Conditional.

Condensation *(Climate)*: The process of changing water vapor to tiny water droplets or ice crystals when the air gets cold enough. It is said the atmospheric moisture has condensed because of cold.

Conditional Fare *(Airlines)*: A fare which entitles a passenger to get a seat on the next available flight when the flight for which the ticket was purchased is full.

Conditioned Water *(Ecology)*: Water treated with certain chemical products to prevent chlorine from dissipating in sunlight. Conditioned water is also made by passage between the poles of a magnet or by injecting a weak electrical signal. Water so treated is used in swimming pools.

Conditions *(Tourism)*: The clause of a transportation or tour contract that specifies the terms of application of the contract. It determines the services that are provided, as well as the circumstances under which the contract may be invalidated in all or in part.

Conditions of Carriage *(Airlines)*: The terms of the contract of transportation with an airline, which cover everything from baggage limitations and indemnity for lose or damage to the amount of compensation the passenger can recover if he/she is injured on the flight. These provisions often vary from airline to airline, although main stipulations are established by IATA or international agreements and treaties. A summary of conditions of carriage appear in the fine print of the ticket. It is sometimes called "General Conditions of Carriage". See also Adhesion Contract.

Conditions of Contract *(Airlines)*: The terms and conditions shown on the passenger ticket and baggage check or on the air waybill relating to the contract of air transportation.

Condo *(Tourism)*: Abbreviation for Condominium.

Condo Vacation *(Tourism)*: A tour product that uses condominium accommodation, usually in a resort area which provides additional amenities such as pools, tennis courts, golf courses, and others.

Condominium *(Hospitality)*: A form of ownership of real estate very popular in travel industry, where accommodations are similar to furnished, private apartments or townhouses available for rent by the day or week. The term also identifies the building or complex containing a number of individually owned flats or houses. See also Time Share.

Condominium Hotel *(Hospitality)*: A hotel that sells individual rooms to residents or investors to be occupied when the owner is not present. The income produced from such rentals provides money to pay the owner's costs and obtain an additional benefit.

Condotel *(Hospitality)*: Abbreviation for Condominium Hotel.

Conducted Tour *(Tourism)*: A pre-arranged travel program, usually for a group, that includes a sight-seeing program and escort service. It is also called an Escorted Tour.

Conductor *(Tourism)*: A person in charge of a tour group who is responsible for the comfort of the group members.

Conductor's Ticket *(Tourism)*: A free ticket that is used for a flight or cruise given by the supplier to the agent that gathered the group, depending on the group size.

CONEX *(GDS)*: Code meaning In connection with.

Confederation of Independent States (CIS) *(Geography)*: The association of independent states which where satellite of the deceased Soviet Union (Armenia, Azerbaijan, Belarus, Georgia, Kazakhstan, Kyrgyzstan, Moldova, Russia, Tajikistan, Ukraine, and Uzbekistan). Since August 26, 2005 Turkmenistan is not a permanent member, but an associate member.

Conference *(Tourism)*: A prearranged meeting for exchange of information or discussion usually performed on a formal agenda.

Conference Center *(Hospitality)*: A property designed like a hotel to host conventions and meetings specifically.

Conference Hotel *(Hospitality)*: A specialized hotel, that primarily books conferences, executive meetings, and training seminars. Nevertheless, a conference center may provide extensive leisure facilities, resembling a hotel operation.

Confidential Tariff *(Tourism)*: Wholesale prices negotiated confidentially for retail companies, who then markup their commission.

Configuration *(Airlines)*: An arrangement or layout of parts or elements in a particular form or figure. Typical example is the configuration of an airplane's interior. See Aircraft Configuration

Confirmation *(Tourism)*: Oral or written acknowledgement by the supplier verifying a booking has been accepted. In general, confirmations are subject to certain conditions.

Confirmation Number *(Tourism)*: An alphanumeric code used by the supplier to identify a booking.

Confirmed Reservation *(Tourism)*: An oral or written statement by the supplier (a carrier, hotel, car rental company, etc.) accepting that a reservation has been received and will be honored. Confirmed reservations may be either guaranteed or non-guaranteed.

Congener *(Hospitality)*: A substance other than alcohol or water that provides flavor and aroma, which is found in wine and new spirit distillates. Congeners may be desirable or undesirable.

Conglomerate *(Hospitality)*: A group of different companies under common ownership run as a single organization.

Congress *(Tourism)*: A large formal meeting or series of meetings of representatives from countries or societies at which ideas are discussed and information is exchanged on matters of common interest or concern. Congresses may be regional, national or international.

Conjunction Tickets *(Airlines)*: A set of two or more airline tickets issued to cover a multi-segment itinerary under a single contract.

Connecting Carrier *(Airlines)*: A carrier which receives passengers, baggage or cargo for onward transportation from the connecting point.

Connecting Flight *(Airlines)*: An air journey requiring passengers to change aircraft and/or airlines at an intermediate stop along the way. See also Connection.

Connecting Point *(Airlines)*: A point where a change of plane takes place from the services of one carrier to the services of the same or a different carrier.

Connecting Rooms *(Hospitality)*: Two or more guestrooms which are next to each other and have private connecting doors that permit guests to access between rooms.

Connection *(Airlines)*: The transference of passengers, baggage or goods from one aircraft to another at an intermediate point of the route, to provide continuing transportation service.

Connecting Services *(Airlines)*: The term indicates that on a given route, the traveler has to change planes and, usually, flight numbers at an airport en route. See also Transfer.

Connectivity *(GDS)*: The data communication process linking global distribution systems to a hotel central reservation system.

Conservation *(Ecology)*: The preservation or restoration of the natural resources, environment and wildlife.

Conservation Biology *(Ecology)*: A branch of Biology that is concerned with preserving genetic variations in that make up the earth's biological diversity. It deals with the effects of humans on the environment and with the conservation of biological diversity inside the ecological unity.

Consignee (CNEE) *(Customs)*: The person or company whose name appears on the air waybill or in the shipment record as the party to whom a seller or shipper sends merchandise and who, upon presentation of necessary documents, is recognized as the merchandise owner. He/she will then declare and pay customs duties.

Consignment *(Customs)*: 1. An arrangement whereby a seller (the consignor) transfers some goods to another legal entity (consignee) who acts as a selling agent and has to pay for it only upon sale. 2. Goods designated under such an arrangement. See Shipment.

Consignor *(Customs)*: Any person who sends goods to himself or to another party in a bill of lading or an equivalent document. A consignor might be the owner of the goods, or an authorized freight forwarder. See Shipper.

Consolidation *(Airlines)*: 1. A business strategy in which a company unifies business activities into a single integral whole. 2. The process of selling the same travel package with identical departure dates through a number of wholesalers, travel agencies or other outlets in order to increase sales.

Consolidation List Message (FHL) *(Airlines)*: A standard Cargo IMP message identifier used to provide a Check-list of House Waybills (HAWB's) associated with a Master Air Waybill (MAWB)

Consolidator *(Tourism)*: A company or individual that forms groups to travel on air charters or at group fares on scheduled flights to increase sales, earn override commissions and reduce the possibility of tour cancellations. Consolidators negotiate bulk contracts at deep discounts from airlines seating inventory (or other travel supplier) and resell services at a markup to travel agencies or travelers directly.

Consortium *(Tourism)*: A group of companies associated to share resources that help them gain market advantages. By extension, it is a group of suppliers offering higher commissions and other incentives to travel agencies.

Constructed Fare *(Airlines)*: A fare that is not published and is obtained by mileage calculation or by the sum of two or more fares and then shown as a single amount. It is always the result of a fare calculation.

Consular Information Sheet *(Tourism)*: A publication of the United States Department of State, which provides basic travel information for each country of the world.

Consular Invoice *(Customs)*: A document certified by a consular official describing a shipment of goods and including information on the consignor, consignee, value, quantity, and nature of the shipment.

Consulate *(Tourism)*: A subsidiary office of a sovereign state in a foreign country that is charged with the representation of the interests of its country and its nationals. It handles visa applications and other business affairs.

Consultant *(Tourism)*: A person with knowledge and experience in a specialized field who provides professional advice or services to companies on a fee basis.

Consumer Show *(Tourism)*: An event to display products for the general public. Consumer Shows target the consumer, as opposed to a Trade Show, which generally targets industry professionals.

Contact Flight *(Air Traffic)*: Navigation in which altitude and flight path can be maintained by visual reference to the ground and its landmarks. See also VFR.

Contactless Smart Card *(Airlines)*: An identification card that contains a chip to transmit stored information to a reader. It does not need to make contact with the reader to be read, or swiped without having to be swiped through a reader. This type of cards provides consumers with more convenience by speeding checkout or authentication processes.

Container *(Airlines)*: A large standard-sized metal box for the transport of goods by road, rail, sea, or air. Those used by airlines are for dry cargo and are rigid, reusable, insulated. All containers must bear manufacturer's specifications. See Unit Load Device.

Containerization *(Airlines)*: The ultimate unitizing of cargo used by both steamship lines and air cargo lines. Containers allow greater cargo protection from weather, damage, and theft and save time and effort.

Contamination *(Ecology)*: The act or process of contaminating something or becoming contaminated by the presence of unwanted or dangerous substances. It is also the unclean or impure state that results from this.

Continental Breakfast *(Hospitality)*: A small morning meal that usually includes rolls or toasts, butter, marmalade and coffee or tea. It sometimes includes fruit juice. Continental breakfasts are mostly offered on a complimentary basis by hotels and motels.

Continental Climate *(Climate)*: A type of climate with a large range between the maximum and minimum monthly temperatures, usually found toward the interior of a large landmass. Regions with continental climate usually experience hot summers and colder winters. Their positions far away from the moderating influence of oceans causes that the soil gain and lose heat much more quickly. This is also the reason why continental climates are often found to be relatively dry. Regions that have continental climates include Siberia, central Russia, Canada and much the northern states of the US. Particularly Siberia, Canada and the northern states of the US experience very large differences of up to 40°C between summertime and wintertime.

Continental Europe *(Geography)*: The continental mass, excluding the surrounding islands (the UK, Ireland and Iceland). Some definitions extend the boundaries of Continent Europe to include Georgia, Armenia, Azerbaijan, and Turkey. The definition might seem simple, but it has profound social and political implications, beyond to the geographical concept.

Continental Plan *(Hospitality)*: A hotel room rate that includes bed and continental breakfast.

Continental Shelf *(Geography)*: It is the edge around a continent's land mass, where the sea is relatively little deep.

Continental USA *(IATA Geography)*: The term is commonly used to refer to the 48 contiguous states located on the central part of the North American Continent, including the District of Columbia, but excluding Alaska, that should be logically included. Common usage has evolved otherwise, excluding that continental state and, of course, Hawaii and the islands on the Caribbean Basin.

Continents of the World *(Geography)*: A continent is a large, continuous mass of land on Earth, with natural geological borders, which are usually separated from others by expanses of water. Depending on how the count is made, there are from 5 to 7 continents. The difference is due to the fact that some people consider Europe and Asia as one continent called Eurasia; some others say North and South America are a single continent; and a few people even assure Europe, Asia, and Africa form a huge continent called Eurafrasia. Continents are generally identified by convention rather than by geographical criteria. The most accepted division of the earth includes seven continents, which are, from the largest to the smallest: Asia, Africa, North America, South America, Antarctica, Europe and Oceania (Australia and other islands).

Continuous Descent Approach (CDA) *(Air Traffic)*: A method by which aircraft approach airports prior to landing in a continuous and gradual decrease of altitude. The process begins many miles from the airport and requires substantial time flying at low altitudes. Aircraft descend in steps and require additional thrust each time they level off. The benefits of CDA include significant reduction in noise impact, reduced emission contamination because of less fuel burn, and shorter flights.

Contour Flight *(Air traffic)*: A flight operating in or around mountainous areas following visual reference to the terrain's contours.

Contour Line *(Geography)*: A line symbol joining points of equal elevation above sea level.

Contour Map *(Geography)*: A map that shows gradations in altitude. The technique to join points of equal elevation allows a contour map to show valleys and hills, and the steepness of slopes.

Contraband *(Customs)*: Merchandises and goods that are illegally imported or exported.

Contract *(Business)*: A legal and enforceable agreement between two or more parties in which there is a promise to do something in return for a valuable benefit known as consideration. A contract requires the inclusion of the following factual elements:
1) An offer;
2) An acceptance of that offer;
3) A promise to perform;
4) A valuable consideration (a promise or any form of payment);
5) A time to perform the object of the contract;
6) Terms and conditions governing the contract.

Contract of Carriage *(Airlines)*: A contract between a carrier and a passenger, the consignor, or the consignee which defines the rights, duties and liabilities of the parties to the contract. It is usually evidenced by standard terms and conditions printed on a document that is attached to the copy of an e-ticket information. It can also be downloaded from major airlines' web sites. Paying for a ticket, filling out a waybill, or the receipt of a Bill of Lading usually constitutes acceptance of a contract of carriage, due to the character of adhesion of this type of agreements. The legal frame of the Contract of Carriage is established by the local aeronautical authority and/or international treaties.

Contract Rate *(Airlines)*: The price charged by carriers selling capacity over a given route to a shipper or forwarder.

Contractor *(Tourism)*: In tourism context, the contractor is a land operator who provides services to wholesalers, tour operators, and travel agents.

Control Law *(Air Traffic)*: The mathematical definition of a system used to control or to change the dynamic response of a system.

Control Tower *(Airlines)*: An airport building from which traffic controllers supervise and direct the movement of aircraft on and around the airport.

Controlled Airspace *(Air traffic)*: An airspace of defined dimensions within which air traffic control service is provided to IFR and VFR flights in accordance with the airspace classification.

CONUS *(GDS)*: A code meaning Continental United States comprising the 48 contiguous states, excluding Alaska, but including the District of Columbia. The term is of primarily usage by government and military.

CONV *(GDS)*: Code meaning Convertible Car.

Convection *(Geography)*: The rising of warm air and the sinking of cool air. When a layer of air receives enough heat from the Earth's surface it moves upward, but when it reaches higher altitudes, it cools and begins to sink. Convection causes local breezes.

Convection Process *(Geography)*: The circular motion of air that results when warm air rises and is replaced by cool air.

Convectional Precipitation *(Climate)*: A type of precipitation produced when moist air, warmed by the surface of the ground, rises, cools, and then falls as precipitation.

Convective SIGMET *(Air Traffic)*: In-flight weather advisory concerning tornadoes, they lines of thunderstorms, embedded thunderstorms, areas of thunderstorms, and/or hail.

Convenience Food *(Hospitality)*: Any packaged dish or food that requires little, quick and easy preparation by the consumer.

Convention *(Tourism)*: 1. A gathering of professionals or individuals who meet at a fixed place and time in order to discuss matters of common interest. 2. Something that is regarded as a normative example. 3. An agreement or contract between two or more parties on a specific object.

Convention and Visitors Bureau (CVB) *(Tourism)*: Local tourism marketing organizations specializing in developing conventions, meetings, conferences and visitations to a city, county or region. Usually they are nonprofit organization, which encourage people to hold meetings, conventions, and trade shows in their city, and promote tourism.

Convention Center *(Tourism)*: A large facility designed to accommodate trade shows and conventions. The term is often used referring to smaller meeting facilities attached to hotels.

Convention on International Civil Aviation *(Organizations)*: See

Chicago Convention.

Conventional Approach (CDA) *(Airlines)*: A method by which aircraft approach airports prior to landing. In conventional approach Air Traffic Control gives clearance from the bottom level of the holding stack (normally an altitude of 6,000 or 7,000 feet) to descend to an altitude of 3,000 feet. The aircraft then fly level for several miles before intersecting the final 3 degree glide path to the runway. While in level flight, the pilot needs to apply additional engine power to maintain constant speed.

Conventional Gear *(Aeronautics)*: An aircraft that has two main landing wheels at the front and a tail wheel or tailskid at the rear.

Conventioneer *(Tourism)*: A person attending a convention.

Convergence *(Climate)*: Wind movement that results in a horizontal net inflow of air into a particular region. Convergent winds at lower levels are associated with upward motion. It is opposite to divergence winds.

Convergence Zone *(Geography)*: Usually refers to a region of the Earth where two prevailing flows meet and interact in the lower atmosphere, resulting in distinctive weather conditions, such as the Polar Front, South Pacific Convergence Zone, and the Intertropical Convergence Zone.

Conversion *(Hospitality)*: The process of changing a property from one brand to another.

Conversion *(Tourism)*: The act of switching from one agent to another.

Conversion Agency *(Tourism)*: An independent travel agency that joins a chain or group resulting in the agency's name change.

Conversion Payment *(Tourism)*: An amount paid by a travel agency to a chain or group as a joining fee.

Conversion Rate *(Tourism)*: The rate at which one currency or commodity can be exchanged for another.

Converter *(Tourism)*: 1. Any technology that is able to change the potential energy in a fuel into a different form of energy such as heat or motion; 2. An electrical device that changes the quantity or quality of electrical energy, allowing appliances designed for one type of current to be used with another.

Convoy *(Tourism)*: 1 A number of land vehicles traveling together orderly moving over the same route at the same time and under one commander, with or without escort protection. 2. A group of merchant ships or vehicles traveling together and usually escorted by warships and/or aircraft.

Co-op Advertising *(Tourism)*: An arrangement whereby a supplier sponsors a part of a travel agency's advertising expenses with the condition that such advertising features the supplier's products.

Co-op Marketing *(Tourism)*: Any marketing program in which two or more partners pool their resources.

Co-op Tour *(Tourism)*: A tour that is sold through a number of wholesalers, travel agents, cooperatives or other outlets in order to increase sales and reduce the risk of tour cancellations.

Co-ordinate *(Geography)*: A reference number and/or letter assigned to a grid on a map or a sign that identifies a position of a point, line, or plane.

COO *(Business)*: See Chief Operating Officer.

Cook, Thomas *(Tourism)*: One of the most influential pioneers of Tourism and Travel Agents activities. He was born in November 22, 1808 in Melbourne, Derbyshire, England. The idea to offer excursions as a tour product arose when he formed a group of 570 temperance campaigners and took them from Leicester to Loughborough, England. He charged one shilling per person for this service, including rail tickets and food for the journey. In 1844 the Midland Counties Railway Company agreed to keep a permanent arrangement with him, on the condition he provided the passengers. The agreement became a successful initiative that led him to start his own business by running pleasure rail excursions. In May 1851 Cook made travel arrangements for over 165,000 people attending the Great Exhibition in London. Four years later, he operated the first excursion abroad for a group he took from Leicester to Calais to attend the Paris Exhibition. By 1860 Cook started his "Grand Circular Tours" of Europe, which took visitors to Switzerland, Italy, Egypt and the United States. The concept of "Inclusive Independent Travel" was later introduced as a method of including transportation, accommodation and food services in a fixed price over a chosen route. He formed a partnership with his only son John A Mason Cook and renamed the business as

"Thomas Cook and Son". In 1866 they launched the "hotel coupon" that was a counterfoil book valid for either a restaurant meal or an overnight hotel stay. In 1865, the agency started organizing tours in the United States, gathering passengers from several cities. The first 222 days "Round the World Tour" operated in 1872, including a coach across North America, a steamship across the Atlantic, a paddle steamer to Japan, and an overland journey across China and India, for a price of 200 guineas. Due to conflicts of interest with his son Thomas Cook retired in 1879 and moved back to Leicestershire, where he died the 18th of July, 1892.

Cook Only Yacht Charter *(Yacht)*: A Bare Boat Charter that includes a cook.

Cooking Wine *(Hospitality)*: A wine of inferior quality to normal drinking wine that is used only for cooking.

Cooling Degree-Day *(Hospitality)*: A measure of the air conditioning needed indoors based upon outdoor temperatures. Cooling degree-days are calculated by deducting - 18.3°C (65°F) from daily mean temperature for that day (DMT-18.3°C = CDD).

Cooperative *(Tourism)*: An organization that joins together individuals willing to increase their buying or negotiating power.

Cooperative Advertising *(Tourism)*: Advertising that promotes and is sponsored by two or more companies or suppliers.

COORD *(GDS)*: A code meaning Coordinate, Coordinating, Coordinated, Coordination.

Coordinated Universal Time (UTC) *(Geography)*: A highly precise time system for worldwide reference, which is maintained by atomic clocks. For non-technical purposes such as specifying time zones, UTC is the same as Greenwich Mean Time. Coordinated Universal Time is expressed using a 24-hour clock and uses the Gregorian calendar. It is used in air and ship navigation, where it is sometimes known by Zulu Time. The international abbreviation UTC is neither English nor French, but it means both Coordinated Universal Time and *Temps Universel Coordonné*.

COP *(Airlines)*: Country of Payment.

COP *(GDS)*: Code for Colombian Peso, the national currency of Colombia.

COPA *(Organizations)*: See Canadian Owners and Pilots

Association.

Copilot *(Airlines)*: A qualified second pilot in an aircraft, who shares the flying duties or relieves the pilot, but is not in command.

COR *(GDS)*: Code meaning Corporate.

Coriolis Effect *(Climate)*: An effect by which a body moving in a rotating frame of reference acts perpendicular to the direction of motion and to the axis of rotation. It is a force which deflects moving bodies to the right in the Northern Hemisphere and to the left in the Southern Hemisphere.

Cork Charge *(Hospitality)*: A fee charged by a restaurant for opening a bottle of wine or liquor brought along by the customer and not purchased from the restaurant. It is also called Corkage.

Corkage *(Hospitality)*: See Cork Charge.

Corn Whiskey *(Hospitality)*: A straight American whiskey that is made from a mash made up of at least 80 percent corn. It may have any age up to two years.

Corporate Agency *(Tourism)*: A travel agency that distinguishes for servicing corporate clients or which is physically located on the premises of a corporation it serves.

Corporate Apartment *(Tourism)*: An apartment owned or rented by a corporation at a condominium for the use of its employees and guests.

Corporate Hotel Chain *(Hospitality)*: A hotel organization that has its own brand and may be managed by the corporate chain or by a conglomerate.

Corporate-owned Locations *(Car Rental)*: Locations that are owned and operated by the Car Rental Corporation, while others can be owned and operated independently.

Corporate Rate *(Car Rental)*: 1. A discount rate available for business travelers, customarily 10% below standard rates. 2. A discount rate negotiated by a corporation applicable to its employees and guests.

Corporate Rate *(Hospitality)*: Reduced accommodation price for staff of companies who have negotiated such rates based on the number of nights the company as a whole occupies the hotel.

Corporate Retreat *(Tourism)*: A corporation event or meeting that is performed usually at a resort or any quiet location where executives and/or employees gather to attend seminars, workshops, training initiatives, or for team building adventures or other professional development topics.

Corporate Social Responsibility (CSR) *(Ecology)*: A private sector's initiative to support social and environmental efforts by integrating the economic, social, and environmental imperatives of its activities. By committing to CRS a company becomes accountable in all its pursuits, with the aim of achieving sustainable development that comprises both economical objectives and socio-cultural and environmental consequences.

Corporate Travel *(Tourism)*: 1. A business trip arranged by a company for business purposes. 2. The department of a travel agency that is responsible for planning and managing business travel and inherent events.

Corporate Travel Manager *(Tourism)*: A middle management position whose main duty is the setting of corporate travel policy and standardizing and supervising the completion and operation of business objectives.

CORR *(GDS)*: Code meaning Correction to previous message.

Corridor *(Air Traffic)*: A defined route through a country's airspace which foreign aircraft are permitted to use.

Cost *(Business)*: The value of resources (money, material, effort, time and utilities consumed) that has been used up to buy, produce, or achieve something, and hence is not available for use anymore. Costs include risks and sometimes opportunities lost in production and delivery of a good or service. All expenses are costs, but not all costs are expenses. In travel context, almost all booking modifications fall into costs.

Cost-benefit Analysis (CBA) *(Business)*: A technique of estimating and comparing short-term and long-term costs and benefits from a financial year for deciding whether to introduce changes. It consists of adding up the value of the benefits of a course of action, and subtracting the costs associated with it. A cost benefit analysis is useful to determine how well, or how poorly, a planned action will turn out.

Cost Center *(Airlines)*: An airline's accounting division that is responsible for managing the cost control.

Cost-effectiveness Analysis (CEA) *(Business)*: A form of economic analysis that measures the net cost of providing a service as well as the outcomes obtained during two or more courses of action.

Cost of Living *(Business)*: An amount of money needed to buy the goods and services to satisfy basic necessities of life (as food, shelter and clothing). Cost of living is not an absolute concept, since it can also mean the cost of maintaining a certain standard of living, beyond the basic necessities.

Cost per Passenger *(Airlines)*: The cost of a segment that is booked, modified or cancelled for each passenger.

Costing *(Tourism)*: The process of estimating all itemized costs of producing or undertaking something, such as a tour package.

Cot *(Tourism)*: 1. A small bed that can be folded up for storage or transport. 2. An abbreviation for Cottage.

COTAL *(Organizations)*: An acronym for Confederation of Tourism Organizations of Latin America. Its primary purpose is the promotion of tourism development to Latin American destinations. Its head office is in Buenos Aires, Argentina.

Cote D'Azur *(Tourism)*: One of the most famous resort areas in the world located in France's southeastern coast of the Mediterranean Sea, at the border with Italy. A distinguished feature of this region is Cannes, city that hosts the annual presentation of the *Palme d'Or*, which attracts movie stars from around the world. It is also called French Riviera.

Coterminous *(Geography)*: Term that qualifies countries sharing a common boundary.

Cottage *(Tourism)*: A small house, typically one in the country, generally used for vacationing. In the hotel business, any small separate unit often designed to look attractive or old-fashioned.

Couch Surfing *(Tourism)*: A slang term for sleeping on sofas while visiting relatives or friends.

Couchette *(Tourism)*: A French term denoting a compartment in a train car that contains beds for basic non-private sleeping accommodation.

Counterfeit *(Tourism)*: A false document or an illegal copy of paper currency.

Country *(Airlines)*: In fares context, it is the country in which travel commences, transaction takes place, bookings are made, modified or canceled, or where payment is made.

Country *(Geography)*: A territory representing a geographic, historic and cultural unity which confers the community members a sense of belonging and the conviction to share the same destiny. The corresponding French term for country is *Bassin de Vie.*

Country Code *(GDS)*: The two alphabetic characters designator assigned to every country; for instance, MX for Mexico, IT for Italy, TH for Thailand, and EC for Ecuador.

Country of Commencement of Transportation *(Airlines)*: The country where the first international travel sector starts.

Country of Payment *(Airlines)*: The country where payment is made by the purchaser to the carrier or its agent.

Country of Origin Minimum Check (COM) *(Airlines)*: In one way journeys, the fare for the component via the country of origin to another country can not be lower than the highest international fare from the point in the country of origin to any ticketed point in the component.

Country of Registry *(Cruise)*: The country under whose maritime laws a ship's ownership is formally registered and whose flag it flies. See also Flag of Convenience.

Country of Residence *(Tourism)*: There is no unanimity in defining the Country of Residence. While some say it is the country where a person has his/her residence for most of the past 12 months or for a shorter period provided he/she intends to return within 12 months to live there, other say that the Country of Residence is where a person has been normally resident for the last three years and where he/she considers to be "home". A temporary residence in another country for purposes of education or short-term employment does not change a person's country of residence.

Country of Unit Origin *(Airlines)*: The country where the point of origin of a pricing unit is situated.

Couples Treatment *(Tourism)*: A treatment that is carried out simultaneously on two persons by two therapists working in a Couples Treatment Room, to enable couples to share the spa experience together.

Coupon *(Airlines)*: Coupons are partial virtual images of E-tickets.

There is an individual flight coupon for each segment of the itinerary. An e-ticket contains an agent coupon, an auditor coupon, a charge form and a passenger receipt.

Coupon *(Tourism)*: A printed and pre-paid voucher to be exchanged for specified services, such as a hotel room or a city tour.

Coupon Broker *(Airlines)*: An illegal practice of persons or companies who buy and resell airline frequent flyer awards, infringing airlines regulations.

Coupon Code *(Car Rental)*: A coupon designator that identifies a unique discount or offer.

Coupon Media *(GDS)*: A code that was used in connection with the "Issued In Exchange For" data element to identify if the flight coupon being exchanged was "P" for paper or "E" for Electronic.

COUR *(GDS)*: Code meaning Courier.

Courier *(Tourism)*: 1. Any person accompanying goods or documents for hand-delivery; 2. An employee of a travel agency to guide and assist a group of tourists along their itinerary. See also Air Courier.

Course *(Tourism)*: 1. The direction in which a plane moves. It is expressed in degrees of the compass; 2. The route along which a ship moves, which is expressed in degrees of the compass; 3. Part of a meal served at one time.

Court de Tennis *(Tourism)*: French term meaning a ground equipped for the practice of tennis, according to regulations defined by the respective Sports Federation.

Courtesy Room *(Hospitality)*: A room that a hotel grants to a guest group for a short time at no additional charge. Typical case is when a resort provides a courtesy room to guests already checked out so they can shower and change clothes before leaving for the airport.

Courtesy Vehicle *(Hospitality)*: A van or bus used by a hotel off the airport to pick up

Cove *(Geography)*: A small bay on the shore of a body of water, especially one that is enclosed by high cliffs. It is smaller than a bay.

Cover Charge *(Hospitality)*: A fixed fee charged by a restaurant or night club over and above the charge of food and beverage. Cover

Charges are often collected by entertaining establishments.

Cover Letter *(Business)*: A business letter attached to other documents or package to explain the contents of what is being sent or provide necessary or additional information

Covered Hatch *(Car Rental)*: A hatchback luggage compartment with a shade or board instead of an enclosed trunk in some smaller vehicles.

CP *(GDS)*: Continental Plan.

CPH *(GDS)*: Three-letter IATA code for Copenhagen, capital city of Denmark.

CPM *(GDS)*: Code meaning Common Point Minimum Check.

CPT *(GDS)*: Three-letter IATA code for Cape Town, important city in South Africa.

CPU *(GDS/ Air Traffic)*: Code for Central Processing Unit, the computer's brain.

CPY *(GDS)*: A code meaning Copy, Copying, Copied.

CR *(GDS)*: Code meaning Change Record.

Cradle Seat *(Airlines)*: A seat in an airline that with neck and lumbar supports that reclines, but does not lie flat. It can be found in business class compartments. See also Flat-bed Seat.

CRC *(GDS)*: Code for Colon, the national currency of Costa Rica.

Cream Ale *(Hospitality)*: A style of beer which is produced by mixing ale with lagered beer, resulting in a smoother, creamier taste and texture, resembling a Kolsch.

Credit Memo *(Business)*: An informal document used for informing the amount of credit a company has with another. It can happen as a result of overpayment.

Crew *(Airlines)*: All the staff members of an airline, ship, or other transport company who work onboard the vehicle.

Crew Tea *(Airlines)*: A jargon term for an alteration in appearance or nature of alcoholic beverages as a means of avoiding prohibitions on alcohol consumption.

Crew to Passenger Ratio *(Cruise)*: The quantitative relation between the number of passengers on a cruise ship divided by the number of crew members. The lower the number, the higher the level of service.

Crewed *(Yacht)*: A Yacht that is hired with crew included.

Crewed Charter *(Cruise)*: A contract in which a yacht or another vessel is hired with crew included. Fully crewed means that the Yacht provides a full time captain and cook on board and sometimes a stewardess or deck hand.

CRM *(Computing)*: See Custom Relationship Management.

CRN *(GDS)*: Code meaning Cash Refund Notice.

CRO *(Hospitality)*: See Central Reservations Office.

Croak Fare *(Airlines)*: A jargon term for an air fare available for persons traveling due to death or sickness of a family member or due to other compassionate reason. See also Bereavement Fare.

Croiseur Fluvial *(Tourism)*: See House Boat.

Cross Ticketing *(Airlines)*: See Back to Back Ticketing.

Cross-border Ticketing *(Airlines)*: An illegal practice of issuing a ticket as if the travel commences in a country different to the actual country of origin. It is intended to take advantage of lower fare or currency structures.

Cross-country Skiing *(Tourism)*: A leisure winter sport for skiing across large distances over relatively flat terrain of the countryside. Narrower skis are used than those for downhill skiing. The sport is popular in many countries with large snowfields, such as Northern Europe, Canada and Alaska.

Crossing the Line *(Cruise)*: A traditional ceremony that takes place among passengers and crew when a ship crosses the equator line for the first time during a cruise.

Croupier *(Hospitality)*: A casino employee who conducts games at gaming tables and collects and pays bets. He is also called a Dealer.

Crown Colony *(Geography)*: A colonial territory controlled by the British Crown represented by a governor exerting authority.

Crow's Nest *(Cruise)*: The lookout's platform built at the masthead of a ship. Sometimes it is constructed with sides and a roof.

CRS *(Airlines)*: See Computer Reservations System.

CRT *(GDS)*: See Computerized Reservation Terminal.

Cruise *(Cruise)*: Any ocean, river or lake tourist navigation that includes scales (ports of call) undertaken for pleasure on board of luxury vessels specially equipped to accommodate hundreds of passengers.

Cruise Broker *(Tourism)*: A travel agent or other person expert in the sale of cruise berths.

Cruise Card *(Cruise)*: A small card given to each adult cruise as a personal ID document for use in charging shipboard purchases, entering their cabin, embarking and debarking the ship.

Cruise Director *(Cruise)*: A person in charge of all onboard entertainment and social events. He is the most visible member of the staff member.

Cruise Fare *(Cruise)*: The price charged for the cruise, excluding port charges and government taxes, gratuities and insurance fees. Hotel accommodation or land packages are optional extras.

Cruise Host *(Cruise)*: A male person recruited by the cruise ship to serve as a dancing and social partner for single ladies on the cruise. He usually travels at a reduced fare.

Cruise Line *(Cruise)*: A company that owns a fleet of cruise ships and operates cruise services.

Cruise Lines International Association (CLIA) *(Organizations)*: The world's largest cruise association dedicated to the promotion and growth of the cruise industry. CLIA was created in 1975 in response to a need for an entity to promote the special benefits of cruising. In 2006 it merged with the International Council of Cruise Lines (ICCL), a sister entity created in 1990. Its objectives are committed to promote all measures that foster a safe, secure and healthy cruise ship environment, educate, train its travel agent members, and promote and explain the value, desirability and affordability of the cruise vacation experience. CLIA is administered by a Ft. Lauderdale-based headquarters staff and is currently composed of 23 of the major cruise lines serving North America.

Cruise-only Agency *(Tourism)*: A travel agency mainly dedicated to promote and sell cruise vacations.

Cruise, Pleasure *(Cruise)*: Pleasure is the essence of a tour cruising. Travelers are naturally exonerated from any task onboard, since comfort, resting and well-being are featured characteristics of a cruise.

Cruise Rate *(Cruise)*: The cost of a Cruise plus port charges, but exclusive of government taxes, insurance and optional extras.

Cruise Ship *(Cruise)*: A large passenger ship designed for vacationers, which makes circle trips with several en route stops, and take on passengers only at the port where the trip begins and ends. Today's cruise ships look like floating resort hotels and feature a variety of activities and entertainment.

Cruise to Nowhere *(Cruise)*: A cruise, typically of short duration with no stops at ports of call and highlighting partying and gambling.

Cruise, Theme *(Cruise)*: A cruise in which entertainment is the central theme, such as music, dancing, gambling, sports, history, etc.

Cruise Tourism *(Tourism)*: An alluring alternative for making holiday tourism in present days. It is offered onboard large ships specially equipped and featuring many entertainment activities. Cruise ships themselves have become global microcosms. With an annual growth of 8 percent cruise tourism has increased at almost twice the rate of tourism overall. It explains the rapid growth of cruise tourism to more and more ports around the world. The Caribbean region continues to attract about half of the world's cruise business. Some islands, such as Barbados, Barbuda, St Vincent and the Grenadines, and the US Virgin Islands receive more cruise tourists than stopover tourists.

Cruising *(Cruise)*: A leisure travel by boat, yacht, or cruise ship that involves living comfortably onboard for a few days, while traveling from place to place for pleasure. Cruising is done on both sail and power boats.

Cruising Area *(Cruise)*: The geographic region where cruise ships operate.

Crystallization *(Climate)*: The process of a substance going directly from a vapor form (water vapor) to a solid (ice) at the same temperature, without going through the liquid phase (water). It is the opposite of sublimation.

CS *(GDS)*: Code meaning Segment Closed.

CSC *(Airlines)*: See Cargo Services Conference.

CSM *(GDS)*: Code meaning Convention Services Manager.

CSML *(GDS)*: Code meaning Child's Meal.

CSR *(Ecology)*: See Corporate Social Responsibility.

CST *(Geography)*: See Central Standard Time

CT *(GDS)*: A Code meaning Circle trip or Central Time.

CTA *(Organizations)*: An acronym meaning: 1. Canadian Transportation Agency; 2. Certified Travel Agent or Associate; 3. China Tourism Association.

CTALT *(Air Traffic)*: Abbreviation for Controlled altitude

CTC *(GDS)*: A code meaning: 1. Contact, Contacting, Contacted; 2. Acronym for Certified Travel Counselor.

CTCA *(GDS)*: Code meaning Contact's Address (home or hotel)

CTCB *(GDS)*: Code meaning Contact's Business Phone.

CTCH *(GDS)*: Code meaning Contact's Home Phone.

CTCP *(GDS)*: Code meaning Phone Nature Not Known.

CTCT *(GDS)*: Code meaning Travel Agent Phone.

CTD *(GDS)*: Code meaning Corporate Travel Department.

CTG *(GDS)*: Code meaning: 1. Cottage; 2. Three-letter IATA code for Cartagena, a tourist destination in Colombia.

CTIE *(Tourism)*: Certified Travel Industry Executive, a certification administered by The Travel Institute.

CTIP *(Tourism)*: Coalition for Travel Industry Parity.

CTM *(GDS)*: See Circle Trip Minimum Check.

CTM *(GDS)*: Code meaning Consolidated Tour Manual.

CTO *(GDS)*: Code meaning: 1. City ticket Office; 2. An acronym for Caribbean Tourism Organization.

CTP *(GDS)*: See Common Ticketed Point.

CTR *(GDS)*: Code meaning Click-through Rate. It is a way to measure how effective advertisements work on the Internet.

CTS *(Air Traffic)*: Controlled speed

Cuisine *(Hospitality)*: A French term for "kitchen" that is meant to define a particular style of cooking..

Cultural Imperialism *(Tourism)*: The practice of one country to exert a power to promote its culture, habits or language in another. The promotion can be made by frontal economic or military influences over smaller, less affluent countries, or it can take the form of a formal policy or a general attitude.

Cultural Tourism *(Tourism)*: Travel designed to experience cultural expressions of a location, with tourists usually becoming immersed in them. By Cultural Tourism visitors seek an encounter with the authentic people they visit. Tourists involved in cultural tourism spend time in rural areas, visiting villages and historical monuments, but also engaging whenever possible with the local inhabitants of a region to learn about the "true way of life" of the destination's inhabitants. In 1985, World Tourism Organization (WTO) provided two definitions of cultural tourism. The first and more specific definition states that this type of tourism consists of "movements of persons for essentially cultural motivations such as study tours, performing arts and cultural tours, travel to festivals and other cultural events, visits to sites and monuments, travel to study nature, folklore or art, and pilgrimages." The second and more general definition includes: "all movements of persons, ... because they satisfy the human need for diversity, tending to raise the cultural level of the individual and giving rise to new knowledge, experience and encounters".

Culturally-based and Heritage Tourism *(Tourism)*: A type of tourism concerned with a country's or region's culture, usually of urban character, that includes visiting historical, cultural environments, the values and lifestyles, heritage, visual and performing arts, traditions and leisure pursuits of the local population and host community.

Culture *Tourism)*: The whole of arts, habits, attitudes, languages, beliefs, institutions, and other manifestations of human intellectual achievements which are common to a group of persons, and configure its social organization and way of life at a particular period of time.

Culture, Mass *(Tourism)*: See Mass Culture.

Culture Shock *(Tourism)*: The trauma people experience when they move into a cultural which may be dramatically different from their home culture.

Cumuliform *(Geography)*: Clouds composed of water droplets that exhibit vertical development. The density of the droplets often blocks sunlight, throwing shadows on the earth's surface. They are classified as low clouds and include all varieties of cumulus and cumulonimbus.

Cumulonimbus *(Geography)*: A heavy dense cloud with considerable vertical extent in the form of massive towers.

Cumulus *(Geography)*: One of the three basic cloud forms (the others are cirrus and stratus). It is also one of the two low cloud types. It develops in a vertical direction from the base up.

CUN *(GDS)*: Three-letter IATA code for Cancun, Mexico.

CUP *(GDS)*: Code for Cuban Peso, the national currency of Cuba.

CUPPS *(GDS)*: Code meaning Common Use Passenger Processing Systems.

CUR *(GDS)*: Three-letter IATA code for Curaçao.

Curator *(Tourism)*: The person responsible for looking after a museum's collection, and for deciding how it should be displayed to the public.

Curb Appeal *(Tourism)*: The good impression how an establishment such as a travel agency makes on a potential customer.

Curbside Check-in *(Tourism)*: The service of an airline that allows the passengers to hand over their luggage at counters outside of the airport terminal building and get their boarding passes.

Curtains *(Hospitality)*: Window clothes made from lightweight materials to allow light filtering through.

CURR *(GDS)*: Code for Currency.

Currency *(Airlines)*: Anything that is widely established as a means of payment or exchange in a particular country. This means of payment is usually called money, term that refers to an abstract unit of account in terms of which the value of goods, services, and obligations can be compared.

Currency Adjustment *(Airlines)*: A necessary adjustment when local currency fares are modified before commencement of travel.

Currency of the Country of Payment *(Airlines)*: The currency in which international fares from the country of payment are expressed.

Currency Restriction *(Airlines)*: Any rule or law regulating the currency circulation inside its own country or out of its territory.

Curtiss, Glenn Hammond *(Aviation)*: An aviation pioneer and founder of the "Curtiss Aeroplane and Motor Company," born in 21 May, 1878 in Hammondsport, New York. Curtiss began his career as a Western Union employee, and became later a bicycle shop owner. Backed by his interest in motorcycles, he began manufacturing motor-bicycles equipped with his own design of a single cylinder internal combustion. Then he started a motorcycle racer activity, setting a world speed record by averaging 64 miles per hour in 1903. In 1907 he set a new record of 136.36 miles per hour on a 40-hp V8 powered motorcycle of his own design. In August 1906, Curtiss met the Wright brothers in Dayton, Ohio, with whom he discussed terms on an eventual association to produce aeronautical motors and propellers. He maintained a patent dispute with the Wright brothers for several years. On 29 May 1910, Curtiss made a flight along the Hudson River, from Albany, to New York City, and ended his adventure flying over Manhattan Island and circling the Statue of Liberty. The deed reported him a $10,000 prize backed by the publisher Joseph Pulitzer. The 137 miles distance was covered in 153 minutes, averaging nearly 55 mph. Curtiss was the first person to receive an air pilot license from the Aero Club of America in June 8, 1911. One year later (1912), Curtiss produced his two-seat "Flying Fish", a large machine classified as a flying boat because it took off and "landed" on water. On July 5, 1929 Curtiss and the Wright brothers decided to merge the "Wright Aeronautical Corporation" with the "Curtiss Aeroplane and Motor Company," forming the "Curtiss-Wright Company." After a fruitful life of 52 years Glenn Hammond Curtiss died in 23 July, 1930 in Buffalo, New York, from post complications of an appendix surgery. He was initiated in the Motorsports Hall of Fame of America in 1990.

CUSS *(Airlines)*: See Common Use Self-Service

CUST *(GDS)*: Code for Customs.

Customer-activated Ticketing *(Airlines)*: A vending machine where passengers can purchase airline tickets with a credit card.

Customized Tour *(Tourism)*: A tour designed to fit specific needs of a particular target market.

Custom Relationship Management (CRM) *(Computing)*: Information applications that allow companies to manage every aspect of their relationship with customers, such as identification, targeting, acquiring, and retaining the best mix of them. Such information is then used in profiling prospects, understanding their needs, and in building relationships with customers by providing the most-suitable products and a very high level of customer service.

Customs *(Customs)*: A government agency in charge of controlling the flow of goods including animals, personal effects and hazardous items in and out of its country. The agency is responsible for imposing levies, fees, fines, and other charges according to local legislation and regulations. The inspection area maintained at an airport or other port of entry is also identified as Customs.

Customs and Border Protection (CBP) *(Customs)*: A US agency created in 2003 by merging the Customs Service, Immigration Inspection Service, Animal Plant and Health Inspection Service and the Border Patrol.

Customs Broker *(Customs)*: A person or agency specialized in inbound customs clearance.

Customs Clearance *(Customs)*: The fulfillment of Customs formalities necessary to allow goods to enter a country or to be exported.

Customs Clearance Agent *(Customs)*: A customs broker assigned to perform customs clearance services for the consignee.

Customs Declaration *(Customs)*: A form that is completed by an arriving passenger detailing the dutiable goods he/she carries.

Customs Duty *(Customs)*: See Duty.

Customs User Fee *(Airlines)*: A fee charged on international air tickets in favor of the customs service of the country of arrival.

Cut-off Date *(Tourism)*: The date by which some action must be taken, or an offer or availability ended. In the US it refers to the date when people must apply for permanent residence if they are listed on the Department of State's monthly visa chart.

CUTE *(Airlines)*: Common Use Terminal Equipment (sharing desk check-in systems).

Cuvée *(Hospitality)*: A blend of wines (from different vintners or different years) which is then re-fermented to make Champagne.

CV *(GDS)*: Container vessel.

CVB *(GDS)*: See Convention and Visitors Bureau.

CVR *(Airlines)*: See Cockpit Voice Recorder.

CWGN *(GDS)*: Code meaning Compact Station Wagon.

CWO *(GDS)*: Code meaning Cash with Order.

CX *(Airlines)*: Two-letter IATA code for Cathay Pacific, the airline of Hong Kong.

CXL *(GDS)*: A code meaning Cancel, Cancelled, Cancellation.

CYBA *(Organizations)*: An acronym for Charter Yacht Brokers Association.

Cybernetics *(Computing)*: The science of communications and automatic control systems using both machines and living elements.

Cyberspace *(Computing)*: The space where all cybernetic data are stored and shared.

Cycle Rickshaw *(Tourism)*: Human-powered vehicle for hire in many Asian urban centers and some western cities, mainly as a tourist attraction. It seats one or two persons. According to the place, it is known by a variety of other names such as "rickshaw" (in India and Bangladesh), "cyclo" (in Cambodia and Vietnam), "trishaw" (in China, Malaysia and Singapore), "pedicab" (in United Kingdom), "bike taxi" (in the United States), "taxi ecologico" (in Mexico), "padyak" (in the Philippines), or "tuk-tuks" (in Thailand).

Cyclic Redundancy Check (CRC) *(Airlines)*: A method of checking data stored on an RFID tag to be sure that it hasn't been corrupted or part of it lost.

Cycling *(Tourism)*: A form of recreation and a sport. Cycling comprises riding bicycles, unicycles, tricycles, quadricycles and other similar "Human Powered Vehicles."

Cyclo *(Tourism)*: See Cycle Rickshaws.

Cyclone *(Geography)*: 1.A low pressure system with rotating and converging winds. The circulation of air is counterclockwise in the Northern Hemisphere and clockwise in the Southern Hemisphere. 2. Any tropical storm system in the Indian Ocean. Cyclones only take place over warm sea waters and extend their influence over isles and continental coasts. It is erroneous to use the term as a synonym with tornado.

Cyclonic Flow *(Geography)*: Winds that blow in and around a cyclone, that is counterclockwise in the Northern Hemisphere, and clockwise in the Southern Hemisphere.

D

D *(Airlines)*: "Delta," name used to designate the letter "D" in the International Phonetic Alphabet

D *(GDS)*: Code meaning: 1. Business Class Discounted; 2. Double Size Bed (with bed code).

Da Vinci, Leonardo *(Airlines)*: Leonardo di ser Piero Da Vinci was born in Vinci, in the region of Florence, in April 15, 1452. He was an Italian genius dedicated to several artistic and scientific disciplines: Mathematician, engineer, inventor, anatomist, painter, sculptor, architect, botanist, musician, poet and writer. Leonardo is defined as the archetype of the "Renaissance Man", whose great curiosity equaled only his ability of invention. Da Vinci is one of the greatest painters of all time and perhaps the most diversely genius of human history. Two of his works, the *Mona Lisa* and *The Last Supper* are thought to be the most famous portraits of all times. As an engineer, Leonardo envisaged ideas for building machines such as a helicopter, a calculator, concentrated solar energy, and other devices. For many years Leonardo was allured by the prodigy of flying, and accomplished many studies on the flight of birds. He produced numerous drawings and plans for the construction of flying machines, including a helicopter and a light glider. Most of them were impractical, excepting the hang glider that was successfully constructed and tested. Leonardo Da Vinci died in May 2, 1519.

Dabble Agent *(Tourism)*: Unfavorable term applied to travel agents or contractors defamed on their professionalism.

Dacha *(Tourism)*: Russian Country Cottage.

Dahabeeyah *(Cruise)*: Vessel resembling ancient sailing boat on the Nile, which is currently motorized boat operating cruises.

Daily *(Airlines)*: Something that happens every calendar day of the week, including Saturday and Sunday.

Daily Mean Temperature *(Hospitality)*: The average between maximum and minimum temperatures of a day.

Daily Program *(Cruise)*: The listing of the day's activities to be performed on a cruise ship.

Daily Rate *(Car Rental)*: The daily rate is the price for a 24-hour period of car rental and applies when a rent does not qualify for a weekly or weekend provision.

Daily Rental *(Car Rental)*: A daily rental is for a 24-hour period. Minimum daily rental is one day, and maximum is four days.

Dais *(Hospitality)*: A raised platform or podium above the surrounding level to give prominence to the persons on it. A dais is used to place the head table at a banquet or a meeting. It is also furnished in a room or hall for a speaker's lectern.

DAL *(GDS)*: 1. Three-letter IATA code for Dallas, Texas, USA. 2. Three-letter IATA code for Dallas Love Field serving the city of Dallas.

DALPO *(GDS)*: Code meaning Do All Possible. It is the same as DAPO.

DAM *(GDS)*: Three-letter IATA code for Damascus, capital city of Syria.

Damper *(Hospitality)*: A device used to modulate the volume of air to pass through an air outlet, inlet, or duct.

Dancercise *(Tourism)*: Aerobic exercise derived from modified modern dance steps.

Dangerous Goods (DG) *(Airlines)*: Articles or substances which involve potential risk to health, safety or to property and that usually require special attention when being transported by air.

DAPO *(GDS)*: Code meaning Do All Possible. It is the same as DALPO.

Dark Beer *(Hospitality)*: A rich and creamy taste beer similar in color to bock but not as sweet. Dark beer gets its color and flavor from malt sprouts roasted at high temperatures.

Dark Tourism *(Tourism):* The term identifies visits to places where tragedies or historical death events occurred and continue to impact current lives. Typical examples of such places are Hiroshima and Nagasaki.

DAT *(Airlines)*: Code for Dangerous Articles Tariff.

Data *(Computing)*: 1. Information that has been organized in such a manner that it is more convenient to move or process by human beings or with a computer. 2. A collection of organized information, such as the results of studies, observation, experience, experiment, or a set of premises, from which conclusions may be drawn.

Data Block *(Air Traffic)*: The information sent by an aircraft's transponder to an air traffic controller's radar scope that moves adjacent to the aircraft's image on the screen.

Data Element *(GDS)*: A sequence of alpha-numeric characters to which a unique meaning is assigned, depending on their specific context such as Flight Designator, Days of Operation, etc.

Data Transfer System (DTS) *(Air Traffic)*: A device for transferring data with avionics, similar to a diskette drive.

Data Source Object (DSO) *(Air Traffic)*: Software that receives data from a physical device, translates the data into standard units, maintains equipment status, and provides a common interface for each variation of a particular device.

Database *(Airlines)*: 1. A structured collection of records or data which can be organized so that its contents are easily accessed, managed and updated. 2. A computer software designed to organize the storage of such information. A computer database relies upon software.

Datalink *(Air Traffic)*: The continuous transmission of the most recent data to/from the airborne and ground systems.

Date of Transaction *(Airlines)*: The date of issuance of tickets, MCOs or PTAs.

Davits *(Cruise)*: A device on a ship that is used for lowering and raising anchors, lifeboats, and cargo pallets. Davits are also a pair of small cranes available on many catamarans and some power boats.

Day at Sea *(Cruise)*: A full day on which a ship remains at open sea, without touching any port.

Day Rate *(Hospitality)*: A special fee charged for a short stay, less than an overnight stay. It often occurs during daylight hours and is sometimes called a Use Rate.

Day Return *(Airlines)*: A return journey in which the passenger goes and comes back on the same calendar day.

Day Spa *(Tourism)*: An establishment where wellbeing and health services are provided. Services vary by provider; however, day spas usually provide beauty, health, and therapeutic treatments without overnight, unless the business establishment is a Resort Spa. Overnight accommodations

Day Tripper *(Tourism)*: Name given to a traveler completing a return trip on the same day. The term is also applied to a person who makes one-day excursions to different places from the same hotel.

Day Use *(Tourism)*: The use of a hotel room for a short period without overnight, but for a fee.

Day Visitors *(Tourism)*: Visitors who complete their travel on the same day. They arrive and leave the same day either for vacation or for business purposes. Typical examples are cruiser travelers visiting ports of call.

Daylight Savings Time *(Geography)*: A regulated adjustment of the clock in order to make better use of daylight hours and intending to increase business time. It is a way of getting more light out of the day by advancing clocks by one hour during the summer. Benjamin Franklin was the first to suggest the adoption of Daylight Saving Time in 1784, but it was not until 1916 when it was accepted by several European counties.

DBA *(GDS)*: Code meaning Doing Business As.

DBL *(GDS)*: Code meaning Double.

DBLB *(GDS)*: Code meaning Double Room with Bath.

DBLN *(GDS)*: Code meaning Double Room without Shower or Bath.

DBLS *(GDS)*: Code meaning Double Room with Shower.

DBML *(GDS)*: Code meaning Diabetic Meal.

DC *(GDS)*: Code meaning Direct Current.

DCA *(Airlines)*: Department of Civil Aviation. Common term used to denote the government agency of a country that is responsible for aviation regulation and inherent traffic rights.

DCA *(GDS)*: Three-letter IATA code for Ronald Reagan National Airport serving the city of Washington D.C.

DCS *(Airlines)*: See Departure Control System.

DCSN *(GDS)*: Code meaning Decision.

De la Cierva Juan *(Aviation)*: A Spanish engineer who invented the autogyro in 1919. For two years since then, he conducted tests that resulted in the successful flight of a helicopter from *Cuatro Vientos* to Getafe, a distance that was covered in 8 hours and 12 minutes.

DEA *(Airlines)*: See Drug Enforcement Administration.

Dead Ahead *(Cruise)*: AN expression meaning a position straight in front of a vessel.

Dead Bolt *(Hospitality)*: A door lock that safes the door by means of a heavy metal bolt.

Dead Calm *(Cruise)*: A climate condition with no winds. Position Zero on the Beaufort scale.

Dead Freight *(Airlines)*: The contracted space of a vessel left partially unoccupied, for which the charterer pays freight charges.

Dead Leg *(Airlines)*: The portion of a trip flown without payload.

Dead Line *(Tourism)*: A date on or before which something must be completed, such as a booking, a payment or a ticketing.

Dead Reckoning *(Airlines/Cruise)*: A method of calculating a plane's or a ship's position, based on speed, direction, and drift, without making reference to sun or stars.

Dead-end Booking *(Airlines)*: A booking transacted on a GDS that is never ticketed. Dead-end bookings can originate in training sessions, or forgetfulness or fraud on the part of the booker.

Deadhead *(Airlines)*: 1. An aircraft or other vehicle travelling without paying passengers or cargo. 2. An airline employee travelling for free.

Deadline, Reservation *(Airlines)*: The number of days needed to have reservations confirmed before the day of departure.

Deadline, Ticketing *(Airlines)*: The number of days before the day of departure or number of hours or days after confirmed reservations by which payment and ticketing must be completed. Issue date of a PTA constitutes the ticketing date.

DEAF *(GDS)*:   Code meaning Deaf Passenger.

Death Slide *(Tourism)*: See Zip Line.

Deadstick *(Air traffic)*: It is a descending aircraft with engine and propeller stopped.

Debark *(Airlines)*: To get off a plane or a passenger ship.

Debarkation *(Airlines/Cruise)*: To exit, or the process of exiting the plane or the ship. The term Disembark is also used.

Debit Memo *(Tourism)*: An advise stating that additional amounts due have to be invoiced.

Debriefing *(Airlines)*: A post-flight meeting for crew members.

Debt-for-nature Swap *(Ecology)*: A financial agreement in which a portion of a developing nation's foreign debt is forgiven in exchange for the debtor country's compromise to invest in the maintenance of natural resources or to protect certain areas in the from harmful development.

Debug *(Computing)*: A slang term which defines the need to troubleshoot problems in a computer program. A bug is a problem. It is often it is also used to denote the correction of mistakes in other contexts.

DEC *(GDS)*: Code for December.

Decanter *(Hospitality)*: A glass container into which wine is carefully poured in order to save the wine from any sediment that may have settled at the bottom of the bottle.

Decanting *(Hospitality)*: The process of gently and carefully pouring wine from the bottle into another container (a decanter), separating it from the sediment in the bottle. The wine is then served from the decanter.

Decelerate *(Air Traffic)*: To slow down. When an airplane comes in to land, it decelerates and rolls to a stop.

Decibel (dB) *(Airlines)*: A unit to express the intensity of a sound or the power of an electrical signal.

Deck *(Cruise)*: Every floor area of a ship. Passenger decks are either named or numbered or both. Some typical deck names are "Lido", "Promenade", "Sun", "Sports", "Sun Deck 11", etc. The average number of decks is between 11 and 14, but some cruise liners have more.

Deck Chair *(Cruise)*: A reclining chair designed for sitting or reclining comfortably.

Deck Plan *(Cruise)*: A multilevel diagram or map showing decks, cabins and public room locations in relation to each other. Crew and staff areas are out of passengers' bounds and are not shown on ship deck plans.

Deck Steward *(Cruise)*: A member of the crew who serves passengers by providing drinks, towels, deck chairs, etc.

Declared Value for Carriage *(Airlines)*: The value of goods or baggage revealed to the carrier by the passenger for determining charges or for establishing the limit of the carrier's liability in case of loss, damage or delay.

Decode *(Airlines)*: The action to substitute a code for a word or phrase.

Decommission *(Cruise)*: A term used to describe the process of removing a ship (typically fishing boats) from active service.

Decompression *(Airlines)*: The sudden reduction in atmospheric pressure in an aircraft's cabin, which makes breathing difficult and can cause loss of consciousness. Decompression activates the automatic deployment of oxygen masks.

Dedicated Line *(Airlines)*: A telephone line set apart for a particular purpose, such as data transference or a fax machine. The term also refers to an electrical line that is used for a single purpose.

Dedicated Self Service Kiosk (DSSK) *(Airlines)*: Same as Airline Self Service Kiosk (ASSK), it is a small installation set up by an air carrier for passengers self service.

Deep-Fat Fryer *(Hospitality)*: An appliance used for cooking foods by immersing them in heated fat. It is often called a Deep Fryer.

Deep Tissue Massage *(Tourism)*: Firm and deep massage using specific techniques to release tensions, blockages and knots in the muscles.

DEF *(GDS)*: Code for Definite.

Default *(Airlines)*: The act of failing to meet a financial obligation, as when a travel agency fails to pay the money for sales made on behalf of an airline. The agency enters in a default condition and is prohibited to keep making business.

Default *(Business)*: The failure of a debtor to meet his/her legal obligations according to the debt contract, or when he/she is unwilling or unable to pay their debt. A default also occurs when a person does not supply the goods or services that are the object of a contract.

Default *(Computing)*: In computing activities, it is a setting or value assigned to a software application, computer program or device that automatically starts when no alternative is specified, outside of user intervention.

Default Protection Plan (DPP) *(Tourism)*: An insurance policy that protects the user against failure to receive products or services, or money refund from a supplier.

Deforestation *(Ecology)*: Permanent removal of trees from a forested area, often done to provide timber or other purpose, without an adequate replanting. This practice has a profound effect on global environmental problems, such as air pollution, global warming, soil erosion, desertification, sedimentation of water courses, alteration of climate and hydrological cycles, alteration of the atmospheric oxygen, and carbon dioxide balance. Deforestation is the cause for the extinction of many species, and the reduction of worldwide biodiversity. It also destroys available nutrients contained in the forest biomass that impoverishes newly cleared lands to support crops for more than a few seasons.

Degree-Day, Cooling *(Hospitality)*: A measure of the air conditioning needed indoors based upon outdoor temperatures. Cooling degree-days are calculated by deducting - 18.3°C (65°F) from daily mean temperature for that day (DMT-18.3°C (65°F) = CDD).

Degree-Day, Heating *(Hospitality)*: A measure of the heating needed indoors based upon outdoor temperatures. Heating degree-days are calculated by deducting the daily mean temperature measure for that day from 18.3°C (65°F). It means 18.3°C (65°F) - DMT = HDD.

DEI *(GDS)*: Code meaning Data Element Identifier.

Dejeuner *(Hospitality)*: A French term meaning Lunch. See also *Petit Dejeuner*.

DEL *(GDS)*: Code meaning: 1. Delete; 2. Three-letter IATA code for Delhi, capital city of India.

Delay *(Air Traffic)*: A controller's failure for an interval of 15 minutes or more to take an action that prevents an aircraft from proceeding to its destination.

Delta *(Airlines)*: Designator for the letter "D" in the International Phonetic Alphabet.

Delivery *(Hospitality)*: A business establishment that delivers goods to customers' domiciles.

Delivery/Collection *(Car Rental)*: An arrangement in which, for an extra fee, some rental companies deliver or collect a vehicle from an office or a hotel. This fee depends upon the distance from the rental location. All deliveries and collections have to be requested.

Delta-Wing *(Aeronautics)*: A triangularly-shaped aircraft wing.

Deltaplane *(Tourism)*: A French term meaning a sport activity in which a pilot flies an unpowered, light, foot-launchable aircraft called a hang glider. The pilot launches him from a cliff or a steep and soars into the air aboard a hang glider. The corresponding English term for Deltaplane is Hang Gliding.

Deluxe *(Hospitality)*: A French term for a top class hotel that has all rooms with a private bath and a high standard of furnishings and luxurious service standards.

Deluxe Tour *(Tourism)*: A tour presumably of the highest quality.

Demand *(Business)*: The desire and ability to purchase goods or services required to satisfy a need.

Demi-pension *(Hospitality)*: A French term meaning Half Pension or Half Board. Also called a Modified American Plan, it includes accommodation plus breakfast and one main meal (lunch or evening meal).

Demo *(Tourism)*: 1. The physical demonstration of how a product works or how a service is performed. 1. Any visual or hands-on device used in a sales presentation.

Demographic Profile *(Business)*: A term used in marketing and broadcasting, to define a demographic grouping of a market segment. It is a set of characteristics employed in research such as age, gender, occupation, income, marital status, place of residence, etc. A demographic profile is useful for determining the time and the place where advertising should be placed so as to achieve maximum results. In ecological context, it helps countries to determine death and birth rates.

Demonstration Effect *(Tourism)*: The trends of local residents for adopting the styles and behavior they observe in tourists and foreign visitors.

Denied Boarding *(Tourism)*: The act of restraining a passenger from boarding a flight for which he/has a confirmed reservation. The impediment can arise from a passenger condition menacing the well-being of other passengers, or from a bumping circumstance.

Denied Boarding Compensation *(Tourism)*: The payment given to passengers bumped from a flight, cruise or land tour with a confirmed reservation not honored by the service provider, as a result of an overbooking. The payment may consist of vouchers, a free trip or hotel accommodations and may be somewhat negotiable.

Denied Boarding Cost *(Airlines)*: The financial impact on a service provider due to bumped passengers, including the loss of reputation.

DEP *(GDS)*: A code meaning Depart, Departure, Departing, Deposit.

DEPA *(GDS)*: Code for "Deportee" (accompanied by an escort).

Depart *(Air Traffic)*: The exit of an aircraft by taking off.

Department of Homeland Security (DHS) *(Tourism)*: The agency created by the U.S. National Strategy for Homeland Security and the Homeland Security Act of 2002 after the 9/11 attacks on the United States. Its core purpose consists of mobilizing and organizing the nation to secure the homeland from terrorist attacks.

Department of State *(Tourism)*: The US government department in charge of foreign affairs. Among other concerns, the Department of State publishes cautions and warnings regarding travel to several places worldwide.

Department of Transportation (DOT) *(Organizations)*: The Department of Transportation is a federal department of the United States government concerned with transportation. It was created by an act of Congress on October 15, 1966, to fulfill the mission to: "Serve the United States by ensuring a fast, safe, efficient, accessible and convenient transportation system that meets our vital national interests and enhances the quality of life of the American people, today and into the future". The DOT absorbed the CAB (Civil Aeronautics Board) in 1985.

Departure *(Air Traffic)*: The number of aircraft takeoffs actually performed by all commercial aircraft.

Departure *(Airlines)*: The day or time the flight on which the passenger is scheduled to leave, as per the booking or the ticket.

Departure Airport *(Air Traffic)*: The airport from which an aircraft takes off.

Departure Control System (DCS) *(Airlines)*: An automated method to complete check-in, load and balance control, and dispatch of flights.

Departure Controller *(Air Traffic)*: An air traffic control person that is responsible for monitoring all departing flights and for guiding departing aircraft to their initial navigational fix.

Departure Tax *(Airlines)*: A government tax charged on travelers when they leave a country by land, sea, or air. It is also the fee collected from a traveler by the host country at the time of departure.

Departure Times *(Airlines)*: Local times shown on timetables on which planes should depart.

Departures *(Airlines)*: The area of the airport used by people for boarding a plane. The airport departure halls consist of two parts, the first part contains the check in desks (landside), and the second part may only be used by people boarding the planes (airside).

Deplane *(Airlines)*: To disembark from an airplane.

Deplate *(Airlines)*: The act of withdrawing the right of a travel agency to issue tickets for an airline. It usually happens when the agency fails to pay moneys to the BSP or ARC.

Depot *(Tourism)*: 1. A Bus or Train terminal. 2. A warehouse for goods or motor vehicles.

Deposit *(Tourism)*: A partial or total advance payment required at the time of booking to secure a room, airplane seat or a tour. Deposits are generally not refundable, but sometimes it can be refunded in full or partially.

DEPT *(GDS)*: Code for "Department."

DEPU *(GDS)*: Code for "Deportee" (unaccompanied).

Dereg *(Airlines)*: Short term for Deregulation.

Deregulation *(Airlines)*: Deregulation means the removal of government controls from an industry or sector. In the airline business, the term is used to refer to the elimination of governments' restrictions on airlines' fares, routes, rules, etc., seeking to allow for a free and efficient marketplace. The first deregulation in the word took place in the United Stated when its government issued the Airline Deregulation Act of 1978 to remove many of the controls on fares, routes, and schedules. It changed the face of civil aviation and introduced a new era in passenger air travel. The effects of the airline regulations are varied, some are positive, while many are negative. Among the several effects of regulation we can mention the following:

- Many airlines abandoned less profitable routes that took passengers to smaller cities;
- Hub-and-spoke routes were multiplied;
- New start-up airlines were allowed to enter the market;
- Fares dropped dramatically and total operating revenues rose to a high for the major national and international airlines;
- Later fare-wars generated an impoverishment of the service quality;
- Many airlines were unable to afford low prices and high operating costs, and went out of the business

DESALT *(Air Traffic)*: Desired Altitude

Description of Goods *(Airlines)*: Description of the nature of the goods sufficient to identify them when required by banks, customs or carriers.

Descend *(Air Traffic)*: To come down under control from a higher to a lower altitude.

Descent *(Air Traffic)*: The action carried out in flying an aircraft from a higher to a lower altitude.

Descent Control *(Air Traffic)*: The air traffic control operation that directs aircraft from the end of their en route flight phase to their approach phase from a higher to a lower altitude.

Desert *(Geography)*: A region characterized by its aridity index greater than 4.0, with an average annual rainfall of 10 inches or less and sparse vegetation, typically having thin, dry, and sandy conditions. There are tropical deserts such as the Sahara and the Central Australian Desert; steppe or tempered deserts such as the Kalahari and the Gran Chaco, and continental deserts such as the Gobi.

Desertification *(Ecology)*: It is the transformation of useful land into a desert environment, with a drop in agricultural productivity of 10% or more. Although desertification is a complex process, scientists think it involves multiple causes, such as overgrazing, soil erosion, prolonged drought, and climate change. Desertification appears at variable rates and does not occur in easily palpable patterns, but advances erratically, forming patches on their borders.

It may intensify a general climatic trend toward greater aridity, or it may initiate a change in local climate. The presence of a nearby desert has no direct effect to desertification. Unfortunately, an area undergoing desertification is brought to public attention only after the process is advanced. Scientists still question whether desertification, as a process of global change, is permanent or how and when it can be stopped or reversed.

Design Theme *(Hospitality)*: A theme established to ensure overall coherence in the design of furnishing and interior decoration.

DES, DESI, DESIG *(GDS)*: Airline terms for Designator Code

Designator *(Airlines)*: The alphabetic and alphanumeric code created by IATA for the purpose of identifying airlines, cities and airports throughout the world.

Designator Code *(Airlines)*: Same as above.

Desired Path *(Air Traffic)*: A way in the space determined by controlled guidance to meet the current destination.

Desired Speed (DESS) *(Air Traffic)*: The velocity determined by guidance control parameters.

DESS *(Air Traffic)*: See Desired Speed.

Dessert Menu *(Hospitality)*: A menu usually separate from the regular menu. It may also show items listed on the regular menu and include dessert specials as well. High quality restaurants often include after-dinner wines, cordials, brandies, and liqueurs on the dessert menu.

Dessert Wine *(Hospitality)*: A wine assigned to be served after dinner with a dessert or as a dessert; dessert wines are often fortified. See also Fortified Wine.

DEST *(GDS)*: Destination

Destination *(Airlines)*: Ultimate city or airport of the journey as shown on the passenger ticket or the geographical zone where tourist activities or a cruise take place. In other words, destination is the ultimate stopping place according to the contract of carriage. A journey can have many destinations but each flight sector has only one.

Destination Airport *(Air Traffic)*: The airport to which an aircraft is flying.

Destination Club *(Tourism)*: A partial ownership similar to a time share. Memberships in destination clubs are expensive and yearly maintenance fees have to be paid to have the right to spend time at properties owned by the club. The purpose of destination clubs is to offer their members a flexible alternative to luxury hotels, second homes and vacation home rentals on a global scale. The properties range from luxury vacation homes to cabins on cruise ships, but all are high-quality and fully serviced.

Destination Location *(Hospitality)*: A type of hotels or resorts offering special features and amenities.

Destination Management Company *(Tourism)*: A company located in the place of destination that operates tours, meetings, transportation arrangements and other services for groups arriving from elsewhere.

Destination Marketing *(Tourism)*: A kind of marketing focused on Tourist destinations, such as a city, country, or region to consumers and trade. They are expertise marketers who know their product in detail.

Destination Marketing Organization (DMO) *(Tourism)*: An entity that is organized to promote and sell tourism to specific destinations.

Destination Spa *(Tourism)*: See Health Resort.

Destination Specialist *(Tourism)*: A person who possesses an expert level of knowledge about a specific tourist destination.

Destination Voyage *(Tourism)*: A trip on a ship that takes passengers from one port to another, without leisure services.

Destination Wedding *(Tourism)*: A wedding that takes place in a popular tourist destination.

DET *(GDS)*: A code for Domestic Escorted Tour.

Detached Interface *(Computing)*: A configuration that allows the computer to perform additional functions, such as writing communications, while primary functions, such as bookings, are in progress.

Deutscher Sekt *(Hospitality)*: An effervescent German wine made from German grapes that resemble Champagne.

Devaluation *(Tourism)*: The declining value of a currency compared to the currencies of other countries. It can be a deliberate government decision or the consequence of other country's currency rising in value.

Developer *(Hospitality)*: The entity that develops, markets, and sells interests in a Resort.

Developer-Owner *(Hospitality)*: The owner of a managed hotel who purchased an existing hotel or developed and retained the property.

Deviation *(Air Traffic)*: A detour introduced to a route making it different to that which was expected.

Device *(Air Traffic)*: A piece of equipment, a subsystem.

Dew Point *(Climate)*: The air temperature level at which condensation takes place.

DFW *(GDS)*: Three-letter IATA code for Fort Worth Airport serving the city of Dallas.

DGR *(GDS)*: Code meaning Dangerous Goods Requirement.

DHS *(Tourism)*: See Department of Homeland Security.

Diagnosis *(Tourism)*: In tourism developing, it is the conclusion on the feasibility of a project that verifies its capability to become real with the use of accurate means and a justified demand. The objectives of a diagnosis are gathering all the information elements on the territory concerned, producing the corresponding guides, and adopting a development procedure that involves local economic actors.

Dialect *(Tourism)*: A variant of a major language, which is peculiar to a specific region or social group. Quite often speakers of different dialects of the same language have difficulty understanding each other.

Diamond Lane *(Tourism)*: See High Occupation Vehicle (HOV) Lane.

Differential *(Airlines)*: An amount charged or credited due to a change in the class of service.

Differential *(Tourism)*: An amount of difference in price, quality, etc. between two or more comparable products or services.

Dig *(Tourism)*: 1. The site of an archeological investigation. 2. An informal way of naming lodgings in the United Kingdom.

Digital Terrain Elevation Data (DTED) *(Air Traffic)*: DTED is a system that was originally developed in the 1970s to support aircraft radar simulation and prediction.

Dine-around Plan *(Tourism)*: 1. A prepaid meal plan that allows guests to choose any restaurant on the hotel premises. 2. A prepaid plan to dine at any of various restaurants in an area, usually owned by the same company.

Diner *(Tourism)*: 1. The dining car on a train. 2. A small and inexpensive roadside restaurant, usually informal.

Dinghy *(Tourism)*: 1. A small boat with a mast and sails, for recreation or racing. 2 A small inflatable rubber boat.

Dinner *(Hospitality)*: The main evening or night meal.

Dinner Cost *(Hospitality)*: The price of a standard night meal that is sold as one menu selection.

Dinner Show *(Tourism)*: A spectacle acted that features dances, theatrical representations or other cultural activities while guests enjoy their dinner.

DIP *(GDS)*: Code meaning Diplomatic.

DIPL *(GDS)*: Code meaning Diplomatic Courier.

Direct Access *(Airlines)*: A program that gives the user the ability of accessing directly into an airline's or other supplier's database to get last-minute information about its products or services availability.

Direct Access Booking *(Airlines)*: A type of booking that allows the user of a CRS to view the schedules, availability fares and other products in the internal display of the Airline Reservation System (ARS).

Direct Billing *(Airlines)*: The method by which a travel agency bills a corporation's employees for their business travel. This method requires the employees to submit an expense accounting to his corporation for the payment or to be reimbursed by the corporation.

Direct Fare *(Airlines)*: The fare between two points without any fare calculation for deviation.

Direct Flight *(Airlines)*: A flight between two geographical points that is identified by a single flight number, not involving a change of aircraft. Contrary to this opinion, it is also admitted that a direct flight might involve change of planes or even change of airlines, provided the flight number does not change. What is clear is that direct flights can include intermediate stops.

Direct Impact *(Tourism)*: The first and immediate effect of tourists' behavior or spending.

Direct Mail *(Business)*: A method of marketing goods or services directly to the consumer through the mall, bypassing intermediaries. Direct mail is considered one of the marketing strategies.

Direct Reference System (DRS) *(GDS)*: It is the section of Global Distribution Systems with wide capacity for text files that provide sales-oriented descriptions of services to encourage a traveler or a travel agent to book the product or service. The Direct Reference System informs about miscellaneous topics, such as new products, service offers, connectivity, commissions and special promotions.

Direct Route *(Airlines)*: The shortest operated route between ticketed points of the travel.

Direct Route Fare *(Airlines)*: The air fare applied over a direct route.

Direct Sell Booking *(Airlines)*: A booking that is made in the participating airline's system.

Direct Spending *(Tourism)*: Any money that directly flows from tourists into the local economy.

Directional Gyro *(Aeronautics)*: A panel instrument providing a gyroscopic reading of an aircraft's compass heading.

Directional Selling *(Airlines)*: The practice by which a travel agency influences to book the services of its preferred suppliers.

Directional Tariff *(Airlines)*: The air fare applied to a fare component as per the rule that fares are applied in the direction of the trip, excepting the components destined to the country of origin of the trip, where fares are applied from the country of origin.

Director of Sales (DOS) *(Hospitality)*: The employee responsible for managing the activities of a Sales Department, in such a manner that the business organization attains its goals.

Dirigible *(Airlines)*: A blimp propelled by mechanical means. It is a type of steerable airship that includes pressure airships (such as blimps), semi-rigid airships and rigid airships (such as zeppelins).

DIS *(GDS)*: Code meaning Discontinued.

Disaster Tourism *(Tourism)*: Travel organized for visiting the scene of a natural disaster as a matter of curiosity.

Disburse *(Tourism)*: To make a payment.

Disclaimer *(Airlines)*: A legal document informing that an intermediary agent acts only as a middleman in the sale of travel products or services and that the liability lies only with the supplier.

Disclaimer of Liability *(Airlines)*: A formal denial of legal and financial responsibility derived from any injury or monetary losses incurred on products or services sold.

Disclosure *(Airlines)*: The act of making something known or the release a provision to access. For example, airlines disclose restrictions on special fares they advertise.

Discontinued Date *(Airlines)*: The date when the validity of an offer or a fare expires.

Discotheque *(Tourism)*: A nightclub where people go for dancing.

Discount Fares or Discounted Fares *(Airlines)*: Promotional fares or other discounted fares of different maximum validity offered by scheduled airlines. They are lower than the fully flexible fares, usually offered for a limited time, in a limited quantity and subject to numerous restrictions.

Discover America *(Airlines)*: The travel marketing campaign promoted by the Travel Industry Association of America, designed to stimulate leisure travel within the U.S territory.

Disembark *(Airlines)*: To get off a plane, ship, or train.

Dishwashing Machine *(Hospitality)*: An appliance for washing, rinsing and drying dishes automatically.

Disk *(Computing)*: A magnetic device used in computers to save files.

Dispatcher *(Tourism)*: An employee of a transportation company who controls the departure of vehicles, who is responsible for their safe operation and efficient service. In transportation by train, the dispatcher coordinates all train movements in his assigned area. In air transportation, the dispatcher is responsible for authorizing the departure of aircraft, ensuring, among other things, that the aircraft's crew has all the proper information necessary for their flight and that the aircraft is in proper mechanical condition.

Display Bias *(GDS)*: An overcome practice in which a GDS displayed its sponsors' flights and fares in first place.

Distance *(Tourism)*: The amount of space between two geographical points. It is a variable that usually affects the price structure of transportation or even of lodging services. All of the tourism journeys are conditioned by distance expressed in kilometers, miles or hours.

Distraction *(Tourism)*: Something that takes somebody's attention away from worries and vexations, provoking pleased interest and distraction.

Distribution *(Tourism)*: 1.The process of delivering products or services from the source to the customers through a channel or a network. Distribution, also called placement, is one of the four mix elements of marketing. 2. The supplier's distribution network itself.

District Sales Manager *(Tourism)*: The individual who is responsible for the performance of sales inside a district region for a business organization.

DIT *(GDS)*:   Code meaning Domestic Independent Tour or Traveler.

Dive Boat *(Tourism)*: A small boat that scuba divers use to reach a diving site or to cover other of their needs. Some of they provide accommodation services.

Dive Travel Industry Association *(Organization)*: An association dedicated to the economic and professional development of all small businesses associated with water sports.

Diversion *(Tourism)*: An activity that diverts or amuses, and serves to make time pass agreeably, taking one's mind off routine.

DKR *(GDS)*: Three-letter IATA code for Dakar, capital city of Senegal.

DL *(Airlines)*: Two-letter IATA code for Delta Airlines.

DLV *(GDS)*: A code meaning Deliver, Delivery, Delivered.

DLX *(GDS)*: Code meaning Deluxe Room.

DLY *(GDS)*: A code meaning Delay, Delaying, Delayed.

DM *(GDS)*: Code meaning District Manager.

DMAI *(Organizations)*: An acronym for Destination Marketing Association International.

DMC *(Tourism)*: See Destination Management Company.

DME *(GDS)*: Three-letter IATA code for Domodedovo Airport, serving the city of Moscow, Russia.

DMO *(Tourism)*: See Destination Marketing Organization.

DNOJ *(Airlines)*: See Double Normal Fare Open Jaw.

DO *(GDS)*: Code meaning Drop-off.

Do Not Disturb *(Hospitality)*: A sign attached to a room's door warning not to disturb guests.

DOC *(GDS)*: Code for Document.

Docent *(Tourism)*: A trained tour guide in a museum or art gallery.

Dock *(Cruise)*: 1. A body of water between two piers or wharves that ships use to enter in ports. 2. A structure built along a waterway so that vessels may load and discharge cargo.

DOCS *(GDS)*: Code for Documents.

DOCS RCVD *(Airlines)*: An abbreviation for Documents Received.

Document Number *(Airlines)*: The identification number of a traffic document. The number of an airline document, such as ticket or air way bill, is formed by the airline code, the form code, the serial number and in some cases, by a check digit.

Documentation *(Airlines)*: The paperwork required to accompany a shipment such as airwaybill, Export Declaration, Health Certificates, etc.

Dog and Pony Show *(Airlines)*: A pejorative expression used to qualify a disastrous business presentation.

Doing Business As (DBA) *(Tourism)*: An expression that denotes a corporation is registered to conduct business under a name different to its usual corporate name. A corporation might be entitled to use several DBA's.

DOM *(GDS)*: Domestic.

Dom Pérignon *(Hospitality)*: A famous champagne brand produced by *Moet et Chardon*. It is said *Dom Pérignon* was a cellar monk of a Benedictine abbey who, by the XVII century, accidentally discovered how to trap the carbon dioxide created in the second fermentation of a sparkling wine.

Dome Car *(Tourism)*: A passenger train car that has a domed plexiglass on top of the car, where passengers can ride and see in all directions around the train. It is also called Bubble Car.

Domecq *(Hospitality)*: A famous sherry producer with vineyards in

Jerez de la Frontera, Spain.

Domestic Agents *(Airlines)*: Travel agencies authorized to sell and issue Traffic Documents only within the country of location of the Agency on behalf of Domestic Airlines in that country. Countries where such type of agents operates are: Australia, Argentina, Brazil, Canada, Chile, Ecuador, Greece, Italy, Mexico, People's Republic of China, Peru, Spain, United Kingdom, and Venezuela.

Domestic Airline *(Airlines)*: An air carrier operating all of its services within its own country.

Domestic Carriage *(Airlines)*: A travel in which, according to the contract of carriage, the points of departure, intermediate stops and destination are within the territory of a sovereign state, as in the travel YVR-YYC-YTO.

Domestic Escorted Tour (DET) *(Tourism)*: Preplanned packages that include the services of a tour escort and are operated within the traveler's own country.

Domestic Fare *(Airlines)*: The air fare charged for a domestic travel.

Domestic Flight Leg *(Airlines)*: A portion of a trip flown between two places of the same country.

Domestic Tourism *(Tourism)*: Tourist activities performed within the traveler's country of residence. It is also called National Tourism.

Domestic Transfer *(Airlines)*: A change of plane from the domestic service of one carrier to another domestic service of the same or different carrier. Usually transfers do not permit stopovers.

Domicile *(Tourism)*: Home of permanent residence, the place to which a person is linked by legal, social or economic reasons. It may or may not be the place where a person actually resides at any one time, but the place where duties are discharged. The domicile is the permanent home to which a person has the intention of returning whenever he/she accomplishes the purpose for which is absent. The definition of domicile is important in determining the legal status of a person.

Door Rate *(Tourism)*: The retail price for accommodation or activity.

Doorknob Menu *(Hospitality)*: A type of room service menu that is ordered by guests selecting what they want to eat and the time they want the food delivered. The menu order is hung outside the door on the doorknob and is collected and taken to the room service department, where orders are prepared and sent to the rooms at the indicated times.

Door-Type Dishwasher *(Hospitality)*: Also called a Single-tank or Stationary-rack Dishwasher, it is a dishwashing machine in which racks of dishes remain stationary while water is sprayed.

Dorm *(Hospitality)*: Abbreviated term for dormitory.

Dormette *(Airlines)*: A French term for an airline seat designed to recline to a sleeping position, almost horizontally. It is also called a *Sleeperette*.

Dormette *(Tourism)*: A French term for a small sleeping compartment on a train.

Dormitory *(Hospitality)*: Large single rooms where many single beds are arranged, with shared bath facilities and little or no privacy. They are common in youth hostels.

DOS *(Hospitality)*: See Director of Sales.

Dosage, Le *(Hospitality)*: In the elaboration of traditional Champagne or wine "champagnized" method, it is the final step in which wine, yeast and/or sugar is added to the cask or bottle to aid secondary fermentation.

DOT *(Organizations)*: An acronym for Department of Transportation.

Dot-matrix Printer *(Computing)*: An old-style printer that forms characters with a series of ink dots.

Double *(Hospitality)*: 1. An expression used to denote a guestroom assigned to be occupied by two persons. A double room may have one double bed, two twin beds, or two double beds. Rooms with two double beds are called a Double Double. 2. In beverage operations, double is a drink prepared with twice the standard measure of alcohol in one glass.

Double Booking *(Airlines)*: A rejected practice of holding reservations for a traveler to the same destination for the same times or dates, on the same carriers but through different travel agencies, when only one will be used.

Double-Double *(Hospitality)*: A hotel guestroom with two double beds.

Double-Decker *(Tourism)*: A two-level bus used in some places for public transportation, or for sightseeing, or other particular purposes.

Double Normal Fare Open Jaw *(Airlines)*: It is a journey consisting of travel from one country and return thereto, comprising not more than two international fare components with a domestic surface break at both origin and turnaround countries. The fare used to calculate the price for this type of journeys is half the normal round trip fare for each fare component.

Double-Loaded Slab *(Hospitality)*: A guestroom floor design in which rooms are located on both sides of a central corridor.

Double-Locked Room *(Hospitality)*: An occupied room locked from inside by the guest with a dead bolt, meaning he/she refuses housekeeping service. Double-locked rooms are not accessible by means of a standard passkey.

Double Occupancy *(Tourism)*: The system in which almost all tour packages and cruise fares are quoted, conditioning the occupation to two persons per room. Most hotels publish their room rates on the basis of two adults to a room.

Double Occupancy Percentage *(Hospitality)*: The occupancy ratio calculated on the basis of two guests per room.

Double Occupancy Rate *(Tourism)*: The individual price charged when two persons share a room, a suite, an apartment, or a cabin. Usually, the rate used for tour groups are based on double occupancy.

Double Open Jaw *(Airlines)*: An Open Jaw trip where the origin point of the outgoing portion is not the destination point of the incoming portion and the destination point of the outgoing portion is not the origin point of the incoming portion.

Douglas, Donald Wills, Sr. *(Aviation)*: An American aircraft builder who was born in Brooklyn, N.Y., April 6, 1892. At the age of 17, Donald Douglas entered the U.S. Naval Academy at Annapolis, Md. He early demonstrated a high interest in aviation and spent much of his time in building and testing model airplanes. In 1914 he received his bachelor's degree in Mechanical Engineering from the Massachusetts Institute of Technology after a study carrier of only two years. He was immediately hired at the same Institute as an assistant professor in aeronautics. From 1915 to 1918 Douglas became involved in several aeronautical jobs, as a consultant, as a chief engineer, and as a chief civilian aeronautical engineer. In 1920 Douglas associated with the millionaire sportsman David R. Davis and formed the "Davis-Douglas Co." to build "The Cloudster." Davis lost interest in the company and sold his shares to Douglas, who incorporated a new company with the name of "The Douglas Co." in July 1921. From 1932 to 1940 he built the models DC-1, DC-2 and DC-3. In 1957 Donald Wills Douglas Sr. resigned as president of the company and his son, Donald Douglas Jr., took over that position. On April 28, 1967, Douglas merged his company with the McDonnell Aircraft Co. and retired. He remained honorary chairman of the new company until his death on February 1, 1981.

Downdraft *(Climate)*: A sudden descent of cool or cold air to the ground, usually with precipitation, and associated with a thunderstorm or shower.

Downgrade *(Tourism)*: The action to move a passenger to a lower grade accommodation or class of service.

Downline *(GDS)*: All the linear information displayed on a schedule below the originating or headline city, such as segments, legs, or cities.

Download *(Computing)*: The electronic transference of a file from a remote computer to a local computer.

Downtime *(Computing)*: Time during which work or operations are stopped as the result of a malfunction, repairs, or alterations to a system, network, machine, or program.

Downtown *(Tourism)*: Term used for the commercial, shopping, administrative and entertainment area of a city.

DPLX *(GDS)*: Duplex.

DPP *(Tourism)*: See Default Protection Plan.

DPST *(GDS)*: Code for Deposit.

DPTR *(GDS)*: Code for Departure.

Draft *(Cruise)*: The measurement in feet of a vertical distance between the waterline and the lowest point of the keel, including the thickness of the hull. Draft determines the minimum depth of water needed to float safely the ship. The usual draft of a ship is about 25 feet

Drag *(Air Traffic)*: The resisting force exerted on an aircraft acting in opposite direction of the airspeed vector projected into a horizontal plane.

Drainage Basin *(Geography)*: The surface area which is drained by a river and its tributaries.

Dram Shop Legislation *(Tourism)*: The term refers to laws that regulate the sale of alcoholic beverages in establishments.

Draperies *(Hospitality)*: A sort of curtains made of heavy material and designed to keep light out. Draperies are better sound absorbers than curtains and keep heat from escaping through windows.

Draw *(Tourism)*: In the context of tourist activities, draw is an amount of money paid regularly to a salesperson that is deducted from his/her commission earnings. It means draw against commission.

Drayage *(Business)*: The charge assessed for transporting goods for short distances, such as within a commercial area or town. It is also called Cartage or Haulage.

Dress Circle *(Tourism)*: A curved and separate section of the auditorium in a theater, concert hall, or opera house, usually the first seating gallery above the orchestra.

Dress Code *(Cruise)*: The set of rules stating the correct manner to dress while onboard a ship, or specifying what type of dress is prohibited. Although the trend is for a more relaxed, casual dress code, one has to be aware on the manner to be dressed for specific places at certain times.

Drift *(Air Traffic)*: Slow and monotonic change in measured data

Drill *(Cruise)*: The training exercise for guests, such as a lifeboat drill on a cruise ship.

Drink Incentive *(Hospitality)*: A promotional offer to sell beverages, such as two drinks for the price of one or half-priced drinks during the so-called "Happy Hours".

Drink Rail *(Hospitality)*: A narrow bar counter, usually located against a wall, where guests can either sit on high stools or stand while drinking.

Drink Size *(Hospitality)*: The amount of alcohol poured into a glass and measured in fluid ounces.

Drive-away Company *(Business)*: A company responsible for transporting automobiles and other vehicles, which hires people to drive such vehicles to their destination.

Drive-in *(Tourism)*: 1. A commercial establishment designed to provide service or products to customers while they remain in their cars in a parking lot. 2. An outdoor theater where people watch movies without leaving their cars.

Driver Profile Form *(Car Rental)*: The paperwork usually filled out prior to arrival, where special services are arranged, such as deliveries at a hotel or after hours pick ups.

Driving Record Addendum *(Car Rental)*: The document a driver may be asked to sign in the U.S. in order to help ensure his/her safety, since Car Rentals only rent to responsible drivers.

Drop Box *(Car Rental)*: It is an after hours drop box that most rental companies have to allow a renter to return his vehicle when the office is closed. If the user needs a drop box at the end of his/ her rental, he/she must notify the reservations agent at the rental counter before picking up the car.

Drop off *(Car Rental)*: The act to return the hired car to a rental company. Usually the car is returned to the same rental office from which it was picked up, although it is possible to deliver the vehicle to a different office if that suits the traveler.

Drop-off *(Tourism)*: The action to transport and leave persons in a specific place.

Drop off Charge *(Car Rental)*: A flat fee that is charged when a rental car is returned at a location other than that where it was received.

DRS *(GDS)*: See Direct Reference System.

DRS Publisher *(GDS)*: It is a multi-channel Publishing Application for Global Distribution Systems for Intranets, Extranets and the World Wide Web.

Drug Enforcement Administration (DEA) *(Organizations)*: An agency of the US Department of Justice responsible to enforce the controlled substances laws and regulations, and to fight drug smuggling and use within the U.S. It also coordinates and pursues U.S. drug investigations abroad. The DEA was created by President Richard Nixon through an Executive Order in July 1973.

Dry *(Tourism)*: A term used to indicate a country or airline where alcohol is forbidden. Some routes of Middle Eastern airlines are dry.

Dry Berthing *(Cruise)*: A method of docking ships between sailing departures.

Dry Dock *(Cruise)*: The operation of emptying the ship of water to enable the performance of maintenance and repair works.

Dry-Hopped *(Hospitality)*: A brewing method in which the hops are soaked in the brew without boiling in order to obtain a lighter and less bitter flavor beer.

Dry Lease *(Airlines)*: The rental of an aircraft without crew, ground staff or supporting equipment. In other words, it is the leasing of a "clean" aircraft.

Dry Weight *(Air Traffic)*: The weight of an engine excluding fuel, oil, and coolant.

DS *(Tourism)*: See Destination Specialist.

DSSK *(Airlines)*: See Dedicated Self Service Kiosk.

DSM *(GDS)*: Code meaning District Sales Manager.

DSO *(GDS)*: Code meaning District Sales Office. May also be called a DMO.

DSPL *(GDS)*: Code for Display.

DST *(Geography)*: See Daylight Saving Time.

DTED *(Air Traffic)*: Digital Terrain Elevation Data. DTED (or Digital Terrain Elevation Data) was originally developed in the 1970s to support aircraft radar simulation and prediction.

DTIA *(Organization)*: An acronym for Dive Travel Industry Association.

DTS *(Air Traffic)*: Data Transfer System

DTT *(GDS)*: Three-letter IATA code for Detroit, Michigan, USA.

Dual Designated Carrier *(Airlines)*: An air carrier that publishes timetables using another airline's code.

Dual Jet Bridges *(Airlines)*: A two-jetway system for boarding an aircraft from the terminal.

Dude Ranch *(Tourism)*: A recreational resort designed to recreate the surroundings of the Old West, including activities such as horseback riding, and varied outdoor activities.

DUE *(GDS)*: Code meaning Due to.

Dumbwaiter *(Hospitality)*: A small hand-operated elevator on which dishes, food, etc., are passed from one room or story of a house to another, as the kitchen to the dining room. It is also a piece of furniture with movable or revolving shelves.

Dump Store *(Tourism)*: A theme park shop located in such a way that everyone taking an attraction passes through it.

DUPE *(GDS)*: Code for Duplicate.

Duplex *(Tourism)*: 1. Separate accommodation rooms sharing walls. 2. A house or apartment comprising two separate dwelling units, or with rooms distributed on two floors.

Duplex *(Computing)*: A communications channel with capacity to transmit data in both directions at the same time. The Half Duplex is a channel capable of transmitting data in both directions also, but not simultaneously.

Durable Goods *(Ecology)*: Manufactured items that have a long life expectancy of three years or more, such as automobiles, furniture and equipment.

Dutiable *(Customs)*: Items subject to duty. Most items traded by international commerce have specific duty rates, which are determined by a number of factors, including place of purchase, manufacture origin, and prime material.

Duty *(Customs)*: A tax levied on almost all imported goods.

Duty-free *(Tourism)*: 1. The exemption from custom duties applied often to goods bought in entitled airport shops just before boarding international trips; 2. total value of merchandise a traveler may bring back to his country without having to pay duty. It is also called Personal Exemption.

Duty-free Exemption *(Customs)*: See Personal Exemption.

Duty-Free Port *(Cruise)*: A port free of customs duty and most customs regulations on goods purchased locally that will be taken out of the country. There may be another type of taxes applied, such as national or local taxes.

Duty-free Shop *(Airlines)*: A shop usually located at an airport, where goods may be purchased free of duty.

Dynamic Lift *(Aeronautics)*: The vertical movement of an airship created by aerodynamic forces acting on the aircraft, as opposed to static lift, which is generated by the buoyancy of lighter-than-air lifting gases.

Duvet *(Hospitality)*: A warm, comfortable coverlet similar to a comforter and/or a quilt. It is composed of two layers of fabric with an insulation substance between, and often over-filled with down feathers

DVD *(GDS)*: Code meaning Divided PNR Message.

DWB *(GDS)*: Code meaning Double Room with Bath.

DXA *(GDS)*: Code meaning Deferred Cancellation Area.

Dynamic Package *(Tourism)*: A tour product customized to meet customers' needs, using a web-based software program or Dynamic Packaging Engine. It is opposed to Static Package.

Dynamic Pressure *(Air Traffic)*: A measure of barometric pressure in the moving air. It is synonymous with Stagnation Pressure, Total Pressure.

E

E *(Airlines)*: "Eco," name used to designate the letter "E" in the International Phonetic Alphabet

E *(GDS)*: Code for "Economy."

E-passport *(Tourism)*: A new type of passport containing a chip that stores electronic information relating the traveler. It is being used in the United States and some other countries,

E-ticket *(Airlines)*: A virtual image that contains full information about travel reservations made for a specific passenger. It replaces the paper tickets and enables automated check-in at the airport. See Electronic Ticket.

E-ticketing *(Airlines)*: See Electronic Ticketing.

EAN *(Tourism)*: See European Article Numbering.

EAN International-Uniform Code Council (EAN-UCC) *(Organizations)*: A supply chain standards family name that includes product barcodes which are printed on the majority of products available in stores worldwide and electronic commerce standards. The EAN International-Uniform Code Council is an entity that was born by the mergence of two organizations related to the same purpose: The global organization EAN International and Uniform Code Council (the Numbering Organization in the

USA that changed its name to GS1 US in 2005).

EAN-UCC *(Organizations)*: An acronym for EAN International-Uniform Code Council.

Earhart, Amelia *(Aviation)*: The first woman to cross the Atlantic Ocean on June 18-19, 1928. The flight was completed on board a Fokker tri-motor called the Friendship. In 1932, five years after Lindbergh's flight across the Atlantic, Amelia became the second person to repeat the feat, and the first woman to do so. She died in 1937, while attempting a round-the-world flight with navigator Fred Noonan.

Early Arrival *(Hospitality)*: The arrival of a guest at the property before the date announced in the reservation.

Early Bird Rate *(Hospitality)*: A discounted rate for booking early.

Early Check in *(Hospitality)*: Anticipated show of a guest at check in counter, before the standard time.

Early Makeup *(Hospitality)*: A term indicating that the guest has reserved an early check-in time and has requested his/her room to be cleaned as soon as possible.

Earth Coordinates *(Air Traffic)*: Coordinates referenced to the earth.

Earth Data *(Air Traffic)*: Environmental data related to the earth at some point of interest. It is usually a function of latitude and longitude.

Earth Eccentricity *(Geography)*: The shape of the Earth's orbit around the Sun. A measure of how elliptical the Earth's orbit is.

EAS *(Tourism)*: See Electronic Article Surveillance.

EASA *(Organizations)*: An acronym for European Aviation Safety Agency.

Eastern Africa *(IATA Geography)*: The territory comprising Burundi, Djibouti, Eritrea, Ethiopia, Kenya, Rwanda, Somalia, Tanzania, Uganda.

Eastern Caribbean *(IATA Geography)*: The territory comprising Anguilla, Antigua, Dominica, Grenada, Montserrat, St Kitts and Nevis, St Lucia, St Vincent and the Grenadines.

Eastern Daylight Time (EDT) *(Geography)*: EDT is 4 hours behind of Coordinated Universal Time (UTC). EDT is used during the summer only in these Canadian territories: Most of Nunavut, most parts east of 90 West and two communities west of 90 West of Ontario, and Quebec. EDT is used during the summer in these US states: Connecticut, Delaware, District of Columbia, Southern/Eastern parts of Florida, Georgia, Indiana (all except for these north-western counties near Chicago), eastern parts of Kentucky, Maine, Maryland, Massachusetts, most of Michigan, New Hampshire, New Jersey, New cork, North Carolina, Ohio, Pennsylvania, Rhode Island, South Carolina, eastern counties of Tennessee, Vermont, Virginia, West Virginia

Eastern Hemisphere *(IATA Geography)*: The region comprising IATA Areas 2 and 3.

Eastern Standard Time (EST) *Geography)*: EST is 5 hours behind of Coordinated Universal Time (UTC). EST is used during winter only in these Canadian territories: Most of Nunavut, most parts east of 90 West and two communities west of 90 West of Ontario, and Quebec. EST is used during winter in these US states: Connecticut, Delaware, District of Columbia, Southern/Eastern parts of Florida, Georgia, Indiana (all except for these north-western counties near Chicago), eastern parts of Kentucky, Maine, Maryland, Massachusetts, most of Michigan, New Hampshire, New Jersey, New cork, North Carolina, Ohio, Pennsylvania, Rhode Island, South Carolina, eastern counties of Tennessee, Vermont, Virginia, West Virginia

Eating Shrimp *(Cruise)*: A Cruise slang term meaning the practice of entertaining travel agents during a Fam Trip.

EB *(GDS)*: A code meaning Eastbound, English Breakfast.

EBT *(GDS)*: Code meaning Electronic Booking Tool.

ECAA *(Organizations)*: An acronym for European Common Aviation Area.

ECAR *(GDS)*: Code for Economy Car.

ECAT *(GDS)*: Code meaning E-Commerce Action Team.

ECBS *(Organisms)*: An acronym for European Committee for Banking Standards.

Eclipse *(Geography)*: A total or partial cutting off the light from one celestial body by the passage of another between it and the observer or between it and its source of illumination. An eclipse happens when the moon blocks the Sun, the Earth's shadow falls on the moon or one star in a binary system obscures another.

Eclipse Chaser *(Tourism)*: A person who travels with the only purpose to observe solar eclipses. Some amazing tours of this type of tourism are organized aboard cruise ships with special eclipse itineraries.

Eco *(Airlines)*: Designator for the letter "E" in the International Phonetic Alphabet.

Eco-certification *(Ecology)*: A procedure designed around a set of criteria to assist tourism operators in mitigating negative environmental, economic, and socio-cultural impacts of tourism, while maximizing the benefits it can provide to the environment and local communities.

Eco-friendly *(Ecology)*: A tourist activity having a beneficial effect on the environment and or on local communities.

Eco-label *(Ecology)*: A sign or seal that informs a product has met a set of environmental, socio-cultural and or economic standards.

Eco-Tourism, Eco Tourism or Ecotourism *(Tourism)*: An environmentally responsible type of tourist activity designed to allow visitors enjoy and appreciate nature and any accompanying cultural features, but minimizing damage risk to the ecosystem. Although different in details, almost all definitions of ecotourism identify it as a special form of tourism that meets three criteria: 1) It cares environmental conservation; 2) It demands meaningful participation of the community; 3) It is a profitable activity that can sustain itself.

Ecological Efficiency *(Ecology)*: The percentage of energy in a biomass that is transferred from one trophic level into the next trophic level.

Ecologically Sustainable Development *(Ecology)*: A type of development in which resources are used at a level that it neither exceeds the carrying capacity of the existing natural capital nor threatens their future availability.

Ecologist *(Ecology)*: A scientist dedicated to the studies of Ecology.

Ecology *(Ecology)*: In general terms, Ecology is a branch of Biology which focuses on the relationships between live organisms and their environment. More specifically, it is the study of the distribution and abundance of life, the interactive relationship of living organisms with one another and with their non-living surroundings, the processes of energy flows and nutrient cycles within communities and ecosystems. It involves such subjects as species abundance, biodiversity, complexity, trophic levels, ecological niches, and structure of communities. The basic units in ecological studies are species, population and community. Ecology is subdivided into three fields of study: Autoecology (relationship of individual species or populations to their environment), Synecology (composition of living communities), and Dynecology (processes of change in related communities). The study concerned with relationships between human groups and their physical and social environments is called Human Ecology, and includes the study of detrimental effects of modern civilization on the environment, with a view toward prevention or reversal through conservation. A political ecology is also identified as the resource of ecologist groups whose objective is the transformation of production and consuming methods in order to safeguard the natural environment.

Economic and Social Council (ECOSOC) *(Organizations)*: ECOSOC was established under the United Nations Charter in San Francisco on 26 June, 1945, as the principal organism to coordinate economic, social, and related work of the 14 UN specialized agencies, functional commissions and five regional commissions. The Council is responsible for promoting higher standards of living, full employment, and economic and social progress; identifying solutions to international economic, social and health problems; facilitating international cultural and educational cooperation; and encouraging universal respect for human rights and fundamental freedoms. To accomplish its mandate, the Council holds a four-week substantive session each July, alternating between New York and Geneva.

Economic Impact *(Tourism)*: The macroeconomic effect on employment and incomes produced by a decision, event, or policy. There are three types of economic impacts: Direct, indirect, and induced. Direct impacts in travel activities are those directly related to tourism, such as the profits of travel providers and the retributions to employees. Indirect impacts take place when purchases of goods and services are made from other companies, resulting in additional profits or earnings associated with the provision of these goods and services. Induced impact occurs, for instance, when employees in the travel industry spend their money on food, cars, homes, and other goods and services, inducing additional economic activities for the providers of these goods and services.

Economy Cabin *(Airlines)*: The section of a plane assigned to travelers holding Economy Class tickets.

Economy Class *(Airlines)*: 1. The cheapest class of normal fares. 2. Coach class, same as Economy Cabin.

Economy Class Fare *(Airlines)*: The full cheap fare established for normal, regular or usual service, generally not restricted by application conditions, such as minimum or maximum stay, stopovers or other special circumstances.

Economy Hotel *(Hospitality)*: A low rates hotel offering few amenities.

Economy Plus *(Airlines)*: An intermediate class of services ranked between coach and business class, featuring more space, better service (meals and drinks) and additional amenities.

ECOSOC *(Organizations)*: An acronym for "Economic and Social Council."

Ecosystem *(Ecology)*: In general terms, an ecosystem is a geographical area of a variable size where plants, animals, and the physical environment all interact together. More specifically, it is the dynamic complex formed by a community of organisms interrelating and interacting with each other and with their physical surroundings, all functioning as a unit. It is a group of biotic and abiotic factors which live together and have mutual relationships. Ecosystems are found in a particular environment, such as a forest, a desert, or a coral reef. They are much smaller than a biome

Ecosystem Services *(Ecology)*: The whole of natural services which are vital for supporting human life, such as the purification of air and water, decomposition of wastes, regulation of climate, restoration of soil fertility, and maintenance of biodiversity.

ECTAA *(Organizations)*: An acronym for European Travel Agents and Tour Operators' Associations.

Ecumene *(Geography)*: A type of region permanently inhabited.

EDCT *(Air Traffic)*: See Expect Departure Clearance Time.

EDI *(Computing)*: See Electronic Data Interchange.

EDIFACT *(Computing)*: See Electronic Data Interchange for Administration, Commerce and Transport.

EDST *(Geography)*: See Eastern Daylight Savings Time.

EDT *(Geography)*: See Eastern Daylight Time.

Educational Tour *(Tourism)*: A tour designed around an educational topic such as studying Naïf art.

Eduventurer *(Tourism)*: A term composed of the word education and adventure referring to a traveler with special interest in adventure travel and educational opportunities at the same time, especially when both themes are combined in a single trip.

EE *(GDS)*: Code shown on a ticket, to indicate fare applied is economy.

EEA *(Organizations)*: An acronym for European Economic Area.

EEC *(Organizations)*: An acronym for European Economic Community.

EEPROM *(Airlines)*: See Electrically Erasable Programmable Read-Only Memory.

EFD *(GDS)*: Three-letter IATA code for Ellington Field serving the city of Houston.

EFF *(GDS)*: Code for Effective.

Effective Date *(Tourism)*: The date on which something becomes valid, such as a fare, or a tour offer.

Efficiency *(Hospitality)*: Any hotel room with a small kitchen and dining area.

EFP *(GDS)*: Code meaning "Equivalent Fare Paid."

EFT *(GDS)*: See Elapsed Flying Time.

EFTA *(Organizations)*: An acronym for European Free Trade Association.

EG *(GDS)*: Code meaning For Instance.

EH *(GDS)*: Global Indicator for a travel within Eastern Hemisphere.

Eighth Freedom of the Air *(Airlines)*: This freedom, also known as "cabotage privilege," gives an airline the right to carry traffic between two domestic points in a foreign country, provided the flight either originates in or is destined to the carrier's home country.

Eiswein *(Hospitality)*: A German term literally meaning "ice wine", a rare German wine which is made only with very ripe grapes that are not harvested until late November. The grapes are left on the vine to freeze, quickly harvest, rush frozen to the presses, and pressed while frozen. Temperatures of -7C are required. The resulting wine is sweet, concentrated and luscious.

EJT *(GDS)*: See Elapsed Flying Time.

El Nino *(Climate)*: A condition caused by the decrease in atmospheric pressure over the Eastern Pacific Ocean, weakening the prevailing western winds that warm waters and creates strange weather patterns worldwide, sometimes causing droughts in South American coasts and flooding in California simultaneously. The effect gets its name from the Spanish *El Niño* for the Christ Child because it is experienced in December.

El Nino Southern Oscillation (ENSO) *(Climate)* Pressure systems in the South Pacific of sudden or unexpected reversal of direction that activate short lasting global changes in climate. Warm waters flowing from the western Pacific move across the ocean and significantly warm the eastern tropical Pacific.

Elapsed Flying Time *(Airlines)*: The actual time spent by an airplane in the air, excluding the time spent taxiing to and from the gate and during transit stops. It is also called Elapsed Journey Time.

Elapsed Journey Time *(Airlines)*: See Elapsed Flying Time.

Elasticity *(Tourism)*: A marketing concept denoting the percentage change in the price of a product (such as a tour package), and the percentage change in demand for that product. Summarily, it is the relationship between pricing and consumer demand.

ELD *(GDS)*: Code meaning Electronic Liquor Dispenser.

Elderhostel *(Tourism)*: It is a Hostel that provides services to senior citizens. It is mostly offered in educational travel programs for seniors, often with accommodation arrangements at universities.

Electric liquor dispenser *(Hospitality)*: An electronic device for serving precise amounts of alcoholic beverages.

Electrically Erasable Programmable Read-Only Memory (EEPROM) *(Computing)*: A method of storing data on microchips in which bytes can be erased and reprogrammed individually. RFID tags that use EEPROM are more expensive than factory programmed tags.

Electromagnetic Interference (EMI) *(Computing)*: Interference caused when the radio waves of one device distort the waves of another, such as cell phones and wireless computers that produce interference with RFID tags.

Electronic Article Surveillance (EAS) *(Computing)*: Simple electronic tags that can be turned on or off. When an item is purchased, the tag is turned off, because an alarm will sound if the tag in on position when the purchaser passes the gate area. EAS tags can be RF-based, or acoustic-magnetic.

Electronic Coupon *(Airlines)*: An electronic Flight Coupon or other value document held in a Carrier's system as a virtual image.

Electronic Data Interchange for Administration, Commerce and Transport (EDIFACT) *(Computing)*: An electronic set of computer interchange standards to create electronic versions of common business documents that work on a global scale, such as invoices, bills, and purchase orders. It is widely used by airlines.

Electronic Mail *(Computing)*: Generally known as "e-mail" or email", it is a communications system enabling people to exchange messages through a computer network.

Electronic Miscellaneous Document (EMD) *(Airlines)*: An electronic record issued by an air carrier or its authorized agent, in accordance with applicable tariffs, for the issuance of Excess Baggage Tickets or Miscellaneous Charges Order.

Electronic Product Code (EPC) *(Airlines)*: A serial code created by the Auto-ID Center to transfer information on an individual item for complementing barcode reading.

Electronic Reservations Service Provider (ERSP) *(Airlines)*: An ARC code that identifies online bookings made for airlines.

Electronic Reservations Service Providers (ERSP) *(Airlines)*: The expression identifies Worldwide Travel Service Providers (excluding the USA), registered with IATA, and established on the Internet or other on-line services to promote reservation information similar to that provided by an IATA Member Airline's system. It is a designator that identifies airline bookings made online.

Electronic Settlement Authorization Code (ESAC) *(Airlines)*: ESAC is an alpha/numeric code that is generated by the Carrier's e-ticket database when a travel agent requests permission, via GDS, to make a change to an e-ticket. The purpose of the code is to confirm that an e-ticket has not been used (in the Carrier's ticketing database) and is available for voiding, refunding or exchanging. The Carrier will grant its permission for the requested change by sending the ESAC code back to the agent via the GDS system.

Electronic Ticket (ET) *(Airlines)*: A paperless airline ticket holding all the travel information and allowing the holder to check-in and fly with just showing a proper ID with photo. The issuer hands a printing that looks like a ticket, but it is actually just a paper passenger receipt. Since E-tickets are system images, they cannot be lost or used by anyone else. A possible disadvantage is that e-tickets on one carrier cannot be honored by another carrier. Effective 1 Jun 2008, paper tickets are eliminated from IATA BSPs and BSP travel agencies only have access to E-tickets.

Electronic Ticket Delivery Network *(Airlines)*: A network of ticket printing machines that are operated by companies selling ticket distribution services on behalf of accredited travel agencies. Nevertheless, an ETDN issues tickets only after an agent generates them.

Electronic Ticket Distribution Network *(Airlines)*: See Electronic Ticket Delivery Network.

Electronic Ticket List *(Airlines)*: A message sent by a ground handler to the operating carrier detailing the electronic coupons that have been placed in flown status.

Electronic Ticket Refund Exchange Authorization (ET/REA) *(Airlines)*: The ET/REA is a non-accountable document that may be printed even on plain paper, to replace the unused flight coupons of an electronic ticket in order to process the exchange or refund of that transaction.

Electronic Ticket Server *(Airlines)*: A computer system that handles requirements from reservation and ground handling systems referred to electronic tickets stored on a linked electronic ticket database.

Electronic Ticketing *(Airlines)*: A computerized system used by airlines following the booking process in which no physical ticket or boarding pass is generated and concludes with the issuance of an electronic ticket. According to IATA, it is one of the most significant opportunities to reduce ticket processing costs, eliminating "the need for paper and allows greater flexibility to the passenger and the travel agent to make changes to the itinerary". Precise steps must be followed when issuing e-tickets. A few of them are detailed as follows:

• *Segments*: In general, the itinerary may contain no more than 16 segments per ticket. An ARNK is considered to be a segment. Open segments are permitted if the itinerary contains at least one confirmed segment.

• *Tickets*: Infants may not travel on an e-ticket. A paper ticket will be issued as required by international tariffs.

• In case of a cancelled-flight, the original carrier must print hard copy tickets before endorsing it to another airline.

• *Agency Eligibility*: To be eligible for electronic ticketing the agency must be registered at any GDS or CRS and must be supported by ATB/OPTAT ticket printers.

• *Cancellations*: Canceling a PNR does not cancel an electronic ticket. An electronic ticket must be voided directly in the GDS up until 11:59p.m. of the business day after the ticket was issued. Travel agents have to update the cancellation records accordingly.

• *Changes to an Electronic Ticket*: Changes are available subject to the fare rules, but the electronic ticket record must always be updated through the exchange process.

• Paper tickets may be exchanged / reissued for a new electronic ticket per tariff reissue policies and rules.

• *Refund*: Electronic refund is processed according to local settlement plan rules. Most airline tickets are nonrefundable. However, after applying the appropriate change fee, any remaining balance may be applied to the purchase of a new electronic ticket.

Electronic Ticketing Data Elements Glossary *(Airlines)*: A document that holds a terms list defining each of the data elements used in Electronic Ticketing EDIFACT messages.

Electronic Ticketing EDIFACT Implementation Guide *(Airlines)*: A document which describes the recommended standards for Electronic Ticketing EDIFACT messages.

Electronic Travel Authority (ETA) *(Tourism)*: A program that issues the equivalent of a visa online which allows to travel to Australia for a short stay. The ETA avoids stamps or labels placed in passports. The Electronic Travel Authority (ETA) is available online from participating travel agencies when making travel arrangements, or through participating airlines, as well as at Australian visa offices overseas

Elevation *(Air Traffic)*: An angle in the vertical plane through a longitudinal axis; height above mean sea level, usually of terrain.

Elevator *(Aeronautics)*: A control surface usually located on the horizontal stabilizer of an aircraft, which is used to control the upward or downward movement of the aircraft's nose.

Elite Qualifying Miles *(Airlines)*: Any credit of mileage applied to the highest status level eligible in a frequent flyer program.

EM *(GDS)*: Code for Emission.

EMA *(Airlines)*: See Extra Mileage Allowance.

Email/ E-Mail *(Computing)*: See Electronic Mail.

EMAN *(GDS)*: Code meaning Economy Car with Manual Transmission.

Embargo *(Airlines)*: 1. A blackout period in which some fares or promotions are not valid. 2. A governmental order restraining the departure of a commercial vehicle from an airport or port, or the prohibition to perform any commercial activity.

Embark *(Tourism)*: The process of entering or boarding a transportation vehicle, such as ship, or a plane.

Embarkation *(Tourism)*: See Embark.

EMD *(Airlines)*: See Electronic Miscellaneous Document.

EMEA *(GDS)*: Code meaning "Europe, Middle East and Africa."

EMER *(GDS)*: Code meaning Emergency Travel.

EMERG *(GDS)*: Code for Emergency.

Emerging Disease *(Ecology)*: A new disease resulting from the evolution or change of an existing pathogenic condition, a known infection extending to a new geographic area, or an unknown pathogenic agent diagnosed for the first time and which involves a significant impact on animal or public health.

Emergency Sickness Plan (ESP) *(Car Rental)*: A plan that provides international renters visiting the U.S. with medical expense coverage to become protected against unexpected illness.

EMI *(Airlines)*: See Electromagnetic Interference.

EMIG *(GDS)*: Code for Emigrant.

Emigrant *(Tourism)*: A person who, by force of the circumstances, leaves the country of his/her residence to settle in another. See also Immigrant.

Emigrate *(Tourism)*: The action of leaving one's country to settle permanently in another.

Emissary *(Tourism)*: A person or an agent who is sent on a mission to represent the interests of another person or a country.

Emissions *(Ecology)*: The gas expelled by an engine burning fossil fuels during combustion.

Empennage *(Aeronautics)*: A French term for an aircraft's tail group, including rudder, fin, stabilizer and elevator.

EMS *(GDS)*: Code meaning: 1. Excess Mileage Surcharge. 2. Emergency medical service.

Empty Leg *(Airlines)*: A segment flown without passengers onboard between two consecutive scheduled stops. It occurs frequently when a charter flight takes passengers in one direction but returns empty rather than waiting for a return load.

En Route *(Airlines)*: A French expression meaning on a route to some place or during the trip to a destination.

En Route Air Traffic Control Services *(Air Traffic)*: Air traffic control services provided to aircraft on IFR flight plans when these aircraft are operating between departure and destination terminal areas.

En Route Center *(Air Traffic)*: See Air Route Traffic Control Center

En Route Chart *(Air Traffic)*: A chart of air routes in specific areas that shows the exact location of electronic aids to navigation, such as radio-direction-finder stations, radio- and radar-marker beacons, and radio-range stations.

En Suite *(Hospitality)*: A French term meaning literally "in the room". It is used in reference to a bedroom constructed with its own toilet and bathroom

Enclave *(Tourism)*: An enclosed area of a country or city, usually occupied by people that are ethnically and culturally distinct from the foreign territory that surrounds it.

Encode *(Airlines)*: 1. The process to substitute a word or a phrase by a short set of letters or numbers known as a code. 2. The action of converting a plain text to equivalent cipher text by means of a code.

Encroach *(Ecology)*: The action of exceeding gradually the proper limits of something or taking possession of what belongs to another. A desert might encroach on a meadow.

Endangered Species *(Ecology)*: The term refers to organisms, animals, plants, or populations that could soon become extinct in all or most of its natural range. The danger can emerge because the species is few in numbers, or threatened by changing environmental or predation causes.

Endangered Species Act *(Ecology)*: The United States federal law that protects the species and their habitats in danger of extinction.

Endemic *(Ecology)*: Something that is native to a place. It is contrary to terms such as exotic, non-native, introduced, alien, and naturalized. But it is not a synonym with indigenous. An endemic species is unique to a place or region, but can not be found elsewhere. An indigenous species is not unique, because it can also be native to other locations.

Endemism *(Ecology)*: The term denotes a phenomenon by which species or a defined group of species are highly adapted to a determined area, inside which they are differentiated by the ecological conditions surrounding the environment. The endemism is particularly important for animals and plants living in an island, because islands represent privileged centers of endemism. An example is the Galapagos Islands.

ENDG *(GDS)*: Code for Ending.

ENDI *(GDS)*: Code meaning End Item.

Endorsement *(Airlines)*: A transfer of authority occurring when a passenger with an international ticket needs to rebook to a carrier other than carrier shown on the ticket.

Energy *(Ecology)*: The thermodynamic quantity equivalent to the ability of a system to do work. Some forms of energy are kinetic, potential, thermal, gravitational, and electrical. According to a thermo-dynamic law, energy cannot be created or destroyed, but only transformed. In an ecological context, the energy circulates by the way of trophic webs. Common units of energy are calories, joules, and ergs.

Energy Efficient *(Ecology)*: An expression relating to the minimal amount of energy required to achieve the maximum yield.

Energy Healing *(Tourism)*: A general term used to describe a series of treatments and practices used to balance the flow of energy and remove energy blockages around the body to increase the flow of chi through the meridians.

Engine *(Aeronautics)*: A machine that uses combustion to create energy. Those used by airplanes are either jet engines or engines that drive one or more propellers.

English Breakfast *(Hospitality)*: A basic meal of cereal, juice, eggs, meats, bread and other beverages. It is common with most hotels in the United Kingdom. This type of breakfast is in risk to disappear due to the offer of buffet breakfasts.

English Channel *(Geography)*: The mass of sea water that separates England from France.

Enhancement *(Tourism)*: An improved feature added to a tour.

Enhancement *(Computing)*: Capabilities that have been added to a software program.

Enology *(Hospitality)*: See Oenology.

Enologist *(Hospitality)*: See Oenologist.

Enophile *(Hospitality)*: See Oenophile.

Enplane *(Airlines)*: To board or get in an aircraft.

ENQ *(GDS)*: A code meaning Enquire, Enquiry, Enquiring, Enquired.

Enrichment *(Tourism)*: Any activity or program that is added to a cruise or tour package in order to enhance the travelers' amusement or information.

Enroute *(Airlines)*: See En Route.

Ensign *(Cruise)*: The flag flown by a ship to show its nationality.

ENSO *(Geography)* See El Nino Southern Oscillation.

Entrée *(Hospitality)*: A French term with two meanings: 1. In the U.S., a dish served as the main course of a meal. 2. In Europe, a dish served as an appetizer before the main course in a formal meal.

Enterprise Resource Planning (ERP) *(Computing)*: A procedure applied by an organization in order to integrate all of its data and processes into a unified system. An ERP system uses multiple components of computer software and hardware to achieve the integration, featuring the use of a unified database to store data for the various system modules.

Entertainment *(Tourism)*: 1. The art of maintaining people amused, especially by performing certain amusement activities. 2. An event, activity or performance designed to entertain an audience.

Entremetier *(Hospitality)*: A French term referring to a kitchen employee who prepares soups, vegetable dishes and egg dishes, but none involving meat or fish.

Entrepreneur *(Tourism)*: A person who starts a business venture and assumes the risk for it.

Entry *(Computing)*: An input made into a computer program.

Entry Fee *(Tourism)*: The price a tourist pays to be admitted to an attraction or the duty charged on a person for entering a country.

Entry Requirements *(Tourism)*: Official documents required from travelers to enter a country, such as passport, visa, vaccination certificates, and proofs of economic solvency.

Entry Visa *(Tourism)*: An authorization issued by a diplomatic representation allowing a foreign traveler entering its country. Usually visas are stamped on the traveler's passport. Australia issues an electronic visa to citizens of certain countries, which is not stamped on the passport. See Electronic Travel Authority.

Environment *(Ecology)*: In general, the term denotes all the external physic or natural conditions that affect an organism. In a more specific meaning, it joins both physical, chemical, natural, components and all biological factors, as well as social and human components. Human species is a part of the environment contributing to its modification. Other definitions describe environment as the systems supporting all earth's forms of life or the solar capital and earth capital.

Environmental Degradation *(Ecology)*: 1. The reduction of an ecosystem's capacity to support its natural living components. 2. The destruction of renewable resources that can become nonrenewable or nonexistent if such misuse is continued. 3. Environment is also degraded when it is polluted, poisoned or otherwise altered, making it less productive, inhospitable, or unusable.

Environmental Impact *(Ecology)*: The direct and indirect consequences of human actions on the natural environment.

Environmental Impact Assessment (EIA) *(Ecology)*: The evaluation process of identifying, predicting and assessing the positive and/or negative influence a project may have on the environment, as well as mitigating the biophysical, social, and other relevant effects of development projects before decisions are taken.

Environmental Protection Agency (EPA) *(Organizations)*: A U.S. entity whose purpose is to protect human health and the environment. EPA is responsible for researching and setting national standards for a variety of environmental programs that will improve the scientific basis for decisions on national environmental issues.

Environmentally Additional Offsets *(Ecology)*: The standards used for assessing whether a project has resulted in greenhouse gas reductions or removals compared to what would have occurred in its absence.

Environs *(Geography)*: The outer adjacent area surrounding a place.

EP *(GDS)*: Code meaning European Plan.

EPA *(Organizations)*: An acronym for Environmental Protection Agency.

EPC *(Airlines)*: An acronym for Electronic Product Code.

EPC Information Service *(Computing)*: A part of the EPC Network, a network infrastructure enabling companies to store data associated with EPCs in secure databases on the Web.

EPCglobal *(Organizations)*: A non-profit organization comprising the Uniform Code Council and EAN International, the two organizations that maintain barcode standards and commercialize EPC technology originally developed by the Auto-ID Center. EPCglobal performs its job by chapters established in different countries and regions.

EPCglobal Network (or EPC Network) *(Computing)*: The Internet-based technology and services enabling companies to recover data associated with EPCs.

EQFP *(GDS)*: Code meaning Equivalent Fare Paid.

EQM *(GDS)*: Code meaning Elite Qualifying Miles.

EQT *(GDS)*: A code meaning Equipment, an aircraft type.

Equator *(Geography)*: The imaginary line that divides the Earth into northern and southern hemispheres.

Equatorial Rain Forest *(Tourism)*: An area located near the equator, characterized by high precipitation, high tree and vegetative growth rates, high humidity, high photosynthetic rates, extreme biodiversity, and absence or shortage of dry season. The equatorial rain forests cover seven percent of the earth's surface, produce much of the oxygen in the Earth's atmosphere and absorb large quantities of carbon dioxide from the air.

Equilibrium *(Airlines)*: A condition of relative balance in which the forces of lift and gravity are equal.

Equinox *(Geography)*: A phenomenon occurring two times a year (around March 21 and September 23) when the sun crosses the equator line equaling the duration of day and night.

EQUIP *(Air Traffic)*: A code meaning Equipment.

Equipment *(Airlines)*: In air navigation, the term denotes the vehicle used to operate commercial flights. In a general sense, the term refers to any tangible personal property that is capitalized, such as computers, copiers, scanners, printers, stereos, televisions, VCR or DVD players, etc.

Equirectangular Projection *(Geography)*: A graph of the earth that represents a land mass in its correct shape but distorting its area.

Equity Club *(Tourism)*: A private organization owned by its members, such as a country club, that is focused on its members' benefit or enjoyment. Equity Clubs make the investments productive and allow members to profit from increases in the club's property values.

EQUIV *(GDS)*: Code meaning Equivalent Amount.

Erosion *(Geography)*: A general geologic term which refers to the gradual wearing down of land by the action of different external factors.

ERF *(Car Rental)*: See Excess Reduction Fee.

ERP *(Tourism)*: See Enterprise Resource Planning.

ERQ *(GDS)*: Code meaning Endorsement Request.

Error Correcting Code *(Computing)*: A code stored on an RFID tag to enable the reader to assess the missing or garbled bits of data.

Error Correcting Mode *(Computing)*: A data transmission mode for correcting automatically errors or missing data.

Error Correcting Protocol *(Computing)*: A set of rules used for reading and interpreting correctly data from the tag.

Errors and Omission Insurance *(Tourism)*: Insurance that covers damages derived from an agent's mistake or omission. It is also called Professional Liability Insurance.

ERSP *(Airlines)*: See Electronic Reservations Service Providers.

ESAC *(Airlines)*: See Electronic Settlement Authorization Code.

ET/REA *(Airlines)*: See Electronic Ticket Refund Exchange Authorization.

Escarpment *(Geography)*: A steep cliff formed by erosion or faulting.

Escoffier, Georges Auguste (1847-1935) *(Hospitality)*: *Georges Auguste Escoffier* is one of the most important leaders in the development of modern French cuisine and a legendary figure among chefs and gourmets. He was also a culinary writer who popularized and updated traditional French cooking methods. He was born in the village of *Villeneuve-Loubet*, in the neighborhood of Nice, in the Provence region, in 28 October 1846. At the age of thirteen he started an apprenticeship at his uncle's restaurant *Le Restaurant Français* in Nice. When he was nineteen, Escoffier was invited by the chef of the *Le Petit Moulin Rouge*, the most fashionable restaurant in Paris at that time, to join his team. In short time he started introducing his initiatives, as simplifying menus. Instead of serving a vast array of dishes all at once, according to the *Service à la Française* (as was the practice), Escoffier imposed his viewpoint to serve dishes in the order they appeared on the menu, that is, according to the *Service à la Russe.* In 1884 Escoffier was assigned as *Directeur de Cuisine* at the Grand Hotel. During the following six years he divided his time between the Grand Hotel in winter and the Hotel National of Lucerne, Switzerland, in the summer. It was precisely here that Escoffier met Cesar Ritz, a famous hotelier and founder of several hotels. It was easy for Escoffier and Ritz to agree in a mutual understanding to form the teamwork that brought about the most significant changes and modern development in the hotel industry. In 1890 the two men moved to the Savoy Hotel in London, from where they established a number of famous hotels, including the Grand Hotel in Rome, and many Ritz Hotels around the world. While in the London Savoy, Escoffier created several famous dishes, such as the "Peach Melba" in honor of the Australian singer Nellie Melba, and the "Tournedos Rossini," in honor of the Italian composer Gioacchino Rossini. In 1903 Escoffier published his most significant book, *Le Guide Culinaire*, a collection of 5,000 recipes. The book is used even today as both a cookbook and textbook for classic cooking. It is said the menu served on the Titanic's final night was created by Escoffier. Between 1904 and 1912 Escoffier was hired to manage the kitchens for ships belonging to the German Shipping Company "Hamburg-Amerika Lines." In one of its journeys, the Kaiser William II congratulated Escoffier, telling him "I am the Emperor of Germany, but you are the Emperor of chefs." Escoffier died on February 12, 1935 at the age of 88 in Monte Carlo, a few days after his wife's death.

Escort *(Tourism)*: A person with travel experience who, representing a tour operator, takes individual visitors or tour groups to see a place or a city.

Escorted Service *(Tourism)*: A prearranged tour program, usually fit for groups, operated with escort service. Fully escorted tours often use additionally local guide services. Euphemistically, the term is also used for social engagements or disguised call girl operations.

Escorted Tour *(Tourism)*: A pre-packaged or sightseeing program that is operated in company of a guide. In a fully-escorted tour, the guide travels with the group along the whole itinerary as a guide or trouble-shooter.

ESP *(Car Rental)*: See Emergency Sickness Plan.

Essential Air Service *(Airlines)*: Official subsidized service for airlines which continued operating in rural areas of the United States after the Airline Deregulation Act of 1978.

Essential Oils *(Tourism)*: Oils extracted from plants and flowers that have specific characteristics, which determine their use, for stimulating or relaxing or even for healing.

EST *(GDS)*: A code meaning: 1. Estimate, Estimating, Estimated, Estimation; 2. Eastern Standard Time.

Estimated Time En Route (ETE) *(Air Traffic)*: The estimated flying time from departure point to destination (from takeoff to landing).

Estuary *(Geography)*: A costal inlet of water reaching inland from a sea or lake and located at the mouth of a river where tides flow in and out mixing fresh water with sea water.

ET *(Airlines)*: See Electronic Ticket.

ET Server *(Airlines)*: See Electronic Ticket Server.

ETA *(GDS)*: A code meaning: 1. Electronic Travel Authority. 2. Estimated Time of Arrival.

ETC *(GDS)*: Code meaning: 1. Etcetera; 2. European Travel Commission.

ETD *(GDS)*: Code meaning Estimated Time of Departure.

ETDN *(GDS)*:   Code meaning Electronic Ticket Delivery Network.

ETE *(Air Traffic)*: See Estimated Time en Route.

Ethanol *(Ecology)*: An oxygenated hydrocarbon that can be burned as a fuel, or blended into gasoline. Conceived as an alternative for a clean fuel, ethanol is a renewable energy source made from corn or other grains. In Brazil ethanol is extracted from sugar cane. When blended into gasoline, ethanol improves the combustion process and reduces the formation of unburned hydrocarbons. Ethanol is also known as ethyl alcohol.

Ethnic Group *(Geography)*: A collectivity sharing common language, history and culture (costumes, social organization principles, etc.) living in a specific space (the territorial unit). The term is derived from the Greek "ethnos", which means people.

Ethnic Menu *(Hospitality)*: Menu that features dishes of a particular nation or ethnic group, such as Japanese, French, or Spanish.

Ethnic Restaurant *(Hospitality)*: A restaurant featuring the cuisine of a particular nation or ethnic group, such as Italian, Mexican, or Chinese.

Ethnic Tourism *(Tourism)*: A type of cultural tourism of particular interest for scientists and anthropologists because of its concepts of authenticity, tradition, and modernity which are all components of social change. Ethnic tourism is of key importance as the tourist industry grows larger and becomes more and more popular. It is said that Tourism is the ultimate journey toward the "Other", and Ethnic tourism sets the path to search for the style of living of other human groups whom are often seen as exotic and strange, but at the same time identified to the visitor.

Ethnocentrism *(Tourism)*: A mindset, belief, or attitude that affirms one's own ethnic group is superior to all others. As a consequence ethno centrists are tendentious to judge other cultures by the standards of their own.

Ethnopharmacology *(Ecology)*: The study of indigenous medicines, the method of production, the medical practices, treatment protocols, etc. utilizing such medicines.

ETL *(Airlines)*: See Electronic Ticket List.

ETOPS *(Air Traffic)*: Extended Two-engine Operations.

ETS *(Organizations)*: An acronym for European Telecommunications Standards Institute.

EU *(GDS)*: A code meaning: 1. A Global Indicator meaning a travel is via Europe; 2. European Union.

EU-US Open Skies Agreement *(Airlines)*: An air transport agreement between the European Union and the United States that allows any airline of the European Union and any airline of the United States to fly between any point in the European Union and any point in the United States. The agreement allows airlines of the United States to fly between points in the European Union, and airlines of the European Union to fly between the United States and non-EU countries like Switzerland. The agreement was signed in Washington, D.C., on April 30, 2007 and became effective on

March 30, 2008.

EUR *(GDS)*: Code for Euro, official currency for the European Union.

Eurafrasia *(Geography)*: See Africa-Eurasia.

Eurailpass *(Tourism)*: A special-fare train ticket that allows the user to either unlimited train travel, or travel for a certain number of days/weeks, in many European countries (except in Britain, where the Britrailpass offers similar travel in England, Scotland, and Wales). The Eurailpass is only available for residents outside Europe.

Eurasia *(Geography)*: A large landmass covering about the 10.6 percent of the Earth's surface, or about 53,990,000 square kilometers. Usually considered as a single continent, Eurasia is formed by the continents of Europe and Asia. Some geographers think the borders used to establish the division between these two continents are somewhat arbitrary. Eurasia, in turn, is part of the landmass of Africa-Eurasia, whereby Asia is joined to Africa at the Isthmus of Suez.

Euro *(Geography)*: The common currency unit used by the member states of the European Economic Community, excepting United Kingdom, Denmark and Sweden, that continue to use their own currency. Outside Europe, Cuba decided in June 1rst, 2002, to accept the Euro instead of the US Dollar for tourism transactions.

Euro-style *(Tourism)*: A term denoting that something happens according to the European fashion. In tourism the term implies that partial or total nudity is permitted, as at a swimming pool. Some resorts feature a Euro-style pool.

Eurobudget Fares *(Airlines)*: Discounted tickets valid for one year and without minimum stay requirement. Nevertheless, once tickets are issued with confirmed reservations, the passenger is not allowed to change dates, unless he pays extra charges.

Eurocentrism *(Tourism)*: A belief in the preeminence of Europe and the Europeans, reflecting a tendency to understand the world according to the values and experiences of European or Anglo-American regions.

Eurocontrol *(Organizations)*: An acronym for European Organization for the Safety of Air Navigation.

Eurodollars *(Tourism)*: Deposits of U.S. dollars at banks outside the United States, which are not under the jurisdiction of the Federal Reserve. Eurodollars are much less regulated than similar deposits within the United States. The term "Euro" does not imply such deposits have to be made in Europe, because a US dollar deposits made in Shanghai or the Caribbean would likewise be deemed as Eurodollar deposits. Neither is there a connection with the euro currency.

Euro Domino Pass *(Tourism)*: An unlimited travel rail ticket for persons who reside in Europe for at least six months, available in first or standard class.

Europe, Geographical *(Geography)*: If observed on a map, Europe looks like an appendix of the Asian continent. In fact, physically and geologically, Europe is the westernmost peninsula of Eurasia, west of Asia. Europe is bounded to the north by the Arctic Ocean, to the west by the Atlantic Ocean, to the south by the Mediterranean Sea, to the southeast by the Caucasus Mountains and the Black Sea. To the east, Europe is separated from Asia by the Ural Mountains, the Ural River, and by the Caspian Sea.

Europe is the second smallest continent of the world, after Oceania, covering about 10,530,750 square kilometers or 6.7 percent of the Earth's surface. But it is also ranked as the third most populous continent (after Asia and Africa) with a population of 715 million or about 11 percent of the world's population. It is predicted that European population will be around 731 million by 2010. The continent comprises 48 countries, among them, the largest (Russia) and the smallest (the Vatican) of the world.

The European continent is traversed by the huge Alpine mountain chain, the Carpathians, the Balkans, and the Caucasus, containing high elevations such as Mt. Elbrus (5,642 meters) in the Caucasus, Mont Blanc (4,807 meters), and the Matterhorn (4,477 meters) in the Alps. The Caspian Sea is Europe's lowest point located at 28 meters below sea level. Europe can be divided into seven geographic regions:

1. Eastern Europe (Estonia, Latvia, Lithuania, Belarus, Ukraine, Moldova, the European portion of Russia, and the Transcaucasian countries of Georgia, Armenia, and Azerbaijan);

2. Scandinavia (Iceland, Norway, Sweden, Finland, and Denmark);

3. The British Isles (the United Kingdom and Ireland);

4. Western Europe (France, Belgium, the Netherlands, Luxembourg, and Monaco);

5. Southern Europe (Portugal, Spain, Andorra, Italy, Malta, San Marino, and Vatican City);

6. Central Europe (Germany, Switzerland, Liechtenstein, Austria, Poland, the Czech Republic, Slovakia, and Hungary); and,

7. South Eastern Europe (Slovenia, Croatia, Bosnia and Herzegovina, Serbia, Montenegro, Albania, Macedonia, Romania, Bulgaria, Greece, and the European part of Turkey).

Among the most important river systems of Europe are, from east to west, the Vistula, the Oder, the Elbe, the Weser, the Rhine, the Thames, the Loire, the Garonne. And from west to east, the Ebro, the Rhône, the Po, the Tevere, the Danube, the Dnieper, the Don, and the Volga.

Europe has a transportation system highly developed. Its rivers and canals provide excellent inland water transportation in Central and Western Europe. The Channel Tunnel constructed under the sea waters, connects Great Britain to France. Some of the world's greatest sea ports and airports are found in Europe, such as Rotterdam (with the huge new *Europort* complex), London, Le Havre, Hamburg, Genoa, and Marseilles among the chief ports; and London, Paris, Frankfurt, Amsterdam and Rome, among the outstanding air gates. The whole continent is a rich complex of destinations, from heritage, to cultural, natural, and sun tourism regions.

Europe Sub-area *(IATA Geography)*: It is the territory comprising the following countries: Albania, Algeria, Andorra, Armenia, Austria, Azerbaijan, Belarus, Belgium, Bosnia and Herzegovina, Bulgaria, Croatia, Cyprus, Czech Republic, Denmark, Estonia, Faroe Islands, Finland, France, Georgia, Germany, Gibraltar, Greece, Hungary, Iceland, Ireland, Italy, Latvia, Liechtenstein, Lithuania, Luxemburg, Macedonia, Malta, Monaco, Montenegro, Morocco, Netherlands, Norway, Poland, Portugal, Romania, Russia (in Europe), Serbia, Spain, Sweden, Switzerland, Tunisia,

Turkey, Ukraine, United Kingdom.

European Article Numbering (EAN) *(Tourism)*: The bar code standard used throughout Europe, Asia and South America.

European Aviation Safety Agency (EASA) *(Organizations)*: A strategic entity of the European Union for aviation safety. Its mission is to promote the highest common standards of safety and environmental protection in civil aviation to keep air transport safe and sustainable. While national authorities are responsible for the majority of operational tasks, such as certification of individual aircraft or licensing of pilots, the Agency evolves common safety and environmental rules at the European level. It monitors the implementation of standards through inspections in the Member States and provides the necessary technical expertise, training and research.

European Committee for Banking Standards (ECBS) *(Organizations)*: The entity was created in December 1992 by Europe's three credit sector associations: The Banking Federation of the European Union, the European Association of Co-operative Banks, and the European Savings Banks Group. The aim of ECBS is to enhance the European technical banking infrastructure by developing standards after identification of clear business and commercial interests.

European Common Aviation Area (ECAA) *(Organizations)*: An agency of the European Union created to change the future structure of air traffic control across Europe. Its aim is to implement more efficient air traffic initiatives, with air traffic control areas based on operational efficiency, not on national borders considerations. It also integrates civil and military air traffic management. The ECAA's purpose is to liberalize the air transport industry by allowing air carriers from an ECAA member state to fly between any airports in all ECAA member states, including cabotage rights. It is expected the market integration between EU and non-EU members will be completed by the year 2010.

European Economic Area (EEA) *(Organizations)*: An European entity created on January 1, 1994 following an agreement between three member states of European Free Trade Association, the European Community, and all member states of the European

Union, in order that country members of the EEA enjoy free trade with the European Union.

European Economic Community (EEC) *(Organizations)*: An organization created in 1958 as the Common Market, on the background of a treaty signed in 1957 by Belgium, France, Italy, Luxembourg, the Netherlands, and Germany. Its main objectives work for the free movement of labor and capital, the abolition of trusts and cartels, and the development of joint and reciprocal policies on labor, social welfare, agriculture, transport, and foreign trade. One of its important achievements is the establishment of common price levels for agricultural products in 1962. In 1968, internal tariffs on trade between member nations were abrogated and a common external tariff was fixed. In summary, it is a bloc of European countries that have adopted common trading rules.

European Environment Agency (EEA) *(Organizations)*: The EEA is an organization that aims to support sustainable development and to help achieve significant and measurable improvement in Europe's environment through the provision of timely, targeted, relevant and reliable information to policy making agents and the public.

European Free Trade Association (EFTA) *(Organizations)*: An European trade bloc created on May 3, 1960 as an alternative for European states non members of the European Union. The EFTA Convention signed on January 4, 1960 in Stockholm provides for the liberalization of trade among the member states.

European Organization for the Safety of Air Navigation (Eurocontrol) *(Organizations)*: An international organization created in 1963, and counting with 38 member states at present. Its main objective is the development of a pan-European Air Traffic Management (ATM) system. The tasks of the EUROCONTROL are the development, and the coordination and planning of air traffic management strategies. Its primary activities comprise the whole air navigation service operations, such as strategic and tactical flow management, controller training, regional control of airspace, safety-proofed technologies and procedures, and collection of air navigation charges. This civil organization has its headquarters in Brussels.

European Plan *(Hospitality)*: An accommodation plan that does not include any meals in the price.

European Telecommunications Standards Institute (ETSI) *(Organizations)*: The European Union communication entity that establishes recommendations of standards to be adopted by member countries.

European Travel Agents' and Tour Operators' Associations (ECTAA) *(Organizations)*: The ECTAA is a group of national travel agents' and tour operators' associations within the European Union which was founded in 1961 according to Belgian laws, as an international non profit organization. At present ECTAA encompasses travel agents' and tour operators' associations of the 27 EU Member States and of Switzerland and Norway. ECTAA is concentrated on the EU policies, which may have an impact on tourism. It acts in coordination with other instances that have an impact on the industry in Europe.

European Travel Commission *(Organizations)*: A non-profit organization which deals with government and educational personnel interested in tourism to Europe. It is responsible for the promotion of Europe as a tourist destination. Its members are the 38 National Tourism Organizations (NTOs) of Europe, whose role is to market and promote tourism to Europe in general, and to their individual countries in particular. Its member states are: Austria, Belgium, Bulgaria, Croatia, Cyprus, Czech Republic, Denmark, Estonia, Finland, France, Georgia, Germany, Greece, Hungary, Iceland, Ireland, Italy, Latvia, Lithuania, Luxembourg, Malta, Monaco, Montenegro, Netherlands, Norway, Poland, Portugal, Romania, San Marino, Serbia, Slovak Republic, Slovenia, Spain, Sweden, Switzerland, Turkey, Ukraine, and United Kingdom. The ETC headquarters are in Brussels (Belgium).

European Union *(Geography)*: The European Union is a collective of twenty seven nations brought together over the last decade to enhance political, economic and social co-operation within the boundaries of the world's smallest, yet most diverse continent. For the list of member states see European Union Member States.

European Union Member States *(Geography)*: Each of the following countries associated to the European Union: Austria,

Belgium, Bulgaria, Cyprus (Greek part), Czech Republic, Denmark, Estonia, Finland, France, Germany, Greece, Hungary, Ireland, Italy, Latvia, Lithuania, Luxembourg, Malta, Netherlands, Poland, Portugal, Romania, Slovakia, Slovenia, Spain, Sweden, United Kingdom of Great Britain and Northern Ireland.

Euroregion *(Organizations)*: A structure adopted between two or more territories located in different European countries to perform some type of transnational co-operation.

Eurotunnel *(Geography)*: See Chunnel.

Event *(Tourism)*: A noteworthy and organized happening that attracts tourists, such as a Fair, a Congress, a Sport Contest, a Concert, or a Ceremony.

Events *(Hospitality)*: The department of a hotel or other business involved in arranging and marketing meetings, conventions, receptions, banquets and other special occurrences.

Events Tourism *(Tourism)*: A type of tourism designed for business travelers attending festivals, fairs or cultural. It also attracts people who are interested in exchanging information and knowledge through Congresses, Incentives, Meetings and Exhibitions.

EWGN *(GDS)*: Code meaning Economy Station Wagon.

EWR *(GDS)*: Three-letter IATA code for Newark International Airport serving the city of New York.

Ex *(GDS)*: Code meaning Departing from.

EXC *(GDS)*: Code for Except.

Excess Baggage *(Airlines)*: The luggage that surpasses the allowed limits for weight, size, or number of pieces a passenger is entitled to carry with him/her.

Excess Baggage Charge *(Airlines)*: An extra charge made by the airline when the traveler's baggage exceeds the limits of free allowance.

Excess Mileage Surcharge *(Airlines)*: A charge applied to an air fare when the actual mileage flown on a route exceeds the maximum permitted mileage for such route.

Excess Reduction Fee (ERF) *(Car Rental)*: A coverage plan applied only in Australia and New Zealand that helps reduce the cost of excess damage to the car. It depends on the vehicle category and the age of the driver. It is similar to Loss Damage Waiver (LDW) in the U.S.

Exchange Order *(Airlines)*: A voucher issued by an airline or its travel agent requesting the issuance of a ticket or the ARC document entitling a travel agent to receive a commission.

Exchange Rate *(Airlines)*: The rate used to exchange a monetary unit into another monetary unit or the rate to exchange a NUC into a monetary unit or vice versa. See also Rate of Exchange.

Exclusive *(Tourism)*: A term referring to a special deluxe tour package that is aimed to a selective clientele, not open to the general public. The term is often used in tour brochures to indicate something is "not included", as a synonym for "excluding".

Excursion *(Tourism)*: An organized journey that departs from a main destination and returns thereto, usually offering optional activities at an added cost.

Excursion Fare *(Airlines)*: A discounted and individual air fare, conditioned to specific airline or route restrictions, such as advance purchase, maximum duration, minimum stay, stopovers, seasons, etc.

Excursionist *(Tourism)*: A traveler who spends less than 24 hours in a destination without overnight. Sometimes the term identifies also a cruise traveler staying on board of the ship. Both the excursionist and the tourist are classified in the visitor category.

Executive Club *(Airlines)*: A private lounge area at an airport, where airlines host their preferred passengers, providing them a set of courteous attentions.

Executive Floor *(Hospitality)*: A floor of a hotel that provides selected service to business or VIP travelers. It is also called a Business Floor or the Tower Concept.

Executive Housekeeper *(Hospitality)*: The head of a hotel's housekeeping department in a lodging property. The executive housekeeper is a member of the management team.

Executive Lounge *(Airlines)*: See Airport Lounge.

Exercise Center *(Hospitality)*: See Fitness Center.

Exhibit or Exhibition *(Tourism)*: A display of goods, equipment, work of art, devices, or skill in a public place.

Exotic *(Tourism)*: A term to denote that something or someone is unusual, romantic, sensual, or erotic. A place can be an exotic destination and a girl can be an exotic dancer.

Expatriate *(Tourism)*: A person who lives in a foreign country.

Expect Departure Clearance Time EDCT *(Air Traffic)*: The time assigned to a plane to inform the pilot when he/she can expect to receive departure clearance. EDCTs are issued as part of Traffic Management Programs, such as a Ground Delay Program (GDP).

Expected Arrival List or Report *(Hospitality)*: A daily report detailing the number and names of guests expected to arrive with reservations.

Expected Departure List or Report *(Hospitality)*: A daily report detailing the number, names and the number of stay-overs of guests expected to depart.

Expediter *(Hospitality)*: A hotel employee who acts as a communication link between kitchen personnel and servers. The expediter collects the orders from the servers and calls them to the appropriate kitchen stations. It is required the expediter know cooking times in order to coordinate the delivery of meals in a sequential order.

Expedition *(Tourism)*: A journey usually prepared to remote areas, sometimes for a scientific purpose, including few amenities.

Expense Account *(Tourism)*: In general, it reflects the costs for goods or services consumed by a company during a given period. In tourism context, it is the account of business expenditures, such as transport, hotel room, meals, and even entertainment, related to the work of an employee while in business travel. An expense account gives an employee the right to be reimbursed for money he/she spent for work-related purposes.

Expenses *(Business)*: The outflow of money or other reductions of assets or increases in liabilities of a business through its operations of delivering or producing goods, rendering services, or carrying out other activities to earn revenue.

EXPL *(GDS)*: Code for Explain.

Export *(Business)*: The process of selling and shipping products from one country to another country or countries for purposes of use or sale in the country of destination.

Export License *(Business)*: A document issued by a governmental office authorizing a person to export a specific quantity of particular commodity to a certain country.

Export Permit *(Business)*: A document issued by a governmental office authorizing the export of specific goods to designated countries.

Exposition *(Tourism)*: A large showcase of industrial achievements, or services of a company, region, or country, usually sponsored by a government or trade group, sometimes international in scope.

Express Check-out *(Hospitality)*: A procedure offered by many hotels in which the bill is settled automatically with the guest's credit card.

Expressway *(Tourism)*: A highway or toll-road with limited-access.

EXST *(GDS)*: Extra Seat.

Extant *(Ecology)*: The term, literally meaning not lost or not destroyed, denotes a species that is still alive and reproducing. In fact, all species that currently live on earth are extant.

Extended Stay *(Hospitality)*: A hotel stay extended for more than seven overnights.

EXtensible Markup Language (XML) *(Computing)*: A globally accepted method of sharing information over the Internet in a way that computers can use, regardless of their operating system.

Extension Tours *(Tourism)*: Fully arranged tours that are offered as an extra to buyers of a primary tour or cruise, to create a longer trip. Extensions can be taken before, during or after the basic travel program.

Extinct *(Ecology)*: Species that once occupied a space and no longer exist on earth, because all of their representatives are dead. It is opposite to Extant.

Extinction *(Ecology)*: An irreversible disappearance of species from the earth due to natural processes or human activity. This phenomenon happens when the environment is modified and the species cannot adapt and successfully reproduce under new conditions.

Extra Day Charge *(Car Rental)*: A charge made by rental companies when cars are returned more than three hours late.

Extra Equipment *(Car Rental)*: Additional equipment required further to regular equipment.

Extra Mileage Allowance (EMA) *(Airlines)*: The concession of additional mileages to be deducted from the Actual Flown Mileage of a route, in order to avoid Excess Mileage Surcharges. The EMA concept is strictly applied to specific routes

Extra Section *(Airlines)*: A supplemental aircraft used to accommodate additional passengers and operated with the same number of a given scheduled flight.

Extreme Sports *(Tourism)*: Extreme sports are activities that are associated with a high degree of danger or risk where any mistake could result in injury or even death. They are nontraditional sports and activities that require participants to combine athletic skill with pronounced risk and are usually done by individuals rather than teams. The term evolved in the 1970s when "extreme sports" was almost exclusively used for hang gliding.

EZE *(GDS)*: Three-letter IATA code for *Ministro Pistarini Airport* (formerly Ezeiza), serving the city of Buenos Aires.

EZS *(GDS)*: Code meaning "easySABRE."

F

F *(Airlines)*: "Foxtrot," name used to designate the letter "F" in the International Phonetic Alphabet

F *(GDS)*: A code meaning: 1.First Class Fare; 2. First Class of Service; 3. Fahrenheit.

F/A *(GDS)*: Code meaning Flight Attendant.

FA *(Air Traffic)*: See Area Forecast.

FA *(GDS)*: Code for Families.

FAA *(Organizations)*: An acronym for Federal Aviation Administration.

FAA Flow Control *(Air Traffic)*: See Ground Delay Program.

FAALC *(Air Traffic)*: Federal Aviation Administration Logistics Center.

FAATC *(Air Traffic)* Federal Aviation Administration Technical Center

Fabric Brightener *(Hospitality)*: Sometimes called an optical brightener, it is a laundry chemical for keeping the original appearance of fabrics and looking new.

FAC *(GDS)*: Code meaning Facility.

Face *(Hospitality)*: The pile of a carpet or the nap of a towel.

Facility *(Tourism)*: A commercial or industrial property, building, structure or plant that is built, installed, or established to perform specific activities or functions, such as an airport, a university, a warehouse or a factory.

Facility Charge *(Car Rental)*: A fee charged by some airports to rental companies for every customer transaction at that airport location.

Factory Programming *(Computing)*: The process of writing the identification number into the silicon microchip of some read-only devices. Data can't be written over or changed.

FAF *(Air Traffic)*: See Final Approach Fix.

Fahrenheit, Gabriel Daniel (1686-1736) *(Climate)*: A German physicist and an instrument maker. Although he lived in Amsterdam most of his life, he spent considerable time in England, where he became a member of the Royal Society. Fahrenheit invented his first two thermometers by 1714. They used alcohol and produced exact readings, but soon they were replaced by mercury, because of its expansion properties. He settled on a temperature scale ranging from 0 to 212, being 32 as the temperature of ice or water freezing, and 212 a point selected by chance, as about the boiling point of water.

Fahrenheit Scale *(Climate)*: A scale used in the United States of America to measure temperature in which water boils at 212 degrees above zero and freezes at 32 degrees above zero.

Fair *(Tourism)*: An event that gathers sales and buyers at a specific place and time with entertainment, rides, and other amusements, where they trade.

Fair Market Value *(Business)*: The right price for a product or service according to a free market offer and demand.

Fait Accompli *(Tourism)*: A French term used to indicate something has been accomplished and can not be reversed.

False Booking *(Airlines)*: Term synonymous with Deadend Booking, which is referred to a booking which is transacted on a GDS but never honored. False bookings can be a case of fraud on the part of the booker.

FAM *(GDS)*: Code for Family, used together with another word, such as fare or trip.

Fam Tour or Fam Trip *(Airlines)*: Literally, Familiarization Tour. A reduced-rate, often complimentary, travel program designed to acquaint airline employees, travel agents, wholesalers, incentive travel planners, or journalists with a destination or a service, in order to stimulate its sale.

Familiarization Trip *(Airlines)*: Same as Fam Trip.

Family Life Cycle *(Hospitality)*: The process of categorizing travelers, according to such variables as age, marital status, and presence and ages of children.

Family of Resorts *(Hospitality)*: A select group of resorts dealing special relationship to make exchange of time share periods easier.

Family Plan *(Tourism)*: Arrangement or rate that allows family members traveling together become entitled to discounts. For example, some lodging properties let children under 12 years stay free in their parents' room.

Family Rate *(Hospitality)*: A special room rate for parents and children occupying one guestroom.

Family Stateroom *(Cruise)*: Specific accommodation configuration usually provided for 4 to 6 passengers in lower beds. This type of accommodation varies according to the provider, but often features convertible sofas, separate sleeping areas, and extra sinks, bathrooms, and/or closet space.

Family Style *(Hospitality)*: A manner of serving meals by which foods are placed on large platters or in large vessels for people to help themselves, rather than serving on separate dishes.

Familymoon *(Tourism)*: A trip taken subsequent to a wedding, typically after a second or third marriage, in which children or other family members are included.

Family-Style Service *(Hospitality)*: Same as Family Style.

Fantail *(Cruise)*: The rear overhang of a ship.

FAO *(Organizations)*: See Food and Agriculture Organization.

FAP *(GDS)*: Code meaning Full American Plan. See also American Plan.

FAR *(Airlines)*: See Federal Aviation Regulations.

Far East *(Geography)*: A term that commonly defines the area comprising East and Southeast Asia.

Fare *(Airlines)*: The amount charged by a carrier for the carriage of a passenger and his allowable free baggage. It is currently published in the airline's tariffs.

Fare *(Hospitality)*: Range of food, for example, the fare served by a restaurant.

Fare, Applicable *(Airlines)*: For fare construction purposes, a fare which is established after the application of all fare construction calculations, subject to the pertinent conditions.

Fare Basis *(Airlines)*: The specific fare which is used for pricing an air travel, according to the level or class of service. The fare base is identified by a specified letter or a combination of letters and numbers. For example: F designates First Class, YH designates Economy Class for High Season, YE30 designates an Excursion Economy Fare valid for a 30 days trip.

Fare Bias *(Airlines)*: An obsolete practice in which a GDS displayed its sponsors' fares in first place.

Fare Break Points *(Airlines)*: The terminal points (origin and destination) of a fare component.

Fare Bucket *(Airlines)*: An assignment of defined number of airline seats at a certain fare.

Fare Calculation *(Airlines)*: The process to obtain a fare for a complex air journey, subject to certain rules and conditions.

Fare Code *(Airlines)*: The code used to make a booking on a GDS according to a specific fare. See also booking code.

Fare Component *(Airlines)*: A portion of an itinerary between two consecutive fare construction points to which an individual fare is applied. If the journey has only one component, the points of origin and destination of the travel are also the fare construction points.

Fare Construction *(Airlines)*: See Fare Calculation.

Fare Construction Points *(Airlines)*: Same as Fare Break Points.

Fare Market Value (FMV) *(Cruise)*: The estimated fair market price (including charges) for a specific cruise journey.

Fare Type *(Airlines)*: The class of fare selected by a traveler for his trip, identified by an alphabetical or alphanumerical code.

Farm Tourism *(Tourism)*: See Agrotourism.

Fast Food *(Hospitality)*: Industrialized meal easily prepared and quickly delivered to consumers.

Fast Food Service *(Hospitality)*: The large segment of the food service industry, which comprises commercial establishments offering drive-through and/or counter service to customers.

Fast Track *(Airlines)*: An express transit facility offered to First and Business Class passengers by some airports.

Fast Travel *(Airlines)*: An IATA project to offer full service to passengers through a range of self-service options, since customer demand for self-service options keeps evolving as technology progresses. Furthermore, the project matches airlines needs to reduce cost of operations while they deliver a set of solutions to enable the passenger manage all appropriate aspects of the departing and arrival processes.

Fastbreak *(Car Rental)*: A quick and easy way to rent a car that is recommended to frequent renters.

Fastbreak Choice *(Car Rental)*: A rental option available at many major U.S. airports, by which customers just confirm their reservation at a lot kiosk, select the car of their choice, and show their driver's license at the exit booth.

Fastbreak Counter *(Car Rental)*: Locations where Fastbreak members show their driver's license to the car rental agent and get their keys.

Fathom *(Tourism)*: A unit used to measure the depth of water that equals six feet.

FBP *(GDS)*: See Fare Break Points.

FCC *(Air Traffic)*: See Federal Communications Commission

FCCA *(Organizations)*: An acronym for Florida-Caribbean Cruise Association.

FCFS *(Air Traffic)*: First Come First Served, meaning a scheduling method.

FCFS *(GDS)*: Code meaning First come, First Served, meaning a booking method.

FCO *(GDS)*: Three-letter IATA code for Fiumicino - Leonardo da Vinci International Airport, serving the city of Rome, Italy.

FCP *(Airlines)*: See Fare Construction Points.

FCS *(Air Traffic)*: Flight Control System.

FCT *(Air Traffic)*: See Federal Contract Tower Program.

FDOR *(GDS)*: Code meaning Four-door Car.

Feasibility *(Tourism)*: An important and basic stage of a project carried out to determine whether it may be done practically and successfully taking in mind such variable as market conditions, competition, available technology, manpower, and financial resources.

FEB *(GDS)*: Code for February.

Federal Aviation Act of 1958 *(Airlines)*: A legislation that transferred the functions from the Civil Aeronautics Administration (CAA) to a new independent body, the Federal Aviation Agency (later called Federal Aviation Administration FAA), keeping the CAA as a US agency.

Federal Aviation Administration (FAA) *(Organizations)*: The United States government organization created to provide for the regulation and promotion of civil aviation in such manner as to promote its development and safety, and to provide for the safe and efficient use of the airspace by both civil and military aircraft. Its mission, according to its own declaration, is to provide the safest, most efficient aerospace system in the world.

Federal Aviation Regulations (FARs) *(Aviation)*: A set of rules and procedures established by the Federal Aviation Administration (FAA) in order to secure safe and orderly air transportation.

Federal Communications Commission (FCC) *(Organizations)*: An independent United States government agency, responsible for regulating interstate and international communications by radio, television, wire, satellite and cable. The FCC's jurisdiction covers the 50 states, the District of Columbia, and U.S. possessions. It was established by the Communications Act of 1934.

Federal Maritime Commission (FMC) *(Organizations)*: An independent agency responsible for the regulation of commercial ocean transportation. The principal statutory provisions administered by the Commission are the Shipping Act of 1984, the Foreign Shipping Practices Act of 1988, section 19 of the Merchant Marine Act, 1920, and Public Law 89-777.

Federal Trade Commission (FTC) *(Organizations)*: A federal agency established for the consumer protection. It was created in 1914 with the purpose to prevent unfair methods of competition in commerce. In 1938 the Commission added other functions to administer a wide variety of other consumer protection laws, including the Telemarketing Sales Rule, the Pay-Per-Call Rule and the Equal Credit Opportunity Act. In 1975, the Congress entrusted the FTC the authority to adopt industry-wide trade regulation rules.

Federation of International Youth Travel Organizations (FIYTO) *(Organizations)*: A leading global membership association and trade forum devoted exclusively to the youth travel industry, promoting youth mobility and protecting the identity of youth travel. It is aimed to enabling its members and the industry's continued growth by providing Business and Trade Networking Opportunities, Marketing Opportunities, Developing and Distributing Key Industry Intelligence, Advocacy for Shaping Legislation. FIYTO collaborates with leading national, official and private tourism organizations.

Fee, Cancellation *(Tourism)*: A penalty amount collected from passengers who fail using their reservations without prior advice to the service provider.

Fee-Based Pricing *(Tourism)*: A compensation method by which a corporation accepts to pay its agency a portion of the commission for the business volume generated by the corporation. The travel agency can negotiate with the corporation to price its services based on the suppliers' net price, plus a mark-up that covers the cost of delivering the service and a profit. Or they can agree the application of booking or transaction fees.

Feeder Airline *(Airlines)*: An air carrier that "feeds" traffic for the national and international carriers besides servicing a local market.

Fermentation *(Hospitality)*: A step prior to distillation, during which a mash consisting of crushed grain, grapes, sugar cane, or other plant product and water are mixed together with yeasts.

Fermented in the Bottle *(Hospitality)*: The second fermentation (the transfer process) that takes place "in the bottle" of champagne or sparkling wine. Sparkling wine is transferred to a vat under pressure for settling, clarifying, fining, and then returned under pressure to the original bottles. This characteristic is shown on the bottle's label.

Fermented in this Bottle *(Hospitality)*: The re-fermentation of champagne or sparkling wine takes place in the bottle in which the champagne or sparkling wine is sold (the traditional champagne method). In this case a legend is shown on the bottle's label.

Ferry *(Tourism)*: Also known as a Ferryboat, it is a form of transport for carrying people, and/or vehicles and other cargo across a body of water, and operates on a regular schedule.

Ferry Flight *(Airlines)*: A flight for the purpose of either returning an aircraft to the base, or delivering an aircraft from one location to another, or moving an aircraft to and from a maintenance base.

Festival *(Tourism)*: A set of artistic representations, cultural events or entertainments focused on a certain subject.

FET *(GDS)*: Code meaning Foreign Escorted Tour.

Fete *(Tourism)*: A French term meaning Party.

FEVE *(Tourism)*: *Ferrocarriles de Vía Estrecha* in Spain (Narrow rails railways).

FFP *(GDS)*: Code meaning Frequent Flyer Program.

FHTL *(GDS)*: Code meaning First Class Hotel.

FIATA *(Organizations)*: An acronym for International Federation of Freight Forwarders Associations.

FIC *(Air Traffic)*: See Flight Information Centers.

Field *(Computing)*: A space allocated for a particular item of information, such as the client's name, address, phone number, destination, travel date, and so on. Each of these items is saved in an individual field.

Fifth Freedom of the Air *(Airlines)*: The freedom to carry traffic (passengers or goods) between two foreign countries on a flight that is either originated in or is destined for the carrier's home country.

FIH *(GDS)*: Three-letter IATA code for Kinshasa, capital city of Congo Kinshasa.

File *(Computing)*: A set of related records on a specific client or destination kept together.

File *(GDS)*: A term referred to: 1. A PNR in a GDS. 2. To enter records into a file.

File Transfer Protocol (FTP) *(Computing)*: A simple way to exchange files or data between computers through a network, such as over the Internet.

FIM *(GDS)*: Code for Flight Interruption Manifest.

Fin *(Aeronautics)*: The fixed part of a vertical airfoil that controls the yaw of an aircraft.

Final Approach *(Air Traffic)*: Last procedures at the end of a flight, immediately before the aircraft touches down.

Final Approach Fix (FAF) *(Air Traffic)*: The geographical position determined by any of the following visual references to the surface: One or more radio NAVAIDS, celestial plotting, or another navigational device, from which the final approach to an airport is executed and which identifies the beginning of the final approach segment.

Finger Scanning *(Tourism)*: A biometric identification accomplished by automatically scanning a person's fingerprints electronically

Finish *(Hospitality)*: A protective coating liquid applied on floors to enhance their appearance.

Finished Product Catering Delivery *(Hospitality)*: Home delivery catering services.

Fiord *(Geography)*: A deep and narrow inlet of the sea, which is caused by the flooding of a glacial valley and usually bounded by cliffs. They are mainly located in Alaska, Norway, and New Zealand. It is also written as Fjord.

FIR *(Air Traffic)*: See Flight Information Region.

FIRAV *(GDS)*: Code meaning "First Available Flight."

Firewall *(Aeronautics)*: A fire-resistant bulkhead that isolates the engine from other parts of an airplane's structure.

Firewall *(Computing)*: A system designed to prevent the access of unauthorized information to or from a private network.

Firm up *(Tourism)*: To give conformity on what has been discussed. A travel agent "firms up" the itinerary before booking seats.

First Carrier *(Airlines)*: The participating airline operating the first sector of the transportation.

First Class *(Tourism)*: A product or service constituting or belonging to the highest or best group in a system of classification, such as airline first class seats or first class hotels. Some suppliers offer an even more expensive class of services named "Luxury". Airlines' first class seats are located up front the aircraft and offer much more room and upgraded cabin service, meals, amenities, etc.

First Class Fare *(Airlines)*: The full normal fare established for the best type of service onboard. Its application is generally not dependent upon any condition or limitation, such as restricted period of ticket validity, minimum stay, stopovers, or other special circumstances.

First-Class Hotel *(Hospitality)*: A hotel type that offers top quality services usually coinciding with five-star classification in the hotel business. First class classification is based on evaluations of hotel amenities, service, customer satisfaction, and "extras" that go beyond standard hotel service.

First Freedom of the Air *(Airlines)*: Also called the Transit Freedom, it is the freedom to overfly a foreign country without landing, en-route from a home country to another country.

First Seating *(Cruise)*: The earlier of various scheduled meals that is served on a cruise ship. It is also called Main Seating.

FIT *(Tourism)*: Code meaning: 1. Foreign Independent Tour; 2. Free Independent Travelers; 3. Fully Independent Tour.

Fitness center *(Hospitality)*: Also called Health Club, Fitness Studio, or Exercise Center, a Fitness Center is a place with facilities and equipment for people to maintain or improve their physical fitness.

Fitness Studio *(Hospitality)*: See Fitness Center.

Five-By-Five (5x5) *(Air Traffic)*: A radio jargon term to affirm that a radio transmission was received clear and loud. This method rates the transmission one to five, with the first figure indicating clearness and the second indicating loudness.

Fix *(Air Traffic)*: A geographical position determined by visual reference to the surface, by reference to one or more radio NAVAIDS, by celestial plotting or by another navigational device.

Fixed Time *(Hospitality)*: In Time-share modality, the guest owns the same week each year. It is guaranteed he/she will be able to use the same week every year provided the maintenance fees are punctually paid.

Fixed-Wing *(Airlines)*: An aircraft's steady wing or whose orientation cannot be changed.

FIYTO *(Organizations)*: An acronym for Federation of International Youth Travel Organizations.

Fjord *(Geography)*: See Fiord.

Flag *(Hospitality)*: In a formal meaning, a flag is a banner to symbolize and identify a country, but informally, it is used to denote a brand, especially in the hotel industry. It is usual to say, for instance, "The service bears the Ypsilon flag." (Ypsilon is a supposed name of hotel chain).

Flag Carrier *(Airlines)*: A carrier (Airline or ship-line) registered under the laws of a country whose government grants it partial or total monopoly over international routes. Maritime laws require that all vessels (aircraft or ships) display the national flag of the country where they are registered.

Flag of Convenience *(Cruise)*: The flag of the country under whose maritime laws ship-owners register their ships for such reasons as to easy or less maritime regulations and low fees and taxes. See also Country of Registry.

Flagged *(Cruise)*: Term meaning registered in a country. For instance, "The cruise ship is flagged in Mauritania."

Flagstaff *(Cruise)*: A vertical pole located at the ship's stern where the flag of the ship's country of registry is hoisted.

Flambé *(Hospitality)*: A French term literally meaning flaming. It is a method of cooking in which foods are splashed with liquor (usually brandy or cognac) and ignited just before serving. This process adds more flavor to the dish.

Flap *(Aeronautics)*: A movable, usually hinged AIRFOIL set in the trailing edge of an aircraft wing designed to increase lift during takeoff or to slow an aircraft during landing.

Flare *(Aeronautics)*: A maneuver performed moments before landing in which the nose of an aircraft is pitched up to minimize the touchdown rate of speed.

Flat *(Hospitality)*: A British term fort apartment.

Flat-bed Seat *(Airlines)*: An airline seat that reclines and offers neck and lumbar support and lies flat. It lies flat for sleeping.

Flat Rate *(Hospitality)*: A fixed room rate negotiated in advance between a hotel and a group that is not subject to any additions or adjustments; but it may include fees for other services. It is also a type of accommodation pricing charged per long billing periods that does not vary according to usage.

Fleabag *(Hospitality)*: A pejorative term to denote an inferior hotel or motel class.

Fleet *(Tourism)*: A group of vehicles operating together under the same ownership and control of one company (airline, cruise line, car rental, etc.).

Fleet Management *(Car Rental)*: It is the management of a company's vehicle fleet including such duties as purchasing, maintaining, inventorying, and selling vehicles.

Flexible Fares *(Airlines)*: Types of fares permitting passengers to make changes to their flights, such as dates, stopovers, and even rerouting.

FLIFO *(GDS)*: Code meaning "Flight Information."

Flight *(Airlines)*: The trip made on an aircraft between the terminal points of a segment with the same Flight Designator.

Flight Attendant *(Airlines)*: Also called steward or stewardess, the flight attendant is an airline's employee who is responsible for the comfort of the passengers on an aircraft. Some of his/her tasks are serving food and drinks, and seeing that safety regulations are obeyed and passengers know what to do in case of emergency.

Flight Characteristic *(Airlines)*: A distinguishing feature of an aircraft relating to its ability to stall or yaw, or its ability to remain stable or controllable at a given speed.

Flight Computer *(Air Traffic)*: A manual slide rule or electronic calculator used to determine wind correction, fuel consumption, airspeed, and other performance calculations during flight planning.

Flight Controls *(Air Traffic)*: Controls in a cockpit for flying an aircraft. They are primary and secondary controls. Primary flight controls are wheel, yoke, cyclic, pedals, throttle, and collective; secondary flight controls are flaps, slats, stabilizer, and landing gear.

Flight, Connecting *(Airlines)*: A flight requiring an intermediate stop to make aircraft's change, and possibly change of airlines.

Flight Coordinator *(Cruise)*: An employee of a cruise line who is responsible to make air travel arrangements for cruise passengers.

Flight Coupon *(Airlines)*: A segment of an Electronic Ticket.

Flight Crew *(Airlines)*: All the airline's employees who perform duties onboard associated with

servicing of passengers, including pilot, co-pilot, and flight attendants.

Flight Data Controller *(Air Traffic)*: An air traffic control employee at an Airport Control Tower responsible to review flight plans, issue approval to pilots and generate the flight data strip before handing the pilot off to Local Control for pushback and taxiing instructions.

Flight Data Recorder (FDR) *(Airlines)*: A device that records flight technical information and the performance of various aircraft systems, such as, aircraft's speed, altitude, heading and other flight parameters. The information stored in a flight data recorder may be used to reconstruct the circumstances leading up to an accident. The FDR is different from the Cockpit Voice Recorder (CVR).

Flight Deck *(Airlines)*: The section of a commercial aircraft, usually known as the cockpit, where pilots work and control it.

Flight, Direct *(Airlines)*: A flight without change of aircraft and identified by a single flight number, even if it includes one or more intermediate stops. See Direct Flight.

Flight Dispatch *(Air Traffic)*: It is a set of coordinated actions accomplished by air traffic control, the flight dispatcher and the pilot. Air-traffic controllers provide separation of aircraft, flight dispatchers manage the aircraft's movement, and pilots fly the aircraft. Together, these professionals form the air safety known as P.A.D., which provides the foundation for air safety.

Flight Dispatcher *(Air Traffic)*: A specialist flight control staff who co-ordinates the departure of commercial aircraft. Dispatchers have very delicate responsibility that is shared with pilots to jointly ensure the safety of every flight. The dispatcher authorizes the flight by issuing a flight release and flight plan, spelling out safety parameters under which the flight is to be conducted, including fuel quantity, route of flight, altitude, severe weather avoidance, type of aircraft, and an alternate airport selection.

Flight Envelope *(Aeronautics)*: An aircraft's performance limits, specifically the curves of speed, altitude, and acceleration that each type of aircraft can not safely exceed.

Flight Information Centers (FIC) *(Air Traffic)*: FICs are Canadian bodies operated by NAV CANADA, which are established to provide maximum assistance to commercial and private aircraft flying over Canadian territory. Pilots obtain any pre-flight information from FICs on the latest weather reports, forecasts, satellite pictures and weather radar, copies of the latest NOTAMs, and file, open, or close a flight plan.

Flight Information Region (FIR) *(Air Traffic)*: A delimited airspace with specific dimensions, where a Flight Information Service is provided. It is a way of regularly dividing the world airspace. Large countries' airspace is subdivided into a number of regional FIRs, while small countries' airspace is typically bounded by a single FIR.

Flight Interruption Manifest *(Airlines)*: A document issued by an airline as a ticket substitution when irregularities occur on a flight restraining passengers to continue their travel.

Flight Kitchen *(Airlines)*: The central kitchen of an aircraft where food for serving passengers is prepared.

Flight Management System (FMS) *(Air Traffic)*: A computerized avionics component built on most commercial and business aircraft in order to assist pilots in navigation, flight planning, and aircraft control functions. It comprises three major components: FMC (Flight Management Computer), AFS (Auto Flight System), and Navigation System including IRS (Inertial Reference System) and GPS.

Flight, Nonstop *(Airlines)*: A direct flight with no intermediate stops.

Flight Number *(Airlines)*: An alphanumerical code identifying a specific airplane's flight. A flight number consists of the two-letter code of the airline plus the numeral three or four-digit code indicating the number of the travel. Examples: LH519, JL1002, AC961.

Flight Operation Officer (FOO) *(Airlines)*: Also known as Flight Dispatcher, he/she is the person at an airport who is responsible for supervising the activities specifically related to air traffic. An FOO has great authority over flights and in some countries, as the USA and Canada, he/she shares legal responsibility with the Commander.

Flight Plan *(Air Traffic)*: A document made up by pilots for approval by Air Traffic Authorities prior to departure, and covering the expected operational details of a flight. Basically, it must contain the following information: Pilot's name and number of passengers on board; type of flight (whether instrument flight rules or visual flight rules); information on departure and arrival points, estimated time en route, and alternate airports in case of emergency. There are both VFR and IFR flight plans. VFR plans are not mandatory.

Flight Planning *(Air Traffic)*: Determining the route and proper method of navigation to be used by the aircraft.

Flight Profile *(Air Traffic)*: The phases of a typical flight that usually consist of preflight, takeoff, departure, en route, descent, approach and landing.

Flight Recorder *(Airlines)*: A crash-proof device that records data referring an aircraft's flight, such as airspeed, heading, and the procedures of the pilot. It is also called Black Box.

Flight Route *(Air Traffic)*: The path or course taken by the aircraft headed to its destination.

Flight Schedule Monitor (FSM) *(Air Traffic)*: A tool for monitoring air traffic demand at airports, which is used by air traffic management specialists.

Flight Service Specialists (FSSs) *(Air Traffic)*: Technician personnel who monitor assigned frequencies to provide pilots with the communications access to obtain and pass flight information, or report emergencies in case the need arises. They also report on aircraft positions and air traffic control clearances in areas where aircraft can not reach air traffic control facility.

Flight Service Station (FSS) *(Air Traffic)*: An air traffic facility created to provide information and services to aircraft pilots before, during, and after flights. FSS differs from Air Traffic Control in the fact that it is not responsible for giving instructions or clearances or providing separation. Some of the most important services offered by Flight Service Stations are: Preflight briefings; weather and notices to airmen; management of flight plans; traffic advisory to aircraft on the ground or in the air; monitoring navigational aids; and providing assistance to aircraft in emergency situations and provides VFR search and rescue services.

Flight Simulation *(Aeronautics)*: A ground tool of Aeronautics employed to train pilots. The simulator creates an environment where pilots see, hear and feel like he/ she were in a real aircraft.

Flight Test *(Air Traffic)*: A tool of Aeronautics in which a real aircraft is flown to gather data to describe the capabilities of that aircraft.

Flight Time *(Air Traffic)*: The time invested since the moment an aircraft first moves under its own power for the purpose of a flight until the moment it comes to rest at the next point of landing.

Flight Tracker *(Airlines)*: A software tool that permits to know in real time the developing position and/or conditions of an airline flight.

Flight-Type Dishwasher *(Hospitality)*: Dishwashing machines in which dishes are placed on carriers that move them through several washing and rinsing chambers.

Floatel *(Tourism)*: A term meaning floating hotel, which denotes a vessel equipped and with suitable facilities to serve as a hotel. It may be permanently moored alongside a platform or not.

Floating Deposit *(Tourism)*: A money deposit that is not refundable and may be switched to cover same services on other dates, or to block bookings or to pay for other packages. It is also called Transferable Deposit.

Floating Week *(Hospitality)*: A type of timeshare ownership where the purchaser has the flexibility of scheduling his vacation with yearly variations in accordance with the resort's guidelines. Usually, resorts only accept requests for specific weeks from owners who have their annual maintenance fees paid. A year-round "float" is most often found in resorts with corresponding similar seasons, such as Hawaii or the Caribbean.

Floatplane *(Tourism)*: An amphibious vehicle with retractable wheels capable of operating on land or sea.

Floodplain *(Geography)*: A portion of normally dry land area that is susceptible to be inundated

by great flows of water from any natural sources.

Floor Person *(Hospitality)*: A casino employee, who supervises gambling operations, resolves disputes and watches for cheaters.

Florida-Caribbean Cruise Association (FCCA) *(Organizations)*: A non-profit trade organization composed of 11 member cruise lines that operate more than 100 vessels in waters of Florida, the Caribbean and Latin America. Its mission is to provide a forum for discussion on legislation, tourism development, ports, tour operations, safety, security and other cruise industry issues. It was created in 1972 and at present comprises the following cruise lines: Carnival Cruise Lines, Celebrity Cruises, Costa Cruise Lines, Cunard Line Ltd., Disney Cruise Line, Holland America Line, MSC Cruises (USA) Inc., Norwegian Cruise Line, Princess Cruises, Regent Seven Seas Cruises, and Royal Caribbean International.

Flotation Device *(Airlines)*: Any object capable of keeping a person afloat in water, such as a life vest, life preserver or even an aircraft's seat cushion.

Floatation Therapy *(Tourism)*: Treatment where the guest floats on the surface of water, which is warmed to body temperature and has heavy salt and mineral content.

Flow, Touristic *(Tourism)*: Displacement of travelers from a place of origin to another, called destination. Mass tourism generates different flow types, and is used to measure the quantity of visitors a destination receives as well as their economic behavior.

Flow Lines *(Geography)*: Arrows drawn on a map or plan to illustrate the movement of people or things.

Flowchart *(Airlines)*: A diagram representing the sequence of activities in process in a system. It is usually displayed through the use of symbols and is sometimes called a Flow Sheet.

FLSOT *(GDS)*: Code meaning Florida Seller of Travel.

FLT *(GDS)*: Code meaning Flight.

Fluvial Cruise *(Airlines)*: A type of cruise operated on river waters.

FLW *(GDS)*: A code meaning Follow, Following, Followed.

Fly by Night *(Airlines)*: A slang expression meaning something or someone operates outside the law or appears shady.

Fly-Cruise Package or Fly/Cruise Package *(Cruise)*: A tour package including cruise and air transportation to and from the port of embarkation.

Fly-Drive Package *(Tourism)*: A tour package that combines air transportation with a rental car. The package may also include hotel room.

Flycruising *(Cruise)*: A flight to a destination where a cruise starts generally included in the travel package.

Flyer *(Tourism)*: A single-sheet printed advertisement for mass distribution.

Flying Casino *(Airlines)*: A project that is currently being developed by the aircraft constructor Airbus to build a passenger airliner of the model A380 equipped to as casino, which supposedly will be ready by 2012.

Flying Food Show *(Hospitality)*: A procedure for delivering cooked meals to guests as soon as it is ready.

FMC *(Organizations)*: An acronym for Federal Maritime Commission.

FMS *(Air Traffic)*: See Flight Management System.

FMV *(Cruise)*: See Fare Market Value.

FOB *(GDS)*: Code meaning: 1. Free on Board; 2. Fresh off the Boat.

FOC *(GDS)*: See Flag of Convenience.

Fog *(Geography)*: A cloud of water droplets that forms just above the ground.

Foghorn *(Cruise)*: A device of sounding signals used for warning ships in fog or darkness. It is found especially on ships, buoys, and coastal installations.

FOID *(GDS)*: Code meaning: 1. Form of Identification; it is an entry used to note the passenger's identification as an SSR. 2. Firearms Owner's Identification. If accepted for transportation, the carrier will require gun owner to show a FOID card.

Fokker, Anthony *(Aviation)*: An aircraft constructor born in Java in 1890. At the age of 20 years, Fokker started an aviation company in Wiesbaden, Germany. His first aircraft, *Spin I* and *Spin II* made short flights and crashed. His third effort, *Spin III*, was operated successfully and was purchased by German military authorities in 1913. Fokker developed a system where the pilot could fire a machine-gun while flying the plane. The system was fitted to the *Fokker E* aircraft. In 1917 he joined Reinhold Platz to form the *Fokker Flugzeug-Werke* company. Anthony Fokker finally settled in the United States where he established the "Fokker Aircraft Corporation." He died in 1939.

Folio *(Hospitality)*: The guest's bill where accommodation and all incidental charges and credits are posted during the guest's stay. It can be a written or an electronic record.

Folklore *(Tourism)*: The term was coined in 1846 by the English writer and archaeologist William John Thoms (16 November, 1803- 15 August 1885) to replace the expression currently used of "popular antiquities." In general terms, folklore is understood as the study of the customs, ceremonies, beliefs, legends, songs and sayings that remain in a social group, and which are transmitted from generation to generation, as part of its popular culture. In this sense, folklore is the expression of spontaneous and traditional culture of peoples.

It is said that folklore has to gather three indispensable characteristics:

1. It must have a spiritual or material function in the society where it occurs;

2. It must not be influenced by other culture manifestations;

3. It must be accepted by the collective group.

The term has evolved to comprise a wider spectrum of study of the cultural characteristics of a given society.

FONE *(GDS)*: Code for Telephone.

FOO *(Airlines)*: See Flight Operation Officer.

Food and Agriculture Organization of the United Nations (FAO) *Organizations)*: A UN agency that leads international efforts to defeat hunger. It serves both developed and developing countries, and acts as a neutral forum where all nations meet at an equality level to negotiate agreements and debate policy. Since FAO is also a source of knowledge and information, it helps developing countries and countries in transition to modernize and improve agriculture, forestry and fisheries practices. It also pursuits to ensure good nutrition for all people worldwide. FAO was created on 16 October 1945 in Quebec, Canada. It was based in Washington, D.C. until 1951, when it moved its offices to Rome, Italy. FAO has 192 members currently.

Food and Beverage Division *(Hospitality)*: The division in a hotel company that is responsible for preparing and serving food and beverages within the property, including catering and room service.

Food and Beverage Manager *(Hospitality)*: The person who is responsible for planning, directing, organizing, and controlling all phases of the food and beverage departments of a hospitality company or cruise ship, and who is in charge of the management of all restaurants, bars, and galleys.

Food Chain *(Ecology)*: A method of describing the energy circulation and the dependence of heterotrophic organisms on other organisms for food, progressing in a series that begins with primary producers (plants) and ends with the largest level of carnivores. It is used for educational purposes only, because real trophic systems resemble webs rather than chains.

Food Dehydration *(Hospitality)*: A technique for dry food preservation, inhibiting microbial activity. There are four types of food dehydration: Sun Drying, Mechanical Drying, Freeze-drying, and Drying During Smoking.

Food Infection *(Hospitality)*: A type of illness caused by bacteria or viruses found in food and later reproduced inside the body.

Food Poisoning *(Hospitality)*: A type of illness caused by germs contained in food, which produce toxic waste products.

Food Web *(Ecology)*: A combination of all the food circulation and feeding relationships existing in an ecosystem. It is represented by an intricate web drawing that illustrates with lines the trophic system, where most prey species are eaten by many different predators, and most predators eat more than one prey item.

Foot Passengers *(Tourism)*: Passengers who travel by walking.

FOP *(GDS)*: A term meaning Fresh off the Plane. It is synonymous with Fresh off the Boat.

Force *(Aeronautics)*: A measurable strength of push or pull in a certain direction.

Force Majeure *(Tourism)*: A French term literally meaning "superior force". It is an event that cannot be anticipated or controlled by humans and for which, nobody is legally responsible. It is also known as an "Act of God" that comprises such occurrences as weather, civil strike, acts of war, labor actions, etc.

Ford, Henry *(Tourism)*: An American automobile builder who was born in July 30, 1863, in Dearborn, Michigan. He grew up on a prosperous family farm, and at an early age, he showed an interest in mechanical things. In 1879, Ford left home for the nearby city of Detroit to work as an apprentice machinist. In 1891, he was hired as an engineer by the "Edison Illuminating Company" in Detroit. Few years later, when he became a Chief Engineer of the company, Ford had the time and money to devote attention to his personal experiments on internal combustion engines. The experiments culminated in 1896 with the completion of his self-propelled vehicle-the Quadricycle. In 1903 he incorporated the "Ford Motor Company," where Henry Ford officiated as vice-president and chief engineer. In 1908 the company launched the Model T, a vehicle that initiated a new era in personal transportation, due to its ability to be easily operated, maintained, and run on rough roads. It immediately became a huge success. By 1918, half of all cars in America were Model Ts. Over the next 19 years, Ford would build 15 million automobiles with the Model "T" engine. With Ford cars people were motivated to go for touring in the country, thus getting involved in contributing to the growth of tourism. Henry Ford died in 1947.

Fordism *(Tourism)*: A manufacturing proposition that aims to achieve higher productivity by standardizing the output, using conveyor assembly lines, and breaking the work into small de-skilled tasks. Fordism seeks to combine machine and worker efficiency as one unit, and emphasizes minimization of costs instead of maximization of profit. The term is named after its famous proponent, Henry Ford, the US automobile pioneer. Apart from the economic implication, Fordism is understood in Tourism as the agent that gave an important contribution to its growth by allowing people to move from one place to another.

Fore *(Cruise)*: The front or bow of the ship.

Fore and Aft (*Cruise*): The length of a ship measured from stem to stern.

Forecast *(Air Traffic)*: A statement of expected future weather occurrences.

Foredeck *(Cruise)*: The area forward of a ship's main deck, between the bridge and the forecastle.

Foreign Air Transportation *(Airlines)*: Transportation between a point in the USA and a point in any foreign country.

Foreign Escorted Tour *(Tourism)*: Tour package arranged for a foreign destination to be operated with the company of a tour escort.

Foreign Exchange Rate *(Tourism)*: The rate of one currency unit expressed in terms of another, which depends on the local demand for foreign currencies, local supply, country's trade balance, strength of its economy, and other such factors. It is also called Rate of Exchange

Foreign Flag Vessel *(Cruise)*: A ship that is owned by a foreign company or that is registered in a country other than the United States.

Foreign Freight Forwarder *(Transport)*: See Forwarder.

Foreign Independent Tour (FIT) *(Tourism)*: An unescorted tour created for individuals or families who take their own travel selections. It is generally used to indicate any independent travel, domestic or international, that does not involve a package tour. It may be designed by a travel agent from separate components such as airfare, hotel and car, adjusted to the traveler wishes. It is also called a "Pre-planned fly-drive".

Forfeit *(Tourism)*: Individual tour Package arranged by a travel agency for a short journey or a small group. It is composed by a set of items, such as airfare, hotel, car or entertainment for a specific time period.

Formal Night *(Cruise)*: The assigned evening when passengers are required to dress formally for dinner. Gentlemen are invited to wear a tuxedo or dark suit and ladies are invited to wear a formal dress to the evening meal.

Fortified Wine *(Hospitality)*: Wine with added alcohol, usually during fermentation. The result is a wine with a minimum of 15

percent and maximum of 24 percent alcohol per volume.

Fortress *(Tourism)*: A large and strong wall with watchtowers built to defend a city from attack.

Fortress Hub *(Tourism)*: A term used to refer to an airport where an airline has a dominant operation presence.

Forum *(Tourism)*: 1. A political and economical centre of the ancient Rome during the Republic. See Roman Forum. 2. A public meeting place, a section of a mass medium where people openly discuss and present their arguments and ideas, or an online message board where information can be shared and discussions can be carried out.

Forward *(Cruise)*: Toward the fore (the front part) or bow of the ship.

Forward Transaction *(Tourism)*: 1. An arrangement that is agreed for actual delivery and payment to occur at a specific date in the future. 2. An agreement for purchasing or selling goods or services for delivery and payment at an agreed date in the future.

Forwarder (FWDR) *(Business)*: An independent business dispatcher appointed by the shipper, and as an agent of the carrier, to process and arrange export consignments overseas for a fee. The firm may ship by land, air, or sea. The forwarder may also handle banking and insurance services on behalf of a client. He is also known as Freight Forwarder or Foreign Freight Forwarder.

Fossil *(Ecology)*: The term usually refers to the mineralized remains or impressions preserved in stone (sedimentary rock) of extinct organisms from past geologic ages.

Fossil Fuel *(Ecology)*: Crude oil, coal, natural gas, or heavy oils originated in plant and animal remains partially or completely decomposed, as a result of exposure to heat and pressure in earth's crust over millions of years.

FOTL *(Tourism)*: See Front of the Line.

Four-Hand Massage *(Tourism)*: Massage performed by two therapists working in synchronised movements on the same person.

Fourth Freedom of the Air *(Airlines)*: The freedom to pick up traffic (passengers or goods) from a foreign country to a home country for commercial purposes.

Foxtrot *(Airlines)*: Designator for the letter "F" in the International Phonetic Alphabet.

FP *(GDS)*: Code meaning: 1. Full Pension; 2. Final Payment; 3. Flight Plan

FPA *(Air Traffic)*: Flight Path Angle.

FQD *(GDS)*: An Amadeus entry to obtain a Fare Quote Display. Typically, it is followed by the pair of cities or airports, slash, the code "A" for airline, the two-letter code for the airline, slash, the date of travel, slash, the type of fare. Example: FDQJFKLHR/ABA/17AUG/R,NUC.

FQM *(GDS)*: An Amadeus entry for Fare Quote Mileage to obtain the flown mileages in a given route. Example: FQMYTOLHRFRAFCO.

FQN *(GDS)*: An Amadeus entry for Fare Quote Note followed by the line number of a fare in a fare quote display. It is used to obtain the rule corresponding to a certain fare.

FQTV *(GDS)*: Code meaning Frequent Traveler.

FR *(GDS)*: Code meaning Forest Road.

FRA *(GDS)*: 1. Three-letter IATA code for Frankfurt, Germany. 2. Three-letter IATA code for Frankfurt am Main International Airport, serving the city of Frankfurt, Germany.

Fractional Ownership *(Hospitality)*: Leisure real estate sold in intervals of more than one week and less than whole ownership. Fractional ownership is usually associated with the luxury segment of vacation ownership, offering greater services and amenities.

FRAG *(GDS)*: Code meaning Fragile.

Franchise *(Hospitality)*: An agreement by which the owner of a trade name, manufacturer or supplier (the franchisor firm) enables a third-party to sell, supply or distribute his products or services in a particular area. Typically, the franchisee can use the trade name of the franchisor and may carry the business on a non-exclusive basis. The franchisor provides training and some marketing tools. The franchise is regulated by a franchise contract, or franchise agreement, that specifies the terms and conditions of the franchise

Franchisee Chain *(Hospitality)*: A number of hotels grouped under the brand of the franchisor that is responsible for their promotion and marketing. The franchisee chain is an independent society which finances the construction of establishments according to the franchisor's patterns and standards.

Franchise Group *(Tourism)*: A group of independently-owned tourism suppliers affiliated with a central marketing organization. A franchise permits the independent supplier to benefit from sharing a common brand in the marketplace, and from having access to a variety of support services.

FRAV *(GDS)*: Code meaning First Available.

Free Baggage Allowance *(Airlines)*: The baggage a passenger can carry with him, without additional payment. It is applied according to the passenger air fare paid, the route and the airline. In some cases, the Piece Concept is applied, allowing the passenger to carry two luggage pieces of a specific size; in other cases, the Weight Concept is applied, where the allowance is usually 20 kilos for Economy Class and 30 kilos for Business and First Class.

Free Hits *(GDS)*: The number of times an agency can access a GDS before incurring in charges.

Free Independent Travelers (FIT) *(Tourism)*: Visitors arriving in a country for holidays who do not purchase pre-arranged package tours and only pay for international airfares. While they stay in the foreign country, they can organize their own travel as they wish.

Free on Board (FOB) *(Business)*: An international commerce practice by which the exporter is responsible for inland freight and all other costs until the cargo is loaded on the vessel or aircraft, and the importer is responsible for ocean or air freight plus the respective insurance.

Free Port *(Tourism)*: A port where merchandise may be stored duty-free, until it is re-exported or sold within that country. Typically tourists buy goods at such ports, without paying taxes.

Free Pouring *(Hospitality)*: A practice in which the bartender simply dispenses an unmeasured amount of alcoholic beverages into the glass. It results in generous servings. It is opposed to Hand-Measured Pouring.

Free Sale *(Airlines)*: The privilege of agencies or tour operators to confirm reservations for dates and products still available without requesting the supplier.

Freeboard *(Cruise)*: The distance measured between the deck and the lowest point of a ship.

Freedom of the Seas *(Cruises)*: The doctrine that establishes unrestricted access of commercial ships to the high seas (international waters) and to waters outside of national territory.

Freedom Rights *(Airlines)*: See Freedoms of the Air.

Freedoms of the Air *(Airlines)*: By 1944 the nature of the postwar airline industry began to concern various countries in regard to the utilization of the skies. While sovereignty was unequivocally affirmed in the Paris Convention on the Regulation of Aerial Navigation (1919) and subsequently by various other multilateral treaties, the United States advocated an "open skies" policy. Great Britain was strongly opposed to the US' viewpoint, arguing that freedom of the skies actually was inapplicable. To settle this impasse, the US convoked in 1944 an International Convention to be held in Chicago in order to establish the framework for all future bilateral and multilateral agreements for the use of international air spaces. Air Service Agreements were signed during that convention, which designed five freedom rights. Four additional freedom rights were augmented later to cover all the possible bilateral negotiations of international air routes. The nine Freedoms of the Air effective at this moment are:

First Freedom: Also called the Transit Freedom, it is the freedom to overfly a foreign country without landing, en-route from a home country to another country.

Second Freedom: The freedom to stop in a foreign country for technical or refueling purpose only. The flight must commence or end in the home country and can land in another country for purposes other than carrying or debarking passengers.

Third Freedom: The freedom to carry traffic (passengers or goods) from a home country to a foreign country for commercial purposes.

Fourth Freedom: The freedom to pick up traffic (passengers or goods) from a foreign country to a home country for commercial purposes.

Third and Fourth Freedoms constitute the basis of the international air traffic, which provides the rights to transport passengers, mail and freight between countries.

Fifth Freedom: The freedom to carry traffic (passengers or goods) between two foreign countries on a flight that is either originated in or is destined for the carrier's home country.

Sixth Freedom: It is a combination of the third and fourth freedoms in which an airline has the freedom to carry traffic between two foreign countries via the carrier's home country. With the hubbing practice of most air carriers, this freedom has become very common.

Seventh Freedom: The freedom to base aircraft in a foreign country to operate international services between two countries outside the home country, establishing an actual "foreign hub".

Eighth Freedom: This freedom, also known as "cabotage" privileges, gives an airline the right to carry traffic between two domestic points of a foreign country, provided the flight either originates in or is destined to the carrier's home country.

Ninth Freedom: The freedom to operate commercial flights between two domestic points in a foreign country. It is also called Full Cabotage or Open-skies privileges.

Freestanding *(Tourism)*: The term refers to something that stands or sets apart. Applied to the tourism activities, it describes an independent organization or business that is not affiliated with any other establishment.

Freestyle Cruising or Free-Style Cruising *(Cruise)*: A policy privileging passengers to choose where and when to dine. Freestyle includes also a wider variety of entertainment and activity options.

Freezer *(Hospitality)*: A storage unit for maintaining food at a temperature of -18°C (0°F) or less.

Freight *(Business)*: All air cargo goods, excluding mail.

Freight Forwarder *(Business)*: See Forwarder.

Freight Status Answer (FSA) *(Business)*: A standard CargoIMP message used to reply to a Status Request (FSR) informing on the current movement status of a shipment.

Freight Status Request (FSR) *(Business)*: Standard CargoIMP message used to request information on the current status of a shipment.

Freight-Ton Mile *(Business)*: The standard measure of air freight activity, consisting of a ton of freight moved one mile.

Freighter *(Business)*: 1. In general terms, it is a vehicle for carrying cargo. More specifically, it is a ship or an aircraft designed for the carriage of cargo. 2. A person employed to receive and forward freight, or one for whom freight is transported.

French Gold Francs *(Airlines)*: Francs consisting of 65.5 milligrams of gold with a fineness of nine hundred thousandths. French Gold Francs were used in the Warsaw Convention as the currency unit to establish the compensation amounts for damages to passengers, baggage and goods.

French Service *(Hospitality)*: An elegant and complex style of food service in which entire platters are brought to the table, where they are carved and portioned at a table-side. Typically it is used in gourmet and high-check-average dining service. It is also known as Tableside or Cart Service. See also British Service and Russian Service.

FREQ *(GDS)*: A code meaning Frequent, Frequency.

Frequency *(Airlines)*: The occurrence rate of a service provision per a time unit, such as the number of flights an airline operates on a given route during a week.

Frequency *(Air Traffic)*: The number of periodic oscillation, vibrations or waves per unit of time, usually expressed in hertz.

Frequency Marketing or Frequency Marketing Program *(Tourism)*: It can be either a marketing plan designed to recompense customers who buy a product or service regularly, or a plan conceived to stimulate customers to by a product or service on a regular basis. A typical example is the Frequent Flyer Program established by airlines.

Frequent Cruiser Program *(Cruise)*: A membership club for frequent cruisers to reward their loyalty. Usually, eligibility begins with the second traveler's cruise with the same cruise line. Some of the program's advantages include cruise discounts, onboard amenities, private cocktail parties, specially-selected cruises, early notification of new itineraries and newsletters or e-mails.

Frequent Flyer *(Airlines)*: A traveler who flies frequently or one who is enrolled in an airline's Frequent Flyer Program.

Frequent Flyer Miles *(Airlines)*: The mileages flown by a traveler in the frame of a Frequent Flyer Program.

Frequent Flyer Program (FFP) *(Airlines)*: A program offered by airlines to promote passenger loyalty by giving them "points" for each mile flown. Participants exchange such points for free travel or upgraded service based on the miles they cumulate with the carrier. They are also entitled to special services, such as airport lounge access or priority bookings. Participation is optional. The first frequent flyer program was created in California by Western Airlines in June 1980. One year later, American Airlines created the first computer based system program AAdvantage, which was presented to the public in May 1, 1981. Lufthansa followed with its mileage program, Miles & More in January 1, 1993.

Frequent Lodger *(Hospitality)*: A person who stays frequently at a particular property or at different properties owned by the same chain, or a person who is enrolled in a hotel's Frequent Lodger Program.

Frequent Lodger Program *(Hospitality)*: A program designed by properties and property chains to win the loyalty of frequent lodgers. Participant members earn credits on the basis of nights stayed and redeem them for free lodging or upgraded services. The program may also offer additional special services. Participation is optional.

Frequent-stay Program *(Hospitality)*: Same as Frequent Lodger Program.

Fresh off the Boat *(Tourism)*: A slang term meaning Just Arrived in The Country, a recent immigrant or a foreigner.

Freshwater *(Ecology)*: Water with content of very low soluble mineral. It is found in lakes, streams, rivers, glaciers, and underground aquifers.

FRI *(GDS)*: Code for Friday.

Friction *(Air Traffic)*: The resistance of fluids (air and water) to the relative motion of a solid body.

Friction *(Geography)*: The turbulent resistance of the Earth on the atmosphere.

Frigobar *(Hospitality)*: Small refrigerator installed in a hotel room.

Fringing Reef *(Geography)*: A type of coral reef which is formed directly offshore with no deep lagoon between it and the shore.

FRM *(GDS)*: Code for From.

Front *(Climate)*: The leading part of an air mass.

Front Bar *(Hospitality)*: A place where guests sit down to consume beverages. The front bar comprises two functional areas for working staff: the backbar (the back wall, for storage and display) and the underbar (the bartender's main working area).

Front Desk *(Hospitality)*: Also called the Reception Desk, it is the main activity area of a hotel, usually located in the hotel lobby. The front desk is the place where guests register, rooms are assigned, and check out is processed.

Front Desk Agent *(Hospitality)*: A hotel employee responsible for registering guests, assigning rooms, and the coordination of room status, preregistration activities, mail, message, and information requests.

Front-Line Agent *(Tourism)*: The employee in a travel agency who is in direct contact with the public.

Front of the Line (FOTL) *(Tourism)*: An expression referring to the most advanced or important position at theme parks.

Front of the House *(Hospitality)*: The functional areas of a hotel or restaurant where employees have extensive contact with customers, such as the front desk of a hotel or the waiting place of a restaurant.

Front Office *(Hospitality)*: A hotel's command post for processing reservations, registering guests, settling guest accounts, and checking guests in and out. It is the same as Front Desk.

Front Office Ledger *(Hospitality)*: See Guest Ledger.

Frontal Precipitation *(Climate)*: A type of precipitation that occurs when a warm moist mass of air is pushed by a cooler body of air.

Frost *(Geography)*: Ice crystal deposits formed of gaseous water when temperature and dew point are below freezing.

Frost Free Period *(Climate)*: A value to show the total number of days between the last expected frost in the spring and the first expected frost in the fall.

FS *(GDS)*: Code meaning Free Sale. Sold on free sale basis.

FSD *(GDS)*: Code meaning Federal Security Director.

FSM *(Air Traffic)*: See Flight Schedule Monitor.

FSS *(Air Traffic)*: See Flight Service Station or Flight Service Specialists.

FT *(Air Traffic)*: See Terminal Forecast.

FTC *(Organizations)*: An acronym for Federal Trade Commission.

FTE *(Tourism)*: See Full Time Equivalent Employee.

FTP *(Computing)*: See File Transfer Protocol.

FUAAV *(Organizations)*: *Federación Universal de Asociaciones de Agencias de Viajes*. The Spanish name for United Federation of Travel Agents' Associations.

Fuel Charge *(Car Rental)*: Amount charged when the car renter does not fill the gas tank.

Fuel Surcharge *(Airline)*: A fee added to an airfare by a carrier to cover the increased cost of fuel.

Full American Plan *(Hospitality)*: See American Plan.

Full Board *(Hospitality)*: Type of accommodation that includes the three daily meals in the price.

Full Bottle *(Hospitality)*: A wine bottle usually containing approximately 25 ounces (750 ml).

Full Bottle Slip *(Hospitality)*: A tool used for controlling the liquor level in a bottle.

Full Day Tour *(Tourism)*: A visit or excursion that is performed in a complete day.

Full Economy/ Business/ First Class Fares *(Airlines)*: Also known as Normal Fares, they are valid for one year and are completely flexible and refundable. Such fares are not conditioned by stopovers, time validity or other conditions.

Full English Breakfast *(Hospitality)*: Also known as "traditional fry-up," it is a type of breakfast consisting of fried bacon and fried eggs; but to be"full English", a number of other ingredients would be expected. A full English breakfast served at a hotel might include a choice of cereal, porridge, kippers; toast and jam or marmalade; kedgeree or devilled kidneys. Scottish, Welsh and Irish breakfasts share some characteristics and ingredients of English breakfasts.

Full Fare *(Airlines)*: Normal Fare of year validity. It is completely flexible and refundable, and is not conditioned by stopovers, time validity and other of the restricted conditions.

Full House *(Tourism)*: A term to indicate that all the seats or rooms of a lodging propriety, a restaurant, or a show place are taken.

Full-Menu Restaurant *(Hospitality)*: A restaurant with more than twelve main-course items on the menu.

Full Night *(Hospitality)*: The stay charge made by a hotel's with a full daily rate, as opposed to a Day Rate.

Full Pension *(Hospitality)*: See American Plan.

Full Prepay *(Car Rental)*: The full rental rate payment required by some suppliers before confirming a vehicle. It does not include taxes or surcharges and is fully refundable.

Full-Service Agency *(Tourism)*: A travel agency that handles all types of travel and tourism services for consumers.

Full Service Agency Location *(Tourism)*: A branch of an agency that provides customers the same services as the head office, such as reservations and ticketing.

Full Service Hotel *(Hospitality)*: A hotel with a full range of services and amenities, including restaurants, meeting facilities, pool, fitness center, business center, etc.

Full Time Equivalent Employee (FTE) *(Hospitality)*: A way to measure a worker's involvement in a project. An FTE of 1.0 means that the person is equivalent to one full-time worker, while an FTE of 0.5 refers to one worker is only half-time. The expression is generally accepted to indicate a "direct", as opposed to contract, full-time employee. An employee can be FTE regular employee, whereas other is a full time contractor.

Fulfillment *(Tourism)*: To bring to an end in a satisfactory manner all the customers' requests.

Fully Appointed Agency *(Tourism)*: A travel agency whose accreditation allows it to sell airline, cruise, and other travel services.

Fully Commissionable *(Tourism):* The expression means a commission applies to the total value of the transaction, not just on selected portions.

Fully Independent Tour (FIT) *(Tourism)*: Packages designed for independent travelers not usually involving group activities at any stage of the trip. A good example is the fly-drive package, including air transportation, car rental and seldom accommodations, meals and/or attractions.

Function Book *(Hospitality)*: The official record used for assigning rooms and controlling other events for meetings at hotels or conference centers.

Function Sheet *(Hospitality)*: See Banquet Event Order.

Functional Image *(Tourism)*: The set of activities that tourists associate with a tourist destination.

Funnel *(Cruise)*: The smokestack in a ship for catching and directing any exhaust particles away from passenger decks.

Funnel Flight *(Airlines)*: A flight on a feeder airline connecting with other flight on a larger aircraft. Funnel flights are common in regional or commuter carriers that feed larger airplanes that continue on to other destinations.

Fuselage *(Airlines)*: The main cylindrical body of an aircraft. It comprises the cockpit, main cabin and cargo compartments. The wings, tail, and landing gear are attached to the fuselage.

FVR *(GDS)*: Code for Favor.

FWD *(GDS)*: A code meaning Forward, Forwarding, Forwarded.

FWDR *(Transport)*: See Forwarder.

FYI *(GDS)*: Code meaning For Your Information.

G

G *(Airlines)*: "Golf," name used to designate the letter "G" in the International Phonetic Alphabet

G *(Air Traffic)*: Acceleration of Earth's gravity.

G Force *(Air Traffic)*: The acceleration of gravity (g), which is approximately 9.81 meters per second.

G.M. *(Tourism)*: A French term for *Gentil Membre* meaning Gentile Member, a guest at a Club Med resort.

G.O. *(Tourism)*: A French term for *Gentil Organisateur* meaning Gentile Organizer, a staff member at a Club Med resort.

GA *(Airlines)*: Two-letter IATA code for Garuda Indonesia Airlines.

GA *(Airlines)*: See General Aviation.

GA *(Air Traffic)*: Go Around.

GA *(GDS)*: Code meaning "Go Ahead."

Gaijin *(Tourism)*: A Japanese term for foreigner. It is not a courteous word for some people.

Galileo *(GDS)*: A Global Distribution System.

Galley *(Cruise)*: The kitchen on a ship.

Gaming *(Tourism)*: The activity of gambling performed on a cruise ship or at a resort casino.

Gangplank *(Cruise)*: See Gangway.

Gangway *(Cruise)*: The movable ramp at a ship's side where people board and disembark at a pier. It is also called a Gangplank.

Gap *(Airlines)*: An open portion of an air trip not traveled by air, but by any other type of surface transportation.

Garden Side Room *(Hospitality)*: A hotel room with a door that opens to a garden.

Garden View Room *(Hospitality)*: A hotel room overlooking a garden, but without access to it.

Garni *(Hospitality)*: A French term denoting a hotel without meal service.

Garnishes *(Hospitality)*: Edible ingredients that are used for enhancing the flavor, texture, shape and general visual appearance of a dish.

GARS *(Car Rental)*: See Government Administration Rate Supplement.

Gasohol *(Tourism)*: An alternative type of automotive fuel derived from grain and corn. It is a blend gasoline and ethanol, in a ratio of 91 percent of gasoline and 9 percent of ethanol.

Gastronome Containers *(Hospitality)*: The set of moveable inserts, pans, containers, wire racks, trays and the like used in hospitality kitchens, which are used for storing and transporting food.

Gastronomy *(Hospitality)*: A term derived from the French *Gastronomie*. Gastronomy is a concept covering a wide and complex range of activities and relationship, related to various cultural components and associated to the Fine Arts and Social Sciences, and even to the Natural Sciences in terms of the digestive system of the human body. Therefore, gastronomy is the art and science of fine cooking, but also the art of eating and fine drinking, in a close relationship between culture and food.

Gate *(Airlines)*: An assigned area at an airport where passengers board or deplane an aircraft.

Gate Rate *(Car Rental)*: The daily rate that is charged if someone turns up and parks at a car

Gateway *(Tourism)*: The first point of entry or the last point of departure in a country, such as an airport or a sea port. It most often refers to a major airport or seaport. It also refers to the port where Customs clearance takes place.

Gateway Airport *(Airlines)*: A facility certified by the aeronautic authority as meeting the suitable conditions and security standards for the operation of commercial international air services. It is usually an airport that serves as a point of entry or departure to or from a country.

Gateway City *(Airlines)*: A city that counts with an airport duly certified as a gateway airport to permit the operation of international flights.

Gateway Fare *(Airlines)*: The fare published to a major gateway city or airport.

GATS *(Organizations)*: An acronym for General Agreement on Trade in Services.

GATT *(Organizations)*: An acronym for General Agreement on Tariffs and Trade.

Gay Friendly *(Tourism)*: Type of tourism supplying services to gay and lesbian travelers.

Gazebo *(Hospitality)*: A small, open-sided structure, usually in a garden, that gives a good view of the surrounding countryside for people sitting on it.

Gazetteer *(Tourism)*: A directory with entries arranged by geographical location, as in a gazetteer of restaurants.

GBA *(GDS):* Code meaning General Booking Agreement.

GBLD *(GDS)*: Code meaning Garbled.

GBTA *(Organizations)*: An acronym for Guild of Business Travel Agents.

GCET *(Tourism)*: See Global Code of Ethics for Tourism.

GCR *(Airlines)*: See General Cargo Rate.

GDB *(GDS)*: Code meaning Guide Dog for the Blind.

GDN *(GDS)*: Code meaning Room with a Garden or with a Garden View.

GDNVW *(GDS)*: Same as above.

GDP *(Air Traffic)*: See Ground Delay Program.

GDP *(Tourism)*: See Gross Domestic Product (earned per capita).

GDS *(GDS)*: See Global Distribution System. See also CRS, Computerized Reservations System.

GDS Hosting *(GDS)*: An arrangement in which an appointed travel agency shares its GDS services with other agencies that do not have a GDS contract. By consequence, affiliated agencies become a sort of branches of the agency with the GDS contract. It is also called Affiliate Hosting.

GDSN *(Organizations)*: An acronym for Global Data Synchronization Network.

GEBTA *(Organizations)*: An acronym for Guild of European Business Travel Agents.

Gemini *(GDS):* A Global Distribution System Company.

GEN *(GDS)*: Code for General.

Genealogy *(Tourism)*: In general terms, Genealogy is the study of the history of a family. More specifically, it involves learning basic information about births, marriages, and deaths in a person's family tree.

Genealogy Tourism *(Tourism)*: It is a type of tourism by which people travel to search out their ancestors and their ancestral homelands. The number of travelers interested in family roots is now increasing.

General Agreement on Tariffs and Trade (GATT) *(Organizations)*: The GATT is a treaty, not an organization that was established on 1 January 1948, after several preparatory sessions. The original document was signed by Canada and 22 other nations. The GATT's main objective is the reduction of barriers to international trade, by reducing tariff barriers, quantitative restrictions and subsidies on trade through a series of agreements.

General Agreement on Trade in Services (GATS) *(Organizations)*: A treaty of the World Trade Organization (WTO) which was created in January 1995 in the frame of the Uruguay Round negotiations. It is aimed to extending the multilateral trading system to services, in the same way the General Agreement on Tariffs and Trade (GATT) provides such a system for merchandise trade.

General Aviation *(Airlines)*: All civil aviation other than common commercial transport that includes personal flying, business flying, instructional flying, and commercial flying such as aerial photography and agricultural spraying.

General Aviation Aircraft *(Airlines)*: Aircraft smaller than large commercial carriers that are used in General Aviation activities.

General Cargo Rate *(Airlines)*: The price an air carrier charges for the transportation of cargo not qualifying for a lower special class or commodity rate.

General Conditions of Carriage *(Airlines)*: When a passenger pays for an air ticket, he is entering into a contract of carriage called Adhesion Contract with the airline. The General Conditions of Carriage are the clauses of that contract, covering all the items associated to the air transportation, such as baggage limitations, compensation for damaged, lost or delayed baggage, liability and amounts of compensation for injuries derived from the operation of the flight. These provisions often vary from airline to airline, although main stipulations are established by IATA or international agreements and treaties. Since air carrier issue electronic tickets, they must print a summary of conditions of carriage for the passenger's knowledge.

General Manager *(Hospitality)*: The chief operating officer of a hotel or a restaurant.

General Sales Agent (GSA) *(Airlines)*: An agent or airline to whom an airline, acting as the principal, delegates general authority to represent it for the purpose of sales of passenger and/or cargo air transportation in a defined territory. The GSA is remunerated with a commission.

Generalized System of Preferences (GSP) *(Customs)*: A trade program that gives duty preferences (free or reduced rates) to some developing countries.

Generic Wine *(Hospitality)*: A blend of wines that appears similar to a particular wine of an already established region.

Gentlemen Host *(Cruise)*: A mature retired gentleman who is employed shipboard to serve as dance partner, conversationalist, and shore excursion escort for single women. They are usually well-traveled people sponsored by a cruise program.

Geocentric Latitude *(Air Traffic)*: Latitude measured with respect to horizontal through the mass center of the earth.

Geographic Center *(Geography)*: The center point of a country measured from the north to the south and from the east to the west.

Geographic Information System (GIS) *(Geography)*: The integrated software used for the input, management, analysis, and display of spatial information.

Geographic Inquiry *(Geography)*: The process by which geographic information is collected, organized, analyzed, and diffused.

Geographic Region *(Geography)*: A territory determined by natural and human factors.

Geographical Africa *(Geography)*: See Africa.

Geographical Europe *(Geography)*: See Europe

Geographical Space *(Geography)*: Although the term involves numerous connotations, many of them ambiguous, in Geography it implies a sense of a vast area which is only delimited by cartographers. In general terms, it can be said that the geographic space encompasses all the spaces that are beyond the human body that may be represented by many different metrics and geometries in many different scales. Geographic space is subjectively defined by human spatial cognition, and objectively, by the physical or geometrical reality. The recognition of the concept of distance is fundamental in human intelligent computation to recognize spaces between geographic objects. By this recognition we could say that space is a measureless ambit where matter is physically elongated and objects and events have positions relative to one another. The concept of space is of great importance for tourism because in regard to it is that touristic activities exist.

Geographic North *(Air Traffic)*: Also called True North, it is a navigational term referring to the direction of the North Pole relative to the navigator's position, namely, the direction of the geographical North Pole from a given point. The direction of true north is marked in the skies by the north celestial pole. Geographical North is different from the Magnetic North.

Geographic North *(Geography)*: The northern axis around which the Earth revolves.

Geographic Territory *(Geography)*: A specific geographical area of land that is owned and controlled by a country.

Geography *(Geography)*: In an etymologic sense, it is the Earth's description. In a broader sense, Geography has the mission to explain the relationship between human beings and their territorial spaces. The essence of Geography deals with the description and analysis of physical and environmental phenomena and their interrelationship with the changing patterns of human populations. But Geography also regards human activities as far as they affect the Earth. As history interprets temporal sequences, so Geography interprets spatial sequences and associations. Geography is divided into several subfields. The most accepted division is that which corresponds to its definition, and comprises Physical Geography and Human Geography. The features of the Earth are the domain of physical geographers and their work includes the research about climates, the formation of landforms, and plant and animal distribution. Human Geography is the study of humans on geographic spaces. Some of its specialties are religion, languages, and cities. Their research is fundamental to our understanding of cultures. Cultural Geography, which is a subdivision of Human Geography, wants to know the reasons why certain groups speak different dialects, organize their cities in a particular way, or practice certain rituals. There will always be something new that Geography can research: New states are created, natural disasters strike populated areas, the world's climate changes, and the communication technology brings people closer together. No doubt that accurate geographical analysis will allow us to understand the world in which we live. Therefore, Geography uses the resources of all the sciences that can help to clarify the interpretation of local and global circumstances of the human condition.

Geography of Tourism *(Geography)*: A branch of Human Geography aimed to study the relationship between man and his environment, identifying and defining the space and its divisions into fractions of territory, regions, cities, etc. The analysis of space is the basic aspect that contributes to the understanding of the complex and dynamic tourist activity.

Geologic Era *(Geography)*: A term used to identify a particular period in the earth's history.

Geology *(Geography)*: The science concerned with the earth's physical history, as registered in the substrate and the fossil records.

Geopolitics *(Geography)*: The study of how geographic, economic, and social factors influence on the politics of a nation.

Geostationary Orbit *(Geography)*: The orbit in which a satellite is fixed at a speed that keeps it exactly above a certain ground position.

Geotechnologies *(Geography)*: Methodic technologies used to carry out geographic studies.

Geotourism *(Tourism)*: Geotourism is a type of tourism enhancing the geographic characters of the place being visited, such as its environment, culture, aesthetics, heritage, and living style of its residents. It shares some common aspects with ecotourism, sustainable tourism, nature-based tourism, and heritage travel. The concept was born in the early 1990's with the purpose to emphasize on the specific geology of a destination.

GFAX *(GDS)*: Code meaning General Facts.

GG *(GDS)*: Code meaning: 1. Group Guaranteed; 2. Go Get, an entry to obtain certain information.

GG Rate *(GDS)*: Code meaning Guaranteed Group Rate.

GI *(GDS)*: Code meaning Global Indicator.

GIG *(GDS)*: Three-letter IATA code for Galeão International Airport, serving the city of Rio de Janeiro.

GIT *(Airlines)*: See Group Inclusive Tour.

GIT *(Car Rental)*: See Goods in Transit Coverage.

Gin *(Hospitality)*: A compounded spirit made of flavored juniper berries. It is classified as dry or heavy. Dry gins are light in flavor and body, while heavy gins are heavily flavored and full-bodied.

Ginger-Flavored Brandy *(Hospitality)*: Neutral and light brown color brandy with the flavor and aroma of ginger root.

GIS *(Geography)*: See Geographic Information System.

GIT *(GDS)*: Code meaning Group Inclusive Tour.

GIT Fares *(Airlines)*: Airfares that apply for groups that include land services in the travel.

Gîte *(Tourism)*: A French term for lodging with facilities to prepare meals.

Giveaway *(Airlines)*: Something given gratuitously by a carrier to the passenger, in addition to the carriage from an airport of departure to another airport of destination.

Glacial *(Geography)*: Term that qualifies something pertaining to a vast period of time when glaciers covered a large part of the earth.

Glacial Spillway *(Geography)*: A type of valley formed by glacial melt water.

Glacier *(Geography)*: A large mass of ice moving slowly.

Glass Cockpit *(Aeronautics)*: A term given to an aircraft's control cabin that has all electronic, digital and computer-based instrumentation.

Glass Rail *(Hospitality)*: An area used by bartenders to set glasses while pouring drinks.

Glider *(Airlines)*: A non-motorized aircraft that is towed to a given altitude where it is set free to glide on air currents. Gliders are mainly used for sport and sightseeing purposes.

Glideslope *(Air Traffic)*: The ideal descent path to a runway that can be electronically detected by radio signals transmitted from the ground.

Global Code of Ethics for Tourism (GCET) *(Tourism)*: The Global Code of Ethics for Tourism is a broad set of principles whose purpose is to give behavior and business guidelines to all parties involved in tourism development, such as central and local governments, local communities, tourism organizations and its professionals, as well as visitors, both international and domestic. The Code was created by a resolution of the UNWTO General Assembly met in Istanbul in 1997. The Global Code of Ethics for Tourism establishes the frame of reference for the responsible and sustainable development of tourism in the world. In its session of July 2001, the ECOSOC adopted a draft resolution on the Code of Ethics and called on the UN General Assembly to give recognition to the Code. The official recognition by the UN General Assembly came on 21 December 2001, through its Resolution A/RES/56/212, by which it further encouraged the World Tourism Organization to promote an effective follow-up of the Code.

Global Data Synchronization Network (GDSN) *(Organizations)*: A section of the GS1 providing an automated, standards-based global environment to enable secure and continuous data synchronization, allowing all partners to have consistent item data in their systems at the same time. Global Registry membership covers multiple sectors across North America, Latin America, Europe and Asia Pacific.

Global Distribution System (GDS) *(GDS)*: An international computer reservation system that accesses many databases where travelers and travel agents can check availability and reserve travel related products like airlines, hotels, car rentals, cruises, rail, etc. all over the world. The travel business is a global marketplace where millions of buyers (travel agents and the public) and sellers (hotels, airlines, car rental companies, etc.) meet together to exchange travel services. GDSs are the tool linking all of them, allowing transactions to be made quickly and easily. The first GDS appeared as early as the 1960s as a way to keep track of flight schedules, availability, and prices. As the mid 1970s GDSs became the first e-commerce companies in the world facilitating business-to-business electronic commerce. GDSs are owned and operated by the airline industry and include systems like Amadeus, Sabre, Galileo, Worldspan, and Pegasus.

Global Indicators (GI) *(Airlines)*: A two-letter code that appears next to the fare and informs the route established for the travel at that fare. Some of the GIs are: WH for travel in the Western Hemisphere, EH for travel in the Eastern Hemisphere, AT for travel via the Atlantic Route, PA for travel via the Pacific Route, AP for travel via the Atlantic and Pacific Route, and TS for Trans Siberian Route.

Global Positioning System (GPS) *(Tourism)*: A satellite navigation system which is used to localize cars, ships or aircraft. Nowadays, the system allows the use of miniature radio receivers on earth to identify one's location within a few feet. Most cruise ships use this system to navigate the world's oceans.

Global Warming *(Ecology)*: A phenomenon by which the overall temperature of the earth's atmosphere, oceans, and landmass is gradually rising. It is widely believed that carbon dioxide and other so-called greenhouse gases released by human activities, notably the burning of fossil fuels are responsible for generating this serious environmental issue.

Globe *(Geography)*: A global representation of the earth.

GM *(GDS)*: Code meaning General Manager.

GMT *(Geography)*: See Greenwich Mean Time.

GNP *(Tourism)*: See Gross National Product.

GNR *(GDS)*: See Guest Name Record.

GO *(GDS)*: Code meaning Value Car Rental Company.

Go Around (GA) *(Air Traffic)*: A basic guidance mode, providing lateral guidance, longitudinal guidance and vertical guidance to climb then to accelerate, while maintaining a wings-level roll.

Go Show *(Airlines)*: A passenger without a pre-existing booking who shows at check-in counter for boarding a flight.

Golden Age Passport *(Tourism)*: A card for persons 62 years or older obtainable from the U.S. National Park Service to for use in unlimited access to the sites it operates.

Golf *(Airlines)*: Designator for the letter "G" in the International Phonetic Alphabet.

Golf *(Tourism)*: A sport activity played on a large open course of grass with 9 or 18 holes. Players use an array of special clubs with long shafts to hit a small ball from a prescribed starting point into the holes. The purpose is to complete the course with the fewer possible strokes.

Gondola *(Tourism)*: 1. A boat with a high bow and stern, very popular in Venice for sightseeing along its channels. 2. A cabin lift used to transport skiers and sightseers. 3. A basket hanging from a balloon system for comfortable lift of passenger.

Gondwana *(Geography)*: It is said two large emerged landmasses existed on the earth 300 million years ago, from Cambrian to Jurassic time, one situated to the north and the other situated to the south. The Southern supercontinent was named Gondwana and hypothetically was composed of South America, Africa, Madagascar, India, Antarctica, and Australia. It was formed after the break up of Pangaea before the Triassic Period, including most of the landmasses which make up today's continents of the southern hemisphere. The Northern part was named Laurasia.

Goods *(Airlines)*: See Cargo.

Goods and Services Tax (GST) *(Tourism)*: A tax much similar to the value added tax levied on the final consumer of goods or services that is charged in Australia, Canada, New Zealand and Singapore. The GST was introduced in Canada on January 1, 1991 and is collected in most of its provinces.

Goods Declaration *(Customs)*: A statement made by the pertinent person in the manner prescribed by Customs applied to the goods that will enter or exit a country.

Goods in Transit Coverage (GIT) *(Car Rental)*: An international term equivalent of the U.S. Personal Accident and Personal Effects (PAE) to cover the renter and the passengers against damages resulting from accident, injury, and loss to personal property.

Gourmet *(Hospitality)*: 1. A French term defining a person who is a critic of food and beverage. 2. A restaurant that provides sophisticated food and beverage.

Government Administration Rate Supplement (GARS) *(Car Rental)*: A fixed per day Admin Rate Supplement tax imposed for U.S. Government rentals.

GOVT *(GDS)*: Code for Government.

GPS *(GDS)*: Code meaning: 1. Three-letter IATA code for the Galapagos Islands in Ecuador; 2. Global Positioning System.

GPST *(GDS)*: Code meaning Group Seat Request.

Grace Period *(Car Rental)*: The amount of time allowed for a renter to bring his car back to the rental agency without being charged for an extra day. Usually car rental companies allow at least 30 minutes of grace.

Grain Neutral Spirit *(Hospitality)*: A colorless, odorless, and tasteless distilled spirit made from a grain mash.

Grand Prix *(Tourism)*: A famous automobile racing that began in France by 1894. With the coming years, Grand Prix motor racing derived into formula racing and Formula One. Nowadays, each event of the Formula One World Championships is called a Grand Prix.

Grand Site *(Tourism)*: A French term for a great place or a great monument. These are natural or architectural spaces protected for a limited number of visitor per year (usually 300,000).

Grand Tour *(Tourism)*: An upper-class extended trip across the European continent that wealthy young people from the British aristocracy made as part of their education, from about 1660 until the arrival of mass rail tourism in the 1840. Grand Tours began in England, could last three or four years, and included the major cultural cities of Italy, France, Germany or all, according to the interests of the sponsoring family. The salons of Paris and the court of Versailles were considered centers where youths could be polished with standards of taste, intellectuality and social patterns. Italy was a preferred destination for its artistic values and its fashionable society. It is believed this is the first time the terms tour and tourist were used. By the end of the Grand Tour era, they were not only young aristocrats who made the trip. The length of the tour decreased to include individual traveling for a purpose other than education, such as for pleasure or even sports. This event is also known as The Grand Tour of Europe or Le Grand Tour.

Grape *(Hospitality)*: A fruit from a vine that is used to make wine.

Grappa *(Hospitality)*: Brandy distilled from the pulpy residue of the wine press.

Gratuities *(Cruise)*: Tips that passengers give to cabin attendants and dining service personnel. Dining gratuities are usually added on the bills, especially on those cruise lines featuring flexible dining hours and dining venues.

Gratuity *(Tourism)*: A voluntary sum of money or gift in addition to the cost of a service, which is given to serving personnel in appreciation for the service provided. It is generally known as a Tip and is called Pourboire in French, Propina in Spanish, and Trinkgeld in German.

Graveyard Shift *(Hospitality)*: The late-night or overnight time shift for employees who work during the night

Gravity *(Air Traffic)*: The natural force that pulls an object toward the earth. An airplane must generate enough lift to counteract the weight of an aircraft.

Gray Water *(Hospitality)*: Wastewater collected from kitchens, bathrooms, tubs, sinks, laundry tubs and or washers that contain chemical or chemical-biological ingredients such as soaps, detergents, etc. It is relatively clean wastewater that can be used to supply needs for landscape water and other non-potable uses.

Greasy Spoon *(Tourism)*: A slang term used to qualify a low-class restaurant or coffee shop that doesn't look particularly clean.

Great Circle Route *(Geography)*: A line drawn on the surface of a globe to show the shortest distance between two places. In sailing, it is the shortest course between two points, following a great circle.

Green *(Ecology)*: Something that is friendly to the environment or something made of recycled materials.

Green Card *(Tourism)*: The identity card issued to noncitizen permanent residents of the United States.

Green Hotel *(Hospitality)*: A green hotel is an environmentally-friendly property whose operation is committed to ecologically sound programs that save water, save energy and reduce solid waste, while saving money, to help protect the earth.

Green-House or Greenhouse *(Ecology)*: A glass structure built to create higher temperatures that assist in the cultivation of plants under controlled conditions.

Green Light *(Air Traffic)*: Approval for landing. An expression from days when aircraft did not have radios, and control towers used a light-gun that beamed various green, red, and yellow signals to communicate with pilots in the air and on the ground.

Green Valley Solano *(Hospitality)*: A region in California, located between Sacramento and San Francisco that produces wines to sell them locally.

Greenhouse Effect *(Ecology)*: A natural effect in which heat reflected by the earth's surface is trapped in the atmosphere by water vapor, carbon dioxide, ozone, and several other gases and then radiated back toward the earth's surface.

Greenhouse Gases *(Ecology)*: Gases laying in the earth's lower atmosphere that produce the greenhouse effect, such as carbon dioxide (CO_2), methane (CH_4), water vapor (H_2O), and nitrous oxide (N_2O) that absorb heat radiated from the surface of the Earth and trap heat from the sun. The increase of these gases in the atmosphere (caused by the burning of fossil fuels, emission of pollutants and deforestation) contributes to global warming.

Greenwashing *(Ecology)*: A false image elaborated to present something as environmental conservative, ecologically sustainable, and/or socio-culturally responsible so as to present an environmentally responsible public image

Greenwich Mean Time (GMT) *(Geography)*: The local time at the 0 meridian passing through Greenwich, England. It is the solar time that is used as a reference unit to calculate the time in all other time zones in the world. GMT is the global time standard that was established in 1884 when delegates from 27 nations met in Washington, DC for the Meridian Conference where they agreed on a system basically the same as that now in use. It is also known as Greenwich Time, Standard Clock Time (SCT), Universal Time and Zulu Time. All airlines operate their schedules in GMT.

Greenwich Time *(Geography)*: See Greenwich Mean Time.

Grenadine *(Hospitality)*: Bright red flavoring syrup blending made of pomegranate, strawberry, and raspberry.

Grid *(Geography)*: A series of lines drawn on a map crossing at right-angles, to create reference areas for location purposes.

Grid References *(Geography)*: A system of grid lines used to create references for location purposes.

Griddle *(Hospitality)*: A cooking appliance heated by burners underneath it.

Grind Player *(Hospitality)*: An infrequent gambler who ventures relatively small amounts of money.

Grogshop *(Tourism)*: A British term for a bar of low class.

Gross *(Business)*: An economic term referring to a total amount of money before deductions.

Gross Domestic Product *(Business)*: The total market value of the goods and services produced by a country's economy for its internal consume during a specific period of time.

Gross Lettings *(Tourism)*: A term used referring to all room renting, including paid and complimentary.

Gross National Product *(Business)*: The total value of goods produced and services provided by a country during a given time period, including gross domestic products, exports, remittances of nationals living outside and income from foreign subsidiaries of local firms.

Gross Profit *(Business)*: The profit resulting from the total revenue and its cost of producing the product or service. These costs can include manufacturing expenses, raw materials, labor, selling, marketing and other expenses. The gross profit is calculated by dividing gross profit by total revenue.

Gross Receipts Meal Tax *(Tourism)*: A tax imposed on a restaurant for its total meal sales.

Gross Registered Tonnage (GRT) *(Cruise)*: The standard way of measuring a cruise ship's interior space. One GRT equals 100 cubic feet of enclosed space. Cruise ships in the 70,000 ton range are considered "Superliners". GRT is also used for calculating the harbor duties.

Gross Sales *(Business)*: The total amount of sales before deducting any expenses for customer discounts, allowances, returns or other post-sale adjustments.

Gross Weight *(Airlines)*: The total weight of an aircraft when it is fully loaded.

GRT *(Cruise)*: See Gross Registered Tonnage.

Ground Arrangements *(Tourism)*: The total of services covering the land portion of a trip, such as lodging, transfers, sightseeing tours, meals, entertainment, etc.

Ground Control *(Air Traffic)*: The tower control of aircraft ground movements at an airport.

Ground Controller *(Air Traffic)*: An operator in the Tower that is responsible for directing and approving the movement of aircraft and ground vehicles on the airport surface.

Ground Delay Program (GDP) or FAA Flow Control *(Air Traffic)*: An air traffic initiative that is applied for the United States Air Space System, when special conditions are given, such as inclement weather, or when the projected traffic demand is expected to exceed the airport's acceptance rate. A GDP usually lasts for several hours, but can vary as conditions change at the controlled area.

Ground Handler *(Airlines)*: An employee of an airline or Handling Organization who is responsible for taking care of passengers during the check-in and boarding process.

Ground Handling *(Airlines)*: The process that deals with passengers and their baggage at an airport during check-in and boarding.

Ground Incursions *(Air Traffic)*: Any occurrence resulting in loss of safe separation with an aircraft taking off, intending to take off, landing or intending to land at an airport caused by an aircraft, vehicle, person, or object on the ground.

Ground Operator *(Tourism)*: A company or individual that makes arrangements to provide local land services, such as hotel accommodations, sightseeing, transfers, and other related services. See also Receptive Operator.

Ground Speed (GS) *(Air Traffic)*: The actual speed at which an aircraft travels over the ground.

Ground Traffic *(Air Traffic)*: All movement of vehicles along the runways, taxiways and pathways of an airport.

Ground Transportation *(Tourism)*: Any system of land transportation using such vehicles as trains, coaches, cars, buses, monorails, trams, etc.

Ground-water *(Geography)*: Water that is stored within the earth that usually supplies wells and springs.

Group *(Tourism)*: An assembly of persons who are the object of a collective transaction. Typically, tourism groups are formed to enjoy better price conditions than individual travelers.

Group Fare *(Tourism)*: A discounted or reduced fare applied to groups, according to some conditions that usually require round-trip travel within a specified time limit.

Group Desk *(Tourism)*: The department or counter of an airline, travel agency, hotel, or other supplier set to handle group reservations and to supply the services its members might require.

Group House *(Hospitality)*: A hotel primarily aimed to the convention and meetings market.

Group Inclusive Tour (GIT) *(Tourism)*: A prepaid tour offered only to groups of a minimum size, with specified components and value.

Group Leader *(Tourism)*: An individual who acts as the link to a tour operator, and is designated to coordinate arrangements for a group. In some cases he/she may also serve as a tour escort.

Group Organizer *(Tourism)*: Any person, travel agent or air carrier who organizes and promotes a pre-arranged group travel.

Group Rate *(Tourism)*: The fare or room rate applicable to people travelling as a group.

Group Reservations *(Hospitality)*:   A block of guestrooms held under an individual or business' name at a particular hotel for specific accommodation of a group for certain dates or range of dates.

Group Sales *(Tourism)*: 1. The product of a marketing effort to sell a group travel. 2. The department of an agency in charge of selling travel services to groups of persons.

Group Size *(Tourism)*: The number of passengers required to qualify as a group.

Group Status Report *(Tourism)*: A document prepared by a tour operator or a supplier that includes detailed information of the list of passengers in a group, accommodations, seat or cabin assignments, payments, and other related services as of the date of the report.

Group Tour *(Tourism)*: A prearranged and prepaid tour program for a group that usually includes transportation, accommodations, attractions, transfers, sightseeing, and meals.

Group Travel *(Tourism)*: A type of journey arranged for holiday-makers or persons identified by a common interest who travel as a collective unity.

Growing Season *(Climate)*: An indicator to determine the number of days in the year with an average temperature above 5.5 degrees C.

GRP *(GDS)*: A code meaning Group, Grouping, Grouped.

GRPF *(GDS)*: Code meaning Group Fare Data.

GRPS *(GDS)*: Code for Groups.

GRT *(Cruise)*: See Gross Registered Tonnage.

GRU *(GDS)*: Three-letter IATA code for serving the city of Guarulhos Internacional Airport Sao Paulo

GS *(Air Traffic)*: See Ground Speed.

GS1 *(Organizations)*: A global organization focused on the design and implementation of multi sector standards and solutions for supply chains worldwide. The GS1 System standards are the most widely used globally. The GS1 System comprises four product areas: 1) Barcodes to automatically identify goods; 2) eCom for automatic electronic transmission of data; 3) GDSN (Global Data

Synchronization Network) by which partners obtain consistent item data in their systems at the same time; and, 4) EPCglobal which uses RFID technology to immediately track items. GS1 was created by the mergence of the Uniform Code Council (UCC), the Electronic Commerce Council of Canada (ECCC) and EAN International in 2005. The GS1 has two headquarters: one in Brussels (Belgium) and another in Lawrenceville, New Jersey (USA), with branch offices in over 100 countries globally.

GSA *(Airlines)*: See General Sales Agent

GSP *(Customs)*: See Generalized System of Preferences.

GST *(Tourism)*: See Goods and Services Tax.

GTAG *(Airlines)*: See Global Tag.

Global Tag (GTAG) *(Airlines)*: A standardization initiative for tracking of baggage, based on radio frequency identification (RFID).

GTD *(GDS)*: Code for Guaranteed.

GTIA *(Organizations)*: An acronym for Golf and Travel Industry Association.

GUA *(GDS)*: Three-letter IATA code for the city of Guatemala, the capital city of Guatemala.

GUAR *(GDS)*: Code meaning Guarantee or guaranteed.

Guarantee *(Tourism)*: 1. A formal way to assure that a product or service will be provided at the agreed specifications. In Cruise terms, a "guarantee" is the cruise line's promise that the passenger will sail on a selected voyage in a specified type of cabin, at an agreed rate no higher than would ordinarily apply for that voyage. 2. The amount paid to guarantee a product or service.

Guarantee for Late Arrival or Guaranteed Late Arrival *(Hospitality)*: A hold placed on a room that assures the hotel will not sell the room to someone else if the guest arrives late. To obtain this guarantee, the guest must provide a credit card number. If the guest fails to appear for the night's stay, the hotel will charge the traveler for the room.

Guarantee Share Fare *(Cruise)*: A price for a single passenger based on the passenger's acceptance to share a cabin with a stranger of the same sex and smoking preference. The rate will be honored even if the cruise line is unable to find a cabin mate.

Guaranteed Group Rate *(Cruise)*: A group rate granted to a travel agency on a negotiated basis, disregarding the number of bookings made.

Guaranteed Payment *(Hospitality)*: An advanced hotel reservation secured by an agreement stating that the guest will pay for the room, even if he fails to arrive. The room will be held all night in a late-arriving state.

Guaranteed Reservations *(Hospitality)*: Same as Guaranteed Payment.

Guaranteed Share *(Cruise)*: Same as Guarantee Share Fare.

Guaranteed Single *(Cruise)*: A guaranteed rate for a single passenger who does not wish to share the cabin with another passenger at a cruise ship.

Guaranteed Tour *(Tourism)*: A tour that will firmly operate unless it is cancelled by the passenger before the time limit.

Guardian *(Tourism)*: A person acting in lieu of parents in the event they are dead or became legally incapacitated.

Gueridon *(Hospitality)*: A small often circular ornate table or stand used in restaurants for displaying certain dishes before serving.

Guest-house *(Hospitality)*: See *Chambre d'hôte*.

Guest Comment Card *(Hospitality):* A short questionnaires that hotels or restaurants ask their guests to fill out. They are used by the property to define current markets and to improve the operation.

Guest History Card *(Hospitality)*: A record of a guest's visits including rooms assigned, rates paid, special needs, and credit rating.

Guest History File *(Hospitality)*: A file that contains guest history cards, which is maintained for marketing purposes.

Guest House *(Hospitality)*: A home that offers rooms for travelers. They operate usually on basis of bed and breakfast.

Guest Information Services *(Hospitality)*: Automated information devices set in public hotel areas to enable guests to obtain information about in-house services and activities.

Guest Lecturer *(Cruise)*: A person (non-permanent employee) who is hired to speak on a particular hobby, skill, or activity in which he/she is considered expert. Typically, lectures deal with history, sports, entertainment, books, etc.

Guest Ledger *(Hospitality)*: An accounts book that keeps individual records of the hotel's registered guests. It provides current status on guest charges and payments. A guest ledger is also referred to as a Front Office Ledger, Transient Ledger, or Room Ledger.

Guest Mix *(Hospitality)*: The composition of a hotel guest clientele, by individuals, groups, business, leisure, and others, who stay at a hotel or patronize a restaurant.

Guest Night *(Tourism)*: A special evening when members of a club are allowed to bring guests to the club.

Guest Name Record *(Hospitality)*: An electronic code assigned to each hotel guest

Guest Profile *(Hospitality)*: The common characteristics qualifying a property's guests. It helps management to identify which market segments the property appeals to and which segments the property wants to attract.

Guest Relations *(Hospitality)*: The hotel department responsible for personal harmonious relationships and goodwill with guests through service and attention to their individual needs. It is in charge of the promotion of in-house products and services, the entertainment of VIPs, and the handling of social functions.

Guest Service Manager (GSM) *(Hospitality)*: The person who is responsible for the guest services department.

Guest Service Representative (GSR) *(Hospitality)*: A hotel employee who provides check-in, check-out, mail, key, message, and information services for guests.

Guest Survey *(Hospitality)*: A questionnaire that is completed by guests for the use of managers to define current markets and to improve the operation.

Guestroom Control Book *(Hospitality)*: A book where the number of guestrooms committed to groups are monitored. It provides the sales office with the maximum number of guestrooms it can sell to groups on a given day, in order that the remaining guestrooms are available for individual guests.

Guestroom Key *(Hospitality)*: A key to open a single guestroom door.

Guestroom Maintenance *(Hospitality)*: A set of activities to keep a room in the best occupying conditions.

Guide *(Tourism)*: 1. A person duly qualified to conduct tours in specific localities or attractions and who is able to share his knowledge with visitors. 2. A sort of Manual for an airline, bus, railroad, or shops listing fares, prices, procedures or descriptions.

Guided Tour *(Tourism)*: A local sightseeing trip conducted by a guide.

Guild of European Business Travel Agents (GEBTA) *(Organizations)*: An organization founded in January 1990, at the stimulation of the Guild of Business Travel Agents Ltd. in Great Britain. GEBTA's main objective is to obtain special advantages for business travelers, both in infrastructure and in cost of travel. The supporting argument is that business travelers use air transport and accommodation facilities more times a year than leisure travelers. The organization has currently seven National Guilds with over 300 members in Germany, Ireland, Italy, the Netherlands, Portugal, Spain, and the United Kingdom.

Gulf *(Geography)*: A large portion of a sea or ocean partly surrounded by land, with a narrow mouth. It is usually larger than a bay.

Gulf States *(IATA Geography)*: Bahrain, Oman, Qatar, and United Arab Emirates.

Gulf Stream *(Geography)*: A warm-water current of the Atlantic ocean that flows from the Northeast of the Caribbean and is extended by the North Atlantic Drift until reaching the British Isles. It passes through the Strait of Florida, and follows the eastern coastlines of the United States and Newfoundland before crossing the Atlantic Ocean. The Gulf Stream influences the climate of the coastal regions it borders.

Gunwale *(Cruise)*: The upper edge or wale of a vessel's or boat's side.

GVA *(GDS)*: Three-letter IATA code for Geneva, important city in Switzerland.

GVU *(GDS)*: Code meaning Garden View.

Gwailo *(Tourism)*: A sort of pejorative Chinese word for a foreigner, mainly a white one, having the implication of "ghost person".

GYE *(GDS)*: Three-letter IATA code for Guayaquil, a seaport in Ecuador.

Gym or Gymnasium *(Hospitality)*: Room or building designed for indoor sport activities.

Gyroplane *(Aeronautics)*: An aircraft, such as a helicopter or autogyro, equipped with wings that rotate about an approximately vertical axis.

Gyroscope *(Airlines/Cruise)*: A device consisting of a rotating heavy metal wheel pivoted inside a circular frame whose movement does not affect the wheel's orientation in space. It is used in compasses and other navigational aids for stabilizing mechanisms on ships and aircraft.

H

H *(Airlines)*: "Hotel," name used to designate the letter "H" in the International Phonetic Alphabet

H *(GDS)*: A code meaning: 1. Economy or Coach Discounted Class; 2. Accompanying the seat code, it means Handicapped Seat; 3. Together with the fare code it means High Season.

HAA *(Geography)*: *Heure Avancée de l'Atlantique.* See Atlantic Daylight Time.

Habitat *(Ecology)*: The place that gathers the conditions to offer a suitable and specific environment where an organism, population, or community can develop its life, such as a forest, desert, or wetlands.

Habilitation *(Tourism)*: In France, the homologation of professional activities permitting a hotel or tourism supplier to organize and sell travel services.

HAC *(Geography)*: *Heure Avancée du Centre.* See Central Daylight Time.

Hacienda *(Tourism)*: A Spanish term for a country house or farm.

HADT *(Geography)*: See Hawaii-Aleutian Daylight Time.

HAE *(Geography)*: *Heure Avancée de l'Est.* See Eastern Daylight Time.

HAI *(Organizations)*: An acronym for "Helicopter Association International."

Halal *(Tourism)*: A meal that conforms to Islamic dietary provisions. Major airlines and cruise ships provide halal meals for Muslim passengers.

Half Bottle *(Hospitality)*: A wine bottle containing around 375 ml (12.5 ounces), equaling two glasses.

Half Pension *(Hospitality)*: A hotel rate for a meal regime that includes breakfast and one main meal, usually dinner. It is also called Modified American Plan (MAP) or *Demi-Pension*.

Half RT Fare *(Airlines)*: The half of a specified or constructed round trip normal or special fare.

Halo Effect *(Airlines)*: The extra business produced by a travel agency privileging the airline that owns the GDS system used by the agency. The agency displays in first place the patronizing airline's flights and tariffs. This practice is now rare, because the so-called "architectural bias" is not accepted.

HAM *(GDS)*: Three-letter IATA code for Hamburg, an important sea port in the north of Germany.

Hand Caddy *(Hospitality)*: A portable container for holding and transporting cleaning supplies usually located on the top shelf of the room attendant's cart.

Hand Controls *(Car Rental)*: Controls available in some rent cars for use by individuals with physical challenges. They must be requested at least 24 hours prior to pick-up, because hand controls require special set-up.

Hand Geometry *(Tourism)*: A biometric system used to identify persons by the shape of their hands. It is not the best identification method, because hand geometry is reliable when combined with other forms of identification, such as identification cards or personal identification numbers. Fingerprinting and Iris Recognition are the preferred technology for high-security processes.

Hand Luggage *(Airlines)*: Baggage that a passenger can carry into the seating cabin, instead of being checked in the cargo compartment of the plane. Its size, type, and weight are restricted to certain limits by the respective airline's regulations. Usually, its weight should not exceed 10 kg and its size (length, width and height) should be no more than 115 cm.

Handicraft *(Tourism)*: Articles fashioned by manual skill.

Handle Tow *(Tourism)*: See Rope Tow.

Handling *(Tourism)*: The set of coordinated and integrated services performed by a company on behalf of another company.

Handling Agents *(Airlines)*: Companies providing contract services to Airlines. They require an IATA numeric code to identify the transportation documents issued on behalf of the Airlines to whom they are contracted.

Hand-Measured Pouring *(Hospitality)*: The dispensing of alcoholic beverages by the use of measuring tools, such as shot glasses or jiggers. It is opposed to Free Pouring.

Hang Glider *(Aeronautics):* An un-powered flying apparatus for a single person, consisting of a rigid frame with a fabric aerofoil stretched over it from which a harnessed rider hangs while gliding down from a cliff or hill. Most modern hang gliders are made of aluminum; however vintage hang gliders are still built with a combination of wood, bamboo, and metal. Control of hang gliders is accomplished by shifting the pilot's mass fore and aft or left or right. Other hang gliders include modern aircraft flight control systems.

Hang Gliding *(Tourism)*: Also called Deltaplane, it is a recreational air sport, although it has also been used in commerce and for military applications. The operator launches him from a cliff or a steep incline and soars through the air by means of a hang glider. The *Fédération Aéronautique Internationale* governs this type of activity.

Hangar *(Airlines)*: An enclosed structure for housing aircraft.

Hansom Cab *(Tourism)*: A two-wheeled covered carriage drawn by a horse, which is used for sightseeing rides.

HAP *(Geography)*: *Heure Avancée du Pacifique.* See Pacific Daylight Time.

Happy Hour *(Hospitality)*: The time of a weekday during which bars, beer joints and other establishments sell alcoholic drinks at a reduced price to bring in customers.

HAR *(Geography)*: *Heure Avancée des Rocheuses.* See Mountain Daylight Time.

Harbor *(Cruise)*: A natural or man-made embayment of a large body of water where ships may shelter from the weather or are stored. Ships or boats dock rest at a harbor while they are loaded or unloaded. It is also written harbour or haven.

Harbor Master *(Cruise)*: The official who supervises the operations of a port.

Harbor Pilot *(Cruise)*: Port official responsible for guiding ships into and out of the harbor.

Hard Copy *(Tourism)*: A printed version of a document, such as an airline ticket or hotel voucher. It is opposed to an image copy (virtual data stored in a computer).

Hard-Dollar Savings *(Tourism)*: Tangible and identifiable savings on travel that is easily identifiable, such as free tickets, reduced rates, or revenue-sharing. It is opposed to savings that is realized from not spending. See also Soft-Dollar Savings.

HAST *(Geography)*: See Hawaii-Aleutian Standard Time.

HAT *(Geography)*: *Heure Avancée de Terre-Neuve.* See Newfoundland Daylight Time.

Hatch *(Tourism)*: A hinged door in an aircraft, spacecraft, or submarine.

Hatchback *(Car Rental)*: A car with a door across the full width at the back end that opens upwards to provide easy access for loading.

Hatchway *(Tourism)*: The opening covered by a hatch.

HAT (Heure Avancée de Terre-Neuve) *(Geography)*: See Newfoundland Daylight Time.

Haul *(Airlines)*: The distance over which passengers and load are transported.

Haulage *(Airlines)*: The charge assessed for transporting goods for short distances, such as within a commercial area or town. It is also called Drayage or Cartage.

Haute-saison *(Tourism)*: A French term for High Season.

HAV *(GDS)*: Three-letter IATA code for Havana, the capital city of Cuba.

Hawaii-Aleutian Daylight Time (HADT) *(Geography)*: HADT is 9 hours behind of Coordinated Universal Time (UTC). HADT is used during summer in this US state: Alaska - Aleutian Islands west of 169.30 West (east of 169.30 West use AKST/AKDT).

Hawaii-Aleutian Standard Time (HAST) *(Geography)*: HAST is 10 hours behind of Coordinated Universal Time (UTC). HAST is used during winter in this US state: Alaska - Aleutian Islands west of 169.30 West (east of 169.30 West use AKST/AKDT).

HAWB *(Airlines)*: See House Air Waybill.

Hawker Stand *(Tourism)*: A counter used in Singapore for outdoor or indoor service of cooked food.

Hawser *(Cruise)*: A large and heavy rope that is used for towing or tying up a ship to the dock.

HAY *(Geography)*: *Heure Avancée du Yukon*. See Alaska Daylight Time.

Hazardous Materials *(Airlines)*: Articles or substances which involve potential risk to human health, to general safety or to property and that usually require special attention when being transported by air. Some of them are: combustible liquids, compressed gases, corrosives, explosives, flammable materials, oxidizers, poisons, radioactive materials, and toxic materials.

Hazardous Materials *(Ecology)*: Materials that are capable of posing a significant risk to the health and the environment.

Hazardous Waste *(Ecology)*: Any waste (solid, liquid, or containerized gas) that can pose an immediate potential hazard to human life or the environment when improperly treated, stored or disposed of. Hazardous wastes can also contribute to an increase in mortality, or an increase in irreversible or incapacitating illness.

HCC *(GDS)*: Code meaning Hotel Clearing Corporation.

HCIMA *(Organizations)*: An acronym for Hotel & Catering International Management Association.

HCP *(GDS)*: Code meaning Handicapped.

HDD *(Hospitality)*: See Heating Degree-Day

HDD *(Computing)*: Hard Disk Drive.

HDL *(GDS)*: A code meaning Handle, Handling, Handled.

Head Count *(Airlines)*: The practice of counting passengers to compare the manifest with the actual number of passengers onboard a plane. It is also known as Nose Count.

Head Tax *(Tourism)*: A fee assessed by some places for each arriving or leaving passenger.

Head Waiter *(Cruise)*: The waiters' supervisor who monitors service and efficiency. The Head Waiter personally prepares or serves specialty items.

Heading *(Air Traffic)*: Direction on a compass that an aircraft is pointed, measured with respect to true north or magnetic north.

Heading Error *(Air Traffic)*: A basic output from guidance to flight director, indicating the difference between actual heading and desired heading.

Headland *(Geography)*: A narrow portion of land jutting into a sea or lake, usually with steep high cliffs. It is generally smaller than a cape.

Health Certificate *(Airlines)*: A document signed by a doctor assigned by an airline attesting a person in health risk is able to travel. It is also a veterinarian document attesting to the good health of an animal ready for air transportation.

Health Club *(Hospitality)*: See Fitness Center.

Health Information *(Tourism)*: Details on specific health risks and requirements in each country for visitor' safe travel.

Health Resort *(Tourism)*: A short term lodging facility with the primary purpose of guiding guests to develop healthy habits, including spa services, physical fitness activities, wellness education, healthful cuisine and special interest programming. Some Health Resorts offer programs which, in addition to the mentioned services, include facilitated fitness classes, healthy cuisine, educational classes and seminars. It is also known as Destination Spa or Resort Spa.

Health Tourism *(Tourism)*: A type of tourism that offers a salutary environment for health vacationing or fitness purposes, for enjoying alternative therapeutic treatments, or for visiting health spas. See also Medical Tourism.

Heat Loss *(Ecology)*: The transfer of heat from inside to outside by means of conduction, convection, or radiation through walls, windows, and other building surfaces.

Heating Degree-Day *(Hospitality)*: A measure of the heating needed indoors based upon outdoor temperatures. Heating Degree-Days are calculated by deducting daily mean temperature for that day from 18.3°C (65°F). It means 18.3°C - DMT = HDD.

Heavier than Air (HTA) *(Aeronautics)*: A series of flight vehicles that require air passing over an airfoil to generate aerodynamic lift, such as airplanes, gliders, helicopters and kites, either piloted or un-piloted.

Heavies *(Airlines)*: See Heavy Aircraft.

Heavy Aircraft *(Airlines)*: A type of aircraft capable of taking off weights of 300 thousand pounds or more.

Heavy Metals *(Ecology)*: Metallic elements that tend to accumulate in the food chain and can damage living organisms even at very low concentrations. Some of them are: antimony, arsenic, cadmium, chromium, lead and mercury.

HEDNA *(Organizations)*: An acronym for "Hotel Electronic Distribution Network Association."

High *(Climate)*: An atmospheric phenomenon of relatively high atmospheric pressure, resulting in clear weather. It is opposite to Low.

Helicopter *(Aeronautics)*: A wingless aircraft that gets its lift from revolving blades driven by an engine about a near-vertical axis which also moves it forthward, backward and allow it to fly.

Helicopter Association International (HAI) *(Organizations)*: A not-for-profit, professional trade association of more than 1400 member organizations in more than 68 countries. Since 1948, HAI provides its membership with services that directly benefit their operations and advances the civil helicopter industry by providing programs to enhance safety, encourage professionalism, and promote the unique contributions made by helicopters to society.

Heliotropism *(Tourism)*: In a literal sense, it means being attracted by the sun. In tourism the term is used to define the displacement of tourists to destinations where sun is the main attraction.

Heliport *(Tourism)*: An area of land, water, or structure used for the landing and takeoff of helicopters, including its buildings and facilities.

Heli-Skiing *(Tourism)*: An excursion by helicopter to skiing areas.

Helm *(Cruise)*: A device used for steering a ship.

Hemisphere *(Geography)*: One of the halves of the Earth when it is divided by the equator line into Northern and Southern parts or when it is divided by a meridian line into Eastern and Western parts.

Hennessy *(Hospitality)*: An old and famed very superior old pale cognac producer that merged with *Möet* and *Chandon*.

Herbalism *(Tourism)*: Therapeutic use of herbs and plant-based medicines in treatments and diets to prevent and cure illness.

Heritage *(Tourism)*: The whole of valued things such as historical buildings and sites that are considered to be of interest and value to present generations.

Heritage Culture *(Tourism)*: A process by which values and facts as well as rules and attitudes relating to knowledge and wisdom are transmitted from one generation to another inside the familiar frame and environment.

Heritage Tourism *(Tourism Industry)*: The travel that is motivated by a desire to experience the authentic natural, historic and cultural resources of a community or region.

Herringbone Setup *(Hospitality)*: A seating arrangement in which chairs are aligned in rows in a V shape and separated by a center aisle, so that they can easily face the head table or speaker. It is also known as Chevron Set-up.

Heterotroph *(Ecology)*: A term derived from Greek, meaning, "eater of others". It is an organism that eats other organisms to fuel its metabolism. Heterotrophs do not produce their food. Animals, including humans, are heterotrophs. It is opposite to an Autotroph organism that produces its own food.

Heure Avancée de l'Atlantique (HAA) *(Geography)*: See Atlantic Daylight Time.

Heure Avancée de l'Est (HAE) *(Geography)*: See Eastern Daylight Time.

Heure Avancée de Terre-Neuve (HAT) *(Geography)*: See Newfoundland Daylight Time.

Heure Avancée des Rocheuses (HAR) *(Geography)*: See Mountain Daylight Time.

Heure Avancée du Centre (HAC) *(Geography)*: See Central Daylight Time.

Heure Avancée du Pacifique (HAP) *(Geography)*: See Pacific Daylight Time.

Heure Avancée du Yukon (HAY) *(Geography)*: See Alaska Daylight Time.

Heure Normale de l'Atlantique (HNA) *(Geography)*: See Atlantic Standard Time.

Heure Normale de l'Est (HNE) *Geography)*: See Eastern Standard Time.

Heure Normale de Terre-Neuve (HNT) *(Geography)*: See Newfoundland Standard Time.

Heure Normale des Rocheuses (HNR) *(Geography)*: See Mountain Standard Time

Heure Normale du Centre (HNC) *(Geography)*: See Central Standard Time.

Heure Normale du Pacifique (HNP) *(Geography)*: See Pacific Standard Time.

Heure Normale du Yukon (HNY) *(Geography)*: See Alaska Standard Time.

HFML *(GDS)*: High Fiber Meal

HFTP *(Hospitality)*: See Hospitality Financial and Technology Professionals.

Hidden-City Ploy *(Airlines)*: A silly and unethical intent to cheat airlines when issuing a round trip ticket assuming that in certain cases a travel via a higher intermediate point could result in a lower fare. Systems automatically detect the higher rated point and reject such practice.

Hidden-City Ticketing *(Airlines)*: Same as Hidden-City Ploy.

High *(Climate)*: An atmospheric phenomenon of relatively high atmospheric pressure resulting in clear weather. See also Low.

High Occupancy Toll (HOT) *(Hospitality)*: A fee sometimes collected for booking during high occupancy periods.

High Occupancy Vehicle (HOV) *(Tourism)*: Any passenger vehicle carrying more than a specified number of passengers. An automobile carrying more than one or more than two people is included in this category that also comprises buses and vans. Automobiles classified as HOVs are also named carpools. Qualification for HOV status varies by locality, and may require more than two passengers.

High Occupation Vehicle Lane *(Tourism)*: A marked highway lane reserved for high occupancy vehicles, in order to move more people in fewer vehicles through congested areas. HOV lanes are conceived for people who share the ride in buses, van pools, or carpools. It is also known as Car Pool or Diamond Lanes.

High Season *(Airlines)*: The time period of the year when travel demand for certain destinations augments considerably, producing an increase on air fares and hotel and rental car rates. Summertime is high season for travel to Europe.

Higher Intermediate Point *(Airlines):* The intermediate point of a route that produces a higher fare from the point of origin than the fare between the point of origin and the fare break point or point of destination.

Highway Neighbors *(Tourism)*: Communities and businesses that are located along the road system.

Highways *(Tourism)*: Very wide roads that carry large volumes of traffic between communities.

Hijack or Highjacking *(Airlines)*: The action of seizing by force any vehicle when it is occupied and traveling. The most common types of highjacking are carjacking, skyjacking, and maritime piracy. Carjacking is the illegal appropriation of a motor vehicle while it is occupied and riding. The driver is forced by an armed carjacker to get out of the car. This is an extremely hazardous crime. Aircraft hijacking (also known as skyjacking or aircraft piracy) is the criminal action to take possession of an aircraft during a flight by an armed group or even a person. Skyjacking is not committed to robber the aircraft or its cargo, but for using the passengers as host as a way to oblige authorities to do something or to force the pilot to fly to a specific destination. Maritime piracy is a robbery perpetrated at sea and rarely on the shore. The purpose in maritime highjacking is the appropriation of goods. It is a criminal action that causes high losses especially in the waters between the Pacific and Indian Oceans. Hijacking is also committed in the Internet technology, typified as Domain hijacking, IP hijacking, Page hijacking, Reverse domain hijacking, Session hijacking, and Thread hijacking, for instance.

Hindenburg *(Airlines)*: Hindenburg LZ 129 was a German zeppelin, the largest rigid aircraft ever built. It was named after Paul von Hindenburg, President of Germany. It operated services during two years, and was destroyed and went into flames while landing at Lakehurst Naval Air Station in Manchester Township, New Jersey, U.S., on 6 May 1937, causing the death of 36 persons. It was the first transatlantic trip of the 1937 season.

Hinterland *(Geography)*: A region behind the coast.

HIP *(GDS)*: Code meaning Higher Intermediate Point Fare Check.

Hire Car *(Car Rental)*: A British term for Rented Car. Also known as Self-drive, U-drive, and You-drive.

History *(GDS)*: A detailed record of the actions and processes that have been done in a booking.

HK *(GDS)*: Code meaning Hold Confirmed.

HKG *(GDS)*: Three-letter IATA code for Hong Kong, tourist and commercial destination in Popular Republic in China.

HKTB *(Organizations)*: See Hong Kong Tourist Board.

HL *(GDS)*: Code meaning Hold List, Have Listed (on waiting list).

HLD *(GDS)*: A code meaning Hold, Holding, Held.

HN *(GDS)*: A code meaning Hold Needing, Have Requested.

HNA *(Geography)*: *Heure Normale de l'Atlantique.* See Atlantic Standard Time.

HNC *(Geography)*: *Heure Normale du Centre.* See Central Standard Time

HND *(GDS)*: Three-letter IATA code for Haneda International Airport, serving the city of Tokyo.

HNE *(Geography)*: *Heure Normale de l'Est.* See Eastern Standard Time.

HNML *(GDS)*: Code meaning "Hindu Meal."

HNP *(Geography)*: *Heure Normale du Pacifique.* See Pacific Standard Time.

HNR *(Geography)*: *Heure Normale des Rocheuses.* See Mountain Standard Time

HNT *(Geography)*: *Heure Normale de Terre-Neuve.* See Newfoundland Standard Time.

HNY *(Geography)*: *Heure Normale du Yukon.* See Alaska Standard Time.

Hobby Tourism *(Tourism)*: A tour package arranged for individuals or groups willing to participate in hobby interests, to meet others with similar interests, or to experience something pertinent to a specific avocation.

HOBIC *(Hospitality)*: See Hotel Billing Information Center.

Hold *(Air Traffic)*: To maintain some aspects of an aircraft's state, such as heading, airspeed, altitude, pitch.

Hold *(Tourism)*: 1. To keep a reservation; 2. The storage compartment of a ship.

Hold Time *(Hospitality)*: The time at which hotel rooms are released for sale if the reservation is not guaranteed. That hour usually is 4:00 or 6:00 pm.

Holding *(Tourism)*: A company that owns or controls other companies on basis of the majority of shares it has. The Holding is not a production concentration, but a capital concentration.

Holding Bay *(Air Traffic)*: Area of the airport where planes are held until they receive the permission to take off.

Holding Pattern *(Air Traffic)*: A sort of circular flight path at an assigned altitude, where aircraft turn around the airport while awaiting further instructions from the air traffic control.

Holding Pen *(Airlines)*: A jargon term for the area at an airport gate where passengers wait.

Holiday *(Tourism)*: Vacation or a day of exemption from labor; a day of amusement and gayety.

Holiday Camp *(Tourism)*: A British expression for a place where people can stay and are entertained on a holiday.

Holiday Travel *(Tourism)*: A trip of specified duration to enjoy a vacation time. Usually, transportation, lodging and food are all provided at an inclusive holiday package.

Hologram *(Computing)*: A three-dimension image generated by laser, which is mainly used to avoid counterfeiting of currency, credit cards and identification.

Hollow Square Setup *(Hospitality)*: A setup for meetings in which seating and tables are arranged in a square or rectangle with an open space in the center.

Home Exchange *(Tourism)*: A strategic method by which people in different cities or countries exchange their personal residences in order to reduce the accommodation costs of a vacation travel. Home Exchanging Travel is an opportunity for anyone with a home or second home to see the world for less. It is often the beginning of lasting friendships. Many exchangers are invited to special family events, such as weddings or anniversary parties.

Home Resort *(Hospitality)*: The resort location where a purchaser owns his/her week, as stated on the purchase agreement. The timeshare ownership is usually tied to the home resort where the owner generally enjoys priority reservation rights.

Homeopathy *(Tourism)*: Holistic healthcare system that treat diseases by using minute doses of natural substances. The treatment was developed by the German physician Dr Samuel Hahnermann (1755-1843).

Homepage *(Computing)*: The first screen set at a web site displaying the table of contents.

Homeport *(Cruise)*: A port of embarkation or debarkation within the country where the cruise line is based.

Homesickness *(Tourism)*: The attitude of longing for home or family experienced by some travelers.

Homestay *(Tourism)*: A lodging option to stay in a private home, which is frequently used when the purpose of travel is learning a foreign language or culture. Home staying is also offered in some countries during fair events of high demand.

Homogeneous Region *(Geography)*: A type of region where particular features are common to all parts of the region.

Hong Kong Tourism Board (HKTB) *(Organizations)*: A government body founded on 1 April 2001. The HKTB has no affiliation to any specific sector or organization within the industry and is able to support the interests of Hong Kong's tourism. The primary responsibilities of the HKTB are the marketing and promotion of Hong Kong as a destination worldwide. The HKTB's mission is to maximize the social and economic contribution of tourism for the community of Hong Kong, and to consolidate Hong Kong's position as a unique, world class and most desired destination.

Honor System *(Tourism)*: A self-service system in which customers help themselves, and then pay for what they bought or used.

Honorarium *(Tourism)*: A reward paid for professional services for which it is not usual to set a price

Horizon *(Airlines)*: The line at which the sky and earth appear to meet. In air navigation, it is the reference line with respect to aircraft body coordinates that help keep the plane horizontal.

Horizontal Stabilizer *(Airlines)*: Also known as a Tail plane, it is the horizontal airfoil of an aircraft's tail assembly that is fixed and to which the elevator is hinged. The horizontal stabilizer is designed to give stability.

Horizontal Tail *(Airlines)*: The horizontal stabilizer and elevator located in the tail assembly of an aircraft.

Hors d'oeuvres *(Hospitality)*: A French term for light meal or snacks served before the main course or at the beginning of the meal.

Horseshoe Setup *(Hospitality)*: A setup for meetings in which seating and tables are arranged in a U shape.

Hospitality *(Tourism)*: The term refers to the relationship between a guest and a host, and the process of performing it in a pleasant, generous, and courteous way. It also refers to the act or practice of being hospitable. The term implies the act of generously providing care and kindness to whomever is in need. The word "hospitality" comes from the Latin root meaning "host" or "hospice."

Hospitality Association of New Zealand (HANZ) *(Organizations)*: A voluntary trade organization of businesses and operators in the hospitality sector. The Association represents over 2,350 members and is committed to adding value to its members via individual membership service and by local and national advocacy. The membership includes: Cafes, Bars, Hotels, Motels, Restaurants, Taverns, Country Hotels, Motor Inns, Off-License premises, Wineries, Catering Businesses, and Serviced Apartment Complexes.

Hospitality Financial and Technology Professionals (HFTP) *(Hospitality)*: The international professional association that serves over 4,800 members working in hospitality. HFTP was founded in 1952. Since then it has been dedicated to providing first-class educational events, networking, certifications and essential resources for professional growth. HFTP is headquartered in Austin, Texas USA and has an office in Maastricht, The Netherlands.

Hospitality Industry *(Hospitality)*: An usual although inaccurate expression to refer to lodging and food service businesses that provide transitional accommodation services. The expression is of common usage in travel and tourism activities referring to the businesses involved in providing short-term accommodation, food and beverages, or entertainment. The activity comprises hotels, restaurants, casinos, catering, resorts, clubs and any other service position that deals with tourists.

Hospitality Room *(Hospitality)*: A room used for welcoming or entertainment of group members.

Hospitality Sales & Marketing Association International (HSMAI) *(Organizations)*: An individual membership organization founded in 1927 that was conceived as a resource for sales and marketing professionals by creating business opportunities and by providing value through educational programs, networking, customer events and research. With more than 8,000 executives recruited from different sectors of the hospitality, travel and tourism activities, such as hotels and resorts, tour operators, restaurants and catering, tourist attractions, cruise and ferry lines, cultural institutions, airlines, travel trade associations, railroad companies, educational institutions, travel agencies, and other suppliers to the industry.

Hospitality Suite *(Hospitality)*: A hotel room or suite, assigned by a company or group for greeting or for the entertainment of those attending a meeting, a conference or convention. It is the same as Hospitality Room.

Host *(Computing)*: The system to which an agent's terminal is connected to accomplish GDS operations.

Host *(Tourism)*: A person who provides information or greeting services. A representative of a tour operator or other supplier who provides escort services.

Hosted Tour *(Tourism)*: A tour in which the main feature is the service of a person, who is always available to carry out some tasks for group members.

Hostel *(Hospitality)*: A low-cost lodging that offers dormitory-style accommodations (dorm rooms of 4 to 8 beds shared by unrelated parties) usually with bathroom facilities shared and communal self-catering (cooking) facilities. It is a very popular type of accommodation among student travelers and backpackers. See Bunkhouse.

Hosteller *(Hospitality)*: The traveler who usually stays at hostels.

Hostelling *(Hospitality)*: The practice of staying at hostels, especially youth hostels, while traveling for pleasure.

Hostelry *(Hospitality)*: A term derived from old French word *hostelerie*. It is used referring to a hostel or an inn.

HOT *(Hospitality)*: See High Occupancy Toll.

Hot Air Ballooning *(Tourism)*: The activity of flying hot air balloons. A type of excursion in which people are carried aloft in a basket suspended from a large balloon filled with heated air. Ballooners enjoy an unequal bird's-eye view.

Hot Deals *(Tourism)*: Special and limited-time promotions offered to customers, such as Last-minute Specials.

Hot Lane *(Tourism)*: A lane on a highway reserved for a heavy volume of traffic.

Hot Line *(Tourism)*: A phone line assigned to provide fast customer service.

Hot Weekly Deals *(Cruise)*: The best offers a cruise can put on the market to attract travelers.

Hotel *(Airlines)*: Designator for the letter "H" in the International Phonetic Alphabet.

Hotel *(Hospitality)*: A large and multi-story building that provides short-term lodging and various personal services, such as meal, laundry, on a commercial basis. To be qualified as a hotel, an establishment must have a minimum of six bedrooms, at least three of which must have private bathroom facilities. It seems the word *hotel* is a transcription of the French word *hôtel*, which at its turn comes from the term *hôte* meaning *host*. It was meant to refer to a townhouse receiving frequent visitors. But the concept is almost as ancient as humankind, because people ever traveled for commerce, family, health, religious, or educational purposes. The first hotels were possibly nothing more than private homes opened to the travelling public. Records are registered on the existence of inns during the Roman Empire, which were located along the road system to serve merchants and first pleasure travelers. European monasteries operated as inns in some regions, during the medieval times. The growth of tourism in the 18th century contributed to the development of hotels. In the following centuries, they were the result of railways and the increasing presence of automobiles. The first notice of a hotel in the United States was recorded in 1607. Tremont was the first modern hotel opened in Boston in 1809. It was followed by the Buffalo Statler, a business hotel that opened in 1908. The Windsor Hotel in Montreal, Quebec, Canada, is considered to be the first grand hotel constructed in Canada by a railway company. It opened in 1878, and closed 1981. Other hotels were constructed and operated by the Canadian Pacific Railway, such as Hotel Vancouver, inaugurated on May 16, 1888, and Banff Springs Hotel that was officially opened on June 1, 1888. Hotels are ranked in classes, according to the services and amenities they offer, along with the location. A general segmentation includes Budget hotels, Business class hotels, and Luxury class hotels.

Hotel and Catering International Management Association (HCIMA) *(Organizations)*: The professional body for managers and potential managers in the hospitality industry. It is committed to bring together the common interests of both the public and private sectors in the provision of food and accommodation services. The HCIMA was created in 1971 as a result of the fusion of the UK Hotel and Catering Institute and the UK Institutional Management Association. The HCIMA has a world-wide membership of around 23,000 associates.

Hotel and Travel Index (HTI) *(Tourism)*: A print publication listing thousands of hotel properties worldwide, which travel agents use as a guide.

Hotel Billing Information Center (HOBIC) *(Hospitality)*: With a HOBIC system, long-distance calls dialed by guests are detected by a local operator who completes the call. The cost of the call is then registered and recorded via a HOBIC teleprinter to make the appropriate charges to the guest's folio.

Hotel Chain *(Hospitality)*: A group of affiliated hotels operating under the same brand and service standards. They are operated by a management company.

Hotel Classification *(Hospitality)*: There is not an official system to classify the hotels. However, the industry uses the term Star as a rating system since André Michelin introduced this pattern by the year 1920. This system uses a range of categories from one to five stars, according to the number and quality of the services provided, such as restaurants, pools, in-room TV, business centers, entertaining, gyms, communication facilities, etc. Nevertheless, there is no standard way of assigning these ratings, and compliance with customary requirements is voluntary. Many attempts have been made (such as those of the WTO and ISO) to persuade hotels to agree on some minimum requirements as world-wide norms so that to establish a system that becomes an internationally recognized and reliable standard. The problem is that many differences stand in the way hotels render the accommodation and food services, even in the same country. For example, a US hotel with a certain rating may provide a facilities level, and quality of service that look very different from a European or Asian hotel, and still, be rated in the same category. A short percentage of hotels in Europe choose to comply with the provisions of the rules established by the Hotels & Restaurants associations.

Notwithstanding, the following guide is noted as a general reference:

• One-Star category includes hotels with limited range of services and amenities, being obliged to apply a high standard of cleanliness.

• Hotels in the Two-Star category offer better accommodation of rooms with private bathroom and telephone.

• Three-Star hotels offer wider rooms with added decoration, furnishing, and TV. They also count with one or more bars or lounges.

• Four-Star category comprises hotels providing more comfortable rooms, excellent cuisine, room service, and other additional services.

• Hotels in the Five-Star classification are luxurious, have a wider range of services and amenities, including swimming pool and sport and exercise facilities.

By the other hand, The Official Hotel Guide, a catalogue published in the US, applies its own criterion and ranks hotels in the following nine categories:

• First: Moderate Tourist Class,
• Second: Tourist Class,
• Third: Superior Tourist Class,
• Fourth: Moderate First Class,
• Fifth: Limited Service First Class,
• Sixth: First Class,
• Seventh: Moderate Deluxe,
• Eighth: Deluxe, and

• Ninth: Superior Deluxe.

In another classification scheme, The Crown Macau casino and the St. Regis Shanghai Hotel both in China, claim for a six star rating, while the Burj Al Arab in Dubai currently characterizes itself as the world's only "7-Star Hotel".

Hôtel de Tourisme *(Hospitality)*: A French expression to define a type of hotel that offers accommodation for tourists or transiting passengers.

Hotel Electronic Distribution Network Association (HEDNA) *(Organizations)*: The HEDNA is a not-for-profit trade association structured to encourage hotel bookings through the use of Global Distribution Systems (GDSs), the Internet and other electronic means. Its objective is to increase hotel industry revenues and to be the best distribution tool. This will be done by: Optimizing the use of current technology, Influencing development of current and emerging electronic distribution channels, Training, and providing an opportunity for open exchange among members. The organization has presently over 200 of the most influential companies in the hotel distribution industry.

Hotel Guest Cycle *(Hospitality)*: The stage sequence that includes pre-sale events, point-of-sale activities, and post-sale transactions, in order to identify the physical contacts and financial exchanges that occur between guests and hotels.

Hotel Management Company *(Hospitality)*: A company that is hired by the company owner to manage its hotel.

Hotel Manager: *(Cruise)*: A person at cruise ships who is employed to supervise the hotel related operations, such as Food and Beverage, Entertainment, Housekeeping, etc.

Hotel/Motel Occupancy Tax *(Hospitality)*: A government tax assessed on hotel rooms and other lodging facilities.

Hotel Package *(Hospitality)*: A package offered by a hotel, depending on the services it usually provides, such as room and breakfast. Resort hotels offer packages consisting of ground transportation, room, meals, sports facilities and other components.

Hotel Register *(Hospitality)*: A book or other record located in a public place of the hotel to allow guests sign it.

Hotel Rep Firm *(Hospitality)*: An independent company that is engaged by a hotel or hotel chain to provide marketing support or group reservations support.

Hotel Representative *(Hospitality)*: A company or individual who acts as the booking channel between hotels and travels agencies, wholesalers, and the public. A hotel representative is paid on a fee basis or by commission. Some hotel reps offer also marketing and other services.

Hotel Voucher *(Hospitality)*: A pre-paid coupon that can be exchanged for lodging at some hotels.

Hotelier *(Hospitality)*: A person involved in the hotel business, such as owners and managers. A hotelier is also called "hotelkeeper."

Hôtellerie Indépendante *(Hospitality)*: A French expression defining hotels that are not depending on hotel chains. They are typically run by family groups.

Hotelling *(Tourism)*: A term referring to an office arrangement for staff that travel very frequently and do not have a permanent assigned office. They are unassigned seating employees who must reserve an office for the times they are not traveling. It is similar, but different to Hot Desking. Hotelling is reservation-based unassigned seating, while Hot Desking is unassigned seating without reservation.

Hotels, Restaurants and Cafés in Europe (HOTREC) *(Organizations)*: HOTREC represents hotels, restaurants and cafés in the European Union. Its mission is to defend the interests of the European hospitality sector before the European Institutions. It was founded in 1982 in Paris under the auspices of the then International Hotel Association, now IH&RA. It moved to Brussels in 1991 and comprises 36 national trade and employer associations and the hotel, restaurant and café industry of 22 countries in the EU.

HOTREC *(Organizations)*: An acronym for "Hotels, Restaurants and Cafés in Europe."

HOU *(GDS)*: Three-letter IATA code for Houston, Texas, USA.

Hourly Charges *(Car Rental)*: Vehicles are rented on a 24-hour basis. Hourly charges apply when a renter returns the vehicle after the expected time of return. If the hourly charge exceeds three hours, a full-day charge is applied.

House Air Waybill (HAWB) *(Airlines)*: A document issued by an international air Freight Forwarder or a Freight Consolidator under the terms of their own tariff.

House Boat or Houseboat *(Tourism)*: A recreational boat resembling a small house or apartment. Usually, a fluvial ship operated by local communities or artisan guilds with capacity for 4 to 10 passengers. In France this type of boats has varied denominations, such as *Coche d'eau, Croiseur Fluvial*, or *Housbo*t.

House Brand *(Hospitality)*: Any brand of liquor served when a guest does not request a specific brand, but a generic one. Usually, it is the retailer's custom brand which they only offer, and the least expensive brand.

House Committee *(Hospitality)*: A group of members that is responsible for monitoring the maintenance and operation of a private clubhouse and its services.

House Flag *(Cruise)*: The corporate flag or ensign, which identifies the company that owns the ship.

House Limit *(Hospitality)*: The credit limit predetermined by management officials for a guest. Casinos establish a house limit for the maximum wager permitted. A hotel's house limit is the maximum amount to which credit will be extended. In restaurants and bars, it is the maximum consumption of food or alcoholic beverages permitted for a single customer.

House Plan *(Hospitality)*: A plan of a property's floor with a diagram that describes function spaces.

Housekeeper *(Hospitality)*: A person employed to take care of the neatness of hotel rooms

Housekeeping Department *(Hospitality)*: The department of a hotel that is responsible for the clean maintenance of rooms and public spaces.

HOV *(Tourism)*: See High Occupancy Vehicle.

HOV Lane *(Tourism)*: See High Occupation Vehicle (HOV) Lane.

Hovercraft *(Tourism)*: An amphibious vehicle or craft capable of traveling on smooth land or water surfaces, by the use of an air cushion formed between the vehicle and the surface.

HPV *(Tourism)*: See Human Powered Vehicles.

HQ *(Air Traffic)*: Headquarters.

HRU *(Cruise)*: Hydrostatic release units.

HS *(GDS)*: A code meaning: 1. Have Sold, 2. Holding Sale.

HSMAI *(Organizations)*: An acronym for Hospitality Sales & Marketing Association International.

HTI *(Tourism)*: See Hotel and Travel Index

HTL *(GDS)*: Code meaning Hotel or Hotel Accommodation

Hub *(Airlines)*: In general terms, a center of activity, commerce or transportation around which events revolve. In air transport, the term identifies a city or an airport in which airlines concentrate their major operations. It is a selected location which receives traffic from many cities and from which traffic is fed to other destinations. Example: Air Canada has its hub in Toronto; Lufthansa has its hub in Frankfurt; American Airlines is hubbed in Dallas, and United Airlines is hubbed in Chicago.

Hub and Spoke *(Airlines)*: A system many airlines have adopted to have their planes in the air, maximizing the profits. It requires the use of a strategically located airport that is the hub, where passengers exchange their flights to and from other cities, called the spokes. The schedule plan for Hub and Spokes demands a very strategic and thorough study.

Hub and Spoke Tour *(Tourism)*: Tours that operate in the scheme of the hub and spoke concept. Tour members travel out of a central place and return to it each day.

Hull *(Cruise)*: The main frame or body of a ship.

Human Capital *(Ecology)*: Human attributes of people that are productive in some economic extent, such as health, strength, education, training, and skills, which are usable in the production, distribution, and sale processes.

Human Factors *(Air Traffic)*: The interaction between people and machines, or the interaction between people, which deals as a real-time element to any simulated operation.

Human Powered Vehicle *(Tourism)*: A type of vehicle for the transport of people or goods in which human muscle power is used. Although it is still used in underdeveloped or inaccessible regions, many forms of human-powered is used for reasons other than transportation, such as for leisure, physical exercise and environmentalism.

Humidity *(Climate)*: The amount of moisture in the environment.

Hunting Tourism *(Tourism)*: A form of leisure travel for the purpose of hunting animal. It is experienced in wild permitted areas or on tracts of land created specially for this objective.

Hurricane *(Climate)*: A weather phenomenon in which a large mass of air moves in spiral course at extremely high speed around a low-pressure area.

Hurricane Season *(Climate)*: The period in the year during which hurricanes occur, usually from June to October in the Caribbean and the Southeastern territory of the United States.

Hush Kit *(Aeronautics)*: A silencer equipment to make aircraft engines more quiet.

HW *(Air Traffic)*: Hardware.

HX *(GDS)*: Code meaning Have Cancelled.

Hydrofoil *(Tourism)*: A ship or boat designed for travels above the water. A special design lifts its hull lifts as speed increases, lessening friction and increasing speed.

Hydrographic Basin *(Geography)*: The space drained by a river course and its tributaries.

Hydrologic Cycle *(Ecology)*: The natural process in which water is collected from the earth's sources, distributed among living organisms and then returned to the environment.

Hydrosphere *(Geography)*: The total of the water on Earth in the form of liquid contained in oceans, lakes, rivers and underground sources. In frozen state, water forms polar ice caps, floating ice caps, and permafrost. Small amounts of water exist in the atmosphere as water vapor. The 71 percent of the Earth is covered by water and only 29 percent is emerged land. That is the feature why the Earth is called a "Blue Planet".

Hydrospeed *(Tourism)*: The European name given to Hydrospeed Riverboarding, which is a board sport activity where the participant is prone on the board with fins on his feet for propulsion and steering.

Hydrospeed Riverboarding *(Tourism)*: See Hydrospeed.

Hydrostatic Release Units *(Cruise)*: Life rafts that are automatically deployed by a device that releases the equipment carried on a ship or aircraft when the ship sinks or the aircraft ditches in the sea.

The mechanism is activated when ambient pressure changes due to the entry into the water and at a certain predetermined depth.

Hydrotherapy Bath *(Tourism)*: A bathtub filled with water jets that pummel and massage all parts of the body.

Hypersonic Flight *(Aeronautics)*: A flight operated at speeds faster than Mach 5, or five times the speed of sound, approximately 3,300 miles per hour. It exceeds a supersonic flight.

Hypoxia *(Airlines)*: An insufficient supply of oxygen in the bloodstream and bodily tissues that results in dizziness, unconsciousness and ultimately death.

I

I *(Airlines)*: "India," name used to designate the letter "I" in the International Phonetic Alphabet

I/S *(Cruise)*: Inside, as of a ship's cabin.

IACC *(Organizations)*: An acronym for International Association of Conference Centers.

IACVB *(Organizations)*: An acronym for International Association of Convention and Visitors Bureaus.

IAD *(GDS)*: Three-letter IATA code for Dulles International Airport serving the city of Washington D.C.

IAFE *(Organizations)*: An acronym for International Association of Fairs and Expositions.

IAH *(GDS)*: Three-letter IATA code for George Bush Intercontinental Airport serving the city of Houston.

IAMAT *(Organizations)*: An acronym for International Association for Medical Assistance to Travelers.

IARS *(Tourism)*: See Interactive Agent Reporting System.

IAS *(Air Traffic)*: Indicated Airspeed.

IAS *(GDS)*: Code meaning Insert a Segment.

IATA *(Organizations)*: An acronym for International Air Transport Association.

IATA Accredited Passenger Agency *(Airlines)*: A non-U.S. travel agency appointed by IATA to sell air transportation and issue Standard Traffic Documents on behalf of IATA Member Airlines.

IATA Accredited Travel Agency *(Airlines)*: See IATA Accredited

Passenger Agency.

IATA Cargo Agent *(Airlines)*: A forwarder or broker who has been approved by IATA to receive cargo, to issue airway bills and collect charges for air shipments on behalf of air carriers.

IATA Carrier *(Airlines)*: A carrier that is a member of the International Air Transport Association (IATA).

IATA e-freight *(Airlines)*: A project launched by IATA in 2004 designed to eliminate the need to produce paper documents for air cargo shipments by replacing them for a simpler, industry-wide, electronic, paper-free environment, named IATA e-freight.

IATA Member *(Airlines)*: Any carrier affiliated to IATA. There are two types of Members: Active Members which are airlines operating international regular services, and Associate Members that are airlines either operating international non-regular services or operating domestic regular services.

IATA Number *(Airlines)*: A numerical code of 8-digits that identifies travel agencies or other bodies involved in the sale of travel.

IATA Rate of Exchange (IROE) *(Airlines)*: The exchange rate set by IATA for fare construction purposes. The IROE is not a banker's rate of exchange, and is used to convert local currency fares to Neutral Unit of Construction (NUC) amounts or to convert total NUC amounts to the currency of the country of commencement of transportation. IROEs are published by IATA four times a year.

IATA Resolution 722g *(Airlines)*: The provision governing the issuance of Electronic Tickets for the Neutral documents. Under Sub paragraph 6.2.3.1 of Electronic Tickets it states: "An ET shall be comprised of the following:
• ET flight coupon(s);
• Paper audit coupon(s) or optionally electronic audit coupon(s);
• Paper agent coupon(s) or optionally electronic agent coupon(s);
• Paper Itinerary/Receipt or optionally electronic Itinerary/Receipt;
• Paper Charge form (optional)".
This means that an Itinerary/Receipt has to be provided. Such an itinerary/ receipt must also meet the requirements of subparagraph 6.2.3.8 in which the specifications are listed. It is not specified though if the receipt must be delivered in paper or electronic form.

If the GDS can secure the delivery in electronic form, i.e. via email, then there is no specific requirement to additionally print a paper copy of this. As long as there is a guaranteed delivery of the Itinerary/Receipt in an electronic form, then the paper form is not needed and could be deactivated. There may be legal issues in some countries that make it mandatory to provide a paper receipt.

IATA-ARC Accredited Travel Agency *(Airlines)*: A travel agency that has been qualified by both IATA and ARC and assigned an identifier number to sell air transport services to retail costumers on a commission basis.

IATA/UFTAA Authorized Training Centers *(Tourism)*: ATCs are organizations authorized to teach one or more of the IATA/UFTAA courses for travel and tourism corporations. Authorization is granted previous verification of instructional expertise in the courses of interest, as well as the institution's overall ability to provide quality training.

IATAN *(Organizations)*: See International Airlines Travel Agents Network.

IATAN Card *(Airlines)*: The only identification card for travel agents issued by IATAN.

IATAN Endorsed Agents *(Tourism)*: U.S. travel agencies (including its Territories and Possessions) accredited by IATAN to sell and issue international airline tickets on behalf of Member Airlines of IATAN's accreditation program.

IATAN Endorsed Location *(Tourism)*: A travel agency in the US that has been qualified by IATAN or other authorized body to sell air transportation services, or an accredited Travel Service Intermediary agency.

IATAN List *(Tourism)*: A list of employees and independent contractors who qualify for travel benefits that is submitted by a U.S travel agency to IATAN.

IATAN Registered Personnel *(Tourism)*: The employees and owners of a U.S. accredited travel agency who are registered in the IATAN List.

IB *(Airlines)*: Two-letter IATA code for Iberia, the airline of Spain.

IBE *(Airlines)*: See Internet Booking Engine.

Iberian Peninsula *(IATA Geography)*: The territory comprising

Spain including Balearic and Canary Islands, Portugal including Azores and Madeira, and Gibraltar.

IC *(Tourism)*: Code for: 1. Identification Cards; 2. Independent Contractor.

ICAO *(Organizations)*: An acronym for International Civil Aviation Organization.

ICAR *(GDS)*: Code meaning Intermediate-size car.

ICC *(Organizations)*: An acronym for International Chamber of Commerce.

ICCL *(Organizations)*: An acronym for International Council of Cruise Lines.

Ice Bin *(Hospitality)*: A container of ice to make drinks located in the underbar.

Ice Machine *(Hospitality)*: A machine that automatically makes cubed or crushed ice.

Ice Pallets *(Climate)*: Winter precipitation in the form of small bits or pellets of ice that rebound after striking the ground or any other hard surface. It is also known as Sleet.

Icebiking *(Tourism)*: A form of recreation and a sport using a bicycle over ice.

Icing *(Air Traffic)*: Any deposit of ice that forms on an aircraft. It can alter the aircraft's weight and flight characteristics.

ICOMOS *(Organizations)*: An acronym for International Council of Monuments and Sites.

ID *(GDS)*: Code for Identification.

Identification Cards (IC) *(Tourism)*: Also called an Identity Card, it is a document designed to verify data of a person's identity. It has the form of a small standard-sized card.

Identification Document *(Tourism)*: Any document containing personal data that serves to identify and individualize a person, such as a Passport, and ID card or a Driving Licence.

Identifier *(Computing)*: A character or group of characters used to individualize an item.

Identity Card *(Tourism)*: An official document which contains personal data associated to the bearer and a photograph that is used to attest reliably to his/her identity.

Identity of Product *(Tourism)*: The product's individuality set by means of its brand, label or mark.

IDL *(Tourism)*: Code meaning: 1. International Driving License; 2. International Date Line.

IDS *(Air Traffic)*: Infrared Detecting Set.

IFR *(Air Traffic)*: See Instrument Flight Rules.

IFTO *(Organizations)*: An acronym for International Federation of Tour Operators.

IFTTA *(Organizations)*: An acronym for International Forum of Travel and Tourism Advocates.

IH&RA *(Organizations)*: An acronym for International Hotel & Restaurant Association.

IFUN *(GDS)*: Code meaning If Unable.

IFWTO *(Organizations)*: An acronym for International Federation of Women's Travel Organizations.

Igloo *(Airlines)*: An air cargo container resembling an Eskimo house.

IGN *(GDS)*: Code meaning Ignore.

IHA *(Organizations)*: An acronym for International Hotel Association.

IIT *(GDS)*: Code meaning Individual Inclusive Tour.

ILO *(Organizations)*: An acronym for International Labor Organization.

ILS *(Air Traffic)*: See Instrument Landing System.

Illegal Connections *(Air Traffic)*: Flight connections that do not comply with the Minimum Connecting Time requirement.

Image *(Tourism)*: In a general sense, image is a visible representation of someone or something. When travelling, people capture certain images of the places they visit. Three types of tourist images are identified:

1. The Global Image, which is the general and subjective perception on the country, region or city;

2. The Cultural Image or the idea on the characteristics individualizing the form of being and way of living of people living in the destination; and,

3. The Experience Image, which supersedes the other two images, derived from the services received.

Imagineer *(Tourism)*: An employee at a theme park, who performs the duties of a designer or engineer.

IMC *(Air Traffic)*: See Instrumental Meteorological Conditions.

Immediate Family *(Tourism)*: The following group of specific relatives: Spouse, children, parents, brothers, sisters, grandparents, grandchildren, parents-in-law, brothers-in-law, sisters-in-law, and sons-in-law.

Immersion Heater *(Tourism)*: A small electrical device used for heating water to make coffee or tea while traveling.

Immigrant *(Tourism)*: A person who goes to a country where he/she was not born in order to settle there.

Immigrate *(Tourism)*: To enter a foreign country to establish a permanent residence there.

Immigration and Naturalization Service (USCIS) *(Organizations)*: A governmental organization that is responsible for the administration of immigration and naturalization functions. It establishes immigration services policies and priorities. Some of its duties include: Adjudication of immigrant visa petitions; adjudication of naturalization petitions; adjudication of asylum and refugee applications; adjudications performed at the service centers, and all other adjudications performed by the INS. USCIS comprises has Headquarters and approximately 250 field offices around the world.

Immunity *(Tourism)*: 1. An exemption from certain regulatory conditions granted to a person under some given conditions, as in diplomatic immunity. 2. A special capacity of resistance to a disease acquired.

IMO *(Organizations)*: An acronym for International Maritime Organization.

IMP *(GDS)*: Code for Important.

Impervious Rock *(Geography)*: A type of rock which water cannot soak through.

Import *(Tourism)*: A product brought into one's country from a foreign country.

Impromptu Travel *(Tourism)*: A travel without booking arrangements for the country of destination prior to travel. It is synonymous with FIT travel.

IMT *(GDS)*: A code meaning Immediate or immediately.

IN *(GDS)*: A code meaning: 1. International, 2. Infant, 3. Hotel Reservation Element to advise the check-in date.

In Bond or In-Bond *(Customs)*: Merchandise held as duty-free goods until they are sold or taken out of the country.

In-Bond Transportation *(Airlines)*: Transporting a transiting cargo shipment without clearing customs.

In-flight *(Airlines)*: A term used to indicate something is provided aboard a flight, as in-flight entertainment, in-flight duty-free shopping, or in-flight magazines.

In-house Sales *(Business)*: Sales that are made to the employees of a company. See also self-sales.

In-Out Dates *(Hospitality)*: Dates that define a hotel guest's permanence.

In Plant *(Tourism)*: A travel agency physically located inside the premises of a corporation it services. See also Corporate Agency.

In-Room Beverage Service System *(Hospitality)*: A computer-based system for the guest self service. It monitors sales transactions and determines inventory.

In-Room Check-Out *(Hospitality)*: A computer-based check-out system accessible by guests, by which they review their folio data and approve and settle their accounts in their rooms.

In-Room Guest Console *(Hospitality)*: A multi-feature device that gathers in one many functions as phone calls, a jack for portable computer use, an alarm clock, radio, remote control for heating, ventilating, and air conditioning, television, and room lights, energy management, and a theft alarm.

In-Room Messaging *(Hospitality)*: A computer-based system that allow hotel guests to receive electronic mail and faxes on their room televisions.

In-Room Movie System *(Hospitality)*: A system for guests' entertainment through an assigned television pay channel.

In Season *(Tourism)*: A term to denote a product or service is available only at certain times of the year.

In Transit *(Airlines)*: En route, in the process of traveling.

In-vehicle Travel Information Systems *(Rental Car)*: Any safety equipment such as cellular phone, global positioning system, digital mapping, and others offered by car rentals.

INAD *(GDS)*: Code for Inadmissible Passenger.

Inaugural *(Tourism)*: The first of a series of operations. However, since Inaugurals are primarily events for publicity, it's common to schedule two or more inaugural flights or two or more cruise inaugural sailings.

Inaugural Flight *(Airlines)*: The first official flight operated by an airline on a new route.

Inaugural Sailing: *(Cruise)*: The first official sailing of a ship with passengers.

Inbound *(Airlines)*: Arriving. The incoming portion of an airline itinerary.

Inbound *(Tourism)*: Term relating to travel services provided to passengers arriving to a location where the travel agent is based.

Inbound Operator *(Tourism)*: A person or company that provides inbound tourism services such as accommodation, transport, activities and attractions on behalf of offshore tour wholesalers or retail travel agents.

Inbound Tour *(Tourism)*: A group of travelers whose trip originates out of the destination, into the operator's country.

Inbound Tour Operator *(Tourism)*: See Inbound Operator and Receptive Operator.

Inbound Tourism *(Tourism)*: Vacation travel that originated elsewhere to the place where services are provided.

Inbound Travel *(Tourism)*: Arrivals of nationals or residents coming from other countries.

Incentive *(Tourism)*: A reward consisting of cash, travel, merchandise, or intangible offered to an employee or customer for achieving a goal or for performing a specified action.

Incentive Commission *(Tourism)*: An additional percentage of commission or an amount offered to a travel agency for achieving a specified volume of sales. See Override.

Incentive House *(Tourism)*: A company that operates incentive travel programs for other companies.

Incentive Tourism *(Tourism)*: A type of tourism arranged jointly by a travel agency and a corporation to stimulate the productivity or reward employees or sales force for achieving specific sales objectives.

Incentive Travel *(Tourism)*: A travel given as a reward for an employee's distinguished accomplishment or to encourage someone to achieve specific goals.

Incidental Charges *(Hospitality)*: Charges on a guest's bill for items other than room and tax, such as food, beverage, phone, laundry, movies, etc.

Incidentals *(Tourism)*: Miscellaneous charges incurred by the participants of a tour, not included in the tour price.

INCL *(GDS)*: A code meaning Include, Including, Included, Inclusive.

Inclement Weather *(Air Traffic)*: Rough, severe or stormy weather.

INCPLT *(GDS)*: Code meaning Incomplete.

Inclusive Rate *(Car Rental)*: A type of car rental rate where the insurance is provided by the rental company. It is opposed to Basic Rate.

Inclusive Tour *(Tourism)*: A pre-arranged tour for groups or individuals consisting of air travel and surface services, such as accommodations, transfers, sightseeing, possibly some meals, etc. offered for a flat price. An inclusive tour rate does not necessarily cover all costs, but only when it is particularly specified so.

Inclusive-Tour Charter (ITC) *(Tourism)*: A type of group excursion that uses a chartered aircraft for the air transportation and has tour services included in the price.

Inclusive Tour Fare *(Tourism)*: A fare specifically established for the use of inclusive tours which conforms certain minimum requirements.

Inclusive Tourism *(Tourism)*: See Inclusive Tour.

Incoming Tourism *(Tourism)*: The type of tourism based on the set of patrimonial elements, equipment, activities and services at a tourist destination offered to foreign visitors.

INCOR *(GDS)*: Code meaning Incorrect.

Incoterms *(Business)*: A codification of terms used in foreign trade contracts according to the International Chamber of Commerce.

IND *(GDS)*: A code meaning Indicate, Indication.

INDEF *(GDS)*: A code meaning Indefinite, Indefinitely.

Independent Contractor (IC) *(Tourism)*: An outside sales representative who performs services for a company on the basis of an agreed fee or percentage. Typical case is a travel agency's IC.

Independent Food Service Operation *(Hospitality)*: The operation performed by an owner of the property that has no chain relationship.

Independent Hotel *(Hospitality)*: A hotel with no chain or franchise affiliation.

Independent Tour *(Tourism)*: An unescorted tour for individuals. The traveler has the option to make his/her own arrangements or to purchase services from a menu offered by a travel agency, without having to get involved in a group.

Independent Travel *(Tourism)*: Trip where the traveler makes his/her own arrangements and design his/her own itineraries.

Independent Traveler *(Tourism)*: The tourist who does not travel with a group and has not purchased pre-arranged package tours. He/she organizes his own travel as it develops.

India *(Airlines)*: Designator for the letter "I" in the International Phonetic Alphabet.

Indian Ocean Islands *(IATA Geography)*: The territory comprising Comoros, Madagascar, Mauritius, Mayotte, Reunion, Seychelles.

Indian Subcontinent *(IATA Geography)*: See South Asian Subcontinent.

Indicated Airspeed *(Air Traffic)*: The aircraft's speed compared to the speed of the wind. It is calculated according to the altitude and density of the wind, and is not an actual speed in respect to the ground, but with respect to the surrounding air.

Indicator *(Geography)*: A number or ratio derived from a series of observed facts that permits to show the presence or state of a condition or trend, as when measuring the economic or social evolution of a place.

Indicator Species *(Ecology)*: Species of plants or animals that serve to predict the living conditions in a particular habitat or an ecosystem that is in risk to be degraded.

Indigenous *(Ecology)*: A term to qualify something originating in and naturally living, growing, or occurring in a region or country.

Indigenous People *(Ecology)*: Original inhabitants or people descendant from the original inhabitants of a geographic region who maintained some or all of their linguistic, cultural and organizational characteristics, prior to colonization.

Indirect Route *(Airlines)*: Any scheduled continuous air route other than a direct route, typically including deviations.

Indirect Route Principle *(Airlines)*: A general rule allowing passengers paying full fares on IATA airlines to deviate from the direct route without an extra payment provided the passenger does not exceed the maximum permitted mileage for the route listed in the tariff.

Indirect Spending *(Tourism)*: The money spent by tourists that is spent again within the local market.

Inductive Coupling *(Airlines)*: An RFID method of transmitting data between tags and readers.

Industry of Tourism *(Tourism)*: Tourism is commonly considered as an Industry. In fact, it is not an industry, because the term qualifies the manufacture of stackable goods, opposing to Tourism, which makes aggregates of non-stackable products. Industry uses raw materials that, by means of a process, are transformed into final products. Tourism does not process any raw material to obtain a finished good. Furthermore the Word Tourism Organization reminds that the use of the term "Industry" referring to the economic activities of tourism is incorrect. Alternative terms such as "activity", "sector" or "system" are suggested.

Industry Strategy Group (ISG) *(Organizations)*: It is an agency responsible for improving the ground safety of aviation in the United Kingdom.

Inertial Navigation System (INS) *(Air Traffic)*: A navigation aid that uses a computerized system and motion sensors to track the position, orientation, direction and speed of movement of an aircraft without the need for external references.

INF *(GDS)*: Code for Infant.

Infant *(Airlines)*: A person who has not reached his/her second birthday at the date of commencement of travel. The specification is useful to determine the fare applicable. Infants usually travel for free.

Infection *(Tourism)*: A disease caused by bacteria or viruses that reproduce inside the body after food ingestion.

Inflation *(Business)*: The tendency experienced by prices to go up.

INFO *(GDS)*: A code meaning Inform, Informing, Informed, Information.

Information technology (IT) *(Computing)*: The engineering technology that deals with the use of computers and telecommunications to store, retrieve and transmit information. It includes all matters concerned with the computer science and technology and with the design, development, and management of information systems and applications.

Infrared Oven *(Hospitality)*: An oven that uses infrared electromagnetic waves to cook food quickly at very high temperatures. It is also called a Quartz Oven.

Infrastructure *(Tourism)*: A general term describing the utilities, facilities and network of transportation services including roads, bridges, water lines, power lines, fire stations, and other sites and facilities that are necessary to the functioning of populated areas.

Inlet *(Geography)*: A small opening or passage that allows entering in enclosed place, a sort of small bay.

Immigration *(Tourism)*: Arrival of people to a country where they are not born.

Inn *(Hospitality)*: A small lodging establishments that provide lodging, food, and drink usually in an ambience of intimacy and charm.

Innkeeper *(Hospitality)*: The Inn's owner or its manager.

Innkeepers Lien *(Hospitality)*: Legal right of hotels to detain guests' property against unpaid bills, if certain circumstances are given.

INOP *(GDS)*: Code for Inoperative.

INP *(GDS)*: Code meaning If not Possible.

INS *(Organizations)*: An acronym for Immigration and Naturalization Service.

INS *(Air Traffic)*: See Inertial Navigation System.

Inside Cabin *(Cruise)*: A cabin not having sea-view windows or portholes.

Inside Passage *(Geography)*: The sheltered channels of British Columbia and southeastern Alaska protected from the Pacific Ocean by forested islands.

Instrument Approach Procedures *(Air Traffic)*: A series of predetermined actions using flight instruments beginning at the initial approach fix to a point from which a landing can be completed.

Instrument Flight *(Air Traffic)*: A flight performed solely by reference to the cockpit instruments during low visibility or bad weather.

Instrument Flight Rules (IFR) *(Air Traffic)*: A set of rules directing a flight under instrument meteorological conditions. Under IFR, an aircraft is required to be in permanent contact with air traffic control facilities.

Instrument Landing *(Air Traffic)*: The use of navigational equipment to direct and land an aircraft. It is typically used during inclement weather.

Instrument Landing System (ILS) *(Air Traffic)*: A method that provides radio-based course and vertical guidance to aircraft approaching a runway.

Instrument Weather Conditions *(Air Traffic)*: Weather conditions with reduced visibility and cloud ceilings that require a pilot to fly by reference to the cockpit instruments.

Instrumental Meteorological Conditions (IMC) *(Air Traffic)*: Meteorological conditions expressed in terms of visibility, distance from cloud, and ceiling, having less than minimums specified for visual meteorological conditions (VMC). It compels the pilot to make an instrumental flight.

Instrumentation *(Aeronautics)*: Hardware to measure and to monitor a system

Instruments *(Air Traffic)*: Tools used to observe, measure and control.

INT *(GDS)*: Code meaning International.

Integrated Services Digital Network (ISDN) *(Hospitality)*: A high-speed telephone line capable of sending large amounts of data quickly.

Interactive Agent Reporting System (IARS) *(Airlines)*: A secure ARC program that is used for submitting weekly sales reports by means of electronic channels. The IARS makes it easy to file and verify ticket sales reports electronically; complete sales reports from any computer that has an Internet connection and browser; print or download sales report transaction lists to spreadsheets or word processing documents; reconcile the agency's IARS transactions with its Back Office; report and reconcile ticket sales data from multiple offices, individually or centrally; get in-depth training, and support via instructor led online training classes or access training videos on ARC's Corporate Web site.

Interactive Conversation *(Computing)*: A system that allows the development of a participative conversation with immediate processing and response and which can involve additional queries and responses.

Intercontinental *(Airlines)*: An airline or network service extended to more than one continent.

Interface *(Computing)*: The program or device that connect two computer systems, two pieces of equipment, or two programs, and that controls the way they work together. By extension, it is also used to refer to the connection between any two systems or organizations. The term interface also describes a program displayed on the screen that interacts with the user.

Interference *(Airlines)*: In general, any occurrence that obstructs the free development of a process. In particular, any unexpected act or fact act that alters or disrupts any normal operation process such as deplaning or re-boarding an aircraft.

Interhome *(Tourism)*: System allowing the exchange of residences to lower the lodging costs. Homes are widely offered on advertisement media, such as a web site, including details, contacts and eventual requirements. Travelers can make direct approaches through dedicated organizations.

Interior Tourism *(Tourism)*: The type of tourism achieved by citizens of a country visiting attractions inside their own country. Foreign visitors staying at a country and traveling inside such country also perform interior tourism.

Interline *(Airlines)*: Mutual agreement between airlines to link their route network and cooperate on several aspects of air transportation business.

Interline Agreement *(Airlines)*: A voluntary and formal agreement between airlines that engage to handle passengers or cargo traveling on itineraries that require more than one carrier. Interline agreements state the rules governing such matters as fares, ticketing, baggage transfers, and so forth. One of the most important points in an interline agreement is, for instance, the Interline e-ticketing (IET) that enables passengers to travel to almost any destination on multiple airlines using just a single electronic ticket (ET). While travelling on multiple air carriers, passengers make arrangements with only one carrier, usually the ticketing airline, and pay only one price for the whole journey.

Interline Carriage *(Airlines)*: The carriage over the routes of two or more air carriers.

Interline Connection *(Airlines)*: A flight on one airline connecting to a flight on another airline.

Interline e-ticketing (IET) *(Airlines)*: An electronic ticket that is issued for air transportation on multi-segment itineraries that require the participation of more than one air carrier. In such a case, an IET agreement is needed between airlines to allow them to carry passengers on each other's flights. IET benefit passengers by allowing them to travel to almost any destination on a single electronic ticket. In case of irregularity, passengers and their baggage are efficiently managed until reaching their final destination.

Interline Transfer *(Airlines)*: Transfer from the service of one air carrier to the service of another air carrier.

Interline Transfer Point *(Airlines)*: The point at which the passenger transfers from the service of one carrier to the service of another carrier.

Interline Transportation *(Airlines)*: Transportation performed using the services of more than one air carrier.

Interlining *(Airlines)*: The action to carry business with the participation of several airlines. See also Interline Agreement.

Intermediate Class *(Airlines)*: A class of service with seating standards which may be superior to those provided on economy/tourist class but less liberal than standards provided in First Class. It is also called Business Class or Executive Class.

Intermediate Landing *(Airlines)*: An unexpected stop by an aircraft that becomes necessary for emergency or safety reasons usually.

Intermediate Stop *(Airlines)*: A scheduled landing of an airplane at an airport located between airports of departure and arrival. Usually passengers do not have to change planes.

Intermodal Transport *(Tourism)*: Transportation that involves multiple forms of transport, as in air and sea, cruise and rail.

Intermodal Tour *(Tourism)*: Tour that uses several forms of transportation to create a diversified and efficient tour package.

International Air Transport Association (IATA) *(Organizations)*: IATA is the international trade association representing the airline industry. It was founded in Havana, Cuba, in April 1945, to replace the original IATA (International Air Traffic Association) founded by six European air carriers in The Hague in 1919, as a regional organization. The 1945 founder members were 57 airlines from 31 countries, mostly from Europe and North America. Today IATA has 240 airlines from more than 130 countries worldwide representing the 94 percent of all international scheduled air traffic. IATA's main objective is to represent and serve the airline business as a prime vehicle for interline cooperation in promoting safe, reliable, secure and economical air service, for the benefit of the world's consumers. According to its own statement, "IATA seeks to improve understanding of the industry among decision makers and increase awareness of the benefits that aviation brings to national and global economies." IATA has introduced some programs to help airlines simplify the processes and increase passenger convenience while reducing costs and improving efficiency. One of these programs is named "Simplifying the Business", a series of five points (E-Ticket, Bar Coded Boarding Pass, RFID baggage, Common Use Self Service CUSS, and e-Cargo), by which airlines approach to the market in a way that is easy to access by the public.

International Airlines Travel Agents Network (IATAN) *(Organizations)*: A subsidiary body of the International Air Transport Association, responsible for accrediting U.S. travel agents for member airlines. It is also a non-profit organization committed to provide a vital link between the supplier community and the U.S. travel distribution network. Its mission consists of promoting professionalism, administering meaningful and impartial business standards, and to providing cost-effective products and services that benefit the travel industry.

International Association for Medical Assistance to Travelers (IAMAT) *(Organizations)*: A non-profit organization established in 1960 that is aimed to advising travelers about health risks, geographical distribution of diseases worldwide, immunization requirements for all countries, and to make competent medical care available to travelers by doctors who speak English besides their mother tongue.

International Association of Conference Centers (IACC) *(Organizations)*: A not-for-profit, facilities-based organization whose mission is to assist members in providing the most productive meeting facilities around the world, that represent the highest-quality venues available to meeting professionals on a global basis. It is focused on providing and promoting market awareness of conference centers. It collects and distributes information on the industry and its trends; provides an exchange of experiences among its members; addresses common problems, needs and opportunities; provides programs and services that assist members in operating more effectively; and responds to the needs and interests of conference center users as determined by the Board of Directors. IACC's Active members are conference centers that comply with the 30 strict standards of the Universal Criteria.

International Association of Convention and Visitors Bureaus (IACVB): *(Organizations)*: A worldwide association of convention and visitors bureaus, based in Washington, DC, that serves as an information exchange, and exerts its collective influence in matters that impact the national and international convention and visitor industries. The key goal of the Association is to position the visitor industry as an important economic generator in member communities.

International Association of Fairs and Expositions (IAFE) *(Organizations)*: A non-profit corporation that is in charge of the organization of state, provincial, regional, and county agricultural fairs, shows, exhibitions, and expositions. Its associate members include state and provincial associations of fairs, associations, corporations, and individuals that are interested in the improvement of fairs, shows, expositions, and similar fields. The IAFE was created in 1885 to manage a small number of fairs; today it represents more than 1,300 fairs around the world and more than 1,300 members from allied fields.

International Atomic Time (TAI) *(Geography)*: The acronym TAI comes from the French denomination *Temps Atomique International*. It describes a high-precision atomic time standard in which a second is defined in terms of atomic events that are known to a high degree of accuracy. It is the basis for Coordinated Universal Time (UTC) which is used for time tracking all over the Earth's surface.

International Carriage *(Airlines)*: The carriage in which, according with the contract of carriage, the place of departure and any place of landing are situated in different sovereign states.

International Carrier *(Airlines)*: An airline or other carrier operating transport services between countries.

International Chamber of Commerce (ICC) *(Organizations)*: ICC is the voice of world business that supports the cause of the global economy as a force for economic growth, job creation and prosperity. ICC activities cover a broad spectrum, from arbitration and dispute resolution to making the case for open trade and the market economy system, business self-regulation, fighting corruption or combating commercial crime. Its International Secretariat based in Paris feeds business views into intergovernmental organizations on issues that directly affect business operations.

International Civil Aviation Organization (ICAO) *(Organizations)*: A United Nations Specialized Agency and the global forum for civil aviation that establishes the principles and techniques of international air navigation and promotes the planning and development of international air transport in terms that ensure safe, orderly growth and sustainable development. To achieve its vision the ICAO works through cooperation amongst its member States and has established the following specific Strategic Objectives:

• Enhance global civil aviation safety and security;

• Minimize the adverse effect of global civil aviation on the environment;

- Enhance the efficiency of aviation operations;
- Maintain the continuity of aviation operations; and,
- Strengthen laws governing international civil aviation.

Created in the frame of the Chicago Convention in November 1944, ICAO has its headquarters in the Quartier International of Montreal, Canada.

International Convention for the Prevention of Pollution from Ships (Marpol) *(Cruise)*: The MARPOL Convention is the main international convention covering prevention of pollution of the marine environment by ships from operational or accidental causes. It is a combination of two treaties adopted in 1973 and 1978 respectively and updated by amendments through the years.

International Council of Cruise Lines (ICCL) *(Organizations)*: A non-profit trade association which represents the interests of 16 passenger cruise lines.

International Council of Monuments and Sites (ICOMOS) *(Organizations)*: An international non-governmental organization of professionals, dedicated to the conservation of the world's historic monuments and sites.

International Date Line (IDL) *(Geography)*: It is a meridian line at 180 degrees longitude running from the North pole to the South Pole in the Pacific Ocean, at which the date changes. By international agreement the date on the east side of the line is one calendar day earlier than on the west side. The actual IDL used is not a straight line; it zigzags around certain populated areas

International Driving License (IDL) *(Car Rental)*: A document required to enable travelers drive in foreign countries. In the U.S. and Canada, it is a reprinting of the local license. Rental car companies at some countries demand having an International Driving Licence, which can be obtained through AAA, CAA or the respective National Automobile Club.

International Federation of Freight Forwarders Associations (FIATA) *(Organizations)*: FIATA in French is named *Fédération Internationale des Associations de Transitaires et Assimilés* and is also known as the *Architects of Transport*. It is a non-governmental organization, representing today an industry that covers approximately 40,000 forwarding and logistics firms that employs around 10 million people in 150 countries. Founded in Vienna, Austria on May 31, 1926, FIATA it influences all over the world.

International Federation of Tour Operators (IFTO) *(Organizations)*: The IFTO is the international trade association representing the tour operator associations of most of the European countries and Turkey, founded in 1970 by a group of established tour operators in the UK and Scandinavia. Its objective is to ensure the long-term success of the organized holiday by influencing opinion formers, legislators and civil servants in the European Union. Its present members are ABTO of Belgium, Atlas Airtours of Croatia, RID of Denmark, AFTA of Finland, CETO of France, DRV of Germany, ANVR of Netherlands, RiN of Norway, ASTOI of Italy, Kompas of Slovenia, AMAVE of Spain, RIS of Sweden, TURSAB of Turkey, and FTO of United Kingdom.

International Federation of Women's Travel Organizations (IFWTO) *(Organizations)*: A worldwide network of professional women in the travel and tourism activities with 26 member clubs in 11 countries on four continents. The membership is made up of travel agents, tour operators, airlines, bus companies, cruise lines, tourism bureaus, hotels and media. The idea for the International Federation of Women's Travel Organizations was conceived by Blanche Berger of California in 1967. Its aim is focused in developing an international network of travel professionals and to enhance their personal and professional growth.

International Flight *(Airlines)*: A flight that arrives from or takes off to another country.

International Forum of Travel and Tourism Advocates (IFTTA) *(Organizatios)*: An international, independent organization created to facilitate professional exchanges in the field of legal issues related to tourism and travel. It was conceived in Jerusalem in November of 1983 at a conference on the legal aspects of Travel & Tourism. The event was hosted by Israel's Tourism Ministry, the Bar Association, and the Hebrew University. In 1985 IFTTA established in San Francisco, CA, a depository containing judicial decisions and articles pertaining to Travel and Tourism. That same year the organization started publishing the IFTTA JOURNAL. The main IFFTA's objectives are: To provide a Forum for the exchange of information on the legal aspects of Travel Law; to provide a worldwide resource of Travel Law information (statutes, case law, etc.); to encourage the establishment of common legal standards for the Travel Industry; to work with educational institutes in fostering research on the legal aspects of Travel; and, to sponsor Conferences on the legal aspect of Travel.

International Hotel Association (IHA) *(Organizations)*: A private organization that comprises the hotel associations operating in all the countries. Its main offices are located in Paris, France.

International Hotel & Restaurant Association (IH&RA) *(Organizations)*: The only global business organization representing the hospitality industry worldwide. Officially recognized by the United Nations, IH&RA comprises approximately 300 thousand hotels and 8 million restaurants, employs 60 million people and contributes with over USD 950 billion annually to the global economy.

International Institute for Peace through Tourism (IIPT) *(Organizations)*: A not-for-profit organization dedicated to promoting tourism initiatives which contribute to international understanding and cooperation. Through initiatives for improving quality of environment and preserving the heritage, IIPT pursues to bring about a peaceful and sustainable world. More than 20 international tourism organizations are founding members, including the European Travel Commission, Africa Travel Association, Caribbean Tourism Organization, International Association of Convention and Visitors Bureaus, Society of Incentive Travel Executives, International Federation of Women Travel Organization, Society for the Advancement of Travel for the Handicapped and others.

International Labor Organization (ILO) *(Organizations)*: An international organization focusing on labor issues and related social matters, bringing together governments, employees and trade unions. The main aspects of its mission are related with social policy, human and civil rights, injustice, hardship, privation, technical cooperation and research. The organization was created in 1919, at the end of the First World War and at present over 170 sovereign states throughout the world are members.

International Maritime Organization (IMO) *(Organizations)*: The IMO was established in 1948 as the United Nations agency concerned with international maritime activities. However the IMO did not enter into full force until 1958. It promotes cooperation among governments and the shipping industry to improve maritime safety and to prevent marine pollution. IMO has its main offices in London, United Kingdom, and perform its duties through five committees supported by technical sub-committees.

International Mileage System *(Airlines)*: A system used for calculating fares applicable to international air transport of passengers, based on the distance flown.

International Organization for Migration (IOM) *(Organizations)*: An agency devoted to fostering human and orderly migration for the benefit of migrants and society. It was established in 1951 to resettle European displaced persons. Its main goals consist of assisting to meet the growing operational challenges of migration management; advance understanding of migration issues; encourage social and economic development through migration, and uphold the human dignity and well-being of migrants. At this moment, 112 states are members.

International Organization for Standardization (ISO) *(Organizations)*: A worldwide federation of national standards bodies. ISO's mission is to promote the development of standardization and related activities in the world with a view to facilitating the international exchange of goods and services, and to developing cooperation in the spheres of intellectual, scientific, technological and economic activity. It was established in 1947 and has a membership of 130 countries.

International Organization of Employers (IOE) *(Organizations)*: An international organization that represents the interests of businesses in the labor and social policy fields. Its mission is the promotion and defense of the interests of employers in international tribunals, so that to create an environment favorable to enterprise development and job generation. The IOE's was founded in 1920 and its present membership consists of 142 national employer organizations from 137 countries from all over the world.

International Phonetic Alphabet *(Airlines)*: A system of words identifying the letters of the alphabet and numbers. See Phonetic Alphabet.

International Sector *(Airlines)*: A part of an air travel for which the departure and arrival points are situated in two different countries. When transoceanic travel is involved in a fare component, such transoceanic sector shall be considered the international sector.

International Society of Hospitality Consultants (ISHC) *(Organizations)*: ISHC is a professional society of consultants in the hospitality industry that was founded in recognition of the public need for competent, unbiased advice, professional guidance and sound judgment on hospitality industry issues. The ISHC's members are highly experienced, professional consultants offering expertise to hotels, restaurants, clubs, and travel related businesses in a wide range of disciplines. They are invited to join ISHC in virtue of their qualifications. At present there are 150 members with 20 percent of them residing outside the United States.

International Society of Travel and Tourism Educators (ISTTE) *(Organizations)*: An international organization of industry professionals in travel, tourism and related fields representing all levels of educational institutions, ranging from professional schools and high schools to four-year colleges and graduate-degree granting institutions. ISTTE is a nonprofit organization dedicated to improving the quality of education and research in the travel, tourism and hospitality industries by promoting the exchange of information, ideas, and outstanding service to its members.

International Tourism *(Tourism)*: Tourism activities performed by people who visit places located in countries out of their country of residence.

International Tourist *(Tourism)*: Any person entering a country other than his/hers for a stay of at least 24 hours and less than 12 months, regardless of the purpose, excepting for residence or work.

International Transportation *(Tourism)*: Any transportation provided by any carrier in which the point of departure and any other points of arrival are situated in the territory of different sovereign countries.

International Travel Bourse *(Tourism)*: Bourse is a French term for market. ITB is a trade fair held in Berlin every year. It is the largest travel trade and consumer show in Europe.

International Union of Railways (IUR) *(Organizations)*: The UIR (UIC from its French name *Union Internationale des Chemins de Fer*), is an international rail transport industry organization. The Union was born in October 1922 with the aim of standardizing industry practices, such as making sure that vehicles are safe, clean, efficient, and economical in fuel consumption. Other of its purposes are: helping to make roads safer and less congested, working for harmonization and simplification of procedures affecting road transport, and striving to lift the barriers to international transport and trade.

Internet *(Computing)*: A network that connects computers world-wide by means of different types of linkage, such as satellite, cable or telephone lines, allowing for the global dissemination of the information.

Internet Booking Engine *(Computing)*: A travel technology program for airlines and consolidators, supporting reservation systems for the global travel, packaging options to combine air plus hotel reservations in one transaction. It also allows online travel providers to meet the specific requirements of their market. The booking process is organized in such a way that travelers assume they are buying one single air and hotel product.

Interpretation *(Tourism)*: The process to educate tourists about the culture and history of the places they are visiting, by means of signs, markers, icons, etc., but also the ability to understand people through their individual beliefs, judgment or interest.

Interpreter *(Tourism)*: A person who serves as communication channel among people who speak different languages.

Interpreter Guide *(Tourism)*: A person capable to guide tourists, making them discover the values or meanings of places or monuments. Excellence in languages and cultural knowledge is required.

Interstate *(Tourism)*: A travel involving different states in a country.

INTL *(GDS)*: Code meaning International.

INTM *(GDS)*: Code meaning Intermediate.

Intoxication *(Hospitality)*: A disease resulting from ingestion of poisonous or toxin-contaminated food, as well as from the consumption of alcohol, with a blood concentration of .10 grams or higher of alcohol per 100 milliliters of blood.

INTR *(GDS)*: A code meaning Interrupt, Interrupting, Interrupted, Interruption.

Intraline *(Airlines)*: A flight on one airline connecting to a flight of the same airline.

Intraline Transportation *(Airlines)*: Carriage using the services of a single carrier.

Intranet *(Computing)*: An inter-connected private network within one organization for the internal sharing of information through the use of Web technologies

Intrastate *(Tourism)*: Travel or commerce confined to the limits of a state.

Intrepreneur *(Tourism)*: Same as entrepreneur: A person who starts a business venture and assumes the risk for it.

Inventory Risk *(Tourism)*: The potential exposure for financial loss a travel agency incurs when it blocks airline seats without having the passengers. It is the same as Risk Inventory.

Invoice *(Tourism)*: A commercial document detailing goods or services provided, which is issued to request payment.

INVOL *(Tourism)*: Abbreviation for Involuntary Denied Boarding.

Involuntary Denied Boarding *(Airlines)*: The action to force a passenger not to board a flight. The reason can be justified or not, but involuntary denied boarding will oblige the airline to pay the highest level of compensation.

IOE *(Organizations)*: An acronym for International Organization of Employers.

IOM *(Organizations)*: An acronym for International Organization for Migration.

Ionosphere *(Geography)*: A complex atmospheric zone of ionized gases that extends between 80 to 640 kilometers (50 and 400 miles) above the Earth's surface. It is located between the mesosphere and the exosphere and forms part of the thermosphere.

IOSA *(GDS)*: Code meaning IATA Operations Safety Audit.

IR *(Tourism)*: Code for Indian Reservation.

IRC *(GDS)*: Code meaning International Route Charge.

Iris Recognition *(Tourism)*: A biometric technique of authentication that uses pattern recognition techniques based on high-resolution images of the irises of an individual's eyes. Iris recognition uses camera technology and subtle IR illumination and is almost never interfered by glasses or contact lenses. The patterns of each human iris are unique, much like fingerprints. It is presently used at airports for security scanning.

Iris Scan *(Tourism)*: Same as Iris Recognition.

Irish Travel Agents Association (ITAA) *(Organizations)*: An organization created in November 1970, due to the merge of two previous organizations, namely the Alliance of Irish Travel Agents and the Irish Provincial Travel Agents. Today it comprises 370 retail travel agents and 22 Tour Operators nation wide.

Irish Whiskey *(Hospitality)*: A whiskey of Ireland made from barley (malted and unmalted) plus oats, wheat, and sometimes a small ratio of rye.

IROE *(GDS)*: See IATA Rate of Exchange.

Iron Compass *(Air Traffic)*: Railroad tracks used by pilots in ancient times as a dependable aid to surface navigation.

Iron Horse *(Tourism)*: A familiar denomination for railroad locomotives.

Ironer *(Hospitality)*: A machine with rollers for ironing linens.

IRREG *(GDS)*: Code meaning Irregular.

IS *(GDS)*: Code meaning If not holding, sell.

IS Category *(Cruise)*: Term used in Carnival Cruise Lines to book an Inside Guarantee Cabin.

ISB *(GDS)*: Three-letter IATA code for Islamabad, capital city of Pakistan.

ISC *(GDS)*: Code meaning Interline Service Charge.

ISDN *(Hospitality)*: See Integrated Services Digital Network.

ISG *(Organizations)*: An acronym for Industry Strategy Group.

ISHC *(Organizations)*: An acronym for International Society of Hospitality Consultants.

Island Hopping *(Tourism)*: A way of visiting many islands in quick succession onboard a cruise.

ISLVW *(GDS)*: Code meaning Island View.

ISO *(Organizations)*: An acronym for International Organization for Standardization.

Isobar *(Geography)*: A line drawn on a weather map to separate areas of different atmospheric pressures.

Isodemographic Map *(Geography)*: A map drawn to represent the size of a population.

Isopleth *(Geography)*: A line which joins areas of equal value.

Isotherm *(Geography)*: A type of isoline (line) which joins points of equal temperature.

ISP *(Computing)*: Internet Service Provider.

Issuing Airline *(Airlines)*: The airline that issues the ticket or airwaybill that will be used for the entire journey. See also Validating Carrier.

Issuing Carrier *(Airlines)*: See Issuing Airline.

IST *(GDS)*: Three-letter IATA code for Istanbul, important city in Turkey.

Isthmus *(Geography)*: A narrow strip of land connecting two larger landmasses, with water on each side.

ISTTE *(Organizations)*: An acronym for International Society of Travel and Tourism Educators.

IT *(Computing)*: See Information technology.

IT *(GDS)*: A code meaning 1. Inclusive Tour; 2. International Tour.

IT Fare *(Airlines)*: A fare that is applicable to an inclusive tour travel.

IT Number *(Tourism)*: Number given to a tour that has met the conditions required.

ITAA *(Organizations)*: An acronym for Irish Travel Agents Association.

ITB *(Tourism.)*: An acronym for International Travel Bourse.

ITC *(Tourism)*: See Inclusive Tour Charter.

Itinerary *(Airlines)*: A list of an airline's flights, showing times, stops, meals, in-flight entertainment, and other related information.

Itinerary *(Cruise)*: A ship's schedule detailing port stops, days at sea and activities.

Itinerary *(Tourism)*: A document showing the planning of a tour travel organized by a tour operator or tour agency with chronological details of the stops, activities and services included, such as hotels, meetings and social events of every stage of the journey.

Itinerary (Print) *(Airlines)*: A document that is part of the Electronic Ticket that contains the information and notices required in accordance with IATA Resolutions 722f and 722g.

ITM *(GDS)*: Three-letter IATA code for Itami International Airport, serving the city of Osaka.

ITO *(GDS)*: Code meaning: 1. Inbound Tour Operators; 2. Industry Training Organizations.

ITX *(GDS)*: Code meaning Inclusive Tour Excursion Fare.

IUR *(Organizations)*: An acronym for International Union of Railways.

IWGN *(GDS)*: Code meaning Intermediate-size Station Wagon.

IX *(GDS)*: Code meaning If holding, cancel.

J

J *(Airlines)*: "Juliet," name used to designate the letter "J" in the International Phonetic Alphabet

J *(GDS)*: Code meaning: 1. Business Class Premium; 2. Together with the fare code, it indicates shoulder season.

JAC *(GDS)*: Code for Jacuzzi.

Jack *(Cruise)*: A small flag flown from the bow to show the ship's nationality.

Jacobs Ladder *(Cruise)*: A rope ladder used to facilitate the boarding of crew or emergency staff. It is released from the deck of a ship while it is at sea.

Jacuzzi *(Hospitality)*: A whirlpool bath with a system of underwater jets that deliver water under pressure in order to massage and invigorate the body.

Jamaica Rum *(Hospitality)*: Full-bodied rum, with heavy rum flavor, pungent bouquet, and dark color.

JAN *(GDS)*: Code for January.

Jannus, Tony *(Aviation)*: Tony Jannus is a character of the early US aviation, the first to pilot a scheduled airline flight with a passenger from St. Petersburg to Tampa, Florida on March 22, 1914. The plane flew at an altitude of 15 feet across the Tampa

Bay in a Benoist biplane seaplane. This fact started him on a transport business carrying passengers always across the Tampa Bay. Although the planes he flew were owned or designed by other people, Jannus was always the center of attention. His personality, good looking, and talent as a speaker made him a popular figure. Tony Jannus died on October 12, 1916 at the age of 27 when the Curtiss H-7 he was testing for the Russia crashed into the Black Sea. His body was never found.

Japan, Korea Sub area *(IATA Geography)*: The territory comprising Japan, North Korea, South Korea.

Japan Association of Travel Agents (JATA) *(Organizations)*: An association approved by the Minister of Land, Infrastructure and Transport according to the Travel Agency Law. The Japan Association of Travel Agents (JATA) has its headquarters in Tokyo and seeks to improve the quality of services provided to travelers to and from Japan. It contributes to the development of travel and tourism activities through a variety of tasks including disseminating information, encouraging cooperation among members, and promoting the development of businesses and legislation that will benefit the membership and the industry at large.

Jargon *(Tourism)*: A special and simplified language that develops as a means of communication among a particular group or among the members of the same profession.

JATA *(Organizations)*: An acronym for Japan Association of Travel Agents.

JATO *(Air Traffic)*: Abbreviation for Jet-assisted takeoff.

Jaunting Car *(Tourism)*: See Carrig.

Jet Engine *(Aeronautics)*: An engine that works by creating a high-velocity jet of air to propel the engine forward.

Jet Lag or Jetlag *(Airlines)*: A temporary physiological alteration following a long journey across several time zones. It is characterized by irritability, fatigue, lethargy, insomnia, and bad concentration, all of them symptoms of the difficulty for adjusting to the time zone of the destination.

Jet Loader *(Airlines)*: A bridge between the terminal building and an aircraft to facilitate the direct and protected boarding of passengers.

Jet Propulsion System *(Aeronautics)*: A method of propelling aircraft that uses the reaction force created when compressed outside air and hot exhaust gases are forced through a jet nozzle.

Jet Port *(Airlines)*: An uncommon synonym for airport.

Jet Ski *(Tourism)*: A trademark for a model of Personal Watercraft.

Jet Stream *(Air Traffic)*: 1. Relatively strong wind currents that are concentrated in a narrow band in the atmosphere, usually found between 6 and 10 miles above the surface. They are usually thousands of kilometers long, hundreds of kilometers wide but only a few kilometers thick, and can aid or hinder a jet flight depending on its direction. 2. The trail of condensation left by a jet flying at high altitude can cause also a Jet Stream.

Jet Way *(Airlines)*: See Jet Loader.

Jetbridge *(Airlines)*: See Jet Loader.

Jetliners *(Airlines)*: Commercial jet aircraft for carrying passengers and/or cargo.

Jetty *(Cruise)*: A wooden or stone pier built to influence the current or to protect the port, often used for the docking of boats and ships.

JFK *(GDS)*: Three-letter IATA code for John F. Kennedy serving the city of New York.

Jigger *(Hospitality)*: A stainless steel device of double-ended cups used for measuring liquids. Each end cup holds a different measure.

Jitney *(Tourism)*: A mode of public transportation comprising passenger cars or vans that operate on fixed routes, according to a flexible schedule. There is currently one jitney service in Laguna Beach, CA. In Puerto Rico operates a mode similar to jitney called a *público*.

JKT *(GDS)*: Three-letter IATA code for Jakarta, capital city of Indonesia.

JL *(Airlines)*: Two-letter IATA code for Japan Airlines.

JNB *(GDS)*: Three-letter IATA code for Johannesburg, important city in South Africa.

Joint Declaration *(Customs)*: A single declaration for the same family members returning to their country of residence.

Joint Charge *(Airlines)*: A charge applied for carriage over the routes of the participating carriers, published as a single amount.

Joint Fare (JT) *(Airlines)*: The fare applied to a travel that is operated by more than one airline and is published as a single amount. The fare is negotiated and then agreed upon by the airlines involved.

Joint Notice of Change *(Airlines)*: A notification form containing information about an agency's legal and financial status that is in process of an ownership change. The notice is submitted to IATA for its records.

Joint Operational Flight *(Airlines)*: A flight on more than one airline operating one or more legs.

Joint Venture *(Tourism)*: A form of strategic business partnership between companies that are sometimes based in different countries, which involves shared ownership, joint management and shared risks and profits. This sort of alliance may strengthen existing businesses through shared expertise, capital, and removal of competition and creation of economies of scale.

JOJ *(Tourism)*: Code meaning Just off the Jet, an expression with similar significance as Fresh off The Boat.

Journée *(Tourism)*: A French term denoting a time period of 24 hours or less (half a day) used for estimating the duration of a trip.

Journey *(Tourism)*: The entirety of travel from point of origin to point of destination, as shown on the ticket.

JRSTE *(GDS)*: Code meaning Junior Suite.

JT *(GDS)*: A code meaning Joint, Joint Fare.

JUL *(GDS)*: Code for July.

Juliet *(Airlines)*: Designator for the letter "J" in the International Phonetic Alphabet.

Jumbo Jet *(Aeronautics)*: Any large, wide-body aircraft propelled by jet engines.

Jumpseat *(Airlines)*: The small fold-down seat on a commercial aircraft that is used by flight attendants. It is also found as one behind the front seat of a limousine, taxi, etc.

JUN *(GDS)*: Code for June.

Jungle Tourism *(Tourism)*: A type of tours performed in the scenery of a sub-tropical forest consisting of trees and scrub which may form an almost impenetrable barrier for tourists. Jungle tours have become a major component of green tourism in tropical destinations.

Junior Suite *(Hospitality)*: A hotel room that includes the bedroom and a separate living area.

Junket *(Tourism)*: A trip of pleasure features taken for business purposes, as when a authorities of a foreign destination invite travel journalists to visit. Or any other legitimate sponsored trip in which the sponsors pay for the travelers' expenses.

Just-In-Time Delivery *(Airlines)*: An operation permitting goods or parts being ordered and received just before the buyer needs to use them.

Junction *(Airlines)*: A place where two or more pathways or routes meet.

K

K *(Airlines)*: "Kilo," name used to designate the letter "K" in the International Phonetic Alphabet.

K *(GDS)*: Code meaning: 1. Economy Coach Discounted; 2. Together with a fare code, it indicates shoulder season; 3. Shown in the weight allowance case of the ticket, it denotes the permitted baggage allowance; 4. Kilobyte, a measure of a computer memory size.

Kapok *(Hospitality)*: Fiber of natural plant used to cram solid mattresses.

Kasbah *(Tourism)*: In North Africa, the older (or native) part of a city or town, often the market area.

Kayak *(Tourism)*: An Eskimo-type boat with a small opening, and propelled by a double bladed paddle for one or two persons. Although it is often used for shooting river rapids, there are also seagoing models.

Kayaking *(Tourism)*: The sport activity which is experienced by utilizing kayaks according to the rules of the corresponding Federation.

KCAL *(Hospitality)*: See Kilocalorie.

KE *(Airlines)*: Two-letter IATA code for Korean Airlines, an airline of South Korea.

Keel *(Cruise)*:   The centerline of a ship's body running from fore to aft.

Key Accounts *(Hospitality)*: Top accounts for which a preferential pricing or attention treatment is applied.

Key Accounts Policy *(Hospitality)*: A corporate stratagem to reward top accounts with preferential pricing.

Key Deposit Receipt *(Hospitality)*: A document sometimes used at certain hotels as evidence that a guest has returned the room key.

Key Informant Survey *(Tourism)*: The accurate information gathered by interviewing people who are likely to have some insight into a problem, such as managers, sales staff, suppliers, and consultants.

KG *(GDS)*: Code meaning Kilogram.

KHI *(GDS)*: Three-letter IATA code for Karachi, important city in Pakistan.

Kilo *(Airlines)*: Designator for the letter "K" in the International Phonetic Alphabet.

Kilo *(Hospitality)*: Short term for Kilogram.

Kilobyte *(Computing)*: A measure of a computer's storage capacity. One kilobyte equals approximately one thousand bytes (exactly 1,024 bytes) or typewritten characters.

Kilocalorie (KCAL) *(Hospitality)*: A unit of a value for producing energy from food when eaten and digested. It equals one thousand calories.

Kilogram (KG) *(Hospitality)*: A unit of weight measure equivalent to one thousand grams, approximately 2.2 pounds.

Kilometer *(Tourism)*: A metric measure of distance, used as standard in most countries, excluding the U.S. Speed, for instance, is measured by kilometers per hour (kph). It is approximately five-eighths of a mile.

Kinesiology *(Tourism)*: A therapeutic technique that uses fingertip pressure to locate weakness in specific muscles and diagnose a problem or a symptomatic illness.

King Bed *(Hospitality)*: A large bed of approximately 78 inches by 80 inches.

King Room *(Hospitality)*: A hotel room with a king-size bed.

Kiosk *(Airlines)*: 1. A workstation designed to provide travel-related services such as the Common Use Self Service (CUSS) kiosks where passengers can issue their boarding passes at an airport. Guest can also checking in or out of a hotel at a kiosk. 2. A small vendor's stall or a public booth to obtain personal or interactive TV information.

KIP *(GDS)*: Code meaning Keep alone if possible.

Kirschwasser or Kirsch *(Hospitality)*: A fruit brandy distilled from cherries.

Kit *(Tourism)*: A set of things, such as a Sales Kit or a Tool Kit.

Kitchenette *(Hospitality)*: Small kitchen that is part of a suite or of an apartment hotel room.

KIX *(GDS)*: Three-letter IATA code for Kansai International Airport, serving the city of Osaka

KK *(GDS)*: A code meaning Confirm, Confirming, Confirmed.

KL *(Airlines)*: Two-letter IATA code for KLM, the airline of the Netherlands.

KL *(GDS)*: Code meaning Confirmed from waiting list.

KM *(GDS)*: Code meaning Kilometer.

Knot *(Cruise)*: A unit of speed representing one nautical mile per hour, or 1.15 land miles per hour. A nautical mile is 6,080.2 feet per hour or 1.85 kilometers per hour. A ship traveling at 15 knots is traveling at about 22 mph or 27.75 kph.

Kosher *(Airlines)*: Special meal for Jewish travelers that is provided by some airlines onboard.

KP *(GDS)*: Code meaning Commission Percentage.

KPH *(Tourism)*: Kilometers-per-Hour. Land speed measurement in most other countries. 50 miles-per-hour equals approximately 83 kilometers-per-hour.

Kroc, Ray (1902-1984) *(Hospitality)*: Founder of McDonald's, whose vision made emphasis on quality, service, cleanliness, and value.

KRT *(GDS)*: Three-letter IATA code for Khartoum, capital city of Sudan.

KSML *(GDS)*: Code meaning Kosher Meal.

KTM *(GDS)*: Three-letter IATA code for Kathmandu, capital city of Nepal.

KUL *(GDS)*: Three-letter IATA code for Kuala Lumpur, capital city of Malaysia.

Kyoto Convention *(Customs)*: An international convention on the simplification and harmonization of customs procedures, which was signed on 18 May 1973, with added Amending Supplements No. 13 of January 1993 and October 1975.

Kyoto Protocol *(Ecology)*: The Kyoto Protocol is named after the city where a treaty was signed by negotiators in December 11, 1997. It is an agreement intended to carry into effect the objectives and principles agreed in the United Nations Convention on Climate Change of 1992. The main purpose of the Protocol aims to stabilizing the atmosphere by compromising the governments to quantified limits on their greenhouse gas emissions, through sequential rounds of negotiations for successive "commitment periods". The first-period, running from 2008 to 2012, require that industrialized nations reduce the emissions of the six main anthropogenic greenhouse gases (carbon dioxide, methane, nitrous oxide, perfluorocarbons, hydrofluorocarbons, and sulfur hexafluoride) by a certain percentage on 1990 levels until the end of the first commitment period in 2012. The initial discussion of the Protocol included broad global participation and signatories, but later it has been more politically charged and has fewer participating parties. As of June 2007, 175 nations were parties to the Kyoto Protocol, representing approximately 60 percent of the global emissions. Although the US is the largest greenhouse gas emitter, it is not a party to the Kyoto Protocol. The President William J. Clinton signed the Treaty, but it was never submitted to the Senate for ratification. Finally, George W. Bush repudiated the Protocol. Australia has also refused to ratify but assures to be committed to fulfill its emissions target and to participate in negotiations on subsequent commitments. Kyoto Protocol entered into force on 16 February 2005, with about 130 countries having ratified it. As of May 2008, 182 parties have ratified the protocol, 36 of which are developed countries that are required to reduce greenhouse gas emissions.

L

L *(Airlines)*: "Lima," name used to designate the letter "L" in the International Phonetic Alphabet

L *(GDS)*: Code meaning: 1. Economy Coach Discounted; 2. Together with a fare code, it means low season.

L. & D. *(GDS)*: Code meaning Loss and Damage.

LA *(Airlines)*: Two-letter IATA code for Lan Chile.

La Niña *(Climate)*: A phenomenon characterized by unusually cold ocean temperatures in the central and eastern tropical Pacific Ocean that impacts global weather patterns. La Niña conditions come and go every few years and can persist for as long as two years. As compared to El Niño, which is characterized by unusually warm ocean temperatures in the Equatorial Pacific, La Niña brings nearly opposite effects. The impacts of El Niño and La Niña are most clearly seen in wintertime. El Niño and La Niña result from interaction between the surface of the ocean and the atmosphere in the tropical Pacific.

LAADR *(Air Traffic)*: Low Altitude Arrival/Departure Routing.

Label *(Hospitality)*: A slip or display of written, printed, or graphic reference that is attached to the immediate container of any substance (as a bottle), or in the case of an article to indentify the brand.

Labor Tourist *(Tourism)*: A person who lives in one country but works in another.

Lady of the Evening *(Tourism)*: A euphemistic term to name a prostitute.

Lager *(Hospitality)*: A light colored bottom-fermented beer. It is usually dry.

Lagering *(Hospitality)*: A German term derived from *Lagerbier* that means "beer to be stored" and denotes the process of bottom fermentation during which the yeast works slowly at the required low temperatures, after which the brew is stored at cold temperatures.

Lagoon *(Geography)*: A small body of water connected to the open sea by coral reefs or sand bars.

LAHSO *(Air Traffic)*: See Land and Hold Short Operations.

Lake *(Geography)*: An inland body of standing water completely surrounded by land; usually but not necessarily fresh water.

LAN *(Computing)*: Local Area Network

Lanai *(Hospitality)*: A guestroom with a balcony or patio, overlooking water or a garden. In Hawaii the term denotes a porch or patio.

Land and Hold Short Operations (LAHSO) *(Air Traffic)*: Operations that control simultaneous takeoffs and landings and/or simultaneous landings when a landing aircraft is able to hold short of the intersecting runway or taxiway or at a designated hold-short point as instructed by the controller.

Land Arrangements *(Tourism)*: The set of travel services provided to a tourist upon his/her arrival at the destination, such as transfers, accommodation, car, sightseeing, and other.

Land Breeze *(Geography)*: A coastal breeze blowing from land to the sea, usually at night when the sea surface is warmer than the adjacent land.

Land Cruise Package *(Cruise)*: A vacation package that combines a cruise and hotel accommodation.

Land Only *(Tourism)*: A price including the whole of ground services, like accommodations, transfers, sightseeing, park tickets, rental care, etc. but excluding air transportation.

Land Operator *(Tourism)*: A company or individual that provides such services as hotel accommodations, sightseeing, transfers and other related services, exclusive of air transportation.

Land-use Map *(Geography)*: A type of color-coded map which shows the use distribution of land.

Land-use Planning *(Ecology)*: A physical and socio-economic process to determine the best use of land in an area with the corresponding effects on different segments of the population.

Landau *(Tourism)*: A fancy and covered carriage with four wheels that is drawn by a horse.

Landfall *(Tourism)*: The land first sighted when making a cruise.

Landing *(Air Traffic)*: To carry out the process of bringing a flight vehicle down to the earth or another surface.

Landing Card *(Tourism)*: A document which must be filled out by passengers prior to arrival. It is then handed to the immigration or customs officers.

Landing Fee *(Airlines)*: A tax that the airlines pay for the right to land an aircraft at an airport.

Landing Gear *(Aeronautics)*: Another word for Undercarriage. It includes wheels, skis, and floats that enable a flight vehicle to land and move about on land, water or other surfaces.

Landing Roll *(Aeronautics)*: The distance from the point of touchdown to the point where the aircraft is brought to a stop or exit the runway.

Landing Sequence *(Air Traffic)*: The order in which aircraft are positioned for landing.

Landing Strip *(Airlines)*: The long, paved strip at an airport from where aircraft takeoff and on where they land.

Landlocked *(Geography)*: A territory that has no access to the sea.

Landlubber *(Cruise)*: A person who knows very little of ships and sailing.

Landmark *(Air Traffic)*: Any object on land such as a building, a monument or a prominent geographical place which is easily seen and recognizable by the pilot during a flight.

Landside *(Tourism)*: The area lying before passport control and security checks with free access.

LANG *(GDS)*: Code meaning Specify Language Spoken.

Larboard *(Cruise)*: An archaic term for Port.

Large Cabin *(Airlines)*: A term to denote an executive or corporate jet, categorized according to a combination of passenger capacity, range, and maximum speed. Usually, a large cabin jet holds between ten to eighteen passengers, has a range of over 5,000 square miles and a maximum speed over 500 miles per hour.

Large Ship *(Cruise)*: A ship of a gross registered tonnage between 65,000 and 100,000 tons. Some examples of this type of ships are Carnival Legend, Celebrity Constellation, Crystal Serenity, Disney Magic, and Coral Princess.

LAS *(GDS)*: Three-letter IATA code for Las Vegas, Nevada, USA.

Laser Obstacle Avoidance (OA) *(Air Traffic)*: A sensor that provides warnings for long, thin objects (like wires).

Last Carrier *(Airlines)*: The participating airline operating the last section of the transportation.

Last-Room Availability *(GDS)*: A feature of an electronic reservation system that provides users with up-to-the minute information about a hotel's available inventory.

Last-Seat Availability *(GDS)*: A feature of an electronic reservation system that provides travel agents with up-to-the minute information about the last remaining seats in a particular flight, either at a certain fare or actually the last remaining seat on an aircraft.

Late Arrival *(Hospitality)*: A notice given by a guest who holds a hotel room reservation that he/she plans to arrive after the designated cancellation time established by the property.

Late Booking Fee *(Tourism)*: A fee collected by some tour operators for travel arrangements made at the last minute. The charge usually covers express delivery of documents and other last minute arrangements would become necessary.

Late Charge *(Hospitality)*: The charge levied to a guest for consumptions made after he/she has settled his/ her account.

Late Check-Out *(Hospitality)*: The allowance given to a guest who is to check out later than the property's standard check-out time.

Latin America *(Geography)*: The term Latin America is used when referring to those territories whose official or national languages come from Latin (namely Spanish, Portuguese, and French). In this sense, the Latin American territory comprises the region which extends from Mexico to the most southern part in South America, *Cabo de Hornos*. But language is not the only element linking Latin-American countries. They are also identified by other values and cultural components, such as history, costumes, religion, art expression and other related features. There is a tendency to confuse Latin America with South America. South America is the continent located to the south of Panama, excluding Mexico, Central America and the Caribbean, and is a part of Latin America. Conversely, Anglo-America is used to refer to areas whose language is English, mainly the United States of America and most of Canada, but also other parts of the Americas, including some islands. Similarly, areas where English is just prominent are considered part of the Anglo sphere.

Latitude *(Geography)*: Imaginary horizontal lines of angular distance, measured in degrees North or South of the equator.

Launch *(Cruise)*: A small boat that takes cruise passengers to and from the shore. It is also called Tender.

Laurasia *(Geography)*: According to a geological theory, about 300 million years ago, all the emerged continents were united into a vast supercontinent called Pangaea. Centuries later, it broke into two land masses, Laurasia to the north, and Gondwana to the south. Laurasia was composed of Laurentia, Baltica, Avalonia (the present territories of North America, Greenland, Scandinavia, Western and Central Europe, and most of Asia). The continents as we know them today began to split apart in the Mesozoic era about 100 million years ago, drifting to their present positions.

Lav *(Tourism)*: Abbreviation for lavatory.

Lavatory *(Tourism)*: A toilet, rest room or washroom.

LAX *(GDS)*: Three-letter IATA code for Los Angeles, California, USA.

Layover *(Air Traffic)*: A temporary cessation of a flight that will resume later.

Layover *(Tourism)*: A trip interruption, sometimes including overnight. It is usually associated with a change of planes or other transportation, due to a misconnection or lack of connecting services.

Layover Scheduled *(Tourism)*: A planned interruption of a journey, usually overnight, either at the passengers request or because of a lack of a connecting service.

LC *(GDS)*: Code meaning Limit sales, the waiting list is closed.

LCAR *(GDS)*: Code meaning Luxury Car.

LCC *(GDS)*: Code meaning Low-cost Carrier.

LCF *(Airlines)*: See Local currency fare.

LDW *(Car Rental)*: See Loss Damage Waiver.

Le Grand Tour *(Tourism)*: See Grand Tour.

Leaching *(Hospitality)*: The loss of cementing consistency caused by the filtration of water through cracks in walls.

Lead-in Price *(Cruise)*: The lowest available price for a travel product namely cabins on a cruise ship.

Lead Time *(Tourism)*: The length of time between the announcement of an event and its occurrence. Similarly, it is the advance time between initiating a tour and its departure date.

League *(Cruise)*: A measure of approximately three miles used for nautical distances.

Leased Space Flight *(Airlines)*: See Blocked Space Flight.

Lectern *(Tourism)*: A small stand or desk with a slanted top used to hold a text for the use of speakers or lecturers at formal meetings. See also Podium.

Lee *(Cruise)*: See Leeward.

Leeward *(Cruise)*: The side of a ship or island that is protected from the wind, as opposite to Windward.

Leg *(Air Traffic)*: A segment of a flight plan. Flight path between two waypoints

Leg *(Airlines)*: A portion of an air travel between two consecutive scheduled points of the route. It is typically used to refer to the outgoing portion of a trip as an Outgoing Leg, or to the incoming portion, as the Incoming Leg.

Lei *Tourism)*: A Hawaiian flower necklace used for welcoming travelers.

Leisure *(Tourism)*: The freedom from time-consuming duties, responsibilities, or activities used for relaxation or recreation. Leisure is sometimes defined as an individual human life as measured by time. But leisure is actually the time of one's life. It means Leisure is both a means and an end, because it allows human beings to do things that can not be achieved through labor, such as those considered spiritual or personal values. The right to leisure is consecrated in the Declaration of Universal Human Rights. Tourism activities are precisely performed during leisure times.

Leisure Park *(Tourism)*: A space organized to offer recreation, cultural or sports activities.

Leisure Tourist *(Tourism)*: A traveler for pleasure, not under any obligations. Leisure tourists are usually visitors to specific destinations or facilities that meet their vacation needs.

Leisure Travel *(Tourism)*: Travel for pleasure as opposed to business travel.

Length of Stay *(Tourism)*: The period of time which people spend in a destination. According to the WTO's definition, a visitor to a destination must stay at least 24 hours and less than one year, to be considered a tourist.

Letter of Agreement *(Tourism)*: A contract in the form of a letter from the buyer to the supplier accepting the terms of the proposal. The document must be signed by both parties for the agreement to become binding.

Letter of Intent *(Tourism)*: A document in the form of a letter from a potential buyer informing about his/her serious intention to do or to obtain something from the seller and agreeing to hold in strict confidence any data of the agreement.

Levee *(Tourism)*: A term derived from the French word *levée* connoting raised. It has the following meanings in English: 1.A formal reception of visitors or guests; 2. A natural or artificial embankment that prevents a river from overflowing; 3. A pier that provides a landing place on a river.

Level Playing Field Policy *(Tourism)*: A supplier policy preventing unfair competition by forbidding travel agents from advertising discounted or rebated fares for the supplier's products.

Lexus Lane *(Tourism)*: A High Occupation Vehicle (HOV) lane also available to single-passenger vehicles for a fee.

LGA *(GDS)*: Three-letter IATA code for La Guardia Airport serving the city of New York.

LGW *(GDS)*: Three-letter IATA code for Gatwick International Airport, serving the city of London, UK.

LH *(Airlines)*: Two-letter IATA code for Lufthansa, the airline of Germany.

LHR *(GDS)*: Three-letter IATA code for the Heathrow International Airport, serving the city of London, UK.

LHTL *(GDS)*: Code meaning Luxury Class Hotel.

Liability *(Airlines)*: It is one of the most significant institutions in the field of law, meaning legal and/or financial responsibility for one's acts or omissions. It is the state of one who is bound in law and justice to do something which may be enforced by action. This liability may arise from contracts either express or implied or in consequence of torts committed. Liability in air transportation is clearly stated in many law and regulation bodies, and is recognized by international treaties and conventions. Warsaw Convention of 1929 primarily deals with air carriers' liability to protect the weaker part of the contract, the user. Failure of an airline to meet that responsibility leaves it open to a lawsuit for any resulting damages. But the suing party (the plaintiff) must prove the legal liability of the defendant showing evidence of the duty to act, the failure to fulfill that duty and the connection (proximate cause) of that failure to some injury or harm to the plaintiff. The plaintiff (passenger, forwarder or passenger's relative) must also demonstrate he/she has accomplished with what is required from him/her as a party of the contract. Compensations for liability are established in the Warsaw System.

Liability Coverage *(Car Rental)*: A type of insurance covering a car renter in the event that damage is inflicted to third parties or properties. It is available as an option for car rentals.

Liability Insurance *(Tourism)*: Insurance that protects a company from legal claims arising out of accidents or losses incurred by customers.

Liability Waiver *(Tourism)*: A unilateral act of one party that results in the surrender of the other party's legal right. In tourism, several of its activities are waived from responsibility, giving the sense that it was agreed by mutual consensus. So, liability waiver is applied by means of a legal document containing a declaration that sets free a supplier from a financial or legal responsibility for eventual damages that might affect a traveler. By signing such a document the traveler acknowledges that he/she is aware of the risks inherent to the trip. See also Waiver.

Licence or License *(Tourism)*: 1. The authorization extended to individuals or companies to conduct certain types of business activities, such as a travel agency, a hotel or a restaurant. 2. A private agreement for a company may use the logo or image symbols of another, as on advertisements. 3. The permit to drive a vehicle.

License Recoupment Fee *(Car Rental)*: A charge made by a rental car company to cover the fees charged by the local or state government.

Licensee *(Tourism)*: A location that is subcontracted to perform activities for the principal, under the supplier's franchise name.

Licensee-owned Locations *(Car Rental)*: The locations owned and operated by a car rental company.

Lido *(Tourism)*: An Italian term for a fashionable beach resort.

Lido Deck *(Cruise)*: Usually the open deck on a cruise ship that surrounds the pool area.

Lie-flat Seat *(Airlines)*: An airline seat that folds flat for sleeping, but keeping a slight angle. See also Flat-bed Seat.

Liebfraumilch *(Hospitality)*: A white German wine of sweet style exported in great quantities thanks to its low price. It is originated in the Rheinhessen region.

Life Preserver *(Cruise)*: A circular floating device to be used by travelers in case of emergency.

Life Vest *(Airlines)*: A buoyant floating article to be worn by travelers to keep them afloat in water in case of emergency.

Lifeboat *(Cruise)*: A small boat carried on vessels that are used to remove passengers from the ships in emergencies. The total capacity of all lifeboats must exceed the total number of passengers and crew members onboard.

Lifeboat Drill *(Cruise)*: A mandatory training of travelers on the cruise ship's emergency procedures to be carried out within 24 hours of sailing.

Lifestyle Hotel *(Hospitality)*: See Boutique Hotel.

Lift *(Airlines)*: The maximum number of airline seats available in a specific time to a defined destination.

Lift *(Aeronautics)*: The aerodynamic force generated by the movement of air across the wings of an aircraft that makes it possible for the plane to fly. With enough lift to overcome its weight, the aircraft rises.

Lift *(Cruise)*: An elevator.

Light-Cabin *(Airlines)*: A term to denote an executive or corporate jet, categorized according to a combination of passenger capacity, range, and maximum speed. Usually, a light cabin jet holds seven passengers, has a range of about 1600 to 2000 square miles and a maximum speed of about 500 miles per hour.

Light Pollution *(Ecology)*: An intrusive light resulting harmful or offensive.

Lighter Than Air (LTA) *(Aeronautics)*: The term refers to aircraft that are less heavy than the air, including balloons, dirigibles of all types (piloted or un-piloted), kites balloons, or aerostats. LTA is also a branch of aeronautics dealing with such type of vehicles.

Ligne *(Tourism)*: A French term for a service of regular transportation.

Lilienthal, Otto *(Aviation)*: Is considered by many to be the true Father of Aviation. He was born in Anklam, Germany, in 1841. He was the first to demonstrate the advantages of curved surfaces for aircraft wings. His glider designs paved the way for many heavier-than-air machines. He died in 1896 piloting one of his biplanes that failed due to a gust of wind.

LIM *(GDS)*: Three-letter IATA code for Lima, the capital city of Peru.

Lima *(Airlines)*: Designator for the letter "L" in the International Phonetic Alphabet.

Limited Availability *(Tourism)*: A limited number of reservations accepted at a certain rate or special offer.

Limited Purpose Card *(Tourism)*: A credit card that can be used only for travel expenditures.

Limited Service Agency Location *(Tourism)*: A travel agency, typically a branch, which is able to take reservations but does not issue tickets.

Limited Service Hotel *(Hospitality)*: A lodging facility that offers limited number of services or amenities, for example no restaurants, pools, meeting rooms, or room service.

Limited-Menu Restaurant *(Hospitality)*: A restaurant with a small offer of food and limited services.

Limo *(Tourism)*: Abbreviation for limousine.

Limousine *(Tourism)*: A large hire vehicle with chauffeur.

LIN *(GDS)*: Three-letter IATA code for Linate International Airport, serving the city of Milan, Italy.

Lindbergh, Charles *(Aviation)*: He was the first person to fly alone across the Atlantic in a custom-built Ryan monoplane, the "Spirit of St. Louis". The most famous airplane flight of the time took ok from Roosevelt Field near New York City to Paris on May 20, 1927, via Nova Scotia and St. Johns, Newfoundland. His onboard equipment consisted of a magnetic compass, an airspeed indicator, and courage to keep his objective toward Ireland. When Lindbergh was seen crossing the Irish coast, the world cheered and eagerly anticipated his arrival in Paris. A crowd over 100,000 people gathered at Le Bourget Field to welcome him. Lindbergh made the flight in less than 34 hours after his departure from New York. Other pilots had crossed the Atlantic before him, but Lindbergh was the first person to do it alone nonstop.

Line *(Cruise)*: A rope for the use on a ship.

Line of Latitude *(Geography)*: An imaginary line which runs parallel to the equator and is measured in degrees north and south of it.

Line of Longitude *(Geography)*: An imaginary line which runs from the Northern Pole to the Southern Pole, and is measured in degrees east and west of the Prime Meridian. See also Meridian.

Linear Scale *(Geography)*: A line on a map that gives equivalent actual distances.

Linen *(Hospitality)*: The total of sheets and towels.

Linen Room *(Hospitality)*: The area in a hotel often considered the headquarters of the housekeeping department, where housekeeping employees report to work, receive room assignments, and make room status reports.

Liner *(Cruise)*: A large ship operating passenger transport services along definite routes and regular schedules.

Liqueur *(Hospitality)*: A distilled, flavored and often sweet beverage with an alcohol content higher than fortified wine, but lower than most liquors.

Liquidated Damages *(Tourism)*: Compensation demanded by one party when the other fails to honor an agreement between the two. This incident usually occurs between travel agents and GDS vendors.

Liquidated Damages Clause *(Tourism)*: A stipulation on the contract between a travel agency and a GDS vendor stating the compensations when one party fails to comply with the contract.

Liquor *(Hospitality)*: A beverage of non sweet and high-alcohol-content such as gin, vodka, rum, and the various whiskeys, including scotch.

Lithosphere *(Geography)*: The solid outer layer of the Earth consisting of the crust and upper mantle. Although its thickness depends on the age, the average lithosphere thickness is of 100 kilometers. It is divided into 12 major plates, the boundaries of which are zones of intense activity that produce earthquakes.

Liveried *(Tourism)*: A person who wears a livery uniform.

Livery *(Tourism)*: A distinctive uniform worn by some employees, such as menservants, doormen or chauffeurs.

Livestock *(Tourism)*: Farm animals grown for personal use or profit.

LL *(GDS)*: Code meaning Limit Sales, Booking has been Waitlisted.

LO *(GDS)*: Code meaning Domestic Transportation Tax.

LO CIGS *(Air Traffic)*: Low Ceilings or Low Clouds.

Load Factor *(Airlines)*: A value showing the percentage of available seats that are filled with paying passengers, or the percent of freight capacity that is utilized to date. Its calculation is complex, and is an indication of the efficient operation of an airline.

Load Factor (g) *(Aeronautics)*: The ratio between lift and weight of an aircraft commonly represented by **g** or **G.** It is a unit of force equal to the force of gravity times one.

Load Lines *(Cruise)*: An imaginary line, sometimes painted line, on the hull of the ship that is used to know when the ship reaches its maximum cargo load. It is also called Plimsoll Line or Waterline.

Loading Apron *(Cruise)*: A conveyable platform that is used on a ship to move vehicles or cargo.

LOC *(Air Traffic)*: See Localizer.

Local Charge *(Airlines)*: A charge applied for carriage over the routes of a single carrier.

Local Control Tower *(Air Traffic)*: A tall building with a glass-enclosed cab on top that is visible at any airport. Local Control Towers are built to provide for a safe, orderly, and expeditious flow of air traffic at an airport and in its vicinity. Each airport's control tower is also known as Local Control.

Local Currency Fare (LCF) *(Airlines)*: Fares and related charges expressed in the currency of the country of commencement of transportation. It is also Called LSF (Local Selling Fare).

Local Fare *(Airlines)*: A fare that applies for transportation over the routes of a single carrier.

Local People *(Ecology)*: People who pertain to a place and who shape the cultural identity of their community through an active role performed on a long time of life.

Local Selling Fare (LSF) *(Airlines)*: See Local Currency Fare.

Locale *(Tourism)*: A place assigned to be the setting for a particular event.

Localizer (LOC) *(Air Traffic)*: The component of an ILS that provides course guidance to the runway.

Location Code *(Car Rental)*: The three-letter IATA codes that identify each car rental city or airport around the globe. If the location is at an airport, the airport code is used for the car rental location code. For example, Miami is MIA, Madrid is MAD, Fiumicino Airport of Rome is FCO.

Location Factors *(Tourism)*: A general term referring to conditions that influence the choice of a company's location.

Locator *(GDS)*: A reference code assigned to a travel booking that enables to locate easily the booking or to recall quickly the information if needed at a later time.

Lodge *(Hospitality)*: A rustic-shape type of small hotel that is usually located in an environment where such activities as fishing, skiing, boating, eco-tours are performed.

Lodger *(Hospitality)*: A term for a guest who stays at a hotel or lodge.

Lodging *(Hospitality)*: The accommodation or hotel room.

Lodging Capacity *(Hospitality)*: The lodging capacity is the simple counting of the total number of the property's beds. Thus the common unit to measure the lodging capacity is the bed.

Lodging Facility *(Hospitality)*: A business dedicated to provide short-term or transitional lodging.

Lodging Industry *(Hospitality)*: Businesses organized to provide accommodation, food and other related services to the public on a nightly or other term range of times, by week, by month, etc.

Log *(Cruise)*: 1. A device used to measure distances traveled on the water. Logs can be electronic devices or paddle wheels mounted on the hull of the vessel. 2. A daily record of a ship's progress on a minute-by-minute or hour-by-hour basis.

Log or Logbook *(Air Traffic)*: A book where a pilot registers his flying achievements, including flight time, takeoffs, landings, maneuvers completed, instructor endorsements, and other actions taken.

Log or Logbook *(Cruise)*: A book in which the boat's records are written, including he time and date of the entry, weather conditions, wind speed and direction, boat position, boat speed and course, and other information and observations.

Logo *(Tourism)*: Abbreviation for Logotype.

Logotype *(Tourism)*: The symbolic representation of a company's trade mark or corporative image. It is a symbol or a word representing the corporation's activity and its identity.

Loisir *(Tourism)*: A French term for leisure.

LON *(GDS)*: Three-letter IATA code for London, capital city of the United Kingdom.

Long-haul *(Airlines)*: Term meaning long distance.

Long-haul Flight *(Airlines)*: A flight with duration of more than 8 hours.

Long-haul Travel *(Tourism)*: A travel of 8 or more hour duration.

Long Journey *(Tourism)*: A travel comprising four overnights or more, as in leisure or health trip.

Longitude *(Air Traffic)*: Position on earth, east or west of the prime meridian that is measured in degrees.

Longitude *(Geography)*: The angular distance measured in degrees East or West of the Prime Meridian.

Longitudinal *(Air Traffic)*: Lengthwise along the center line of an aircraft in the direction of the long axis.

Longshoreman *(Cruise)*: A worker who loads and discharges cargo at a wharf or dock side. It is a common name in the USA for stevedore.

Long-Term Stay *(Hospitality)*: The stay for a long period of time not qualified for transitory stay.

Loo *(Tourism)*: A British abbreviation for toilet.

Look-to-book Ratio *(Tourism)*: The comparison between the number of people who visit a travel agency and the number of people who actually make a purchase. It is also the ratio between the number of visits to a travel agency's web site and the number of business it brings.

LOS or LoS *(Tourism)*: Length of Stay. The amount of time a tourist spends in a particular place.

Loss Damage Waiver (LDW) *(Car Rental)*: A contractual declaration that relieves car renters of financial or legal responsibility if the car is damaged or stolen while under rental contract. A variation of Loss Damage Waiver is the Collision Damage Waiver employed by some car rental companies.

Loss Leader *(Tourism)*: A product or service advertised or sold at an invitingly low price with the purpose to attract customers who will buy other, more profitable products or services that compensate the low price offered.

Lounge *(Airlines)*: A place in the airport where travelers can spend time before they board the plane.

Lounge Car *(Tourism)*: A railroad passenger car with a bar, tables and lounge chairs for serving refreshments and drinks in an environment of comfort. It is also called Bar Car or Club Car.

Love Hotel *(Hospitality)*: A term of a slightly disreputable connotation that defines a hostelry serving people wishing to engage in romantic liaisons.

Low *(Climate)*: An atmospheric phenomenon of relatively low atmospheric pressure, with frequent presence of rain or stormy weather.

Low-cost Carrier *(Geography)*: An airline category usually defined by low prices but also by low service standards.

Low Fare Search *(GDS)*: A detailed check for the lowest available fare that is applicable to bookings already made.

Low-impact Aerobics *(Tourism)*: A gentle form of aerobics with marching or gliding movements which lowers stress and the possibility of injury.

Low Season *(Airlines)*: The period of the year when prices of tickets and other travel services decline because the demand is at its lowest point to a destination. It is also known as Off-peak or Off-season.

Lower Bed *(Cruise)*: A single bed, the lower of two bunk beds in a cruise stateroom placed at the conventional height from the floor.

Lowest Available Fare *(Airlines)*: The current, lowest airfare available for purchase at the search time.

Lowest Fare *(Airlines)*: The lowest of the published airfares for a pair of cities.

Lowest Fare Guarantee *(Tourism)*: A travel agency's promise to obtain the lowest fare available when the reservation is confirmed. It is a risky compromise that agencies usually avoid.

Lowest Logical Airfare *(Airlines)*: The lowest fare that meets the parameters of a corporation's travel policy.

Loyalty Marketing *(Tourism)*: The whole of the actions aimed to have travelers purchasing the company's services in a repeated way.

Loyalty Programmes or Programs *(Tourism)*: Also known as Frequent Flyer or Frequent Lodger, these are reward programs that encourage business travelers to use the same airline or hotel chain for all their travel arrangements.

LPB *(GDS)*: Three-letter IATA code for La Paz, the capital city of Bolivia.

LRA *(Tourism)*: Acronym of the motor coach industry for Local Receptive Agent.

LRO *(Tourism)*: Acronyms of the motor coach industry for Local Receptive Operator.

LSF *(GDS)*: Code meaning Local Selling Fare.

LT *(GDS)*: Code meaning Local Time.

LTA *(Aeronautics)*: Lighter-than-air craft, generally referring to powered blimps and dirigibles, but often also including free balloons.

LTR *(GDS)*: Code for Letter.

Luggage *(Airlines)*: Baggage carried aboard an airplane by the passenger, as opposed to being checked and carried in the baggage compartment.

Luggage Tag *(Airlines)*: A small identifying label showing the destination and flight details of the baggage. Tags are also provided to note the name and contact information of the bags' owner.

Luncheon *(Hospitality)*: A light midday meal.

LUX *(GDS)*: Code meaning Luxury.

Luxury Class *(Airlines/ Hospitality)*: The highest seat or accommodation category, consequently, the most expensive.

Luxury Hotel *(Hospitality)*: A hotel with high room rates that features exceptional service and amenities.

Luxury Restaurant *(Hospitality)*: A restaurant featuring fine dining and employing well-trained, creative chefs and skilled food servers.

Lymphatic Drainage Massage *(Tourism)*: A massage that uses a gentle, pumping technique to stimulate lymphatic circulation and drainage, thus detoxing and reducing water retention.

M

M *(Airlines)*: "Mike," name used to designate the letter "M" in the International Phonetic Alphabet

M *(GDS)*: Code meaning: 1. Economy, coach class discounted; 2. As a code shown close to the fare amount denotes the fare construction was based on the Mileage System Calculation.

M.S. *(Cruise)*: Abbreviation for Motor Ship.

M/M *(GDS)*: Code meaning Mr. and Mrs.

MAAS *(GDS)*: Code meaning Meet and Assist.

Mach *(Aeronautics)*: The term MACH with a number represents the speed ratio of an object, as an aircraft, compared to the speed of sound in the surrounding medium in which it moves.

Mach Number *(Aeronautics)*: Ratio of airspeed to the local speed of sound Mach 1 is the speed of sound under current atmospheric conditions.

Madero, Francisco *(Airlines)*: The first president of a country to make an air journey. He was a president of Mexico and the feat occurred on November 30, 1911 over the plains of Balbuena close to Mexico City. The flight was operated by the French pilot George Dyot.

Macro Region *(Geography)*: Grouping of Tourist Regions into a larger regional marketing entity.

MAD *(GDS)*: Three-letter IATA code for Madrid, capital city of Spain.

Maglev *(Tourism)*: A term for Magnetic Levitation, relating to high-speed rail technology that allows a train to travel suspended on a magnetic cushion above a magnetized track. Since the travel is free of friction, the train can develop high speeds.

Magma *(Geography)*: A liquid and incandescent rock which rises from volcanoes to the surface of the earth where it cools and solidifies.

Magnetic Compass *(Aeronautics)*: The most common liquid-type compass that is possible to calibrate to compensate magnetic influences within the aircraft.

Magnetic Course *(Air Traffic)*: It is equal to Compass Course plus or less a deviation.

Magnetic Field *(Air Traffic)*: A space where magnetic lines of force exist.

Magnetic Heading *(Air Traffic)*: Direction of the aircraft relative to magnetic north. A Magnetic Heading Sensor provides this heading data.

Magnetic North *(Air Traffic)*: The magnetic North pole, located near 71° North latitude and 96° West longitude that attracts a magnetic compass which is not influenced by local magnetic attraction, as opposed to Geographic North. It is the direction to which a compass points. The magnetic fields of the planet are not exactly in line with the north and south poles.

Magnetic Variation *(Air Traffic)*: Observed differences between true north and magnetic north, varying with position.

MAGVAR *(Air Traffic)*: Abbreviation for Magnetic Variation.

MAIB *(Cruise)*: The Marine Accident Investigation Board in the United Kingdom.

Maid Service *(Hospitality)*: Cleaning services provided in an accommodation property.

Maiden Voyage *(Cruise)*: The first sailing of a ship which is not precisely an Inaugural Sailing.

Mail *(Airlines)*: All types of material communications carried on one aircraft, including General Post Office Mail, Diplomatic Mail, Company Mail (an airline's mail). Nowadays the term also identifies electronic email, which obviously, is not an object of transport.

Mailing Address *(Business)*: 1. The location at which a person or company receives his/her correspondence. 2. The electronic address to send and receive emails.

Main Gear *(Aeronautics)*: The landing gear

underneath   the   fuselage   of   an   aircraft.

Main Seating *(Cruise)*: The earlier of two scheduled meal times served in the ship's dining room. It is also called First Seating.

Mainline *(Tourism)*: 1. Each of the roadways for a highway, excluding connections and local roads that run parallel to an expressway. 2. That track of a railroad for point to point train traffic, exclusive of switch tracks, branches, yards and terminals.

Mainline Flight *(Airlines)*: A flight that is operated by aircraft of the main organization, rather than by a subsidiary, a regional alliance airline, pr a regional code-share air carrier. Example: A flight operated by United Airlines but rather than one operated by United Express.

Maison de la France *(Tourism)*: French expression referring to an office created to promote French tourism in foreign countries.

Maitre d' *(Hospitality)*: See Maitre d'hotel.

Maitre d'hotel *(Hospitality)*: A French term literally meaning "master of the hotel" that defines the person who supervises the waiters at a restaurant and is in charge of assigning customers to tables. He/she is also responsible for the day-to-day operation of the restaurant, including the quality of food preparation and service

Maitre d' or Restaurant Manager *(Cruise)*: The Maitre d' is an employee who is responsible for the day-to-day operation of the restaurants in a cruise, including the quality of food preparation, presentation, service, and guest seating.

Major Airline or Major Carrier *(Airlines)*: An airline with annual operating revenue of more than one billion dollars.

Mal de mer *(Cruise)*: A French term for seasickness.

MALIAT *(Airlines)*: See Multilateral Agreement on the Liberalization of International Air Transportation.

Malt *(Hospitality)*: Any grain that after sprouting is dried to prevent further development. It is used in brewing and distilling processes.

Malt Beverage *(Hospitality)*: A beer, ale, stout, and porters containing 0.5% or more of alcohol, brewed or produced from malt, wholly or in part, or from any substance thereof.

Malt Liquor *(Hospitality)*: A brew made from straight malt that has a definite malt flavor, an appearance slightly darker than regular beer, and usually higher alcohol content, ranging from 3.2 percent to 8 percent by weight.

Malt Whiskey *(Hospitality)*: A whiskey similar to Straight Malt Whiskey, but differentiated in the age. When the label says "Malt Whiskey", it may have an age of up to two years. Straight Malt Whiskeys usually are a minimum of two years old.

Management Contract *(Hospitality)*: An agreement in which a property's owner acquires the services of a separate company to operate the hotel.

Management Report *(Tourism)*: A summary issued for a corporate client by travel agencies or travel suppliers documenting all travel items, such as air transportation, hotel stays, or car rental during a given period.

Mandatory Traffic Advisory Frequency (MTAF) *(Air Traffic)*: An obligatory communication service required from airports which do not have a control tower. MF airports operate scheduled passenger service of an insufficient traffic to support a control tower. The flight information service is provided by a specialist monitoring the frequency, with aircraft pilots following standard procedures. Untowered airports are common in Australia, Canada, Norway and the United Kingdom. MTAF is also known as Mandatory Frequency (MF) or Air/Ground.

Manifest *(Airlines)*: A final and official document listing all passengers and/or cargo aboard an aircraft or a ship.

Manual *(Tourism)*: 1. A handbook including instructions on specific topics; 2. A car with a manual transmission; 3. A computer guide to develop certain skills.

MAP *(GDS)*: Code meaning Modified American Plan.

Map Projection *(Geography)*: A flat representation of the earth's surface that is projected on to a piece of paper.

Map Scale *(Geography)*: A ratio that compares a distance measured on a map to the actual distance between the locations identified by the map.

MAPS *(Air Traffic)*: An abbreviation for Meteorological and Aeronautical Presentation System.

MAR *(GDS)*: Code for: 1. Maracaibo, a commercial city in

Venezuela; 2. March.

MARAD *(Cruise)*: An abbreviation for Maritime Administration.

Marathon *(Tourism)*: The term is after the place in southeastern Greece that was the site of an important Athenian military victory over the Persians in 490 B.C. A legend says that a Greek messenger named Pheidippides was sent to Athens to announce that the Persians had been defeated in the Battle of Marathon. The messenger covered the entire distance without stopping, running a race that collapsed him upon his arrival in the Senate. The term marathon is used to refer to a foot race of 26 miles, 385 yards, the distance run by the Phidippides to announce the Greek victory. Nowadays, it is a long-distance running race, keeping the original distance of 26 miles 385 yards, equivalent to 42.195 km.

Marbellisation *(Tourism)*: A French term which defines a type of space totally specialized in tourism, sensitive to become saturated. The concept introduces the occupation problem when the demand is extremely high. This phenomenon is manifested in different points of the Mediterranean basin, like Marbella and Palma de Majorca. It is synonymous with Balearization.

Mardi Gras *(Tourism)*: A French term referring to a carnival held on Mardi Gras, often celebrated at some cities with costumes, parades, balls, and other festivities. The most notable Mardi Gras celebrations take place in New Orleans. See also Carnival.

Marina *(Tourism)*: A dock facility for private yachts or sailboats, offering fuel and other related services, sometimes even eating locations.

Maritime Climate *(Climate)*: Also called Oceanic Climate and Marine West Coast Climate is a type of climate usually found along the west coasts at the middle latitudes of all the world's continents, and in southeastern Australia. Maritime Climates are characterized by a narrow annual range of temperatures but do not have the extremely dry summers of Mediterranean climates.

Mark-up or Markup *(Tourism)*: The percentage or amount added to the net price of tour packages as a commission component, to determine the selling price. The final selling price is thus the sum of wholesale or purchase price plus the markup.

Market *(Tourism)*: A group of people living in a geographical place and sharing some demographic and consuming characteristics who are potential buyers of products or services.

Market Driven Conservation Model *(Ecology)*: A model thought to protect bio-diversity through promotion of sustainable tourism.

Market Segment *(Tourism)*: A portion of the total consumer market that is selected according to specific parameters.

Market Share *(Tourism)*: The percentage of the total volume of sales achieved by a company in a specific circumscription, compared to all sales of similar products made by other companies.

Marketplace *(Tourism)*: A travel trade event where tourism suppliers schedule appointments with travel trade buyers.

Marketing *(Tourism)*: A process comprising a set of activities of promoting, selling and distributing a product or service with which the producer intends to meet the needs and wants of a defined market.

Marketing Carrier *(Airlines)*: The airline that deals with marketing activities. Its code is shown on the electronic flight coupons of code share transportation.

Marpol *(Cruise)*: See International Convention for the Prevention of Pollution from Ships.

MARS *(GDS)*: Code meaning Multi-access Reservations System.

Martial Arts *(Tourism)*: Forms of combat and self-defense techniques often practiced as sport or fitness programs.

Mass Culture *(Tourism)*: The sum of knowledge, values, and manners of behaving that are disseminated via the mass media (Press, radio, TV) and other cultural means. Mass culture is a recent phenomenon associated to the notion of "consumption societies", because mass media usually have the power to influence on the tastes and habits of a consumer group on behalf of a favored group. Mass culture concept is thought to be a factor for standardizing the culture. If all of the social groups think and behave in a similar way, all of them become standardized.

Mass Extinction *(Ecology)*: A widespread event in which major groups of species are vanished over a relatively short period when compared to normal extinction rates.

Mass Tourism *(Tourism)*: The travel by a large number of people at a wide scale. Tourism in its origins was an activity of elite. It became accessible for mass travelers, when laborers conquered their right to leisure time, achieved discretionary income, and counted on reliable and inexpensive modes of transportation such as the train, the automobile and the airplane.

Mass Tourists *(Tourism)*: Travelers who participate in wide-scale travel designed for large numbers of people.

Masseur *(Tourism)*: A French term related to a man whose work is giving massages professionally.

Masseuse *(Tourism)*: A French term related to a woman whose work is giving massages professionally.

Master Account *(Tourism)*: The specific group's guest account that is paid by the sponsoring organization.

Master Air Waybill (MAWB) *(Airlines)*: The carrier's air bill issued to cover a consolidated shipment presented by a forwarder or consolidator.

Master Bill *(Airlines)*: The bill containing all items provided by the supplier to be paid by the operator.

Master Caution *(Air Traffic)*: A signal which indicates that one or more caution lights have been activated.

Master Folio *(Hospitality)*: A bill comprising all charges for the members of a group.

Master Key *(Hospitality)*: A key that can open all guestroom doors.

Master Warning *(Air Traffic)*: See Master Caution.

MAT *(GDS)*: Material.

Material Recovery Facility (MRF) *(Ecology)*: A specialized plant where recyclables are separated, processed and stored. These materials are then sent on to re-processors.

MATS *(GDS)*: Code meaning Military Air Transport Service.

Maturing *(Hospitality)*: The process of aging wine or whiskey. Wine aging is usually associated with maturing in the bottle to obtain its full-bodied reds such as red Bordeaux or Burgundy. The aging of whiskey in oak barrels develops its characteristic taste, color, and aroma.

MAX *(GDS)*: Maximum.

Maximum Authorized Amount *(Tourism)*: The largest sum of money a travel agency authorizes its bank to withdraw from its account in order to settle the weekly sales report.

Maximum Permitted Mileage (MPM) *(Airlines)*: The maximum amount of miles a passenger can travel at the published fare. Each direct fare is published in the air tariffs together with its respective Maximum Permitted Mileage. The term is associated to the system used to calculate fares for complex flight itineraries on the basis of the mileage flown.

Maximum Stay *(Airlines)*: The maximum time a passenger can stay at his/her destination in order to qualify for a specific airfare. This is one of multiple conditions that affect special and promotional air fares. The Maximum stay requirement depends on the type of the fare.

MAXR *(GDS)*: Code meaning Maximum Room Rate Desired.

MAY *(GDS)*: Code for May.

Mayday *(Airlines)*: A radio signal word used for emergency cases. By extension, it is also used in any other difficult situation.

MBR *(GDS)*: Code meaning Mini bar.

MCD *(GDS)*: Code meaning Multiple Carrier Designator.

McDonnell Douglas *(Aviation)*: The Company McDonnell Douglas was a major U.S. aerospace manufacturer and defense contractor, which produced a number of famous commercial and military aircraft. McDonnell Douglas Corporation was founded by James Smith McDonnell and Donald Wills Douglas by a merging formed on April 28, 1967. One of its stellar products was the wide body DC-10 that marked an era. In 1997 McDonnell Douglas merged with Boeing to form "The Boeing Company."

McDonnell, James Smith *(Airlines)*: James Smith McDonnell was born in Denver, Colo., April 9, 1899 and grew up in Little Rock, Arkansas, where his father, also named James McDonnell, was a successful cotton merchant. In his youth James S. McDonnell delivered the "Arkansas Gazette" on horseback. In 1917 he graduated from Little Rock High School and served briefly as a private in the Army. Shortly after, he attended Princeton University, obtaining a degree with honors in Physics in 1921. In August 1923, McDonnell was commissioned as a second lieutenant in the Army Air Service Reserve. He was one of six volunteers to make the first airplane parachute jump. He then enrolled at Massachusetts

Institute of Technology and obtained a Masters Degree in aeronautical engineering in 1925. In 1928, McDonnell established his own company to build the single Doodlebug plane, but he did not succeed and spent the next 10 years working for several aircraft companies, ending as a chief engineer with the "Glenn L. Martin Aircraft Co." In 1938 McDonnell resigned from Martin and started again an own company. On July 6, 1939, he incorporated the "McDonnell Aircraft Corp." in St. Louis, Missouri. For the next three decades, the company was the leading producer of jet fighters and built the first spacecraft to carry an American into orbit. In 1967, his company merged with the major company "Douglas Aircraft Co.," taking over as chairman and chief executive officer of the new "McDonnell Douglas Corp." James Smith McDonnell remained chairman of the board of directors until his death on Aug. 22, 1980.

MCO *(GDS)*: Code meaning: 1. Miscellaneous Charges Order; 2. International Airport serving the city of Orlando.

MCT *(GDS)*: Code meaning Minimum Connecting Time.

MDT *(Geography)*: See Mountain Daylight Time.

MDW *(GDS)*: Three-letter IATA code for Chicago Midway Airport serving the city of Chicago.

Meal Plan *(Hospitality)*: An accommodation program that includes a certain number of meals per day.

Meal Plan *(Tourism)*: A tour option that offers a prepaid meals plan at pre-selected restaurants in the destination area.

Meal Sitting *(Cruise)*: Pre-selected times for meals. It is one of the designated meal times on a cruise ship, which generally are two for each meal.

Mean Sea Level (MSL) *(Air Traffic)*: The height of sea surface water level averaged between high and low levels, computed from the tidal oscillations over a long period.

Mechanical Oven *(Hospitality)*: An oven with moving mechanical parts for easier cooking. Some of these types are the revolving oven, traveling-tray oven, and rotary oven.

MED *(GDS)*: Code for Medical.

Medical Certificate *(Airlines)*: A note issued by a doctor on his letterhead to attest the health condition of a passenger in case of illness.

Medical Tourism *(Tourism)*: A term initially describing the practice of traveling to another country to obtain health care. Medical services can include elective procedures as well as complex specialized surgeries, such as cosmetic surgeries, dental surgery, joint replacement, cardiac surgery, and even in-vitro fertilization and other assisted reproductive technology treatments. Such treatments typically include associated leisure aspects. It is also called Medical Travel, Health Tourism or Global Healthcare.

Medical Travel *(Tourism)*: See Medical Tourism.

Medieval Age *(Tourism)*: A period in the European history extended from the fall of the Roman Empire by the middle the 5th century (400-476 AD) to the dawn of the Renaissance in the 16th century (1453-1517 AD). The Middle Age is a tumultuous period characterized by struggles, invasions, migration, the dominant role of the Catholic Church and the strengthening of the power of its pope, and the presence of kingdoms that amalgamated barbarian, Christian, and Roman cultures with political interests. Many nation-states were born during the Medieval Age. It saw the rise of humanism in the Italian Renaissance, the division of Roman Christianity in the Reformation, and the beginnings of European expansion overseas. It produced the Empire of Charlemagne and the appearance of thousands of knights who joined to develop the Crusade wars. The medieval architecture reached its climax in the 13th century with the emergence of Gothic style that characterizes many buildings, among churches, castles, universities, and public houses. Many and varied were the factors that caused the decline of the middle Ages, including weakening of national governments, the discredit of the papal power, the retrogression of medieval theology and philosophy, and a generalized collapse of the economy. The Medieval theme interests the activity of tourism as far as it concerns to cultural travel.

Medium-haul Flight *(Airlines)*: An air travel of between 4 and 8 hours duration.

Meditation *(Tourism)*: Method of deep breathing and concentration. It relieves stress and pain and reduces blood pressure.

Meet and Greet *(Tourism)*: A service provided to meet and assist travelers upon arrival in a place or at the airport. The assistance deals with entrance formalities, collecting baggage, and obtaining transportation.

Meeting Fare *(Airlines)*: A fare negotiated with an airline for a group of people who travel to attend a meeting or convention.

Meeting Planner *(Tourism)*: A company or individual who gathers specialized know-how for planning and organizing conventions, congresses and other business meetings.

Meeting Rate *(Hospitality)*: The hotel rate available for guests who will attend a meeting.

Mega Agency *(Tourism)*: A travel agency big enough to produce very large volume sales nationwide.

Mega Airlines *(Airlines)*: In fact there are no mega airlines, due to limitations established by anti-monopoly laws. People think of large air carriers or a holding of them as being mega airlines. The term should not be confused with alliances that are global strategies to optimize airlines' resources.

Mega Restaurant *(Hospitality)*: A large restaurant that enjoys the patronage of numerous clienteles.

Megacarrier *(Airlines)*: See Mega Airlines.

Megaship *(Cruise)*: A large cruise ship with a capacity of over 2,000 passengers.

MEL *(GDS)*: Code meaning: 1. Minimum Equipment List; 2. Melbourne, important city in Australia.

Member (IATA Member) *(Airlines)*: Any carrier affiliated to IATA. To be an IATA Member an airline has to operate regular international services. There are two types of members: Active Members, which are airlines operating international regular services, and Associate Members that are airlines operating non-scheduled international services or regular domestic services.

Member Sales Offices (MSO) *(Airlines)*: A city or airport ticket sales office operated by an IATA Airline.

Memory *(Computing)*: 1. The amount of data that can be stored on a hard disc or on any external storing device; 2. The amount of data that can be stored on the microchip in an RFID tag.

Menu Engineering *(Hospitality)*: A process employed to analyze the entire menu and measure its profitability.

Mercator Projection *(Geography)*: A description of the earth which represents land masses in their correct shapes, as it would appear if projected on a cylinder wrapped around the earth. The method was designed by Gerhardus Mercator, a cartographer and geographer of the 16ᵗʰ century.

Merchant Model Pricing *(Tourism)*: A system used by suppliers to sell services to travel agents at a net price in order they will be able to set a retail price by adding a markup.

Merger *(Tourism)*: The legal process in which one company merges to another or acquires its property.

Meridians *(Geography)*: The imaginary lines of longitude on a globe running from the Northern Pole to the Southern Pole, and measured in degrees East and West of the Prime Meridian. See also Line of Longitude.

Metal *(Airlines)*: A slang term for airplane, which is common in the United States.

Metal Detector *(Airlines)*: A hand-held or walk-through device used at airport security checkpoints for detecting hidden metal objects.

METAR *(Air Traffic)*: Acronym that is thought to mean *Meteorologique Aviation Routine* in French. It is a term used in FAA pilot briefings and weather reports. The format was not adopted by USA and Canada until 1 July 1996.

Meteorological Information *(Air Traffic)*: A document containing information on weather, prognostics, meteorological conditions and any other related data.

Meteorologist *(Air Traffic)*: A person who studies and forecasts the weather.

Me-Too *(Airlines)*: The name chosen by a group of European airlines that sell travel products directly to the public, bypassing travel agents.

Metro *(Tourism)*: A subway system built for public rail transportation.

Metroliner *(Tourism)*: An Amtrak faster service of a train line that runs from New York to Washington.

MEX *(GDS)*: Three-letter IATA code for Mexico City, Mexico.

Mezzanine *(Tourism)*: An intermediate floor just above the ground floor. Similarly, it is the balcony level above the orchestra in a theater.

MF *(GDS)*: A code meaning: 1. Mandatory Frequency; 2. Monday through Friday; 3. Main Floor.

MGA *(GDS)*: Three-letter IATA code for Managua, the capital city of Nicaragua.

MGR *(GDS)*: Code for Manager.

MH *(Airlines)*: Two-letter IATA code for Malaysia Airlines.

MIA *(GDS)*: Three-letter IATA code for Miami, Florida, USA.

MICE *(Tourism)*: An acronym for "Meetings, Incentives, Conventions and Events."

Michelin André *(Tourism)*: A French industrialist (16 January 1853–4 April 1931) who, in 1888 founded the "Michelin Tyre Company" with his brother Édouard in the city of Clermont-Ferrand. Michelin was the first to publish the Michelin Guides with the purpose to promote tourism by car, thereby supporting his tire manufacturing operation. At the age of 33 André abandoned his career as an engineer to take over his grandfather's farm equipment business. By the late 1880s, cycling was becoming a popular form of transportation and hobby. Backed by Dunlop's invention of inflatable tires, Michelin Brothers developed a number of prototypes. In 1891, they obtained a patent for a detachable tire. The major contribution of Andre Michelin in tourism is the publication of a series of guides known up to date as the Michelin Guides.

Michelin Guides *(Tourism)*: The Michelin Guide or *Le Guide Michelin* is a series of guide books published annually for several countries in the world. The first edition of a guide to France was published in 1900 with the purpose to help drivers maintain their cars, find decent lodging, and eat well while touring. It included addresses of places of interest for travelers, such as gasoline distributors, garages, tire stores, and public toilets. The guide was distributed free until 1920. The oldest guide is the Michelin Red Guide, a well-known European guide for hotels and restaurants, awarding the Michelin stars. There are also the "Green Guides" for travel and tourism, and several newer publications such as the *Guide Voyageur Pratique* for independent travelers, the *Guide Gourmand* that lists good-value eating-places, the *Guide*

Coup de Coeur for a special type of hotels. Nowadays there is a "Red Guide" covering France, Austria, Netherlands, Belgium, Luxemburg, Italy, Germany, Spain, Portugal, Switzerland, the United Kingdom and Ireland. Individual editions are published for several European cities, Tokyo, San Francisco, Los Angeles, and Las Vegas.

Michelin Stars *(Tourism)*: Michelin thought it would be important to rate the services of the properties he was advertising. He then created a rating system based on a number of stars assigned according to the service and the property's features. Three stars were the equivalent of a "Worth the Trip" qualification; two stars, "Worth a Detour"; one star, "Interesting". The Michelin method of stars now comprises five typical scales and is not considered a suitable system to categorize service properties.

Microsecond *(Air Traffic)*: One millionth of a second.

Microjets *(Airlines)*: A small aircraft propelled by jet engines, with seating capacity for two to four passengers. They are mainly used for air taxi services.

Microbrewery *(Hospitality)*: A small beer maker that produces no more than 15,000 barrels of beer and ale a year. They usually sell and distribute their production.

Microwave Oven *(Hospitality)*: An oven that uses very short electromagnetic waves to cook food.

Mid Atlantic Fares *(IATA Geography)*: Those fares which are applicable for journeys between Mid Atlantic Area and points in Areas 2 and/or 3 via the Atlantic Ocean.

Mid Atlantic Sub Area *(IATA Geography)*: The territory comprising Anguilla, Antigua and Barbuda, Aruba, Bahamas, Barbados, Belize, Bermuda, Bolivia, Cayman Islands, Colombia, Costa Rica, Cuba, Dominica, Dominican Republic, Ecuador, , El Salvador, French Guiana, Grenada, Guadeloupe, Guatemala, Guyana, Haiti, Honduras, Jamaica, Martinique, Montserrat, Netherlands Antilles, Nicaragua, Panama, Peru, St Kitts and Nevis, St Lucia, St Vincent and the Grenadines, Suriname, Trinidad and Tobago, Turks and Caicos Islands, Venezuela, Virgin Islands (British).

Mid-office System *(Tourism)*: The part of a computer system assigned to management, differencing from the GDS and accounting functions that are front office and back office sections, respectively.

Mid-Price/Extended-Stay Hotels *(Hospitality)*: Hotels that are aimed to persons needing to stay in an area for a week or longer. This type of guestrooms have more living space than regular hotel guestrooms, may also have cooking facilities, and tend to be less expensive than guestrooms in full-service or all-suite hotels.

Middle East Sub Area *(IATA Geography)*: The area comprising Bahrain, Egypt, Iran, Iraq, Israel, Jordan, Kuwait, Lebanon, Oman, Qatar, Saudi Arabia, Sudan, Syria, United Arab Emirates (Comprised of Abu Dhabi, Ajman, Dubai, Fujasirah, Ras Al Khaimah Sharjah, Umm al Qaiwain), Yemen.

Mid-Range Service *(Hospitality)*: A modest but sufficient level of service that appeals the largest segment of the traveling public. A mid-range property may offer uniformed service, airport limousine service, and food and beverage room service, a specialty restaurant, coffee shop, and lounge, and special rates for certain guests.

Mid-size Cabin *(Airlines)*: A flexible designation to denote an executive or corporate jet, categorized on a combination of passenger capacity, range, and maximum speed. Usually, a mid-size cabin jet holds between six to nine passengers, has a range of over 3,000 to 3,800 square miles and a maximum speed of about 550 miles per hour.

Midship *(Cruise)*: The longitudinal center part of a ship. The term is also used to denote something is in or toward the middle of the ship. Cabins located in midship usually are more expensive because they experience less motion during rough seas.

Midweek *(Airlines)*: Any day between Monday to Friday or Monday to Thursday. The code for midweek fares is the letter "X". On routes where the day of the week affects the fare, the rule shows how "midweek" is defined.

Migration *(Tourism)*: The movement of individuals or groups from one area to another or from the country of residence to another where they were not born.

Mike *(Airlines)*: Designator for the letter "M" in the International Phonetic Alphabet.

MIL *(GDS)*: Three-letter IATA code for Milan, and industrial city in Italy.

Mildew *(Hospitality)*: An odorous fungus that grows on bathroom surfaces, shower curtains, doors, and humid walls.

Mileage Allowance *(Car Rental)*: The amount of miles that entitles a car renter to drive a specified distance at no charge before a mileage surcharge takes effect

Mileage Based Pricing *(Airlines)*: An air fare calculation system based on the comparison between the actual amount of miles flown and the maximum permitted mileage in a fare component. If the sum of miles for all ticketed sectors is equal or lower than the MPM, the fare for the component is the published fare. If the sum of miles for all ticketed sectors is higher than the MPM, an excess percentage has to be found in order to charge the same excess percentage to the fare. It is also known as Mileage System.

Mileage Charges *(Car Rental)*: The charge assessed for each mile a rental car is driven beyond the terms of the agreement, unless the reservation or rental contract mentions unlimited mileage.

Mileage Run *(Airlines)*: A multi-segment airline trip offered by airlines to fly during special promotion periods for the purpose of increasing frequent flyer miles.

Mileage System *(Airlines)*: See Mileage Based Pricing.

Millibar *(Geography)*: A unit to measure the atmospheric pressure, which is equal to one thousandth of a bar (a Bar is a unit of pressure equal to a million dynes per square centimeter). The average atmospheric pressure of the Earth is 1013 millibars at sea level.

Military Aviation *(Aviation)*: The operation of aircraft by the Armed Forces.

Military Operations Area (MOA) *(Air Traffic)*: Airspace that is established for the purpose of separating military training activities from IFR traffic. MOA can be identified on a VFR sectional chart

Military Passenger *(Airlines)*: Any member of the army forces serving out of his country and travelling on a commercial air carrier.

Milk Run *(Tourism)*: A slang term to denote a trip that makes many stops along the way.

Millennium Development Goals *(Ecology)*: They are a set of purposes established by the United Nations aimed to humankind's

welfare. They are eight goals comprising the following topics:
1. Eradicate extreme poverty and hunger and achieve significant improvement in lives of at least 100 million slum dwellers, by 2020;
2. Achieve universal primary education at all levels by 2015;
3. Promote gender equality and empower women;
4. Reduce by two thirds the mortality rate among children under five years;
5. Improve maternal health, reducing by three quarters the maternal mortality ratio;
6. Combat and begin to reverse the spread of HIV/AIDS, malaria and other diseases;
7. Ensure environmental sustainability, by integrating the principles of sustainable development into country policies and programs; and
8. Develop a global partnership development.

MIN *(GDS)*: Code meaning: 1. Minute, 2. Minimum.

Minibar *(Hospitality)*: A small refrigerator that can be stocked with liquor, beer, wine and snacks. The items that are consumed are charged to the hotel bill.

Mini-Lease Rate *(Car Rental)*: Rental rates offered by some car rental companies including substantial discounts over monthly rates. To be entitled to this rate, the user must rent a car for a minimum of 32 consecutive days or a maximum of 330 days.

Minimal Impact *(Ecology)*: The control established on human behavior or activities, which is designed to reducing or mitigating the negative impacts of human beings on the environment to minimum levels.

Minimum Connecting Time (MCT) *(Airlines)*: The minimum time necessary to connect from one flight to another, as legally required for a reservation. These times vary according to the airport and the type of connections.

Minimum Equipment List (MEL) *(Airlines)*: A list of aircraft equipment required to be in good working condition before the aircraft may take off with passengers.

Minimum Group Size *(Tourism)*: Minimum number of passengers required to qualify the group for a fare.

Minimum Land Package *(Tourism)*: The minimum price of land services that is required to qualify for a special air fare.

Minimum Room *(Hospitality)*: A hotel room with the lowest rate.

Minimum Tour Price (MTP) *(Tourism)*: The minimum selling price for the tour calculated as the air fare plus an amount for land arrangements.

Mini-Suite *(Cruise)*: Typically, a large passenger cabin that offers separate sleeping and sitting areas.

MINIT *(Air Traffic)*: An abbreviation for Minutes in Trail. It is a specified interval between aircraft that is expressed in time.

MINR *(GDS)*: Code meaning Minimum Room Rate Desired.

Minshuku *(Hospitality)*: A lodging business in Japan usually run by a family group. It is a bed-and-breakfast inn, similar to a ryokan, but with fewer amenities and a cheaper price.

MIS *(GDS)*: Code meaning Management Information System. See Mid-office System.

Miscellaneous Charges Order (MCO) *(Airlines)*: A document issued by a carrier or its agent requesting the issuance of an appropriate Passenger Ticket and Baggage Check, or the provision of services to the person named in the document.

Mise en Bouteille a la Proprieté *(Hospitality)*: A French expression literally meaning "bottled by the owner" (at the vineyard). It is sometimes found on the label of French wines of vine growers who bottle their own wines.

Mise en Bouteille au Domaine *(Hospitality)*: A French expression literally meaning "bottled at the place" (or residence). It is often found on the labels of French wines of vine growers who bottle their own wines.

Mise en Place *(Hospitality)*: A French expression literally meaning "to put in place." It is typically related to the stage of pre-service preparation, including setting the tables.

MISS *(GDS)*: A code meaning Miss, Missing, Missed.

Mission Objectives *(Air Traffic)*: Goals to be accomplished during a specific mission, including flight plan, NRPs, legs, and a plan on how to accomplish these objectives.

MIT *(Air Traffic)*: An abbreviation for Miles in Trail. It is a specified interval between aircraft expressed in nautical miles.

MITA *(Airlines)*: See Multilateral Interline Transportation Agreements

Mitigating Negative Impacts *(Ecology)*: To cause a lessening or alleviation of negative behavior or activities. See also Minimal Impact.

Mixer *(Hospitality)*: An appliance used to knead, whip, emulsify, slice, mix, beat, grind, or chop different types of solid food, solid food and liquid(s), or two or more different liquids. It is commonly known as a blender.

MLM *(Tourism)*: See Multi-level Marketing.

MNL *(GDS)*: Three-letter IATA code for Manila, capital city of Philippines

MNM *(GDS)*: Code meaning Minimum.

Mobile OnAir *(Airlines)*: Onboard mobile connection service that is available on one of Air France's A318 aircraft since December 17th, 2007. With Mobile OnAir passengers are enabled to use their own devices and mobile phones to send and receive emails, exchange text messages and make and receive voice calls.

MOD *(GDS)*: Code meaning Moderate Room.

Moderate *(Hospitality)*: A type of hotels offering accommodation, on-site restaurants, bar, and perhaps conference rooms, as well as the basic services.

MODIF *(GDS)*: A code meaning Modify, Modifying, Modified, Modification.

Modified American Plan (MAP) *(Hospitality)*: A room rate that includes daily breakfast and one meal, usually dinner.

MODR *(GDS)*: Code meaning Moderate Room Rate.

Moist-Heat Cooking *(Hospitality)*: Cooking method using water or any other liquid.

Moisture *(Air Traffic)*: The water vapor content in the atmosphere, or the total water, liquid, solid or vapor, in a given volume of air.

MOM *(GDS)*: Code for Moment.

MOML *(GDS)*: Code meaning Muslim Meal.

MON *(GDS)*: Code for Monday.

Monitor *(Air Traffic)*: The action performed by traffic controllers observing aircraft in their respective airspace to assure safety.

Monitor *(GDS)*: See Computerized Reservation Terminal.

Monocropping *(Ecology)*: The activity of planting and maintaining a monoculture.

Monoculture *(Ecology)*: An unnatural agricultural system consisting of cultivating a single crop.

Monohull *(Cruise)*: Any conventional sailboat or powerboat with just one hull.

Monoplane *(Aeronautics)*: An airplane with one set of wings. Most aircraft built today have only one set of wings and are classified as monoplanes.

Monsoon *(Climate)*: A term that identifies seasonal winds in southern Asia reversing their direction according to the seasons, bringing wet and dry conditions depending on the direction.

Montgolfier Brothers *(Airlines)*: The brothers Joseph Michel Montgolfier (Born the 26th of August, 1740) and Jacques-Étienne Montgolfier (Born the 6th of January, 1745) were the inventors of the *Montgolfière, Globe Airostatique* or European hot air balloon. They succeeded in launching the first human ascent into the sky. He was Joseph who first intended to build a flying device. He recruited his brother to balloon building, convinced to have discovered the method to perform such idea. The two brothers built a big balloon model. Unfortunately, they were not able to keep control of their craft due to the great lifting force they lost on its very first test flight on 14 December 1782. The device floated nearly 2 kilometers and then was destroyed after landing by suspicious passersby. The Montgolfier brothers decided to make a public demonstration of a balloon as a way to claim their right to its invention. They flew a globe-shaped balloon on 4 June 1783 at *Annonay*, in front of a group of dignitaries and public. The flight covered 2 kilometers (about 1.2 miles), lasted 10 minutes, at an estimated altitude of 1.600 to 2.000 meters. The notice of this success quickly reached Paris. The following test was set for September of the same year, but this time, they wanted to search about the effects of flight into the upper atmosphere on living creatures. The king proposed to launch two criminals, but the inventors decided to send animals first. The test was accomplished on 19 September, 1783, using the *Aerostat Réveillon* with the first living creatures in a basket attached to the balloon. These creatures were a sheep called *Montauciel*, a duck and a rooster. The flight was a complete success performed before the King Louis XVI of France and Queen Marie Antoinette, and a huge crowd gathered at the royal palace in Versailles. The flight took approximately eight minutes, covered two miles, and reached an altitude of about 1500 feet. The animals survived the trip unharmed.

Upon this success, Etienne started the construction of a 60,000 cubic foot balloon for the purpose of making flights with humans. The balloon was tested by *Pilâtre de Rozier*, a twenty-six-year-old physician, who offered his services. This was the first free flight manned by humans accomplished by Pilâtre, together with an army officer, *François Laurent, Marquis D'Arlandes* on 21 November 1783. The flight took off from the *Parc de Château de la Muette* near the *Bois de Boulogne*, and landed between the windmills, outside the city ramparts, on the *Butte-aux-Cailles*. The pioneer pilots flew 25 minutes at about 3,000 feet above Paris covering a distance of nine kilometers. Numerous and sensational experiments came later. Jacques-Étienne died the 2 of August 1799 and Joseph died in June 26, 1810.

Monthly Rate *(Car Rental)*: A rate set to rent a car for a minimum of 28 consecutive days or a maximum of 31. Monthly rentals usually offer substantial discounts over weekly rates.

Montreal Protocol No.4 *(Airlines)*: A Protocol signed at Montreal on 25 September 1975 to amend the "Convention for the Unification of Certain Rules Relating to International Carriage by Air" known shortly as the "Warsaw Convention." The Montreal Protocol is considered to be the culmination of almost a half century of efforts to increase, and later to eliminate, the low limits of liability applicable under the 1929 Warsaw Convention when passengers are killed or injured in international air carrier accidents or baggage and merchandise are lost or damaged. The most important changes are related to the Limitation of Liability, Willful Misconduct, and Failure to Issue a Ticket or Waybill, and the provision for Carriers Trade Electronically. These significant new benefits include:

1. The elimination of the limits of liability applicable under the Warsaw Convention when passengers are killed or injured in international air carrier accidents. Under the Protocol, survivors of

international aircraft accidents and the families of accident victims will have access to courts in seeking damage compensations for the losses they suffered. The Protocol requires air carriers to pay compensations up to approximately USD 141,000 of proven damages on behalf of accident victims, without regard to whether the airline was negligent.

2. Provisions on code sharing clarify that when an accident occurs, a passenger may recover from either the airline operating the aircraft at the time of the accident, or the airline whose code is carried on the passenger's ticket.

3. Air cargo carriers and shippers can take advantage of technological innovations currently available, to facilitate the processing of international air cargo.

Monument *(Tourism)*: An object constructed by a community to keep the memory of a person or of an event.

Moor *(Cruise)*: To secure a ship to a dock with cables or ropes.

Morse Code *(Airlines)*: A telegraph code system in which letters and numbers are represented by standardized sequences of short and long elements that can be formed by sounds, marks or pulses. These elements are typically known as "dots" and "dashes" (short and long signals). The Morse Code is in effect today and it is said it will remain as a highly reliable communication means during difficult communications conditions. Morse code can be transmitted as electrical pulses along a telegraph wire, as an audio tone, or as a mechanical or visual signal. It was invented by Samuel F. B. Morse.

Morse, Samuel F.B. *(Airlines)*: An American painter of portraits and historic scenes (Apr 27 1791 - Apr 2 1872) who was the inventor of the Code Morse and the founder of the National Academy of Design. He knew little about electricity but in 1832 he assumed that pulses of electrical current could transport information over wires, and four years later he built the first working telegraph.

Mortality Rate *(Ecology)*: The number of deaths in a human population measured in a unit of time. The mortality rate is usually measured in units of deaths per 1,000 individuals per year.

Motel *(Hospitality)*: A small lodging facility generally found just off highway exits that usually offer sole occupancy of a bedroom.

It is also referred to as motor hotel where parking is provided at or near the room.

Motor Coach or Motorcoach *(Tourism)*: A large multi-seat bus that is comfortable and well-powered and is used for transporting tourists and their luggage over long distances, as opposed to scheduled transportation for individual passengers.

Motor Court *(Hospitality)*: See Motel.

Motor Home *(Tourism)*: A recreational self-motored vehicle that is equipped with complete living accommodation. Its French name is *Auto Caravane*.

Motor Hotel *(Hospitality)*: See Motel.

Motorbike *(Tourism)*: A small motorcycle that is easy to operate.

Motorboat *(Tourism)*: A power boat of 65 feet in length or less, which is equipped with an inboard or outboard engine.

Motorcoach Broker *(Tourism)*: An individual licensed and bonded by the U.S. Interstate Commerce Commission to operate motorcoach tours in the United States and, in some cases, Canada. Also known as a Tour Broker.

Motorcoach Tour *(Tourism)*: A group tour in which the principal mode of transportation is by motorcoach.

Motorcoach Tour Operator *(Tourism)*: A company that creates tours in which group members are transported via motorcoach to their destination, covering itinerary activities, and back.

Mountain *(Geography)*: It is a land mass rising abruptly to a large height from the surrounding level and occupying a minimum surface of some square kilometers. They are classified either in attention to their height or according to their geologic history. A first criterion divides mountains in medium size and high size. Medium size mountains range between 800 and 2,500 meters and high mountains have an altitude over 2,500 meters. Medium mountains are covered by forests, pasturage and are snowed only during the winter. High mountains are crowned by glaciers and snow. As per the second criterion, mountains are old or young.

Mountain Daylight Time (MDT) *(Geography)*: MDT is 6 hours behind of Coordinated Universal Time (UTC). MDT is used during winter in these Canadian provinces: Alberta, a few eastern communities of British Columbia, Northwest Territories and

Lloydminster in Saskatchewan. MDT is used during winter in these US states: Navajo Nation in Arizona, Colorado, most of the state of Idaho, some Western counties of Kansas, Montana, Western counties of Nebraska, New Mexico, South-Western parts of North Dakota, Parts of Malheur county in Oregon (rest of Oregon is PST/PDT), Western bounties of South Dakota, El Paso and Hudspeth in the west of Texas, Utah, Wyoming.

Mountain Standard Time (MST) MST is 7 hours behind of Coordinated Universal Time (UTC). MST is used during winter in these Canadian provinces: Alberta, a few eastern communities of British Columbia, Northwest Territories and Lloydminster in Saskatchewan. MST is used during winter in these US states: Navajo Nation in Arizona, Colorado, most of the state of Idaho, some Western counties of Kansas, Montana, Western counties of Nebraska, New Mexico, South-Western parts of North Dakota, Parts of Malheur county in Oregon (rest of Oregon is PST/PDT), Western counties of South Dakota, El Paso and Hudspeth in the west of Texas, Utah, Wyoming. MST is used all year: Most of Arizona and Sonora.

Mountain Tourism *(Tourism)*: Mountains are the most important destinations for global tourism after beaches and islands. Their attraction power is varied: the climate and clean air, topography, scenic beauty, local traditions, simple lifestyles, and the opportunities to practice sports that only can be played in steep slopes or winter snow. Due to these facts, mountain tourism is a diverse phenomenon, involving a great variety of activities. The benefits tourism can bring to mountain communities are evaluated against negative environmental, cultural, and economic impacts.

Mountain Wind *(Geography)*: Cool, heavy air that sinks and blows down a mountain slope.

MOV *(GDS)*: A code meaning Move, Moving, Moved.

Movement *(Tourism)*: The departure or arrival of a vehicle.

Moving Sidewalk *(Tourism)*: A mechanical band or moving ramp that are designed to carry people and goods horizontally or along slight inclines. They are mainly found in long corridors at airports and are also called Travelators.

MOW *(GDS)*: Three-letter IATA code for Moscow, capital city of

Russia.

MPD *(GDS)*: Code meaning Multiple Purpose Document.

MPH *(GDS)*: Code meaning Miles per Hour.

MPM *(GDS)*: Code meaning Maximum Permitted Mileage.

MS *(Cruise)*: Code meaning Motor Ship, a designation for many cruise liners.

MSA *(Geography)*: Metropolitan Statistical Area.

MSCN *(GDS)*: A code meaning Misconnect, Misconnected, or Misconnecting.

MSG *(GDS)*: Code for Message(s)

MSL *(Air Traffic)*: See Mean Sea Level.

MSHDL *(GDS)*: A code meaning Mishandle, Mishandling, or Mishandled.

MSO *(Airlines)*: See Member Sales Offices.

MST *(Geography)*: See Mountain Standard Time

MSY *(GDS)*: Three-letter IATA code for New Orleans, Louisiana, USA.

MT *(GDS)*: Code meaning Mountain Time.

MTAF *(Air Traffic)*: See Mandatory Frequency.

MTG *(GDS)*: Code for Meeting.

MTP *(Tourism)*: See Minimum Tour Price.

MTS *(Cruise)*: Code for Motor Turbine Ship.

MUC *(GDS)*: Three-letter IATA code for Munich, an important city in the southern part of Germany.

Multi-access System *(GDS)*: A GDS capable to access the system of a supplier, an airline or hotel.

Multi-level *(Tourism)*: Something that has more than one floor or level, be it a building or a marketing process.

Multi-level Marketing (MLM) *(Business)*: A promotion and sales system for a business that markets its products directly to consumers by means of relationship referral and direct selling. The associated people to the business are independent and unsalaried salespeople who are compensated a commission proportional to the volume of sales generated through the people they have recruited into their independent distribution network. Many business of this type have resulted fraudulent or at least, inoperative. The system is also called Network Marketing.

Multi Sector *(Tourism)*: A sector of a journey that includes one or more transit stops.

Multi-Taxi *(Air Traffic)*: Many aircraft trying to taxi at once, creating congestion.

Multihull *(Cruise)*: A term denoting a catamaran or trimaran. It is a classification for yachts having more than one hull which is extensively used by charter industry professionals.

Multilateral Agreement on the Liberalization of International Air Transportation (MALIAT) *(Airlines)*: A Multilateral Agreement negotiated between 31 October and 2 November 2000 at Kona, Hawaii, and signed at Washington D.C. on 1 May 2001 by Brunei Darussalam, Chile, New Zealand, Singapore and the United States of America, with the purpose to promote open skies for air services arrangements. The Protocol provides for parties to exchange seventh freedom passenger and cabotage rights. The key features of the MALIAT are: Open route Schedule, open traffic rights including seventh freedom cargo services, open capacity, multiple airline designation, third-country code-sharing, and a minimal tariff filing regime. The New Zealand is the depositary state for the Agreement and Protocol.

Multilateral Interline Traffic Agreements (MITA) *(Tourism)*: According to the IATA definition, it is "an agreement whereby passengers and cargo use a standard traffic document (i.e. passenger ticket or air waybill) to travel on various modes of transport involved in a routing in order to reach a final destination." It establishes the rules followed by airlines when collecting money and issuing documents for carriage on each others' services, as well as the Cargo Claims Procedures Agreement, and the Multilateral Interline Service Charge Agreements, Passenger and Cargo.

Multiple Guest Splits *(Hospitality)*: Charges that are divided among the members of a group.

Multipropriété *(Hospitality)*: A French term for Time-Sharing.

Murphy Bed *(Tourism)*: A bed found in some hotel rooms or in cruise cabins that is designed to fold up or swung into a closet or cabinet when not in use. Where offered in cruise accommodations, a Murphy bed is typically used for the third or fourth occupants of the stateroom.

Museum Tourism (*Tourism*): A type of cultural tourism that is designed for people who have interest in visiting museums. It is performed by very trained and educated staff. Some of the most popular Museum tours are organized to visit the Louvre in Paris, El Prado in Madrid, British Museum in London, the Vatican in Rome, the Modern Art Museum in New York, just to mention a few.

Must (*Hospitality*): The juice or other parts of the grape produced by crushing and pressing the grapes. After this process the must goes to fermentation.

Muster (*Cruise*): To assemble passengers and/or crew to their assembly areas in the event of an emergency at sea.

Muster Drill (*Cruise*): A safety demonstration conducted by members of the ship's staff who instruct passengers about the route to and location of their muster station, use of their life savers, and other important safety information. The muster drill is usually conducted before or within 24 hours after the cruise departure.

Muster Station (*Cruise*): The location where groups of passengers are asked to report in the event of an emergency at sea. Muster stations are either interior public rooms or open deck or promenade spaces that are familiar to passengers. The crew staff assigns a muster station to every passenger.

MV (*Cruise*): A code meaning Motorized Vessel.

MVD (*GDS*): Three-letter IATA code for Montevideo, the capital city of Uruguay.

MX (*Airlines*): Two-letter IATA code for Mexicana de Aviacion, an airline of Mexico.

MXN (*GDS*): Code for *Nuevo Peso Mexicano*, national currency of Mexico.

MXP (*GDS*): Three-letter IATA code for Malpensa Airport, serving the city of Milan, Italy.

MY (*Cruise*): Motorized Yacht.

N

N (*Airlines*): "November," name used to designate the letter "N" in the International Phonetic Alphabet.

N *(GDS)*: Code meaning: 1. No Smoking Zone; 2. Together with the air fare it indicates a night fare.

NA *(GDS)*: A code meaning Not Available, Not Applicable, No Answer, Need Alternative.

NABTA *(Organizations)*: An acronym for National Association of Business Travel Agents.

NAC *(GDS)*: Code meaning No action taken.

NACA *(Organizations)*: An acronym for National Air Carrier Association.

NACOA *(Organizations)*: An acronym for National Association of Cruise-Oriented Agencies.

NACTA *(Organizations)*: An acronym for National Association of Commissioned Travel Agents.

NAFTA *(Business)*: See North American Free Trade Agreement.

Named Storm *(Cruise)*: A tropical weather system that is baptized with an alphabetical name by government weather services.

NanoBlock *(Computing)*: A term used in Alien Technology to describe tiny microchips with a width of three human hairs.

Nansen Passport *(Airlines)*: Internationally recognized identification document that is issued to refugees. It is named after Fridtjob Nansen, a Norwegian humanitarian statesman.

Napery *(Hospitality)*: Table linens.

NAR *(GDS)*: Code meaning New Arrival Information.

Narrow Body *(Aeronautics)*: Commercial aircraft with a fuselage cabin measuring from 3 to 4 meters (10 to 13 ft) and a single center aisle, along which seats are located. The maximum capacity of narrow-body aircraft is 250 seats. If seating less than 100 passengers, they are considered regional airliners. Some types of narrow body airplanes are Airbus A320 family, Boeing 707, Boeing 727, Boeing 737, Boeing 757, McDonnell Douglas DC-9, McDonnell Douglas MD-80/MD-90, and Fokker F28.

NAS *(Air Traffic)*: See National Airspace System.

NASA *(Air Traffic)* Acronym for National Aeronautics and Space Administration.

National *(Tourism)*: A person who has citizenship of a country, either by birth or by naturalization. Something that is owned or maintained for the public benefit by the national government, such as National Parks. A carrier, such as an airline or a cruise line that is registered in a country showing the flag carrier condition. Any corporation owned by national stockholders.

National Aeronautics & Space Administration (NASA) *(Air Traffic)*: NASA was created by the U.S. President Dwight D. Eisenhower in 1958 as a response to the Soviet Union's launch of the first artificial satellite in 1957. President John F. Kennedy focused NASA and the nation on sending astronauts to the moon by the end of the 1960s. In its early years it conducted purely scientific research and worked on developing applications for space technology, combining both pursuits in developing the first weather and communications satellites. After Apollo, NASA concentrated on creating a reusable ship to provide regular access to the space: the Space Shuttle that was first launched in 1981. In 2000, the United States and Russia established permanent human presence in space aboard the International Space Station, a multinational project representing the work of 16 nations. NASA"s mission is to pioneer the future in space exploration, scientific discovery and aeronautics research. NASA conducts its work in four principle fields, called mission directorates: Aeronautics, Exploration Systems, Science, and Space Operations. Though nearly 50 years old, NASA is only beginning the most exciting part of its existence.

National Air Carrier Association (NACA) *(Organizations)*: An aviation trade association promoting the national and international interests of the members and representing their interests before the Congress of the United States and the many U.S. Government agencies that have an oversight on the U.S. Aviation Industry. It was incorporated in the State of Delaware on January 3, 1962. Its mission is aimed to: Promote among the members the highest degree of operational safety and efficiency; advance and maintain with Congress, government agencies, and the traveling public an enlightened understanding of the member's goals and problems; influence in a proper manner the laws and regulations promulgated on the industry; promote the national and international aviation interests of all the members; and, bring members' representatives into closer personal and professional relations with each other, with government and with other industry leaders.

National Airspace System (NAS) *(Air Traffic)*: The common network of US encompassing airspace, air navigation facilities (equipment and services, airports or landing areas), aeronautical charts (information and services), rules, regulations and procedures, technical information, and human and material resources. Included are system components shared jointly with the military.

National Airline *(Airlines)*: An airline with annual operating revenues between USD100 million and USD1 billion. The term also denotes a flag carrier owned or controlled by a state.

National Association of Business Travel Agents (NABTA) *(Organizations)*: Travel agents who specialize in servicing corporate and business accounts in the United States and provide travel services for businesses and organizations holding out-of-town meetings and conventions. It promotes members' awareness of practical methods of servicing and increasing their accounts; prepares detailed descriptions of convention facilities, hotels, restaurants, tour operators, and tourist attractions for members, and organizes family trips for members to visit destinations and view convention facilities.

National Association of Commissioned Travel Agents (NACTA) *(Organizations)*: A trade group and leading association for independent travel agents, cruise oriented agents, home based travel agents and outside sales travel agents. It was incorporated in 1987 to offer its travel agent members numerous benefits and services.

National Association of Cruise-Oriented Agencies (NACOA) *(Organizations)*: A professional trade group of travel agencies who sell primarily cruises, and tours sometimes. The Vision of NACOA is to be a premier association for cruise oriented travel retailers by promoting cruise vacations, uniting cruise retailers, providing educational programs, and creating a forum for Cruise Agents & Cruise Lines.

National Carrier *(Airlines)*: See National Airline.

National Oceanic and Atmospheric Administration (NOAA) *(Organizations)*: A scientific U.S. government agency that is centered in keeping the public informed of the changing environment around them. NOAA's products and services support economic vitality and affect more than one-third of America's gross domestic product. Its services enclose daily weather forecasts, severe storm warnings, climate monitoring, fisheries management, coastal restoration, and maritime commerce. It was founded in 1807.

National Park *(Tourism)*: A relatively large area of public land containing representative examples of major natural regions, features, or scenic, recreational, scientific, or historical importance. A national park is typically an area of natural beauty, chosen for the conservation of flora, fauna and scenery, and for recreation, if this does not conflict with the conservation objectives of the parks and their landscapes. National park ecosystems are protected by governments against and are not heavily altered by humans. Activities such as hunting, mining, commercial fishing and agriculture are all controlled within national parks.

National Telecommunications and Information Administration (NTIA) *Organizations)*: A bureau of the U.S. Department of Commerce. It is the President's principal adviser on telecommunications and information policy issues. NTIA performs telecommunications research and engineering, including resolving technical telecommunication issues for the Federal government and private sector. It administers infrastructure and public telecommunication facilities.

National Tour Association (NTA) *(Organizations)*: A trade organization of tourism professionals involved in the growth and development of the packaged travel industry. It is committed to providing business opportunities and professional education in an environment where members can promote relationships with one another. The NTA members are tour operators that develop and sell travel packages, and tour suppliers who provide the package components for tour operators and can fall into one of the following categories: hotels, attractions, restaurants, airlines, cruise lines, railroads, and sightseeing services. Its headquarters are in Lexington, KY, USA

National Tourism *(Tourism)*: A type of tourism practiced inside the boundaries of the country where tourists reside. It is also called

Domestic Tourism.

National Tourism Office *(Tourism)*: A government agency responsible for accomplishing national goals and public policy with respect to tourism, and for providing information services to international travelers.

National Wildlife Refuge *(Tourism)*: A land or water area protected to provide habitat for wild animals and birds, located within the National Wildlife Refuge System. These refuges are limited to recreational practices. Almost all of them use the words National "Wildlife Refuge", "Wetland Management District", or "Wildlife Management Area" in their names.

National Wildlife Refuge System *(Tourism)*: A network of certain protected areas of land or water in the United States, which is reserved to protect wildlife and wildlife habitat. The system is administered by the U.S. Fish and Wildlife Service and consists of over 500 refuges across the nation.

Native Species *(Ecology)*: Species that have evolved in a specific area or habitat or are indigenous or occur naturally in it.

Natl *(Tourism)*: National.

NATO Alphabet *(Airlines)*: See Phonetic Alphabet.

Natural Attraction *(Tourism)*: A natural feature that excludes human intrusion and that attracts tourists.

Natural Resources: *(Ecology)*: Resources supplied by nature that are used for human needs, such as nutrients and minerals that are found in the soil and deeper layers of the earth's crust. They are divided into renewable and nonrenewable.

Natural Resources Canada (NRCan) *(Organizations)*: A department of the Canadian government, which is responsible for ensuring a responsible development of natural resources, energy, minerals and metals, and forests. It also uses its expertise in earth sciences to build and maintain an up-to-date knowledge base of earth sciences, mapping and remote sensing.

Natural Selection *(Ecology)*: One of several steps through which evolution occurs. It is the process described by Darwin's theory of evolution that favors certain types of genes and disfavors others when the population is exposed to an environmental change or stress. By this process some organisms live and reproduce and others die before reproducing. The result is a population with a greater proportion of organisms better adapted to certain environmental conditions. The process is entirely guided by the interaction of organisms with their environment.

Natural Wine *(Hospitality)*: The product of grape fermentation without the addition of alcohol, sugar or other additives.

Nature-based Tourism *(Tourism)*: Leisure travel organized for tourists who are willing to enjoy natural attractions while getting involved in a variety of open-air activities.

Nature Tourism *(Tourism)*: Leisure travel that is made to places where people can experience and enjoy nature. Tourists become often engaged in varied outdoor activities. Nature tourism is carried out in a manner that promotes the protection of natural and human communities and consideration for those who will inherit our world.

Naturism *(Tourism)*: A manner of practicing leisure tourism going without clothes, usually in a communal setting or in designated areas, in the belief that nudity is a healthy natural state

Naturopathy *(Tourism)*: Holistic approach that believes in the body's ability to heal itself. It uses treatments to encourage the body's self-healing mechanisms. It is also known as Natural Medicine.

Nautical Chart *(Cruise)*: A map of navigable waters, pointing depths and hazards.

Nautical Mile (NM) *(Cruise)*: A distance equal to 6,082.2 feet as opposite to a land mile that measures 5,280 feet. It equals 1.852 meters.

NAV Canada *(Air Traffic)*: A private and non-profit organization that operates Canada's civil Air Navigation Service (ANS). In 1996 Transport Canada entrusted NAV Canada the duty of managing a safe, orderly and expeditious flow of air traffic in Canadian airspace. It is headquartered in Ottawa, Ontario, directs about 1,400 ground-based navigation aids across the country, and employs around 2,000 air traffic controllers, 800 flight service specialists and 700 technologists.

NAVAID *(Air Traffic)*: See Navigational Aid.

Navigable *(Cruise)*: Term denoting that waters are open to commercial shipping.

Navigation *(Tourism)*: The set of skillful actions and science to direct the course of a ship, aircraft of spacecraft.

Navigation *(Air Traffic)*: A system, usually software, in which the primary purpose is to generate position relative to a coordinate frame, usually fixed earth frame, such as latitude and longitude.

Navigation Aid *(Air Traffic)*: Any device or process that helps with navigation, such as a VOR station or a position update.

Navigation Lights *(Cruise)*: A series of bright lights required from a ship during night navigation to prevent risks. See Running Lights.

Navigation Reference Point (NRP) *(Air Traffic)*: A point, usually fixed in earth coordinates.

Navigational Aid or Navaid *(Air Traffic)*: Any visual or electronic device external to a vessel or an aircraft, intended to provide guidance information or position data for aircraft in flight. Such aids can be lighthouses, buoys, fog signals, and day beacons.

NB *(GDS)*: Code for Northbound.

NBO *(GDS)*: Three-letter IATA code for Nairobi, capital city of Kenya.

NBR *(GDS)*: Code for Number.

NBTA *(Organizations)*: See National Association of Business Travel Agents.

NC *(GDS)*: A code meaning: 1. No connection; 2. No Charge.

NCO *(GDS)*: Code meaning New Continuation Information.

NDT *(Geography)*: See Newfoundland Daylight Time.

NEC *(GDS)*: Code for Necessary.

NEG *(GDS)*: Code for Negative.

Negative *(Airlines)*: As a reply to a message, it means acknowledging but letting know the answer is negative.

Negotiated Rate *(Tourism)*: An air fare or hotel rate that has been set through a negotiation between the provider and the client. Negotiated rates apply to a specified time period and for specific travelers.

Nested Excursions *(Airlines)*: See Back to Back Fares.

Net *(Tourism)*: A short term for referring informally to Internet.

Net Amount *(Tourism)*: The amount payable to a supplier after deducting commissions or markups.

Net Fare *(Tourism)*: The fare at which a provider sells a service to a travel agent, without commissions and taxes.

Net Group Rate *(Tourism)*: A wholesale rate applied for a group to which the agent or operator adds a mark-up.

Net Profit *(Tourism)*: The earnings after all expenses have been deducted.

Net Rate *(Tourism)*: The rate at which a provider sells a service to a travel agent, without commissions and taxes.

Net Revenue *(Tourism)*: See Net Profit.

Net Weight *(Airlines)*: The actual weight of goods exclusive of containers and/or packaging.

Net Wholesale Rate *(Tourism)*: A rate marked-up by the wholesale agent for a tour, which covers distribution, promotion, and retail rate, but not commissions for the retailer

Network *(Business)*: 1. Any interconnected combination of pathways joined together to form a system, such as a network of air routes, roads, railways, etc. 2. A group of stations (computers, servers, telephones, or other components) connected to exchange information. 3. An interconnected system of people, acquaintances, or business associates for the easy flow of data and the use of resources between one another.

Network Marketing *(Business)*: See Multi-level Marketing.

Networking *(Business)*: A practice of marketing consisting of using one contact to reach other potential customers. Networking is one of the key strategies for certain types of businesses.

Neutral Spirit *(Hospitality)*: An alcoholic spirit purified in the still to a minimum of 95 percent of absolute alcoholic purity, at which point it has no important taste and little body. Neutral spirits are used to make blended whiskey and are the base for many cordials and liqueurs.

Neutral Unit of Construction (NUC) *(Airlines)*: A common denominator used to calculate the total air fare for multi-segment journeys in which individual local selling fares are applied. Since it would be impossible to add amounts with different currency denominators, the local selling fares are substituted by NUC amounts which then are added as a sole amount. This total amount is converted to the local currency of the country where the trip starts, by using de IATA rate of exchange (IROE).

New England Rum *(Hospitality)*: Full-bodied rum produced in the United States from molasses shipped from the West Indies.

Newfoundland Daylight Time (NDT) *(Geography)*: NDT is 2 hours and 30 minutes behind of Coordinated Universal Time (UTC). NDT is used during summer in this Canadian province: Newfoundland and Labrador, except most of Labrador (the mainland part).

Newfoundland Standard Time (NST) *(Geography)*: NST is 3 hours and 30 minutes behind of Coordinated Universal Time (UTC). NST is used during winter in this Canadian province: Newfoundland and Labrador - except most of Labrador (the mainland part).

Newberry, Jorge Alejandro *(Airlines)*: Jorge Newbery was an Argentine pilot and engineer, one of the first Latin American aircraft pilots in history. He was born in Buenos Aires in 1875. By the beginning of the 20th century Newbery had flown air crafts four times across Argentina, but until 1907 he had not been in any. In 1907 he flew the aerostatic globe *Pampero* accompanied by Aaron de Anchorena. In 1908 Jorge's brother, Eduardo Newbery, died in an aerostat accident, one of the first casualties in Argentine aviation history. By 1910, aircraft began to arrive in Argentina, and Newbery became interested in them. When Argentina became the first Latin American country to have a militarized air force in 1912, Newbery was one of its promoters. In 1913 he accompanied the German pilot Heinrich Lubbe in his flight from Buenos Aires to Colonia, Uruguay, setting a world record of a flight over the sea. Jorge Newbery died by cause of an air crash in Mendoza, while intending to cross the Andes in 1914. Buenos Aires' second largest airport, the *Aeroparque Jorge Newbery*, is named after him.

Next Generation Air Transportation System *(Airlines)*: A program of the Department of Transportation of the United States adopted to design an advanced technology system that will avoid flight delays, increase capacity, and decrease security risks. It is also known as NextGen Initiative.

NextGen Initiative *(Airlines)*: See Next Generation Air Transportation System.

NFDC *(Air Traffic)*: Code for National Flight Data Center.

NGO *(GDS)*: Three-letter IATA code for Nagoya, important city in Japan

NH *(Airlines)*: Two-letter IATA code for All Nippon Airways.

NIBS *(GDS)*: Code meaning Neutral Industry Booking System.

Niche Cruise *(Cruise)*: A market segment of the cruise industry featuring special and differentiated characteristics that is aimed to a specific sector of the market. Typical examples are adventure or ecological itineraries that are operated in smaller or unconventional vessels.

Niche Cruising *(Cruise)*: See Niche Cruise.

NIL *(GDS)*: Code meaning None, nothing.

Nimbostratus *(Geography)*: A principal cloud type, gray colored, often dark, with a diffuse appearance due to more or less continuously falling rain or snow.

Ninth Freedom of the Air *(Airlines)*: The freedom to operate commercial flights between two domestic points in a foreign country. It is also called Full Cabotage or Open-skies Privilege.

NKG *(GDS)*: Three-letter IATA code for Nanjing, important city in the Popular Republic of China.

NM *(Cruise)*: See Nautical Miles.

NML *(GDS)*: Code for Normal.

NN *(GDS)*: Code meaning Need, needing, needed.

NO *(GDS)*: A code meaning: 1. No Action Taken (on segment). 2. Not Operating Flight.

NO ADC *(GDS)*: Code meaning No Additional Collection.

No Cook Yacht Charter *(Tourism)*: A charter with captain only, without a cook, stewardess or deck hand. Captain only charters are available on bare boat yachts. It is also called Captain Only Yacht Charters

No Frills *(Airlines)*: A sort of "bare bones" service, as an airline flight that provides nothing else than only the basic service without additional amenities.

No Frills Airlines *(Airlines)*: A name given to "Budget" or "Low Cost" Airlines.

No Go *(Tourism)*: An expression meaning Not possible. It also denotes a cancelled service or flight.

No Host Bar (No-host Bar or Nohost Bar) *(Hospitality)*: Also known as "A la Carte Bar" or "Cash Bar", the term refers to a bar service at a social event where guests have to pay for beverages. It is opposed to a hosted bar where drinks are paid for by the host. By extension, there are a "No Host Bar and Menu" and a "No Host Dinner."

No Name *(GDS)*: 1. Name element missing in a reservation; 2. A product or service of an unknown brand or without brand identification.

No Show *(Airlines)*: A passenger who doesn't arrive for a flight due to reasons other than missed connections and fails to cancel the reservation.

No Show *(Hospitality)*: A guest who fails to notify the hotel when he/she does not show for check in and has not cancelled his/her stay, thereby incurring in a penalty.

No Show Charge *(Airlines)*: The charge made by reason of the failure to use a reserved seat either through failure to arrive at the airport at the time fixed by the airline or through arriving improperly documented or otherwise not ready to travel on the flight.

No Show Charge *(Hospitality)*: The charge made by reason of the failure to use a reserved accommodation through failure to arrive at the hotel at the check in time fixed by the hotel or through failing in giving advice on the cancelation.

No Show Fee *(Car Rental)*: The charge made for not using a reserved vehicle when it is not cancelled within 24 hours of pick up.

No-tell Motel *(Hospitality)*: A cheap lodging place that is used for clandestine romantic liaisons.

NOAA *(Organizations)*: An acronym for "National Oceanic and Atmospheric Administration."

NOCN *(GDS)*: Code meaning No Connection.

Noise Abatement Procedures *(Air Traffic)*: An action taken in order to reduce aircraft engine noise over populated areas.

Noise Pollution *(Ecology)*: Harmful or offensive sounds that are unreasonably intrusive. Maximum noise levels for humans must not exceed 85 decibels, for a maximum period of six continuous hours.

NOJ *(GDS)*: Code meaning Normal Fare Open Jaw.

Non Affinity Group *(Tourism)*: A travel group formed by travelers who do not share a common affinity.

Non-biodegradable *(Ecology)*: Products or substances that are not able to be consumed or broken down by biological organisms, such as plastics, aluminum, and many chemicals used in industry and agriculture.

Non-commissionable *(Tourism)*: A travel product priced without a commission or markup for the travel agent, or a product or service that does not generate a commission, such as taxes and surcharges..

Non-IATA Carrier *(Airlines)*: Any carrier that is not a member of IATA.

Non-Perishable Food *(Hospitality)*: Food product that resists spoilage and damage unless improperly handled and stored, namely sugar, flour, spices, and dry beans.

Non Ref *(Airlines)*: Abbreviation for Non-refundable.

Non-Refundable *(Airlines)*: A notation made on a ticket advising that no moneys will be returned in case the trip is cancelled by the passenger. This is a usual condition for cheap fares.

Non-Scheduled *(Tourism)*: A transport service with no regulated frequency, and departure and arrival times.

Non-Scheduled Flight *(Airlines)*: Any flight operating not subject to a fixed timetable of regular departure and arrival times.

Non-Sked *(Tourism)*: See Non-scheduled.

Non Stop Flights *(Airlines)*: Flights that depart from one airport and arrive in another without landing at any intermediate point.

Non-Towered Airport *(Air Traffic)*: An airport not directed by air traffic control. Pilots fly into and out of these airports using standard operating procedures to avoid one another.

Non-Transferable *(Airlines)*: One of the characteristics of air tickets is that they cannot be used by anyone else. They must be used only by the person to whom it is issued.

Nonrevenue *(Tourism)*: Passengers or guests, who do not pay for the services they receive, namely travel company employees.

Nonstop *(Airlines)*: Term referring to a flight not stopping enroute, that is, a single transport segment with no intermediate stops.

Nontoxic *(Ecology)*: A product not showing potentially harmful characteristics for the consumer.

Nonrenewable Resource *(Ecology)*: A resource that exists in a limited amount in the earth's crust and can not be renewed, such as copper, coal, and oil. They are also classified as exhaustible resources because men are extracting and using them at a much faster rate than they were formed.

NOOP *(GDS)*: A code meaning No Operate, No Operation, Not Operating.

Nordic *(Geography)*: A term used to define something related to the Scandinavian countries (Denmark, Finland, Iceland, Norway, Sweden).

NOREC *(GDS)*: Code meaning No Record.

Normal Fare *(Airlines)*: A type of air fare valid to complete the journey in the period of one year, not subject to restrictions and allowing unlimited stopovers en route. Normal fares can be Economy, Business or First Class Fares.

Normal Fare Open Jaw *(Airlines)*: Travel from one country and return thereto comprising not more than two international fare components with a domestic surface break in one country, either at unit origin or unit turn around, or a surface break at both unit origin and unit turnaround and for which the fare is assessed as a single pricing unit using half trip normal fares.

Normal Round Trip *(Airlines)*: A journey that starts and ends in the same point comprising two fare components for which the fare is assessed using half trip normal fares.

North America *(IATA Geography)*: The area comprising Alaska, Canada, Continental USA, Hawaii, Mexico, Saint Pierre and Miquelon.

North America, Geographical *(Geography)*: It is the northern portion of the landmass known as the Americas. It has the shape of a triangle having the base resting on the Arctic zone and the vertex on the Gulf of Mexico. It is surrounded by the Arctic Ocean in the North, by the Atlantic Ocean in the East, by the Caribbean Sea in the Southeast, and by the Pacific Ocean in the West. The Isthmus of Panama separates it from South America, and the Strait of Bering separates it from Asia. North America is the third largest continent on the earth, covering an area of about 27,328,190 square kilometers or 10,545,177 square miles, including its insular territory. The islands are numerous, the most important of which are the Bermudas on the Atlantic Ocean; the Aleutians, the Alexander Archipelago, Queen Charlotte and Moresby on the Pacific Ocean. Since Greenland is located on the same tectonic plate, it is also part of North America, as well as Central America and the Caribbean. As of October 2006, its population was estimated at over 514,600,000 inhabitants. It is the fourth continent in population following Asia, Africa, and Europe.

North America is divided into four great regions:

1. The raised and relatively flat plateau of the Canadian Shield in the northeast;

2. A varied region in the east, that includes the Appalachian Mountains, the Atlantic coastal plain, and the Florida peninsula;

3. The Great Plains running from the Gulf of Mexico to the Canadian Arctic; and,

4. The mountainous west region that includes the Rocky Mountains, the Great Basin, California and Alaska.

Each of these geographical elements is subdivided into other sub-regions. High mountains are found in North America. Mount McKinley or Denali in Alaska is the highest mountain in the North American continent, with a height of 6,194 meters (20,320 feet); Mount Logan, Canada's highest mountain and the second-highest in North America with 5,959 meters (19,551 feet); the Pico de Orizaba or Citlaltépetl (in aboriginal language), the highest mountain in Mexico and the third highest in North America with 5,636 meters (18,490 feet), the Popocatépetl, an active volcano with 5,636 meters; Mount Elbert, the highest peak in the Rocky Mountains with 4,421 meters, and Mount Whitney in California with 5,680 meters.

North American rivers are large, the most important of which are: The Mackenzie, the longest river in Canada (1,200 miles or 1,800 km), the Yukon, that remains frozen most of the year (1,265 miles or 2.035 km), St. Lawrence, a 760 miles (1,225 km) passage between the Atlantic Ocean and the Great Lakes; Mississippi, the major river of North America (2,339 miles or 3,765 km); Missouri, the longest river in the United States (2,500 miles or 4,023 km); Ohio, one of the major affluent of the Mississippi River (975 miles or 1,569 km); Rio Grande, one of the longest rivers in North America (1,885 miles or 3,034 km); Colorado (1,450 miles or 2,333 km), a river that begins in the Rocky Mountains of northern Colorado and ends in the Gulf of California; the Columbia (1,152 miles or 1,857 km), a fast-flowing river that begins in the Canadian Rockies of southeast British Columbia and ends in the Pacific; and Fraser (850 miles or 1,368 km), a Canadian river empting its water into the Strait of Georgia, just south of Vancouver.

North America houses the Great Lakes, also called Laurentian Great Lakes. They are a chain of freshwater lakes located in eastern North America, on the Canada-United States border. They form the largest group of freshwater lakes on Earth comprising Lakes Superior, Michigan, Huron (or Michigan-Huron), Erie, and Ontario. They are also called "Inland Seas" or "Canada and the United States Third Coast".

North America has a great variety of tourist attractions, both natural and cultural. A particular mention, among natural destinations, deserve the diversity of National Parks, such as Banff National Park, Jasper National Park, Kluane National Park and Reserve, and Algonquin Provincial Park in Canada; Yosemite National Park, Everglades National Park, Yellowstone National Park, Mount Rushmore National Memorial, Grand Canyon National Park, Death Valley National Park, and Hawaii Volcanoes National Park in the United States. Mexican places such as Chichén Itzá, Palenque, Teotihuacán, Uxmal and Tulum are archeological parks of a rich historic and cultural heritage. North American urban tourism is represented by many places, the most outstanding of which are Quebec, Toronto, Boston, New York, Washington, Chicago, New Orleans, Los Angeles, San Francisco, the city of Mexico, Guadalajara, Oaxaca and Puebla. For the practice of leisure tourism travelers go to the beaches of Florida, Santa Monica, Venice Beach, Hawaii, Acapulco, Cancun and Puerto Vallarta. Among the most important commercial cultural attractions of North America are Kennedy Space Center Visitor Complex, SeaWorld Orlando, Walt Disney World, and Disneyland.

North American Free Trade Agreement (NAFTA) *(Business)*: The trade bloc in North America created by Canada, Mexico, and the United States in January 1, 1994. As of 2008 it remains the largest trade bloc in the world in terms of combined GDP of its members. Over a 15-year period NAFTA eliminated the majority of tariffs on products traded among the three members and gradually phased out other tariffs. Restrictions were to be removed from many categories, including motor vehicles, computers, textiles, and agriculture. The treaty also protects intellectual property rights (patents, copyrights, and trademarks), and outlines the removal of investment restrictions among the three countries. Provisions regarding worker and environmental protection were added later as a result of supplemental agreements signed in 1992.

North American Route Program (NRP) *(Air Traffic)*: A set of rules and procedures intended to provide an improved adaptability for flight planning within published guidelines.

North and Central Pacific Fares *(Airlines)*: Fares that are applicable for travel between points in the Area 1 and Points in Area 3 (except South West Pacific Sub-area) via the Pacific Ocean.

North Atlantic Fares *(Airlines)*: Those applicable for travel between the North America Area and points in Areas 2 and/or 3 via the Atlantic Ocean.

North Atlantic Sub-area *(IATA Geography)*: The area comprising Canada, Greenland, Mexico, Saint Pierre and Miquelon, USA (including Alaska, Hawaii, Puerto Rico and Virgin Islands US).

Northern Lights, The *(Airlines)*: A colorful geomagnetic and electric display visible near the North Pole, known as "Aurora Borealis".

Northern South America *(IATA Geography)*: The territory comprising Ecuador, Colombia, Venezuela, Guiana, Surinam and Guyana.

Nose Gear *(Aeronautics)*: The landing gear nearest the nose of the aircraft, usually located under the cockpit.

Nose Count *(Airlines)*: Also known as "Headcount" it is an infrequent physical counting of passengers made by a flight attendant in order to compare a manifest with the actual number of passengers onboard.

NOSH or NOSHO *(GDS)*: Code meaning No show.

NOSHOW *(Airlines)*: A passenger who doesn't show up to take the flight that he/she is booked on. It is the same as No Show.

NoTAM or NOTAM *(Air Traffic)*: See Notices to Airmen.

Notel *(Hospitality)*: 1. An illegal lodging operating short-term bed and breakfast services. 2. A term denoting no-television or no-telephone services are provided.

Notice to Airmen (NOTAM or NoTAM) *(Air Traffic)*: A NOTAM is an informative notice related to conditions not known in advance or change in any component of the National Airspace System. NOTAMs are issued by qualified authority to alert aircraft pilots of any hazards en route or at a specific location. Among other subjects NOTAMs can be referred to: Temporary Flight Restrictions, closed runways, inoperable radio navigational aids, air-shows, military exercises, parachute jumps, kite flying, temporary erection of obstacles near airports, etc. Notice to Airmen that is created and transmitted by government agencies under guidelines specified by Annex 15 entitled "Aeronautical Information Services" of the Convention on International Civil Aviation.

Notification of Arrival *(Airlines)*: A written notice sent to the consignee informing on a shipment's arrival.

NOTR *(GDS)*: Code meaning No traffic rights.

NOV *(GDS)*: Code for November."

November *(Airlines)*: Designator for the letter "N" in the International Phonetic Alphabet.

NPTA *(Organizations)*: An acronym for National Passenger Traffic Association.

NR *(GDS)*: A code meaning: 1. No rate; 2. No Payment Required.

NRC *(GDS)*: Code meaning No Record Passenger.

NRCan *(Organizations)*: An acronym for Natural Resources Canada.

NRCF *(GDS)*: Code meaning Not Reconfirmed by Passenger.

NRP *(GDS)*: Code meaning Non-revenue passenger.

NRP *(Air Traffic)*: A code meaning: 1. Navigation Reference Point; 2. North American Route Program.

NRS *(GDS)*: Code meaning No Rate Specified.

NRT *(GDS)*: Three-letter IATA code for Narita International Airport, serving the city of Tokyo.

NSML *(GDS)*: Code meaning No-salt Meal.

NSSA *(GDS)*: Code meaning No Smoking Seat.

NSSB *(GDS)*: Code meaning No Smoking Bulkhead.

NSST *(GDS)*: Code meaning No Smoking Seat.

NSSW *(GDS)*: Code meaning No Smoking Window Seat.

NST *(Geography)*: See Newfoundland Standard Time.

NTA *(Organizations)*: An acronym for Canadian National Transportation Agency.

NTA *(Organizations)*: An acronym for National Tour Association.

NTBA *(GDS)*: Code meaning Names to Be Announced.

NTI *(GDS)*: Code meaning Need Ticketing Information.

NTIA*(Organizations)*: An acronym for National Telecommunications and Information Administration.

NUC *(GDS)*: See Neutral Unit of Construction.

Nudism *(Tourism)*: A manner of practicing leisure tourism going without clothes as a social practice at specially secluded places. See also Naturism.

Nutrient *(Ecology)*: Any food or element absorbed by an organism for its living, growth, and reproductive needs.

Nutritional Consultation *(Tourism)*: A consultation with qualified nutritional professionals to review eating habits and dietary needs. Taking into account lifestyle, food intolerances, appetite control and weight goals, the nutritionist may design a nutritionally balanced program to help attain optimal health and weight.

NV *(Cruise)*: Nuclear Vessel.

NW *(Airlines)*: Two-letter IATA code for North West.

NWS *(Air Traffic)*: National Weather System.

NXT *(GDS)*: Code for Next.

NYC *(GDS)*: Three-letter IATA code for New York, New York, USA.

NZ *(Airlines)*: Two-letter IATA code for Air New Zealand.

O

O *(Airlines)*: A code for "Oscar", name used to designate the letter "O" in the International Phonetic Alphabet.

O *(GDS)*: Code meaning: 1. Stopover, if shown on the route display of a ticket; 2. On a ticket and close to the fare type it indicates shoulder season.

O&D Traffic *(Airlines)*: Origin and destination traffic. An expression used for referring to passengers who embark or disembark a flight at a particular stop, to differentiate from those passengers remaining onboard for another destination.

O/B *(GDS)*: Code meaning On board.

O/S *(Cruise)*: Code referring to an insider cabin of a ship.

O/R *(Airlines)*: Code for Owner's risk.

O.r.b. *(Airlines)*: Abbreviation for Owner's risk or breakage.

O.R. Det. *(Airlines)*: Abbreviation for Owner's risk of deterioration.

O.R.F. *(Airlines)*: Abbreviation for Owner's risk of fire or freezing

O.R.L. *(Airlines)*: Abbreviation for Owner's risk of leakage

O.R.W. *(Airlines)*: Abbreviation for Owner's risk of becoming wet

OA *(Air Traffic)*: Code for Obstacle Avoidance.

OAT *(Air Traffic)*: Code for Outside Air Temperature.

OBJ *(GDS)*: Code meaning Object, Objecting, Objected.

Objective *(Tourism)*: The setting of levels on what an organization wants to achieve along a period of operation. It is the quantification of goals.

Obscuration *(Air Traffic)*: Any phenomenon in the atmosphere, excluding precipitation, which reduces horizontal visibility.

Obstacle Avoidance (OA) *(Air Traffic)*: Flight cues designed to avoid obstacles, such as terrain, buildings, and power lines.

OCC *(GDS)*: Code meaning Occupied.

Occupancy *(Hospitality)*: The percentage of available rooms occupied for a specific period.

Occupancy Rate *(Airlines)*: The occupancy ratio of the number of airline seats or cargo space occupied for a given period of time. This ratio is obtained by dividing the number of occupied seats by the total number of seats available for sale during the same period.

Occupancy Rate *(Cruise)*: The percentage of occupied cabins expected to be filled in a ship during a specific time period. The percentage is obtained by dividing the number of occupied cabins by the total number of cabins available for sale during the same period.

Occupancy Rate *(Hospitality)*: A property's percentage of occupied rooms or the percent of hotel rooms expected to be occupied during a specific time period. This percentage is obtained by dividing the number of occupied rooms by the total number of rooms available for sale during the same period.

Occupancy Report *(Hospitality)*: A report prepared each night by a front desk agent listing the rooms occupied that night and listing the guests expected to check out the following day.

Occupied *(Hospitality)*: A room status term denoting a guest is currently registered to a room.

Ocean Liner *(Cruise)*: A large ship operating passenger transport services along definite routes and regular schedules.

Oceans *(Geography)*: An ocean is a large body of salt water constituting a principal part of the hydrosphere and covering about the 71 percent of the earth's surface. Oceans contain the 97 percent of hydraulic resource of the planet and are weather regulators. There are four oceans: Arctic Ocean, Atlantic Ocean, Indian Ocean and Pacific Ocean. According to the International Hydrographical Organization (Spring 2000), there is a fifth Ocean, the Southern or Antarctic Ocean, surrounding the Antarctic continent. All of them are connected one to each other.

Oenology *(Hospitality)*: The science of wine and winemaking.

Oenologist *(Hospitality)*: A person who is dedicated to the science of winemaking.

Oenophile *(Hospitality)*: A person who enjoys tasting or drinking wine.

OCF *(GDS)*: Code meaning Ocean front.

OCNFT *(GDS)*: Code for Oceanfront.

OCNVW *(GDS)*: Code meaning Ocean View.

OCT *(GDS)*: Code for October.

OCV *(GDS)*: Code meaning Ocean view, usually in reference to a hotel room.

OECD *(Organizations)*: An acronym for Organization for Economic Co-operation and Development.

Off-airport *(Car Rental)*: Expression to denote something is not in the airport area, but close by. Typically, rental car companies have off-airport locations.

Off Airport Location *(Car Rental)*: The counter or premises of a rental car company located out of the terminal building, but usually close to it.

Off-Line *(Airlines)*: A term used to describe a company that has no operations in the market or to define a service operated by other carrier. An off-line air carrier is an airline that sells in a market where it does not operate.

Off-Line Point *(Tourism)*: A place that has no transport services. It is out of a transport network.

Off-Peak *(Tourism)*: An air fare or a hotel rate applied to a season of less travel demand. Off-Peak fares and rates are usually lower during these times.

Off-Peak Season *(Airlines)*: See Low Season.

Off Point *(Airlines)*: Station of disembarkation.

Off-Premise Location *(Airlines)*: A location that is not administered by an airline where automated tickets are issued, such as an approved location of a passenger sales agent or a commercial account.

Off-Premise Ticket *(Airlines)*: The term refers to a ticket that will be issued by travel agents as described in Resolution 722a.

Off-Premise Transitional Automated Ticket (OPTAT) *(Airlines)*: A term that was used to define an automated ticket able to be issued by travel agents, as described in Resolution 722a. It was a multi-coupon ticket.

Off-Season *(Tourism)*: See Off-Peak or Low Season.

Offer *(Business)*: 1. The action of presenting or providing a product or service for sale. 2. The maximum quantity of products or services an economic agent would like to sell for a specific price in a market during a given period.

Office des Transports du Canada (OTC) *(Organizations)*: See Canadian Transportation Agency.

Officers *(Cruise)*: The Deck Officers. In order of command they are: Captain, Staff Captain, Chief Officer, and First Officer(s). The Captain is first in command of the ship. The Staff Captain, as second in command, is fully capable of assuming command of the ship, when necessary. The Chief Officer is responsible for supervising the maintenance and supplies for the ship. Finally, the First Officers are responsible for maintaining staffing of the bridge, even while the ship is in port.

Offline Airline or Offline Carrier *(Airlines)*: An airline that sells its services in a market where it has no operations. An offline carrier uses the flights of another airline to connect to its network services.

Offline Connection *(Airlines)*: The change of aircraft at an intermediate point that also involves a change of airline to expedite the onward destination flight.

OJ *(GDS)*: Code meaning Open Jaw Trip.

OK *(GDS)*: Code meaning Confirmed. Shown on a ticket it means the booking and the seat are confirmed.

Old-growth Forest *(Ecology)*: Virgin and old forest of trees that are hundreds, sometimes thousands, years old. They are the rich forest biomes hosting the widest arrays of microhabitats and broad biodiversities.

Old West *(Tourism)*: The term used to identify the Western region of the United States that is assumed existed during the period of its settlement, by the nineteenth century. By extension, anything related to the atmosphere and culture of the Western states of the lawless period.

Omnibus *(Tourism)*: A term of infrequent use for a bus or motor coach.

On Airport Location *(Car Rental)*: The counter or premises of a car rental company that is located in the airport terminal building.

OnAir *(Airlines)*: A program created in 2005 by SITA and the aircraft manufacturers Airbus, in order to develop and operate in-flight passenger communication services. With OnAir, passengers are able to use their own portable electronic devices, including laptop computers, mobile phones, Smartphones and Personal Digital Assistants (PDAs), as well as the airline's in-seat equipment, to communicate in-flight, just as they do on the ground. Onboard communication services enable airline passengers to use their own devices and mobile phones to send and receive emails, exchange text messages and make and receive voice calls. Some European airlines are already offering the service onboard..

On Line Charge *(Airlines)*: A charge applied for carriage over the routes of a single carrier. It is the same as Local Charge.

On-line Connection or On Line Connection *(Airlines)*: A change of aircraft that does not involve a change of airlines. Passengers change from the aircraft of a carrier to another aircraft of the same carrier.

On-Line Transfer *(Airlines)*: Transfer from the service of one carrier to other service of the same carrier.

On-Line Transfer Point *(Airlines)*: Any point at which the passenger transfers from one service of a carrier to other service of the same carrier.

On Request *(Airlines)*: 1. Booking status represented by the code "RQ", meaning the confirmation is not yet given. 2. A type of service that needs to be prearranged, such as a vegetarian meal or a wheel chair on an airline.

On Request *(Car Rental)*: Some special services that have to be confirmed manually by an operations agent. A credit card is necessary to request these types of services, but the client is not charged until the rental is confirmed. Last minute reservations are also considered "on request".

On The Rocks *(Hospitality)*: A drink served in a glass with ice in it.

On Vouchers *(Tourism)*: A type of service provided against prepaid coupons or similar travel documents that cover its expenses.

Onboard *(Airlines)*: Inside the plane.

One Way Subjourney *(Airlines)*: Part of a journey wherein travel from one country does not return to such country and for which the fare is assessed as a single pricing unit using a one way fare.

One Way Subjourney Check for Normal Fares (OSC) *(Airlines)*: The sum of fares for two or more consecutive contiguous price units may not be lower than the direct throughfare published. This rule is only applicable to journeys comprising several subjourneys to which normal OW fares are applied.

One Way Trip or One-Way Trip *(Airlines)*: A type of trip where the point of origin of the travel is different to the point of arrival. It has no return leg. According to IATA definition, one way trip is considered any journey which, for fare calculation purposes, is not a complete round or circle trip entirely by air.

One Ways (*Car Rental*): In rental car terms, a one way occurs when the car is dropped off at a location that differs from the place it was picked up. There are two types of car rental one ways: domestic (within a country) and international (outside of country). Usually domestic one ways are free of charge, but a fee will be charged for making an international one way.

One-way Rental *(Car Rental)*: See One Ways.

Online Carrier *(Airlines)*: An airline that provides immediate access to its data base through a computerized reservation system.

Online Connection *(Airlines)*: A change of planes that does not involve a change of airlines.

Online Reservation System *(Hospitality)*: An internet based system used by hotels allowing hotel guests to check availability and make reservations at the hotel.

Online Transfer (*Airlines*): A change from the service of one carrier to another service of the same carrier.

ONOJ *(Airlines)*: See Origin Normal Open Jaw.

OOJ *(Airlines)*: See Origin Open Jaw.

OP *(GDS)*: Code meaning Other Person.

Open *(Airlines)*: Term shown on a ticket for sectors without reservation.

Open Bar *(Hospitality)*: A bar at any social event where the drinks are served free of charge and without restrictions. It is opposite to cash bar

Open Jaw *(Airlines)*: A gap, a surface portion of a flight either at the origin or at the turn around area.

Open Jaw Trip *(Airlines)*: A formal definition of an open-jaw journey would describe it as a journey with two fare components in which the outbound point of arrival and the inbound point of departure are not the same, and/or the outward point of departure and the inward point of arrival are not the same. In more simple words, open-jaw journey is a travel consisting of two fare components with a surface break at the turnaround, at the origin, or both at the turnaround and origin areas. There are three exceptions to the "domestic surface break" conditions:

1. For travel origination in Canada or the USA, the surface break may be between countries in the European Subarea, provided travel in both directions is via the Atlantic Ocean;

2. Canada and the USA are considered one country;

3. Scandinavia (Denmark, Norway and Sweden) is considered one country.

Open Pay *(Tourism)*: A payment that is subject to negotiation.

Open Rate *(Tourism)*: A rate of payment that will be determined by negotiation.

Open Return *(Airlines)*: The incoming portion of an air travel for which no return booking has been specified. It is applicable only to normal fare journeys.

Open Seating or Open Sitting *(Cruise)*: Access permitted at any time to unoccupied tables in the ship's dining room, as opposed to specific table assignments. It works on a first-come basis.

Open Seating Plan *(Airlines)*: An airplane seating method allowing the seat assignation in the order passengers arrive at the gate. Other seating assignment methods are "back-to-front system," "reverse pyramid system," "rotating zone system," and "Wilma."

Open Segment *(Airlines)*: A segment or sector of an itinerary for which specific booking has not been requested. It is applicable only to normal air fare journeys.

Open Skies *(Airlines)*: An international air transport agreement negotiated between two countries (sometimes multi-lateral) under which the party countries allow unrestricted overflight and landing rights to one another. It implies the elimination of aerial surveillance of military installations, and minimizes government intervention.

Open Skies Agreement EU-US *(Airlines)*: See EU-US Open Skies Agreement.

Open System *(Ecology)*: A living organism system that exchanges both matter and energy with the environment.

Open Ticket *(Airlines)*: A very infrequent case of a valid ticket issued without specific reservations.

Open Water *(Cruise)*: Part of the sea far from land coasts or rougher seas, where a cruise ship experiences greater motion.

Open-jaw Ticket *(Cruise)*: A ticket issued for any type of open jaw air journey.

Operating Carrier *(Airlines)*: The airline that is currently providing a carriage or other incidental services inherent to such carriage. The Operating Carrier is frequently different to the Marketing Carrier.

Operation *(Airlines)*: The action performed by a transport vehicle travelling from point to point.

Operational Leg *(Airlines)*: A flight leg which is physically operated and identified by its Airline Designator and Flight Number.

Operations *(Air Traffic)*: The takeoffs and landings at an airport.

Operations *(Tourism)*: Performing the practical work of operating a tour or travel program. Usually involves the in-house control and handling of all phases of the tour, both with suppliers and with clients.

Operations Manager *(Tourism)*: Individual in charge of performing the practical and detailed work of tour operations.

Operator *(Airlines)*: Any company providing airline, cruise line, railway, hotel, car rental or other related services. It is a general term involving contractor, tour operator, wholesaler, or a combination of any or all.

OPNS *(GDS)*: Code meaning Operations.

Opposing Forces *(Aeronautics)*: Forces that push or pull in the opposite direction.

OPT *(GDS)*: A code meaning: 1. Option; 2. Optional date.

OPTAT *(Airlines)*: A code for Off Premise Transitional Automated Ticket.

Optical Brightener *(Hospitality)*: See Fabric Brightener.

Option *(Tourism)*: A tour feature extension or other element requested by tourists to complete a tour.

Option Date *(Airlines)*: Limit date on which payment must be made to secure a reservation and avoid cancellation.

Option or Hold *(Cruise)*: A tentative booking which is placed in the passenger's name pending receipt of his/her contract, sailing resume and payment of a deposit. An option is usually in effect for 5 to 10 days (depending upon the company) and provided payment and documents are received within time allowed.

Optional *(Tourism)*: Any feature or service not pertaining to the basic package, which may be added at the traveler's request for an additional cost.

ORD *(GDS)*: Three-letter IATA code for O'Hare Airport serving the city of Chicago.

Organic *(Ecology)*: All living organisms and products that are uniquely produced from living organisms, such as wood, wool, leather, and sugar.

Organization of Economic Co-Operation and Development (OECD) *(Organizations)*: An inter-governmental organization focusing on economic matters which bring together the 30 most developed countries in the world. The Organization aims to building strong economies in its member countries, improve efficiency and market systems, expand free trade and contribute to development in industrialized as well as developing countries. It was founded in 1947 as the Organization for European Economic Co-operation (OEEC), which was formed to administer American and Canadian aid under the Marshall Plan for reconstruction of Europe after World War II. The change to the present scheme was made in 1961. It is sometimes referred to as the "Rich Man's Club".

Orient, The *(Tourism)*: A term historically used in Western culture to refer to Asia or the Far East.

Orient Express *(Tourism)*: A legendary train of luxury service through Europe, which has captured the imagination of aristocrats, spies, film stars and writers. It extended its way through majestic scenery to destinations such as Paris, Rome, Venice, Vienna, Budapest, Prague and Istanbul. Its route has been modified very frequently, while several routes have used the name. The current Orient Express does not serve Paris or Istanbul and the Paris-Vienna service was operated for the last time on 8 June 2007. According to the operator, it includes a stylish collection of international travel experiences aboard the most glamorous and elegant trains around the world.

Orientation *(Air Traffic)*: Direction in reference to a coordinate frame

Orientation *(Tourism)*: A briefing held for tourists to provide basic information and guidance.

ORIG *(GDS)*: A code meaning Origin, Original, Originate, Originated, Originating.

Origin *(Airlines)*: The place where a journey commences as shown on the ticket or on the Airway Bill.

Origin Normal Open Jaw (ONOJ) *(Airlines)*: A journey consisting of travel from one country and return thereto, comprising not more than two international fare components with a domestic surface break in the country of origin. Prices for such trips are assessed using half normal round trip fares.

Origin Single Open Jaw (OSOJ) *(Airlines)*: A trip where the outward point of departure in the country of unit origin and the inward point of arrival in the country of unit origin are different. Prices for such trips are assessed using half normal or special round trip fares.

Origin Open Jaw (OOJ) *(Airlines)*: See Origin Single Open Jaw.

Originating Flight *(Airlines)*: A flight that starts the air transportation departing from the point of origin.

ORL *(GDS)*: Three-letter IATA code for Orlando, Florida, USA.

ORML *(GDS)*: Code meaning Asian Meal.

ORY *(GDS)*: Three-letter IATA code for Orly International Airport, serving the city of Paris, France.

OS *(GDS)*: Code meaning Outside Sales, as in Outside Sales Representative.

OS Category *(Cruise)*: On some Cruise Lines, OS is an "Outside Guarantee" cabin. When the traveler books this cabin category he/she will be guaranteed accommodation in an outside cabin.

OSA *(GDS)*: Three-letter IATA code for Osaka, important industrial city in Japan.

OSC *(Airlines)*: See One Way Subjourney Check for Normal Fares.

Oscar *(Airlines)*: Designator for the letter "O" in the International Phonetic Alphabet.

OSI *(GDS)*: Code meaning Other Service Information.

OSL *(GDS)*: Three-letter IATA code for Oslo, capital city of Norway.

OSOJ *(Airlines)*: See Origin Single Open Jaw.

OTC (Office des Transports du Canada) *(Organizations)*: See

Canadian Transportation Agency.

Other Charges *(Airlines)*: Charges with no relation to fares, such as taxes, fees, etc., excluding excess baggage charges.

Other Service Information *(GDS)*: Informative notes attached as OSI to a PNR which do not require attention by the airline.

OTHS *(GDS)*: Code meaning Other Services (Different to OSI and SRS).

OTS *(Air Traffic)*: Code meaning Out of service.

OUT *(GDS)*: Code meaning Check out date, or departure date, as from a hotel.

Out of Door Costs *(Hospitality)*: Charges for incidentals such as Internet access, in-room entertainment or an in-room safe.

Out Plant *(Tourism)*: A travel agency branch located on the premises of a corporate client to facilitate reservations but which is not able to issue tickets. Ticketing is handled at another location.

Outbound *(Tourism)*: A term to denote a travel or flight goes out of the country of residence.

Outbound or Outward Portion *(Tourism)*: The first part of an itinerary or journey departing from the point of origin.

Outbound Operator *(Tourism)*: A tour company or individual providing services to travelers who depart from their place of residence to other destinations. An outbound operator either operates the tours by him/herself, or he/she commission the services of an inbound operator to handle local arrangements at the destination.

Outbound Tourism *(Tourism)*: It is defined as tourism involving residents of a country travelling to another country, where services are provided by an outbound tour operator. The country where tourists originate their trip is known as the generating market or country.

Outbound Travel *(Tourism)*: The departure leg of a journey.

Outfitter *(Tourism)*: A business providing appropriate transportation and/or equipment necessary for the practice of some range of wilderness activities, such as white-water rafting, trekking, camping, etc.

Outlook Briefing *(Air Traffic)*: A weather briefing requested by a pilot six or more hours prior to departure that provides weather information to help him determine the feasibility of the flight.

Out-of-Order *(Hospitality)*: A room status term indicating a room cannot be assigned to a guest due to maintenance, refurbishing, deep cleaning, or other reasons.

Outrigger *(Airlines)*: A structure attached to an aircraft or other vehicle or machine to stabilize it or to support something.

Outrigger Canoe *(Tourism)*: A sea going vessel (Polynesian style) with an extending arm to prevent it from upsetting.

Outside Agent *(Tourism)*: A person who usually is not part of the organization and is engaged in outside sales.

Outside Air *(Hospitality)*: Air taken from outside the building envelope to be processed by the building's mechanical systems.

Outside Air Temperature (OAT) *(Air Traffic)*: The temperature just outside the aircraft.

Outside Cabin *(Cruise)*: A cabin with windows or portholes or occasionally a private terrace offering an exterior view.

Outside Sales *(Tourism)*: A department whose task is the developing of business through direct solicitation of potential customers out of the retail location.

Outside Salesperson or Sales Representative *(Tourism)*: A travel agency employee or free sale person who sells travel and is not based primarily in the agency location most of the time.

Outskirts *(Geography)*: The outlying areas of a city or town.

Outsource *(Tourism)*: The practice to have a service performed or a function completed by persons outside of a company, because they are specialists in some field.

Oven *(Hospitality)*: Any appliance with a heated chamber for cooking food.

Over Flights *(Air Traffic)*: A flight over a given area, especially a flight of military aircraft over foreign territory.

Overboard *(Cruise)*: A term to indicate something or someone is off the side of a ship into the water, when it is at sea.

Overbooking *(Tourism)*: 1. The practice of booking more airline seats than are available on a specific flight, to protect occupancy against no-shows passengers; 2. The airline practice extended to the hotel industry consisting of taking more reservations than there are rooms available in the expectation that no shows will balance the number of reservations actually used below maximum occupancy.

Overcast *(Air Traffic)*: A weather description for clouds depicting a low ceiling of continuous clouds.

Overconsumption *(Ecology)*: It is a situation in which the consumption per capita is so high that sustainability is not achieved, even in spite of a moderate population density. It is also thought that overconsumption is a condition by which some people consume more than they need at the expense of those who can not meet their basic needs. Whatever the case, overconsumption attempts against the earth's present and future life-support systems for humans and other forms of life.

Overfishing *(Ecology)*: Capturing fishes of certain species in an amount that does not permit to replenish the species, leading to commercial extinction.

Overhead *(Airlines)*: 1. The compartment located above the aircraft's seats where hand luggage is located. 2. The ongoing expense of operating a business such as rent and salaries.

Overhead Bin *(Airlines)*: Enclosures located above head level of aircraft's seats used for storage of hand baggage.

Overland *(Tourism)*: Transportation or services that take place on land.

Overnutrition *(Ecology)*: A type of diet that unbalances human health due to high consumption of calories, saturated fats, salt, sugar, and processed foods, and so low in vegetables and fruits that the consumer runs high risks of diabetes, hypertension, heart disease, and other health hazards.

Overpouring *(Hospitality)*: The excessive use of alcohol than is recommended in the standard recipe.

Override or Override Commission *(Tourism)*: An extra commission paid by suppliers to agents as a bonus for productivity when a certain volume sales are achieved.

Oversale *(Tourism)*: The practice to sell aggressively more seats of hotel rooms than available, in order to protect the occupation against no shows. See Overbooking.

Oversell *(Tourism)*: See Oversale, overbooking.

Overstay *(Hospitality)*: The stay of a guest beyond the dates booked.

Oversupply *(Tourism)*: The excessive offer of airline seats or hotel rooms at a given period.

OW or O/W *(GDS)*: Code meaning One-way.

OX *(GDS)*: Code meaning "Cancel if requested segment is available, otherwise hold."

OX *(Airlines)*: Code used with a fare type indicating a one way excursion fare.

Oxygen Mask *(Airlines)*: A breathing device in aircraft that is hooked up to oxygen tank and deploys automatically when the interior atmosphere is decompressed. A mask that covers the mouth and nose, and is

Oxygen Therapy *(Tourism)*: In spas it typically describes a wide range of treatments, including hyperbaric oxygen therapy, the therapeutic use of ozone and hydrogen peroxide.

OZ *(Airlines)*: Two-letter IATA code for Asiana Airlines, an airline of South Korea.

Ozone Layer *(Ecology)*: An atmospheric layer located at 15 to 50 kilometers (10 to 30 miles) above the Earth's surface, which contains a high proportion of oxygen that concentrates as ozone. It acts as a filtering mechanism against incoming ultraviolet radiation from the sun. In the 1980s it was realized that industrial pollutants such as CFCs were damaging the ozone layer and that holes had appeared in it, especially over the Antarctic. Some specialized organizations are now committed in several programs to control the destruction of the ozone layer caused by pollution generated in human activities.

Ozone Steam Bath *(Tourism)*: Individual steam cabinet in which about 99 per cent oxygen and one per cent ozone is pumped into the cabinet and mixed with steam.

P

P *(Airlines)*: "Papa," name used to designate the letter "P" in the International Phonetic Alphabet

P *(GDS)*: Code for First Class Premium.

P&L *(GDS)*: Code meaning Profit and Loss.

P/U *(GDS)*: Code meaning Pick up.

PA *(GDS)*: A Global Indicator for travel via the Pacific Ocean.

PAC *(GDS)*: Code meaning Personal Accident Coverage. See also PAI, PIP.

Pacific Asia Travel Association (PATA) *(Organizations)*: PATA is an organization gathering private and public sector bodies involved in tourism in the Pacific Asian region. PATA's mission is to promote the growth, value and quality of Pacific Asia travel and tourism for the benefit of its membership. It was founded in 1951 and consists of 38 national government members, over 50 state and local tourism bodies, 65 airlines and cruise lines, and more than 2,000 travel industry companies including hotels. For total, 17,000 travel professionals forming 79 PATA Chapters located throughout the world.

Pacific Daylight Time (PDT) *(Geography)*: PDT is 7 hours behind of Coordinated Universal Time (UTC). PDT is used during summer in these Canadian provinces: Yukon, British Columbia, except for these eastern communities: Cranbrook, Golden, and Invermere which are in the MST/MDT zone. PDT is used during summer in these US states: California, Western counties and North part of Idaho, Nevada, Oregon, except most of Malheur County, Washington.

Pacific Standard Time (PST) *(Geography)*: PST is 8 hours behind of Coordinated Universal Time (UTC). PST is used during winter in these Canadian provinces: Yukon, British Columbia, except for these eastern communities: Cranbrook, Golden, and Invermere which are in the MST/MDT zone. PST is used during winter in these US states: California, Western counties and North part of Idaho, Nevada, Oregon, except most of Malheur County, Washington.

Pacing *(Tourism)*: A way to make travel arrangements, in such a manner that enough time is assigned to each activity.

Package *(Tourism)*: A bundle of travel products, such as air transportation, accommodation, rental car, meals, entertaining activities, etc. that is booked and sold as an all-inclusive unit price, not by components.

Package Tour *(Tourism)*: A prearranged tour that includes pre-paid transportation, accommodations and/or some combination of other tour elements, such as meals, transfers, sightseeing or car rental. It has a unique price involving all the tour elements, a predetermined length of time and other features. Nevertheless, it can also offer options for separate purchase. A package tour includes one or more destinations.

Package Traveler *(Tourism)*: A person who makes and purchases pre-arranged travels.

Packaged Terminal Air Conditioning Unit (PTAC) *(Hospitality)*: A self-contained air conditioning unit that provides heat or cooling. It is generally installed through the wall.

Packager *(Tourism)*: A company or an individual that organizes and promotes a tour including prepaid transportation and related travel services, such as hotel, transfers, car rental, sightseeing, etc. and usually destined to more than one place.

PAD *(Air Traffic)*: The set of coordinated actions performed by **P**ilots, **A**ir traffic controllers, and Flight **D**ispatchers. See Flight Dispatch.

Padyak *(Tourism)*: See Cycle Rickshaws.

PAE *(Car Rental)*:   See Personal Accident and Personal Effects Insurance.

Page *(Tourism)*: The action of calling a person in public places, as a hotel or an airport, by means of a public addressing system.

PAHO *(Organizations)*: An acronym for Pan-American Health Organization.

PAI *(Car Rental)*: See Personal Accident Insurance.

Paid Occupancy Percentage *(Hospitality)*: A ratio that indicates the hotel occupancy of rented rooms. It is calculated by dividing the number of rooms sold by the number of available rooms.

Paleoecology *(Ecology)*: A branch of Ecology that is concerned with ancient ecosystems and the interactions that took place within them.

Pallet *(Airlines)*: A platform where cargo is secured and transported aboard the aircraft.

Pallet Extender *(Airlines)*: A metal or cardboard device that helps to increase the pallet's capacity.

Pan-American *(Tourism)*: A term denoting that something concerns to all of the regions of the Americas (North, Central, and South

America).

Pan-Asian *(Tourism)*: A term denoting that something comprises or involves the entire Asian continent.

Pan-American Health Organization (PAHO) *(Organizations)*: An international public health agency dedicated since more than 100 to improve health and living standards of the countries of the Americas. It is the specialized organization for health of the Inter-American System that acts as the Regional Office for the Americas of the World Health Organization, and is recognized as part of the United Nations system. Its mission consists of leading strategic collaborative efforts among Member States and other partners to promote equity in health, combating disease, and improving the quality of the lives of the peoples of the Americas. Its head offices are located in Washington, DC.

Pangea *(Geography)*: A supercontinent that is supposed existed prior to the Triassic period, about 250 million years ago. It included all the emerged landmass of the earth that centuries later separated to form Laurasia and Gondwana continents. The name Pangea (Pan = All; Gea = Land) was given by the German scientist Alfred Wegener in 1920. Evidences of the existence of Pangaea have been found by the fossil presence of similar and identical species on continents that are now great distances apart.

PANIBS *(IATA Geography)*: The territory comprising Pakistan, Afghanistan, Nepal, India, Bangladesh, Bhutan, and Sri Lanka. See South Asian Subcontinent Sub-area.

Papa *(Airlines)*: Designator for the letter "P" in the International Phonetic Alphabet.

PAR *(Air Traffic)*: A code meaning: 1. Precision Approach Radar; 2. Preferred Arrival Route; 3. Paris, capital city of France.

Parador *(Tourism)*: A type of hotel accommodation offered in a historical Spanish style building, such as a castle, a monastery or a farm.

Parish *(Geography)*: A geopolitical division of a state or territory, equivalent to a county.

Parlor Car *(Tourism)*: A train car where comfortable seating and/or food service are offered in a living room style.

Part Charter *(Airlines)*: The section of an airline's scheduled flight that is sold as if it were a charter in its own right.

Part Load Charter *(Airlines)*: A part of an aircraft's load that is discharged at one destination, while other part or parts are off-loaded at different destinations.

Partial Prepay *(Car Rental)*: A deposit required to confirm a vehicle reservation at some car rental companies, instead of the full payment. The balance is then paid directly to the car rental agent at the delivery of the vehicle. The deposit is fully refundable in the event the renter cancels the reservation on time.

Participating Carrier *(Airlines)*: An air carrier that participates in a multi-segment transportation under the ticket or airwaybill conditions.

Partner Tickets & Fares *(Airlines)*: A term used for promotions where an airline offers discounted fares for husbands, wives, partners flying on the same flight as the main traveler. Documentary evidence has to be provided.

Partners *(Car Rental)*: A term denoting the car rental's business partners that include Travel Agents, Online Affiliate Sponsors, and some hotel, airline and credit card companies.

Partnership *(Business)*: A legal structure of having a business ownership by two or more persons who are personally liable for all business debts.

Pass *(Geography)*: A passage between mountains that facilitates the construction of roads or any other communication facility.

Pass *(Tourism)*: A ticket or permit handed over to enter or to be in a certain place.

PASS *(GDS)*: Code meaning People Access Security System.

Pass Card *(Tourism)*: An identification card that U.S. citizens use to cross the country border instead of a passport.

Passage Contract *(Cruise)*: Detailed terms of liability and conditions determining the services that are provided by a cruise operation.

Passenger *(Tourism)*: Any person carried or to be carried on an aircraft or a ship for a price he/she pays and with the carrier's consent. The concept of Passenger differs from the concept of Traveler. A passenger is a traveler who pays a fare and adheres to the carrier's terms and conditions to have the right to be transported. A traveler is a person who moves from one place to another by his/

her own means or by using a vehicle. A traveler can be transported against a price or without payment. Travelers are, for instance, crew members who travel under the terms of a labor contract, or a stowaway that illegally boards a plane without the consent of the carrier, without paying and not passing through immigration procedures.

Passenger Coupon *(Airlines)*: The part of the Passenger Ticket and Baggage Check that constitutes the passenger's evidence of the contract of carriage.

Passenger Facility Charge (PFC) *(Tourism)*: A tax set on passengers for using an airport's facilities, which is usually added to the cost of the air fare.

Passenger Information List (PIL) *(Airlines)*: Also known as Flight Manifest, it contains the list of all persons on board and other related details such as special meals, additional assistance requirements, and/or other information.

Passenger Mile *(Airlines)*: A statistical concept representing one airline passenger traveling one mile. The value is obtained by multiplying the total number of miles flown by the total number of passengers carried.

Passenger Name Record (PNR) *(GDS)*: Also called a Personal Name Record, it is a file on a Global Distribution System where all the information relating to a specific booking of a specific person is stored.

Passenger Sales Agent *(Tourism)*: Any travel agent who sells services to travelers.

Passenger Service Agent *(Airlines)*: An airline employee responsible for assisting passengers at check-in and boarding procedures.

Passenger Service Representative *(Airlines)*: An airline employee whose duty is providing information and other services to travelers, such as connection information or wheelchair assistance.

Passenger Ship *(Cruise)*: A passenger ship that is authorized to carry over twelve passengers for cruises lasting from a few hours to a few days.

Passenger Space Ratio *(Cruise)*: A statistical measure to obtain the theoretical amount of public space assigned to each passenger on a cruise ship. The higher the passenger space ratio, the roomier the ship.

Passenger Terminal Indicator *(Airlines)*: See Passenger Service Indicator.

Passenger Ticket *(Airlines)*: It is the same as the Electronic Ticket.

Passenger Traffic Manager *(Airlines)*: 1. An airline manager who is based in an airport. 2. A person in a corporation who is in charge of travel arrangements for the company's employees.

Passenger, Adult *(Airlines)*: A person who is 12 years of age or older.

Passenger, Child *(Airlines)*: A person who has reached his/her second birthday but not his/her 12th birthday at the date of commencement of transportation, who pays the applicable child fare. This designation is used in travel industry to determine fares and other rates. The precise definition varies from carrier to carrier and from hotel to hotel.

Passenger, Infant *(Airlines)*: A person who has not reached his/her second birthday at the date of commencement of travel. The designation is used to determine applicable fares. Infants often travel for free. Under 2 years of age.

Passenger, Senior *(Airlines)*: A person over 62 years of age.

Passive Booking *(GDS)*: A booking entered in a GDS that does not produce a ticket issue. It is typically used by agents to generate itineraries or to introduce notes.

Passive Segment *(GDS)*: A segment entered in a GDS that does not produce a ticket issue.

Passive Solar *(Ecology)*: A method that uses sunlight to generate energy, omitting active mechanical systems. Sunlight is converted into usable heat or ventilation flow. It also stores heat for future use.

Passive Tourism *(Tourism)*: A type of leisure travel in which the main activity consists of seeing and observing rather than getting involved in other activities. Example: Bird watching or going for sightseeing or to a theater.

Passport *(Tourism)*: A document issued by a national government attesting to his or her identity and ability to travel freely. It is required from international travelers but does not give them the right to enter a country.

Password *(GDS)*: An alphanumeric entry used to identify individuals, enabling them the use a reservation system, a computer, a computer network or a similar system.

Pastime *(Tourism)*: An interest or activity that one pursues in his/her spare time to occupy pleasantly one's time and thoughts, such as a hobby.

PATA *(Organizations)*: An acronym for Pacific Asia Travel Association.

Patch *(Cruise)*: An adhesive scrap that is applied to the skin to prevent or reduce the effects of seasickness.

PATCO *(Organizations)*: An acronym for Professional Air Traffic Controllers Organization.

Pathway *(Tourism)*: A route connecting places.

Patois *(Tourism)*: A French term for a language or a dialect other than the dominant language.

Pattern *(Air Traffic)*: The path of aircraft traffic around an airport, at an established height and direction. Patterns are supervised by radio by air traffic controllers.

Pavilion *(Tourism)*: An exhibit hall as part of an exposition or a section of a building.

PAWOB *(GDS)*: Code meaning Passenger Arriving without Baggage.

PAX *(GDS)*: An abbreviation for Passenger or Passengers.

Payload *(Airlines)*: The total load of an aircraft including paying passengers, cargo and mail.

PC *(GDS)*: A code meaning: 1. Public Charter; 2. Personal Computer.

PCTC *(GDS)*: Code meaning Passenger Contact.

PDA *(Computing)*: See Personal Digital Assistant.

PDM *(GDS)*: Code meaning Possibly Duplicated Message.

PDQ *(GDS)*: A code meaning "Pretty than Quick" to denote Immediately, As Soon as Possible.

PDR *(GDS)*: Code meaning People's Democratic Republic.

PDT *(Geography)*: See Pacific Daylight Time.

PDW *(Car Rental)*: Personal Damage Waiver. See Collision Damage Waiver.

PDX *(GDS)*: Three-letter IATA code for Portland, Oregon, USA.

Peak Fare *(Airlines)*: A higher fare that applies during periods of maximum demand for a destination.

Peak Season *(Airlines)*: Period of the year when travel and hotel occupation increases, pushing the prices up.

PEC *(Car Rental)*: See Personal Effects Coverage.

Pedal *(Aeronautics)*: A flight control operated by pushing with feet, primarily to control yaw via the rudder in fixed-wing aircraft or thrust to tail rotor in rotary-wing aircraft. Pedals are automatically controlled in modern aircraft.

Pedicabs *(Tourism)*: A type of rickshaw commonly used in London as a mode of urban transportation. See Rickshaws and Cycle Rickshaws.

Penalty Fare *(Airlines)*: An air fare that is subject to a fee charge in the event the passenger changes the itinerary or cancels the reservation.

Penetration *(Airlines)*: The ability of a radio frequency to pass through non-metallic materials. Low-frequency systems have better penetration than UHF systems.

Peninsula Booth *(Hospitality)*: An exhibit setup allowing two or more standard units to be placed back to back with aisles on three sides.

Pension *(Hospitality)*: A Spanish term for a small hotel or boarding house.

Pension Complète *(Hospitality)*: A French term for American Plan.

Penthouse *(Hospitality)*: 1. The top floor of a hotel or an apartment or suite located on it; 2. A cabin located on the top deck of a cruise ship.

People Mover *(Tourism)*: See Automated People Mover.

PEP *(Car Rental)*: See Personal Effects Protection.

Per Diem *(Tourism)*: 1. A Latin term denoting an amount of money allotted to cover an employee's daily expenses during a travel; 2. The cost of a cruise per person and per day.

Perishable Food *(Hospitality)*: A food product that spoils if not protected by special processing or preservation techniques. Perishable foods include most products used daily in a food service facility, such as meats, poultry, fish, shellfish, eggs, dairy products, and most fruits and vegetables.

Perishables *(Airlines)*: Any cargo products, such as fresh fruit and vegetables that lose natural or commercial value if their transportation is delayed.

Permafrost *(Geography)*: Soil, silt or rock found in areas perpetually cold. It remains frozen year-round until the local climate changes by cause of continental drift toward the equator or global warming.

Permanent Residence *(Tourism)*: Residence and domicile are terms frequently used as synonymous. A person can have two or more places of residence (a city house and a country cottage, for example), but only one domicile. Residence means just living in a place, but domicile means living in that place with the purpose to make it a permanent home. In consequence, the term permanent residence can signify the place where a person lives for long periods of time when he/she is absent of his/her domicile or can be used erroneously to define his/her domicile.

Permanent Resident *(Tourism)*: An immigration law term referring to a person who has the status in a country usually less than citizen but more than a visitor. See Permanent Residence.

Perpetual Tourism *(Airlines)*: A strange type of tourism accomplished by wealthy persons who travel constantly without a fixed stay, some of them for tax purposes or to avoid being resident in any country. Such individuals are always on holiday.

Personal Accident and Personal Effects Insurance (PAE) *(Car Rental)*: A type of coverage that protects the renter and passengers against expenses resulting from accident, injury, as well as damage or loss to personal property.

Personal Accident Coverage (PAC) *(Car Rental)*: Also called Personal Injury Protection (PIP), it is an insurance providing coverage against accidental death and medical protection for the driver and his passengers.

Personal Accident Insurance (PAI) *(Car Rental)*: See Personal Accident Coverage.

Personal Choice Dining *(Cruise)*: A term used in some cruise lines to describe their onboard dining program whereby passengers have the freedom to choose where and when to dine.

Personal Digital Assistant (PDA) *(Computing)*: Also known as a hand computer, it is a device that can store data in a similar way as a personal computer. It sometimes substitutes a laptop and will be useful with OnAir applications.

Personal Effects Coverage (PEC) *(Car Rental)*: An insurance that covers the belongings in a rented car in the event they are stolen or damaged.

Personal Effects Protection (PEP) *(Car Rental)*: Another way to refer to Personal Effects Coverage.

Personal Exemption *(Customs)*: The total value of merchandise a traveler may bring back to his country without having to pay duty.

Personal Injury Protection *(Car Rental)*: See Personal Accident Protection.

Personal Name Record *(Cruise)*: See Passenger Name Record.

Personal Watercraft *(Tourism)*: A small, lightweight craft looking like a motorcycle that is used for recreational purposes on lakes or near-shore waters. It is designed to be either sat-on or stood-on, is usually jet-propelled, and is driven by means of handlebars and squeeze throttle.

PETC *(GDS)*: Code meaning Pet in Cabin.

Petit Dejeuner *(Hospitality)*: A French term for Breakfast.

PEX or Pex Fare *(Airlines)*: Restricted Instant Purchase Fare. It is a special air round trip fare that must be purchased as soon as the reservation is confirmed. Once the ticket has been purchased, changes can not usually be done. It is a very restricted type of fare.

PF *(Hospitality)*: A French code for Prix Fixe (Price Fixed).

PFC *(Airlines)*: See Passenger Facility Charge.

PFCS *(Air Traffic)*: A code for Primary Flight Control System.

PHL *(GDS)*: Three-letter IATA code for Philadelphia, Pennsylvania, USA.

Phonetic Alphabet *(Airlines)*: It is a system adopted by airlines for voice radio or any wire or wireless communication, consisting of using a word or name to represent each of the letters of the alphabet. The first letter of the word represents the letter. The alphabet was developed by the International Civil Aviation Organization (ICAO) and was adopted by the North Atlantic Treaty Organization

(NATO) in 1950, and by many other organizations, including the International Telecommunication Union (ITU), the International Maritime Organization (IMO), the Federal Aviation Administration (FAA), and the American National Standards Institute (ANSI). The Phonetic Alphabet, also called NATO Alphabet, is currently as follows: **A**lfa, **B**ravo, **C**harlie, **D**elta, **E**cho, **F**oxtrot, **G**olf, **H**otel, **I**ndia, **J**uliet, **K**ilo, **L**ima, **M**ike, **N**ovember, **O**scar, **P**apa, **Q**uebec, **R**omeo, **S**ierra, **T**ango, **U**niform, **V**ictor, **W**hisky, **X**-ray, **Y**ankee, **Z**ulu.

Photo Gallery *(Cruise)*: A gallery that displays photographs of passengers taken by photographers onboard a ship.

Photo Safari *(Tourism)*: A tour designed for tourists who want to see wildlife sites where they impress their experience in photographs.

PHS&T *(Airlines)*: A code to define the action of Packaging, Handling, Storing and Transporting.

PHX *(GDS)*: Three-letter IATA code for Phoenix, Arizona, USA.

Physiotherapy *(Tourism)*: A rehabilitative therapy that aids to recover from injury, surgery or disease. Treatments can include massage, traction, hydrotherapy, corrective exercise and electrical stimulation to help relieve pain, increase strength and improve mobility.

Phytosanitary Inspection Certificate *(Airlines)*: A certificate issued by a Department of Agriculture showing that specific goods have been inspected and are free of harmful pests and plant diseases.

Phytotherapy *(Tourism)*: Healing through plants, using herbs, aromatic essential oils, seaweed and floral extracts. It can be applied through several methods such as massages, wraps, water and steam therapies, inhalation treatments and the drinking of herbal teas.

PiC *(Air Traffic)*: See Pilot in Command.

Pick Up *(Car Rental)*: A term used by Car Rental companies referring to the act of receiving a hired car at the rental company location or at the place assigned.

Pidgin *(Tourism)*: A simplified form of speech resulting from the mixture of two or more languages used in limited contact situations between people who have no common language. It has a very limited vocabulary and a simplified grammar. Typical examples of pidgin are Creole, Papiamento and Lingua Franca. Creole is a language that began as a pidgin but later became the mother tongue; Papiamento or Papiamentu is a mixture of Dutch, Portuguese, African and Spanish spoken in the Netherlands Antilles, and Lingua Franca is a mixture of Italian with Provençal, French, Spanish, Arabic, Greek, and Turkish, formerly spoken on the eastern Mediterranean coast.

Pidgin English *(Tourism)*: Any combination of English with a local language, giving by result a type of English linguistically simplified, with a rudimentary grammar and a limited vocabulary.

Piece Concept or Piece System *(Airlines)*: One of the two methods that airlines apply to baggage allowances. Piece Concept is usually used for flights to/from North America that helps the passenger to define the number of pieces he/she can take free of charge. It is defined as two pieces of luggage, disregarding the class of service. Each of the pieces must not exceed 32 kg. The weight of the pieces cannot be added in order to balance the total weight. If one piece is more than 32 kg, the passenger will be charged an excess baggage fee, even though the other piece is weighs 18 kg, for instance. Each piece is also limited to a size (length, width and height) not exceeding 158 cm for Economy Class and 203 cm for Business Class. Outsize baggage also causes extra charged, depending on the airline.

Pier *(Cruise)*: A structure built out into the water that is used as a landing place for ships or boats and for mooring them.

Pier Head Jump *(Cruise)*: The practice of booking last minute with the intent to get a lower rated cabin.

Pier Pickup *(Cruise)*: The collection of cruise tickets and related documents at the pier prior to boarding the ship, instead of an early delivery at home or at the business address.

PIL *(Airlines)*: See Passenger Information List.

Pilâtre de Rozier, Jean Francois *(Airlines)*: On November 21, 1783, a young man from *Lorraine* named *Jean-François Pilâtre de Rozier* (1754-1785), ascended the skies of Paris on board a strange machine invented by the brothers *Etienne* and *Joseph Montgolfier*. *Pilâtre de Rozier* was a French chemistry and physics teacher, and one of the prominent pioneers of the early aviation. He was born the 30th of March, 1754 in Metz, Germany. At the age of eighteen years he traveled to Paris, where, some years later, he witnessed the flight of a sheep, a cock, and a duck from the front courtyard of the Palace of Versailles on board a balloon (September 19, 1783). His encounter with the *Montgolfier* brothers marked his destiny from that very moment. After tireless tests in October, he made the first manned flight of the human history on 21 November 1783, accompanied by the *Marquis d'Arlandes*. They made a 15-kilometers flight which was covered in 25 minutes from the *Château de la Muette* to the *Butte-aux-Cailles,*. Pilâtre de Rozier made several other flights until he died in June 15 1785, in an attempt to fly across the English Channel, in the company of *Pierre Romain.*

Pilgrimage *(Tourism)*: A journey organized to visit a place featuring a religious shrine or to accomplish certain religious acts or promises.

Pilot *(Airlines)*: A person licensed to conduct an aircraft during a flight and to remain in control of it.

Pilot *(Cruise)*: A person licensed to conduct a ship into and out of a port.

Pilot *(Tourism)*: The action to operate, control, or guide a flight vehicle or a ship from within the vehicle.

Pilot House *(Cruise)*: A booth from where the crew operates the steering mechanism of a ship.

Pilot Pressure *(Air Traffic)*: See Dynamic Pressure.

Pilot Program *(Business)*: A small-scale test of a system or methodology used to assess the viability or to determine suitability of a project, prior to committing significant large-scale capital.

Pilot Report (PIREP) *(Air Traffic)*: Any news reported by a pilot to the nearest ground station on actual weather conditions encountered by an aircraft en route. The information is then encoded and relayed to other weather offices and air traffic service units.

Pilot in Command (PiC) *(Air Traffic)*: The pilot responsible for the operation and safety of an aircraft during flight time.

Pilotage *(Air Traffic)*: A method of navigation in which the pilot, flying at low altitudes, uses visual references and compares symbols on aeronautical charts with surface features in order to conduct the vehicle.

Pilsner *(Hospitality)*: A light and mellow lager with a dry flavor and a light color, made from hops grown in the area around Pilsen, Czech Republic.

Pinisi *(Cruise)*: A two-masted Indonesian sailing vessel for 12 to 18 passengers, used for soft-adventure tours.

Pinot Blanc *(Hospitality)*: A pleasant, medium-bodied white wine of the Pinot family made around the world, mainly at the Alsace region.

Pinot Gris *(Hospitality)*: A grayish to pinkish color wine of the Pinot family made in Alsace, Italy and Germany.

Pinot Noir *(Hospitality)*: One of the best red grapes used to make some of the best red wines and good varieties of white wine. The grapes grow in the Burgundy region of France, Germany, the USA, Australia and New Zealand.

PIP *(Car Rental)*: Personal Injury Protection, see Personal Accident Protection.

PIR *(Airlines)*: See Property Irregularity Report.

PIREP *(Air Traffic)*: See Pilot Report.

Pitch *(Airlines)*: The distance between seats of an aircraft, one in front of the other. It is a measurement that, if greater the pitch, the more leg space for travelers. See also Seat Pitch.

Pitch *(Cruise)*: The rise and fall of the ship's bow while it is at sea.

Pitch Pressurized Aircraft *(Airlines)*: An aircraft kept at a specific atmospheric pressure to facilitate passengers and crew breath normally.

Plan *(Airlines)*: A project comprising a set of objectives to be achieved in a specific period of time, including the necessary means to assess it.

Plate *(Airlines)*: A sort of metal piece once used to stamp the name of the agency issuing an airline ticket.

Plate Service *(Hospitality)*: The basic service style in which foods are put on plates in the kitchen and carried to each guest directly. It's opposed to the Table Service.

Plateau *(Geography)*: A large surface area raised above adjacent land.

Plating Away *(Airlines)*: The practice of stopping issuing tickets for an airline that is financially unstable and risking to discontinue flight operations.

Platter Service *(Hospitality)*: See Plate Service.

Pleasure Cruise *(Cruise)*: Pleasure is the essence of a tour cruising, since comfort, resting and well-being are featured characteristics of a cruise. Travelers are naturally exonerated from any task onboard.

Plimsoll Line *(Cruise)*: See Load Lines.

PLS, PLZ *(GDS)*: Codes meaning Please.

PLVW *(GDS)*: Code meaning Pool View.

PM or P.M. *(Airlines)*: Post Meridiem. The time between 12 noon and 12 midnight. The term PM is used in most travel schedules in the USA.

PMS *(GDS)*: Code meaning Property Management System.

PMV *(GDS)*: Three-letter IATA code for Porlamar, a beach destination in Margarita Island, Venezuela.

PNR *(GDS)*: See Passenger Name Record.

POA *(GDS)*: Three-letter IATA code for Porto Alegre, an important city in Brazil.

Pod *(Airlines)*: A sort of seating module in premium class that provides privacy and usually a flat-bed seat.

Pod Propulsion *(Cruise)*: An advanced and high-tech engine system aiming to a high maneuvering capability, low noise and vibration, and low fuel consumption. There are fixed and rotating models. It is also known as "Azimuthing Pod Propulsion".

Podium *(Hospitality)*: A platform set for speakers or lecturer addressing to a public.

POE *(GDS)*: Code meaning Point of Embarkation.

Point *(Tourism)*: A term used to designate an airport, a city, a village or other stop on an itinerary, which is used as a unit for the application of fares and rates.

Point of Embarkation *(Cruise)*: The port from where a cruise ship sails.

Point of Origin *(Airlines)*: The airport where an air travel commences.

Point of Sale System (POS) *(Hospitality)*: A computerized system that interfaces outlets such as restaurants or gift shops with the property management system (PMS), which enters orders and maintains varied accounting information.

Point of Turnaround *(Airlines)*: The farthest geographical fare break point from the Pricing Unit point of origin, where the return trip is assumed to begin.

Point to Point *(Airlines)*: An operation between two cities, without intermediate stops.

Point to Point Fares *(Airlines)*: Fares applicable to flights connecting a pair of cities by means of direct flight.

Point-to-point Flights *(Airlines)*: Flights using commercial aircraft to fly directly from one city to another.

Polar Circle *(Geography)*: Any of the two parallels of latitude located at 66°33' N and 66°33' S, each at a respective distance from a pole of the earth, which is equal to about 23 degrees 27 minutes.

Polar Climatic Zone *(Climate)*: An area of the earth located north of the Arctic Circle and south of the Antarctic Circle, having cool or cold temperatures around the year.

Polar Projection *(Geography)*: A representation of the earth which covers the polar regions of a selected hemisphere, including always the North or South Pole.

Political Asylum *(Airlines)*: Refuge given by authorities of one country to a citizen of another country, endeavoring to protect him/her from arrest or persecution.

Pollution *(Ecology)*: The contamination of ecosystems and the atmosphere through the discharge of harmful substances derived from human activities, in such a way that affects the health, survival, or activities of humans or other living organisms.

Polyglot *(Tourism)*: A person who speaks several languages.

Pond *(Geography)*: A small body of water surrounded by land. They are often artificial and are found in parks and gardens.

Pool Deck *(Cruise)*: The deck where the swimming pool of a cruise ship is located.

Pool Route *(Airlines)*: A route on which two air carriers share equally agreed revenues and facilities.

Poop Deck *(Cruise)*: A type of deck built at the rear of some ships.

Population *(Ecology)*: A group of interbreeding organisms that interact and live in the same place at the same time and that are able to reproduce between them.

Population Ageing *(Ecology)*: The effect occurring when the median age of a country or region rises by slowing birth rates and extending life

Population Change *(Ecology)*: The ration by which the size of a population increases or decreases. It is equal to births plus immigration less deaths plus emigration.

Population Density *(Ecology)*: The number of organisms living in a specified area.

Population Dispersion *(Ecology)*: The pattern in which the members of a population are arranged throughout its habitat.

Population Distribution *(Ecology)*: A variation of population density over a particular geographical area.

Population Pyramid *(Geography)*: A graph showing the distribution of a human population according to age and sex.

Port *(Cruise)*: The place where a ships docks. It also describes the left side of a ship looking towards the forward end/front of the vessel.

Port *(Hospitality)*: A fortified sweet wine from Portugal.

Port à sec *(Cruise)*: See Dry Berthing.

Port Authority *(Airlines)*: A local entity that is responsible for ruling and controlling transportation facilities such as airports, ship ports, bus terminals and so forth. It is usually in charge of various airports and/or ocean cargo pier facilities, transit sheds, loading equipment warehouses for air cargo, etc.

Port Charges or Port Taxes *(Cruise)*: Charges levied by local government authorities on departing or visiting cruise passengers.

Port Cochere *(Hospitality)*: A covered entranceway designed to protect hotel guests from bad weather or to accommodate cars.

Port-Intensive *(Cruise)*: A term defining a cruise itinerary that visits many ports, with few days at sea. It also describes ports of call that offer particular tourism opportunities.

Port of Call *(Cruise)*: Each of the ports at which a ship stops, facilitating the visit to an island or city.

Port of Discharge *(Cruise)*: Port where a vessel off-loads passengers and discharges cargo.

Port of Entry *(Cruise)*: The port at which ships or passengers enter a country.

Port of Loading *(Cruise)*: The port where cargo is loaded aboard the vessel.

Port Side *(Cruise)*: The left side of a ship, when facing the front.

Porter *(Tourism)*: A person handling baggage. See also Skycap.

Porter *(Hospitality)*: A malt beverage named for the English porters who first served it.

Porterage *(Tourism)*: The job of handling baggage.

Porthole *(Cruise)*: A window in the side of a ship that is usually round or with rounded corners. Some of them can be opened, others are fixed shut.

Portion *(Hospitality)*: A standard amount of food or beverage served for one person.

Portion Cost *(Hospitality)*: A standard food cost for an item that is sold as a single menu selection.

Portside *(Cruise)*: The left, or port side of the ship.

Posada *(Hospitality)*: A small Spanish-style hotel in the country.

Posh *(Tourism)*: A British term for elegant or high-class.

POS *(GDS)*: Code meaning Positive.

Positive Control *(Air Traffic)*: The separation of all air traffic within designated airspace by air traffic control.

Position *(Air Traffic)*: Location, usually in reference to the earth's coordinates of latitude and longitude.

Position Update *(Air Traffic)*: To cause navigation sensors, devices, or algorithms to reset position to value known to be more accurate due to inaccuracies.

Positioning *(Tourism)*: The action to move aircraft or ships from one place to another.

Positioning *(Business)*: A marketing goal to position a product or corporation in a privileged level of productivity or image in comparison to other products or corporations.

Positive Space *(Tourism)*: An expression denoting a seat or room that is confirmed and can be actually occupied.

POSS *(GDS)*: Code meaning Possible.

Post-Convention Tour *(Tourism)*: A tour or excursion that will operate after a convention or a meeting ends.

Postal Code *(Business)*: Also known as Zip Code or Area Code, it is a numeric or alphanumeric combination that is used to identify specific regions of a country for the purpose of directing mail.

POT *(GDS)*: Code meaning Point of Turnaround.

Potability *(Hospitality)*: Quality that makes water suitable for drinking.

Potable *(Hospitality)*: A beverage that is safe to drink.

Potable Water *(Hospitality)*: Water that meets quality standards and/ or is safe for consumption in drinking, eating and/or cooking.

Potentially Renewable Resource *(Ecology)*: A resource that, in theory, can last indefinitely without reducing the available supply.

Pourboire *(Tourism)*: Tip in French.

Pousse-Cafe *(Hospitality)*: A liqueur that is offered to drink after-dinner.

Poverty *(Ecology)*: A simple definition describes poverty a status of a person that makes impossible for him/her to meet essential items as food, clothing, and shelter that are needed for a proper living. The "Copenhagen Declaration on Social Development" of 12 March 1995 describes poverty as "…a condition characterized by severe deprivation of basic human needs, including food, safe drinking water, sanitation facilities, health, shelter, education and information." Thus, when people are unable to eat, go to school, or have any access to health care, they are in poverty, regardless of their income. However, statistical methods to measure and quantify poverty usually are based on income or consumption values. At the conclusion of the World Summit for Social Development that adopted the Copenhagen Declaration ll7 heads of State or Government gave their world of honor to make the conquest of poverty, the goal of full employment and the fostering of stable, safe and just societies their overriding objectives. Thirteen years have past and the number of starving people is frightfully increasing.

Pow Wow *(Tourism)*: A Native American festivity converted into a tourist attraction. The term is also used to define a meeting arranged to conclude a business or make decisions.

Power of Attorney *(Business)*: A written document signed by a person giving another person the power to act as the grantor's agent in conducting the signer's business, including signing papers, checks, title documents, contracts, handling bank accounts and other activities in the name of the person granting the power. There are two types of power of attorney: a) general power of attorney, which covers all activities, and b) special power of attorney, which grants powers limited to specific matters.

Power Loading *(Airlines)*: The Gross Weight of an airplane divided by the rated horsepower, computed for Standard Air Density.

Power Port *(Airlines)*: An electrical outlet provided at an aircraft's seat for varied purposes.

PP *(GDS)*: Code meaning: 1. Prepaid, 2. Per Person.

PPDO *(GDS)*: Code meaning Per person in Double Occupancy.

PPH *(GDS)*: Code meaning Passengers per Hour.

PPPN *(Hospitality)*: Code meaning Per Person per Night. It denotes the price for each person per night.

PPR *(GDS)*: Code meaning Passenger Profile Record.

PR *(GDS)*: Code meaning: 1. Public Relations; 2. Philippine Air Lines.

PRC *(GDS)*: Code meaning People's Republic of China.

Pre-Convention Tour *(Tourism)*: A tour or excursion offered to operate before a convention or meeting starts.

Pre-Booked Travel *(Tourism)*: Travel services (airfares, accommodation, activities, attractions or transport) paid for prior to arrival in the destination.

Precision *(Air Traffic)*: Measure of exactness, possibly expressed in number of digits.

Precision Approach Radar (PAR) *(Air Traffic)*: A ground-radar-based instrument approach providing both horizontal and vertical guidance.

Preclearance *(Tourism)*: Provision of customs and immigration procedures in a foreign country of departure to ease the demand for such facilities in the country of arrival.

Predator *(Ecology)*: Any carnivorous animal that hunts, kills, and eats other animals in order to survive, or any other destructive organism that behaves in a similar way. A predator is usually situated in a lower level of a trophic web.

Preferred Practices *(Tourism)*: Policies and practices that are considered beneficial in dealing with the travel trade (tour operators, travel agencies and wholesalers).

Preferred Supplier *(Tourism)*: A supplier whose products or services are sold most by a travel agent due to specially negotiated prices or higher commissions.

Preferred Supplier Agreement *(Tourism)*: An arrangement between a company and a supplier by which the company's employees are entitled for discounts or other advantages in exchange for the company's compromise to use the products and services of the supplier.

Preflight *(Air Traffic)*: The check and preparation of the aircraft before takeoff.

Preformed Group *(Tourism)*: A compatible group of members sharing a common interest or organizational affiliation that exists prior to the operation of a tour travel, such as civic clubs, senior citizen groups, and numerous types of associations.

Premiere Class *(Tourism)*: Any product or service qualified as first-class.

Premium Class *(Tourism)*: A term used to define an airline business class or first class that is superior to the basic class, as in Premium Business Class or Premium First Class. It is also used to distinguish any accommodation type.

Premium Economy *(Tourism)*: An improved version of economy class offering additional amenities.

Pre-Mix *(Hospitality)*: A commercially prepared mix available for cocktails, such as a Bloody Mary mix that needs only the addition of vodka.

Prepaid *(Tourism)*: A product or service paid in full in advance.

Prepaid Ticket *(Airlines)*: Ticketing method in which the payment is made in one place for a travel that will commence in another.

Prepaid Ticket Advice (PTA) *(Airlines)*: A transaction by which one person or company in one location pays for the air transportation of someone else who will commence the air travel in another place. The traveler receives an advice on the transaction from the issuing airline and picks up the booking information and the e-ticket copy from the airline's counter. PTAs may involve domestic or international reservations and must be processed at least 24 hours prior to the scheduled departure time, excluding Saturday, Sunday, and federal or state legal holidays. PTAs may be used for the prepayment of tickets, excess baggage charges, transportation taxes, and incidentals expenses directly related to the transportation covered by the Prepaid Ticket Advice, but shall not be used for the transmittal of funds.

Pre-Printed Document Number *(Airlines)*: A number or numeric code that is printed on the traffic document at the time of its manufacture.

Preregistration *(Tourism)*: A service typically offered to conventioneers to facilitate room assignments and convention related arrangements prior to their arrival.

Preserve *(Tourism)*: A territory designated by a government in order to protect animal life, vegetation and natural resources.

Press Release *(Tourism)*: A public relations announcement issued by a company for the use of news media and other targeted publications for the purpose to generate or encourage publicity about the company's developments.

Pressure *(Air Traffic)*: Barometric Pressure.

PREV *(GDS)*: Code meaning Previous.

PRF *(GDS)*: Code meaning Partial Refund Message.

Price Fixing *(Business)*: An unlawful practice to agree on restricting prices within certain limits in order to avoid competence, or the illegal intent to control pricing within an industry by alerting companies each other to proposed changes in the pricing structure. It is also known as Price Signaling

Price Quotation *(Tourism)*: An invoice prepared in advance by the seller stating the price of goods or services to be sold.

Price Signaling *(Business)*: See Price Fixing.

Pricing Unit *(Airlines)*: A journey or part of a journey for which a fare is assessed (priced) as a separate entity. It can be ticketed separately.

Pricing Unit Concept *(Airlines)*: A method to calculating air fares by splitting the journey in units that can be priced separately. The combination of such fares usually results in low prices, mainly when half round trip special fares are used.

Primary Airport *(Airlines)*: In the U.S. it is a commercial airport that embarks more than 10,000 passengers per year.

Primary Flight Control System (PFCS) *(Air Traffic)*: The most basic part of the flight controls operated by a pilot, including fixed wing, yoke, cyclic (rotary wing), pedals, throttle, and collective.

Primary Producers *(Ecology)*: Organisms in an ecosystem that make organic material from inorganic material. In other words, primary producers make their own food from inorganic components and form the bottom tier in a trophic system. In most of the cases they are photo synthetically active organisms, such as plants, cyanobacteria and a number of other unicellular organisms. They are also called Autotroph.

Prime Codes *(Airlines)*: Fare basis codes are composed of one or more characters. The first character is called the Prime Code. It is always a letter that identifies the class to which the fare applies or the fare's booking code, such as Y, M, B, S, etc.

Prime Meridian *(Geography)*: The 0 (Zero) degree line of longitude which circles the earth from north to south, passing by the English location named Greenwich.

Principle of Least Effort *(Tourism)*: A concept to seek the shortest possible route assigned to a journey between two places.

Private Island *(Cruise)*: An island or beach property offering an array of beach and water sports that is leased or owned by a cruise line for the use of its cruise passengers.

Prix Fixe (PF) *(Tourism)*: A French term meaning literally Price Fixed, which is commonly used in Europe to designate several course meals that are offered at a fixed price.

PRM *(GDS)*: Code meaning Premium.

PRO *(GDS)*: Code meaning Promotional.

Product *(Tourism)*: Usually known as a Tourism Product, it is a commercial component of a package, such as lodging, attraction, sightseeing, transfer, and even the complete package itself.

Productivity Based Pricing *(GDS)*: An inducing action accomplished by a GDS company to stimulate agencies to make the maximum use of its services to get entitled for a better price.

Professional Air Traffic Controllers Organization (PATCO)

(Organizations): An independent labor union in the United States, currently representing air traffic controllers who work in private sector control towers. PATCO was created in 1968 and has been later reformed.

Professional Liability Insurance *(Car Rental)*: See Errors and Omissions Insurance.

Profile *(Tourism)*: A detailed record about a traveler's personal data and preferences that is kept on file by a travel agency or supplier.

Profit And Loss Statement *(Tourism)*: An accounting notice informing on the company's revenues and expenses.

Proforma Invoice *(Tourism)*: See Price Quotation.

Prohibited Area *(Air Traffic)*: Airspace within which no aircraft may operate without the permission of the aeronautical authority.

Prohibited Items *(Customs)*: Items that are not allowed to enter into a country under any circumstances.

Project *(Tourism)*: A specific and methodic design to represent a reality to happen in the future according to some strategies and pre-established objectives. A project is a work of prospective facts.

Project for a Tourist Development *(Tourism)*: A project to perform activities that meet the touristic needs of a market or a supplier.

Projected Flight Path *(Air Traffic)*: The predetermined set of movement that an aircraft will make or will follow in the airspace.

Promenade *(Cruise)*: 1. A French term for a leisure stroll for amusement; 2. The deck on a ship where lifeboats, davits, deck chairs, joggers, and strollers are located.

Promenade Nordique *(Tourism)*: A French expression defining the practice of Nordic ski over well known places with easy ground conditions such as virgin snow and short distances.

Promissory Note *(Tourism)*: A written promise to pay a certain amount of money on a specific date or at the time stated by the provider.

Promo *(Tourism)*: Abbreviation for promotion or promotional.

Promoter *(Tourism)*: A company or individual that assumes the responsibility to encourage public acceptance and purchase of a product or service.

Promotion *(Tourism)*: The act of performing specific communication techniques to bring a product or service to a potential clientele.

Promotional Fare *(Airlines)*: A special fare incorporating a discount designed to increase an air travel volume.

Proof of Citizenship *(Tourism)*: Any document that verifies a person's citizenship, such as passports, driving licences, birth certificates, etc.

PROP *(GDS)*: A code meaning: 1. Property, 2. Proprietor, 3. Propeller.

Propeller *(Aeronautics)*: A device on engine that propels the aircraft by the backward thrust of air.

Property *(Hospitality)*: Any lodging facility, such as a hotel or motel.

Property Irregularity Report (PIR) *(Airlines)*: A document used to register information on damaged or lost baggage. It is filled out by passengers who do not receive their baggage or when they receive it in an improper condition upon arrival of the flight, and as soon as the failure is noticed.

Property Management System (PMS) *(Hospitality)*: A computerized program for administering hotel inventories and for managing the hotel operations. It interfaces with other internal systems, such as guest billing, telephone, entertainment, etc.

Propfan *(Aviation)*: A term used to describe new technology propeller family.

Proportional Fare *(Airlines)*: A published amount used to obtain an unpublished throughfare by adding it to a published fare. See also Add-on fare.

Proposal *(Tourism)*: A formal written document making a business offer including specifications on prices, type of services, modality of the service, terms and conditions, etc.

Proprietary Booking Engine *(Hospitality)*: An internet reservation system permitting a hotel to take reservation on their own website without paying a fee to a GDS.

Proprietary Club *(Tourism)*: A for-profit organization that sells memberships to the general public, such as country club, tennis or health club.

Propulsion System *(Aeronautics)*: A mechanism on an aircraft used to propel the aircraft through the air by providing thrust.

Prorate *(Airlines)*: A method of calculating the proportional income for an airline participating in air transportation performed by several carriers.

Prospect *(Tourism)*: A potential customer who meets certain buying conditions.

Prospecting Cycle *(Business)*: The stage of a marketing process to reach qualified prospective customers. The prospecting program must incorporate a range of marketing tactics that will bring prospects closer to a decision to purchase a product or a service.

PROT *(GDS)*: Code meaning Protected Reservation.

Protected Area *(Ecology)*: Private or public bodies of land and water selected to protect biodiversity, cultural heritage, natural heritage, or recreational values.

Protected Commission *(Tourism)*: A type of commission to be paid even if the service is not provided.

Protocol *(Computing)*: A set of software conventions that governs network communications by providing applicable rules for its operation.

Protocol *(Tourism)*: The set of formal rules describing the ceremonies and etiquette practices that must be observed by diplomats and heads of state in diplomatic protocols. Protocol is also related to the proper form for conducting at certain business meetings.

Prototype *(Airlines)*: The first version of an aircraft or that is used for testing and demonstration purposes only.

Provincial Standard Time *(Geography)*: A Canadian time zone. See Atlantic Standard Time.

Provisioned Charter *(Cruise)*: A boat or yacht that is chartered including food, fuel and other provisions, but excluding crew.

Prow *(Cruise)*: The foremost part of a ship.

Proximity Sensor *(Aeronautics)*: A device that detects the presence of an object and sends signals to another device.

PSA *(GDS)*: Code meaning Passenger Service Agent.

PSBL *(GDS)*: Code meaning Possible.

Pseudo Agent *(Tourism)*: Someone who pretends to be a travel agent, possibly with fraudulent intentions.

Pseudo ARC Number *(Tourism)*: An alphanumeric designator adopted by suppliers to identify travel agencies that do not have an ARC number.

Pseudo City Code *(GDS)*: A code identifying a travel agency location.

Pseudo PNR *(GDS)*: A record stored in a GDS which is not an airline reservation.

PSGR *(GDS)*: Code meaning Passenger.

PSNT *(GDS)*: Code meaning Present.

PSPT *(GDS)*: Code meaning Passport Number.

PSR *(GDS)*: Code meaning: 1. Passenger Service Representative; 2. Passenger Space Ratio.

PST *(Geography)*: See Pacific Standard Time.

PT *(GDS)*: A code meaning: 1. Pacific Time, 2. Port Taxes, 3. Physical Training.

PTA *(GDS)*: Code meaning Prepaid Ticket Advice.

PTAC *(Hospitality)*: See Packaged Terminal Air Conditioning Unit.

PTHSE *(GDS)*: Code meaning Penthouse.

PTM *(GDS)*: Code meaning Passenger Traffic Manager.

PTP *(GDS)*: Code meaning Point-to-point.

PTT *(GDS)*: Code meaning "Post, telegraph, and telephone."

PTY *(GDS)*: Three-letter IATA code for the city of Panama, the capital city of Panama

PU *(GDS)*: Code meaning Pricing Unit.

Published Fare *(Airlines)*: Any of the fares listed in the carrier's tariff. It is synonymous with direct fare.

Public Bar *(Hospitality)*: A bar where bartenders prepare alcoholic beverages for service to guests and general public.

Public Charter *(Tourism)*: Any vehicle (aircraft, ship, yacht, bus) capable to be leased by the general public for particular purposes.

Public Special Fare *(Airlines)*: A type of fare that is not normal, whose application is subject to fulfilling some conditions and restrictions. Although is improper, they are usually known as promotional fares. Some types of special fares are the excursion fares, Pex and Apex.

Published Charge *(Airlines)*: The amounts that are specifically announced in any carrier's fare publication.

PUC *(Airlines)*: Code for Pricing Unit Concept.

Puddle Jumpers *(Airlines)*: See Commuter Airlines.

Pull *(Aeronautics)*: In physics terms, it relates to the force that causes a mass to accelerate in the direction of the source of power. In simpler terms, it is the force that brings something closer.

Pullman *(Tourism)*: A luxurious passenger car on a railroad for sleeping, dining or meeting.

Pullman Berth *(Airlines)*: A sleeping compartment on a Pullman train.

PUP *(GDS)*: Code meaning Pick up.

Purser *(Airlines)*: An officer aboard an aircraft who is responsible for the well-being of the passengers, and is in charge of the accounts and money.

Purser *(Cruise)*: An administrative officer aboard a ship who is responsible for providing some services to guests and crew, including mail, information, check cashing, safety deposit boxes, tickets, transactions, and so forth.

Purveyor *(Tourism)*: Any company or individual that supplies provisions as a supplier, seller, or circulator of a product or service.

Push *(Aeronautics)*: In physics terms, it relates to the force that causes a mass to move forward. In simpler terms, it is the force used to move something ahead.

Push Factor *(Tourism)*: Any cause that motivates people to change their condition in a way that is not fully suitable.

Pushback *(Air Traffic)*: The action of an aircraft leaving the gate area before taxiing.

Pusher *(Aeronautics)*: A propeller mounted in back of an engine, pushing an aircraft through the air, as opposed to a Tractor configuration.

PVR *(GDS)*: Three-letter IATA code for Puerto Vallarta, Mexico.

PWC *(Tourism)*: Code for Personal Watercraft.

PWCT *(GDS)*: Code meaning Passenger Will Contact.

PX *(GDS)*: Code for PEX Fares, which are Restricted Instant Purchase Fares.

Pylon *(Aeronautics)*: The part of an aircraft's structure which connects an engine to either a wing or the fuselage.

Pyramid of Biomass *(Ecology)*: A diagram representing the biomass at each trophic level in a food web. Primary Producers are located in the bottom of the pyramid, while predators are located at its top.

Q

Q *(Airlines)*: "Quebec," name used to designate the letter "Q" in the International Phonetic Alphabet

Q *(GDS)*: Code for Economy coach Discounted Class of Fare.

QADB *(GDS)*: Code meaning Quadruple Room with Bath.

QADN *(GDS)*: Code meaning Quadruple Room without Bath or Shower.

QADS *(GDS)*: Code meaning Quadruple Room with Shower.

QD *(GDS)*: Code meaning Quadruple Room.

QF *(Airlines)*: Two-letter IATA code for Qantas Airways.

QINB *(GDS)*: Code meaning Quintuple Room with Bath.

QINN *(GDS)*: Code meaning Quintuple Room without Bath or Shower.

QINS *(GDS)*: Code meaning Quintuple Room with Shower.

QTE *(GDS)*: Code meaning Quote.

Quad *(Hospitality)*: A room suitable to guest four persons.

Quadraplane, Quadruplane *(Aeronautics)*: An aircraft having four or more wingforms.

Qualifying *(Tourism)*: In marketing, it is the process of selecting prospective customers meeting certain conditions.

Qualifying Code *(Tourism)*: An alphanumeric designator to define a special fare on a ticket, or the alphanumeric code to identify a promotion or level of amenities on other travel document.

Qualifying Rental *(Car Rental)*: A condition that determines something meets the aptitude for a rental business.

Quality *(Tourism)*: Quality is sometimes a matter related either to subjective feelings or to objective facts. It has been defined as the condition with zero defects or defections, an attribute to distinguish something or someone among others. But companies for-profit are customer-oriented; therefore, when speaking of quality, they are concerned on how customers feel and react about a product or service. Quality becomes, then, a combination of actions and outcome when the expectations and needs of customers are met. The touristic product is intangible and its quality does not appear until it is consumed.

Quality Assurance *(Tourism)*: The process of checking the set of services arranged for a customer, in order to insure its accuracy.

Quality Group *(Tourism)*: A group of travelers for whom quality is the factor determining their travel. They disregard prices and usually ask for first-class services and accommodations.

Quarantine *(Tourism)*: 1. A period during which a ship is forbidden to have contact with the shore when it is suspected it carries a contagious disease. 2. The isolation of persons or goods to prevent the spread of pests or disease. 3. A place where restrained persons or goods are put in isolation.

Quarter Deck *(Cruise)*: The deck at the stern of a cruise ship located above the upper deck, from where the Captain addresses the whole crew.

Quaternion *(Aeronautics)*: A system of representing an aircraft's attitude by measuring the angle of aircraft center line with respect to three axes plus rotation about centerline.

Quarters *(Cruise)*: Officer, crew and staff accommodations onboard a ship.

Quartz Oven *(Hospitality)*: See Infrared Oven.

Quay *(Cruise)*: A pier.

Quebec *(Airlines)*: Designator for the letter "Q" in the International Phonetic Alphabet.

Queen *(Hospitality)*: A bed of approximately 60 by 80 inches.

Queen Room *(Hospitality)*: A hotel room with a queen size bed.

Queue *(GDS)*: A communication area or subsystem within a network computer system where a PNR is routed to a specific destination, such as a travel agency.

QUIN *(Hospitality)*: A hotel room suitable for five persons.

Quota *(Tourism)*: A maximum number allotted or a proportional part assigned.

Quote *(Tourism)*: 1. To state the price for a product or service. 2. To speak or write a text of another person.

R

R *(Airlines)*: "Romeo," name used to designate the letter "R" in the International Phonetic Alphabet

R *(GDS)*: Code once referred to Supersonic Class.

RA *(Air Traffic)*: Radio altitude.

R&R *(GDS)*: Code meaning: 1. Rest and relaxation; 2. Rehabilitation; 3. Recreation.

RAC *(GDS)*: Code meaning Rack Rate.

Rack Card *(Tourism)*: A brochure sized 4" x 9" containing tourism or package information that is displayed in racks.

Rack Rate *(Hospitality)*: The official standard price established and posted by a hotel, attraction or rental car, but not used by tour operators who typically negotiate rates. Hotel rooms are rarely sold for the rack rate unless the property is virtually full or a special event is taking place. Rack rates are sometimes set artificially high and are used as a basis to calculate a variety of discounts.

Racking *(Hospitality)*: The process of transferring wine from one cask or barrel to another in order to separate wine from the sediment or its lees at the bottom.

Racking Policy *(GDS)*: The order of preference to display suppliers' brochures in a travel agency racks.

RADAL or RADALT *(Air Traffic)*: Codes for Radio Altimeter.

Radar *(Air Traffic)*: The term is an abbreviation for Radio Detecting and Ranging. It is a device which measures the time interval between transmission and reception of ultra-high frequency radio pulses that is used to determine an object's direction and distance.

Radar Altimeter *(Air Traffic)*: A device that senses aircraft's height above the terrain. The altitude is monitored to provide a low altitude warning during terrain following and landing operations.

Radar Altitude *(Air Traffic)*: Height with respect to the terrain below.

Radar Approach Control Facility (RAPCON) *(Air Traffic)*: A terminal ATC facility that uses radar and non-radar capabilities to provide approach control services to aircraft arriving, departing, or transiting airspace controlled by the facility. This facility provides radar ATC services to aircraft operating in the vicinity of one or more civil/military airports in a terminal area.

Radar Controller *(Air Traffic)*: An air-traffic controller who is proficient in the use and interpretation of radar, computer, communications, and other sensor systems for the control of aircraft circulation in an airspace sector assigned to him/her.

Radar Feeds *(Air Traffic)*: Electronic data that are transmitted at regular intervals to a radar scope or system.

Radar Hand-off Controller *(Air Traffic)*: A person who supports the radar and assist controllers during peak air traffic flow.

Radar Surveillance *(Air Traffic)*: An observation by radar of a specific geographical area for the purpose of performing certain radar functions.

Radar Weather Report (RAREP) *(Air Traffic)*: A weather report issued each hour describing areas of precipitation along with information on the type of precipitation, its intensity, direction and speed.

Radiation Fog *(Air Traffic)*: Fog characteristically resulting when radiated cooling of the earth's surface lowers the air temperature near the ground to or below its initial dew point on calm and clear nights.

Radio Detection and Ranging *(Air Traffic)*: See Radar.

Radio Frequency *(Air Traffic)*: A frequency that is useful for radio communication with aircraft, usually between 10 kHz and 300,000 MHz.

Radio Frequency Identification (RFID) *(Airlines)*: Radio Frequency Identification is a technology incorporated into a silicon chip embedded in a tag which emits a radio signal that can be read at a distance without needing to see the item. Radio Frequency Identification (RFID) is the technology that is being applied to baggage tagging and tracking. Tags can be "talked to" or "written to", allowing the status of an item to be updated as it is processed.

Radio Navigation *(Air Traffic)*: Navigation relative to radio station, providing relative bearing, range, lateral deviation, and glideslope, for example.

Radome *(Air Traffic)*: A detachable nose cone made of plastic-type material, used to cover and protect an airplane's radar antenna.

Raft *(Tourism)*: The most basic floating structure of wood, cork, or air-inflated rubber for conveying goods or people over bodies of water.

Rafting *(Tourism)*: An adventure tour activity using a raft to navigate a river or other bodies of water. This leisure sport became popular since the mid 1970s.

Raid Nordique *(Tourism)*: A French expression used for defining a journey from one to more days over an easy terrain and with light equipment.

Rain Check or Raincheck *(Tourism)*: A voucher or ticket for future use given to spectators at an outdoor event, as a baseball game or concert that has been postponed or interrupted by rain or other reason.

Rainshadow *(Climate)*: A climatic term for a dry area on the leeward side of a mountain.

RALT SEL *(Air Traffic)*: Abbreviations for Radar Altitude Select.

Rally *(Tourism)*: A long-distance automobile race run on public roads, with numerous checkpoints along the route.

RAM *(Computing)*: See Random Access Memory.

Ramjet *(Aeronautics)*: A type of jet engine in which fuel is burned to produce a high-velocity propulsive jet. It needs to be accelerated to high speed before it can become operative.

Ramp *(Airlines)*: Any paved area around a hangar or runway for parking airplanes. It is a specific area on an airport or heliport intended to accommodate aircraft for purposes of loading or unloading passengers or cargo, refueling, parking, or maintenance.

Ramp Agent *(Airlines)*: An airline's employee, who brings, loads and unloads baggage, cargo, and food supplies on the aircraft.

Rampers *(Airlines)*: Ramp personnel at an airport who service an aircraft upon its arrival and while the plane is parked waiting for the next departure.

Random Access Memory (RAM) *(Computing)*: It is the place in a computer where the residing operating system, applications, programs and other data can be accessed easily by the computer's processor.

Range (RGE) *(Air Traffic)*: 1. The total distance a signal can be received via radio communications; 2. The total distance an aircraft can fly using a given rate of fuel consumption and without refueling.

Range *(Cruise)*: The maximum distance a ship type can sail without refueling.

Range *(Hospitality)*: A food service appliance with a flat cooking surface for frying, grilling, sautéing, etc.

Range Oven *(Hospitality)*: A small oven located beneath a range, used for roasting and baking or as a food warmer.

Ranger *(Tourism)*: An official at a National Park in the United States.

Rapid Return *(Car Rental)*: A rental car service available at most major U.S. airports for just dropping off the car in a return lot.

RAREP *(Air Traffic)*: See Radar Weather Report.

Rate Access Code *(GDS)*: A code used for displaying hotel rates or other service negotiated prices that are only available for certain companies or categories of traveler.

Rate and Service Structure *(Tourism)*: The whole scheme of prices charged, and the services and amenities provided by a carrier.

Rate Assignment *(Hospitality)*: See Automatic Room.

Rate Desk *(Airlines)*: An airline's desk set to quote fares for travel agents and passengers. Usually fares quoted to travel agents are those which are not published by GDS systems.

Rate Hike *(Tourism)*: A price increase.

Rate of Exchange *(Tourism)*: See Foreign Exchange Rate.

Rate of Exchange (ROE) *(Tourism)*: See IATA Rate of Exchange.

Rate of the Day *(Hospitality)*: The rack rate displayed in a hotel pricing system for a specific day.

Rate of Roll *(Aeronautics)*: A measure of the speed with which an airplane can turn around its long axis, or roll. It is generally expressed in degrees per second

RBD *(GDS)*: Code meaning Reservations Booking Designator.

RCFM *(GDS)*: A code meaning Reconfirm, Reconfirming, Reconfirmed.

RCPT *(GDS)*: A code meaning Receipt, Reception.

RCU *(Air Traffic)*: A code for Radio Control Unit.

RCVD *(GDS)*: Code meaning Received.

RDB *(GDS)*: Code meaning Reply to Duplicate Booking Enquiry.

RE *(GDS)*: A code meaning: 1. Regarding; 2. In Regard to; 3. About.

Read, A. C. *(Aviation)*: A.C. Read was a U.S. officer who commanded a crew with which he made a transatlantic flight from Newfoundland to Portugal via the Azores islands, on May 16 1929 on board the flying boat NC-4. They arrived in Plymouth, England, on May 31.

Read-back *(Air Traffic)*: The instance of repeating a message in order to confirm its correctness.

Reader *(Airlines)*: A device that reads magnetic or bar coded bands.

Read-only tags *(Airlines)*: Tags containing data that cannot be changed unless the microchip is reprogrammed electronically.

Real Time *(Computing)*: Time in a computational process which runs at the same rate as a physical process.

Rebate *(Tourism)*: 1. The deduction or return of funds issued to a client, as a portion of a travel agent's commission. 2. The amount of money so returned.

Rebooking *(Airlines)*: A change of reservation not requiring a ticket reissuance.

REC *(GDS)*: Code meaning Record.

Recall Commission Statement *(Airlines)*: An ARC document by which an airline retrieves a commission already paid for a ticket that has been refunded to the passenger.

Receiving Agent *(Tourism)*: A travel agent who provides tour services to incoming travelers, such as transfers, accommodation, sightseeing and similar.

Receiving Carrier *(Airlines)*: The carrier that receives passengers or merchandise in a connecting point for onward transportation.

Reception *(Tourism)*: 1. An event organized to greet a person or a group of persons; 2. Synonymous with hotel front desk.

Receptive Operator *(Tourism)*: A tour operator or travel agent operating services to incoming visitors in particular destinations on behalf of travel organizers and tour operators. Some receptive operators confine their services to the community and area in which they are based, while others provide services in entire regions. See Inbound Operator.

Receptive Region *(Tourism)*: It is a large area receiving touristic flows that features multiple destinations and is located close to principal emitter centers. In French it is called *Bassin Touristique*.

Receptive Service Operator *(Tourism)*: See Receptive Operator.

Receptive Services *(Tourism)*: The set of services provided by a receptive operator or receiving agent to incoming visitors in a particular destination.

Receptive Tourism *(Tourism)*: See Incoming Tourism.

Recheck System *(GDS)*: An automated GDS application that is programmed to carry continuous checks for the lowest fares on a route.

Reciprocity *(Airlines)*: A courteous practice for a government to extend similar concessions to a foreign government. Freedoms of the air are usually negotiated on reciprocity basis.

Recline *(Airlines)*: The back inclination of an airplane's seat. Recline is measured either by inches or by degrees. The higher the figure, the further the seat can recline back.

RECON *(GDS)*: Code meaning In Reference to Conversation.

Reconnaissance *(Airlines)*: The action to fly over an area and look closely to gather information about it.

Reconciliation *(Tourism)*: The instance of matching one account set of records against another.

Reconfirm *(Tourism)*: To confirm repeatedly as on an airline booking.

Reconfirmation *(Airlines)*: A requirement for passengers to advise a carrier on their intention to use the space reserved.

Record *(GDS)*: The information about a booking stored under a PNR.

Record Locator or Record Locator Number *(GDS)*: One of the elements of an airline reservation consisting of an alphanumeric code that uniquely identifies a booking or a PNR in a GDS.

Recreation *(Tourism)*: An activity that people fulfill for pleasure or relaxation during their leisure time.

Recreation Center *(Tourism)*: A building where meetings are held, sports are played and other activities are carried. It is available for the public.

Recreation Management *(Tourism)*: The process or set of tasks aimed to maintain and administer the services, facility conditions and personnel work to run recreational activities in the optimum level of performance.

Recycled *(Ecology)*: Products usually made of post-consumer materials that have passed through a cycle of change or treatment.

Recycling *(Ecology)*: A series of actions allowing materials, which could become solid waste, to be collected, separated, processed and returned to the market to be reused in the form of raw materials or finished goods.

Red Book *(Tourism)*: A Michelin guide that publishes lists of restaurants and hotels. It is so called because of its color that distinguishes it from Michelin guides of tourism.

Red Eye *(Tourism)*: A slang term referring to a person with lack of sleep, as when the traveler lands at an airport after an overnight flight.

Red-Eye Flight *(Airlines)*: A late-night and long flight, usually one that arrives early in the morning.

Red Light District *(Tourism)*: A part of a city assigned by local authorities or custom for sex-related businesses.

REF *(GDS)*: Code meaning Reference, Referring to.

Referral *(Tourism)*: A person recommended to a travel agent by another customer.

Referral Agent/Agency *(Tourism)*: A travel agency that refers business to another travel agency in return for a commission or fee.

REFG *(GDS)*: A code meaning Refrigerating, Refrigeration.

Reflexology *(Tourism)*: The application of finger-point pressure to reflex zones on the feet, hands and ears to re-establish the flow of energy through the body.

Refreshment Break *(Hospitality)*: A period between work sessions during which coffee or other refreshments are served.

Refrigerator *(Hospitality)*: A chilled unit used to maintain the quality of food.

Refuge *(Tourism)*: 1. A place that provides protection as for mountain climbers. 2. In France it is a collective and simple lodging for alpinists, typically located at a mountain.

Refugee *(Tourism)*: A person displaced for safety reasons, by war, natural disasters or political causes.

Refund *(Airlines)*: The return of payment to the purchaser of all or a portion of a fare rate or charge for unused carriage or service.

Refund/Exchange Authorization (REA) *(GDS)*: An authorization given by a system provider to report a refund, exchange or transaction to a BSP office.

Refund/Exchange Notice *(Airlines)*: An ARC form to process adjustments in money due to the ARC or to a travel agency.

REG *(GDS)*: A code meaning Region, Regional.

Regatta *(Tourism)*: A boat race or a series of boat races and festivities arranged by a sailing organization. It is usually an event for unpowered water craft; however, there are also regattas for powerboats. The term was first used in Venice to name some boat races on the Grand Canal.

Regimes of Flight *(Air Traffic)*: A method of placing aircraft into different categories based on their speeds. The regimes of flight are subsonic, transonic, supersonic and hypersonic.

Region *(Geography)*: A land area which is similar at its interior, but different from surrounding areas. It is determined by such characteristic factors as ethnic, climate, production, topography, government, etc. It is a territory of interest to people for whom one or more distinctive traits are used as the basis for their identity.

Regional Airline *(Airlines)*: A U.S. airline with annual operating revenues under USD100 million. They serve a defined area of a country and are also called commuter airlines or feeder airlines.

Regional Carrier *(Airlines)*: A U.S. airline with annual revenues of less than $100 million whose service generally is limited to a particular geographic region. It is the same as Regional Airline.

Regional Getaway Guests *(Hospitality)*: Guests who check into a nearby hotel in order to enjoy some days away from children or disturbances.

Regional Jet *(Airlines)*: A small jet powered aircraft usually serving smaller airports. Its maximum passenger capacity is 50 seats.

Regional Sales Manager *(Tourism)*: A company's employee who is responsible for leading sales activities for the company in a specific geographic area via the selected channels.

Regionalism *(Tourism)*: A way of speaking, acting or behaving that is particular to a region. Sometimes it is an exaggerated way of valuating one region's importance over another.

Regionalization *(Geography)*: The administrative division of a country into smaller units with significant delegated powers.

Registered Luggage *(Airlines)*: Baggage that travels in the same flight as the passenger, free of charge if it fits into the allowance limits, and is handed by the traveler for the temporary care of the air carrier.

Registered Traveler Program *(Airlines)*: A security pilot program that was launched by the Transportation Security Administration (TSA) in partnership with selected airlines and airports across the country. The program was developed since 2002 but it was recently tested in 2005 on a voluntary basis to expedite passenger and baggage security screening at some US airports. It works like this: The program is set to work like this: A traveler submits the driver's license number, the previous home address for the past five years, the Social Security number, an alien registration number (permanent foreign residents only), a current credit card to the government through one of the private companies qualified by TSA. They also capture images of the passenger's irises and fingerprints and take a photograph to complete the documentation. After the traveler gets his/her boarding pass, the passenger goes to a special line with a kiosk that is supposed will allow travelers expedited passage through airport security. The Registered Traveler was adopted to replace the Computer Assisted Passenger Prescreening System (CAPPS) and the canceled CAPPS II counter-terrorism system.

Registry *(Cruise)*: It is the formal registration of a ship's ownership, which is also referred to the country it is registered. Due to some regulatory reason or for tax purposes, many cruise ships are registered in foreign countries. Some countries offer the best registering conditions, such as Panama, Liberia, The Bahamas and Norway. If it happens someone is wedded at sea, his/her wedding is registered in the nation of the ship's registry. See also Country of Registry.

Regular Fare *(Airlines)*: A full-price fare such as normal Economy, Business or First Class that is not subject to restrictions and has one year validity.

Reiki *(Tourism)*: A healing technique based on ancient Tibetan teachings that consists of placing the hand palms over, or on, various areas of the body for a few moments to energize and balance the body, mind and spirit. They assure it helps to treat both physical and emotional problems.

Reissue *(Airlines)*: The issuance of a new ticket that occurs by cause of a change of plans, dates, routes, flights, etc. that may involve additional fare collection, penalties or fees. It is an alteration to an original ticket which cannot be done through revalidation and requires issuance of a new ticket.

Related Charges *(Airlines)*: Charges that are somehow related to the air transportation, such as cancellation penalties, non-refundable amounts, rebooking and rerouting charges, weekend surcharges, or excess baggage charges.

Relative Humidity *(Climate)*: The ratio of the existing amount of water vapor in the air at a given temperature to the maximum amount that could exist at that temperature. In other words, it is the ratio between absolute humidity and humidity capacity at a given temperature. It is usually expressed as a percentage.

Release *(Hospitality)*: A clause usually included in contracts between a hotel and tour operators in which a dead-line is fixed to cancel the reservations without a penalty.

RELET *(GDS)*: A code meaning "In reference to your letter."

Reliever Airport *(Air Traffic)*: A commercial airport assigned by the US FAA to diminish congestions at primary airports.

Religious Tourism *(Tourism)*: A type of tourism featuring visits to sanctuaries or religious events.

Relocation Guests *(Hospitality)*: Individuals or families temporarily relocated to places different to their habitual residences, until a permanent housing is found.

REMF *(GDS)*: Code meaning "In reference to my phone call."

REML *(GDS)*: Code meaning "In reference to my letter."

Remote Communications Outlets (RCO) *(Air Traffic)*: Remote air navigation radio transceivers that are used to expand communication capabilities of Flight Information Centers (FIC) and Flight Service Stations (FSS).

Remote Sensing *(Geography)*: A study about the earth's surface using data and pictures gathered by recording or real-time sensing devices installed in aircraft, spacecrafts or satellites.

Remote Ticketing *(Tourism)*: The practice of making a reservation at one location and issuing the ticket at another. This was a usual practice before e-tickets were introduced. Now, once electronic tickets are issued, they are available anywhere.

REN *(GDS)*: Code meaning Refund Exchange Notice.

Rendezvous *(Air Traffic)*: The meeting of aircrafts in the air, for refueling or other mission purposes.

Rendezvous *(Tourism)*: A French term defining a meeting planned at an agreed time and place. Quite often it is a romantic or social nature meeting. It also designates the place where such a meeting is held.

Rendezvous Approach *(Air Traffic)*: To approach a planned rendezvous point.

Rent a Car *(Tourism)*: A Car Rental, Rent-a-car or Car Hire Company is a firm that rents automobiles, vans and trucks for short time periods for a fee. The business is organized around a network of numerous locations situated near airports or in city areas. Their main customers are travelers who are out of their home town.

Rent It Here; Leave It There *(Car Rental)*: A practice receiving a hired car in a city and dropping it in another.

Rental Agreement *(Car Rental)*: An agreement signed between the car renter and the user stating the terms of usage and the pertinent requirements, such as insurance coverage, dates, car size and type, etc.

Rental Period *(Car Rental)*: The time during which the user is responsible for the rental car. Rental periods are designated in 24 hour intervals, although some rental companies will require a minimum of days.

REORG *(GDS)*: Code meaning Reorganize.

Repeat Customer *(Tourism)*: A customer who buys products or services repeatedly at the same business place.

Reportable Accident *(Airlines)*: An aircraft accident involving death, or which leads to incapacity for work, or one that causes extensive damage to an aircraft. Such accidents must be reported to the aeronautic authorities.

Repositioning *(Cruise)*: The act of moving a cruise ships from a home port to another for all or part of a season, usually at a specific time of year. This is a strategy that maximizes efficiency of use. A typical case of cruise repositioning is the movement of vessels from the Caribbean to Alaska and vice versa.

Repositioning Cruise *(Cruise)*: Same as above.

REPR *(GDS)*: Code meaning Representative.

Representative Fraction Scale *(Geography)*: A type of map scale which is expressed in a fraction or ratio form, such as 1:10, 000 and which indicates the number of times a distance on the ground is greater than the same distance on a map. In this example, one measure unit on the map represents 10,000 measure units on the ground.

REQ *(GDS)*: A code meaning Require, Requiring, Required, Requirement.

Reroute *(Airlines)*: The issuance of a new ticket covering transportation to the same destination, but via a different routing than that designated on the original ticket. It could also be the acceptance of the original ticket for transportation to the same destination but via a different routing. It may or may not involve additional collection. In the case of transportation of goods it is the route to be followed as altered from that originally specified on the AWB.

RES *(GDS)*: Code for Reservation.

RES or RESTN (*GDS***)**: Codes for Restriction.

Res Vendor *(Airlines)*: A GDS business company or a company's sales agent.

Rescission *(Hospitality)*: A term used in time share business meaning a period of time during which a consumer has the right to cancel a purchase contract and obtain a full refund of his/her deposit with no penalty. It is sometimes called a "cancellation" or "cooling off" period.

Reservation *(Tourism)*: An arrangement to set aside an airline seat, a hotel room, a cruise berth or other accommodation for guaranteed use of a specific person at a later time, often on the basis of a deposit payment. See also Booking.

Reservation *(Geography)*: A tract of public land set apart for a special purpose, such as its exclusive use by an ethnic minority living within its borders.

Reservation Deadline *(Airlines)*: The number of days needed to have reservations confirmed before the day of departure.

Reservations *(Airlines)*: A term equivalent to Booking, meaning the allotment of seating in advance, sleeping accommodation or cabin cruise for a passenger. It is also the allocation of a space or weight capacity for baggage or goods.

Reservations *(Hospitality)*: A guestroom or other room space that is held under an individual or business' name at a particular hotel for a specific date at a specific rate.

Reservations Agent *(Tourism)*: The person at a travel agency who is responsible for all aspects of processing reservations.

Reservations Bookings Designator *(GDS)*: The code used in reservation messages to identify individual reservations.

Reservations Department *(Hospitality)*: Hotel department where telemarketing personnel take reservations over the phone, answer questions about facilities, quote prices and date availability, and sell to callers who are shopping around.

Residence *(Tourism)*: Although domicile and residence are usually used as if they were the same, they are not synonymous, even if the residence and the domicile are in the same place. Residence is the place where a person lives temporarily, without the intent to make it his/her permanent home. A person has merely a bodily presence in a residence, while domicile requires the intention to make it his/her permanent home.

Resident *(Tourism)*: A person living in a country of which he/she is or is not a citizen.

Rack Oven *(Hospitality)*: A convection oven into which special racks filled with trays of food are rolled.

Resident Manager *(Hospitality)*: The manager in charge of the rooms division and sometimes also in charge of security.

Residential *(Hospitality)*: A small lodging house or a type of accommodation at private homes rather than commercial buildings.

Resolution 722g *(Airlines)*: See IATA Resolution 722g.

Resort *(Tourism)*: 1. A hotel development, tourist complex, apartment building, condominium, condo-hotel, townhouse or the like, offering a broad range of leisure and amenity facilities, which are designed to provide a total vacation or recreation experience. All the services are usually included under one-price umbrella. Their class range can also vary from budget/economy to luxury. 2. A place, city, a town or beach known for its leisure attractions, where recreation services for vacationers are provided. A resort is usually a scenic area of great natural attractions with a compound of buildings and facilities established to provide accommodation and food in an environment of entertainment and a relaxing.

Resort Fee *(Hospitality)*: An amount charged by some hotels for the use of resort amenities, whether the guests use them or not.

Resort Hotel *(Hospitality)*: A hotel usually located in an outstanding vacation place that has facilities to offer amenities, leisure activities, fine dining and exceptional service.

Resort Spa *(Tourism)*: See Health Resort.

Resource Manager *(Business)*: A person who is responsible for the implementation of outdoor oriented activities and or business operations on public lands.

Responsibility Clause *(Tourism)*: A notice informing that an intermediary agent acts only as a middleman in the sale of travel products or services and that the liability lies only with the supplier.

Responsible Tourism *(Ecology)*: A type of tourism that is achieved by persons who make responsible vacation choices to limit the extent of the sociological and environmental impacts their vacation may cause.

Rest Area *(Tourism)*: A parking area on a highway with amenities such as rest rooms, vending machines, or full restaurant service for allowing travelers to rest without leaving the highway.

Restaurant *(Hospitality)*: A retail business designed to serve prepared food to customers. The term covers today a very wide range of restaurant types, such as fast food, cafés, pubs, casual style dining, bistros, brasseries, and fine dining. It seems the prototype appeared in the 11th century in Kaifeng, China, during the first half of the Song Dynasty (960–1279). There are evidences on the existence of a type of restaurants in ancient Roman times, while inns and taverns are the precursors known in the medieval Europe, aimed at travelers. By the 16th century, Englishmen of all classes used to dine out at local taverns, where meals, wine, ale, and tobacco, were offered at a fixed price. The entry was generally restricted to men. Some other varieties were opened in Spain at the beginning of the 18th Century, but the real first European restaurant is believed was started by a person named A. Boulanger in Paris in 1765. He offered soups and a choice of dishes rather than the standard *table d'hôte* dinner. He likely coined the word "restaurant," a French term for "something that restores". After the French Revolution, restaurants became commonplace in France and the business type was extended all over the world.

Restaurant Manager *(Cruise)*: See Maitre d'.

Restaurateur *(Tourism)*: A person who owns or manages a restaurant.

Restocking Fee *(Hospitality)*: An additional amount charged by some hotels to refill the minibar's stock.

Restricted Area *(Air Traffic)*: An airspace within which the flight of aircraft is subject to restriction, although not wholly prohibited.

Restricted Access *(Tourism)*: A feature determining a place or business is not open to everyone.

Restricted Articles *(Airlines)*: Restricted articles are those also known as Dangerous Goods or Hazardous Materials involving a risk for human health, the property or the general safety. Most of this type of articles is forbidden for air transportation, and, if accepted, they require extreme handling cares.

Retail Agency *(Tourism)*: A travel company that sells directly to the public.

Retail Travel Agent *(Tourism)*: An individual qualified to arrange and sell transportation and other related services directly to the public.

Retailer *(Tourism)*: A business organization, such as travel agencies and airline locations that promote and sell travel to individual consumers.

Retinal Scan *(Tourism)*: A method of biometric identification that uses the unique patterns on a person's retina to identify them. Do not confuse with another ocular-based technology, such as iris recognition.

Retroactive *(Tourism)*: A term denoting something has back effect in the past prior to the execution or announcement, as a retroactive fare increase.

Return Subjourney Check (RSC) *(Airlines)*: Fare check applicable to Round Trips or Circle Trips comprising several Subjourneys, whose fares are obtained by using half round trips.

Return Journey or Return Trip *(Airlines)*: Any journey that brings a traveler back to the country where the air transportation commenced. The category includes round, circle, open-jaw, and round the world trips.

Return Subjourney *(Airlines)*: A part of a journey where travel commences in a point or country and returns thereto and for which the fare is assessed as a single pricing unit using half round trip fares.

Reunion Tours *(Tourism)*: See Alumni Rates.

REV *(GDS)*: Code meaning Revenue.

Revenue Management *(Business)*: The method of pricing the available inventory to optimize revenue at differing price points over the time, for different market segments or from different sources of funding. See also Yield Management.

Revenue Participation *(Business)*: A system where employees participate in part of the profit left in the business at the end of the accounting period, after deductions and appropriations are made.

Revenue Passenger Mile (RPM) *(Airlines)*: An income concept based on one fare-paying passenger carried one mile. It is the statistical unit used in the airline business to measure profitability in passenger traffic.

Revenue per Available Room *(Hospitality)*: An income ratio that is obtained by dividing the total sum of income from room rentals during a specified period by the number of rooms available for rent during the same period. It measures the financial performance of a hotel business.

Revenue Sharing *(Tourism)*: A method by which a travel agency shares its commission with a corporation. See rebate.

Reverse Auction *(Hospitality)*: Reverse auctions allow selling companies to compete for the best price, while buying companies to post items they want to buy.

Reverse Pyramid System *(Airlines)*: An airplane seating method in which coach seats are filled in phases, starting with window seats at the rear of the plane, followed by middle seats, finally aisle seats. See also Back-to-front System, Open Seating Plan, Rotating Zone System, and Wilma.

Reversers *(Air Traffic)*: System for breaking aircraft during landing roll.

RevPAR *(Hospitality)*: A term for "revenue participation" referring to a statistic used to measure the revenue per available room. It is obtained by dividing the total hotel room revenue by the total rooms available to rent for a day or a period.

Rewards *(Airlines)*: The benefits business travelers get for the frequent use of the same airline or hotel chain in the frame of a "Frequent Flyer" or "Frequent Lodger" program. Such rewards can be free flights, tickets to leisure destinations, holiday discounts, gift certificates, hotel accommodation and more.

REYF *(GDS)*: Code meaning "In reference to your phone call."

REYL *(GDS)*: Code meaning "In reference to your letter."

REYM *((GDS)*: Code meaning "In reference to your message."

RFD *(GDS)*: Code meaning Refund.

RFI *(GDS)*: A code meaning: 1. Request Further Information; 2. Request for information.

RFID *(Airlines)*: See Radio Frequency Identification.

RFID Tag *(Airlines)*: See Radio Frequency Identification.

RFU *(Air Traffic)*: A code meaning Radio Frequency Unit.

RG *(Aeronautics)*: Retractable Landing Gear.

RGE *(Air Traffic)*: See Range.

RGLR *(GDS)*: Code meaning Regular.

RHYA *(GDS)*: Code meaning "Release for handling by your agency."

RIB or R.I.B. *(Cruise)*: Code for Rigid Inflatable Boat.

Richter Scale *(Aeronautics)*: A magnitude scale that records the intensity of earthquakes, registering the amount of seismic energy that is released by an earthquake.

Rickshas *(Tourism)*: See Rickshaws.

Rickshaws *(Tourism)*: A mode of transport powered by humans originated in Asia, where they were used for the social elite. They are a type of two-wheeled cycle pulled by a runner, with capacity for one two persons. They are common in Asian cities, but are also used in some western cities like New York and London, where they are called "pedicabs." The term "rickshaw" is an adaptation of the Japanese word *jinrikisha* meaning "human-powered vehicle" (jin = human, riki = strength, sha = vehicle).

Rigging *Cruise)*: The entire set of ropes, lines, masts, and sails that form the propulsion system of a ship.

Right of Search *(Cruise)*: The right to stop a ship to verify if it is violating any maritime law.

Right of Way *(Cruise)*: The right of passing vessels in a channel in order of precedence or proceeding.

Ring-laser Gyro *(Air Traffic)*: A gyroscope based on a laser beam instead of a rotating mass.

RIO *(GDS)*: Three-letter IATA code for Rio de Janeiro, a tourist destination in Brazil.

Riptide *(Geography)*: A strong current of turbulent water in the sea or a strong surface current flowing outwards from a shore that involves a risk for swimmers.

Risk Car *(Car Rental)*: See Buyback Car.

Risk Inventory *(Tourism)*: The potential exposure for financial loss a travel agency incurs when it blocks airline seats without having the passengers. It is the same as Inventory Risk.

Ritz, Cesar *(Hospitality)*: Cesar Ritz was a Swiss hotelier born in Niederwald, Switzerland, on 23 February 1850. He enjoyed an unchallenged fame as the "King of Hotelkeepers", and is considered up to date the father of Hotel business. He organized and managed some of the most luxurious hotels of the so called *Ancien Regime*. It is said he invented the sentence "The customer is always right" that explains his devotion to his guests' desires. By 1884 Ritz met August Escoffier, a famous cook and gourmet chef. Together they formed a teamwork that brought about the most significant changes and modern development in the hotel system. In 1890 the two men moved to Savoy Hotel in London, from where they established a number of famous hotels, including the Grand Hotel in Rome, and many Ritz Hotels around the world, as in Madrid, Cairo and Johannesburg. Ritz died in Kussnacht, near Lucerne, Switzerland, on 26 October 1918.

Riviera *(Tourism)*: It is an Italian name given to a narrow coastal strip which lies between the Ligurian Sea and the mountain chain formed by the Maritime Alps and the Apennines, over the Gulf of Genoa. It is divided into two main sections: the *Riviera di Ponente* and the *Riviera di Levante*. The Riviera is famous for its mild climate, the charm of its old fishing ports and the beauty of its landscape. The most famed parts of this region are the *Riviera delle Palme* and the *Riviera dei Fiori* on San Remo. Many towns in the area are internationally known, such as Portofino, Bordighera and Cinque Terre. By extension, the term also defines the rocky costs of *Côte d'Azur.*

RJ *(GDS)*: Code meaning Regional jet.

RLNG *(GDS)*: Code meaning Releasing.

RLOC *(GDS)*: Code meaning Record Locator.

RLSD *(Air Traffic)*: Code for Released.

RLSE *(GDS)*: Code meaning Release.

RMKS *(GDS)*: Code meaning Remarks.

RMO *(GDS)*: Code meaning Regional Marketing Organization.

RMS *(Air Traffic)*: Code for Root Mean Square.

RMT *(GDS)*: Code meaning In reference to my telex.

RNAV *(Air Traffic)*: An abbreviation for Area navigation device.

RNG *(Air Traffic)*: See Range.

RNP *(GDS)*: Code meaning Reduce Number in Party.

RO *Airlines)*: Two-letter IATA code for TAROM, the airline of Romania.

Road Feeder Service (RFS) *(Airlines)*: Surface transportation arranged by an air carrier to or from one airport to another.

Road Tax *(Car Rental)*: A tax levied on registered cars by some European countries to raise money to restore and maintain the roads.

Road-pricing *(Car Rental)*: A process in Great Britain to track vehicles by satellites and to tax them according to the distance and date they are driven.

Roadside Assistance *(Car Rental)*: A towing service of rental companies in case the car becomes unable to be driven during a rental. The phone number for roadside assistance is usually either in the glove box or on the keychain.

ROC *(GDS)*: Code meaning Record of Charge.

Rodeo *(Tourism)*: An entertaining exhibition of cowboy skills, such as riding wild horses and roping calves.

ROE *(GDS)*: Code meaning Rate of Exchange.

ROH *(GDS)*: Code meaning Run of the House.

ROK *(GDS)*: Code meaning Republic of South Korea.

Roll *(Cruise)*: The side to side motion of a ship while at sea.

Roll *(Airlines)*: A rotational motion in which the aircraft turns around its longitudinal axis.

Rollaway *(Hospitality)*: A bed that can be folded and rolled from place to place used to accommodate another guest, as in a triple room.

ROM *(GDS)*: Three-letter IATA code for Rome, capital city of Italy.

Roman Bath *(Tourism)*: Historically a series of rooms and pools of different temperatures used by ancient Romans. Today it refers to whirlpool bathing areas with benches for more than one person.

Roman Forum (Forum Romanum) *(Tourism)*: It was the political and economical centre of Rome during the Republic. It emerged as such in the 7th century BCE and maintained this position well into the Imperial period. The Forum Romanum is located in a valley surrounded by several Hills: The Palatine, the Velia, the Quirinal, and the Esquiline. In its time the Forum had many central political, religious and judicial buildings, such as the Regia, which was the residence of the kings; the Curia, a meeting place of the Senate; and the Comitium and the Rostra, where public meetings were held. Some of its major temples and sanctuaries are the Forum, the Temple of Castor and Pollux, the Temple of Saturn and the Temple of Vesta.

Romantic Road *(Tourism)*: A German tourist itinerary from the River Main to the Alps that features medieval castles. It is said it was the Romans who built the road. And this is quite true, because from Füssen to Augsburg is extended the Via Claudia Augusta that was used by Romans in 47 AD. Along 360 kilometers the Romantic Road connects more than two dozen towns in South Germany, all of which star unique sceneries. The best known are Rothenburg ob der Tauber, the Baroque city of Würzburg, Füssen, Augsburg, the city silver, the small but delightful town of Dinkelsbühl, Bad Mergentheim with its Castle of the Teutonic Order and Feuchtwangen. The stellar features are precisely the towns that exercise the real power of attraction along the Romantic Road.

Romeo *(Airlines):* Designator for the letter "R" in the International Phonetic Alphabet.

Room Attendant's Cart *(Hospitality)*: A lightweight vehicle used by room attendants for moving cleaning supplies, linen, and equipment needed to fulfill their cleaning duties.

Room Block *(Hospitality)*: A number of rooms reserved for members of a group who plan to stay at a hotel.

Room Data Card *(Hospitality)*: A card used to record information concerning the information of individual guestrooms.

Room Inspection *(Hospitality)*: A detailed verification of cleanliness and maintenance status of guestrooms.

Room Ledger *(Hospitality)*: See Guest Ledger.

Room Night *(Hospitality)*: A statistical unit of occupancy of a hotel room occupied for one night.

Room Occupancy Sensor *(Hospitality)*: A device operating with infrared light or ultrasonic sound waves that sense the physical occupancy of a room. Such sensors turn on devices and appliances such as lights, air conditioning, and heating whenever a guest enters the room, and turn these devices and appliances off when the guest leaves.

Room Occupancy Tax *(Hospitality)*: A government charge on hotel rooms, which is added to the guest's bill.

Room Only *(Hospitality)*: A hotel rate including accommodation but no food.

Room Rack *(Hospitality)*: A card index system that is constantly updated to show occupied and vacant rooms.

Room Rate *(Hospitality)*: The price a hotel charges for overnight accommodation.

Room Service *(Hospitality)*: The meal or beverage service to guests in their guestrooms. Also the department that is responsible for such service.

Room Service Menu *(Hospitality)*: A menu offering a limited number of meal and beverage items for guests at their hotel rooms or cruise cabins.

Room Status *(Hospitality)*: The information about current and future availability of guestrooms. Current availability is given by the housekeeper, while future availability is determined through reservations information.

Room Status Discrepancy *(Hospitality)*: A situation reflecting differences between the housekeeping department's information and that produced by the front desk.

Room Tax *(Hospitality)*: See Room Occupancy Tax.

Roomette *(Tourism)*: A single compartment for passengers on a train sleeping car with a fold-down bed and a toilet. The term roomette was coined by 1937, when such accommodations were constructed by the Pullman Company for its routes in North American.

Rooming List *(Hospitality)*: A list of a group guests and their lodging arrangement presented to a hotel prior to their arrival. The rooming list specifies the needs for doubles, twin-bedded rooms, singles, and triples.

Rooms, Adjoining *(Hospitality)*: Rooms that are separated by a wall but are not connected.

Rooms, Connecting *(Hospitality)*: Rooms that share a wall and are connected by a private door.

Rooms Activity Forecast *(Hospitality)*: A report containing information on anticipated arrivals, departures, stay over, and vacancies. Managers use this forecast to determine staffing needs at the front desk and in housekeeping areas.

Rooms Allotment Report *(Hospitality)*: A report that summarizes rooms allocated by future date.

Rooms Availability Report *(Hospitality)*: A report that lists, by room type, the number of daily available rooms.

Rooms Checklist *(Hospitality)*: A list used for preventive maintenance of guestrooms, detailing all the items in the room, needs for repair, lubrication, adjustments, or cleaning activity to be performed.

Rooms Discrepancy Report *(Hospitality)*: See Room Status Discrepancy.

Rooms Division *(Hospitality)*: The largest, and usually most lucrative division in a hotel comprising four departments: front office, reservations, housekeeping, and uniformed service.

Rooms History Report *(Hospitality)*: A computer-based report detailing the revenue history and use of the guestrooms, room by room type.

Rooms Productivity Report *(Hospitality)*: A report ranking room types by percentage of occupancy and by percentage of total rooms revenue.

Rooms Status Report *(Hospitality)*: See Room Status.

Rope Tow *(Tourism)*: Also called a ski tow or handle tow, it is a mechanized system offering a continuous moving rope to pull skiers up a slope.

Roster *(Tourism)*: A list of persons on duty at a specific moment.

Rostrum *(Tourism)*: Any platform, stage or similar device used for public speech. See also Podium.

Rotary Engine *(Aeronautics)*: A power plant that rotates on a stationary propeller shaft. It was invented by Adams-Farwell Co in1896 for the use in buses and trucks, and was later perfected by French engineers for aircraft engines in 1914.

Rotary Wing *(Aeronautics)*: A helicopter.

Rotating Zone System *(Airlines)*: An aircraft seating plan in which coach seats are filled in alternating block of seats at the rear of the plane, then at the front, then at the rear again and so forth.

Rotational Motion *(Aeronautics)*: The turning of an object, like an airplane, around an axis, or a propeller around a hub.

Rotational Dining *(Cruise)*: A program in which passengers eat at different restaurants during the cruise.

Rotorcraft *(Aeronautics)*: A heavier-than-air aircraft that depends mainly on the lift generated by one or more rotors for its support in flight. The category includes helicopters and gyroplanes.

Round the World Fares *(Airlines)*: A type of fares for Round-the-world Trips that are calculated with normal fares. Also special fares offered by airlines and airline alliances for travels with a reduced price itinerary and a reduced number of stopovers.

Round the World Trip *(Airlines)*: Travel from the point of origin and return thereto, which involves only one crossing of the Atlantic Ocean and only one crossing of the Pacific Ocean. A round-the-world trip comprises two or more fare components, must include stops in each of the three IATA Areas and must keep the same directional sense.

Round Trip *(Airlines)*: A type of journey comprising only two fare components that commences in one point and returns thereto. The fare calculation method is the same for the outgoing fare component as well as for the incoming component. In most of the cases, the price for the outgoing component is the same as for the incoming component.

Route *(Tourism)*: 1. An air way that connect cities or airports in an air travel; 2. A road connecting several points in a journey.

Route Indirect *(Airlines)*: See Indirect Route.

Route, Through *(Airlines)*: See Through Route.

Routing *(Airlines)*: A general term to denote the carrier and/ or the cities and/or class of service and/or type of aircraft via which transportation is provided between two points. It is a list of consecutive segments of an air trip in operational sequence between the point of origin and the point of destination.

Royalty *(Business)*: 1. A fee paid to a company or an individual to have the right to use its property, mainly their intellectual property; 2. A tax, usually a fixed amount, on charter flights charged by some governments before granting the operation rights.

RPK *(GDS)*: Code meaning Revenue Passenger Kilometer. See Revenue Passenger Mile.

RPM *(GDS)*: Code meaning Revenue Passenger Mile.

RPRT *(GDS)*: Code meaning Report.

RPT *(GDS)*: A code meaning Repeat, Repeating, Repeated.

RQ *(GDS)*: Code meaning On request. Shown on a ticket, it indicates that a seat has been requested but confirmation has not been received or the request is "waitlisted".

RQID *(GDS)*: Code meaning Request If Desired.

RQR *(GDS)*: Code meaning Request for Reply.

RQST *(GDS)*: Code meaning Request.

RR *(GDS)*: Code meaning Reconfirmed.

RRTES *(Air Traffic)*: An abbreviation for Reroutes.

RS *(GDS)*: Code meaning Reserved Seat.

RSA *(GDS)*: Code meaning Reservations Sales Agent.

RSC *(Airlines)*: See Return Subjourney Check.

RSD *(GDS)*: Code meaning Release for Sale Date.

RSM *(GDS)*: Code meaning Regional Sales Manager.

RSO *(GDS)*: Code meaning Receptive Service Operator.

RSVP *(Tourism)*: An acronym representing the French phrase *Repondez s'il vous plait* that literally means Respond if you please. Such a term is usually included in written invitations to social events. Etiquette procedures demand a response.

RT *(Air Traffic)*: Receiver-transmitter combined in a single line unit.

RT *(GDS)*: Code meaning: 1. Round Trip or Return Trip; 2. An Amadeus entry to retrieve a PNR. It should be followed by a slash and the name of the passenger, e.g. RT/NEVILLE.

RTG *(GDS)*: Code meaning Routing.

RTRN *(GDS)*: Code meaning Return.

Rudder *(Aeronautics)*: An airfoil located on the tail of an airplane that pivots vertically and controls left-to-right movement.

Rudder *(Cruise)*: A vertical plate or board plate mounted at the stern of a vessel that is used to steer the boat.

Rum *(Hospitality)*: A type of liquor distilled from the fermented juice of sugar cane or molasses. Rum is produced in many countries. Its quality depends on the climate and soil of the place it is made.

Run of the House or Run-of-House (ROH) *(Hospitality)*: A hotel room type which is assigned at the discretion of the hotel shortly before the guest's arrival, rated at a lower price.

Running Lights *(Cruise)*: A series of colored lights that announce a ship's presence during the night.

Run-of-Ship *(Cruise)*: A cabin assigned at the last moment, giving the cruise line the ability to shift accommodations as needed.

Runway *(Air Traffic)*: A long paved surface at an airport designated for the landing and takeoff of aircraft along its length.

Runway Capacity *(Air Traffic)*: The maximum number of operations that can be handled on a particular runway.

Runway Configuration *(Air Traffic)*: The arrangement of approach and takeoff runways.

Runway Incursion *(Air Traffic)*: Any occurrence at an airport involving an aircraft, vehicle, person, or object on the ground that creates a collision hazard or results in loss of separation with an aircraft taking off, intending to take off, landing or intending to land.

Runway Visual Range (RVR) *(Air Traffic)*: Horizontal visual range that is based on the measurement of a transmissometer made near the touchdown point of the instrument runway and is reported in hundreds of feet.

Rural Tourism *(Tourism)*: A type of tourism in which visitors have leisure in a country environment and who perform activities relating to the country, country people or agriculture.

RUSHR *(GDS)*: Code meaning Rush Reply.

Russian Service *(Hospitality)*: A method of serving food in the order dishes appear on menu. See also British service and French Service.

Run-up Area *(Air Traffic)*: An area located just before the takeoff line of a runway where aircraft await clearance.

RVR *(Air Traffic)*: See Runway Visual Range.

RVSM *(Air Traffic)*: A code for Reduced Vertical Separation Minimum

RW *(GDS)*: Code meaning Round-the-world Trip.

RWM *(GDS)*: Code meaning Round-the world Minimum Check.

RWY *(Air Traffic)*: A code for Runway.

RWY CONFIG *(Air Traffic)*: Abbreviation for Runway Configuration.

Rye Whiskey *(Hospitality)*: A whiskey produced from a grain mixture containing at least 51 percent rye.

Ryokan *(Hospitality)*: A type of traditional Japanese inn or small hotel providing food and lodging, which dates from the Edo Era (1603-1868), when they served travelers along Japan's highways. They are surrounded by landscaped gardens and its floors are usually covered with tatami.

RYR *(GDS)*: Code meaning In reference to your.

RYT *(GDS)*: Code meaning In reference to your telex.

S

S *(Airlines)*: "Sierra," name used to designate the letter "S" in the International Phonetic Alphabet

S *(GDS)*: Code meaning: 1. Economy coach class; 2. Smoking area in the aircraft.

S&T *(GDS)*: Code meaning Shower and Toilet.

S.S. *(Cruise)*: Abbreviation for Steam Ship.

SA *(Airlines)*: Code meaning: 1. Surface Aviation Weather Reports; 2. South African Airways; 3. Space Available.

Sabre *(GDS)*: A Global Distribution System.

SAC *(Airlines)*: See Settlement Authorization Code.

SAD *(GDS)*: Code meaning Shared Airline Designator.

Safari *(Airlines)*: A type of adventure tourism, originally organized for hunting and typically in Africa. Nowadays it is a trip aimed to viewing and photographing wildlife, which generally uses off-road vehicles and tent-like accommodations.

Safety of Life at Sea (SOLAS) *(Cruise)*: The whole of international procedures convened to ensure safety aboard ships, which includes the design, construction methods and materials, life safety equipment, fire protection, and safety training of all cruise ships and staff. All major cruise lines abide by all SOLAS requirements.

SAI *(GDS)*: Code meaning System Assisted Instruction.

Sail and Stay Program *(Tourism)*: A combination of a cruise with a short stay at a shore destination, after which the passenger rejoins the cruise ship for the remainder of the cruise.

Sailboat *(Tourism)*: A small wind-powered water vessel.

Sailing Time *(Cruise)*: The scheduled hour at which the ship clears the dock for sailing.

Sailplane *(Airlines)*: An unpowered, soaring aircraft capable of maintaining level flight for long periods of time after release from tow and of gaining altitude using wind currents. It is opposed to a Glider.

SAL *(GDS)*: Three-letter IATA code for San Salvador, the capital city of El Salvador.

Sales by Beverage Server Report *(Hospitality)*: A report produced by sophisticated automated beverage systems indicating the total sales of each beverage served during a shift.

Sales by Major Beverage Category Report *(Hospitality)*: A report produced by automated beverage systems indicating the expected beverage income by the most common beverage categories (liquor, beer, wine, etc.).

Salinization *(Ecology)*: Accumulation of salts in soil that can convert the soil unable to support plant growth.

Salon *(Tourism)*: 1. A professional exhibition presenting a range of products in different categories; 2. A special reception room at a hotel or aboard a cruise ship.

Same Day Visitor *(Tourism)*: Usually an excursionist or traveler who does not need lodging accommodation in the place he/she visits.

Sampan *(Tourism)*: A small Chinese vessel whose main use is for fishing or transportation, although it can frequently be used as a permanent shelter on inland waters.

Sand Storm *(Air Traffic)*: A strong and low level wind carrying sand particles through the air.

Santos-Dumont, Alberto *(Aviation)*: A Brazilian pioneer of early aviation, who was born in Palmyra, Brazil, on 20 July 1873 and died in Sao Paulo on 23 July 1932. Most of his contributions to aviation took place while he was living in Paris, France, where arrived at the age of 18 years. Once established in Paris, he dedicated his time and money to designing, building, and flying dirigible balloons. In March 23, 1898 Santos-Dumont made his first flight on board of a 750 cubic meters balloon from the *Parc de Vaugirard* to the *Parc La Ferrière*, flying a distance of 100 kilometers in about three hours. On 19 October 1901 he won the *Deutsch Prize* of 100,000 francs offered by a wealthy oil-man named *Henry Deutsch de la Meurthe* by taking off from Saint-Cloud, and flying his steerable balloon Number 6 around the Eiffel Tower. The noteworthy achievement was completed in 29 minutes and 30 seconds in the presence of members of the *Aeroclub de France*. This aerial conquest brought him international renown. Santos-Dumont was the first to make a pre-scheduled flight using a powered heavier-than-air aircraft in Paris on 23 October 1906. It was an unusual craft named *Oiseau de Proie* that he flew standing up in the field of *Bagatelle*, over a short distance of 60 meters. In the summer of 1908 Wilbur Wright made some demonstrations near Paris showing the value of full controllability and true maneuverability with coordinated turns. These were lessons that Santos-Dumont applied to his light built *Demoiselle* monoplane with which he found success in fixed-wing aviation. For his many contributions, *Alberto Santos-Dumont* is honored in Brazil as the "Father of Aviation".

SAO *(GDS)*: Three-letter IATA code for Sao Paulo, the industrial city of Brazil.

SAR *(GDS)*: Code meaning "Special Administrative Region", the official Chinese term for Hong Kong.

SAR *(Air Traffic)*: Search and Rescue.

SARS *(Tourism)*: See Severe Acute Respiratory Syndrome.

SASC *(IATA Geography)*: See South Asian Subcontinent Sub-area.

SAT *(GDS)*: Code meaning Saturday.

Satcom *(Air Traffic)*: An abbreviation for Satellite Communications System.

Satellite *(Air Traffic)*: An object that orbits a celestial body, such as a moon. The term is generally used in reference to the manufactured objects that orbit the earth, either in a geostationary or a polar pathway. Manufactured satellites gather such information as weather upper air temperatures and humidity, temperatures of cloud tops, land, and ocean. Some of them monitor the movement of clouds to determine upper level wind speeds, tracing the movement of water vapor. They also monitor the sun and solar activity, and relay data from weather instruments around the world.

Satellite Agent *(Tourism)*: A travel agent or independent contractor who furnishes business to a main office from a separate location.

Satellite Ticket Printer *(Airlines)*: A branch of an IATA or ARC-accredited agency equipped with a ticket printer that is connected to the main office.

Satellite Ticket Printer Network (STPN) *(Tourism)*: A network of ticket printers placed in position for use in hotels or other locations by an IATA/ARC accredited agency, by which it sells and distributes its services to the satellite ARC agencies.

SATH *(Organizations)*: An acronym for Society for Accessible Travel & Hospitality.

SATO *(Airlines)*: See Scheduled Airline Ticket Offices.

Saturday Night Stay *(Airlines)*: The airline requirement for a minimum stay over a Saturday night during a trip in order to qualify for the lowest fare.

SATS *(Aeronautics)*: See Small Aircraft Transportation System

Saturate *(Air Traffic)*: To treat or to charge something to the point where no more can be absorbed, dissolved, or retained. In meteorology, it is referred to the amount of water vapor in a volume of air.

Saturation Point *(Air Traffic)*: The point when the water vapor in the atmosphere is at its maximum level for the existing temperature.

SATW *(Organizations)*: See Society of American Travel Writing.

Sauna *(Hospitality)*: A dry bath using heat steam that causes the person in it to perspire.

Savanna *(Geography)*: A tropical or subtropical grasslands region with scattered trees. It is one of the Earth's biomes associated with dry regions with heavy rainy seasons and continuously high temperatures.

SAW *(Airlines)*: See Surface Acoustic Wave.

SB *(GDS)*: A code meaning: 1. Southbound, 2. Steamboat, 3. School Bus.

SC *(GDS)*: Code meaning Schedule Change.

Scale *(Geography)*: The ratio existing between the distances measured on a map and the actual distances measured on the surface of the earth.

Scandinavia *(IATA Geography)*: The area comprising Denmark, Norway, Sweden. For international fare calculation, Scandinavian countries are considered to be one single country.

SCAR *(GDS)*: Code meaning Standard car (full-size).

Scattergraph *(Geography)*: A type of graph which relates two variables by means of plotted points.

Scenic Route *(Tourism)*: An especially attractive and usually secondary road.

SCH *(GDS)*: Code meaning Scheduled Service.

Scheduled *(Airlines)*: A condition denoting an operation is subject to regular frequencies, departure and arrival times.

Scheduled Airline *(Airlines)*: An air carrier that operates on fixed routes with established frequencies and regular time tables, and between specific places.

Scheduled Airline Ticket Offices (SATO) *(Airlines)*: Companies that provide contract ticketing services to IATA Member Airlines. They require IATA numeric codes to identify the transportation documents issued on behalf of the airlines by which they are contracted.

Scheduled Carrier *(Airlines)*: See Scheduled Airline.

Scheduled Flights *(Airlines)*: Regular flights operating according to fixed routes with departure and arrival regulated times, subjected to regular frequencies.

Schedules Information Standards Committee (SISC) *(Organizations)*: An IATA body that is responsible for the development of standard schedules data procedures and formats for the exchange of schedule information, maintained within the Standards Schedules Information Manual (SSIM).

Schengen Agreement *(Geography)*: A treaty signed in Luxembourg in June 1985 by France, Germany, the Netherlands, Belgium and Luxembourg to gradually abolish immigration controls at their common frontiers. Nowadays, they are thirteen European countries that standardize matters such as entry requirements for non-European Union citizens, asylum matters, and cooperation on police and judicial matters. The agreement is so named for the city in Luxembourg where it was signed.

Schengen Countries *(Geography)*: Originally they were only five the countries that signed the "Schengen Treaty." At present, they are 15 Schengen countries, all in Europe. They are: Austria, Belgium, Denmark, Finland, France, Germany, Iceland, Italy, Greece, Luxembourg, Netherlands, Norway, Portugal, Spain and Sweden. All these countries except Norway and Iceland are European Union members.

Schoolroom Setup *(Hospitality)*: A seating arrangement for a meeting where tables are lined up on both sides of one or more aisles, with all chairs set in single rows behind the tables and facing the front.

Science Tourism *(Hospitality)*: A type of ecotourism in which tourists travel with scientists and students to help with scientific work at various sites throughout the world.

SCL *(GDS)*: Three-letter IATA code for Santiago, the capital city of Chile.

Scooter *(Tourism)*: A small motor bike available for rent at some vacation spots.

Scotch *(Hospitality)*: A distinctive whiskey made in Scotland with at least 80 proof of alcohol content, manufactured in compliance with British laws.

Screamer *(Tourism)*: A slang term for an unruly and impolite passenger.

Screen *(Tourism)*: The action of inspecting passengers, documents, or baggage.

Screen Scraping *(GDS)*: The practice of extracting information from a GDS to use it on another technological medium.

Screener *(Airlines)*: An employee responsible for inspecting passengers, documents, or baggage at an airport.

Screening *(Airlines)*: The act of examining passengers, passenger documents, or baggage. See Screen.

Script *(GDS)*: A GDS attribute that guides an agent through the booking process.

Scud *(Air Traffic)*: Low fragments of clouds, usually *stratus fractus*, that are unattached and below a layer of higher clouds, such as nimbostratus or cumulonimbus. When observed from a distance, they are sometimes mistaken for tornadoes.

Scupper *(Cruise)*: An opening or hole in a ship's side or deck to drain water back into the sea.

SDQ *(GDS)*: Three-letter IATA code for Santo Domingo, the capital city of Dominican Republic.

SDR *(GDS)*: Code meaning Special Drawing Right.

SDU *(GDS)*: A code meaning: 1. Satellite Data Unit; 2. Santos Dumont Airport, serving the city of Rio de Janeiro.

SEA *(GDS)*: A Code meaning: 1. South East Asia Sub-area; 2. Seattle, Washington, USA.

Sea Bands *(Cruise)*: A product resembling a bracelet that is worn on the wrists and operates via acupressure. Wearers claim that seasickness can be avoided by their use, thus eliminating the need for drugs.

Sea Breeze *(Geography)*: A coastal breeze blowing from sea to land, caused by temperature difference when the land surface is warmer than the sea surface.

Sea Fog *(Geography)*: A type of advection fog which forms in warm moist air cooled to saturation as the air moves across cold water.

Sea Legs *(Cruise)*: The skill some people have to move easily around a ship, without suffering seasickness or loss of balance.

Sea Level *(Geography)*: The height or level of the sea surface at any time, used as a reference for elevations above and locations below.

Sea View *(Hospitality)*: The location viewing the sea from a hotel room.

Seaboard *(Cruise)*: The coast or the area close to the sea.

Seagoing *(Cruise)*: Something that has the ability to travel on open seas.

Seamen's Fares *(Cruise)*: Discounted air fares applied to seamen when travelling to embark or disembark a ship.

Seaplane *(Airlines)*: An airplane with boat-hull fuselage and equipped with floats for water takeoffs and landings. It is also called Flying Boat or Floatplane.

Seasickness *(Cruise)*: A temporary illness caused by the body's balance being disrupted affecting sea passengers.

Season *(Geography)*: A period in the year characterized by defined climatic features, such as winter, spring, summer, fall, dry season and rainy season.

Season *(Tourism)*: A delimited period in the year when the traffic flow or demand influences on the cost of air transportation or on accommodation rates. Three main seasons are distinguished in air travel business: Low or Basic, High or Peak and Shoulder. Low is a quiet season of low occupancy and basic fares and rates, High is a busy season of peak occupancy and higher fares and rates, and Shoulders are in-between seasons of intermediate occupancy and intermediate fares and rates.

Seasonal Fares *(Airlines)*: Air fares that change according to the seasonal travel flow. The applicability of economy and discounted fares depend on the date the traveler starts his/her trip. Transoceanic fares depend on the seasonal date the passengers cross the ocean.

Seasonality *(Tourism)*: A feature of periodic travel demand determining the price levels for air transportation or hotel accommodation.

Seasonality Codes *(Airlines)*: Characters used as secondary codes in a fare basis denoting the season to which the fare is applied. Example: H, K, J for High, Low, Shoulder seasons respectively.

Seat, Bulkhead *(Airlines)*: See Bulkhead Seats.

Seat Kilometer *(Airlines)*: One air seat flown one kilometer. It is a European way to measure an airline's performance standards, such as revenue or expenses per available seat kilometer.

Seat Mile *(Airlines)*: One air seat flown one mile. It is a statistical unit used to measure an airline's performance standards, such as revenue or expenses per available seat mile.

Seat Pitch *(Airlines)*: The distance measured in inches between seats in an aircraft's passenger cabin, when both seats are in an upright position. The higher the pitch, the higher is the comfort.

Seat Plans *(Airlines)*: Diagrams of an aircraft's passenger cabin showing seat locations.

Seat Recline *(Airlines)*: The reclining space between seats, measured in inches or degrees from the front to the rear.

Seat Rotation *(Tourism)*: The method of moving travelers from one seat to another for the purpose of giving everybody the opportunity to access the more comfortable seats.

Seat Width *(Airlines)*: The space measured in inches from one side of a seat to the side of another seat.

SEATA *(Organizations)*: An acronym for South East Asia Travel Association.

Seating *(Cruise)*: The specified time shift at which a passenger has his/her meals.

Seating Plans *(GDS)*: Diagrams of the interior of an aircraft allowing the selection of seating locations.

Seating Times *(Cruise)*: See Seating.

Seatmate *(Airlines)*: An immediate neighbor passenger on an airplane.

Seaward *(Cruise)*: A term that denotes the ship is traveling in the direction of the sea.

Seaway *(Cruise)*: A selected traffic route in the ocean or an inland waterway.

Seaworthy *(Cruise)*: Something that is able to float safely and can be used for sea travel.

Second Freedom of the Air *(Airlines)*: The freedom to stop in a foreign country for technical or refueling purpose only. The flight must commence or end in the home country and can land in another country for purposes other than embarking or debarking passengers.

Second Sitting *(Cruise)*: The later of two meal seating shifts on a cruise ship.

Second-tier Airports *(Airlines)*: Small cities airports with limited service.

Secondary Codes *(Airlines)*: Fare basis codes consist of one or more characters. The first character is called the Prime Code. The characters that follow are called Secondary Codes. Secondary codes consist of a single character or a group of characters that identify the fare type and restrictions such as maximum stay, seasonality and day of the week, such as E30 for Excursion 30 day's maximum stay. A fare basis code may have one or more secondary codes.

Secondary Inspection *(Airlines)*: A separate and more detailed screening of some passengers at an airport. It is accomplished by a sample selection or when somebody looks suspicious. It is also called Secondary Screening.

Secondary Screening *(Airlines)*: See Secondary Inspection.

Sectional Chart *(Air Traffic)*: An aeronautical chart designed for visual navigation of slow or medium speed aircraft.

Sector *(Airlines)*: A portion of a leg or segment in a journey or the distance between two ground points within a route.

Sector *(Air Traffic)*: Airspace that is split up into small manageable pieces with vertical and horizontal boundaries.

Sector Bonus *(GDS)*: An extra commission paid for booking specific airline sectors within limited periods of time.

Security *(Airlines)*: A screening point where passengers are checked before boarding an airplane.

Security Deposit *(Car Rental)*: The amount of money blocked on a charge account during a rental period, which is released when the car is returned in the same condition it was rented and with the same amount of gas.

Security Surcharge *(Airlines)*: An additional charge collected on an airline ticket for security inspections at airports.

SEDM *(GDS)*: Code meaning Schedule Exchange Data Message.

Segment *(Airlines)*: A portion of the journey between boarding and disembarking points that may comprise one or more sectors.

Segment *(Business)*: A selected demographic portion of the total market.

Segmentation *(Tourism)*: The act of establishing categories of travelers in a market, according to their needs, desires, preferences and behavior. These typologies can use one or all of multiple parameters.

Séjour *(Tourism)*: A French term for journey involving at least one night accommodation.

SEL *(GDS)*: Three-letter IATA code for Seoul, capital of the Republic of South Korea.

SELCAL *(Air Traffic)*: Abbreviation for Selective Calling system (used primarily with HF)

Self-catering *(Hospitality)*: A term referring to a hotel accommodation where guests have the means to take care of their own meal needs and laundry.

Self-drive *(Car Rental)*: See Hire Car.

Self-Drive Itinerary *(Tourism)*: An itinerary of travel arrangements for an independent traveler driving a rented car.

Self Sales *(Business)*: See In-house Sales.

Selling Away *(Tourism)*: The habit of selling the products or services of one supplier while rejecting the products or services of another.

Selling Fare *(Airlines)*: A fare that can be sold without restrictions.

Semi-Independent Travelers (SIT) *(Tourism)*: Visitors going to a destination on holiday who purchase a partially pre-planned travel package.

Semi-Perishable Food *(Hospitality)*: Foods that have a longer life than perishable foods, such as nuts, apples, potatoes, and waxed vegetables such as cucumbers. However, they should be stored under recommended time-temperature combinations.

Seminar *(Tourism)*: An educational, cultural or socio-cultural meeting of a group of persons regarding a specific work, a study or a reflection theme. The term denotes also a corporative training meeting.

Senior or Senior Citizen *(Tourism)*: A person who has reached certain age (usually 62) and is entitled for discounts on fares and rates. The age at which a person becomes a "Senior" varies from one supplier to another and can be ranged between 50 to 65 years of age.

Sensor *(Airlines)*: A device that responds to a physical stimulus and produces an electronic signal. Sensors are increasingly being combined with RFID baggage tags to detect the presence of a stimulus at an identifiable location.

SEP *(GDS)*: Code for September.

Sequencing *(Air Traffic)*: A method of placing aircraft safely and efficiently into a line of smoothly flowing air traffic.

Server *(Computing)*: A computer of great capacity that stores files and data which are retrieval by other computers.

Servi-bar *(Hospitality)*: A term used by some European hotels for minibar.

Service Ceiling *(Air Traffic)*: The height above sea level at which an aircraft with normal rated load can no longer climb more than 30 meters (100 feet) per minute under standard air conditions.

Service Bar *(Hospitality)*: A small bar where bartenders prepare alcoholic beverages for serving present guests.

Service Charge *(Air Traffic)*: A system of service charges on aircraft operators levied by some institutions to recover the costs of air navigation facilities and services, such as NAV Canada.

Service Charge *(Airlines)*: An amount charged by airlines on discounted or non-revenue tickets.

Service Charge *(Business)*: 1. A monthly fee charged by banks for processing transactions and handling checking accounts. 2. The fee charged to cover the costs for providing personal services.

Service Charge *(Hospitality)*: A gratuity usually paid in restaurants and hotels as remuneration for services. It is usually charged on the bill for distribution among service employees.

Service Charge *(Tourism)*: A charge levied by travel agencies for providing non-commissionable services. It is also called Service Fee.

Service Compris *(Tourism)*: A French expression literally meaning "service included" that denotes the service requires no additional tipping.

Service Fee *(Tourism)*: See Service Charge.

Service non Compris *(Tourism)*: A French expression literally meaning "service not included", which denotes an additional tip is expected.

Service Providers *(Tourism)*: Companies or independent individuals who perform certain activities or render certain services in favor of a third party.

Service Station *(Hospitality)*: A small work island located in a dining room.

Services *(Tourism)*: A term referring to intangible products that are not goods (tangible products), such as transportation, and all types of valuable actions, or efforts performed to satisfy a need or to fulfill a demand. Sometimes services are difficult to identify because they are closely associated with a good. Distinctive features of services are that:

1. No transfer of possession or ownership takes place when services are sold;

2. Services can not be kept in stock or transported;

3. Services come into existence at the time they are bought and consumed the moment they are produced, because they are instantly perishable.

The service production corresponds to the tertiary sector of the Economy. Tourism is a part of the service activities.

Settlement Authorization Code (SAC) *(Airlines)*: A code number generated by the Validating Carrier authorizing the BSP to settle specified coupon or coupons upon final use by another Carrier or agent.

Seventh Freedom of the Air *(Airlines)*: The freedom to base aircraft in a foreign country to operate international services between two countries outside the home country, establishing an actual "foreign hub".

Severe Acute Respiratory Syndrome (SARS) *(Tourism)*: A highly contagious respiratory disease that is caused by a virus. It was first reported in Asia in 2003 and spread worldwide over several months before the outbreak ended. SARS can be life-threatening, with symptoms include high fever, headache, body aches, dry cough, and pneumonia.

Severe Thunderstorm *(Climate)*: A thunderstorm with winds measuring 50 knots (58 mph) or greater, 3/4 inch hail or larger, or tornadoes. Severe thunderstorms may also produce torrential rain and frequent lightning.

Severe Weather *(Climate)*: Any destructive weather event, usually applied to localized storms, such as blizzards, intense thunderstorms, or tornadoes.

Severe Weather Avoidance Plan (SWAP) *(Air Traffic)*: A plan aimed to minimize the effect of severe weather on traffic flows in impacted terminal and/or ARTCC areas.

Severe Weather Watch Bulletin *(Air Traffic)*: An aviation weather report that identifies areas of possible severe thunderstorms or tornadoes.

Sex Tourism *(Tourism)*: Travel made by people wanting to get engaged in sexual activities.

SFML *(GDS)*: Code meaning Sea Food Meal.

SFO *(GDS)*: Three-letter IATA code for San Francisco, California, USA.

SG *(GDS)*: Code meaning School Group.

SGL *(GDS)*: Code meaning Single.

SGLB *(GDS)*: Code meaning Single room with bath.

SGLN *(GDS)*: Code meaning Single room without bath.

SGLS *(GDS)*: Code meaning Single room with shower.

SGMT *(GDS)*: Code meaning Segment.

SGN *(GDS)*: Three-letter IATA code for Ho Chi Minh (Saigon), capital city of Vietnam.

SHA *(GDS)*: Three-letter IATA code for Shanghai, important tourist destination in the Popular Republic of China.

Shakedown Cruise *(Cruise)*: A cruise performed with the sole purpose of testing the ship's systems, mechanical functioning and human work proficiency. Sometimes the cruise takes passengers at a discounted fare.

Shangri-La *(Tourism)*: The tale on a fictional earthly paradise known as Shangri-la is among the most enduring myths in the world. It was described by British author James Hilton in his novel "Lost Horizon" published in 1933. Shangri-la was supposed to be a permanently happy land, isolated from the outside world, where the ravages of time and history have been held back and where human beings lived in harmony with nature, and where the wisdom of the planet is saved for future generations. It would be a harmonious valley, gently guided from a lamasery, enclosed in the western end of the Kunlun Mountains. The word also evokes the imagery of exoticism of the Orient. The story of Shangri-La is based on the concept of Shambhala, a mystical city in Tibetan Buddhist tradition. Many places claim the right to be the scenario for Shangri-La's legend, such as the Buddhist Himalaya between northern India and Tibet, the Chinese southern region of Kham in southwestern Yunnan province, the legendary Kun Lun Mountains in Tibet, the Hunza Valley in northern Pakistan, and Bhutan.

Shared Code Carrier *(Airlines)*: An airline that has a code share agreement with other air carriers and is listed on a GDS under the code of such carriers.

Shell *(Tourism)*: An empty space in a supplier's pre-printed brochure or flyer where a travel agency can print, stamp or stick its own logo and address.

Shell Letter *(Tourism)*: A letter paper pre-printed with logo or illustrations with enough space left to type or print a communication text.

Shiatsu *(Tourism)*: A massage that uses finger pressure, and also pressure from the hands, forearms, elbows, knees and feet on outpoints bringing the benefit of calm and relaxation.

Shift Manager *(Hospitality)*: The manager in charge of a hotel, restaurant or casino during a period of time, usually a six- to eight-hour shift.

Shinkansen *(Tourism)*: A network of railway system in Japan using high-speed passenger trains operated by four Japan Railways

Group companies. The construction of the first segment of 2,459 kilometers (1,528 miles) of the Tokaido Shinkansen between Tokyo and Osaka started in 1959. The line opened on 1 October 1964, just in time for the Tokyo Olympic Games. In less than three years the line reached the mark of 100 million passengers on 13 July 1967. The one billion passengers' record was attained in 1976. The initial speed of 210 km/h (130 mph) has been already exceeded. At present the system links most major cities on the islands of Honshu and Kyushu with running speeds of up to 300 km/h (188 mph), although run speed tests of 443 km/h (275 mph) have been made for conventional trains. The Tokaido Shinkansen is the world's busiest high-speed train line carrying around 375 thousand passengers per day. The bullet-nose is the classic appearance of these trains that use tunnels and viaducts to go through and over obstacles, rather than around them, as the tunnel connecting the islands of Honshu and Hokaido that runs under the ocean.

Ship to Shore *(Cruise)*: A radio system used for communications from ships at sea.

Shipboard Account *(Cruise)*: A daily itemized account of a passenger's onboard purchases, such as alcoholic beverages, shore excursions, gift shop purchases, and Internet charges.

Shipment (SHPT) *(Airlines)*: Goods tendered to an air carrier by one consignor at one time and at one address, to be forwarded to one consignee at one destination, as recorded on one airway bill.

Shipper (SHPR) *(Airlines)*: Also known as the Consignor, the shipper is a company or individual who originates the shipment of goods. The term also describes an exporter.

Shipper Containers *(Airlines)*: Containers which are owned or leased by the shipper.

Shipper's Letter of Instruction (SLI) *(Airlines)*: The document where the shipper or his agent gives instructions for preparing documents and cargo forwarding.

Shoji *(Hospitality)*: A Japanese term describing a translucent rice-paper screen in a wooden frame used as a sliding partition or door in traditional Japanese houses or in Japanese style hotels.

Shopper *(Tourism)*: A slang term for a person who asks a travel agent for quotes, information and advice, but who never makes an actual booking. This type of person is also called Tireckicker.

Shore Excursions *(Cruise)*: Tours available at ports of call operated by independent tour companies to cruise passengers. They are purchased as an option for an additional charge when visiting ports of call or before starting the cruise.

Shore Excursion Manager *(Cruise)*: A cruise employee whose responsibilities are the promotion, arrangement, and supervision of shore excursion programs organized by independent operators on behalf of the cruise line.

Short Haul *(Airlines)*: A short distance over which passengers and/or load are transported. It is a term used to define a limited length and duration flight (of less than 4 hours) often to, from, or between second-tier airports.

Shortest Operated Mileage (SOM) *(Airlines)*: In the mileage system of computing fares, it is the shortest distance, using non-stop sector mileages, between any pair of points on an itinerary.

Short-haul Travel *(Airlines)*: Air travel of less than 4 hours duration. See Short Haul.

Shoulder Season *(Airlines)*: A period in the year between high and low seasons, when prices to certain destinations are between their highest and lowest, and the demand for travel or accommodation is lower than that of the high season but higher than that of the low season.

Shoulder-Wing *(Aeronautics)*: A mid-wing monoplane with its wing mounted directly to the top of the fuselage without use of Cabane Struts.

Showboat *(Tourism)*: A boat where that provides music or other type of entertainment is provided.

SHPR *(Airlines)*: See Shipper.

SHPT *(Airlines)*: See Shipment.

SHSN *(Climate)*: See Snow Shower.

SHTL *(GDS)*: Code meaning Second Class Hotel.

Shuttle *(Tourism)*: A vehicle moving back and forth over short routes on a frequent schedule that provides free transportation service.

Shuttle Bus *(Tourism)*: A short-run bus transfer usually provided free of charge, operating on a frequent schedule between a hotel and the airport and vice versa, or between the airport and a car rental agency and vice versa.

SI *(GDS)*: A code meaning: 1. Service Information; 2. Supplementary Information.

SIA *(GDS)*: Three-letter IATA code for Xian, ancient capital city of the Popular Republic of China.

Side Trip *(Airlines)*: An air travel originating in or destined to any intermediate point of a fare component which is charged as a separate pricing unit.

Side-by-Side Suite *(Hospitality)*: A suite that consists of two joined small compartments.

Sideslip *(Air Traffic)*: A movement of an aircraft in which a relative flow of air moves along the lateral axis, resulting in a sideways movement from a projected flight path.

Sidestand *(Hospitality)*: A service stand used for holding tableware provisions, such as condiments, dairy products, ice, and some beverages for easy access. It is also called Station.

Sidework *(Hospitality)*: Setup and cleanup work that must be completed before opening a dining room or after closing it, including restocking server supply stations, furnishing tables, filling salt and pepper shakers, etc.

Sierra *(Airlines)*: Designator for the letter "S" in the International Phonetic Alphabet.

SIG *(GDS)*: A code meaning Signature, Signed.

Sightseeing *(Tourism)*: A term literally meaning "see what is worth seeing" which was coined by Baedeker guides in the 19th century. Its concept is now used referring to sights of visits that are of touristic interest or worth to be seen, such as a city tour.

SIGMET *(Air Traffic)*: See Significant Meteorological Information.

Signal Data Converter (SDC) *(Aeronautics)*: A device that converts unique signals to a standard protocol.

Significance Criteria *(Hospitality)*: Criteria generally expressed in both dollar and percentage differences, used to determine which variances are significant.

Significant Meteorological Information (SIGMET) *(Air Traffic)*: In-flight advisory concerning severe icing, severe and extreme turbulence, widespread dust storms, or volcanic ash lowering visibility to less than three miles.

Silence Cloth *(Hospitality)*: An oil cloth or other padded material placed under the tablecloth to absorb noise.

Silent Commerce *(Computing)*: A generic term covering all business solutions enabled by tagging, tracking, sensing and other technologies, including RFID, which give humans everyday intelligent and interactive tools. When combined with Internet connectivity, they form a new infrastructure that enables companies to collect data and deliver services without human interaction.

Silk Road *(Tourism)*: It is the name given to the route followed by ancient caravans that traveled for trade between China and Europe. It linked not only China with European countries, but also with the Indian Kingdom and the empires of Persia and Syria. Travelers using the Silk Route did not take a single route; they crossed Central Asia via several different branches and passing through different settlements. All the routes started in Changan. The northern route headed up the Gansu corridor, passed through Yumen Guan and crossed the neck of the Gobi desert to reach the Tianshan Mountains and the Taklimakan desert. The southern route headed Dunhuang, passed through the Yang Guan and the southern edges of the Taklimakan desert, to reach the Karakorum and Kunlun ranges. The northwestern route used passes through the Tianshan and Pamir ranges. Numerous other routes were also used to a lesser importance. Whichever the route taken, it passed though one of the most hostile and inhospitable lands in the world, named at that time as the "Land of Death." Silk was not the only product merchants traded, although it was the most remarkable for the people of the western lands. Many other commodities were also traded, such as gold, ivory, and exotic animals and plants. In the current days, there is increasing number of people interested in visiting these desolate places. For this reason Chinese authorities are making efforts to protect the remaining sites and to restore them.

Silver Dart *(Airlines)*: The Silver Dart was the flying machine constructed by the Canadian Aerial Experiment Association and was used to operate the first flight in Canada that took off the ice at Baddeck, Nova Scotia on February 23, 1909. The pilot was one of its designers, the intrepid John A.D. McCurdy.

Simplifying the Business (STB) *(Airlines)*: Simplifying the Business is an "industry-wide" program involving five key initiatives led by IATA. They are:

1. 100 percent Electronic Ticketing (ET) by May 31, 2008. After May 31, 2008, IATA will stop distributing paper tickets,
2. Bar Coded Boarding Passes (BGBP),
3. Common Use Self-Service Check-in (CUSS),
4. RFID (Radio Frequency Identification Tags) for Baggage Management, and
5. IATA E-freight, planned to be 100 percent by 2010.

The transition to ET involves great advantages, such as no more paper stock to manage or printers to maintain, no more airline fees for using paper tickets, better customer service over a wider area, no more lost tickets, automatic tracking of unused tickets, and no more safes.

Bar Coded Boarding Passes enable fast, convenient check-in by enabling the passenger to print the boarding pass in a home printer and/or check-in using a Common Use Self-service Kiosk and proceed directly to the gate. Bar Coded Boarding Passes use IATA industry standard 2D bar codes that enable their use on interline journeys and take advantage of the efficiencies offered by the industry's conversion to 100 percent electronic ticketing. By the end of 2008 airlines will become BCBP capable and by the end of 2010 the usage will be at its 100 percent level.

CUSS stands for Common Use Self Service. It is a shared kiosk offering convenient passenger check-in whilst allowing airlines to maintain branding and functionality. As kiosks can be located throughout the airport, congestion is alleviated and passenger flow improved. IATA assures that 130 airports will be capable to offer CUSS facilities in 2008.

Radio Frequency Identification (RFID) is a technology that will be applied to baggage tagging and tracking. It consists of a silicon chip embedded in a tag which emits a radio signal that can be read at a distance without needing to see the item. Tags can be "talked to" or "written to", allowing the status of an item to be updated as it is processed.

IATA e-freight was launched in 2004, designed to eliminate the need to produce and transport paper documents for air cargo shipments by moving to a simpler, industry-wide, electronic, paper-free environment.

Simple Syrup *(Hospitality)*: It is syrup made simply from sugar and water. It is a sweetener used in cold drinks instead of granulated sugar for its shorter dissolving time.

Simplex *(Air Traffic)*: Single frequency for both transmitting and receiving communications. It generally implies a push-to-talk function and verbal procedures.

Simulation *(Aeronautics)*: The use of a computer to calculate and visualize the effects of a given process.

Simulator *(Aeronautics)*: A device used to train pilots creating an environment that is as close as possible to reality. In flight simulators, engineers create a cockpit environment identical to the one in a real airplane. In a flight simulator a pilot will see, hear and feel like he/she is in a real aircraft.

Since Major Overhaul (SMOH) *(Airlines)*: The operating hours or time remaining on an engine.

SIN *(GDS)*: Three-letter IATA code for Singapore.

Sine *(Airlines)*: A code created to identify a travel agency in a GDS.

Single *(Hospitality)*: A hotel room occupied by one person.

Single Bed *(Hospitality)*: A bed approximately 36 inches by 75 inches that accommodates one person.

Single Entity Charter *(Airlines)*: An aircraft or any other vehicle that is chartered to a single company or group for its exclusive use. It is also a non-scheduled flight for carrying the cargo of a specific shipper.

Single Occupancy *(Cruise)*: A cabin designed to accommodate two or more passengers, but which is actually occupied by one person at a charge of a Single Supplement.

Single Supplement *(Tourism)*: The additional charge applied to a cabin or hotel room occupied by one guest.

Single-Factor Region *(Geography)*: A region which is determined by only one defining feature.

Sink *(Air Traffic)*: The speed at which an aircraft loses altitude, especially of a glide in still air under given conditions of equilibrium.

Sinking Speed *(Air Traffic)*: See Sink.

SIPP *(Car Rental)*: Abbreviation for Standard Interline Passenger Procedures.

SIPP Codes *(Car Rental)*: See Standard Interline Passenger Procedure Codes.

SISC *(Organizations)*: An acronym for Schedules Information Standards Committee.

SIT *(Tourism)*: See Semi-Independent Travelers.

SITA *(Organizations)*: An acronym for *Societe Internationale Telecommunications Aeronautiques*.

Situational Awareness *(Air Traffic)*: Situational awareness provides the pilots with information relative to the current surroundings, such as other aircraft, obstacles or threats in the immediate area.

SITE *(Organizations)*: An acronym for Society of Incentive Travel Executives.

Site Guide *(Computing)*: The page giving information on the contents of a web site.

Site Inspection *(Tourism)*: A visit to a hotel property or other establishment in order to evaluate its services before the initiation of a meeting, a congress or a conference.

Sitting *(Cruise)*: See Seating.

Sixth Freedom of the Air *(Airlines)*: It is a combination of the third and fourth freedoms in which an airline has the freedom to carry traffic between two foreign countries via the carrier's home country. With the hubbing practice of most air carriers, this freedom has become very common.

Size Category *(Cruise)*: Term referring to Ship sizes that ranges the following categories: Small (less than 40,000 tons), Medium (45,000 to 65,000 tons), Large (65,000 to 100,000 tons) and Very Large (over 100,000 tons).

SJO *(GDS)*: Three-letter IATA code for San José, the capital city of Costa Rica.

SJU *(GDS)*: Three-letter IATA code for San Juan, the capital city of Puerto Rico.

Slang *(Tourism)*: Informal words and expressions adopted for communication of a particular group of people as replacements for standard usage that is not considered appropriate for formal speech.

SK *(Airlines)*: Two-letter IATA code for Scandinavian Airlines System.

Skal International *(Organizations)*: An international association of travel and tourism professionals around the world, promoting global tourism and friendship. Its members meet at local, national, regional and international levels to discuss items of common interest. The first Club was founded in 1932 in Paris by travel managers, but the idea to form an international goodwill and friendship entity strengthened and in 1934 it resulted in the creation of the *Association Internationale des Skal Clubs*, nominating *Florimond Volckaert*, who is considered the Father of Skal, as its first President. At present Skal International has approximately 22,000 members in 500 Clubs throughout 90 countries, having its General Secretariat headquartered in Torremolinos, Spain. Skal's membership is open to managers or executives directly involved in tourism management, sales and promotions, in specified travel and tourism businesses, airlines, cruise lines, railways, travel agents, tour operators, hotels, governments and non-government tourism organizations, and travel media.

SKD *(GDS)*: Code meaning Schedule.

SKED *(GDS)*: A code for Schedule, Scheduled.

Ski *(Tourism)*: The sport of gliding over the snow on a pair of long wood strips bound one on each foot. It is said skis were already used in Sweden around 4,000 to 5,000 years ago as a means of transportation. The term is a Norwegian word used for the first time in 1840 by his inventor *Sondre Nordheim*. The sport made its debut during a 17 kilometers competition held at Holmenkollen near Christiania (Oslo) in 1892.

Ski Lift *(Tourism)*: A mechanism comprising a set of seats or bars hanging from a moving cable that moves skiers up a slope.

Ski Tow *(Tourism)*: See Rope Tow.

Skids *(Airlines)*: A runner used on an aircraft landing gear instead of tires.

Skiff *(Cruise)*: The term defines various types of small sailboat.

Skipper *(Cruise)*: An officer who is licensed to command a cruise ship or the master of the ship. It is also referred to the naval officer in command of a military ship.

Skipper *(Hospitality)*: A slang term to denote a guest leaving without paying.

Sky Cover *(Air Traffic)*: The amount of the celestial dome that is hidden by clouds and/or obscurations.

Skycap *(Airlines)*: A person who helps passengers with his/her baggage at an airport.

Skyjacking *(Airlines)*: The illegal action to take control of an airplane by threat or violence during a flight. It is synonymous with Air Piracy. See also Highjack.

Slant Range *(Air Traffic)*: Direct line distance, not along the ground.

Slats *(Aeronautics)*: Special surfaces attached to or actually part of the leading edge of the wing that are extended to produce extra lift during takeoff or to help stopping during landing.

Sleep Aboard (SAB) *(Yacht)*: The option offered by most boat companies before bare boat sailing vacation begins. This means the person hiring the yacht may sleep aboard (at a reduced rate) while still docked on company premises. There may be times during high season when there is no "sleep aboard" option.

Sleep-around Plan *(Hospitality)*: An accommodation method by which guests spend part of their stay at a nearby hotel or all-inclusive resort of the same organization, so they enjoy different experiences.

Sleeper *(Hospitality)*: A slang term for a room actually available for sale that is believed to be occupied.

Sleeper *(Tourism)*: The Sleeping Compartment aboard a train.

Sleeper Berth *(Airlines)*: An aircraft seat with an almost horizontal reclining angle that provides conditions to sleep.

Sleeper Class *(Tourism)*: A category of accommodation aboard a train that includes sleeping arrangements such as a sleeper, sleeperette, roomette, or similar.

Sleeperette *(Tourism)*: 1. A small sleeping compartment aboard a train; 2. Sleeping Berth.

Sleeping Car *(Tourism)*: See Sleeper.

Sleeping Policeman *(Tourism)*: A speed bumper on roads or streets.

Sleet *(Climate)*: See Ice Pellets.

SLI *(Car Rental)*: See Supplemental Liability Insurance.

Slice and Dice *(Airlines)*: The term describes how to fragment or segment an itinerary into separate pricing units.

Slicer *(Hospitality)*: An appliance that has a spinning disk with a knife-sharp edge for cutting food.

Slip *(Air Traffic)*: A way to lose altitude hurriedly or slide into a final approach during a heavy wind.

Slip *(Cruise)*: The space on a dock at which a ship or boat is moored, as a docking space at a marina.

Slipstream *(Aeronautics)*: The flow of air driven backward by a propeller or downward by a rotor.

Slivovitz *(Hospitality)*: Fruity brandy, distilled from plums that is soft, pleasant, with mellow plum fragrance.

Sloe Gin *(Hospitality)*: A red liqueur with delicate bouquet and tangy fruity flavor resembling wild cherries.

Sloop *(Cruise)*: A sailing vessel with one mast, a jib, and a fore and aft mainsail.

Slot *(Aeronautics)*: A long and narrow gap in a wing, usually near the leading edge that improves airflow at high angles of attack for slower landing speeds.

Slot *(Airlines)*: A parking space assigned to planes for sequence positioning at an airport.

Slotted Flap *(Aeronautics)*: A flap that, when depressed, exposes a slot and increases airflow between itself and the rear edge of the wing.

Slots *(Airlines)*: The scheduled time for takeoff or landing allocated to an aircraft movement on a specific date at an airport.

SLPR *(GDS)*: Code meaning Sleeperette.

Slush *(Climate)*: Snow or ice on the ground that has been reduced to a softy watery mixture by rain and/or warm temperatures.

SM *(GDS)*: Code meaning Sales Manager.

SMA *(Airlines)*: See Surface Movement Advisor.

Small Aircraft Transportation System (SATS) *(Aeronautics)*: A plan proposed by NASA to develop technology that will provide a new framework for the transportation system.

Small Ship *(Cruise)*: A ship with a gross registered tonnage (GRT) of less than 40,000 tons.

Smart Card *(Airlines)*: A plastic card about the size of a credit card with an embedded microchip which can be programmed to perform multiple functions, such as personal data storage including passport and travel information, electronic cash payments, telephone calling, and other applications. Smart Cards were introduced in 1999 to help prevent card crime and are recognized by the gold colored contact plate on the front of the card. Although they work in the same way as other cash cards, they are much more secure than other credit or debit cards.

Smart Label *(Airlines)*: A barcode label that contains an RFID transponder and is able to store information and to communicate with a reader.

SMERF *(Hospitality)*: An acronym for "Social, Military, Educational, Religious, and Fraternal" that defines the market segments for the sale of specific services and meeting facilities.

Smog *(Climate)*: A term defining a noxious mixture of smoke and fog which pollutes the air at low layers.

SMOH *(Airlines)*: See Since Major Overhaul.

Smoke *(Airlines)*: Small particles produced by combustion that are suspended in the air.

Smokestack *(Cruise)*: A ship's flue for catching and directing any exhaust particles away from passenger decks.

Smorgasbord *(Hospitality)*: A Swedish-style buffet meal with a variety of hot and cold dishes.

SMRY *(GDS)*: Code meaning Summary.

SMSA *(GDS)*: Code meaning Smoking Aisle Seat.

SMST *(GDS)*: Code meaning Smoking Seat.

SMSW *(GDS)*: Code meaning Smoking Window Seat.

SN *(GDS)*: Code meaning Serial Number.

Snow *(Climate)*: An atmospheric solid precipitation in the form of translucent ice crystals generally of hexagonal form. Those crystals often fall from stratiform clouds where they are formed by water drops slowly frozen. The quantity of falling snow depends on the season, the altitude and orientation of the ground. And its quality varies in function of the atmospheric conditions. Wind, for instance, is a prevailing factor.

Snow Banner *(Climate)*: A plume of snow blown off a mountain crest, resembling smoke blowing from a volcano.

Snow Shower (SHSN) *(Climate)*: Frozen precipitation in the form of snow, characterized by its sudden beginning and ending. It is reported as SHSN in an observation and on the METAR.

Snow Tourism *(Tourism)*: One of the numerous types of Tourism of Sports that takes advantage of the snow and environment for recreation and leisure activities. Some of the snow tourism activities are Snowmobiling, Downhill, Nordic Skiing, Ski Touring, Curling, Skating, Tobogganing & Snow Shoeing, and Snowboard.

Snowbird *(Tourism)*: A slang term for a person traveling from a northern region to a southern region during the winter.

Snowboard *(Tourism)*: A device resembling a surf board used on ski slopes.

Social Host or Hostess *(Cruise)*: The most visible crew member in charge of the ship's staff assisting in various activities and functions onboard.

Social Structure *(Ecology)*: Organizational patterns of a human society in its economic or political interrelation elements.

Societe Internationale de Telecommunications Aeronautiques (SITA) *(Organizations)*: The world's leading service provider of IT business solutions and communication services to the air transport industry. It is completely owned by the air transport community. SITA manages complex communication solutions for its air transport, government and GDS customers over the world's most extensive communication network, complemented by consultancy in the design, deployment and integration of communication services. SITA has two main subsidiaries: OnAir, which is leading the race to bring in-flight mobile telephony to the market, and CHAMP Cargo systems, the world's only IT company solely dedicated to air cargo. SITA also operates two joint ventures providing services to the air transport community: Aviareto for aircraft asset management and CertiPath for secure electronic identity management. SITA offers services for over 600 members and around 1,800 customers in over all the countries worldwide and territories. Its corporate offices are located in London, Brussels and Geneva, with eight regional offices in the world.

Society for Accessible Travel & Hospitality (SATH) *(Organizations)*: An educational nonprofit membership organization founded in 1976 having the mission to raise awareness of the needs of all travelers with disabilities, remove physical and attitudinal barriers to free access and expand travel opportunities in the United States and abroad. Members include travel professionals, consumers with disabilities and other individuals and corporations who support its mission.

Society of American Travel Writing (SATW) *(Organizations)*: The Society for American Travel Writing was created in 1994 by Beth L. Lueck (University of Wisconsin-Whitewater) and Jeffrey Melton (Auburn University Montgomery), as an affiliated society of the American Literature Association. The society's members share an interest in the literature and culture of travel. The SATW fosters interest and scholarship in travel writing by American authors or about America by hosting panels at professional conferences, particularly the annual conference of the American Literature Association, and by pursuing other appropriate activities.

Society of Incentive Travel Executives (SITE) *(Organizations)*: Founded in 1973, SITE is the only international, not-for-profit, professional association devoted to the pursuit of excellence in incentives. SITE provides educational seminars and information services to those who design, develop, promote, sell, administer, and operate motivational programs as an incentive to increase productivity in business. The SITE Strategic Plan has thee main objectives:

1. To raise the global awareness level of the effectiveness of performance improvement and, in the process, elevate SITE to a position of industry preeminence;

2. To enhance member value; and

3. To provide and promote business to business opportunities between members, strategic alliances and Future contributions.

Currently SITE has over 2,100 members in 87 countries, with 35 local and regional chapters. Members represent corporate executives, incentive companies, destination management companies, travel and event planners, official tourist organizations, transportation companies, hotels and resorts, cruise lines, trade publications, and supporting organizations such as restaurants and visitors attractions.

Soft Adventure *(Tourism)*: An outdoor touristic activity involving a low level of risk or physical effort.

Soft Departure *(Cruise)*: A departure date with relatively few bookings.

Soft-dollar Savings *(Tourism)*: Savings made by simply not spending money or by saving time. See also Hard- dollar Savings.

Soft Opening *(Hospitality)*: A business opening of a new hotel, which may not be fully booked and that has not formally announced the event.

Soft Sailing *(Cruise)*: A cruise sailing with relatively few passengers.

Soil Erosion *(Ecology)*: The wearing away and loss of topsoil by the action of water, strong wind, ice, or other geologic agents.

Soiree *(Tourism)*: A French term for an evening dance party or an evening event.

SOJ *(GDS)*: Code meaning Single Open Jaw.

Solar Radiation *(Ecology)*: The electromagnetic radiation emitted by the sun.

Solar Year *(Geography)*: The period of time required for the earth to make one complete revolution around the sun, measured between two vernal equinoxes and equal to 365 days, 5 hours, 48 minutes, 45.51 seconds. It is also called Astronomical Year or Tropical Year.

SOLAS *(Cruise)*: See Safety of Life at Sea.

Sole Proprietorship *(Tourism)*: A business, such as a travel agency, owned and managed by one person or that in which, for tax purposes, a sole proprietor and his/her business are one tax entity, meaning that business profits are reported and taxed on the owner's personal tax return. The main downside of a sole proprietorship is that its owner is personally liable for all business debts.

Solid Waste *(Ecology)*: Any discarded material including solid, liquid, semi-solid or gaseous material resulting from industrial and commercial operations, and from community material.

Solstice *(Geography)*: The point in the Earth's ecliptic at which the sun is farthest from the equator. The summer solstice falls in June 20 or 21 in the northern hemisphere and in December 21 or 22 in the southern hemisphere, and vice versa for the winter solstice.

SOM *(GDS)*: Code meaning Shortest Operated Mileage.

Sommelier *(Hospitality)*: A French term to denote a person specialized in wines and who is responsible for wine in a restaurant.

Son et Lumière *(Tourism)*: A French expression meaning literally "sound and light" which is used to define a form of entertainment performed by the enhanced means of music and the artful lighting.

SOS *(Cruise)*: A traditional acronym meaning "Save our souls", which is used as an international signal of help demand in distress emergencies.

Sound *(Geography)*: A long passage of water wider than a strait that separates an island from the mainland or connects two larger bodies of water.

Sounding *(Cruise)*: The depth of the sea as measured beneath a ship.

Sour Mash *(Hospitality)*: A term referring to straight whiskeys. Sour mash identifies a production process, distinguished from the "sweet mash" technique of distillation that has nothing to do with the taste of the whiskey.

Sous Chef *(Hospitality)*: An assistant chef or cook.

South America, Geographical *(Geography)*: South America is one of the two continents of the Americas, entirely located in the Western Hemisphere and most of it in the Southern Hemisphere. It is bounded on the north by the Caribbean Sea, on the north and east by the Atlantic Ocean, on the west by the Pacific Ocean and on the northwest by Central America (part of North America). South America has an area of 17,854,130 square kilometers (6,900,000 square miles), around 14% of the Earth's surface, ranking the fourth largest continent on the earth. As of 2007, its population was estimated at more than 371 million or 6 percent of the world's people, the fifth most populated continent after Asia, Africa, Europe, and North America. South American coastline is mostly regular, except in the extreme south and southwest, where it is indented by numerous fjords. The islands are relatively few. The most important of them are the Galápagos in Ecuador, Easter Island and Juan Fernandez Islands in Chile, the Falkland Islands which are claimed by Argentina as the Islas Malvinas, and Fernando de Noronha Archipelago in Brazil. Smaller islands are located on the northern South American continental shelf.

South America is a spectacular continent boasting many marvels of landscape, wildlife, geographic formations and natural wonders, such as the Andes, the world's longest mountain range and the second in height; the Amazon Rainforest, the largest in the world; the Amazon River, by many considered the largest river in the world; Angel Falls in Venezuela, the highest waterfall; the Galapagos in Ecuador that are the most bio-diversified islands; the highest navigable lake in the world, Lake Titicaca; the highest capital city, La Paz, Bolivia; and so forth. South America is organized around four large land masses: The Andes mountain range, the Guiana Shield, the Brazilian Massif and the Patagonian.

The western region of South America is dominated from the northern coast to the tip of Tierra del Fuego by the Andes mountain system. It is 7,240 kilometers long, measures an average of 241 kilometers wide, has a medium height of 3,660 meters, and covers an area of 1,845,000 square kilometers. Many Andean volcanoes are alive and form part of the Pacific Rim of Fire. The greatest peak is Aconcagua on the border of Argentina and Chile, raised at 6,960 meters as the highest peak in the Western Hemisphere. The second is Huascarán (6,768 meters) in the Peruvian Andes. One of the most important elevations is the Chimborazo (6,310 meters) in the Ecuadorian Andes. It is said that, if measured from the center of the Earth, the Chimborazo would be the highest mountain of the planet, because of its position near the equator line.

The Guiana Shield is located in northeast South America, covering an area of 2,000,000 square kilometers and extended over the territories of Guyana, Suriname, French Guiana, Colombia, Venezuela and Brazil. The higher elevations on the shield are called the Guiana Highlands, where the impressive *tepuis,* such as the Roraima, are found. The Guiana Highlands are also the source of some of the world's most spectacular waterfalls such as Angel Falls, Kaieteur Falls and Kuquenan Falls.

The Brazilian Massif covers most of the Brazilian territory. The Amazonia is the enhancing part of this region. It is a wonderland for botanists, scientists, ecologists, anthropologists, archaeologists, bird watchers, and tourists in general. It is responsible for 50 percent of the renovated oxygen on Earth, and its hydrographic basin contains more than one fifth of the fresh water reserves on the planet. The Amazonia's flora and fauna are the most exuberant of the world with thousands of century old trees that are the habitat for over 15,000 species of animals.

The Patagonian Plateau is a semiarid plateau that covers nearly the entire southern portion of mainland Argentina. With an area of about 673,000 square kilometers (260,000 square miles), it is a vast area of steppe and desert that extends south from latitude 37° to 51° S. Although soils here are generally fertile, climatic constraints limit agricultural usefulness.

The largest river of the world in terms of water volume discharged into the sea is the Amazon, traversing almost the continent from west to east, in a distance of 6,565 kilometers (4,080 miles). Its total drainage basin covers about 7,045,800 square kilometers (2,722,000 square miles) and encompasses about one-third of the South American area. Other large rivers draining South America to the Atlantic are: The Orinoco in the northern lowland, the São Francisco River draining the northeastern Brazil, and the Paraguay-Paraná system in the south. South America has few large lakes, the largest of which are Lake Titicaca and Lake Poopó in Bolivia, and Lake Maracaibo in Venezuela.

In reason of its marvelous nature scenery, South America has an endless number of touristic attractions. Just to name a few, following is a short list of them:

• Galápagos Islands, called the world's greatest living laboratory, the islands support a fantastic array of wildlife that is unique on the earth;

• The rain forest region forming Venezuela's Canaima National Park with its *tepuys* and the Angel Falls with 979 meters height;

• The Iguazu Falls that drop between 60 to 80 meters (197 to 262

feet) into the river below, forming a series of 275 cascades;
• Machu Picchu, a pre-Columbian Inca site located in the Valley, at 2,400 meters above sea level, is the symbol of the Inca Empire;
• Quito, the capital city of Ecuador, a mixture of colonial style and modern architecture;
• Rio de Janeiro and its multiple beaches and cultural expressions;
• Buenos Aires is a European-style Metropolis.

South America Sub Area *(IATA Geography)*: The territory comprising Argentina, Bolivia, Brazil, Chile, Colombia, Ecuador, French Guiana, Guyana, Panama, Paraguay, Peru, Suriname, Uruguay, and Venezuela.

South Asian Subcontinent Sub-area *(IATA Geography)*: The territory comprising Afghanistan, Bangladesh, Bhutan, India, Maldives, Nepal, Pakistan, and Sri Lanka. The subarea is also known as PANIBS.

South Atlantic Fares *(Airlines)*: Those fares applicable for journeys between points in the South Atlantic subarea and points in Areas 2 and/or 3 via the Atlantic Ocean.

South Atlantic Sub-area *(IATA Geography)*: The territory comprising Argentina, Brazil, Chile, Paraguay, and Uruguay. This is also distinguished as the ABCPU subarea.

South East Asia Sub-area *(IATA Geography)*: The territory comprising Brunei, Darussalam, Cambodia, China, Chinese Taipei, Christmas Island, Cocos (Keeling) Islands, Guam, Indonesia, Kazakhstan, Laos, Malaysia, Marshal Islands, Micronesia, Mongolia, Myanmar, Northern Mariana Islands, Palau, Philippines, Russia (in Asia), Singapore, Tajikistan, Thailand, Turkmenistan, Uzbekistan, and Vietnam.

South East Asia Travel Association (SEATA) *(Organizations)*: SEATA is a non-profit membership association for travel professionals who take care of the traveling public, the people of the region and the environment. Its aim is to promote true responsible tourism to South East Asia by means of quality, honesty and transparency.

South Pacific Fares *(Airlines)*: Those which are applicable for travel between points in Area 1 and points in South West Pacific via the Pacific Ocean.

South West Pacific Sub-area *(IATA Geography)*: The territory comprising American Samoa, Australia, Cook Islands, Fiji, French Polynesia, Kiribati, Nauru, New Caledonia, New Zealand, Niue, Papua New Guinea, Samoa, Solomon Islands, Tonga, Tuvalu, Vanuatu, Wallis and Futuna Islands, including intermediate islands.

Southern Africa *(IATA Geography)*: The territory comprising Botswana, Lesotho, Mozambique, Namibia, South Africa, and Swaziland.

Southern Lights, The *(Geography)*: See Aurora Australis.

SP *GDS)*: Code meaning Special Operations.

Spa *(Hospitality)*: 1.A resort facility offering massage services, hydrotherapy, exercise, steam baths, etc., which are usually located on areas rich in mineral springs, hot springs and the like. It is said the name is taken after the town of Spa in Belgium, but it is also thought the name is an acronym for *sanitas per aqua*, meaning "health through water". 2. A room or area in a hotel property that is equipped with such services as steam baths, saunas, massage, and so forth.

Spa Cuisine or Spa Food *(Tourism)*: Light, healthy meals, often organic that are typically low in calories, fat and salt.

Spa Menu *(Tourism)*: Selection of treatments and therapies offered by the spa.

Spa Package *(Tourism)*: Two or more treatments offered together. It can include lunch or refreshment and use of the spa facilities.

Space *(Airlines)*: A generic term used to denote a hotel room, an air seat, a cruise cabin, or a restaurant table when processing a reservation.

Space, Geographical *(Geography)*: See Geographical Space.

Space Available (SA) *(Tourism)*: 1. On a ticket it means a seat is not confirmed, but subject to availability; 2. The expression is used in reference with any remaining travel room, seats or lodging.

Space Standby *(Tourism)*: Seats or accommodations that will be able for use only after all confirmed customers have been served.

Space Law *(Airlines)*: A body of agreements governing the exploration and use of outer space, developed since the first launching of a satellite into space in 1957. Space law is a part of international law, has grown under the auspices of the United Nations. In 1963 the UN issued a declaration stating that the exploration and use of outer space would be for the benefit of all humankind; that no sovereignty could be claimed in space; and that nations launching objects would be responsible for damages caused by them. Four years later, in 1967, this treaty went into effect, embodying the mentioned principles and adding a prohibition on the military use of space and a provision for the inspection of installations on celestial bodies. A new treaty was issued by the UN in 1979 on use of the moon's resources.

Space Ratio *(Cruise)*: A ratio representing the cubic space occupied by a passenger. It is obtained by dividing the Gross Registered Tonnage by the number of passengers.

Space Tourism *(Tourism)*: A recent tourism initiative still in its developing phase that intends to take adventure travelers into the outer space, offering such unique experiences as the thrill of looking at Earth from space and the opportunity to watch celestial bodies from a closer platform. Numerous locations are targeting the space tourism industry by spaceports already being built in California, Oklahoma, New Mexico, Florida, Virginia, Alaska, Wisconsin, Esrange in Sweden, Singapore and the United Arab Emirates. Three are the most important current projects aimed to close accomplishments. The Russian Space Agency I perhaps the pioneer providing flights for Space Adventures to the International Space Station aboard a Soyuz spacecraft. Even if space tourism opportunities are still limited and expensive (USD20 million per person) Soyuz flights are fully booked until 2009. Virgin Galactic, a division of Virgin Group, is the first private space tourism company planning to have passenger service on its first spacecraft the VSS Enterprise supposed to begin operations by 2009 at an initial price of USD200,000. The third outstanding initiative is the "Project Enterprise," which was launched by the German TALIS Institute in 2004. Its purpose is to develop a rocket propelled space plane until 2011, carrying one pilot and up to five passengers into a suborbital trip. Several smaller prototypes will be developed in order to proof the concept, before the definitive space plane will be constructed. Its main launch site will be an airport near Cochstedt, Germany.

Spar *(Aeronautics)*: A principal section of the wing structure of an airplane, going from tip to tip.

SPCL *(GDS)*: Code meaning Special Class of rental car.

Special Drawing Rights (SDR) *(Airlines)*: A fictitious unit of currency that international air travel industry has adopted to devise international air fares and to establish the amounts for liability compensation. The Special Drawing Right (SDR) was created as a new international reserve asset by the International Monetary Fund (IMF) in 1969, since it was proved the current key reserve assets (gold and the U.S. dollar) became inadequate for supporting the expansion of world trade and financial development. The SDR is neither a currency, nor a claim on the IMF, but it is a potential claim on the freely usable currencies of IMF members. Today, the SDR has only limited use as a reserve asset, and its main function is to serve as the unit of account of the IMF and some other international organizations. In 1975 the international carriers used the SDR as a means to update the compensation amounts that were originally established in Gold Francs in the Warsaw Convention. It occurred in the frame of the Montreal Protocols.

Special Event Tour *(Tourism)*: A tour designed around a particular event, such as the Calgary Estampede, Kentucky Derby, Mardi Gras, or Rose Bowl Parade.

Special Fare *(Airlines)*: Any fare other than the normal fares, which is subject to several conditions of application.

Special Group Fares or Rates *(Tourism)*: Prices per person including a discount on group bookings.

Special Instructions *(Cruise)*: Directions for handling or delivering a shipment.

Special Interest Group *(Tourism)*: A group built around a common interest shared by the group members on a specific subject or activity.

Special Interest Group Tour *(Tourism)*: A tour designed to appeal members of clubs, associations and similar entities who share common interests. Such tours usually include visits to places and events of their special interest.

Special Operations *(Tourism)*: Specific types of motorcoach services, such as transfers to/from the or to/from a place of special events.

Special Service Requirement (SSR) *(Airlines)*: A request for special services needed for the well being and comfort of the passenger, such as special diets meals, wheelchairs, etc. It is a booking element included in the PNR at the time of the reservation.

Special Traffic Management Program (STMP) *(Air Traffic)*: A program issued to regulate arrivals and/or departure procedures at airports that are in areas where special events are taking place.

Special Use Airspace (SUA) *(Air Traffic)*: Airspace of defined dimensions identified by an area on the surface of the earth where activities are confined because of their nature and/or where limitations may be imposed on aircraft operations that are not a part of those activities.

Specialty Cars *(Car Rental)*: Popular specialty cars for rent including convertibles, mini vans and 12-passenger vans.

Specialty Menu *(Hospitality)*: A menu that differs from the regular menu, usually designed for holidays and other special events or for specific guest groups.

Specialty Restaurant *(Hospitality)*: A theme restaurant featuring defined types of food.

Specialty Vehicle *(Tourism)*: A series of vehicles suitable for the practice of certain sports or activities, such as jet skis and all-terrain vehicles.

Specified Fare *(Airlines)*: A fare specifically set out in a tariff.

Species *(Ecology)*: A group of individuals having common characteristics such as appearance, general behavior, and genetic structure, which are capable to interbreed with one another.

Speed Brakes *(Aeronautics)*: Surfaces mounted on the wing or fuselage which can be extended into the airflow to create more drag and slow the aircraft. They are also known as Air Brakes.

Speed Bump *(Tourism)*: See Sleeping Policeman.

Speed of Sound *(Aeronautics)*: The speed at which sound waves travel through a medium. Although speed of sound is commonly measured in the air, the speed of sound can be measured in virtually any substance. As measured in the air, the speed of sound is 344 meter per second (1230 km/h or 770 mph) when the medium is dry and the temperature is of 21 °C (70 °F). The speed of sound in liquids and non-porous solids is higher than that in the air.

SPF *(Ecology)*: Sun protection factor, a measure of the protection provided by sunblock lotions.

Spiff *(Tourism)*: A limited time bonus offered by a supplier to encourage travel agents to book more of its services.

Spinner *(Airlines)*: A slang term used for passengers who have duplicate assignment of the same seat.

Spirit *(Hospitality)*: An alcoholic beverage containing a significant amount of distilled ethanol.

SPK *(GDS)*: Three-letter IATA code for Sapporo, important city in northern Japan.

Split *(Tourism)*: A term referred to a division into parts or pieces that has been previously agreed, such as a split commission, a split service, a split charter, etc.

Split *(Hospitality)*: A half bottle of wine containing about six ounces (187 ml), suitable for serving one person.

Split Charter *(Tourism)*: A charter where a number of consignments are carried to the same destination as partial loads that are treated as a single entity charter.

Split Payment Transaction *(Tourism)*: A transaction in which full payment is made in two or more parts, each by a different means, as when paying part by cash and part by a credit card, or by two different credit cards.

Split Service *(Hospitality)*: A food service method in which courses are served separately. This method helps maintain food quality and safety because each course is served when it is ready, eliminating short-term holding in the kitchen.

Split Ticketing *(Tourism)*: The issuance of separate tickets for a single journey, intended to obtain a lower fare, as when issuing two one-way tickets instead of a round-trip ticket.

SPML *(GDS)*: Code meaning Special Meal.

Spoiled Seat *(Airlines)*: An airline seat that remains empty on a flight causing a loss of revenue for the airline.

Spoiler *(Aeronautics)*: A long, movable, narrow plate located on the top of the wing used to change the airflow around a wing to reduce lift and increase drag.

Sponson *(Aeronautics)*: A short, wing-like protuberance on each side of a seaplane to increase lateral stability.

Sport Tourism *(Tourism)*: A type of tourism accomplished for the purpose of attending a specific sport event or to get engaged in a particular sport activity. Sport-oriented travel is nothing new (Romans and Greeks traveled to and participated in numerous sports events) but has become increasingly common in the tourism segment over last years. Likewise, the number of vacation destinations offering sport facilities has grown hugely. Cruise ships, hotels, theme parks, and communities all use sports as a marketing tool to appeal a specific target market, while nations and cities contend for the right to host sporting events, such as the World Football Cup, the Olympic Games or various championship series.

Sports Bar *(Hospitality)*: A pub type or restaurant that shows live sport events in television monitors.

Spouse Fares *(Airlines)*: A type of discounted air fare offered for husbands, wives or partners flying on the same flight as the business traveler.

Spumante *(Hospitality)*: An Italian term for sparkling wine.

SPT *(GDS)*: Code meaning Single Parent Tour.

SQ *(GDS)*: Code meaning: 1. Space Requested; 2. Singapore Airlines.

Squall *(Geography)*: A sudden attack of strong winds with speeds increasing to at least 16 knots (18 mph) and sustained at 22 or more knots (25 mph) for at least one minute.

Squall Line *(Air Traffic)*: A narrow band or line of active thunderstorms that is not associated with a cold front.

Squawk *(Air Traffic)*: A four-digit number which is dialed into his transponder by a pilot to identify his aircraft to air traffic controllers.

Squitter *(Air Traffic)*: The transmission of a specified reply format at a minimum rate without the need to be interrogated (transponders).

SR *(GDS)*: Code meaning Senior, Seniors.

SRO *(GDS)*: A code meaning Standing Room Only, typically in a theater.

SRVS *(GDS)*: Code meaning Serves, Servicing.

SRY *(GDS)*: Code meaning Sorry.

SS *(GDS)*: A code meaning: 1. Sold; 2. Supersaver Fare, when used with a fare type; 3. Steamship.

SSB *(Air Traffic)*: Single sideband. A highly efficient form of radio transmission used in HF communication transceivers.

SSCI *(Airlines)*: An abbreviation for Self-Service Check-In.

SSCVR *(Air Traffic)*: An abbreviation for Solid State Cockpit Voice Recorder.

SSIM *(GDS)*: Code meaning Standard Schedules Information Manual.

SSM *(GDS)*: A code meaning: 1. Segment Status Message; 2. Standard Schedules Message

SSR *(GDS)*: Code meaning Special Service Requirement.

SSSS *(Airlines)*: A code sometimes noted on a boarding pass warning that the passenger bearing it looks somehow suspicious.

SST *(GDS)*: Code meaning Self-service Terminal.

ST Category *(Cruise)*: A code used by some cruise lines denoting a "Suite Guarantee" cabin.

STA *(Air Traffic)*: A code meaning Scheduled Time of Arrival.

Stability *(Air Traffic)*: The condition of an aircraft when it is steady. A motion of an aircraft is said to have stability, or be stable, when it returns to that motion after a disturbance, without the pilot having to move the controls.

Stabilizer *(Air Traffic)*: The fixed part of a horizontal airfoil that helps to provide stability for an aircraft. Stabilizers are like the feathers of an arrow, which keep it pointed in the right direction. As opposed to the movable parts of the aircraft, which are the Elevators.

Stabilizers *(Cruise)*: Retractable devices looking like wings that extend from the sides of most all cruise vessels to reduce roll and produce a more stable ride. Stabilizers are usually pulled in at night in order to reach faster speeds when traveling between ports of call.

Stack *(Cruise)*: See Smokestack.

Stacking *(Air Traffic)*: The condition of an aircraft that is flying in large circles at two or more levels waiting for permission to land. This occurrence is frequent at busy airports.

Staff Captain *(Cruise)*: The official who is second in command on a cruise ship.

Stagnation Pressure *(Air Traffic)*: See Dynamic Pressure.

Stair Tower *(Cruise)*: A stairway on large cruise ships that connects several decks.

Stall *(Air Traffic)*: Sudden loss of lift when a wing or airfoil fails to generate enough lift to keep the plane stable and causing it to drop. It results when a wing exceeds its angle of attack, the airflow is disrupted, and the wing no longer produces lift, with sudden drop and possible loss of control.

Standard Atmosphere *(Air Traffic)*: It is the standard atmosphere established by the International Civil Aeronautical Organization (ICAO) for calibration of aircraft instruments. The presumed terms for standard atmosphere are: a mean sea level temperature of 15°C, a standard sea level pressure of 1,013.25 millibars or 29.92 inches of mercury, and a temperature lapse rate of 0.65°C per 100 meters up to 11 kilometers in the atmosphere.

Standard Atmospheric Pressure *(Air Traffic)*: For aviation purposes, 29.92 inches (1013.2 millibars) or 14.7# per square inch.

Standard Briefing *(Airlines)*: A complete and concise weather report including preparatory instructions, NOTAMS, military activities, flow control information, and other relating items.

Standard Clock Time *(Geography)*: See Greenwich Mean Time.

Standard Hotel *(Hospitality)*: A tourist or economy class hotel.

Standard Interline Passenger Procedure Codes *(Car Rental)*: A set of one-letter codes used to determine the category and features of the car that is being rented. These codes are formed by 4 letters to designate size, type, transmission and air conditioning (a/c), respectively. A quick description is displayed below:

First Letter Car Size	Second Letter Car Type	Third Letter Transmission	Fourth Letter Air Conditioning
M-Mini E-Economy C-Compact I-Intermediate S-Standard F-Full Size P-Premium L-Luxury X-Special	B-2 door C-2 or 4 door D-4 door F-Four Wheel Drive K-Truck T-Convertible W-Wagon X-Special	A-Automatic M-Manual	N-No A/C R-Has A/C

Standard Passenger Capacity *(Cruise)*: The optimum number of passengers determined by the manufacturer or operator of a vessel or vehicle.

Standard Rate Turn *(Air Traffic)*: A turn in which the heading of an aircraft changes 3° per second, or 360° in two minutes.

Standard Room *(Hospitality)*: The average rate room at a hotel.

Standard Temperature *(Air Traffic)*: For aviation purposes, 15°C (59°F).

Standard Terminal Arrival Route (STAR) *(Air Traffic)*: An ATC preplanned Instrument Flight Rule (IFR) arrival procedure published for pilots' use in graphic and textual form. STARs provide transition from the enroute structure to an instrument approach fix/arrival waypoint in the terminal area.

Standby *(Airlines)*: A term used to define the condition of a passenger who is not entitled to a firm reservation as in heavily discounted and conditioned fares or on a space-available basis tickets.

Standby Passenger *(Airlines)*: A passenger who boards a flight subject to space availability at departure time and only after all passengers having reservations and all paying passengers without reservations have boarded the flight. The Status Reservation code for such tickets is SA

STAR *(Air Traffic)*: See Standard Terminal Arrival Route.

Star Service *(Hospitality)*: A method to qualify the service at many hotel and cruise ship properties. It is not completely reliable due to its subjective character.

Starboard *(Cruise/Airlines)*: A nautical term for the right-hand direction or side of a ship or aircraft looking towards the front.

Starboard Side *(Cruise)*: See Starboard.

State Data *(Air Traffic)*: Data defining aircraft parameters, such as position, velocity, attitude.

State Rental Surcharge *(Car Rental)*: A tax levied by some states on car rentals.

Statement Scale *(Geography)*: A type of map scale which is written in words and numbers, such as 1 cm to 5 km.

Stateroom *(Cruise)*: A guest cabin aboard a ship. Another term for a cabin aboard a ship.

Static Package *(Tourism)*: A tour product, consisting of several elements, but without options for customization. It is opposite to Dynamic Package.

Static Wire *(Airlines)*: A wire used to ground an aircraft by drawing off static electricity that can be a potential fire hazard during refueling.

Station *(Airlines)*: A place to which a Location Identifier has been assigned.

Station *(Hospitality)*: A small place or table set for dining room staff's work.

Station *(Tourism):* A regular stopping place on a transportation route, as in a railroad, a bus route or an aircraft route.

Status *(Air Traffic)*: An indicator of how well a system or subsystem is working

Statute Mile *(Cruise)*: A unit of linear measure equal to 5,280 feet. There are 0.87 nautical miles in one statute mile and 1.15 statute miles in one nautical mile.

Stayover *(Hospitality)*: A room status term indicating a guest is not checking out but will remain at least one more night.

StB *(Airlines)*: See Simplifying the Business.

STCR *(GDS)*: Code meaning Stretcher Passenger.

STD *(GDS)*: A code meaning: 1. Scheduled Time of Departure. 2. Standard (as for a room). 3. Sexually-transmitted Disease.

Steam Beer *(Hospitality)*: A malt beverage brewed originally in

San Francisco, California. It receives a second fermentation which produces a creamy foam and high carbon dioxide content.

Steam Cooker *(Hospitality)*: An appliance that cooks food by the direct or indirect application of steam, resulting in a minimum of nutrient loss. It is also called steam-cooking equipment.

Steam Jacketed Kettle *(Hospitality)*: A steam cooker in which steam does not come into direct contact with food. The steam is jacketed or trapped within the kettles' walls.

Steam Room *(Hospitality)*: Tiled room with benches in which steam is generated at high pressure and temperature to open pores, eliminate toxins and relax the body. It can be infused with the aroma of essential oils.

Steam Tunnel *(Hospitality)*: Laundry equipment that moves articles on hangers through a tunnel where they are steamed as they are moved through.

Steamer *(Cruise)*: A ship that is powered by steam.

Steerage *(Cruise)*: Non advisable way of sea travel, made in an uncomfortable class, although at a very low price.

Stem *(Cruise)*: The leading edge of a ship's bow or prow.

Stem to Stern *(Cruise)*: An expression used to describe something extends from the front to the rear of a ship. It also suggests a thorough action completed.

Step-on Guide *(Tourism)*: A freelance guide who joins a tour bus to give an informed overview of the city or attraction to be toured.

Stepped Descent *(Air Traffic)*: A process by which aircraft descend by decreasing altitude in a series of stages prior to landing. See also Continuous Descent.

Sterile Filtration *(Hospitality)*: A process in which the fermentation of wine and beer is stopped and the product is passed through filters fine enough to remove yeasts, bacteria, and other microorganisms.

Sterilization *(Hospitality)*: A process that destroys virtually all microorganisms and their spores. One of the sterilization methods is by heating in a large container which is pressurized according to the food product.

Stern *(Cruise)*: The rearmost portion of a ship.

Stern Thruster *(Cruise)*: A propeller that is mounted at the rear of a vessel to get greater maneuverability at slow speeds.

Stevedore *(Cruise)*: A worker who loads and discharges cargo at a wharf or dock side. See also Longshoreman.

Steward *(Tourism)*: A ship's officer who is responsible for the care of passengers and who manages provisions and dining aboard a ship.

Steward *(Airlines)*: An attendant on an airplane who serves passengers and takes care of them.

Stewardess *(Airlines)*: A female flight attendant.

STG *(GDS)*: Code meaning Student Travel Grant.

Stiff *(Tourism)*: A slang term for avoiding deliberately tipping a service person.

Still *(Hospitality)*: An apparatus used in alcohol distillation process.

Stir Method *(Hospitality)*: A method of mixing cocktails that consists of stirring with a bar spoon for a proper mixture.

STMP *(Air Traffic)*: Special Traffic Management Program. It is a reservation program implemented to regulate arrivals and/or departures at airports that are in areas hosting special events.

STN *(GDS)*: Code meaning Station.

STO *(GDS)*: Code meaning: 1. Stockholm, capital city of Sweden; 2. Studio.

STOL *(Aeronautics)*: A type of aircraft designed for short takeoffs and landings in limited space.

StolPort *(Airlines)*: A land strip at an airport assigned to accommodate short take-off and landing aircraft.

Stopover *(Airlines)*: A voluntary interruption of the travel in an intermediate point. Usually a stopover occurs when a passenger arrives in an intermediate point and is not scheduled to depart within 24 hours of arrival; but it can also happen when a passenger interrupts his journey in an intermediate point an does not continue to the onward destination on the first available flight of the carrier of his/her choice. Stopovers add significant costs to an air fare.

Stow *(Tourism)*: A term used in the airline and cruise activities to instruct passengers for storing personal items in specific places as in the overhead bins.

Stowaway *(Tourism)*: A passenger who hides on an airplane or a ship intending to travel illegally and without paying.

STP *(GDS)*: Code meaning: 1. Stop; 2. Satellite Ticket Printer.

STPC *(GDS)*: Code meaning Layover at Carrier's Expenses.

STPN *(GDS)*: Code meaning Satellite Ticket Printer Network.

Strait *(Geography)*: A narrow channel connecting two larger bodies of water.

Straight Up *(Hospitality)*: Any drink served without ice. It is also called a Neat.

Straight Whiskey *(Hospitality)*: An alcoholic distillate of a fermented mash of grain, characterized by its taste, body, and aroma. It is bottled as it comes from the barrel in which it has matured.

Strategy *(Business)*: A careful plan or method that gather a set of coordinated actions for achieving an end. It can be defined as the art to prepare an action. A strategy performance requires that all the interdependent elements are taken into account as well as the formulation of a process.

Stratocumulus *(Geography)*: A low cloud of predominantly horizontal development in gray and/or whitish appearance.

Stratosphere *(Geography)*: The stratosphere is an Earth's layer located just above the troposphere, and below the mesosphere. It is very stable and characterized by low moisture content and absence of clouds. The stratosphere is situated in a range between about 10 km (6 miles) and 50 km (31 miles) altitude, although at the poles it starts at about 8 km (5 miles) altitude. Commercial airliners usually cruise at an altitude near 10 km in temperate latitudes, in the lower layers of the stratosphere.

Stratus *(Geography)*: A low, gray cloud layer with a fairly uniform base.

Streetcar *(Tourism)*: A sort of bus running on rails and moved by electric power used for public transportation in some cities.

Streetmosphere *(Tourism)*: A term resulting from the combination of "street" and "atmosphere" that describes the environment produced by street entertainers such as musicians or jugglers.

Stretch Limo *(Tourism)*: A limousine enlarged by the addition of an extra space between the driver's seat and the passenger area.

Stretched Vessel *(Tourism)*: A cruise ship that has been equipped with new parts or sections after manufacture, to increase its passenger capacity.

Stripped Package *(Tourism)*: A tour product meeting the minimum requirements for an IT qualification.

Student Visa *(Tourism)*: A type of visa granted to travelers who plan to attend an accredited educational institution during a specific period of time.

Student & Youth Travel Association (SYTA) *(Organizations)*: A non-profit, professional trade association that promotes student and youth travel and seeks to promote integrity and professionalism among student and youth travel service providers. SYTA members are Tour Operators, Travel Agencies and supplier organizations (Hotels, Restaurants, Attractions, Airlines, Destination Marketing Organizations, etc.) that are committed to professionalism and integrity in student and youth travel. Membership can be Active (Tour Operator & Travel Agencies) or Associate (Hotels, Restaurants, Attractions, Airlines, Destination Marketing Organizations, etc.). The organization has its headquarters in the metro Detroit, Michigan area.

Studio *(Hospitality)*: A one or two room apartment or efficiency with a combined living and sleeping area.

STVR *(GDS)*: Code meaning Stopover.

Style of Life *(Tourism)*: The way of living, the code of conduct of a social group. Quite often the style of life is associated to material priorities rather than to values and individual development.

SU *(GDS)*: Used with a fare SU indicates the traveler must stay over a Saturday night at his destination.

SUA *(Air Traffic)*: Code meaning Special Use Airspace.

Sub Recipe *(Hospitality)*: A recipe that is included as an ingredient within a standard recipe record.

SUBJ *(GDS)*: Code meaning Subject.

Sublimation *(Climate)*: A transition from the solid state to gas phase without passing by an intermediate phase of liquid. It occurs at temperatures and pressures below the sp-called "triple point".

Subsidiary *(Tourism)*: A company wholly owned or controlled by another main company.

Subsonic *(Aeronautics)*: An aircraft flying at a velocity lower than the speed of sound. Many of the commercial airplanes do not fly above the speed of sound.

Subtropical *(Geography)*: A region located between the tropical and temperate regions. It is an area between 35° and 40° North and South latitude of semi-permanent high pressure.

SUBTTL *(Airlines)*: An abbreviation for Subtotal NUC.

Suburban Hotel *(Hospitality)*: A hotel usually smaller than a downtown hotel, which is located in the environs of a city.

Subway *(Tourism)*: An underground railway system built for urban mass transportation. It is also an underground pedestrian passageway.

Suite *(Hospitality)*: A hotel accommodation with more than one room that includes a sitting room, and sometimes a kitchen.

Suite Hotel *(Hospitality)*: A hotel whose sleeping rooms have separate bedroom and living room or parlor areas, and perhaps kitchenettes.

Summit *(Tourism)*: The action of climbing to the highest point of a mountain.

SUN *(GDS)*: Code meaning Sunday.

Sun Deck *(Cruise)*: The open area on the upper deck of a ship used for sunbathing.

Sunday Rule *(Tourism)*: A rule for a type of fare requiring the passengers commence the return travel from the point of turnaround not before 00:01 hour on the Sunday following the day of outbound departure. The traveler must stay over a Saturday night at his destination.

Sundries *(Tourism)*: A set of small personal articles (toiletries or grooming).

Sunstroke *(Tourism)*: A bodily heat stroke caused by an over exposure to the sun.

SUP *(GDS)*: Code meaning Superior Room.

Supercomputer *(Computing)*: An especial computer designed to receive, process and display very large amounts of data very quickly.

Supercooled Water *(Hospitality)*: Water that has been cooled below the freezing point, but is still in a liquid state.

Super-elite *(Tourism)*: A level of a frequent flyer program above the elite level. Super-elite programs are available by invitation only.

Super-jumbo Jet *(Aeronautics)*: An aircraft designed to carry more than 500 passengers.

Supercharged *(Aeronautics)*: Method for increasing the power of an aircraft engine.

Superior Room *(Hospitality)*: A hotel room better than the standard, with more amenities or a better location.

Superapex (AB) *(GDS)*: Abbreviation meaning Advance Purchase Excursion Fares. They are very restricted fares.

Superliner *(Tourism)*: A term used to define a large luxury cruise vessel or a luxury train.

Superpex (SX) *(GDS)*: Abbreviation meaning Very Restricted Instant Purchase Fares.

Supersaver *(Airlines)*: A type of low discount airfare available but heavily restricted.

Supersonic *(Aeronautics)*: An aircraft faster than the speed of sound. Its speed of flight ranges between 750 mph and 1500 mph, greater than Mach 1.0. A typical example of a supersonic aircraft was the Concorde that could fly from New York to London in less than two hours. After it ceased operating in 2003, the majority of supersonic aircraft today are military or experimental aircraft.

Supersonic Flight *(Aeronautics)*: Any flight at speeds greater than the speed of sound.

Supersonic Transport *(Aeronautics)*: See Supersonic.

Superstructure *(Cruise)*: The part above the waterline of a cruise ship.

SUPL *(GDS)*: Code meaning Supplementary.

Supl Info *(Tourism)*: Abbreviation meaning Supplementary Information.

Supplement *(Tourism)*: An additional charge on regular fares or rates required to grant services not included in the regular price.

Supplemental Airline or Carrier *(Tourism)*: An airline whose operations are not subjected to scheduled departure and arrival times. It is a charter operator.

Supplemental Liability Coverage *(Car Rental)*: See Supplemental Liability Insurance below.

Supplemental Liability Insurance (SLI) *(Car Rental)*: An extra automobile liability coverage that protects all authorized drivers of the rental car against third-party bodily injury and property-damage claims.

Supplier *(Tourism)*: Any company that provides travel, accommodation, entertainment, transportation, sightseeing and/or related services to the traveling public.

Supply Chain Management *(Tourism)*: The management activity to ensure that products and services are offered in the right quantities, in the right locations, and at the right time, in order to maximize resource productivity and minimize waste and system-wide costs while satisfying customer needs.

SUR *(GDS)*: Code meaning Surface (Transportation made by ship, rail or bus).

Surcharge *(Tourism)*: An additional fee charged for the provision of certain additional features or because of special circumstances.

Surety *(Tourism)*: An agreement or obligation used to guarantee the performance or completion of an activity or service.

Surf *(Geography)*: The waves that break upon the ocean shore.

Surface *(Tourism)*: A portion of an air travel that is not flown. The surface transportation is covered by means of any other type of land vehicle, such as a train, a bus, or an automobile.

Surface Acoustic Wave (SAW) *(Airlines)*: A technology used for unique automatic identification in which low power microwave radio frequency signals are converted to ultrasonic acoustic signals.

Surface Analysis Chart (SA) *(Airlines)*: An aviation weather chart used to show air pressure patterns, high and low pressure areas, fronts, and station models.

Surface Aviation Weather Reports (SA) *(Air Traffic)*: A report that provides pilots with an observation of surface weather and includes a detailed information on sky conditions and ceiling, visibility, weather obstructions, pressure, temperature and dew point, wind information, station reporting, and time of report.

Surface Sector *(Airlines)*: A sector between two intermediate points of the fare component where travel is via a vehicle other than an aircraft. In the case of a mileage fare, the ticketed mileage between the origin and destination of the surface sector is usually included in the TPM calculation of the through fare component. In the case of a routing fare, both the origin and destination of the surface sector should be on the specified routing. The fare over the surface sector is covered by the through fare component.

Surface Movement Advisor (SMA) *(Airlines)*: In the USA, a joint FAA and NASA project to help current airport facilities operate more efficiently.

Surfing *(Tourism)*: A sport consisting of riding the sea waves using specially designed boards.

Survey *(Tourism)*: A research performed on basis of questionnaires aimed at discovering and interpreting the consumers' attitudes or behaviors.

Survivability *(Air Traffic)*: A subsystem's ability to detect and counterfight hostile environments and actions.

Sustainability *(Ecology)*: The capability of a system to survive for a specified time.

Sustainable Agriculture *(Ecology)*: A method of growing crops and raising livestock by the use of organic fertilizers, water conservation, and minimal use of non-renewable fossil-fuel energy.

Sustainable Development *(Ecology)*: A form of economic development that does not deplete or degrade natural resources upon which present and future economic growth and life depend. It is a responsible type of development that meets the needs of the present without compromising the ability of future generations to meet their own needs. The notion of sustainable development has been imposed as a necessity since 1980. The first definition was introduced in 1987 by the World Commission for the Environment.

Sustainable Living *(Ecology)*: Living in such a way that it does not take more potentially renewable resources from the natural world than can be replenished naturally.

Sustainable Society *(Ecology)*: A society that manages its economy and population size by working with nature to avoid irreparable environmental damages. It is a society that satisfies the needs of its members without depleting earth capital and thereby jeopardizing the prospects of current and future generations of humans and other species.

Sustainable System *(Ecology)*: A system that survives and attains its full expected lifetime.

Sustainable Tourism *(Tourism)*: According to the World Tourism Organization it is the management of all resources in such a way that economic, social, and aesthetic needs can be fulfilled while maintaining cultural integrity, essential ecological processes, biological diversity, and life support systems. The Report Brundtland entitled "Our Common Future" imposed the concept of Sustainable Tourism in 1987. And the World Conference on Sustainable Tourism held in Lanzarote, Spain in 1990 adopted a declaration affirming that Sustainable Tourism should be performed on basis of durability, economically sustainable at long term and coordinated with local plans of social and ethic development.

Sustainable Yield or Sustained Yield *(Ecology)*: The highest rate at which a potentially renewable resource can be used without reducing its available supply.

SV *(GDS)*: Code meaning Sailing Vessel.

SVC *(GDS)*: Code meaning Service.

SVO *(GDS)*: Three-letter IATA code for Sheremetyevo International Airport, serving the city of Moscow, Russia.

SVRL *(GDS)*: Code meaning Several.

SVRWX *(Air Traffic)*: Severe Weather.

SVW *(GDS)*: Code meaning Sea View.

SW *(GDS)*: Code meaning Software.

SWAP *(Air Traffic)*: See Severe Weather Avoidance Plan.

SWB *(GDS)*: Code meaning Single Room with Bath.

Swedish Massage *(Tourism)*: Massage in which oils are applied to the body with techniques including effleurage, friction and vibration.

Swept-wing *(Air Traffic)*: A wing in which both the leading and trailing edges are slanted backward, to reduce air resistance at high speed.

SWIFT Code *(Business)*: An alphanumeric code used by the banking system to identify a financial institution. Swift Codes are used to make international wire transfers.

Swing Shift *(Hospitality)*: The work period extending from 4 p.m.

to 12 midnight.

Swing-Wing *(Aeronautics)*: A wing whose horizontal angle to the fuselage centerline can be adjusted in flight to vary aircraft motion at differing speeds.

SWP *(IATA Geography)*: See South West Pacific.

SX *(Airlines)*: Used with a fare type, it means Superpex fare. They are very restricted Instant Purchase Fares.

SXF *(GDS)*: Three-letter IATA code for Schoenefeld International Airport, serving the city of Berlin.

SXM *(GDS)*: Three-letter IATA code for Saint Martin.

SYD *(GDS)*: Three-letter IATA code for Sydney, the most important city in Australia.

Symbiotic *(Ecology)*: A term referring to a component or member of a system of symbiosis.

Synchro *(Aeronautics)*: Any device capable of converting mechanical position into an analog electronic signal.

Synthesizer *(Air Traffic)*: Frequency synthesizer, an electronic circuit capable of generating multiple frequencies from a single crystal oscillator.

System *(Tourism)*: A group of independent but interrelated elements comprising a unified whole. Tourism is a typical example of system. Instead of being an industry, tourism is a complex whole resulting from the combination of various interrelated elements, such as transportation, accommodation, entertainment, etc. Each of these elements is at its turn, a subsystem comprising respective composing elements. As a whole, tourism is a vast system of production, distribution and consumption as well.

System *(Ecology)*: A group of units so combined as to form a whole.

System One *(GDS)*: An independent Global Distribution System.

System Provider *(Airlines)*: See Computer Reservations System.

System-wide Revenue *(Hospitality)*: The total amount of revenue obtained at all of a hotel company's locations, both company-owned and franchised.

SYTA *(Organizations)*: An acronym for Student & Youth Travel Association.

T

T *(Airlines)*: "Tango," name used to designate the letter "T" in the International Phonetic Alphabet.

T *(GDS)*: Code for Economy coach discounted fare.

T&D *(Business)*: An abbreviation meaning Training and Development.

T&E *(Business)*: An abbreviation meaning Travel and Entertainment.

TA *Airlines)*: Two-letter IATA code for Taca International S.A., the airline of the Central American countries.

TA *(GDS)*: Code meaning Travel Agent.

TA *(Air Traffic)*: A code for Traffic Advisory (TCAS).

TAAD *(Tourism)*: An abbreviation meaning Travel Agent Automated Deduction

Tab *(Hospitality)*: A small addition, as in a restaurant.

Table Assignment *(Cruise)*: A specified assignment of table and seating at a meal shift.

Table d'hote *(Hospitality)*: A French term meaning literally "table of the host" used to describe a full-course meal with limited choice of dishes at a fixed price.

Table d'hôte menu *(Hospitality)*: A menu offering two or more course choices with pre-set prices.

Table Lectern *(Hospitality)*: A raised table to hold a speaker's papers.

Table Service *(Hospitality)*: A type of service in which guests are served food while seated at a table.

Table Skirt *(Hospitality)*: A piece of linen used to cover the sides of the table.

Table Tent *(Hospitality)*: A folded card placed on a restaurant table to display specials or promotions.

Tableside Service *(Hospitality)*: See French Service.

Table Top Display *(Hospitality)*: A portable display that is used on top of a table.

TAC *(GDS)*: Code meaning Travel Agency Commission.

TACAN *(Air Traffic)*: See Tactical Air Navigation Aid.

TACAN Station *(Air Traffic)*: A ground-based station with a radio that continuously transmits navigational signals on an assigned frequency to determine the range and position to a radio station with a TACAN transmitter. TACAN stations constitute a global navigation system for civilian and military aircraft operating at L-band frequencies (1 gigahertz).

Tachometer *(Aeronautics)*: A device for measuring an aircraft's angular velocity.

Tactical Air Navigation Aid (TACAN) *(Air Traffic)*: TACAN is a type of radio air navigation aid of ultra-high frequency system that provides air crew with continuous positioning and distance information from the aircraft to the station. The TACAN operates in combination with a TACAN ground station, but can also operate as both the interrogator and transponder with another aircraft equipped with TACAN.

Tactical Discounting *(Tourism)*: The routine of offering reduced prices in a limited amount in order to attract additional purchasers from a targeted market.

TAF *(Air Traffic)*: See Terminal Airport Forecast.

Tag *(Airlines)*: An attached stick used to identify and track baggage.

Tai Chi *(Tourism)*: Series of graceful movements that combine mental concentration with deep, controlled breathing and balance that contribute to bring about relaxation and good health.

Tail Numbers *(Airlines)*: The registration number of an aircraft painted on its fuselage or tail.

Tailplane *(Airlines)*: See Horizontal Stabilizer.

Takeoff *(Air Traffic)*: The process of using the power of the engines to accelerate an airplane along a runway until the aircraft breaks contact with the ground.

Takeoff Roll *(Air Traffic)*: The part of takeoff where the aircraft's landing gear is still in contact with the ground.

Tandem bicycle *(Tourism)*: A bicycle built to carry two persons.

Tango *(Airlines)*: Designator for the letter "T" in the International Phonetic Alphabet.

Tapas *(Tourism)*: Spanish snacks served with wine at a bar or at a *tasca*.

Target *(Air Traffic)*: In the traffic controllers' language, an aircraft appearing on an air radar scope.

Tariff *(Airlines)*: A term used for any listing of fares, rates, charges, prices, etc. The term Tariff is most frequently used in reference to fare listings for international transportation by air, sea or land. Air carriers particularly publish tariffs compiling fares rates, charges and/or related conditions of a carrier.

Tariff *(Customs)*: Lists of duties charged by governments on imports or exports.

Tariff Rules *(Airlines)*: Also known as Notes, they are the general terms and conditions applicable to each air fare.

Tarmac *(Air Traffic)*: The paved area of an airport where planes wait, take off or land.

TAS *(Air Traffic)*: See True Air Speed.

Tasca *(Hospitality)*: A Spanish term to define a tavern or bar that offers *tapas* and wine.

TAT *(GDS)*: Code meaning Transitional Automated Ticket.

Tatami *(Hospitality)*: A straw mat, used especially in Japanese homes or traditional lodges as a floor covering.

TATCA *(Air Traffic)*: An abbreviation for Terminal Air Traffic Control Automation

Taxi *(Air Traffic)*: The journey of an airplane under its own power on the surface of an airport. Aircraft usually taxi between its loading point and takeoff point and from its landing position to its unloading point. The term also describes the movement of helicopters with wheels on the surface.

Taxi Ecologico *(Tourism)*: See Cycle Rickshaws.

Taxiway *(Air Traffic)*: A way or paved surface at an airport which allows aircraft to travel between runways and other airport locations such as hangars or terminals.

Taxonomy *(Ecology)*: The classification of living organisms according to a pre-determined system hierarchical factors and relationships.

TBA *(GDS)*: Code meaning To Be Announced.

TBO *(Airlines)*: An abbreviation for Time Between Overhaul.

TBD *(Air Traffic)*: An abbreviation meaning To Be Determined or To Be Documented.

TBF *(GDS)*: Code meaning Total Body Fitness.

TBF Travel *(Tourism)*: A travel accomplished to participate in total body fitness events.

TBR *(Air Traffic)*: An abbreviation meaning To be Resolved.

TBS *(Air Traffic)*: An abbreviation meaning To Be Supplied.

TC *(GDS)*: Code meaning Tour Conductor.

TCA *(Air Traffic)*: See Terminal Control Area.

TCAS *(Air Traffic)*: See Traffic Collision Avoidance System.

TC1 *(IATA Geography)*: See Area 1.

TC2 *(IATA Geography)*: See Area 2.

TC3 *(IATA Geography)*: See Area 3.

TCN *(Air Traffic)*: Code for Tacan.

TCP *(GDS)*: Code meaning To Complete Party.

TCNP *(Air Traffic)*: Code meaning Tacan Point-to-Point

TC's *(Airlines)*: Code meaning Transfer Connections.

TD *(GDS)*: Code meaning Ticket Designator.

TDA *(GDS)*: Code meaning Today.

TDD *(Car Rental)*: See Telecommunications Device for the Deaf.

TDOR *(GDS)*: Code meaning Two-door Car.

TECH *(GDS)*: Code meaning Technical.

Technical Landing or Stop *(Air Traffic)*: A landing for non-traffic purposes, as for refueling. Passengers cannot embark or disembark at this point.

Technology *(Aeronautics)*: The scientific study that involves the generation of knowledge and processes, development of devices, methods and techniques to foster systems that solve problems and expand human capabilities. Its practical application extends to commerce or industry activities.

Technotourisme *(Tourism)*: A French term referring to a type of tourism that requires heavy equipment, infrastructure and large investment for its operation. It is opposed to Ecotourism which is considered to be a light kind of tourism.

Telecommunications Device for the Deaf (TDD) *(Car Rental)*: A device service available upon request at the moment of reserving the vehicle.

Telecommute *(Computing)*: A way of working at home while linked to the office by a computer.

Telecommuter *(Computing)*: A person who works at his/her home using a computer linked to his/her office.

Teleconference *(Computing)*: The live exchange of information to geographically dispersed downlink sites via telephone, computer network connection, or satellite. It is a an audio conference with one or both ends of the conference sharing a speaker phone, by which group of persons participate actively. Today's audio teleconferences use over dial-up phone lines with bridging services that provide the necessary equipment for the call.

Teleferic *(Tourism)*: A cable car system consisting of a passenger cabin and a set of air cables that pull it from one place to another.

Telegraph *(Airlines)*: A communication system used to send coded messages by wire. It uses a special language developed by Guglielmo Marconi at the beginning of the 20th century.

Telemarketing *(Business)*: A method of direct marketing used by companies to advertise and sell their products and offer their services. It is usually performed by a team of salespersons who contact prospective customers over the phone, by fax or via Internet means. There are professional telemarketers or call centers that companies hire to contact potential customers on their behalf.

Telematics *(Computing)*: The science of using computers in concert with telecommunications systems to transmit and store information data from machine to machine. It is a mix of resources and services that includes dial-up service to the Internet and all types of telecommunications systems and networks to transport data. One of its most popular applications is in the Global Positioning System.

Temperature *(Climate)*: In physics, temperature is a measure of the energy in a substance. The more heat energy is concentrated in the substance, the higher is the temperature. The Earth receives a slightest amount of the energy the sun produces. Notwithstanding, as the surface warms, it also warms the air above it. Temperature is one of the elements forming a climate. It is the degree of heat or cold measured in the atmosphere on a definite scale by means of a thermometer.

Temperate Climatic Zones *(Geography)*: These are areas of the earth of mild climates, without extreme temperatures. There are two temperate zones, respectively located between the Tropic of

Cancer (at about 23.5 degrees north latitude) and the Arctic Circle (at about 66.6 degrees north latitude) and between the Tropic of Capricorn (at about 23.5 degrees south latitude) and the Antarctic Circle (at about 66.5 degrees south latitude).

Temperature-dew Point Spread *(Climate)*: The difference between air temperature and dew point temperature. Surface temperature and dew point spread are important in anticipating the formation of fog.

Temperate Zones *(Geography)*: See Temperate Climatic Zones.

Temperature Controlled Cargo *(Airlines)*: Any cargo that requires special controlled temperatures during the carriage.

Temperature Index *(Climate)*: A comparative value indicating the number of degrees above or below a temperature of reference, such as a long-term average.

Temperature Inversion *(Climate)*: A temperature condition in which a mass of cold air is trapped beneath a mass of warm air.

TEMPO *(GDS)*: Code meaning Temporary, Temporally.

Temps Universel Coordonné *(Geography)*: See Coordinated Universal Time.

TEN *(GDS)*: Code meaning Ticket Exchange Notice.

Tender or Launch *(Cruise)*: A small vessel that moves cruise passengers to and from the shore when the ship is anchored.

Tent *(Tourism)*: A collapsible shelter of material stretched held up by poles and held down by stakes in the ground.

Tequila *(Hospitality)*: A Mexican liquor distilled from the fermented juice of the blue variety of the agave plant.

Terminal *(Airlines)*: A building or buildings designed to accommodate the embarking and disembarking activities of air carrier passengers. By extension, the train or bus stations where routes end or start.

Terminal Airport Forecast (TAF) *(Air Traffic)*: A weather report generated at a particular airport, predicting the weather conditions at that airport area. It is issued four times a day and includes usually wind direction and speed, visibility, sky conditions, cloud cover and cloud type, wind shear indications, and precipitation.

Terminal Control Area (TCA) *(Air Traffic)*: An assigned zone around and above busiest airports requiring special skills from the pilot and special aircraft and communication conditions.

Terminal Forecast (FT) *(Air Traffic)*: Predictions of future weather (up to 24 hours) at a particular airport.

Terminal Points *(Airlines)*: The origin and destination points of a fare component.

Terminal Radar Approach Control Facility (TRACON) *(Air Traffic)*: An Air Traffic Control facility that uses radar and non-radar capabilities to monitor and direct air traffic through the approaching, descending, departing, climbing, or transiting phases of a flight.

Terminal Radar Service Area (TRSA) *(Air Traffic)*: The airspace surrounding designated airports where ATC provides radar vectoring, sequencing, and separation on a full-time basis for all IFR and VFR aircraft.

Terminating Flight *(Air Traffic)*: A flight, identified by a Flight Number, ending at certain station.

Terms and Conditions *(Tourism)*: The information included in a tour or cruise document detailing the conditions in which the service is performed, especially the liability and responsibility limitations.

Terms and Conditions of Carriage *(Airlines)*: Terms and Conditions of Carriage are stipulations contained in an air carrier's tariff that are applied by the carrier to all of its passengers regardless of the fare paid. They are in fact the clauses of the air transportation contract, which explain the benefits and limitations associated to the service provided by air carriers. Terms and Conditions of Carriage refer such subjects as limitations or restrictions on free baggage allowance; compensation for lost, delayed or damaged luggage; compensation for denied boarding, and the carrier's rules concerning the carriage of persons with disabilities or minors. Since airlines do not issue paper tickets any more, they are obligated to print the terms and conditions of carrier for the passenger's knowledge. Terms and Conditions of Carriage are regulated by IATA Resolution 724, Attachment A, and the legal notices provided for in Resolution 724, Attachments B and C, Resolution 724a, 724b and Resolution 745.

Terra Incognita *(Geography)*: A Latin expression meaning an unexplored territory.

Terrain *(Geography)*: The contour of the earth regarding its topographical features or fitness for a certain use.

Terrain Avoidance (TA) *(Air Traffic)*: Flight operated in such a manner that aircraft maintain a constant barometric altitude but avoiding obstacles, even thin objects (like wires).

Terrain Following (TF) *(Air Traffic)*: A basic guidance mode that provides vertical guidance to maintain a selected radar altitude above the terrain. Pilots try to maintain a constant height above the terrain, usually in the range of 100-1,000 feet.

Terrain Referenced Navigation (TRN) *(Air Traffic)*: A navigation mode based on comparison of barometric altitude and radar altitude with a map.

Terrestrial Radiation *(Geography)*: The total infrared radiation emitted by the earth and its atmosphere.

Terrorism *(Tourism)*: A political action of individuals of organized minorities using terror and violence as a means of coercion. Terrorism is one of the fiery enemies of Tourism.

Test Pilot *(Air Traffic)*: A pilot who is specially trained to test aircraft.

Tetrahedron *(Air Traffic)*: A ground-based, free-rotating, triangular-shaped wind direction indicator generally placed near a runway.

TFC *(GDS)*: A code meaning: 1. Taxes, Fees and Charges; 2. Traffic.

TGC *(GDS)*: Code meaning Travel Group Charters.

TGU *(GDS)*: Three-letter IATA code for Tegucigalpa, the capital city of Honduras.

TGV *(GDS)*: An acronym meaning *Train de Grande Vitesse*, name given to the French high-speed train system.

Thai Massage *(Tourism)*: Traditional massage from Thailand that involves a combination of stretching and gentle rocking, and uses a range of motions and acupressure techniques.

Thalassotherapy *(Cruise)*: Therapeutic method consisting of a hot bath with sea water, seaweed, sand or sea mud that help remove toxins and increase circulation when used in association with bioclimatic conditions under medical supervision. It is a therapy featured by several cruise ships.

The Air Cargo Tariff (TACT) *(Airlines)*: Rates, rules and regulations published for international air shipments.

The Fifth Utility *(Tourism)*: A jargon term for GPS technology or devices.

The Grand Tour *(Tourism)*: See Grand Tour.

The   International   Air   Cargo   Association   (TIACA) *(Organizations)*: TIACA is an association organized to advance the interests of the air cargo industry and strengthen its contribution to world trade expansion. Its objectives are aimed to support and assist progressive liberalization of the global market and easier, enhanced trade between developing and developed economies.

The International Ecotourism Society (TIES) *(Organizations)*: The world's oldest and largest ecotourism organization committed to promoting the principles of ecotourism and responsible travel. TIES gather members in over 90 countries, as the global source of knowledge and advocacy in ecotourism. Focused on the aim of uniting conservation, communities and sustainable travel, TIES promotes responsible travel to natural areas for conserving the environment and improving the well-being of local people.

Theater Setup *(Hospitality)*:   A meeting configuration as in a theater, where seats are arranged in rows facing front.

Theft Protection *(Car Rental)*: Type of insurance that covers the renter in the event the vehicle is stolen but does not cover belongings inside the vehicle.

Thematic Map *(Geography)*: A type of map showing a particular topic or theme, such as climate.

Thematic Park *(Tourism)*: An amusement space offering cultural or entertainment attractions related to specific themes or based on defined characters or situations. In a theme park all the entertainments go with the theme of the park, for example Magic Kingdom in Walt Disney World. The concept of thematic parks was conceived by Walt Disney and requires a sophisticated technology and specially trained staffs.

Theme Cruise *(Cruise)*: A cruise in which entertainment is the core attraction. It offers or suggests a specific onboard theme, such as music, dancing, gambling, sports, history, etc.

Theme Park *(Tourism)*: See Thematic Park.

Theme Party *(Hospitality)*: An event that organizes food service, entertainment, and decorations around a central theme.

Theme Restaurant *(Hospitality)*: A restaurant designed with a combination of decor, atmosphere and menu around a particular theme such as a sport, an era atmosphere, a style of music, or a character. Usually theme establishments are operated in a theatrical fashion.

Thermal Baths of Caracalla *(Tourism)*: See Caracalla Thermal Baths.

Thermal Neutron Analysis *(Airlines)*: A technology used for screening baggage.

Thermal Waters *(Tourism)*: Natural water with particular mineral characteristics, generally glowing of a spring or geyser. Its temperature is above the local average air temperature and is used in some pathologic treatments.

Thermosphere *(Geography)*: The atmospheric layer located between the mesosphere and the exosphere, between 85 and 500 kilometers above the Earth's surface, in which temperature steadily increases with height. It includes all of the exosphere and most of the ionosphere.

THF *(GDS)*: Three-letter IATA code for Tempelhof Airport, serving the city of Berlin.

Third Freedom of the Air *(Airlines)*: The freedom to carry passengers, goods and mail from the airline's home country to a foreign country for commercial purposes.

Third Party *(Tourism)*: Any person who acts on behalf of another person.

Third Party Booking Engine *(Hospitality)*: An internet site with a large data basis of lodging facilities that provides a booking engine where travelers can search for availability and reserve a room. The properties are not affiliated with the site and pay a commission for the business generated by third parties.

Third World *(Geography)*: A subjective term used to qualify developing countries in comparison with the self called first world countries. The French demographer Alfred Sauvy coined the expression (*tiers monde* in French) in 1952 by analogy with the "third estate". At that time, there was a group of countries that neither belonged to the industrialized capitalist world nor to the industrialized communist bloc. It was necessary, then, to create a concept that would comprise such countries as an entity with common characteristics, such as poverty, high birthrates, and economic dependence on the advanced countries. The term, nevertheless, implies that the third world is exploited, much as the commoners of France (the third state) before and during the French Revolution. But now, the third world term has no application, as no application has the "second world" identified in the communist bloc that does not exist anymore. The actual world situation is that the world is divided into two groups of nations: The first, characterized by its high industrialized and technological development quite often built over the depending relationship with the other group, and the second group which is marked by highly dependent economies devoted to producing primary products for the developed world and to provide markets for their finished goods. The truth behind this condition is a well orchestrated plan to maintain the current situation for the well being of the wealthy group.

THR *(GDS)*: Three-letter IATA code for Teheran, capital city of Iran.

Thread Count *(Hospitality)*: A method used in hotels to measure the quality of bed sheets. The higher the thread count, the finer the sheet.

Threatened Species *(Ecology)*: Wild species that may be still abundant but are in risk of danger because of a decline in numbers.

Three Holer *(Airlines)*: A slang term to denote a three engine aircraft.

Three Letter Codes *(Airlines)*: The language of the airline business has to be concise and precise to expedite communications. For that reason, IATA introduced a coded language. Some of the terms used are three letter codes to denominate cities, airports and currencies. For example, the three letter code for Beijing, China is BJS; Buenos Aires, Argentina is coded BUE; the three letter code for John F. Kennedy airport is JFK; the Japanese currency (Yen) is coded JPY; the three letter code for the Sterling Pound is GBP.

Throttle *(Air Traffic)*: A flight control operated by moving manually fore or aft.

Throttle Cue *(Air Traffic)*: A longitudinal flight director cue for fixed-wing aircraft, primarily to control speed by changing power.

Through Cargo *(Airlines)*: Cargo that stays on board at a stopping place en-route for ongoing carriage on the same flight.

Through Charge *(Airlines)*: The total amount charged from point of origin to point of destination.

Through Fare or Throughfare *(Airlines)*: Fare applicable for travel between two consecutive construction points via intermediate points. It is synonymous with Published Fare or Direct Fare.

Through Passenger *(Airlines)*: A passenger who remain on board at a stopping place while enroute to the final destination.

Through Route *(Airlines)*: The total route from point of departure to point of destination.

Through Service *(Airlines)*: A flight that stops at intermediate points not requiring a change of planes.

Throughput *(Air Traffic)*: The amount of aircraft flying through the airspace system in a given period.

Throwaway *(Tourism)*: It is something made to be discarded after use, but in tourism it is a part of a tour package that is paid for but is not used. Somehow, it is discarded.

THRU *(GDS)*: A code for Through

THRU FLT *(Airlines)*: An abbreviation meaning Direct Flight.

Thrust *(Aeronautics)*: The force produced when air is pushed rearward by jet engines or propellers, thus pushing an aircraft forward. It is defined as the forward reaction to the rearward movement of a jet exhaust.

THTL *(GDS)*: Tourist Class Hotel.

THU *(GDS)*: Code for Thursday.

THX *(GDS)*: Code for Thanks.

TIA *(Organizations)*: An acronym for Travel Industry Association of America.

TIAC *(Organizations)*: An acronym for Travel Industry Association of Canada.

TIACA *(Organizations)*: An acronym for The International Air Cargo Association.

Ticket (*Airlines*): The Electronic Ticket issued by or on behalf of an air carrier, which includes Conditions of Contract and notices.

Ticket Agent (*Airlines*): Any person or company that is involved in the sale of air transportation.

Ticket Association (*Airlines*): The process that associates an existing ticket with an existing booking (PNR) or check-in record. Sometimes the itinerary on the associated ticket does not match exactly with that in the booking or check-in record.

Ticket Designator (*Airlines*): A code usually referring to a discounted fare.

Ticket on Departure (*Airlines*): A ticket that will be picked up by the passenger at the airport check-in counter. It is a usual practice with Prepaid Ticket Advice.

Ticket Swiping (*Airlines*): An illegal practice of reimbursing unused nonrefundable tickets to agents instead of doing to the original payer when refund is applicable. Most unused tickets are not refundable, but some of them are reroutable.

Ticketed (*Airlines*): A PNR booking for which a ticket has been issued.

Ticketed Point (*Airlines*): Each of the points of the route as shown in the passenger ticket.

Ticketed Point Mileage (TPM) (*Airlines*): The distance between every subsequent pair of cities on an itinerary. It is also the sum of all the partial mileages of a fare component.

Ticketing (*Airlines*): The process of pricing and issuing tickets for an air transportation already booked.

Ticketing, Back-to-Back (*Airlines*): See Back-to-Back Ticketing.

Ticketing Deadline (*Airlines*): The number of days before the date of departure or number of hours or days after confirmed reservations by which payment and ticketing must be completed. Issue date of a PTA constitutes the ticketing date.

Ticketing, Hidden-city (*Airlines*): See Hidden-city Ploy.

Ticketing Time Limit (*Airlines*): An expression referring to the time by which a passenger must pay for his ticket for a confirmed reservation as required by the carrier.

Ticketless Travel (*Airlines*): The travel a passenger makes under an electronic ticket, case in which there is no more paper ticket.

Tipping *(Tourism)*: The practice of giving tips. Tipping is common, and even expected in some countries, such as the United States, but is rare in others, such as France. In some other, such as China, tipping can be considered an offense or an illegal act.

Tidal Flat *(Geography)*: A type of shoreline which is exposed when the water withdraws at low tide.

Tidal Wave *(Geography)*: An anomalous destructive wave generated by a storm, earthquake, or other natural event.

TIDS *(Airlines)*: See Travel Industry Designator Service.

TIDS *(Airlines)*: See Travel Intermediary Designator Service.

Tie-in *(Tourism)*: The method of linking products or promotions, as when frequent travelers earn air miles by using a particular hotel accommodation.

Tie-up *(Tourism)*: 1. A transitory halt in business; 2. A temporary stop in traffic caused by accident or congestion; 3. A cord to secure small boats.

TIES *(Organizations)*: An acronym for The International Ecotourism Society.

Tilt Rotor or Tiltrotor *(Aeronautics)*: An aircraft with tilting rotors for fixed-wing flight or rotary-wing flight that is tilted from a horizontal alignment for takeoff and landing, to a vertical alignment for level flight.

Tilt-wing *(Aeronautics)*: Wing that can be rotated so as to facilitate landing or taking off an aircraft in short distances.

Time and Mileage *(Car Rental)*: A term to define the time and mileage included in the basic rental price. Airport fees, taxes and/or surcharges are calculated separately.

Time Share *(Hospitality)*: A form of shared property ownership in which a person purchases from a specialized promoter the right to occupy a part of a property such as a condominium in a resort area, during a specified time unit (usually one week) each year. This right can be transferred, leased, sold or exchanged for accommodation in another property of the same company.

Time Sharing or Time–sharing *(Hospitality)*: See Time Share.

Time Zone *(Geography)*: Each of the artificial divisions of the world east and west of the Prime Meridian, which is the universal standard time. There are 24 time zones usually extended across fifteen degrees of longitude, each representing a different hour of the day. However, time zones are not of equal size; political and geographical factors can generate irregularly-shaped zones that follow political boundaries or that change their time seasonally. For instance, while Canada is divided into five time zones (Atlantic, Eastern, Central, Mountain and Pacific), China has adopted only one time zone for its wide territory.

Tip *(Tourism)*: Any gratuity, gift or a small sum of money offered for a service provided. It is synonymous with Gratuity.

Tipping *(Tourism)*: The action to tip.

Tirekicker *(Tourism)*: A slang term to denote a person who asks for travel information or quotations but who never has the intention to book.

TKNO *(GDS)*: Ticket number

TKS *(GDS)*: Code meaning Thanks.

TKT *(GDS)*: A code meaning: 1. Ticket, 2. Ticket Total.

TKTD *(GDS)*: Code meaning Ticketed.

TKTL *(GDS)*: Code meaning Ticket Time Limit.

TLV *(GDS)*: Three-letter IATA code for Tel Aviv, important city in Israel.

TMS *(Air Traffic)*: See Traffic Management System.

TMW *(GDS)*: Code meaning Tomorrow.

TN *(GDS)*: Code meaning Telephone Number.

TNOJ *(GDS)*: Code meaning Turn around Normal Fare Open Jaw.

TO *(GDS)*: Code meaning: 1. Town Office; 2. Tour Order.

TOD *(GDS)*: A code meaning: 1. Time of delivery; 2. Total Overall Dimensions of Luggage; 3. Ticket on Departure (for PTA cases).

TOE *(GDS)*: Code meaning Ticket Order Exception.

Tokaji Aszu *(Hospitality)*: A famous sweet wine from Hungary.

Tolerances *(Air Traffic)*: A term for allowed error in measurements.

Toll Call *(Tourism)*: A phone call out of the local dialing area, or long distance call.

Toll Road *(Tourism)*: A road system that charges a fee.

Toll Transponder *(Car Rental)*: An electronic device attached to a car's windshield that enables the electronic collection of highway tolls.

Tonnage (*Cruise*): The carriage capacity of a cruise ship.

Tool (*Aeronautics*): A device or process that is used to do some kind of work, such as a handheld calculator, or a marketing strategy.

Tools of Aeronautics (*Aeronautics*): Processes that use special devices to perform research in aeronautics, such as CFD, Wind Tunnel Testing, Flight Simulation and Flight Test.

TOP (*GDS*): Code meaning Tour Operator Program.

Topographic Map (*Geography*): A detailed and scaled map of the surface features of a place that gives the features' relative positions and elevations.

Topographic Profile (*Geography*): An outline of a landscape as seen from a side.

Topographical (*Air Traffic*): The whole of maps and charts representing the surface features of a region.

TOR (*GDS*): Code meaning Time of Receipt.

Tornado (*Geography*): A violently rotating column of air into a funnel cloud that often reaches the surface of the earth. It is the most destructive of all storm-scale atmospheric phenomena capable of causing great destruction. They can occur anywhere in the world, but are most frequent in the United States in the large area enclosed by the Rocky Mountains and the Appalachians.

Torque (*Air Traffic*): Twisting and gyroscopic force acting in opposition to an axis of rotation.

Torrid Zone (*Geography*): The part of the Earth's surface that lies between the Tropic of Cancer and the Tropic of Capricorn. It is characterized by a hot climate. See also Tropical Climate Zone.

Torture Class (*Airlines*): A slang term to define a low-service and uncomfortable economy class of an airline.

TOT (*GDS*): Code meaning Transient Occupancy Tax.

Total Body Fitness (*Hospitality*): A training regimen designed to prepare the body for multi-sport events.

Total Choice Dining (*Cruise*): A cruise term that describes the onboard dining program whereby passengers are offered multiple dining times rather than the traditional "first and second seating".

Total Overall Dimensions (TOD) (*Airlines*): The combined measure of length, width, and depth of a piece of luggage that is used to determine whether a piece qualifies as a hand bag for the bins or has to be carried in the baggage compartment.

Total Pressure *(Air Traffic)*: See Dynamic Pressure.

TOTL *(GDS)*: Total.

Touch-and-Go *(Air Traffic)*: Landing practice wherein an aircraft does not make a full stop after a landing, but proceeds immediately to another take-off.

Touchdown Zone *(Air Traffic)*: 1. The first 3,000 feet of runway for fixed wing aircraft beginning at the threshold. 2. The portion of the helicopter landing area or runway used for landing of rotary wings and vectored thrust aircraft.

Tour *(Tourism)*: Any pre-arranged journey to take individuals or groups on a trip or an excursion all the way around a particular area including the visiting of a number of places and sometimes amusement or entertainment for travelers to enjoy.

Tour Basing Fare *(Airlines)*: A reduced-rate excursion fare available to travelers who also buy land services as part of pre-paid tours or packages.

Tour Broker *(Tourism)*: See Motorcoach Broker.

Tour Catalog *(Tourism)*: A publication made by tour wholesalers listing all of their tour products.

Tour Conductor *(Tourism)*: A professional staff member of the agency who is in charge of a group of passengers and/or who personally escorts them for all or part of the itinerary. It is also called Tour Escort, Tour Leader or Tour Manager.

Tour Conductor Pass *(Airlines)*: A free pass that is issued for the tour escort based on a specific number of bookings.

Tour Departure *(Tourism)*: The date when the tour operation starts departing from the place of origin of the travel.

Tour Desk *(Tourism)*: A counter at a hotel for the arrangement of tours and excursions.

Tour Development *(Tourism)*: A marketing activity designed to create tour programs to local or foreign destinations.

Tour Documents *(Tourism)*: The set of tickets, vouchers, itineraries, instructions, and related information handed to travelers by a tour company.

Tour Escort *(Tourism)*: See Tour Conductor.

Tour Guide *(Tourism)*: A professional who possesses in-depth knowledge of an area's attractions and takes people on sightseeing excursions of limited duration.

Tour Itinerary (*Tourism*): The itinerary for a tour detailing the day-by-day or event-by-event activities.

Tour Leader (*Tourism*): See Tour Conductor.

Tour Letters (*Tourism*): Pre-designed paper containing artwork and/or illustrations used to overprint letter texts.

Tour Manager (*Tourism*): See Tour Conductor.

Tour Manual (*Tourism*): A set of information about a destination including geographic data, its attractions, accessibility, accommodation facilities, special events, etc. It is very useful for marketing organizations planning to attract visitors to their destinations.

Tour Operator (*Tourism*): A company that specializes in the planning (including creation and design) and operation of inclusive vacation tours, which are sold directly to the public or through travel agents. Tour operators usually perform tour services by themselves, but sometimes they subcontract the operation.

Tour Operator Rates (*Tourism*): Discount rates offered to tour operators by tourism suppliers.

Tour Organizer (*Tourism*): A commissionable passenger sales agent or an airline employee who is responsible to make travel arrangements for an inclusive tour group. The tour organizer neither creates nor operates the tour; he/she only finds people to form the group.

Tour Series (*Tourism*): The stopovers of a motorcoach travel where passengers have prearranged services.

Tour Shells (*Tourism*): Brochures pre-designed with artwork, graphics and/or illustrations but without text. The individual tour information and itinerary details are overprinted by tour operators, travel agents or wholesalers.

Tour Supplier (*Tourism*): A company or individual that provides the travel trade with a specific component or service, product, attraction or activity.

Tour Vouchers (*Tourism*): Documents issued by tour operators that are exchanged for tour services such as accommodation, transfers, meals, sightseeing, and other related services. They are also called

Coupons.

Tour Wholesaler *(Tourism)*: A company that creates tour packages by assembling individual components bought to suppliers, prices them as a unit, and sells them through travel agents to the public. Wholesalers usually do not sell tours at retail and typically do not operate them.

Tour-based Fare *(Tourism)*: See Tour Basing Fare.

Tourinaut *(Tourism)*: A recent term resulting from the fusion of the words "tourist" and "astronaut," invented to describe a participant in space tourism.

Tourism *(Tourism)*: It is thought Tourism is a word derived from the term "Touring" that appears for the first time in England by 1811. The World Tourism Organization (WTO) adopted a definition of tourism in the International Conference held in Ottawa, in 1991, as "the activities of persons travelling to and staying in places outside their usual environment for not more than one consecutive year for leisure, business or other purposes." It has to be added that travelers must not be linked by any profitable activity to their destination places. Tourism has also been defined as a set of phenomena resulting from the travel and stay of persons foreign to the places they visit, which tend to satisfy a cultural necessity of visitors. Tourism gathers a group of production and consumption activities

Another definition of tourism states that it is a service activity or system comprising a number of tangible and intangible elements, and the production and consumption components around persons who leave their own environment for a variety of reasons, such as pleasure, health, business, religious, sports, attendance to events, etc. The tangible elements include transport systems (airways, railroads, motorcoach, sea vessels, and now, spacecraft), hospitality services (accommodation, food and beverages), and related services such as tours, souvenirs, banking, insurance and safety and security. The intangible elements include rest and relaxation, culture, escape, adventure, new and different experiences. Considering the three categories of economic activities, Tourism is part of the Tertiary Sector of Economy, which involves the provision of services to other businesses and final consumers.

Mining and fishing activities constitute the Primary Sector, while the Secondary Sector comprises manufacturing and the production of primary goods.

Tourism Base *(Tourism)*: The set of resources, infrastructure, and other amenities that attract leisure visitors in a region, providing well-being and enjoyment during their stay.

Tourism, Commercial *(Tourism)*: See Commercial Tourism.

Tourism, Cruise *(Tourism)*: See Cruise Tourism.

Tourism, Cultural *(Tourism)*: See Cultural Tourism.

Tourism Development *(Tourism)*: The long-term process of preparing the conditions for the arrival of tourists, including planning, building, and managing attractions, transportation, accommodation, services, and facilities that make their stay happy and comfortable.

Tourism Enclave *(Tourism)*: Self-contained resort complex that caters to all the needs of tourists who arrive as part of a tour or other type of package.

Tourism, Health *(Tourism)*: See Health Tourism.

Tourism, Incoming *(Tourism)*: See Incoming Tourism.

Tourism Industry *(Tourism)*: See Industry of Tourism.

Tourism, Ethnic *(Tourism)*: See Ethnic Tourism.

Tourism, Events *(Tourism)*: See Events Tourism.

Tourism, Incentive *(Tourism)*: See Incentive Tourism.

Tourism, Interior *(Tourism)*: See Interior Tourism.

Tourism, International *(Tourism)*: See International Tourism.

Tourism, Medical *(Tourism)*: See Medical Tourism.

Tourism, Mountain *(Tourism)*: See Mountain Tourism.

Tourism, Museum *(Tourism)*: See Museum Tourism.

Tourism, National *(Tourism)*: See National Tourism.

Tourism, Nature *(Tourism)*: See Nature Tourism.

Tourism, Outbound *(Tourism)*: See Outbound Tourism.

Tourism Planning *(Tourism)*: The process of preparing a set of activities and choices associated with tourism development.

Tourism Product *(Tourism)*: See Product and Tourist Product.

Tourism, Receptive *(Tourism)*: See Incoming Tourism.

Tourism, Religious *(Tourism)*: See Religious Tourism.

Tourism, Rural *(Tourism)*: See Rural Tourism.

Tourism, Snow *(Tourism)*: See Snow Tourism.

Tourism, Sport *(Tourism)*: See Sport Tourism.

Tourism Supplier *(Tourism)*: A tourism business provider, such as an airline, a hotel, a bus, etc.

Tourism, Sustainable *(Tourism)*: See Sustainable Tourism.

Tourism, Urban *(Tourism)*: See Urban Tourism.

Tourism, Winter *(Tourism)*: See Winter Tourism.

Tourist *(Airlines)*: Synonymous with coach or economy class on an airplane.

Tourist *(Tourism)*: Anyone who spends at least one night and less than one year away from home, for any of the classified purposes as either holiday (recreation, leisure, sport and visit to family, friends or relatives), business, official mission, convention, or health reasons. As defined by the World Tourism Organization, a tourist is someone who travels at least eighty kilometers (fifty miles) from home for the purpose of recreation. A tourist must not be engaged in profitable activities.

Tourist Card *(Tourism)*: A document that replaces a visa to allow visitors to enter a country, usually for a short duration stay.

Tourist Destination *(Tourism)*: In theory, any geographical space could become a tourist destination. Such category, however, requires a place gathering specific components that configure the tourist offer and help position the place in the broad range of the demand. Among those components are the own natural or cultural attractions, accessibility, infrastructure, equipment and relative services together with a vocation to respond to the market trends and necessities.

Tourist Fare *(Airlines)*: See Economy Fare.

Tourist Flow *(Tourism)*: Displacement of travelers from a place of origin to another, called destination. Mass tourism generates different flow types, and is used to measure the quantity of visitors a destination receives as well as their economic behavior.

Tourist, International *(Tourism)*: See International Tourist.

Tourist Marketing *(Tourism)*: Series of systematic efforts orderly performed with the purpose to promote and sell tourist products and services intending to match consumers' needs and wants.

Tourist Profile *(Tourism)*: A document that gives basic information about a country, which would be of tourist interest, such as climate, food, and customs.

Tourist Tax *(Tourism)*: A tax assessed by some governments on tourism activities.

Tourist Trap *(Tourism)*: A pejorative term to qualify tourist attractions offering bad taste or poor value services. It also refers to tourist destinations that have become over-promoted.

Tourist Product *(Tourism)*: The set of tangible (as places) and intangible components (as services) that gather conditions to appeal tourists, aspiring to satisfy their needs and likes. By extension, touristic product is also any place equipped for developing tourist services, such as a hotel or any tourist attraction.

Tourist Geography *(Geography)*: A branch of Human Geography aimed to study the geographical location of tourism processes and the relationship of tourists with the external features of the destination. It begins with the analysis of the natural and cultural elements forming the geographical context of the destination. And is centered on the linkage between tourists and the places they visit.

Tourist Territory *(Geography)*: A territory with touristic potential, taking into account supply and demand conditions, competition and market trends. It defines the basis for a tourism development strategy coordinated by the various local players concerned. It is the space orderly modified by man attempting to exploit its natural or artificial resources.

Tower *(Air Traffic)*: A terminal facility that uses air and ground communication systems, visual signaling, and other devices to provide ATC services to aircraft operating in the vicinity of an airport or on the movement area. The tower staff authorizes aircraft to land or takeoff at the airport controlled by the tower or to transit the class D airspace area regardless of flight plan or weather conditions (IFR or VFR).

Tower *(Hospitality)*: Hotel floor configuration in which guestrooms are located around a central vertical core.

Tower Concept *(Hospitality)*: See Exclusive Floor.

Tower Controller *(Air Traffic)*: Any tower employee who is responsible for issuing takeoff and landing clearances and for monitoring all traffic within a five-mile radius and up to an altitude of 2,500 feet.

Towering Cumulus *(Geography)*: Rapidly growing cloud cumulus in which height exceeds width.

TP *(GDS)*: Code meaning Theft Protection.

TPE *(GDS)*: Three-letter IATA code for Taipei, capital city of Taiwan.

TPM *(GDS)*: Code meaning Ticketed Point Mileage.

TPI *(GDS)*: Code meaning Travel Price Index.

TPL *(GDS)*: Code meaning Triple.

TPM *(GDS)*: Code meaning Ticketed Point Mileage.

TR *(GDS)*: Code meaning: 1. International Transportation Tax; 2. Tour.

Trace Detector *(Airlines)*: A security device at an airport checkpoint that detects dangerous chemicals.

Track (TRK) *(Air Traffic)*: The actual flight path of an aircraft over the surface of the Earth.

Track Handle *(Air Traffic)*: A device to move a cursor in two axes on a display, similar to a mouse

Tracking *(Airlines)*: A carrier's system of tracing shipments from origin to destination.

TRACON *(Air Traffic)*: See Terminal Radar Approach Control.

TRACTOR *(Aeronautics)*: A propeller mounted in front of its engine, pulling an aircraft through the air, as opposed to a Pusher configuration.

TRAD *(GDS)*: Code meaning Trace and Advice.

Trade *(Airlines)*: Trade is the business of buying, selling or bartering goods, but in air transport activities the term is used to define a market area or a specific route served by carriers.

Trade Mission *(Tourism)*: A group tour for persons traveling with a business rather than a vacation purpose. Trade missions are usually planned for business or government representatives who travel to explore new foreign markets for their products or for widening current business opportunities.

Trade Name *(Business)*: The legally registered name of a company's product or service.

Trade Show *(Tourism)*: A business-to-business exhibit or exposition at which companies display and show their products and services to prospective customers. It is generally an industry-specific event not open to the public and differing from a "Consumer Show" in that a trade show targets the professional industry, while a consumer show targets consumers.

Trade Show Exhibitors Association (TSEA) *(Organizations)*: A not-for-profit association established to enhance the expertise of professionals in exhibit and event marketing, to provide education, information, advocacy, and professional advancement to exhibitors and event planners across all industry sectors. It is based in Chicago, Illinois.

Traditional Fixed Seating *(Cruise)*: An evening dining program that offers passengers the possibility to dine at the same time, as opposed to "Anytime Dining" program.

Translational Motion *(Aeronautics)*: Motion along a straight line, such as an axis. Translational motions of aircraft are forward and back along the longitudinal axis, side to side along the lateral axis, and up and down along the vertical axis.

Traffic *(Tourism)*: 1.The action of making business by selling, buying or bartering products or services. 2. The circulation of vehicles in a great volume. The term is used in air traffic referring to the circulation of aircraft. 3. In computing, the number of persons visiting a web site.

Traffic Alert and Collision Avoidance System (TCAS) *(Air Traffic)*: A system installed in commercial aircraft to alert pilots to the presence of other aircraft. Advanced versions of TCAS also advise pilots on actions to take to avoid aircraft getting too close.

Traffic Bubble *(Airlines)*: An unusual increase of passengers volume passing through an airport that may be provoked by a temporary fare decrease among airlines serving that airport.

Traffic Collision Avoidance System (TCAS) *(Air Traffic)*: A system that provides warnings of other nearby aircraft.

Traffic Conference Areas *(Airlines)*: The geographical divisions of the world adopted by IATA for the purpose of establishing the fare structures according to traffic and particular interests inside each region. Traffic Conferences, coded TC, are three and are called Areas:

- TC1 or Area 1 comprising North and South America, the Caribbean, Greenland and the adjacent islands in the Atlantic and Pacific Ocean, as far as Palmyra, an island of the Hawaiian Archipelago;
- TC2 or Area 2 comprising Europe to the west of the Ural Mountains, Africa and the Middle East plus the surrounding islands;
- TC3 or Area 3 comprising Asia, Australasia and the Pacific islands not included in TC1.

Traffic Conferences (*Airlines*): See Traffic Conference Areas.

Traffic Document *Airlines*): Tickets, Miscellaneous Charges Orders, Multi Purpose Documents or any other accountable traffic document.

Traffic Management System (TMS) *(Air Traffic)*: A method that allows accession, integration and management of real-time information generated by multiple data sources, such as airline, airport operations, ramp control, and air traffic control tower. The system is used to establish and update data values for every aircraft operation, to facilitate information sharing, and improve taxi queuing.

Traffic Pattern *(Air Traffic)*: The traffic flow assigned for aircraft landing at, taxiing on, or taking off from an airport.

Traffic Rights (*Airlines*): See Freedoms of the Air.

Traffic Situation Display (TSD) *(Air Traffic)*: A device used by Traffic Management specialists to keep track of the position of aircraft and to determine the traffic demand on airports and sectors.

Trail *(Tourism)*:   A marked path for hikers through woods or hinterland.

Trail Bike *(Tourism)*: A sturdy bicycle with wide tires and horizontal handlebars, often used for off-road cycling as along dirt trails. It is also called Dirt Bike or Trail Bike.

Train *(Tourism)*: It is a type of public transportation for passengers and freight consisting of a series of cars coupled together that move along a track. Trains are pulled by a locomotive that in its origins was powered by water steam. Modern locomotives are powered by diesel fuel or by electricity supply. The guide ways are usually conventional rail tracks, but might also be monorail or magnetic levitation. There is today a wide variety of train types, such as atmospheric railways, monorails, high-speed railways, maglev, rubber-tired underground, funicular and cog railways. Atmospheric railways are propelled by air pressure; monorails move on a single beam system; high-speed trains operate at faster speed than the traditional types; magnetically levitating trains or maglev move over an air cushion and use magnetic forces; rubber-tired underground is a form of rapid train with a combined traction of wheels and rubber tires; funiculars or cliff railways are a type of lifts which are moved up and down by a pair of tram-like vehicles on steel rails; cog railway or rack railways are toothed rack rails. Currently, train systems compete with airlines in some countries, as in Japan and France, using high speed trains. The Japanese Shinkansen runs at an average speed of 300 km/h (188 mph), while the French TGV (Train à Grande Vitesse) has achieved a 574.8 km/h (356 mph) testing speed in 2007.

Training Fare (*Airlines*): A negotiated air fare applicable to corporate employees who travel for training purposes.

Trajectory Synthesis (*Air Traffic*): Software that gives the controller a four dimensional view of how the many lines of incoming aircraft can be positioned into one line of arrival aircraft.

Tram (*Tourism*): A streetcar running on a railway.

Tramp Steamer (*Cruise*): A cargo vessel not operating on regular routes that sometimes carries passengers.

Trampoline (*Tourism*): A lightweight fabric or woven netting stretched between two hulls of a catamaran (or three hulls of a trimaran) at the bow of a yacht which acts as a safety net for sailors when on the forward hulls.

Tramway (*Airlines*): A railway for streetcars.

Trans-canal (*Cruise*): A cruise passing through the Panama Canal.

Transatlantic (*Tourism*): A flight or cruise service that crosses the Atlantic Ocean. Since transatlantic travel is heavily served by airplanes, ships are no longer operating passenger services to cross the Atlantic Ocean.

Transatlantic Fares (*Airlines*): Fares for flights between points in Area 1 and points in Area 2 and/or Area 3 via the North, Mid or

South Atlantic Ocean.

Transatlantic Sector *(Airlines)*: The term is used in connection with North Atlantic Fares to denote the portion of the journey covered by a single flight coupon, from the last point of departure in Area 1, to the first point of arrival in Area 2 and vice versa.

Transceiver *(Air Traffic)*: A device that both transmits and receives radio waves.

Transcon *(Airlines)*: Abbreviated term for Transcontinental.

Transcontinental *(Airlines)*: A term used for flights extending across a single continent.

Transfer *(Airlines)*: A change from the service of one carrier to another service of the same carrier (online transfer) or to the service of another carrier (interline transfer).

Transfer *(Tourism)*: Land transportation service from the arrival terminal of a carrier (air, rail, bus, ship, boat) to other terminal, hotel, airport, mall or another place and vice versa. Transfers can be by private car or motorcoach and escorted or unescorted.

Transfer Cargo *(Airlines)*: Cargo arriving at an airport on one carrier and continuing its journey by another carrier.

Transfer Connection *(Airlines)*: The change of flights at an airport enroute to the ongoing destination. There can be more than one transfer connection in an air route.

Transfer Manifest (TRM) *(Airlines)*: The document produced by the transferring carrier upon transfer of interline cargo, which is endorsed by the receiving carrier as a receipt for the consignment transferred.

Transfer Point *(Airlines)*: Any point at which a passenger transfers from the services of one carrier to another service of the same carrier or to the service of another carrier.

Transferable Deposit *(Tourism)*: See Floating Deposit.

Transferring Carrier *(Airlines)*: The participating carrier transferring passengers or consignment to another carrier at a transfer point.

Transient *(Tourism)*: Any person who is not a permanent resident and is passing through a place for only a short stay.

Transient Hotel *(Hospitality)*: A hotel offering services to business guests staying for short periods. Its busiest occupancy is Monday through Thursday.

Transient Ledger *(Hospitality)*: See Guest Ledger.

Transient Occupancy Tax *(Hospitality)*:   A government tax on hotel rooms and other lodgings.

Transit *(Airlines)*: An enroute stopping place where passengers and cargo remain on board.

Transit Cargo *(Airlines)*: Cargo arriving at a point but not entering the country and departing by another flight.

Transit Flight *(Airlines)*: A flight identified by a Flight Number during an enroute landing at a particular station.

Transit Information *(Air Traffic)*: A warning to a pilot on the aircraft that can be close to his/her route.

Transit Passengers *(Airlines)*: Passengers on board a flight at an enroute stop or connecting passengers to/from other scheduled flight/s.

Transit Point *(Airlines)*: Any stop at an intermediate point on the route which is not for a stopover purpose.

Transit Stop *(Airlines)*: An intermediate stop on a flight where the plane will only be on the ground for an hour or so. Sometimes passengers deplane the aircraft, but usually they remain on board.

Transit Time *(Airlines)*: The time an aircraft remains in transit at a station.

Transit Visa *(Tourism)*: A visa issued for a limited-term to allow passengers transit the issuing country's territory.

Transition Zone *(Geography)*: An area where the characteristics of one region gradually blend into the characteristics of the next.

Transitional Automated Ticket (TAT) *(Airlines)*: A form of automated ticket, used in the past which was issued by airline offices.

Transmissible Disease *(Tourism)*: A disease that is able to spread from one person to another by air, water, food, of body fluids.

Transmit *(Air Traffic)*: To radiate radio frequency energy.

Transmitter *(Air Traffic)*: A device used to transmit.

Transonic *(Air Traffic)*: An aircraft that develops a velocity between nine tenths (0.9) and one and four tenths (1.4) times the speed of sound.

Transpacific *(Airlines)*: Air transportation performed between points in Area 1 and points in Area 3 via the Pacific Ocean.

Transpacific Fares (*Airlines*): Fares applicable to flights between points in Area 1 and points in Area 3 via North Central or South Pacific.

Transpacific Sector (*Airlines*): The portion of travel covered by a single flight coupon from the point of departure in Area 1 to the point of arrival in Area 3 and vice versa.

Transponder (*Air Traffic*): An electronic device aboard an airplane that responds to ground-based signals to provide air traffic controllers with the aircraft's identity as well as aircraft's position on an ATC radar screen.

Transport Canada (*Organizations*): The federal governmental department which has the mission to develop and administer regulations, policies and services to assure an affordable, efficient, secure, integrated and environmentally friendly transportation system for Canada and Canadians. It is based in Ottawa and has many locations across Canada.

Transportation (*Airlines*): See Carriage.

Transshipment (*Airlines*): The unloading of cargo from one flight and loading onto another for onward carriage.

Trattoria (*Tourism*): A restaurant or café featuring Italian food.

Travel Advisory (*Tourism*): An official warning delivered by the U.S. State Department to inform that special caution should be taken in a country where political unrest, natural disaster, or other special situation can be found. These warnings are frequently not objective because of misinformation or for not using reliable information sources.

Travel Agency (*Tourism*): An IATA or ARC appointed company, which is full time devoted to the marketing of travel related services. Travel agencies are retail businesses that sell travel services to end-user customers on behalf of third party travel suppliers, such as airlines, hotels, tour companies, and cruise lines on a commission or fee basis. They are also called Travel Bureaus.

Travel Agent (*Tourism*): A company or an individual person qualified to become engaged in selling travel services, issuing travel documents and providing other related services to travelers at the retail level on a commission basis.

Travel Agent Number *(Airlines)*: A unique number issued by IATA, ARC or both to identify accredited travel agencies. It is also called ARC Number or ARC-IATA Number. Identifying numbers issued by CLIA to its members might also be considered Travel Agent Numbers.

Travel and Tourism Research Association (TTRA) *(Organizations)*: An association created to facilitate access to numerous sources of information to support members' research efforts. Its aims consist of educating members in research, marketing and planning skills through publications, conferences and networking. It encourages professional development through award programs that foster growth of travel and professional research in the travel and tourism industry.

Travel Bureau *(Tourism)*: A term sometimes used as a synonymous for Travel Agency

Travel Club *(Tourism)*: A sort of travel agency organization that offers vacation packages at reduced prices to its members in return of an annual membership fee.

Travel Consultant *(Tourism)*:   An alternative denomination for travel agent.

Travel Counselor *(Tourism)*: Same as Travel Consultant above.

Travel Documents *(Cruise)*: The set of paper documents required for a cruise travel, such as cruise tickets, air tickets, passports, visas, etc.

Travel Industry Association of America (TIA) *(Organizations)*: A non-profit trade organization of companies and government agencies representing all segments of the U.S. travel industry. Based in Washington, D.C., TIA is a public voice and political liaison for the entire industry that advocates with the U.S. government to ease travel procedures. TIA promotes increased travel to and within the United States through marketing initiatives. It also promotes a wider understanding of travel and tourism as a major industry that contributes to the economic, cultural and social well-being of the nation. TIA stimulates travel industry cohesion and provides communications forums for industry leaders' objectives, and provides resources to develop and execute programs that benefit the travel activity.

Travel Industry Association of Canada (TIAC) *(Organizations)*: TIAC is the voice of Canadian tourism. It was founded in 1930 to encourage the development of tourism in Canada. Today it serves as the national private-sector advocate for this industry, representing the interests of the tourism business community nation-wide. It works to ensure that tourism keeps developing as a strong, competitive, and sustainable growth industry.

Travel Industry Designator Service (TIDS) *(Airlines)*: An IATA numeric code assigned to certain categories of non-IATA/IATAN travel agencies (excluding U.S.A.) as identification means in industry reservation systems when selling air transportation and services.

Travel Intermediary *(Tourism)*: Any company or individual acting as intermediary between the travel product suppliers and travelers.

Travel Intermediary Designator Service (TIDS) *(Airlines)*: See Travel Industry Designator Service.

Travel Manager *(Tourism)*: See Corporate Travel Manager.

Travel Mission *(Tourism)*: A marketing activity performed in foreign countries by public or private representatives of a destination with the purpose to explore new markets for such destination. It usually includes presentations, media activities and trade information.

Travel Partner *(Tourism)*: A travel supplier that accepts to take part in a marketing program carried out by another travel supplier.

Travel Philanthropy *(Tourism)*: See Altruistic Travel.

Travel Retailers Universal Enumeration (TRUE) *(Tourism)*: A Code number assigned by IATAN to external registrars within the U.S.A.

Travel Sales Intermediaries (TSI) *(Airlines)*: Non-ticketing travel agencies in the US with assigned IATA numeric codes used for identification in the industry reservation systems when selling air transport and services.

Travel Service Intermediary Agency (TSIA) *(Tourism)*: An accredited travel sales intermediary that is engaged in the sale or brokerage of travel-related services or the provision of such services to the general public.

Travel Trade *(Tourism)*: A term describing the full range of agents that operate as intermediaries in the travel and tourism industry. These typically include tour operators, wholesalers, receptive operators, travel agents, and group leaders.

Travelator *(Tourism)*: See Moving Sidewalk.

Traveler or Traveller *(Tourism)*: A person who moves from his home place to any other place. The term is not synonymous with tourist because a traveler is not involved in any tourist activity. The traveler is the antecedent of the tourist.

Traveler's Checks *(Tourism)*: An internationally redeemable preprinted draft purchased in various denominations from a bank or traveler's aid company and used for unconditional payment upon the purchaser's endorsement against the original signature on the draft. Traveler's Checks are protected against loss or theft and can be usually replaced with no major trouble. The use of credit cards has made them less important than they were formerly. However, they are useful when not all credit or debit cards carried are accepted. They are also spelled Traveller's Checks and called Traveler's Cheques or Traveller's Cheques.

Traveler's Cheques *(Tourism)*: See Traveler's Checks.

Traveller's Checks *(Tourism)*: See Traveler's Checks.

Traveller's Cheques *(Tourism)*: See Traveler's Checks.

Travelog *(Tourism)*: See Travelogue.

Travelogue *(Tourism)*: A documentary film or illustrated lecture about the attractions of a specific travel destination or about personal travel experiences.

Travelshopper *(Airlines)*: A simplified version of the Worldspan GDS.

Travolator *(Tourism)*: A moving walkway for pedestrians, typically used in airports or shopping malls. The walkways are often supplied in pairs, one for each direction.

TRBL *(GDS)*: Code meaning Trouble.

Tree Line *(Geography)*: The latitude establishing the limit north of which trees do not grow.

Trek *(Tourism)*: A long and difficult journey on foot.

Trekking *(Tourism)*: A term adopted in 1970 to define a type of adventure travel to mountainous regions including lodging in tents or other nominal accommodation. It is performed under the responsibility of professional guides and allows the discovery of great landscapes with a sustained physical effort not involving any harm.

Trend Line *(Geography)*: A line on a graph showing the general relationship between two variables being graphed.

Trend Monitoring *(Aeronautics)*: Continuous computerized observation of turbine engine performance used to detect early signs of wear.

Triathlon *(Tourism)*: An athletic sports event that combines swimming, cycling, and running over various distances.

Tribal Tourism *(Tourism)*: Travel to learn more about people who are indigenous to a region. It may include attending rituals, ceremonies, and visits to specific sites.

Trimaran *(Tourism)*: A three hulled ship or boat which runs parallel to one another, having often the middle hull shorter than the two outer hulls. Trimarans are not numerous and are used in the Caribbean for scuba diving.

Trip *(Tourism)*: Any journey for some purpose and more than 80 miles from the traveler's home, including or not an overnight stay.

Triple *(Hospitality)*: A hotel room for three persons.

Trishaw *(Tourism)*: A three-wheeled vehicle pulled by a runner, common in China, Singapore and Malaysia. It is used for tourist purposes and remains a strong icon of the local cultural history. See Cycle Rickshaw.

TRK *(Air Traffic)*: See Track.

TRNG *(GDS)*: Code meaning Training.

Trolley *(Tourism)*: A streetcar.

Trophic *(Ecology)*: An organism pertaining to a particular nutrition web.

Trophic Chain *(Ecology)*: An illustration of the linear trophic arrangement, where one organism foods the following.

Trophic Level *(Ecology)*: A stage in a food chain or web grouping organisms of the same type of consumers, such as primary producers (plants, the lowest trophic level), herbivores, carnivores, omnivores.

Tropic of Cancer *(Geography)*: The northern parallel of maximum solar declination, approximately 23°27'N latitude.

Tropic of Capricorn *(Geography)*: The southern parallel of maximum solar declination, approximately 23°27'S latitude.

Tropical Storm *(Geography)*: A tropical cyclone in which the maximum sustained surface winds are from 39 miles per hour (34 knots) to 73 miles per hour (63 knots). At this point, the system is given a name to identify and track it.

Tropical Climatic Zone *(Geography)*: An area of the earth located around the equator between the Tropic of Cancer (23.5 degrees north) and the Tropic of Capricorn (23.5 degrees south). It occupies about forty percent of the land surface of the earth, and is the home to almost half of the world's population. Its temperature is warm or hot temperatures all year, over 20°C (68°F). It is also known as Torrid Zone or The Tropics.

Tropics *(Geography)*: See Tropical Climatic Zone.

Tropopause *(Geography)*: The transition zone between the troposphere and the stratosphere, in which the atmospheric temperature tends to stabilize, and the air ceases to cool at -56.5°C (-70°F), becoming almost completely dry. It marks the vertical limit of most clouds and storms.

Troposphere *(Geography)*: The lowest layer of the atmosphere with a thickness that ranges from about 10 to 20 kilometers (about 6 to 12 miles) over the equator. It contains around the 75 percent of the atmosphere's total mass and is the layer where temperature generally decreases with increasing altitude, where clouds form, precipitation occurs and convection currents activate.

TRN *(Air Traffic)*: Terrain Referenced Navigation.

TRPN *(GDS)*: Code meaning Triple room without Bath or Shower.

TRPT *(GDS)*: Code meaning Transport.

TRPB *(GDS)*: Code meaning Triple with Bath.

TRPN *(GDS)*: Code meaning Triple without Bath.

TRPS *(GDS)*: Code meaning Triple room with Shower.

TRSA *(Air Traffic)*: See Terminal Radar Service Area.

TRUE *(Airlines)*: See Travel Retailer Universal Enumeration.

True Airspeed (TAS) *(Air Traffic)*: The speed of an aircraft along its flight path, in respect to the body of air (air mass) through which the aircraft moves. It is showed only under standard sea-level conditions.

True Altitude *(Air Traffic)*: The exact distance above sea level.

True Heading *(Air Traffic)*: Heading of the aircraft relative to the true north.

True Latitude *(Geography)*: A map projection term which specifies a particular area on a map without distortion.

True North *(Air Traffic)*: The northern direction of the axis of the Earth, or the Geographic North, as opposed to the Magnetic North.

Trundle Bed *(Hospitality)*: A bed that can be rolled out for use from under another bed, and that can be rolled in for storage when not in use.

Trunk Carrier *(Tourism)*: A major airline carrier covering a wide network.

Truth-in-advertising *(Marketing)*: A moral and sometimes legal requirement of being honest with advertising, in order to provide accurate descriptions of products and services offered.

TRVL *(GDS)*: Code meaning Travel.

TS *(GDS)*: Global Indicator for a travel via Trans Siberian route.

TSD *(Air Traffic)*: See Traffic Situation Display.

TSEA *(Organizations)*: An acronym for Trade Show Exhibitors Association.

TSI *(Airlines)*: See Travel Sales Intermediaries.

TSI Card *(Tourism)*: A photo identification card bearing staff of IATAN-approved agencies that do not issue air tickets.

TSIA *(Tourism)*: See Travel Service Intermediary Agency.

TSS *(Cruise)*: Turbine Steam Ship.

TST *(GDS)*: Code meaning Transitional Stored Ticket Record.

TSTMS *(Air Traffic)*: An abbreviation for Thunderstorms.

Tsunami *(Geography)*: A Japanese term for a series of unusually large sea waves that appear when the ocean body is rapidly displaced by a seaquake, underwater explosions, landslides, underwater earthquakes, large asteroid impacts, or volcanic eruption under water.

TTB *(GDS)*: Code meaning Timetable.

TTL *(GDS)*: Code meaning Total.

TTRA *(Organizations)*: An acronym for Travel and Tourism

Research Association.

Tube *(Tourism)*: A British slang term for the London Underground service.

Tubing *(Tourism)*: A simple type of sport consisting of floating down a gentle waterway in an inflated car chamber tube.

TUE *(GDS)*: Code meaning Tuesday.

Tug Boat *(Cruise)*: A small powerful vessel, used for towing or moving larger vessels in such places as harbors and the Panama Canal.

Tuk-tuk *(Tourism)*: See Cycle Rickshaws.

Tune *(Air Traffic)*: To set the operating frequency or channel for a device.

TUR *(GDS)*: Code meaning Tour.

Turbofan *(Aeronautics)*: A type of jet engine in which a certain portion of the engine's airflow bypasses the combustion chamber.

Turbojet *(Aeronautics)*: An aircraft with a jet engine whose power is solely the result of its jet exhaust.

Turboprop *(Aeronautics)*: An aircraft that uses a jet engine in which the energy of the jet operates a turbine that drives the propeller.

Turbulence *(Climate)*: The irregular and instantaneous motions of air which is caused by random fluctuations in the wind flow. It can result from thermal or convective currents, differences in terrain and wind speed, along a frontal zone, or variation in temperature and pressure.

Turbulence *(Airlines)*: An airplane moves through air that is itself moving in a similar way to moving water. Turbulence onboard is felt when air currents vary, and the airplane flies rapidly from one current to another. So, the disagreeable sensation comes from the aircraft crossing a barrier between different currents. But aircraft also generate turbulences when they pass through the air; that one is named Wake Turbulence.

Turbulence Mode *(Air Traffic)*: Flight control system mode in which pilots program a softer response to air sudden upsets.

Turn *(Airlines)*: A complex process at an airport including landing a plane, deplaning passengers and luggage, embarking new passengers and luggage, and departing again. The number of turns a plane makes per day affects the airline economy. The quicker the turns, the more optimized are the planes.

Turnaround *(Airlines)*: 1. The process of refueling and re-provisioning a plane to have it ready for another flight. 2. The time spent by an aircraft between landing and taking off. The term is also applied to ships.

Turnaround Point *(Airlines)*: The farthest geographical location from the travel point of origin, where the outbound portion of the travel ends and where the inbound portion of the travel commences. It is the point which has the highest MPM with respect to the point of origin of the travel. See also Point of Turnaround.

Turnaround Single Open Jaw (TSOJ) *(Airlines)*: A trip where the outward point of arrival in the country of unit turnaround and the inward point of departure in the country of unit turnaround are different. It is a return trip comprising two fare components whose fare is calculated by using half normal or special round trip fares.

Turnaround Time *(Airlines)*: Time required for disembarking and embarking passengers, offloading and uploading cargo, cleaning the plane, refueling, maintaining and supplying it.

Turndown Service *(Hospitality)*: The practice of preparing a hotel room for bedtime by folding back the blanket and sheet, turning on lights to a low level, turning on the radio, and sometimes by putting a mint on the pillow or a cordial on the night stand.

Turnover *(Tourism)*: 1. The frequent rotation of staff by dismissing employees, resignation or retirement. 2. The intermittent change of clientele basis because some customers stop doing business while others approach.

Turnpike *(Tourism)*: See Toll Road.

TV *(GDS)*: A code meaning: 1. Turbine Vessel; 2. Television.

TWB *(GDS)*: Code meaning Twin Room with Bath.

Twenty-four Hour Clock *(Tourism)*: A mode of registering the time by using successively all 24 hours of the day. It is used extensively worldwide, except in the U.S.

Twin *(Hospitality)*: A hotel room with two twin beds.

Twin Bed *(Hospitality)*: A bed of approximately 39 inches by 75 inches.

Twin Bedded Room *(Hospitality)*: A hotel room with two individual beds.

Twin-double *(Hospitality)*: A hotel room with two double beds. It is also called a Double-double.

Twist *(Hospitality)*: A strip of lemon peel twisted over a drink to flavor it with lemon oil (often followed by dropping the twisted peel into the drink).

TWNB *(GDS)*: Code meaning Double room with bath, twin beds.

TWNN *(GDS)*: Code meaning Double twin bedded room without bath or shower.

TWNS *(GDS)*: Code meaning Double twin bedded room with shower.

Two-class *(Tourism)*: A term used to describe a transportation system with two separate types of accommodation or service, such as coach and first class on an airplane or train.

TWOV *(GDS)*: Code meaning Transit Without Visa.

TWR *(GDS)*: Code meaning Tower.

TXT *(GDS)*: Code meaning Text.

TYO *(GDS)*: Three-letter IATA code for Tokyo, capital city of Japan.

Typhoon *(Geography)*: The name given to a tropical cyclone with sustained winds of 74 miles per hour (65 knots) or greater, which occurs in the western North Pacific Ocean. This same type of tropical storm is known as a hurricane in the eastern North Pacific and North Atlantic Ocean, and as a cyclone in the Indian Ocean.

U

U *(Airlines)*: Code meaning "Uniform", name used to designate the letter "U" in the International Phonetic Alphabet.

U *(Airlines)*: On a ticket indicates it is for a shuttle service and no reservation is required.

U-drive *(Car Rental)*: See Hire Car.

U.S. Waters *(Geography)*: A distance of 12 nautical miles surrounding the coasts of the U.S. and its territories; ships operating in such waters must adhere to certain U.S. laws and regulations.

UA *Airlines)*: Two-letter IATA code for United Air Lines Inc.

UATP *(GDS)*: Code meaning Universal Air Travel Plan.

UBOA *(Organizations)*: See United Bus Owners of America.

UC *(GDS)*: Code meaning Unable to Confirm or To Accept Request. The flight is closed.

UCCCF *(GDS)*: Code meaning Universal Credit Card Charge Form.

UCT *(Air Traffic)*: Code for Universal Coordinated Time

UFO *(GDS)*: Code meaning Unidentified Flying Object.

UFTAA *(Organizations)*: See United Federation of Travel Agents' Associations.

UHF *(Air Traffic)*: See Ultra High Frequencies.

UIO *(GDS)*: Three-letter IATA code for Quito, the capital city of Ecuador.

UK *(GDS)*: Code meaning United Kingdom.

ULD *(Airlines)*: Abbreviation for a Unit Load Device.

Ultra-high frequency (UHF) *(Air Traffic)*: Radio frequencies between 300 and 3,000 MHz (3 GHz).

Ultralight *(Aeronautics)*: A single-occupant aircraft operated for sport or recreational purposes. It does not require official registration, an airworthiness certificate, or pilot certification.

UM *(GDS)*: Code meaning Unaccompanied Minor.

UMA *(Organizations)*: An acronym for United Motorcoach Association.

UM08 *(GDS)*: Code meaning Unaccompanied Minor 8 years old.

UMNN *(GDS)*: Same as above: Unaccompanied Minor, where NN should be replaced by the child's age.

UMNR *(GDS)*: Code meaning Unaccompanied Minor.

UN *(GDS)*: 1. Code meaning Unable; 2. An acronym for United Nations Organization.

UNA *(GDS)*: Code meaning Unable.

Unaccompanied Minor *(Airlines)*: A child or infant who is not accompanied by an adult and requires the application of a specific procedure and care.

Unaccompanied Baggage *(Airlines)*: Baggage that is carried separately in cargo compartment.

Unchecked Baggage *(Airlines)*: Baggage other than checked baggage, which is kept under the passenger's custody.

UNCTAD *(Organizations)*: See United Nations Conference on Trade & Development.

Underbar *(Hospitality)*: The primary working space for the bartender.

Undercarriage *(Aeronautics)*: The part of an aircraft that provides support while the aircraft is on the ground. It includes wheels, shock absorbers and support struts. There is one undercarriage unit under the nose of the aircraft and another approximately midway back, under the fuselage. Undercarriage normally includes rubber tires, but may have skis for landing on snow or floats for landing on water.

Undercarriage Strut *(Aeronautics)*: A part of an airplane's structure, which supports the landing gear. It is designed to resist distortion.

Undercurrent *(Tourism)*: A current that flows under another current at a different speed or in the opposite direction. In beach areas they are highly hazardous because they can drag unaware swimmers out to sea.

Underdeveloped *(Geography)*: A term used to qualify a country that has a relatively low level of economic development. It is said that country has not reached its maturity state.

Underdevelopment *(Geography)*: The condition for a country of being underdeveloped. Underdevelopment is not only the result of a wrong conduction of economic policy, but mainly a product of the vocation division introduced for states into two groups: dominant, industrialized and suppliers of finished goods the first; and depending, providers of prime products and consumers of finished products the second. Within development theory, the concept of underdevelopment suggests that wealthy countries have held back the development of so-called "third world" countries. Tourism in third world destinations reinforces dependency, lacks involvement of local decision makers, leads to negative socio-cultural impacts, and is frequently controlled for the economic benefit of foreign investors.

Understay *(Hospitality)*: A guest who checks out before his/her expected departure date.

Undertow *(Tourism)*: See Undercurrent.

Underway *(Cruise)*: A ship in motion. Once the ship has left the pier or lifts its anchorage, the ship is considered "underway".

Unducted Fan *(Aeronautics)*: An engine that uses the basic core of a jet engine to drive fan-like blades which produce the major thrust component of the engine.

UNEP *(Organizations)*: An acronym for United Nations Environment Program.

UNESCO *(Organizations)*: An acronym for United Nations Educational, Scientific and Cultural Organization.

UNICOM *(Air Traffic)*: See Universal Communication.

UNIDO *(Organizations)*: An acronym for United Nations Industrial Development Organization.

Uniform *(Airlines)*: Designator for the letter "U" in the International Phonetic Alphabet.

Unimproved Airport *(Air Traffic)*: An airport with runways made of grass, dirt, or gravel, instead of concrete or asphalt.

Uninterrupted International Air Transportation *(Tourism)*: Any flight that includes a scheduled stop of less than twelve hours in the territory of the United States.

Uninterruptible Power Supply *(Computing)*: A device equipped with a battery pack connected to the computer's power line. When a power fluctuation occurs, the battery pack is triggered to compensate for any energy deficiencies and provide the computer with a continuously stable energy source.

Unique Selling Proposition (USP) *(Business)*: A unique selling proposition is a unique and most saleable feature of a product that makes it different than any other and that a competitor cannot claim. It is a marketing concept that was first proposed as a theory of an ideal model among successful advertising campaigns of the early 1940s.

Unit Destination *(Airlines)*: The ultimate stopping place of a pricing unit.

Unit Load Device (ULD) *(Airlines)*: A type of cargo equipment used for cargo loading and transportation on board of the aircraft. They are designed to load large quantities of freight, luggage, and mail bundled into a single unit. ULDs come in two forms: pallets and containers. Pallets are rugged sheets of aluminum with rims designed to lock onto cargo net lugs. Containers are fully enclosed containers made of aluminum or a combination of aluminum and plastic. Some have refrigeration units built-in for the transportation of specific goods. They are also known as cans and pods. Aircraft loadings can be made up of all containers, all pallets, or a mix. Unit Load Devices have become a key element of high efficiency in air transport on wide-body aircraft and specific narrow-body aircraft for they save ground crews time and prevent flight delays.

Unit Origin *(Airlines)*: The Initial starting point of a pricing unit.

Unit/Week *(Hospitality)*: A timeshare estate, interest, or license entitling the owner to occupy accommodations for such specific periods of time at a Resort.

United Federation of Travel Agents' Associations (UFTAA) *(Organizations)*: The UFTAA was originally created in Rome, Italy, on 22 November 1966, as a result of a merger of two large world organizations, FIAV and UOTAA, recognizing the need to unify travel agencies and tour-operators into a single international federation. In 1989 UFTAA moved its General Secretariat from Brussels to the Principality of Monaco and started its operation as a Confederation on January 1st, 2003. At present, UFTAA is integrated by 114 members and affiliate associations in 121 countries. UFTAA's purposes are: To be an international forum for the world travel business encompassing incoming and outgoing tour operators, travel and tourism agencies, suppliers and other entities of international scope; the strengthening of the world travel and tourism industry and a sustainable tourism; to be a research and information centre for the support of the Federations' members; to work and to offer information for technological development; to organize world congresses of travel agents and other meetings necessary to the exchange and transmission of knowledge.

United Kingdom *(Geography)*: UK comprises the following territories: England, Wales, Scotland, Isle of Man, Northern Island and the Channel Islands.

United Motorcoach Association (UMA) *(Organizations)*: UMA began as the United Bus Owners Association (UBOA) that became UMA in 1996 to reflect more accurately the group it represents. Today it is an association of motorcoach owners and industry suppliers from all across North America and representing companies in England, Belgium and France. The purpose of this Association is to protect and promote the interests and welfare of privately owned common carriers of passengers by motorcoach.

United Nations Conference on Trade & Development (UNCTAD)
(Organizations): It is an agency that promotes the development and friendly integration of developing countries into the world economy. Its main goals are to promote the trade, investment and development opportunities of developing countries, and to help them face challenges arising from globalization to become integrated into the world economy, on an equitable basis. The present UNCTAD members are 188 states.

United Nations Educational, Scientific and Cultural Organization (UNESCO) *(Organizations)*: The UNESCO is a specialized United Nations agency that was founded on 16 November 1945. UNESCO promotes international co-operation among its 193 Member States and six Associate Members in the fields of education, science, culture and communication.

United Nations Environment Program (UNEP) *(Organizations)*: An UN's program committed to the protection of the environment, by inspiring, informing and enabling nations and people to improve their quality of life without compromising that of future generations. The UNEP was created as a result of the 1972 Stockholm Conference on the Human Environment, having the appearance of an environmental conscience of the United Nations system. Its headquarters are in Nairobi, with an office in Paris. The organization is led by an Executive Director and a Governing Council composed of 58 members selected on the following basis: 16 seats for Africa; 13 seats for Asia; 6 seats for Eastern Europe; 13 seats for Western Europe and other States; and 10 seats for Latin America.

United Nations Industrial Development Organization (UNIDO)
(Organizations): A specialized agency of the United Nations created in 1966 that helps developing countries and economies in transition to fight against marginalization. UNIDO implements knowledge, skills, information and technology to promote productive employment, a competitive economy, a sound environment, as well as cooperation at global, regional, national and sectional levels. UNIDO is also committed to the application of the Montreal Protocol for the elimination of ozone depleting substances (ODS)

and the Stockholm Convention for the elimination of persistent organic pollutants (POPs).

United Nations Organization (UN/UNO) *(Organizations)*: The UN is an inter-governmental organization focused on world peace, and aimed to facilitating cooperation in international law, international security, economic development, social progress and human right issues. The United Nations was established on 24 October 1945 by 51 countries to replace the League of Nations. It is based on a territory regarded as international within New York City and is integrated by 192 sovereign states. The UN's main purposes are:

• To maintain international peace and security;

• To develop friendly relations among nations;

• To cooperate in solving international problems and in promoting respect for human rights;

• To be a centre for harmonizing the actions of nations.

The United Nations has six main organs. Five of them (the General Assembly, the Security Council, the Economic and Social Council, the Trusteeship Council and the Secretariat) are based at UN Headquarters in New York. The sixth, the International Court of Justice, is located at The Hague, Netherlands. The UN is financed from assessed and voluntary contributions from member states and has six official languages: Arabic, Chinese, English, French, Russian, and Spanish.

United States Department of Transportation (DOT) *(Organizations)*: See Department of Transportation.

United States Tour Operator's Association (USTOA) *(Organizations)*: A professional association representing the tour operator industry of the U.S. It is composed of companies whose tours and packages encompass the entire globe and which conduct business in the U.S. USTOA was founded in 1972 by a small group of California tour operators concerned about tour operator bankruptcies. In 1975, USTOA became a national organization with headquarters in New York.

Universal Air Travel Plan *(Tourism)*: See Air Travel Card.

Universal Communication (UNICOM) *(Air Traffic)*: A common radio frequency (usually 121.0 MHz) used at non-tower airports for local pilot communication.

Universal Postal Union (UPU) *(Tourism)*: A specialized agency of the United Nations established as a primary forum for cooperation between postal-sector players. It fulfils an advisory, mediating and liaison role, and renders technical assistance to its 191 country members. It sets the rules for international mail exchanges and makes recommendations to stimulate growth in mail volumes and to improve the quality of service for customers. The main UPU's objective is to develop social, cultural and commercial communication between people through the efficient operation of the postal service. Its headquarters are located in Berne, Switzerland.

Universal Product Code (UPC) *(Tourism)*: The barcode standard used in North America. It is administered by the Uniform Code Council.

Universal Time *(Geography)*: See Greenwich Mean Time.

UNK *(GDS)*: Code meaning Unknown.

Unlimited Mileage *(Car Rental)*: A method of renting a car for driving anywhere, any number of mileages, without incurring any per mile charges. This is the best way to go, as it sets the driver free of time and distance.

Unmanaged *(Tourism)*: A customer who is not covered by a negotiated rate plan for hospitality or car rental services.

UNO *(Organizations)*: See United Nations Organization.

Unrestricted Fare *(Airlines)*: The standard level of air fares that include maximum flexibility. Such fares are not subject to any applicability condition and are fully refundable without a penalty fee. Types of unrestricted fares are Economy, Business and First class normal fares.

Unrestricted Rate *(Hospitality)*: The highest hotel room price that excludes any special discounts. See also Rack Rate.

Unscheduled *(Tourism)*: A term used to denote a flight or operation that is not subordinate to a timetable or time plan.

Unspoiled *(Tourism)*: A term describing tourist destinations that keep their natural beauty and conditions because they are unknown and unexploited.

Unstable Air *Geography)*: The phenomenon that occurs when a part of a rising air becomes less dense than the surrounding air.

Since it does not cool as quickly as the surrounding environment, it continues to rise on its own.

Unused Ticket *(Airlines)*: Nonrefundable tickets that have not been used for some reason. Depending on the fare, some unused tickets can be reissued by paying a surcharge. See also Ticket Swiping.

UNWTO *(Organizations)*: An acronym for World Tourism Organization (United Nations World Travel Organization)

Upgrade *(Airlines)*: The action to move a traveler from an airplane class of service to another of superior level either on a voluntary or involuntary basis. Some Frequent Flyer Programs include Upgrading Rewards.

Upgrade *(Car Rental)*: A promotion sometimes run by car rentals to offer a car class upgrade for the normal price.

Upgrade *(Hospitality)*: The action to move a guest from a type of room to a better accommodation.

Upper/lower *(Tourism)*: Terms used in connection to bunk beds or berths at ship cabins or railway compartments.

Upscale *(Tourism)*: Something that is designed for a greater volume of customer affluence.

Upsell *(Tourism)*: A term used to define the skill to sell more or best services than those requested.

UPU *(Organizations)*: An acronym for Universal Postal Union.

Upwind *(Air Traffic)*: In the direction of the wind.

Upwind Leg *(Air Traffic)*: A flight path parallel to the runway in the direction of landing.

Urban Heat Island *(Tourism)*: A buildup of heat in the atmosphere above an urban environment which is created by buildings and other energy consumers, such as vehicles.

Urban Recreation *(Tourism)*: Urban recreational activity that takes place in an urban environment, such as shopping, visits to heritage sites, museums, movie theatres, music events, and indoor sports. People participating in urban activities are either urban residents, day visitors from other areas, or tourists.

Urban Tourism *(Tourism)*: Urban Tourism is that which is offered by many cities, on the basis of their historic, cultural, monumental, heritage or entertainment and recreational facilities, in order to attract tourists and business investment.

URL *(GDS)*: Code meaning Universal Resource Locator, which is the address of a web site.

US *(GDS)*: Code meaning: 1. Unable to accept request, have waitlisted; 2. US Airways.

US Territories *(IATA Geography)*: The overseas territories of the United States of America including, but not limited to: American Samoa, Baker Island, Guam, Howland Island, Jarvis Island, Johnson Atoll, Kingman Reef, Marshall Islands, Micronesia, Midway Islands, Northern Mariana Islands, Palau, Palmyra Islands, Saipan, Swains Island, Wake Island.

USA *(Geography)*: United States of America, the country comprising 50 states, the District of Columbia, Puerto Rico and the US Virgin Islands.

USD *(Airlines)*: Code for United States Dollar.

Useful Load *(Air Traffic)*: The weight comprising crew, passengers, fuel, baggage, cargo, and mail. It is calculated by deducting Basic Operating Weight from Maximum Ramp Weight.

User-friendly *(Computing)*: A device, hardware or software designed in such a way as to be easy to operate.

U-shape Setup *(Hospitality)*: A meeting arrangement in which tables are aligned in U-shape, with chairs on the outer side of the U.

USP *(Marketing)*: See Unique Selling Proposition.

USS *(Tourism)*: United States Ship.

USTAR *(Tourism)*: United States Travel Agent Registry.

USTDC *(Tourism)*: United States Travel Data Center.

USTOA *(Organizations)*: An acronym for United States Tour Operator's Association.

UT *(GDS)*: Code meaning Universal Time.

UTC *(GDS)*: Code meaning Unable to Contact.

UTC *(Geography)*: Universal Time Coordinate. See Coordinated Universal Time.

UTDN *(GDS)*: Code meaning Unattended Ticket Delivery Network.

Utilization Rate *(Car Rental)*: The percentage figured on a system-wide or local basis of vehicles in use during a specified period of time.

UTR *(GDS)*: Code meaning Unable to Reach.

UTV *(GDS)*: Code meaning Universal Travel Voucher.

UU *(GDS)*: Code meaning Unable to Confirm, have waitlisted

V

V *(Airlines)*: Code meaning "Victor," name used to designate the letter "V" in the International Phonetic Alphabet.

V *(GDS)*: Code for Economy coach discounted.

V-Berth *(Cruise)*: A berth aboard a yacht situated at the bow and following the contour of the boat into an inverted V shape.

V-shape Setup *(Hospitality)*: See Chevron Setup.

VAC *(Aeronautics)*: A code meaning Volts Alternating Current.

Vacancy *(Hospitality)*: A term used at hotels and motels to inform empty rooms are available for rent.

Vacant *(Hospitality)*: A room status term indicating a room has been cleaned and is ready for occupation.

Vacation *(Tourism)*: 1. Leisure paid time away from work dedicated to rest, travel, recreation or pleasure. In a legal sense, vacation is the period of paid time between the end of one term and the beginning of another, which employers are required to give employees. The length of vacations is dependent on the length of service and provisions of the local laws or collective agreement. 2. Vacation is also a scheduled period during which the activities of courts, schools, or other regular entities and businesses are suspended.

Vacation Family Houses *(Tourism)*: Non profit lodgings which offer facilities for family members taking holidays together with appropriated collective services.

Vacation Club *(Hospitality)*: A term used to describe various types of timesharing that usually involve the use or access to more than one resort location, and other vacation and travel services.

Vacation Hangover *(Tourism)*: The letdown, sort of exhaustion following a holiday period.

Vacation Ownership *(Hospitality)*: The expression describes a method of use and/or sharing ownership of vacation real estate in which vacationers purchase the right to occupy a condominium, apartment or other type of vacation accommodation for a period of time every year (usually one week). It is also known as Timeshare.

Vacationer *(Tourism)*: Any person who takes or is on a vacation devoting his time to pleasure, travel, recreation or relaxation rather than work.

Vacationist *(Tourism)*: See Vacationer.

Vaccination *(Tourism)*: The inoculation with a relatively harmless virus to produce immunity to certain diseases.

Valet *(Hospitality)*: An employee in a hotel who performs personal services for guests, as in valet parking.

Validating Carrier *(Airlines)*: The issuing airline whose numeric airline code is reflected in the electronic transaction for the flight/value coupon(s).The Validating Carrier shall be the controlling and authorizing airline for Electronic Ticketing transactions. See also Issuing Airline.

Validity *(Airlines)*: A condition referring to the length of time during which an air ticket or an air fare is valid for the passenger to receive the transportation service. Each type of fare has its own validity time. Normal fares are valid for one year, while promotional and special fares are limited to the validity noted for each individual fare.

Validity Dates *(Airlines)*: The dates determining the validity period for a fare or offer.

Valise *(Airlines)*: A small piece of luggage.

Valley Wind *(Geography)*: A wind that is formed during the day by the heating of the valley ground. It blows in the opposite direction of a mountain breeze.

Valuation Charge *(Airlines)*: A charge on the baggage transported, based on the declared value of such baggage.

Value Added Tax (VAT) *(Tourism)*: A form of taxation for the purchase of goods and services. It can be refunded in some countries under certain circumstances to foreign visitors after their visit. Value Added Tax that is charged on car rentals is not refundable.

Value-based Pricing *(Business)*: The practice of pricing a product with different amounts, depending on how each customer values that product.

Value-plus Model *(Business)*: A business strategy that combines low price offers with amenities and service to obtain outcomes that are valued better-than-average.

Value Season *(Airlines)*: Low or Shoulder seasons during which lower fares or rates are offered.

Van *(Tourism)*: Vehicles of varied types, which are larger than a car but smaller than a bus.

Van Pools *(Tourism)*: See High Occupancy Vehicle.

VAPS *(Air Traffic)* See Visual Approaches.

Variable Costs *(Tourism)*: The costs of operating a business that vary over time, are volume sensitive, and are directly related to the sales of goods or services such as costs of goods, shipping, sales commissions, rent, heat and electricity.

Varietal Wine *(Hospitality)*: A wine produced from a single variety of grape.

Variometer *(Air Traffic)*: A panel instrument, often as simple as a tiny ball in a vertical tube, registering subtle movements of aircraft.

VAT *(GDS)*: Code meaning Value Added Tax.

VCE *(GDS)*: Three-letter IATA code for Venice, a tourist destination in Italy.

VCP *(GDS)*: Three-letter IATA code for serving the city of Viracopos Airport Sao Paulo

VDT *(GDS)*: Code meaning Video Display Terminal.

Vector *(Air Traffic)*: A heading issued to an aircraft by ATC to provide navigational guidance by radar.

Vector Forces *(Aeronautics)*: The term is referred to the four forces that make aircraft fly. Those forces are: thrust, drag, gravity or weight, and lift. Thrust is the force generated by the engines. It is directed forward along the axis of the engine and moves the aircraft through the air. Drag is the aerodynamic force that opposes an aircraft's motion. It is generated by every part of the airplane. Gravity or weight is the force directed downward from the center of the airplane's mass towards the center of the earth. Lift is the component of aerodynamic force generated to oppose the gravity force by the motion of the airplane through the air. Lift is directed perpendicular to the flight direction; most of it is generated by the wings.

Vector Line *(Air Traffic)*: A course line that is predicted for a specified number of minutes assuming the aircraft's course does not change.

Vegetable Fruit *(Hospitality)*: A vegetable, such as a tomato, that is classified as a fruit because it contains the ovary of the plant.

Vehicle Class *(Car Rental)*: The car type defined by the passenger in the reservation. Car classes can be: Small (compact and economy), Medium (intermediate and full-size), Large (premium and luxury), SUV (intermediate, standard and full-size) and specialty (convertibles, mini vans and 12-passenger vans).

Vehicle License Fee *(Car Rental)*: A fee taxed to have the right of licensing the vehicle to others. This is a common practice in Europe.

Vehicle Licensing Cost Recovery Fee (VLCRF) *(Car Rental)*: At select locations this fee is sometimes charged to renters for vehicle registration and licensing fees.

Velocity Vector *(Air Traffic)*: Vector signaling the aircraft's true Speed.

Velocity *(Air Traffic)*: Speed. The speed of an object headed in a certain direction. It is the rate of motion in relation to time.

Velocity East *(Air Traffic)*: Aircraft velocity in true east direction

Velodrome *(Tourism)*: A stadium built for bicycle racing.

Velocity North *(Air Traffic)*: Aircraft velocity in true north direction

Vending *(Hospitality)*: The hotel area equipped with vending machines.

Vendor *(Hospitality)*: Any supplier of travel products or services.

Ventilation *(Hospitality)*: The process of supplying air to or removing air from an interior space.

Veranda or Verandah *(Cruise)*: A roofed-porch or balcony outside of a building intended for leisure. Verandas are also provided at some cruise ship staterooms.

Verification *(Tourism)*: The process of establishing the truth and accuracy of an action, as for a reservation.

Vertical Acceleration *(Air Traffic)*: Aircraft acceleration in a direction vertical to the earth.

Vertical Axis *(Air Traffic)*: The axis extending straight up and down through the center of gravity of an aircraft. The vertical axis is perpendicular to the longitudinal and lateral axes. It is sometimes called the "Z" axis.

Vertical Exaggeration *(Geography)*: An indicator which shows the number of times the vertical scale is greater than the horizontal scale on a cross-section profile.

Vertical Fin *(Aeronautics)*: A stabilizer that is part of the vertical tail structure of an airplane.

Vertical Stabilizer *(Aeronautics)*: The vertical part of the tail. The vertical stabilizer helps to increase the stability of the aircraft. It is also known as a Fin.

Vertical Takeoff and Landing (VTOL) *(Air Traffic)*: Aircraft that are able to make vertical takeoff and landing. They are not limited to helicopters, since there are other aircraft types with such ability.

Vertical Velocity *(Air Traffic)*: The aircraft speed in earth vertical direction.

Vertigo *(Tourism)*: A sensation of whirling caused by a fear of heights.

Very High Frequency Omni Directional Range (VOR) *(Air Traffic)*: A ground-based navigation aid that transmits very high frequency navigation signals, which is used as the basis for navigation in the National Airspace System. The VOR periodically identifies itself by Morse Code and may have an additional voice identification feature for transmitting instructions or information to pilots.

Very Large Ship *(Cruise)*: A ship in excess of 100,000 gross registered tons (GRT). Some very large ships are the Carnival Conquest, the Golden Princess, and Royal Caribbean's Navigator of the Seas.

Vessel *(Cruise)*: A generic term to define a craft able to navigate on the water.

VFR *(Air Traffic)*: A code for Visual Flight Rules.

VFR *(Tourism)*: Visiting Friends or Relatives, a trip for 1 to 365 days.

VFR Controllers *(Air Traffic)*: Airport Control Tower staff who occupy the most commanding visual position on the airport so that they can see all of the approach, departure and maneuvering areas. They are responsible for ensuring the safe separation and movement of departing, landing and taxiing aircraft. Controllers must be able to quickly remember important information, such as the registration numbers of aircraft, their types and speeds, positions in the air, and also the location of navigational aids in the area.

VGML *(GDS)*: Code meaning Vegetarian Meal.

VHF *(Air Traffic)*: A code meaning Very High Frequency Radio Equipment.

VHF Omni-directional Range (VOR) *(Air Traffic)*: A ground-based electronic navigation aid transmitting very high frequency navigation signals around 360 degrees, oriented from magnetic north. The VOR periodically identifies itself by Morse Code and may have an additional voice identification feature.

VHF Omnirange (VOR) *(Air Traffic)*: See VHF Omni-directional Range.

Via *(Airlines)*: A Latin term meaning by way of. Used together with an airline code it denotes a fare or journey is applicable to that airline.

VIA Rail *(Organizations)*: An independent Canadian corporation established in 1978 to operate trains in all regions of Canada over a network covering the country from the Atlantic coast to the Pacific coast. It operates 480 trains per week, including 300 in southern Quebec and southern Ontario, and runs over 14,000 kilometers of track serving some 450 Canadian communities. The company offers the most complete passenger service with domed observation cars, berths, roomettes and luxury suites. It has been ranked as one of the Great Trains of the World.

Victor *(Air Traffic)*: Designator for the letter "V" in the International Phonetic Alphabet.

Victor Airway *(Air Traffic)*: An airway system based on the use of VOR facilities.

Video Display Unit (VDU) *(GDS)*: See Computerized Reservation Terminal.

Video Display Terminals (VDT) *(GDS)*: See Computerized

Reservation Terminal.

Videoconference *(Computing)*: A meeting arrangement to allow participants who are in different geographical locations get linked by computer network connection, or a video system transmitted by satellite. The participants can see motion video images of each other. It is a mass articulation of a group of persons who appear to be in the same room together, and remote machines of highly sophisticated technology. Today's videoconferences can be held from one's own computer or even in a mobile setting.

VIE *(GDS)*: Three-letter IATA code for Vienna, capital city of Austria.

Villa *(Hospitality)*: A Spanish word for country-home, often used in the hotel business to denote a cottage or a small separate suite.

Vin Mousseux *(Hospitality)*: A French term meaning literally "foamy wine". It is used to characterize wines made in France outside of the Champagne district.

Vinotherapy *(Tourism)*: The therapeutic use of wine and grapes in beauty and health treatments.

Vintage *(Hospitality)*: The year of yield of grapes or wine or the year in which a wine was bottled.

Vintage Year *(Hospitality)*: The year in which the grapes for a wine were grown.

VIP *(GDS)*: Code meaning Very Important Person.

VIP Lounge *(Airlines)*: See Airport Lounge.

Virtual Airport *(Airlines)*: The system by which airline passengers can check-in at places other than the airport, where customer self service kiosks are provided.

Visa *(Tourism)*: A stamp or text imprinted in a passport authorizing the bearer to visit a country for specific purposes and for a specific length of time.

Visa Expediter *(Tourism)*: A person or company procuring the achievement of visas on a fee basis.

Visa Service *(Tourism)*: A service to expedite the processing of a visa.

Visa Support *(Tourism)*: Any documentation that can favor actively the approval of a visa, such as a letter of invitation or an evidence of confirmed bookings.

Visa Waiver Program (VWP) *(Tourism)*: A program established for certain countries to allow nationals of specific countries to enter for short stays without a visa.

Visibility *(Air Traffic)*: A measure of the opacity of the atmosphere, and therefore, the greatest distance one can see prominent objects with normal eyesight.

Visit Fares *(Airlines)*: A type of discounted economy fares designed for domestic flights in one country of destination. The tickets have to be obtained in conjunction with international air tickets and must be paid for prior to the starting date.

Visit USA *(Airlines)*: A program of individual fares available only to foreign travelers to visit the United States. They offer unlimited travel at reduced domestic fares within a specified time period and are subject to conditions of application that vary from one carrier to another.

Visit USA Fares *(Airlines)*: See Visit USA. Also referred to as VUSA fares.

Visitor *(Tourism)*: Any person visiting a foreign country for vacation or business reasons.

Visitors Centre *(Tourism)*: A travel information bureau located at a destination and operated by a tourism promotion, convention or commercial organization.

Visitor's Visa *(Tourism)*: A visa issued for tourist purposes.

Vistadome *(Tourism)*: A car on a train that allows viewing the passing countryside.

Visual Approaches (VAPS) *(Air Traffic)*: Approaches conducted under Instrument Flight Rules that authorizes the pilot to proceed visually to the airport. It is usually used in conjunction with Visual Separation

Visual Flight Rules (VFR) *(Air Traffic)*: A set of regulations governing the procedures to guide flights during periods of good visibility and limited cloud cover, under which a pilot may operate an aircraft by visual reference to the environment outside the cockpit. In such a condition, the pilot does not need to contact air traffic controllers and is responsible for maintaining safe separation from obstacles such as terrain, buildings, and other aircraft.

Visual Flight *(Air Traffic)*: A flight made by referencing the horizon and other outside visual landmarks.

Visual Flight Rules (VFR) *(Air Traffic)*: Rules that govern the procedures for conducting flight under visual conditions. The term is also used to indicate weather conditions that comply with specified VFR requirements. The expression is also used by pilots and controllers to indicate a type of flight plan. In most cases, the visual condition must be of about 3 miles of visibility plus other parameters in regard to clouds.

Visual Meteorological Conditions (VMC) *(Air Traffic)*: Meteorological conditions expressed in terms of visibility, distance from clouds, and ceiling equal to or better than specified minima.

Visualization *(Tourism)*: Technique that involves focusing the mind by consciously creating a mental image of a desired condition to bring about change.

Vitis Labrusca *(Hospitality)*: A variety of grape vine, native to North America that grows in colder areas.

Vitreous China *(Hospitality)*: Common material from which toilets are made.

VLA *(GDS)*: Code meaning Villa.

VLF *(Air Traffic)*: Code meaning Very Low Frequency

VFR *(Air Traffic)* Code meaning Visual Flight Rules

VMC *(Air Traffic)*: See Visual Meteorological Conditions.

Vodka *(Hospitality)*: Clear colorless liquor made of neutral spirits distilled from a mash.

Voice Analyzer *(Airlines)*: A device for security measure at airports capable to detect lying in a system of "yes" or "no" answers to questions.

Voice Mail *(Hospitality)*: A system that is part of the telephone equipment provided for hotel guests and staff to retrieve messages left by a caller.

Void *(Airlines)*: A term frequently used in travel industry for "null" or "useless".

VOL *(Air Traffic)*: Term meaning Volume. It is used to inform that the volume of aircraft exceeds the airport's capacity.

Volatile Organic Compounds (VOC) *(Ecology)*: Hydrocarbons released from burning fuel as well as vapors from paints and cleaning solvents. When released into the atmosphere these vapors react upon the sun and heat to combine with Nitrogen Dioxide (NOx) and form the ozone.

Volume Incentive (*Tourism*): An extra commission or other stimulus offered by a supplier to a travel agency for achieving a certain sales goal.

VolunTourism (*Tourism*): See Volunteer Tourism.

Volunteer Tourism (*Tourism*): A type of tourism in which tourists volunteer to get involved in certain kind of activities that contribute to aiding or alleviating the material necessities of some social groups or by helping restore the surrounding environments. It is also called VolunTourism or Voluntourism.

Voluntourism (*Tourism*): See Volunteer Tourism.

VOR (*Air Traffic*): See Very High Frequency Omni-directional Range.

VOR Receiver (*Air Traffic*): A cockpit device that receives VOR signals and allows pilots to select and maintain their magnetic compass course.

VOR Station (*Air Traffic*): A ground station that transmits VOR signals.

Vortices (*Air Traffic*): See Wingtip Vortices.

Voucher (*Tourism*): A pre-paid document with a monetary value issued to a client by a tour operator or travel agent, which is exchanged for goods or services. It is commonly used with independent packages and tours. The first coupon of this kind was created by Thomas Cook in 1867. It is also called an exchange order.

Voyeurism (*Tourism*): An immoral practice of a person who obtains sexual stimulation from observing unsuspecting individuals who are partly undressed, naked, or engaged in sexual acts, or (more generally) a person who watches other people's private lives.

VRO (*GDS*): Three-letter IATA code for Varadero, a beach destination in Cuba.

VSBY (*Air Traffic*): An abbreviation for Visibility.

VSI (*Air Traffic*): A code meaning Vertical Speed Indicator. It is a panel instrument that measures the rate of climb or descent in feet-per-minute.

VTOL (*Air Traffic*): See Vertical Take Off and Landing.

VUSA *(GDS)*: Code meaning Visit USA.

W

W *(Airlines)*: Code meaning "Whiskey", name used to designate the letter "W" in the International Phonetic Alphabet.

W *(GDS)*: Code meaning: 1. Economy coach Premium; 2. Together with a fare code it indicates a weekend fare; 3. Window Seat Request.

W/C *(GDS)*: Code meaning Will Call.

W/fac *(GDS)*: Code meaning With Facilities.

W/o fac *(GDS)*: Code meaning Without Facilities.

WAC *(Air Traffic)*: See World Aeronautical Charts.

Wait List or Waitlist or Wait-Listing *(Airlines)*: List produced when there are no more ready available spaces. Passengers requesting a reservation are listed, waiting for people to cancel reservations for a flight that is sold out.

Waitlist Segment *(Airlines)*: A segment that is not confirmed for a specific flight because seating was not available at the time the reservation was requested.

Waiver *(Tourism)*: In essence, a waiver is a unilateral act of renounce or relinquishment of a legal right, claim or privilege. If this renounce is voluntarily surrendered, it is considered an express waiver. In travel, law waiver is used in numerous contexts as in insurance coverage, liability or penalty.

Wake *(Air Traffic)*: Tumultuous currents of air trailing from the side and behind an aircraft in flight. The heavier the aircraft and the more concave the wing surfaces, the greater the wake turbulence. Wake turbulence is a threat to all aircraft flying behind other aircraft.

Wake *(Cruise)*: Also called wake turbulence, it is a streak of foamy turbulent water generated by a vessel.

Walked *(Hospitality)*: A term used to describe the situation when a traveler arrives at a hotel with a reservation but finds that no rooms are available. In such a case, the hotel pays for the traveler's accommodation at another hotel.

Walkie-talkie *(Tourism)*: A portable radio for transmitting and receiving communication within a limited range.

Walk-In *(Tourism)*: A customer who enters a travel agency's office without previous advice.

Walk-In Guest *(Hospitality)*: A guest who arrives at a hotel without a reservation.

Walk-In Refrigerator or Freezer *(Hospitality)*: A large refrigerator or freezer used in big kitchens for storing perishable items.

Walking a Guest *(Hospitality)*: See Walked.

Walking a Tour *(Tourism)*: Moving a traveler from a facility to another, because a service or product is not available.

Walk-up *(Airlines)*: A passenger who purchases a last time ticket, usually at the airport ticket counter.

WAN *(Air Traffic)*: Code for Wide Area Network.

Wanderlust *(Tourism)*: A German term literally meaning "wander desire" that is used to refer to a great desire to travel.

WAPTT *(Organizations)*: An acronym for World Association for Hospitality and Tourism Education and Training.

War Risk *(Tourism)*: Potential aggressive actions against civil ships or aircraft by a belligerent country or terrorist group.

War Risk Insurance *(Tourism)*: A type of insurance issued by marine underwriters against war-like operations specifically described in the policy. Besides the war risk, the war risk insurance covers also losses from derelict torpedoes and floating mines placed during former wars. It is issued even as a safeguard against unforeseen warlike developments.

Warning *(Air Traffic)*: A signal which alerts the operator to a dangerous condition requiring immediate action.

Warning Area *(Air Traffic)*: Airspace of defined dimensions extending from 3 nautical miles outward from the coast of the USA, where hazardous activities are performed, which may be harmful to non-participating aircraft. The purpose of such warning area is to warn pilots of the potential danger.

Warsaw Convention *(Airlines)*: An international multilateral agreement signed at Warsaw on 12 October 1929 as "The Convention for the Unification of Certain Rules Relating to International Carriage by Air". It is considered to be one of the most important instruments of private international law conceived to create a legal framework to foster an orderly development of international civil aviation. It sets the conditions of international transportation by air and deals with requirements regarding ticketing of passengers and carrier limitations of liability on cases of accident, or damage or loss of baggage. While complete unification of law was impossible to attain, the Warsaw Convention laid down certain vitally important rules for international carriage by air. In summary, the Warsaw Convention states the following:

1. It obligates carriers to issue passenger tickets;

2. It orders carriers to issue baggage checks for checked luggage;

3. It instructs carriers to issue air way bills for the transportation of goods;

4. It establishes liability limits in case of dead or injury to passengers due to an accident on international flights;

5. It introduces liability limits for loss or damage to checked baggage and hand luggage.

6. It spells out the procedures for claims and restitution.

Originally signed in 1929 by 31 states, currently 105 signatory nations have adhered to it.

Warsaw Convention System *(Airlines)*: The "Convention for the Unification of Certain Rules Relating to International Carriage by Air," signed at Warsaw on 12 October 1929, or that Convention as amended by the Hague Protocol of 1955, whichever may be applicable to the carriage. The Warsaw Convention of 1929 was adopted when civil aviation was in its early stages. It became necessary to adopt a set of rules to protect the young airline industry from potentially ruinous liability claims. That need was attained by imposing limits on financial liability of air carriers, based on the precedents existing in maritime law at that time. Later on, the development of aviation demanded also the updating of its legal frame. Over the last decades the Warsaw Convention has derived into what is commonly referred to as the "Warsaw Convention System", due to a series of amending Protocols and supplementary instruments gradually adopted. Warsaw Convention System consists of:

1. The original Warsaw "Convention for the Unification of Certain Rules Relating to International Carriage by Air of 12 October

1929";
2. The "Hague Protocol to Amend the Convention for the Unification of Certain Rules Relating to International Carriage" of 28 September 1955;
3. The Montreal Additional Protocols I, II, III and IV of 25 September 1975;
4. The Guadalajara "Convention Supplementary to the Warsaw Convention for the Unification of Certain Rules Relating to International Carriage by Air Performed by a Person Other than the Contracting Carrier" of 18 September 1961;
5. The "Supplemental Montreal Inter-Carrier Agreement" of 1966 (CAB 18900) relative to a journey to, from or via an agreed stopping place in the USA;
6. The "Supplemental IATA Inter-Carrier Agreement on Passenger Liability" of 1995;
7. In most cases the "IATA Conditions of Contract"; and
8. The Conditions of Carriers to which the IATA Conditions of Contract refer.
The Warsaw Convention System rules are difficult to apply in practice, because it often becomes complicated to determine which Warsaw or Warsaw related instrument or instruments apply for a given case. Another problem appears when trying to define which state has ratified which instrument. Different judicial interpretations contribute to additionally complicate the Warsaw System provision.

WAS *(GDS)*: Three-letter IATA code for Washington D.C., USA.

Wash-in, Wash-out *(Air Traffic)*: A method of increasing lift by increasing (Wash-In) or decreasing (Wash-Out) the angle of incidence on the outer part of an airplane wing to counteract the effects of engine torque.

Waste Management *(Ecology)*: Set of duties and actions of administering procedures, systems and services for the collection, handling, treatment (including recycling) and disposal of all sorts of wastes produced in an area or company.

Wastewater *(Ecology)*: Water containing waste materials or pollutants dissolved in it. Black water and gray water contaminated by contact with waste are types of wastewater. Wastewater is highly dangerous for human and animal health, but for plants as well.

Waste-to-energy *(Ecology)*: The burning of municipal solid waste to produce energy.

WATA *(Organizations)*: An acronym for "World Association of Travel Agents."

Watch List *(Airlines)*: List of names of suspicious persons held in database by law enforcement or governmental agencies for intense security screening at airports. Persons watch listed can be denied boarding or even arrested under given circumstances.

Water Closet *(Hospitality)*: Term synonymous with toilet.

Water Park *(Tourism)*: A theme park designed around water rides and activities such as water slides, pools, wave pools, water cannons, jet sprays, ground geysers, cascading waterfalls and others.

Water Parks Cruising *(Tourism)*: Ships are bigger than ever and cruise lines strive today to add more and more onboard activities to keep passengers happily entertained. Major cruise lines are presently offering "Onboard Water Parks" at their news ships including racing slides, whirlpools, surf simulators, jet sprays, water cannons, etc.

Water Park Resort *(Tourism)*: A hotel located in a water park or in an adjacent area. Accommodation at such hotels facilitates the admission to the water park.

Waterfront *(Tourism)*: The part of land facing the sea or on the edge of a body of water. Also the harbor area of a city or town.

Waterline *(Cruise)*: The line that water reaches along the hull of the ship. It changes depending on the ship's characteristics and the load. The waterline is normally painted to assist in determining the floating level of the ship.

Waterpark Hotel *(Hospitality)*: A hotel that offers large recreational water components, such as multiple pools, slides, toboggans or other water related venues.

Watershed *(Geography)*: 1. A region drained by a river, a system of rivers or a stream. 2. A ridge or a mountain dividing two drainage areas.

WATS *(GDS)*: Code meaning Wide Area Telephone Service.

Wave Pool *(Tourism)*: A large swimming pool equipped with a mechanism for producing artificial waves.

WAW *(GDS)*: Three-letter IATA code for Warsaw, capital city of Poland.

Waxing *(Tourism)*: Temporary hair removal method by the application of warm or cool wax on to areas of unwanted hair.

Waypoint (WYPT) *(Air Traffic)*: A geographical reference on the ground, predefined as a point of interest for the flight, an approach definition, or progress reporting purposes.

Waypoint Approach *(Air Traffic)*: To approach a waypoint

WB *(GDS)*: Code meaning Westbound.

WC *(GDS)*: Code meaning Water Closet (toilet).

WCA *(Air Traffic)*: Code meaning Warning, Caution, Advisory

WCHC *(GDS)*: Code meaning Wheelchair (when the passenger is immobile).

WCHR *(GDS)*: Code meaning Wheelchair (when the passenger can walk).

WCHS *(GDS)*: Code meaning Wheelchair (when the passenger cannot negotiate stairs).

Weather *(Geography)*: The general term used to describe the atmosphere conditions at a specific time including temperature, humidity, wind, precipitation, clouds, and sunshine.

Weather Advisories *(Air Traffic)*: Updated weather reports available to pilots during the enroute phase of a flight.

Weather Chart *(Air Traffic)*: An outline map that shows weather patterns.

Weather Deck *(Cruise)*: The uppermost deck of a ship that is exposed to the outside air.

Weather Depiction Chart *(Air Traffic)*: A simplified version of a surface weather chart used for flight planning and determination of general weather conditions. It also helps pilots to quickly locate areas of adverse weather. Weather depiction chart reports are issued every 3 hours.

Weather Forecast *(Air Traffic)*: A computer generated assumption as to what the weather will be at a particular time in a particular area.

Weather Report *(Air Traffic)*: A report of the state of the atmosphere at a specific time and with respect to its effect on life and human activities. It includes brightness, cloudiness, humidity, precipitation, temperature, visibility, and wind.

Weather Side *(Cruise)*: The side of a ship exposed to the dominant winds.

Weather Tourist *(Tourism)*: A person whose travel target is the observance of meteorological events.

Web *(Tourism)*: Popular term for World Wide Web.

Web *(Ecology)*: Also called Food chain, Food Networks or Trophic Networks, it is a graph describing the feeding relationship between species within an ecosystem. The relationships of organisms with each other are represented by arrows linking them and representing the direction of biomass transfer within a web. It also shows how the energy from the producer is transferred to the consumers.

WED *(GDS)*: Code for Wednesday.

Wedge *(Hospitality)*: The part of a fruit, usually lime or lemon, used for garnish in food and beverage operations.

Weekday *(Airlines)*: Any day from Monday to Thursday.

Weekday Fare *(Airlines)*: An airline fare valid for travel from Monday thru Thursday. They are identified by the code "X" and are lower that weekend fares.

Weekday Rate *(Car Rental)*: A 24-hour period. The weekday rate applies when a rental does not qualify for a weekly or weekend day provision. Minimum weekday rental is one day, and maximum is four consecutive days.

Weekend *(Airlines)*: The period of the week from Friday to Sunday.

Weekend Break *(Tourism)*: A short holiday package in the United Kingdom of two or three days.

Weekend Fare *(Airlines)*: An airline fare valid for travel from Friday to Sunday. They are identified by the code "W" and are higher than Weekday Fares.

Weekend Rental or Weekend Rate *(Car Rental)*: Some car rental companies offer promotions for weekends. To qualify for a weekend rate the traveler must pick up his car any time after 12:00 noon on Thursday and return it by 11:59 p.m. (one minute before midnight) the following Monday.

Weight *(Aeronautics)*: The force of gravity acting on an object.

The weight force pulls an aircraft toward the Earth and must be overcome by a combination of lift and thrust.

Weigh Anchor (*Cruise*): To weigh anchor means to take up or lift the anchor off the sea bed when getting underway or "under weigh".

Weight Concept or Weight System *(Airlines)*: One of the two methods that airlines apply for the baggage allowances. When weight concept is applied, the allowance is expressed in the amount of kilos permitted to carry without an extra charge. The general free baggage allowance is 20 kg for Economy Class, 30 kg for Business Class and First Class. These standards apply only to adults and children, since passengers paying infant fares are not entitled to free baggage allowance.

Weight on Wheels (WOW) *(Air Traffic)*: An expression to indicate whether the aircraft has weight on its wheels, meaning airborne or on the ground. Weight on wheels can be detected by a sensor on the wheels, computed from other state data, or a combination of systems.

Well Brand *(Hospitality)*: Any generic brand of liquor served when a guest does not specify the brand.

Well Drink *(Hospitality)*: A drink made from an inexpensive house brand of liquor, usually kept in a "well" (an enclosed space) below the bar where customers cannot see the labels.

Wellness Tourism (*Tourism*): A type of tourism in which activities and travelers' main motivation is to preserve or promote their health. Wellness Tourism is designed around a comprehensive service package including physical fitness, beauty care, healthy nutrition, diet, relaxation, meditation, mental activity, and education. The accommodation is usually arranged at specialized hotels that provide appropriate professional know-how and individual care.

Western Africa (*IATA Geography*): The territory comprising Angola, Benin, Burkina Faso, Cameroon, Cape Verde, Central African Republic, Chad, Congo (Brazzaville, Côte d'Ivoire, Democratic Republic of Congo (Kinshasa), Equatorial Guinea, Gabon, Gambia, Ghana, Guinea, Guinea Bissau, Liberia, Mali, Mauritania, Niger, Nigeria, Sao Tome and Principe, Senegal, Sierra Leone, Togo.

Western Hemisphere (WH) *(IATA Geography)*: The entire territory of Area 1.

Western Hemisphere Travel Initiative (WHTI) *(Tourism)*: A U.S. law that requires all travelers, including U.S. and Canadian citizens, to present a valid passport or another travel document when travelling to, through or from the United States from within the western hemisphere. It is being implemented in stages by mode of transportation. For the time being, the WHTI disposition issued in January 2007 concerns air travel only, while norms for land or water port entries will be impost effective June 1, 2009.

Wet Bar *(Hospitality)*: The area of a small bar or counter for mixing alcoholic drinks that has a sink with running water.

Wet Landing *(Cruise)*: The arrival in a beach on a small boat that requires passengers to step into the shore water.

Wet Lease *(Airlines)*: The leasing arrangement of an aircraft including the provision of crew and supporting services, such as ground support equipment, fuel and related aids, or at least one crewmember. Wet Lease can not act on code-sharing arrangements.

Wet Wings *(Aeronautics)*: Method for containing fuel in the wings without using rubber fuel cells.

WH *(GDS)*: Global Indicator for a travel within Western Hemisphere.

Wharf *(Cruise)*: A dock where ships lie to load and unload.

Whiskey *(Airlines)*: Designator for the letter "W" in the International Phonetic Alphabet.

Whiskey (Whisky) *(Hospitality)*: The generic term for a family of spirits made from grains, such as Scotch, Irish, American (bourbon), and Canadian whiskey. There is a great variety of whiskeys, each having unique characteristics according to the grain used, fermentation process, distillation, and processing after distillation.

Whistle Stop *(Tourism)*: A slang term to denote a very short stop en route.

White-knuckle Flyer *(Airlines)*: A slang term for a person who is fearful to fly.

Whitewater *(Geography)*: It is formed in rapids, when

a river's gradient drops enough to form an unstable current. The water appears white and spumous. The term is also used for less-turbulent but still agitated flows.

Whitewater Kayaking *(Tourism)*: The sport of paddling a kayak on a whitewater river. It is accomplished in a range of water flows, from gently moving water to dangerous whitewater.

Whitewater Rafting *(Tourism)*: A recreational activity using inflatable rubber boats to travel down rivers with rapids. The term "whitewater" also has a broader meaning, applying to any river or creek that has a significant number of rapids.

White-Water Sledging *(Tourism)*: See Hydrospeed.

WHO *(Organizations)*: See World Health Organization.

Wholesale Net Rates *(Tourism)*: Rates that are offered by service providers to wholesalers including a discount off retail prices.

Wholesaler *(Tourism)*: A company that usually creates and markets inclusive tours and FITs for sale through travel agents. Wholesalers usually do not sell to the final consumer; they deal primarily with retailer travel agencies.

Wholesaler Rate *(Tourism)*: A price for a product or service excluding commissions, which is offered to tour operators and packagers.

WHTI *(Tourism)*: See Western Hemisphere Travel Initiative.

Wide-body *(Airlines)*: A type of aircraft with a fuselage diameter of 5 to 6 meters (16 to 20 ft) and more than one aisle in the passenger cabin to accommodate from 200 to 600 passengers. They are usually configured with multiple travel classes. Typical examples of wide body aircraft include the Boeing 747, 767 and 777; McDonnell Douglas MD11; the Airbus Industries' A300, A310, A330, A340 and A380. Technically, any aircraft may be considered a wide body.

WILAD *(GDS)*: Code meaning Will Advise.

WILCO *(GDS)*: A code meaning: 1. Will Contact; 2. Will comply (with).

WILCON *(GDS)*: Code meaning Will Contact.

Wildlife *(Ecology)*: The term comprises all non-domesticated plants, animals, and other living creature, wild by nature, living in their natural environment, on land the majority of their life cycle.

Wildlife Tourism *(Tourism)*: A type of tourism that is focused on wildlife viewing. It is a variation of the large category of Nature Tourism.

WILFO *(GDS)*: Code meaning Will Follow.

Wilma *(Airlines)*: A method of boarding an airplane in which all window seats are filled first, then middle seats, and finally aisle seats.

WILRE *(GDS)*: Code meaning Will Report.

Wind *(Geography)*: Air in motion relative to the surface of the Earth, from an area of high pressure to an area of low pressure.

Wind Chill *(Climate)*: A type of cold wind resulting from a combination of temperature and wind. It can be life threatening because it rapidly drives down the body temperature.

Wind Chill Factor *(Climate)*: 1. The rate of heat loss from exposed human body by the action of moving air combined with the environment temperature. 2. An index combining the effect of temperature and wind to know the weather status.

Wind Direction *(Air Traffic)*: The direction from which the wind is blowing. It is reported with reference to true north and expressed to the nearest 10 degrees, or to one of the 16 points of the compass.

Wind Shear or Windshear *(Air Traffic)*: A violent and sudden change in wind speed of wind resulting in a tearing or shearing effect which can be fatal for an aircraft in process of landing.

Wind Shift *(Air Traffic)*: The term is applied to a change in wind direction of 45 degrees or more, which takes place in less than 15 minutes.

Wind Speed *(Air Traffic)*: The rate of the motion of the wind on a unit of time that can be measured in knots, nautical miles or kilometers per hour.

Wind Surf *(Tourism)*: A sea sport performed with a person standing on a surfboard with an attached sail.

Wind Tunnel *(Aeronautics)*: A tubular passage in which high-speed movements of air or other gases are produced. It is used as a probationary aeronautical tool to test objects such as engines, aircraft, airfoils and rockets placed inside the wind tunnel to investigate the airflow around them and the aerodynamic forces acting upon them.

Wind Tunnel Testing *(Aeronautics)*: A tool of Aeronautics used to test objects such as engines, aircraft, airfoils and rockets placed inside the wind tunnel and using instruments to gather data while air is blown by the model. Wind tunnel testing is used to investigate the effects of airflow and aerodynamic forces that affect them.

Wind Tunneling *(Aeronautics)*: See Wind Tunnel Testing.

Windjammer *(Cruise)*: A large cruise ship powered by wind and sails resembling a merchant ship of the late 19th century.

Windlass *(Cruise)*: A lifting device used to raise and lower a ship's anchor, usually located on the forecastle head of the ship.

Windward *(Cruise)*: The ship's side from which the wind blows.

Windward *(Geography)*: The geographic position on the side of a relief feature facing the prevailing winds.

Wine *(Hospitality)*: The fermented juice of grapes, which also comprises a range of other juicy fruits such as blackberry. The term extends also to other fermented drinks such as rice wine and ginger wine. There are four basic types of wine: Still (that is non-sparkling), Sparkling or effervescent, Fortified (in which alcohol has been added to stop the fermentation), and Aromatic (flavored with herbs).

Wine/Culinary tourism *(Hospitality)*: A type of tourism whose main appeal consists of experiencing good food and wine.

Wine Steward *(Hospitality)*: See Sommelier.

Wing *(Aeronautics)*: Each of the two parts of an airplane that are attached to the fuselage. Wings are shaped in such a way that they provide lift for the airplane. There are four basic types of wings: Straight, sweep, delta, and variable sweep.

Wing Fence *(Air Traffic)*: Term used by some aircraft manufacturers for the vertical structures at the outside ends of the wings of some of their jets, instead of winglet.

Wing Loading *(Air Traffic)*: The maximum take-off gross weight of an aircraft divided by its wing area.

Winglet *(Aeronautics)*: A nearly vertical structure at the wingtip of the aircraft designed to reduce drag by inhibiting turbulence.

Wingtip Vortices *(Air Traffic)*: Circular patterns of air created by the movement of an airfoil through the air when generating lift.

Winter Tourism *(Tourism)*: A seasonal type of Sports Tourism very similar to Snow Tourism in respect to activities performed. As a formal term, it refers to a sport played on snow or ice, but informally can refer to sports played in winter that are also played year-round like basketball. The main winter sports are ice hockey and figure skating, sledding events such as bobsleigh, skiing (Alpine and Nordic) and snowboarding. Other common winter sports include snow-blading, monoskiing, skwal and tobogganing.

WIPO *(Organizations)*: See World Intellectual Property Organization.

Wire Transfer *(Business):* Transmission of funds via an electronic system from one bank to another, which is commonly used to make payments to foreign suppliers.

Within Mileage *(Airlines)*: Verification carried to know whether the actual flown mileage for a route including deviations fits in the maximum permitted mileage. If it fits, the published fare is charged; otherwise, the fare will be increased to the percentage of mileage deviation.

WK *(GDS)*: Code meaning Week.

WK *(GDS)*: Code meaning Was Confirmed.

WL *(GDS)*: Code meaning Waitlist.

WLG *(GDS)*: Three-letter IATA code for Wellington, capital city of New Zealand.

WND *(Air Traffic)*: A code for Wind.

WOM or WoM *(Airlines)*: Word of Mouth. The oral comments customers make to others about a product, a service or a tour experience.

Workshop *(Airlines)*: A seminar or meeting of persons joined to explore a subject or to develop a skill or technique.

World Aeronautical Charts (WAC) *(Air Traffic)*: Types of charts providing topographic information about land areas of the world at a size and scale convenient for navigation by moderate speed aircraft. Such information includes cities and towns, main roads, railroads, important landmarks, drainage and relief, as well as visual and radio aids to navigation, airports, controlled airspace, restricted areas, obstructions, and pertinent data.

World Association for Hospitality and Tourism Education and Training (AMFORHT) *(Organizations)*: An organization created at Nice in 1969 under the French name of *Association Mondiale pour la Formation en Hôtellerie et Tourisme* as part of the same movement which created WTO. They were aimed to define, develop, promote and adapt world tourism training to the needs and evolution of the tourism industry. Its is supported by International Organizations dealing with tourism such as WTO, ILO, IHRA, UFTAA, and its work is based on the world congresses of Brussels, Geneva, Budapest, Lisbon, Toronto, Havana, Costa-Rica that are considered as milestones in the history of professional tourism training.

World Association for Professional Tourism Training (WAPTT) *(Organizations)*: See World Association for Hospitality and Tourism Education and Training.

World Association of Travel Agents (WATA) *(Organizations)*: Eight professional travel agents from France, Italy, Belgium and Switzerland met in Geneva on May 5, 1949 to create an international body to improve and rationalize the organization of international tourism. The purpose has worked helping business exchanges prosper. At present the World Association of Travel Agencies (WATA) is a worldwide organization of travel agencies dedicated to the enhancement of the professionalism and profitability of member agents through mutual cooperation and global networking. Its members are committed to the highest standards of business ethics and quality of service. The headquarters of the organization is in Switzerland.

World Health Organization (WHO) *(Organizations)*: A specialized agency of the United Nations that promotes technical cooperation for health among nations. It performs programs to control and eradicate disease and is committed to improving the quality of human life. The objective of WHO is the attainment by all peoples of the highest possible level of health. It was founded in 1948 and presently has 192 members.

World Intellectual Property Organization (WIPO) *(Organizations)*: WIPO is the UN agency responsible for the protection of intellectual property throughout the world, and for the administration of various multilateral treaties dealing with the legal and administrative aspects of intellectual property. WIPO was created by the Paris Convention of 1883 and was reorganized by the Berne Convention of 1886. Finally, in 1893 both bureaus united to form an international organization called the United International Bureau for the Protection of Intellectual Property. In 1974 it became a specialized agency of the UN. WIPO's members are currently 182 sovereign states.

World Trade Organization (WTO) *(Organizations)*: A global international organization dealing with the rules of trade between nations. Its goal is helping to conduct the business of producers of goods and services, exporters, and importers. The WTO was founded by Uruguay Round negotiations on 1 January 1995. Its main offices are located in Geneva, Switzerland, and presently WTO has a membership of 151 countries.

World Travel & Tourism Council (WTTC) *(Organizations)*: WTTC is the only organization representing the private sector in all parts of the Travel and Tourism system worldwide. Its mission is to raise conscience of the full economic impact of Travel and Tourism. Governments are encouraged to make the activity's potential available by adopting the Council's policy framework for sustainable tourism development. WTTC was founded in 1990 and is formed at present by the presidents, chairs and CEOs of 100 of the world's foremost companies in all sectors of the industry, including accommodation, catering, entertainment, recreation, transportation and other travel-related services. Its main offices are located in London, UK.

World Tourism Organization (WTO or UNWTO) *(Organizations)*: The WTO is a specialized agency of the United Nations Organization and the leading international body in the field of tourism. It serves as a global forum for tourism policy issues and a source of tourism technology. It includes 157 countries and territories and more than 300 Affiliate Members representing the private sector, educational institutions, tourism associations and local tourism authorities. The organization is based in Madrid and maintains regional representatives in Africa, the Americas, East Asia and the Pacific, Europe, the Middle East and South Asia. One of its main roles is the development of responsible, sustainable and universally accessible tourism, paying particular attention to the interests of developing countries. The Organization promotes the use of the "Global Code of Ethics" for Tourism as a tool to maximize the positive economic, social and cultural effects of tourism among member countries, tourist destinations and businesses, as well as fully attainment of benefits, while minimizing its negative social and environmental impacts.

World Travel and Tourism Council (WTTC) *(Tourism)*: The WTTC is formed by executives from all sectors of the tourism industry, including accommodation, catering, cruises, entertainment, recreation, transportation and travel-related services. Its vision is to make of tourism a strategic economic and employment priority to move towards open and competitive markets, to pursue sustainable development, and to eliminate barriers to growth.

World Travel Guide *(Tourism)*: A yearly publication that provides detailed information on most of the countries in the world, with news on currency, transportation, climate, visa and passport requirements, sightseeing opportunities, etc.

World Travel Market (WTM) *(Tourism)*: World's largest travel trade exhibition, which takes place in November each year in London.

World Youth Student and Educational Travel Confederation (WYSE) *(Organizations)*: An organization that was formed in 2006, by the merging of the Federation of International Youth Travel Organizations (FIYTO) and the International Student Travel Confederation (ISTC). At present it has over 550 members representing the global community of youth travel, student travel, cultural exchange and international education specialists. With a network of 5,000 locations in 118 countries, WYSE members provide international travel and educational experiences for more than 10 million students and youth each year.

World Wildlife Foundation (WWF) *(Organizations)*: One of the largest environmental organizations in the world that was born in 1961. Currently there are more than 2,000 WWF conservation projects underway around the world. Its objective is focused to stop the degradation of the planet's natural environment and to build a future in which humans live in harmony with nature. It is intended to be achieved by conserving the world's biological diversity; by ensuring that the use of renewable natural resources is sustainable, and by promoting the reduction of pollution and wasteful consumption.

Worldspan *(GDS)*:   An independent GDS service provider.

WORM *(Airlines)*: An abbreviation meaning Write Once, Read Many. Applicable to a RFID bag tag that can be written to only once, thereafter, the tag can only be read.

Wort *(Hospitality)*: The sweet solution of ground malt or other grain before or in process of fermentation used to produce beer and distilled malt liquors. Sweet wort becomes brewed wort, later fermenting wort and finally beer.

WOW *(Air Traffic)*: See Weight on Wheels.

WPT *(Air Traffic)*: See Waypoint.

Wright, Wilbur and Orville *(Aviation)*: The Wright brothers, Wilbur (born 16 April 1867, dead 30 May 1912) and Orville (born 19 August 1871, dead 30 January 1948), were two American mechanics, the first to carry to completion the world's first successful airplane flight. Although other people before them had built and experimented aircraft, they are fairly credited for inventing aircraft controls that made fixed wing flight possible. The historical flight using a powered machine heavier than the air took place on 17 December 1903 in Kitty Hawk, North Carolina. Two years later, they developed their flying machine into the first practical fixed-wing aircraft. None of the Wright brothers got married, maybe due to their heavy work, as one can deduct from the Wilbur's witty remark the he "could not support a wife and a flying machine". Wilbur died by cause of a typhoid fever at the age of 45 years. Orville became president of the Wright Company, but since he was not skilled for business, he sold it in 1915. His last flight as a pilot was performed in 1918, after which he got retired. Orville Wright died of a heart attack at the age of 77 years.

WTM *(Tourism)*: See World Travel Market.

WTO *(Organizations)*: An acronym for "World Tourism Organization."

WTRVW *(GDS)*: Code meaning Water View.

WTTC *(Organizations)*: An acronym for "World Travel & Tourism Council."

WWF *(Organizations)*: An acronym for "World Wildlife Foundation."

WX *(Air Traffic)*: Code meaning Weather.

WX DEV *(Air Traffic)*: Code meaning Weather Deviation.

WYPT *(Air Traffic)*: See Waypoint.

WYSE *(Organizations)*: An acronym for "World Youth Student and Educational Travel Confederation."

X

X *(Airlines)*: Code meaning "X-ray," name used to designate the letter "X" in the International Phonetic Alphabet.

X *(GDS)*: Code meaning: 1. Connection; 2. Together with a fare type code, it indicates a Midweek Fare.

X Category *(GDS)*: On some cruise lines "X" is a "Balcony Guarantee" cabin.

XA *(GDS)*: Code meaning Animal and Plant Health Inspection Fee.

XBAG *(GDS)*: Code meaning Excess Baggage.

X-band *(Air Traffic)*: Frequency range in which most general aviation weather radars operate.

XL *(GDS)*: Code meaning Cancel Listing.

Xenophobia *(Tourism)*: An unreasonable fear or hatred of strangers or foreigners. This irrational phenomenon is also present in contemporary tourism, mainly manifesting as hostile attitudes of residents towards tourists.

XF *(GDS)*: A code meaning: 1. Cancelled phone; 2. Passenger Facility Tax.

XL *(GDS)*: A code meaning: 1. Cancel; 2. Cancel Waitlist.

XLD *(GDS)*: Code meaning Cancelled.

Xmas *(GDS)*: Code meaning Christmas.

XN *(GDS)*: Code meaning Cancelled Name.

XO *(GDS)*: Code meaning Exchange Order (followed by a number).

Xpond *(Air Traffic)*: Abbreviation for Transponder.

XR *(GDS)*: Code meaning Cancellation Recommended.

X-ray *(Airlines)*: 1. Designator for the letter "X" in the International

Phonetic Alphabet. 2. A baggage screening technology.

XS *(GDS)*: Code meaning Cancelled Segment.

XSEC *(GDS)*: Code meaning Extra Section or Flight.

XTN *(GDS)*: Code meaning Extension.

XX *(GDS)*: Code meaning Cancellation Confirmed.

XY *(GDS)*: Code meaning Immigration INS Fee.

Y

Y *(Airlines)*: Code meaning "Yankee," name used to designate the letter "Y" in the International Phonetic Alphabet.

Y *(GDS)*: Code for Economy or Coach Class.

Y Category *(Cruise)*: On some cruise lines "Y" is an Outside Guarantee cabin.

Y Discount Fare *(Airlines)*: See Selling Fare.

YA *(GDS)*: Code meaning Young Adult.

Yacht *(Cruise)*: A large and often luxury sail boat used for private cruising, racing or other non-commercial purpose.

Yacht Club *(Cruise)*: A private club located near a large body of water, whose main purpose is to provide facilities such as marinas to boat owners.

Yankee *(Airlines)*: Designator for the letter "Y" in the International Phonetic Alphabet.

Yaw *(Aeronautics)*: A rotational motion in which the aircraft turns around its vertical axis. This causes the aircraft's nose to move to the pilot's right or left.

Yaw *(Cruise)*: A ship's temporary turn or deviation in its strait course.

YC *(GDS)*: Code meaning Customs User Fee.

YDA *(GDS)*: Code meaning Yesterday.

YEA *(GDS)*: Three-letter IATA code for Edmonton, Alberta, Canada.

YEG *(GDS)*: Three-letter IATA code for Winnipeg, Manitoba, Canada.

Yeast *(Hospitality)*: A type of living organism that converts starches or other sugars into glucose.

YHA *(Organisms)*: An acronym for "Youth Hostels Association."

Yield *(Airlines)*: The calculation of income produced on the activities performed by airlines. It is the average revenue per paid passenger mile or revenue ton mile, expressed in cents per mile.

Yield Management *(Airlines)*: The set of actions aimed to maximizing the revenue by raising or lowering prices in respect to demand. Also known as revenue management, it is the process airlines use to set fares, adjusting prices up or down with the purpose of finding the mix of seat prices that produces the highest revenue.

Yield Management *(Hospitality)*: A process or strategy that hotel operators use to maximize their hotel room revenue by achieving the right balance between room rates and occupancy that generates the most revenue.

Yield Management *(Tourism)*: A complex pricing system that allows travel companies to maximize profits by charging varying rates over time for comparable products.

Yin and Yang *(Tourism)*: Yin is the universal energy force whose characteristics are feminine, cold, dark, quiet, static and wet. Yang is masculine, warm, bright, dynamic and dry. In Traditional Chinese Medicine true balance and health are achieved only when these two opposing forces are in balance.

YL *(GDS)*: Code meaning Your Letter.

YMQ *(GDS)*: 1. Three-letter IATA code for Montreal, Quebec, Canada. 2. Three-letter IATA code for Mirabel International Airport serving the city of Montreal.

Yoga *(Tourism)*: An ancient Hindu practice comprising focused deep breathing, stretching and toning the body, using various postures, pursuing to reach full physical, mental and spiritual potential.

Yogwan *(Hospitality)*: A traditional and cheap Korean lodge.

Yoke *(Aeronautics)*: The control wheel of an aircraft, having similar properties of an automobile steering wheel. In fixed-wing aircraft it is mounted on a column between the operator's legs, and is operated by pushing and pulling with hands.

Youth Fare *(Airlines)*: A type of airfare available for young people. To be qualified for this discounted fare, the passenger has to be in the range from 12 years of age to 22 or 25 years of age, according to carrier's regulations.

Youth Hostel *(Hospitality)*: An inexpensive accommodation featuring dormitory-style accommodations, very popular among student travelers.

Youth Tourism *(Tourism)*: A type of tourism focused on the youth and student market, including some special air fares and accommodation promotions worldwide.

YOW *(GDS)*: Three-letter IATA code for Ottawa, Ontario, Canada.

You-drive *(Car Rental)*: See Hire Car.

YR *(GDS)*: Code meaning Your.

YTO *(GDS)*: Three-letter IATA code for Toronto, Ontario, Canada.

YTZ *(GDS)*: Three-letter IATA code for Toronto City Centre Airport serving the city of Toronto.

YUL *(GDS)*: Three-letter IATA code for Dorval International Airport serving the city of Montreal.

YVR *(GDS)*: Three-letter IATA code for Vancouver, British Columbia, Canada.

YY *(GDS)*: Two-letter code used when the air carrier is unknown

YYC *(GDS)*: Three-letter IATA code for Calgary, Alberta, Canada.

YYZ *(GDS)*: Three-letter IATA code for Pearson International Airport serving the city of Toronto.

Z

Z *(Airlines)*: Code meaning "Zulu," name used to designate the letter "Z" in the International Phonetic Alphabet.

Z *(Air Traffic)*: Zulu Time. Another term used to designate Coordinated Universal Time (UTC), the standard time of reference to every place in the world.

Z Category *(Cruise)*: On some cruise lines, "Z" is an Inside Guarantee cabin.

Z-plane *(Aeronautics)*: Z-plane is used in control systems engineering in the design of control laws. See Also Z Transform.

Z transform *(Aeronautics)*: Z transforms are commonly used by system engineers to describe avionics systems.

Z-time *(Airlines)*: See Zulu Time.

Zebra *(Tourism)*: Zone on a street drawn with parallel white lines for pedestrian traffic.

Zenith *(Geography)*: The highest point in the sky directly above a given position or an observer.

Zephyr *(Geography)*: A Greek term for a slight wind or gentle breeze.

Zeppelin *(Airlines)*: A generic term for any rigid and lighter-than-air passenger airship, derived from the name of its inventor, Ferdinand Graf von Zeppelin (1838-1917). The first aircraft of this type flew in 1900 near Friedrichshafen, Germany.

Zeppelin, Ferdinand von *(Airlines)*: Count von Zeppelin was the inventor of the rigid cigar-shaped dirigible or airship balloon that is named after him. He was born on 8 July 1838, in Konstanz, Germany. Having become a member of the Prussian army, he went to the United States in 1863. While in Minnesota, he made his first balloon flight. Once back in Germany, he dedicated to the design and construction of airships. After retiring from the Prussian army in 1891, Zeppelin founded an airship factory at Friedrichshafen, Luftschiffbau-Zeppelin, where engine-powered dirigibles would be designed and constructed. One of his airships operated the first commercial air service for passengers in 1908. The innovative airships were used during World War I air raids over the Great Britain and France, but were found vulnerable. Ferdinand von Zeppelin died on March 8, 1917.

Zero - Call or 0 - Call *(Hospitality)*: A telephone call placed with an operator's assistance by dialing 0.

Zero Entry Pool *(Tourism)*: A swimming pool with sloping contours sometimes with a section covered with sand to resemble a beach.

Zero Population Growth (ZPG) *(Tourism)*: A condition in a given place where the birth rate (plus immigration) equals the death rate (plus emigration). By consequence, its population does no longer increase.

Zero-zero *(Air Traffic)*: A term used to describe a weather condition without ceiling or visibility.

Zimbro *(Hospitality)*: A European herb used in the distillation of Gin.

Zip Code *(Tourism)*: An acronym for "Zone Improvement Plan" consisting of a numeric or alpha-numeric code used by the post office services to facilitate the delivery of mail.

Zip Line (*Tourism*): A system consisting of an inclined wire holding a suspending seat where a person is moved down by action of gravity. It is used at some rain forest places, as part of the tourist attraction

ZOC (*Air Traffic*): Code for Zone of Confusion

Zodiac (*Geography*): The annual cycle of twelve stations of celestial longitude extended along the Earth's ecliptic. The zodiac is accepted as the first known celestial coordinate system.

Zone Lighting (*Tourism*): Lighting designed to facilitate traffic from one space to another.

Zoning (*Tourism*): A method in tourism of establishing particular zones in order to regulate land uses by separating them on the bases of specific environmental features such as wetlands, archaeological and historic sites.

Zoo (*Tourism*): See Zoological Park.

Zoological Garden (*Tourism*): See Zoological Park.

Zoological Park (*Tourism*): A park-like place in which wild animals are displayed alive in closed areas, so that people can view them.

Zoonosis (*Ecology*): A disease of animals, such as rabies, that can be transmitted to humans.

ZP (*GDS*): Code meaning Flight Segment Tax.

ZRH (*GDS*): Three-letter IATA code for Zurich, important city in Switzerland.

Z-time (*Airlines*): See Zulu time.

Zulu (*Airlines*): Coordinated Universal Time (UTC) also known as Greenwich Mean Time (GMT).

Zulu (*Airlines*): Designator for the letter "Z" in the International Phonetic Alphabet.

Zulu Time (*Geography*): See Greenwich Mean Time.

BIBLIOGRAPHY

BARRADO, Diego y CALABUIG, Jordi, *Geografía Mundial del Turismo*, Madrid: Editorial Síntesis S.A., 2001.

BOULLÓN, Roberto, *Planificación del Espacio Turístico*, México: Editorial Trillas, 3ª. Edición, 2003.

BRAGA, Rogério, *Diccionario de Turismo*. Sao Paulo: Inovação, 2003.

CASTILLO, Carlos and BOND, Otto F., *The University of Chicago Spanish-English English-Spanish Dictionary*, New York: Pocket Books, 2002.

COLLIN, Simon, *Dictionary of Wine*, London: Bloomsbury Publishing, 2004.

COLLINS, Harper, *Canadian Ringbinder Dictionary*, Toronto: Harper Collins Publishers, 2003.

COWIE A.P., MACKIN R., McCAIG I.R., *Oxford Dictionary of English Idioms*, New York: Oxford University Press, 1993.

FLAVIAN, Eugenia, FERNANDEZ, Gretel Eres, *Minidicionário Espanhol Português, Português Espanhol*, São Paulo: Ática, 2002

GOODWIN, Mark and COGLIANESE, Lou, *Dictionary for the Avionics Domain*, Owego NY: IBM Federal Systems Company.

GURRÍA Di-BELLA, Manuel, *Introducción al Turismo*, México: Editorial Trillas, 7ma. Edición, 2004.

HOUGHTON MIFFLIN COMPANY, *The American Heritage Dictionary of Phrasal Verbs*, Boston: Houghton Miffin Company, 2005.

IATA Aviation Training and Development Institute, *Geography in Travel Planning Course Foundation*, Montreal: IATA, 2002.

IATA Aviation Training and Development Institute, *Geography in Travel Planning II, Course Consultant*, Montreal: IATA, 2002.

IATA/SITA, *Passenger Air Tariff Training Extract*, Montreal: IATA, 2005

MARTÍNEZ ALMEIDA, Homero, *Procedimientos de Cálculo Tarifario*, Quito: Editorial Screen, 1989.

MARTÍNEZ ALMEIDA, Homero, *El Contrato de Transporte Aéreo Internacional*, Quito: Editorial Screen, 1992.

MARTÍNEZ ALMEIDA, Homero, *Tráfico Aéreo Internacional, Manual de Cálculo Tarifario*, Quito: Editorial Monsalve, 1998.

MARTÍNEZ ALMEIDA, Homero, *Geografía Universal Aplicada a la Industria de Viajes*, Quito: 2005.

MERRIAM-WEBSTER, *The New Merriam-Webster Dictionary*, Springfield Massachusetts: Merriam-Webster Inc. Publishers, 1989.

MERRIAM-WEBSTER, *The Merriam-Webster Thesaurus*, Springfield Massachusetts: Merriam-Webster Inc. Publishers, 1989.

NOVELLI, Marina, *Niche Tourism: Contemporary Issues, Trends, and Cases*, Elsevier: Butterworth Heinemann, 2005

OXFORD UNIVERSITY, *Oxford Thesaurus of English Dictionary*, Italy: Second Edition Revised, Editor Maurice Waite, Printed by Legoprint S.p.A., 2006.

OXFORD UNIVERSITY, *Oxford English Reference Dictionary*, New York: Edited by Judy Pearsall and Bill Trumble, Second revised Edition, Oxford University Press Inc. 2002.

RANDOM HOUSE, *Webster's Easy English Dictionary*, New York: Edited by Gerard M. Dalgish, Published by Random House, 2001.

REY, Alan, Le Robert Micro, *Dictionaire de la Langue Française*, Montreal: Troisème Édition, 1998.

SPEARS, Richard A, *Dictionary of American Idioms and Phrasal Verbs*, New York: McGraw Hill, 2005.

WARD, Douglas, *Complete Guide to Cruising and Cruise Ships*, Berlitz, 2007

WEB SITES

http://www.acha/es/bddoc/glosarios/aeropuertos.ehtm
http://www.chez.com/geotourisme/
http://www.hometravelagency.com
http://www.iata.org
http://www.icao.org
http://www.laguia.com.ve/informativas/gastronomia/html/glosario/
   html/
http://www.lanyon.com
http://www.oag.com
http://www.OneLook Dictionary Search
http://www.rci.com
http://www.tiac-aitc.ca
http://www.traveltradesmart.com
http://www.worldcargoalliance.com
http://en.wikipedia.org

Printed in the United States
132737LV00003B/105/P